T0291283

Air Transport and Tourism

Air Transport and Tourism: Interrelationship, Operations and Strategies is a comprehensive textbook covering all major aspects of air transport from operational and managerial perspectives, as well as exploring the intricate relationship that exists between the air transport and tourism industries.

The book introduces and provides in-depth coverage of the complexities of the airline industry and the tourism industry and the ways in which they are connected and impact on each other, for example, the destination–airport–airline nexus, and the roles of air transport and airlines in tourism and vice versa. Emphasis is placed on current and future trends, the impact of COVID-19, sustainability and environmental challenges throughout. Comprehensive coverage of airline operations, strategic management and planning, airport operations and air transport information technology is also provided, offering a practical viewpoint on these vital aspects of the subject.

This will be the ideal introductory textbook for students of tourism and hospitality studying courses in aviation and air travel.

M.R. Dileep is a noted tourism academic, author and columnist. He has been an academic in travel and tourism for over two decades, working as Vice-Principal at Pazhassiraja College (University of Calicut, Kerala, India), and worked with the Ministry of Higher Education (CAS Salalah), Sultanate of Oman, and as Head of Tourism at Kerala Institute of Tourism and Travel Studies (KITTS). He has written a number of research publications and conference presentations and six books. His qualifications include MTA, MPhil, PhD and IATA Diplomas in Air Transport and Cargo.

Ajesh Kurien is an expert in airport ground handling with over 15 years of experience in the area and is currently working as Operations Trainer for National Aviation Services (NAS), Kuwait, the fastest-growing aviation services provider in the Middle East, India and Africa. He was involved in the design and development of the Passenger Ground Services Course for IATA. He holds a Master of Tourism Management from Madurai Kamaraj University, Tamil Nadu, India, and a diploma in IATA air fares and ticketing and has completed IATA Advanced Train the Trainer Course and IATA Instructional Techniques Course.

Air Transport and Tourism

Interrelationship, Operations and Strategies

M.R. Dileep and Ajesh Kurien

Routledge
Taylor & Francis Group

LONDON AND NEW YORK

First published 2022
by Routledge
2 Park Square, Milton Park, Abingdon, Oxon OX14 4RN

and by Routledge
605 Third Avenue, New York, NY 10158

Routledge is an imprint of the Taylor & Francis Group, an informa business

British Library Cataloguing-in-Publication Data
A catalogue record for this book is available from the British Library

Library of Congress Cataloging-in-Publication Data
A catalog record has been requested for this book

ISBN: 9780367683269 (hbk)
ISBN: 9780367683207 (pbk)
ISBN: 9781003136927 (ebk)

DOI: 10.4324/9781003136927

Typeset in Frutiger
by codeMantra

Contents

Contents

Contents

Contents

Contents

Contents

Figures

Figures

Tables

Preface

The inextricable link between air transport and tourism has been evolving since the end of the Second World War, and it is anticipated to reach higher levels in the decades to come as well. While upholding a symbiotic relationship, air transport and tourism have been adding newer dimensions into the realm of their coexistence. Aviation has recorded phenomenal growth since its beginning in the early years of the 20th century, and its evolution as the domineering mode of transport by the last quarter of the same era resulted in establishing its social and economic significance. Indeed, air transport is a feature of modern travel and is part and parcel of social life of the people in this technologically and socially advanced era. Along with the growth of air transport, particularly after the Deregulation that occurred in the 1970s, tourism too has recorded remarkable growth and turned to be one of the largest economic sectors in the world. Their mutual dependence makes the tourism system more complex, and the various industrial elements require the smooth air transport services in order to perform their functions. Currently, more than half of the international tourists depend on air transport for their travel to destinations. Certainly, airlines, the most important element in the air transport system, are instrumental in channelizing tourism demand and their presence is inevitable in the accessibility of some regions and destinations that are otherwise difficult to access. Airports are becoming increasingly relevant in the sphere of tourism, and they are trying to be integral in the destination mix. While the new business models in the airline sector rewrite the role of air transport in tourism, the travel experience is getting increasingly significant in the overall tourist experience. Against this backdrop, an attempt is done to unravel the growing and intense relationship existing between tourism and air transport.

This book, titled "Air Transport and Tourism: Interrelationship, Operations and Strategies", has been written as a comprehensive textbook that covers almost all aspects associated with the relationship between air transport and tourism, along with describing the operational and managerial perspectives of air transportation from a tourism perspective.

There are eighteen chapters in the book, which starts with an introduction on the linkage between air travel and tourism and the significance of air transportation in the process of tourism. The following chapter provides an overview of air transport and the interrelationship among the elements in the air transportation system. The third chapter introduces the basic concepts of tourism along with outlining the structure of the sector. The next chapter comprehends the trends in the contemporary air transport sector. All those significant aspects covered in it are correlated with the evolution of tourism as well in that chapter. The chapter on COVID-19 and its impacts on aviation provides details on the vulnerability of the air transport and tourism sectors to crises, the impacts of the global pandemic on the tourism and air transportation sectors, and the "New Normal" trends seen in those sectors as part of their struggle to recover from the severity of the COVID-19 impacts.

The sixth chapter illustrates the roles played by air transport in tourism. The description includes the way air transport gets involved in the evolution of tourism in destinations, tourism demand addition, benefiting tourists and invigorating dynamism in the tourism sector, and the role it plays in offsetting seasonality. The following chapter identifies the regulations that are there in the realm of air transportation that enable the smooth and safe international air travel, and the role those regulations and policies play in the growth of tourism across the world. The eighth chapter deals with the concept, types and business models in tourism along with a briefing on the relevance of airline types on tourism. The airport concept is introduced in the next chapter, and the customers and products of it are familiarized through it. Airport ownership, socio-economic relevance and the emerging concepts of airport are also dealt with in detail in that chapter. The following chapter elucidates the collaboration and dependence existing between a tourist destination and air transport elements such as airport and airline. The specific roles an airport takes up in the development and growth of a destination are also elaborated in it.

The eleventh chapter is a unique one, which describes the significance of aircrafts in tourism. Various types of aircrafts are introduced in the chapter. The recreational role of aircrafts in tourism in destinations is discussed in detail. Moreover, the role played by the advancements in aircraft technology in the evolution of modern tourism is expounded well in that chapter. As stated before, tourism and air transport do have a symbiotic relationship, which points out that tourism too contributes to the evolution of air transport, and that is the focus of the next chapter. While discussing the role of tourism in the growth of air transport, the scope for increasing dynamism, quality enhancement, network expansion, etc., is described in detail. The catalytic role of tourism in the expansion of air transport is discussed well in it. The following chapters deal with planning in the airline at different levels, which includes fleet planning, network planning, schedule planning, fleet assignment, aircraft routing and crew planning and scheduling. Operations within an airline organization, including the details of airline operations control, flight planning and dispatch, load control planning, maintenance control, station operations control, passenger processing, boarding and arrival procedures, and disruptions and delay management, are explained. The traveller-oriented strategies and practices by airlines constitute the core of the fifteenth chapter. In addition to some of the key aspects of airline promotion, airline economics, dynamic pricing, revenue management and the customer relationship management practices in airlines are described in detail in that chapter. The next chapter consists of airport structure and operations.

Information and communication technology is swiftly altering the airline operations and services, and that is the focus of the seventeenth chapter. Various information systems used by airiness and airports are detailed in it. Also, the use of information technology in airline product distribution, along with the trends in electronic travel distribution, is explained. The book ends with a chapter on the impacts of air transport as well as tourism, the contribution of those sectors to climate change, ameliorating measures, the challenges faced by the air transport sector, and the revival hope of both the sectors in the post-COVID era.

The contents and details included in this book would certainly enlighten the working professionals in the tourism, air transportation and hospitality sectors. Moreover, this is prepared as an invaluable resource for the students of aviation, travel, tourism, hospitality and transport management courses.

Acknowledgements

First and foremost, we humbly tender our wholehearted gratitude to God Almighty for the blessings He has bestowed upon us and for giving us the strength and wisdom to achieve this dream.

Certainly, this book is the product of our combined efforts. It is brought to fruition through hard work, patience and perseverance along with the support we received from a large number of people. We are extremely fortunate to enjoy the strong support of family, colleagues, well-wishers and friends.

I, Dileep, have immense pleasure in acknowledging all my colleagues and friends at Pazhassiraja College (Wayanad, Kerala, India), Kerala Institute of Tourism and Travel Studies (KITTS, Thiruvananthapuram) and the College of Applied Sciences (Ministry of Higher Education), Sultanate of Oman. Also, I am happy to express my thanks to all the office bearers and members of the Indian Tourism and Hospitality Congress (ITHC), which is a professional body of tourism academics in India. Many of my students who are now in different parts of the world in different positions have been encouraging me to do better. I personally thank all of them. Moreover, my friends always inspired my accomplishments and I am grateful to them. And, most particularly I am indebted to my family members and relatives. I owe heartfelt thanks to all of them for their unconditional support and care, especially my wife, Soorya A. N.; son, Gautham Krishna; father, Mr Madhavakurup; mother, Mrs Radhika Devi; father-in-law, Mr V. K. N. Panicker; and mother-in-law, Mrs Ambika Devi.

I, Ajesh Kurien, would like to acknowledge with thanks the support and love of my family – my parents, K G Kurien and Annamma; in-laws, Mathew and Mary; wife, Jisha; daughter, Ardra; and son, Ron Mathew. They all keep me going, and this book would not have been possible without them.

I am especially indebted to Dr. M.R. Dileep, who has given me this wonderful opportunity with the guidance throughout.

To every organization that I am honoured to be a part of, thank you for letting me serve and for being a part of the amazing team members of Air India Charters Ltd. (AICL), Cochin; Qatar Aviation Services (QAS), Doha; and Bird Worldwide Flight Services (BWFS), Cochin. I especially want to thank my present employer National Aviation Services (NAS), Kuwait, and the Group CEO Mr. Hassan El-Houry, an aviation industry expert and author.

Acknowledgements

I extend my sincere gratitude to Mr. Mohammed Omar Al-Habash, Group Training and Development Director, National Aviation Services (NAS), Kuwait, who has been supportive of my career goals and who worked actively to provide me with the protected time to pursue those goals. I am grateful to all my friends and colleagues whom I have had the pleasure to work and interact with.

Chapter 1

Air transport and tourism: an introduction

Learning outcomes

After studying this chapter, you would be able to:

- Describe the concept of air transportation.
- Identify the instances that led to the evolution of modern aviation and tourism.
- Relate travel in the process of tourism.
- Derive the intricacies existing between transport, particularly air transport, and tourism.
- Comprehend the growing travel propensity, hypermobility and tourism.

1.1 Introduction

The human desire to fly has been there since time immemorial. Even in the early history, instances of varied attempts to fly are seen. Such attempts continued, and some of those paved the way for the emergence of mechanized flying. In fact, people had to wait until the 20th century to make air travel possible in a smooth and comfortable manner. Begun in the first decade of the last century, aviation has grown by leaps and bounds and turned into a huge industry with wide socio-economic ramifications. The phenomenal success of air transport is particularly due to the consistent advancements in the aviation technology because of rigorous attempts to improve. Currently, this is the most rapid transport system, which generates incredible economic growth, results in a large number of employment opportunities and facilitates international trade and tourism. Of late, the commercial air transport network is with more than 1,400 scheduled airlines, 26,000 aircrafts in service, 3,900 airports and 173 air navigation service providers (ATAG, 2017). Moreover, out of the total employment of 62.7 million jobs created by this sector, 9.9 million are generated directly in the industry (IHLG, 2017). Moreover, an efficient air transport system is a determinant in the socio-economic progress of a country. Along with the exponential rise of air transport as a major mode of transportation, the air travel propensity has permeated deep into various societies all over the world. Consequently, air travel became accessible to more sections of the society compared to the early stages of modern aviation. Once, air travel was restricted to a few, the rich and the aristocratic. Now, it is a mass transport system having billions of users availing its services annually. Although there is a stalemate in the air transport system due to the pandemic, the sector is poised for further growth, and the predictions in the growth of air transportation are awesome, which is described in the following sections.

By the second half of the last century, air transport became significant in tourism, and of late, the majority of the international tourists now depend on the mode of air transport for their onward and return journeys. Almost in the same era, tourism too got into a new stage of evolution, often remarked as the beginning of modern tourism. Both the sectors have grown together to become large economic sectors in the world towards the end of the 20th century, and more often, both are represented together in the tourism literature. As stated by Page (2009),

> Tourism has become one of the most visible signs of human movement at a global level, benefiting from increased prosperity, a desire to travel and the benefits which new transport technology has brought to aid increased accessibility of destinations to tourists and other travellers.

While air transport has evolved into a mass mode of transportation mainly due to the technological advancements and the deregulation process began in the USA in the late 1970s, tourism gained the pace in its growth due to a wide range of reasons. Yet amongst the reasons, the rise of air transport as an increasingly affordable option for long-haul travel turned to be a major one. Taleb Rifai, the former secretary general of the UNWTO, stated that

> The extraordinary growth of international tourism over the last decades – from 25 million tourists in 1950 to 990 million in 2011 – is as much due to advances in air transport as to growing wealth in industrialized and emerging countries and the forces of globalization. Over half of all international tourists currently arrive to their destinations by air and UNWTO expects 23 million more tourists to take to the skies each year between now and 2030.
>
> (Rifai, 2012/UNWTO Global aviation report)

In the new millennium, the new airline business models and the increasing rate of dynamism in it, along with a number of other factors, spurred tourism growth further to become one of the top five economic sectors in the world. There exists an inextricable link between both the sectors, and it is of paramount importance to discuss deeply the interrelationship between both the sectors. This book has been envisaged as one that comprehends the interactions and interrelationships between tourism and air transport.

1.2 Air transportation

Air transportation is certainly one of the most significant components of the global transport system, and the significance has predominance in the long-haul travel. Moreover, it has remarkable significance in the world's socio-economic impacts. Usually, transportation is classified based on the medium in which the process of movement takes place. In air transport, the vehicle used for the movement is aircraft, mostly. Helicopters, hot air balloons, gliders, jets, etc. can also be used for the movement. Air transport represents the mode of transport using aerial vehicles for moving people, mail and cargo from one place to another. It enables the people to travel through air to a distant place so quickly. In addition, it enables people to send cargo or similar consignments to another location in the fastest possible manner. The term "air transportation" is used to denote the commercial transportation of cargo and passengers. Basically, it conveys the mobility of people and cargo by air. The difference between air transportation and aviation is that the latter is an umbrella term involving all aspects of air travel, whereas the term "air transportation" denotes mainly the commercial transportation of people, mail and cargo from one place to another. Air transportation, simply, is the system in which the air transport activities are undertaken, in order to enable the movement of people, mail and cargo using aircrafts of varied kinds. It is a transportation system for transporting goods and passengers by air. Industries in this system provide "air transportation of passengers and/or cargo using aircraft, such as airplanes and helicopters" (North American Industry Classification System/ www.bls.gov). Air transport services constitute the most visible component of aviation as well. The predominant view of air transport is related to the use of the service of "common carriers", which are used in the context of public transport. While analysing air transport from a marketing point of view, it can be seen as an intermediate good as most of the people use it as a means to achieve some other purpose (O'Connor, 2001). For example, when tourists fly to a destination, they may have an objective to have a happy vacation; the air trip is largely or entirely a means to this objective.

Commercial air transport is getting increasing significance due to its inherent characteristics. As mentioned above, speed is the most important factor that makes it more special in the long-haul travel. Being the fastest mode of transportation, it is the most suitable means where time is an important factor. Its speed is many times more than that of most of the other modes of transportation. Latest aircrafts are speedier as well. Military aircrafts are featured with speed. Some of the latest such aircrafts have a top speed of more than 2,500 mph. In addition, there are planes being developed with a speed of more than 5,000 mph. However, in commercial transportation, flights of 900 km/h, on an average, are in use. The speed can increase tremendously in the future, which can stimulate air travel propensity further. As per latest reports, supersonic commercial aircrafts are being designed that can fly at a speed of 1,450 mph and that can make the trip from New York to London in three hours and 15 minutes. This sector also provides very regular services along with high level of comfort. Most of the operations within air transport are highly time-bound, and efficient system of functioning makes it possible.

1.3 Evolution of air transportation

Though there have been many instances of attempts to fly using different objects in different eras in the written history, the modern aviation began only in the early 20th century. It was on 17 December 1903, using the flight "Flyer One First flight" by Orville Wright, with the help of Wilbur Wright, flew a distance of 39 metres (120 ft.) for the duration of 12 seconds at Kitty Hawk, North Carolina, which paved the way for the emergence of an innovative transport system in the world. From then onwards, innovations and developments emerged at regular intervals. All such contributed to the evolution of a great industry, which changed the way that people move from place to place. Many instances can be noted in the history of aviation, and only a few are pointed out here. In the first decade of the last century itself, aircraft manufacturing company was started – that too just four years after the first successful experimental flight of an aircraft. In 1905, Gabriel and Charles Voisin started the world's first aircraft manufacturing company in France. In 1909, Louis Blériot crossed the English Channel in a monoplane.

In 1914, St. Petersburg-Tampa Airboat Line organized the first scheduled passenger air transport, from St. Petersburg in Florida in the USA. The first airmail route in the United States was established in 1918 between New York City and Washington DC, and in the same year, US Post Office Department took over the entire airmail service. World wars contributed greatly in the evolution of aviation as rigorous experiments and researches were undertaken during the war years to improve the air transport capability. Newer technologies were introduced and experimented during the wars. In Europe, the use of aircrafts for various purposes, particularly for the war purposes, was predominant. For instance, Bartsch (2018) noted that "…at the beginning of the war in 1914, the Great Britain possessed only twelve military aeroplane; by the war's end in November 1918, there were 22,000 aeroplanes".

As air transport gained increased significance, an urge was there to have some agencies to initiate regulations and guidelines for the smooth and efficient air transport all over the world. The International Air Traffic Association was formed in 1919 at The Hague, Netherlands, with the objective of forming a common understanding about international air transportation. Soon, many airlines were born. Examples include Qantas (1920), Imperial Airways (1924), Lufthansa (1926) and Air France (1933). By the time, in 1925, the United States had introduced the Kelly Act, which is a Contract Air Mail Act that authorized the postmaster general to enter into contracts with private persons or companies for the airmail transportation. Soon, the US government passed the Air commerce Act in 1926. Passenger service became popular in the United States by the mid-1920s. The experimental flight by Charles Lindberg in 1927 across the Atlantic was a revolutionary occurrence in the early history of modern aviation. In between, many events occurred with the objective of standardizing various aspects associated with flying on international routes. Paris Convention (1919) was a major one, in which 27 states signed the convention relating to the Regulation of Aerial Navigation in Paris. Madrid Convention (1926), Havana (Pan-American) Convention (1928) (the first multilateral convention), etc. are some other major events held before the Second World War (Bartsch, 2018). Later, after the Second World War, Chicago Convention (1944) was organized. It reaffirmed the system of bilaterally negotiated "traffic rights" between nations and gave birth to the International Civil Aviation Organization

Table 1.1 Second World War and Aviation Development

The contribution of the Second World War in the advancement of aviation is summarized as follows:

- Availability of experienced pilots in large numbers
- Aviation got increased awareness amongst the public
- Increased awareness of the weather
- More maps and knowledge of foreign terrain
- Availability of a large number of airfields in more parts of the world
- A large collection of surplus aircraft designs, flying techniques and other knowledge suitable for the evolution of aviation sector
- The development of jet aircrafts

Source: Modified from Gee et al. (1997).

(ICAO) as a UN agency in order to guide and regulate global civil aviation. In the next year, International Air Transport Association (IATA) was formed with the intention of smooth and efficient commercial air transportation. Bermuda Agreement was undertaken in 1946, which set the pattern for most other traffic rights agreements. Jet aircrafts were introduced in between, and in 1955, Pan American Airways gave orders for Boeing and Douglas jets. The Boeing 707, the pioneer jet engine model, went into service in 1958. Late 1960s saw the entry of supersonic aircraft, and in 1968, British Aircraft Corporation (BAC)/Aerospatiale introduced Concorde with a speed up to 2,400 kph and a range of 7,000 km.

Deregulation, partially liberating the air transport sector from the stringent regulatory network, was one of the most important milestones in the history of aviation, after the Second World War. This was initiated in the United States in 1978 due to the situations prevailing in the air transportation environments. In the highly regulated environments, airlines faced many issues and challenges. Airline capacity increased but demand did not increase at the same pace, which caused a mismatch between capacity and demand. Due to regulations, airlines faced issues to add as well as remove routes. A steep hike in the aviation fuel price due to the formation of Organization of the Petroleum Exporting Countries (OPEC) increased the cost of operations. There was no scope for price competition. Profitability became a matter of concern for many airlines. Airlines had to acquire new fleets to remain competitive, which led to financial issues. Airlines were forced to lure customers by an increased flight frequency with cabin service. Government's stringent regulations became a burden for the airline industry as profitability remained a major concern. These are some aspects that contributed to the decision favouring deregulation. In 1977 itself, cargo airlines were liberated from regulation in the United States. The focus of deregulation was to allow the marketplace to determine the airlines' business decisions and to ease controls over airline fares and routes in order to encourage greater competition and better services. The new initiative also aimed to have competition to gain efficiency, innovation, price competitions and more service options; and all such together can result in instilling managerial efficiency that can result in attracting more capital as well, along with other advantages. Deregulation resulted in dramatic changes in the airline industry. Given below are some of the major effects of deregulation.

- Immediate expansion of routes and networks of existing airlines
- Entry of a number of new airlines and consequent rise in competition
- Complex fare structure emerged
- Discounts were offered according to demand
- Airfares got reduced
- Air travel demand surged
- Emergence of loyalty schemes
- Increase in airline productivity
- Increase in air transport employment
- Region-based airlines could expand service to other regions
- Trunk airlines started growth through introducing "Hub and Spoke" system
- Financial issues loomed large over the airline business
- Mega airlines emerged by multilevel mergers and acquisitions
- Emergence of "open skies agreements"
- Entry of low-cost carriers (LCCs) with much lower fare increased

Privatization became a buzzword in the airline sector, and soon some of the government owned or controlled companies were fully or partially privatized. As competition increased, to increase the number of travellers and to create loyalty amongst passengers, airlines started to adopt the **Frequent Flyer Programme (FFP)**. American Airlines began it in 1981. FFP became a key measure of attracting and retaining travelling customers. **Open skies** agreements were also begun in the United States by making agreements with other countries. It provides a free market for aviation services and offers more benefits to the passengers, shippers

Table 1.2 An Overview of Stages since Deregulation in the USA

Stages	Developments and Changes
1978–1981: Quick emergence of new competitors	A number of new airlines (more than 80) entered into the market, high price competition and consequent lowering of price levels, increase in passenger flow, attempts to defend the market shares of major airlines.
1982–1985: Strategies of major airlines to remain competitive	Cost reduction strategies to compete with price reductions, increasing horizontal integration due to mergers, and the emergence of alliances and competing in the market with diverse strategies including adopting hub and spoke network, expansion of computer reservation systems, profit maximization through yield management and bonus programmes using customer loyalty.
1986–1990: Emergence of regional monopolies	Upper hand of individual airlines in regional hubs, mergers and market exits lead to structural simplification and extreme concentration.

Source: Adapted from Maurer (2006).

and the economy of the country, on a wide scale. As financial crisis continued, many airlines have been merged, taken over or gone out of business; the surviving airlines had to look for other strategies to remain competitive. To ensure economic viability, many airlines aimed at being involved in cross-border alliances, partnerships and other cooperative arrangements. Alliances remain a major category amongst them. Star alliance, Sky team and One World are some of the major airline alliances in the world currently. Of late, the airline industry has become a major player in the global transport system.

1.4 Tourism: a phenomenon emerges out of travel

Tourism in this modern world turned to be a social activity of immense significance to the socio-economic spheres of human life. Having evolved from an activity restricted to the "rich and aristocratic", it has become affordable to many other segments of societies across the world. It has grown almost steadily since the end of the Second World War; tourism expanded because of the deliberate developmental efforts by the respective authorities as well as the dynamism in the industry, and transformations took place in the environments around the tourists. As of now, it is one of the largest economic sectors in the world, and as per 2019 status, it contributes US$8.9 trillion to the world's GDP, which amounts to 10.3% of global GDP (WTTC, 2020).

Certainly, the terms "travel" and "tourism" are used interchangeably often to denote the movement of people from one place to another for visiting, primarily, and to return to the origin place. Yet, while considering it as one of the largest economic sectors, the term "tourism" is used as a comprehensive one to encompass a range of industries that provide the services and products to cater to the travelling population. Moreover, the measurement of the various aspects of this type of movement of people is done considering that process using the term "tourism", internationally.

There are two prime reasons to denote that the tourism phenomenon evolves out of travel. The first aspect is that tourism has evolved as a major socio-economic sector in the world from the basic urge of people to move that has been there since the early era of the evolution of human beings and has grown over the last several centuries. Therefore, from a historical perspective, travel is the root cause of tourism. In the past, journeys were not comfortable and with myriad safety issues, yet they

> were undertaken and this implies some strong motivating factors. However, it is only in the last 150 years, as travel has become more affordable and less difficult, that some of those who travelled were prepared to openly admit that pleasure was one of the motivations for their journeys.
>
> (Mason, 2009)

In the history of tourism, there had been the tendency of travel by people for specific purposes including the quest of seeking knowledge, relaxing, engaging in religious activities and the like. This urge is continuing, but it was expanded remarkably to include a large spectrum of purposes. Currently, tourism as a social activity occurs due to the travel of millions of people to and from different locations situated across the world. This travel quest got newer dimensions at different occasions in the history of tourism. The modern tourism is now increasingly seeking experiential tourism experience, though still major sections of the tourists engage in mass tourism by visiting established attractions that provide a visiting experience rather.

The second aspect is that travel is fundamental in the process of tourism (Dileep, 2019). Tourism occurs when people take part in travel and stay for at least one day in the place visited. While we consider tourism from a spatial perspective, a specified area is designated for travel as shown in the Leiper's model of the tourism system. In the same, a region is referred to as transit route region (TRR), which encompasses activities of travel from the place of origin to the destination, and vice versa (Leiper, 1979). In order to substantiate the role of travel in tourism, a few definitions from different periods are considered below. Earlier, in 1941, tourism was defined by Hunziker and Krapf (1941) as "the sum of Phenomena and relationships arising from the travel and stay of non-residents in so far as it does not lead to permanent residence and is not connected to any earning activity". This specifies that travel is fundamental in the process of tourism, and the movement is to a different place than the place of residence and not for taking part in a remunerative activity. Later, Leiper also indicates similar conditions in considering travel as tourism. According to it, tourism "is a system involving the discretionary travel and temporary stay of persons away from their usual place of residence for one or more nights, excepting tours made for the primary purpose of earning remuneration from points enroute" (Leiper, 1979). After a decade, Davidson (1990) indicated the role of travel in tourism using the definition "it is about people being away from their own homes, on short term, temporary visits, for particular purposes". The description by Goeldner and Ritchie (2003) is more comprehensive with specifying the travel experience to get from the trip. According to them "Tourism is a composite of activities, services, and industries that deliver a travel experience: transportation, accommodations, eating and drinking establishments, shops, entertainment, activity facilities, and other hospitality services available for individuals or groups that are traveling away from home" (Goeldner & Ritchie, 2003). Lately, UNWTO defines it as "…a social, cultural and economic phenomenon which entails the movement of people to countries or places outside their usual environment for personal or business/professional purposes" (UNWTO Glossary of tourism terms). This definition specifies the movement of people from their usual environment to a place outside it, which stipulates the nature of place to where the travel has to take place. Moreover, travel is used for any type of movement from a place to another, whereas tourism-related movement is limited to certain purposes and with a specific set of conditions. After discussing the importance of travel in tourism, it can be implicitly stated that travel is inherent in tourism and an essential component of the tourism system. Apparently, the absence of travel makes tourism non-existent, which reveals that the phenomenon "tourism" emerges out of travel.

1.5 Evolution of tourism

History of tourism is several centuries old as it "…has been around in one guise or another for a very long time. There is little doubt that there were tourists among the Greeks and Romans" (Weiss, 2004). The origin of the word "travel" is seen in its earliest form of *travail*, meaning a painful and laborious effort (Holloway, 2006). Later, trade became a prime factor for travel to distant places, and the invention of the "wheel" stimulated the travel tendency greatly. "Inns" were built on long routes, and thus, the organized hospitality had a humble beginning. Invention of money by Sumerians (Babylonia) during 4000 BC and the usage of it in business transactions helped the travel to grow. Phoenicians were probably the first real business travellers in the modern sense. Soon, the sailor stage emerged as a result of the consistent efforts of men to move to farther places and across the oceans. The curiosity to experience the outside world really initiated travel amongst men. Along with Babylonians, Egyptians and the Greek too have a recorded history of travel to distant places. Leisure travel is reported to begin during 1500 BC when Egyptians began to travel to visit the pyramids. In fact, the emergence of the Roman Empire put an indelible mark in the history of tourism. By 5th century BC, Athens had become an important destination for travellers visiting major sights like Parthenon. Inns were established in major towns and seaports. Romans created an excellent network of roads, transportation and communication system to manage the vast empire, which helped "travel" too. A number of developments were there during that period that spurred the evolution of leisure tourism during the Roman era.

The downfall of the Roman Empire brought a setback to tourism development. For several centuries (between 5th and 15th century AD), tourism experienced sluggish growth, and it is referred to as the "dark stage" of tourism. "Renaissance", originated in Italy after 1350, reached its peak during Elizabethan times. The social and religious innovative thoughts changed the concept of leisure, to a certain extent, and eventually led to the concept of using leisure time more productively. These changes are reported to have contributed to the rise of the industrial society. The holiday concept emerged slowly. Religious travel was undertaken during then (the Middle Ages). In addition, religious travel to even outside the countries was in trend.

Europe had risen with the emergence of the "renaissance" by the 15th century. Italy became the intellectual capital of Europe, and education, politics, economics and other sciences reached a top-notch level as there were a number of stalwarts in each field in that country. By the mid-1600s, coaches were operating regularly in Britain, especially between London and Oxford. Different types of coaches were in use soon. In addition to "inns", lodging or "chambers" were also available to visitors on rent. By the early 19th century, horse-drawn omnibuses were in regular service in the main cities of Europe. The concept of "grand tour" began in Europe by then. It was a traveller's circuit to key destinations and places in Europe to visit, mainly by the wealthy aristocratic and privileged classes in pursuit of education, culture and pleasure (Page, 2009). These tours were for a long duration, even up to three years. The reasons for undertaking the grand tour were also diverse, including career, education, culture, literature, health, science, business and economics. Soon, the grand tour expanded to include leisure travel as well, where pleasure-seeking young men travelled mainly to France and Italy, primarily to cities like Paris, Venice and Florence. British travellers also ventured into other destinations of Europe.

The rise of the industrial revolution led to different changes in the various spheres of human life. Mechanization began and production rates multiplied.

Plenty of changes took place as a result of industrialization. Holidays became common, and people increasingly started to move to other locations for leisure purposes. The introduction of the steam engine, the railways, the steam ship etc. made travel easier, faster and stimulated travel amongst people. In 1841, Thomas Cook led an initiative to organize a trip from Leicester to Loughborough, in which 570 people participated, and the success of it enabled him to commence a tour operation business. This paved the way for a new sector that spurred the growth of leisure tourism. Soon, a number of tour operation companies were started, with various forms of innovations, all of which greatly contributed in the evolution of tourism. During the late 19th century and early 1990s, the imperial trade of many European countries created more demand for business travel. The growing rail transportation was another factor that pushed tourism forward.

Growth of tourism continued during the early years of the 20th century, but the world wars stalled its progress severely. Air travel began by then. By the 1920s, many cruise liners were successfully carrying cruise tourism, focusing on business and pleasure activities. Though tourism was sidelined, transportation, infrastructure and technology advanced well during that time. Automobile cars became a major mode of transportation, and that contributed in the rise of leisure tourism. Rail transport significance started to decrease by the beginning of commercial air transport services. The Second World War also slowed down the growth of international tourism. Yet, with the technological breakthroughs in aircraft design achieved during and after the Second World War, air services proved to be a viable alternative to shipping in international travel. Access to new forms of transport, particularly road-based, in the inter-war periods opened up more non-rural areas for tourism.

Tourism had a phenomenal growth since the end of the Second World War. Multiple factors contributed to the growth of tourism since 1950. Rise in economic standards, advancements in air transport technology, better international understanding and peace, etc. stimulated the growth of tourism. Transportation improvements were mainly in terms of speed, safety and comfort. Introduction of jet aircrafts, wide body jets, evolution of high-speed trains, emergence of larger aircrafts, arrival of cruise tourism, etc. stimulated tourism. Development of new forms of accommodation establishments, like self-catering, second home, etc. also contributed in tourism's growth. The advancements in information technology and the spread of liberalization were two other prominent factors that propelled the evolution of tourism to the next level. Thus, modern tourism is established by its phenomenal transformation from being an activity preserved for the rich classes to a mass phenomenon. The traverse through the history of tourism reveals an important fact that advancements in transportation at different periods have had immense share in the rise of tourism into one of the largest industries in the world.

1.6 Transportation: a vital element in the tourism system

In continuation of the above discussion on the significance of travel in the tourism process, transportation is indeed inevitable in the tourism system. Various aspects of transportation have indubitable contribution in the tourism experience. Certainly, transportation was a prime reason for the dramatic evolution of tourism since the days of the commencement of railways, particularly in the Europe. We know that the organized tour operation process began with the use of rail service way back in the 1840s by the legendary Thomas Cook. The influence of transportation in the growth of tourism, according to Page (2009): "Without transport and its associated infrastructure, human mobility for the purpose of tourist travel would not occur, and certainly not on the massive scale which is documented in current statistics and reviews of tourism performance…". At every stage of tourism development, the effect of advancement in transportation can be seen. In 19th century, when organized tourism began, the role played by steam engine ships and rail services had an extreme significance. In the 20th century, aviation played a great role. For instance, by the introduction of wide-bodied aircrafts in commercial air transport, tourism gained an impetus. Charter airline's rise in Europe gave momentum for leisure travel amongst the Europeans. Deregulation in the air transport made the long-haul travel more accessible to both business and leisure tourists. Emergence of cruise tourism could widen the scope of leisure tourism further. Altogether, the development of transportation, transportation vehicles, infrastructure and the advent and use of new technologies in the transport sector accelerated the development of tourism. Earlier, transportation was considered a necessity for undertaking the travel phenomenon. The current trend reveals that the same has a multitude of roles to play. Dileep (2019) identified a range of such roles transport plays in tourism such as

- facilitator of tourism growth;
- link between the destination and the tourism markets;
- provision of mobility and access within a destination;
- provision of mobility within tourist attractions;
- a recreational travel option;
- act as a primary attraction;
- link between two or more host destinations;
- determinant in tourist satisfaction;
- contributor in tourist attractiveness;
- determinant in destination success and
- significant contributor in tourism's socio-economic benefits.

Transportation ensures accessibility, which is a basic requirement for a tourist place to become a destination. Prideaux (2000) argues that the provision of transport infrastructure is a prerequisite for tourism development. Nowadays, multimodal transport systems are ensured by competitive destinations to enhance the level of accessibility at international level. This accessibility has multiple dimensions for tourist destinations. It demands good connectivity with other major cities from far and wide. Apart from air connectivity, possible land- and water-based transport connectivity can enhance the level of a destination's accessibility. Within the destination, the transport system has to be efficient. Well-connected road networks constitute a prerequisite for tourism development. After reaching a destination, the internal movement has to be smooth, convenient, comfortable, attractive, interesting and with adequate speed. Moreover, when other destinations are nearby, it is always better to have good connectivity with those destinations as well in order to increase tourism inflow. Transportation thus has so much of significance for a destination, and therefore, it is a key component in the Resort Development Spectrum (Prideaux, 2000a). The quality of connectivity and transport system within the destination can certainly be a matter of concern in the tourist experience for the visitors of the place. This is relevant to almost all the destinations except some niche tourism destinations which are either ecologically sensitive or demand adventurous trips.

Some of the recently succeeded mega destinations like Dubai have turned to be tourist hotspots within the span of a few decades, primarily with the catalytic role played by the global connectivity and world-class transport infrastructure developed by them. Kaul (1985) opines that the transportation network has a significant role in the successful creation and development of new destinations along with ensuring a healthy growth of the existing ones. As connectivity increases, convenience, frequency, affordability, options, etc. too increase, which makes the destinations increasingly competitive. Tourist transport has not only the importance in the TRR as propounded by Leiper (1979), but, as stated before, it is equally significant within the destination as well as between and within some attractions. According to Litman (2008), there are a number of factors that can enhance the accessibility of destinations. They are quality of transportation modes, network connectivity strength, affordability, level of mobility, intra-mode linkages in the transportation system, transport demand, availability of information, mobility substitutes like technological solutions that can replace physical travel, transportation management, land-use factors, prioritization of travel activities and the value of inaccessibility or isolation.

A successful international tourist destination can have a well-connected transport network within it, with extended links to international points, and it can look like the cardiovascular system with blood vessels extending throughout the body. In such a system, as if blood being transported everywhere, the vehicles of different kinds are distributed all over the system of tourism within the destination.

1.7 Symbiotic relationship between air transport and tourism

Tourism and air transport are mutually dependent, and there exists a symbiotic relationship between both the sectors (Forsyth, 2010). Growth in tourism is always positive for the air transport sector as it can experience an increase in demand. Bieger and Wittmer (2006) emphasized that "tourism is a driving factor for and, in some cases, a stimulator of change in air transport…". The major tourist destinations, particularly the urban destinations, stimulated air transport demand greatly and strengthened the air transport supply remarkably. As demand is recording consistent growth and the same trend is forecasted, the destinations will be pressurized to expand the air transport infrastructure as well. Once better infrastructure is implemented, all forms of airline services, such as LCCs, full-service carriers (FSCs) and charter airlines, see the scope of increased services.

While the air transport infrastructure enhances, the tourism also starts growing, which simultaneously causes an increase in the travel demand to the destination.

At a global scale, the desire to travel by air and reach far-away destinations has increased, amongst others, due to higher discretionary incomes, improved levels of education, population growth, and urbanisation. Because of historic trends and due to key socio-economic drivers pointing in this direction, continued growth might seem plausible and destination's investments into tourism warranted.

(Becken & Carmignani, 2020)

Currently, a majority of the international tourists use air transport for moving to their destinations. According to Air Transport Aviation Group (ATAG, 2018), 57% of international tourists travelled between the origin point and the destination using airline services. Tourism at the destination can have a boost in tourist arrivals and, in addition to international tourism, domestic tourism can also be benefited greatly, particularly in countries that are geographically vast. Intra-regional tourism can get a boost as what happened in the case of Europe in the 1960s and 1970s when charter airlines experienced a boom. The movement of tourists amongst countries within Europe was high due to charter airline services. The same effect happened when LCCs were established in Europe. Moreover, as an after-effect of the deregulation process, there was a stiff competition in the international air transport market, which caused a price war and consequent lowering of travel cost. Subsequently, air transport became increasingly affordable which drove long-haul tourism to flourish. Significance of air transport increases with the distance to be covered between the origin point and the destination (Papatheodorou & Zenelis, 2013). The farther the destination from the origin place, the greater the significance for air transport. Therefore, air transport can play a vital role in the long-haul tourism. This trend continued, and air transport became the primary mode of transport in international tourism. However, the recent statistics show that air transport has been playing an increasing role in the short-haul, regional tourism and domestic tourism. A study by Donzelli (2010) about the link between airlines and tourism in the South of Italy reveals that those regions that are mainly served by LCCs record a faster growth of tourism activities compared to those regions, which are mainly served by FSCs.

Thus, the advancements as well as the evolution of both the sectors due to a multitude of reasons complemented each other to grow further and got inextricably interconnected to surge ahead. These aspects are discussed in detail in Chapters 7–9.

1.8 Air transport events that spurred the growth of tourism

Significance of air transport in tourism in a considerable manner began after the end of the Second World War, particularly since the bilateral regulations were started and got shaped in proper form for the smooth and safe international air travel. Moreover, there was a consistent growth in air transportation since the end of the Second World War, and IATA summarizes the growth scenario during the first three decades after 1945 in the following manner.

International air transport grew at double-digit rates from its earliest post-1945 days until the first oil crisis in 1973. Much of the impetus for this growth came from technical innovation. The introduction of turbo-propeller aircraft in the early 1950s, transatlantic jets in 1958, wide-bodied aircraft and high by-pass engines in 1970 and later, advanced avionics were the main innovations. They brought higher speeds, greater size, better unit cost control and, as a result, lower real fares and rates. Combined with increased real incomes and more leisure time, the effect was an explosion in demand for air travel.

(IATA/history, growth and development)

While automobiles stimulated tourism in the first half of the 20th century, air travel became the stimulator in the post-world war era. Weiss (2004) pointed out the same: "Air travel added another dimension, the ability to deliver large numbers of visitors to specific locations in far less time than the train or car".

Every decade since the 1950s had remarkable progress in air transportation, which eventually strengthened tourism to evolve into a modern form. The aviation sector gained much improvement in terms of its technology as a result of the technological experiments and developments that happened during the Second World War. The Second World War proved to be not only an arms race but also a technology race, which resulted in high-quality aviation as well (Mindell, 2015). Jet engine aircrafts were introduced during that time. Commercial air transportation got a fillip by the use of jet engines. Soon, in Europe, charter tourism began, which gave a boost to leisure tourism. IATA's establishment in 1945 as a successor to the International Air Traffic Association helped in the streamlining of many of the commercial aspects of air transportation. The Chicago Convention and the consequential development of ICAO paved the way for better cooperation and understanding amongst the nations in terms of international air transport and ensured uniformity in civil aviation regulations, standards, procedures and organization. This enabled international air transportation to be smoother and safer. As international travel increased, credit cards were introduced during the 1950s, began by the American Express first, followed by the Bank America Card (today's Visa Card) and Master Charge (today's Master Card), which stimulated international travel further (Poon, 1993).

The 1960s was of much significance for charter tourism as it began a trend in Europe by then. Charter flights started to get equal rights as that of scheduled flights (Renshaw, 1997). Europe, particularly, has seen a remarkable growth in leisure tourism since then. Introduction of computer reservation system (CRS) in air transportation was another major incident that stimulated international tourism to grow. CRSs were entered into the scene by the introduction of SABRE in 1960 by American Airlines, probably the first transaction processing system (TPS) in the world (Dileep, 2011). Soon it became a trend in the airline industry, and other major CRSs also emerged without much delay. Due to this, airline product distribution improved a lot and progressively, the accessibility of air travel products enhanced greatly as the travellers could buy flight seats from more convenient locations and without much hassle.

The next decade generated an increased role of air transport in tourism, and in the same, one of the major milestones in the history of aviation took place. Air transportation was one of the most regulated sectors and the services provided were under strict regulations of the authorities. By 1978, the United States began the deregulation process, and it resulted in remarkable changes in the industry. The impacts of deregulation in air transportation are already discussed above in this chapter. A lot of dynamism emerged in the market, and people from more sections of the society started to travel by air. Moreover, wide-bodied aircrafts were being increasingly used in commercial transportation, which also contributed in making the long-haul travel dearer to the people. There was considerable rise in the long-haul tourism by then. The increase in speed and comfort made people fly to farther destinations. Frequent flyer schemes led to repeat purchases of same airline seats by the potential customers. As LCCs grew, regional and domestic tourism also enhanced. The trend of deregulation continued in Europe first and then to other regions as well, which led to flourishing of tourism in many other regions across the world. Airlines formed alliances too, which enabled the FSCs to cooperate to compete with the growing prevalence of LCCs, and due to them, network carriers could provide more services and connectivity than LCCs. This helped tourism as well, by having increased options for business tourists, and leisure tourists got a large array of options for multicentre tours spanning over days. Furthermore, in the 1970s the jet aircraft really started being able to carry more passengers and increased profit and made flights cheaper. This revolutionized the travel propensity, and air travel started penetrating deeper into the society. Though emerged decades ago, open skies policy negotiations have been a trend until now, and those certainly impacted tourism greatly by opening up increased air transport options. Airport privatization and the emergence of competition amongst airports constitute another reason for the growth of tourism since this sector has been trying to expand, increase services and facilities as well as enhance the attractiveness. As this sector faces dynamism, it influences the quality and scope of services of air transportation, which eventually stimulate tourism in one or the other way.

In between, globalization took place, which instilled demand in the air transport sector. Subsequently, air transport infrastructure expanded and air travel became more convenient, affordable and attractive. As a result, and due to globalization effects, business travel growth gained momentum, which led to the rise of business tourism greatly. Globalization, air transportation and business tourism have an inextricable link, and each of them supports one another. In the new millennium, the trend continued and air transport was recording an incredible growth. September 11 terrorist attacks in the United States stalled the progress of air transportation for a short term, which led to a crisis in the tourism sector as well. Soon, both the sectors recovered and then, towards the end of 2010s, the global economic recession again had a negative role in the progress of both the sectors. Within a couple of years' time, they were in growth trajectory again and have been registering a remarkable growth rate. Unfortunately, one of the worst crises in the recent history of humankind, coronavirus pandemic, paralysed those sectors devastatingly for months.

1.9 Increasing travel propensity

As technology is advancing at a tremendous pace, people and societies across the world are highly networked. Latest developments in information and communication technology and the advancements in transport always act as catalysts in it. The transformation in air transport, particularly since the deregulation, has a great role in it. Along with these advancements, coupled with a range of other socio-economic determinants, people have become highly mobile. This increasing mobility has contributed in the progress of tourism as well. Travel propensity is a term used to indicate the tendency of people in a particular population to engage in tourism. Simply, travel propensity is defined as the "willingness of a person to become a tourist" (Kožić et al., 2014). It is further clarified as the "percentage of a population that actually engages in tourism" (Boniface & Cooper, 2009). With respect to the increasing mobility of people, some people have a tendency to partake in travel at a high frequency level, and this phenomenon is often cited as hypermobility. Khisty and Zeitler (2001, p. 598) define hypermobility as "...the maximization of physical movement...". The tendency of travel at a high rate is also termed as "liquid modernity" (Bauman, 2007). Whether it is hypermobility or liquid modernity, the principal reason for the growth in it, particularly since the end of the Second World War, is certainly air transport. From a critical context, hypermobility has been associated with a small share of the wealthy society having extreme travel propensity, and they contribute a major share in the environmental consequences of air transport, particularly in the global climate change.

Cooper et al. (2008) described the use of travel propensity to indicate the penetration of travel tendency in a population. They argued that it is the most useful indicator of effective or actual demand of tourists and can quantify the penetration of tourism trips in a population. The measures such as net travel propensity, gross travel propensity and travel frequency are used to quantify the travel propensity of a given population. The first one, net travel propensity, shows the percentage of the population that takes at least one tourism trip in a given period of time. The number of trips a person is undertaking is not considered in it. The second one, gross travel propensity, accounts for the percentage of trips taken by the population in a given period. If you divide gross travel propensity by net travel propensity, travel frequency can be found, which tells about the frequency of the population taking trips during a stipulated period of time.

Socio-economic factors always influence the travel propensity. The developed countries do have increased propensity due to primarily the prevailing socio-economic circumstances. Better education, lifestyle, economic standards, better health parameters, etc. can boost travel propensity. Favourable macroenvironmental factors altogether have a positive correlation with travel propensity. Increasing transport facilities always enhance the mobility of the people. Travel cost is another factor, and air transport demand is featured with elasticity of demand. Increasing distance has an inverse relationship with travel propensity in general. Increasing the rate of incentive travel, paid holiday, etc. too have an influence on travel tendencies. Favourable political environments, positive bilateral agreements with foreign countries for air transport, easier travel facilitations and requirements, too, have a positive effect. Rising crises of varied kinds, including terrorism activities and natural calamities, always challenge the travel propensity by posing safety and security issues. Travel propensity of developing countries has been growing consistently over the years, and many emerging countries have recorded quick expansion in the national travel propensity rates. China, India, Brazil, Indonesia, etc. have witnessed a dramatic rise in the demand for air travel during the last two or three decades, and the same trend is poised to continue in the years to come as well.

1.10 Conclusion

Tourism and air travel are inherently connected. They are the catalyst for world's economic development. The advancements in air transport and information and communication technology, along with the use of latest marketing strategies, have enhanced the quality and affordability of air travel substantially, over the last five decades or so, and it resulted in the remarkable growth of air travel demand, particularly on longer routes (Organization for Economic Cooperation and Development, 1997). The ICAO is the UN agency that guides and regulates global civil aviation. The IATA was formed to promote the smooth and efficient commercial aviation. Airline deregulation began in the United States in 1978, which resulted in a sweeping positive economic impact in the coming years in the form of reduced airfares and a lift of the entry controls. The European Union, certain South and Central American nations, United Kingdom and Australia have taken a similar approach. Open skies agreements provide a free market for aviation services and offers more benefits for the passengers, the shippers and the economy of the country, on a wide scale.

Post Second World War, tourism had a phenomenal growth due to the rise in economic standards, advancements in air transport technology, better international understanding and peace, etc. The boom in LCCs along with the FSCs and charter airlines boosted the air travel and tourism industry considerably. The increasing mobility has contributed to the increasing travel propensity in tourism. As a very sensitive industry, the outbreak of the coronavirus (COVID-19) in 2019 hit air travel and tourism hard, yet they are on the path to survival.

Sample questions

Short/medium answer-type questions:

- Conceptualize air transportation.
- What are the major events in the history of aviation that led to the evolution of modern air transportation?
- Describe the way deregulation transformed air transportation.
- Evaluate the role of travel in tourism.
- Give a brief account of the evolution of modern tourism.
- Describe how transportation is significant in tourism.
- "Tourism and air transportation share a symbiotic relationship": Comment upon the statement.
- Find out the factors that contribute to the growth of travel propensity.

Essay type questions

- Elucidate the relationship between travel, transportation and tourism.
- Discuss in detail the evolution of air transportation and tourism.

Suggested readings

Cook, A.R., Yale, L., & Marqua. (2007). *Tourism: The Business of Travel*, 3rd Edn. New York: Pearson Education.

Dileep, M.R. (2019). *Tourism, Transport and Travel Management*. London: Routledge.

Graham, Anne, & Dobruszkes, Frederic. (Eds.). (2019). *Air Transport – A Tourism Perspective*. Oxford: Elsevier.

Ivanova, Maya Georgieva. (2017). *Air Transport – Tourism Nexus: A Destination Management Perspective*. Varna: Zangador.

Page, J.S. (2009). *Transport and Tourism Global Perspectives*, 3rd Edn. Essex: Pearson Education.

Papatheodorou, Andreas, & Forsyth, Peter. (Eds.). (2008). *Aviation and Tourism: Implications for Leisure Travel*. Hampshire: Ashgate.

Rhoades, Dawna L. (2014). *Evolution of International Aviation: Phoenix Rising*. London: Routledge.

Chapter 2

Air transport

Learning outcomes

After reading this chapter, you would be able to:

- Identify the factors that contributed to the growth of air travel worldwide.
- Define aviation and distinguish between aviation types.
- Describe the structure of air transportation system.

2.1 Introduction

On 17 December 1903, when Wilbur and Orville Wright succeeded with their experimental flight of a heavier-than-air aerial vehicle, it was just an accomplishment of a long-cherished dream of flying, rather than as an effort to commence a transportation system of global significance. However, it paved the way for the beginning of aviation that eventually led to the evolution of air transportation, which currently is one of the most important components of the global transport system. Moreover, it has a remarkable significance in the world's socio-economic impacts now. Air transportation represents a system of transportation that enables the movement of people, mail and cargo using aircrafts of varied kinds. Generally, it is referred to the commercial transportation activities using aerial vehicles. It had a humble beginning in the early years of the evolution of aviation, and the commercial aspects of it came later when it was started to use for the purpose of mail and passenger transportation. In the USA, the focus of air transportation in the beginning was mainly on mail services, and then it evolved into passenger service, along with cargo service as a sideline service. Later, it became an inevitable mode of transport across the world, and the significance of it has been growing remarkably, except in a few occasions of crises, over the last several

DOI: 10.4324/9781003136927-2

decades. As the global network of air transport widened remarkably, people from anywhere can think of a travel to any location in the world at the highest pace in the most comfortable manner using the services of air transport. Air transportation can connect more people and places than ever before. This, along with the increasing rate of accessibility, led to the feel of shrinking of the globe, and the freedom to fly is more accessible for people. Having a commercial aircraft like A380 that can fly at a speed more than 1,000 km/hr, reaching a long-haul

Table 2.1 Air Transport: Benefits

General benefits	Employment
• It drives economic and social progress • Connects people, countries and cultures • Provides access to global markets • Generates trade and tourism • Creates links between developed and developing nations • Contributes to sustainable development	• It supports 65.5 million jobs • Direct employment: 10.2 million jobs • Airlines, airports and Air Navigation Service Providers (ANSPs) employ 9.1 million • The civil aerospace sector employs 1.2 million • Indirect employment: 10.8 million via purchases of goods and services, 7.8 million through spending by industry employees and 36.7 million through its catalytic impact on tourism

Economic benefits	Social benefits
• The only worldwide rapid transportation system which makes it essential for global business and tourism • Total global economic impact is $2.7 trillion (including direct, indirect, induced and the catalytic effects of tourism) • It transported approximately 4 billion passengers in 2017 • Carried 62 million tonnes of freight in 2017 • Daily value of goods sent by air is now $17.5 billion • 57% of international tourists travel by air	• Broadens people's leisure and cultural experiences by enabling them to access to destinations across the globe • Improves living standards and alleviates poverty through tourism • Often serves as the only means of transportation to remote areas promoting social inclusion • Contributes to sustainable development by - Facilitating tourism and trade - Generating economic growth - Creating jobs - Increasing tax revenues • Facilitates the delivery of emergency and humanitarian aid relief • Swift delivery of medical supplies, organs for transplantation

IATA/ATAG, Fact Sheet: Aviation Benefits Beyond, Bordershttps://www.iata.org/pressroom/facts_figures/fact_sheets/Documents/fact-sheet-economic-and-social-benefits-of-air-transport.pdf, and Aviation Beyond Borders, https://www.aviationbenefits.org/media/166344/abbb18_full-report_web.pdf

destination will not be a tiring task. Both passenger and cargo transportation sectors are recording tremendous growth. On an average, air traffic is continuing to double every 15 years (Airbus/www.airbus.com). This necessitates the continuous efforts to improve the air transport infrastructure all over the world.

Air transportation, in addition to the role in the passenger and goods from place to place, has so much of socio-economic significance. According to the World Bank,

> Air transport is an important enabler to achieving economic growth and development. Air transport facilitates integration into the global economy and provides vital connectivity on a national, regional, and international scale. It helps generate trade, promote tourism, and create employment opportunities.
> (The World Bank/www.worldbank.org)

As of 2018, commercial air transportation alone carries more than 4,500 million passengers generating revenue more than 600 billion US dollar (IATA/www.iata.org). It generates millions of employment opportunities and revenue in billions of dollars. According to IATA, as of 2018, "the global air transport sector supports 65.5 million jobs and $2.7 trillion in global economic activity" (IATA Press Release No: 56/2018). Expansion of air transport in a region can be an indicator of economic progress over there. The increased air transportation can help in increased trade, investments, export activities and the like. The destination enters into the network of global air transportation, and it can have a catalytic role on the development of tourism over there. Due to the possible multiplier effects as part of an increase in air transport in a destination, the society over there can experience better opportunities, lifestyle and social well-being, along with the economic progress. The socio-economic significance of air transportation will not be restricted to that destination alone, but it can be extended to the entire region and even to the country at large. The benefits of air transport are listed in Table 2.1.

2.2 Air travel: growth

Commercial air transportation began just more than a century ago, carrying a single passenger on board. In 1914, on the New Year eve, the world's first scheduled passenger airline service took off, operating between St. Petersburg and Tampa, Florida in USA. The first passenger was none other than the former Mayor of St. Petersburg, Mr. Abram C. Pheil. Since then, it has been growing remarkably. Currently, the number of air travellers using commercial air transport services has crossed 4 billion. According to International Air Transport Association (IATA, 2018) in 2017, "system-wide, airlines carried 4.1 billion passengers on scheduled services, an increase of 7.3% over 2016, representing an additional 280 million trips by air". Moreover, IATA also predicts that by 2037, the number of air travellers may double to 8.2 billion. IATA's 20-Year Air Passenger Forecast reveals that "Over the next two decades, the forecast anticipates a 3.5% Compound Annual Growth Rate (CAGR), leading to a doubling in passenger numbers from today's levels" (IATA, 2018a). The growth in air travel is phenomenal as it is becoming increasingly significant in almost all economies in the world. Advancements in technology, changes in social conditions and the amendments in commercial air transport regulations were the major reasons behind the phenomenal evolution of air travel. Certainly, there are a number of other reasons, which spur the growth in air travel. For instance, the Boeing Global Market Overview reveals that the next two decades will see a remarkable growth in air travel particularly due to the factors such as strong economic growth, growing middle classes, increasing consumer spending on services and evolving airline business models (Boeing, 2018). Majority of those factors are economic determinants that can usher the growth of air travel. Changes in the economic power of middle-class population in many countries, especially in the developing countries, will certainly contribute a great share in the growth of air travel.

Air travel has seen a steep decline in demand once in a while due to the sudden fluctuations in the economic conditions. However, the sector remained resilient and could bounce back in short durations. Occasional market shocks were visible at regular intervals. Apart from economic reasons, a range of other reasons also caused steep declines in air travel demand. For instance, 9/11 terrorist attack in the United States dampened the global air transport sector severely. It took many months to recover fully and to regain the growth status. Oil price shocks, spread of communicable diseases, wars, safety and security issues, etc. marred the growth of air transport at regular intervals over the last several years. Yet, the air traffic continued cumulative growth and evolved significantly. The current crises due to the pandemic impacted the sector harshly, and the impacts are yet to be assessed completely.

Boeing's Current Market Outlook specifies the various influences on a region's air travel growth into three categories, namely economic activity, ease of travel and local market factors. The economic activity includes national and regional GDP development; per-capita income and population trends; labour-force composition; and international trade, economic and investment links. Ease of travel is another factor that can witness different types of experience improvements. More open air service agreements between countries, liberalized domestic market regulation, emerging technology, business model innovation and airline-network improvements are some of the common reasons seen in the category of ease of travel. Local market factors include various factors that are specific to particular regions/countries. For instance, while Chinese air travel market is growing significantly, US domestic air market growth is seen a paltry progression as the sector has already reached the maturity stage and the load factors were already high, and little headroom was left for traffic growth (Boeing, 2016).

Leisure travel is a major category in air travel. A significant share of air travellers are tourists, which consists of both leisure and business travellers. Growth in international tourism certainly contributed greatly to the evolution of air transport in the post Second World War era. The contribution of air transport in tourism is remarkable, and both share a symbiotic relationship. If we analyse the international tourism transport statistics, it will be evident that the share of air transport has been increasing for the last several years and the same of the rest of the modes of transportation has been decreasing. Majority of the international tourists, both leisure and business, now depend on air transport for reaching the destination and returning to the origin place. UNWTO reports that air and land (road and rail) are the most widely used means of transport by the international tourists. In 2016, 55% of the international tourists used air transport, whereas 41% of them used land-based transportation. Four percent of international tourists used water transport for reaching destinations and for returning (UNWTO, 2017). There are a number of reasons for the phenomenal growth of tourism in the same era. Of them, a consistent progress of the economic circumstances of various societies across the world is a major one that resulted in increased discretionary income level. The urbanization, penetration of economic development into many more countries after the end of colonization and the emergence of new economic giants are the other related factors that facilitated the growth of tourism. Other most significant factors were the phenomenal evolution of transport technology and the rising of air transport as the leading transport mode across the world. Consistent advancements in aviation technology and corresponding increase in comfort, speed and safety of air transport became stimulating factors for the evolution of tourism to further heights.

Increased political stability and peace among sovereign nations after the Second World War was another major reason why people started to cross the borders for visiting other countries. Changing attitude of local population towards tourism; increase in accessibility, and affordability of transport; increased government involvement for tourism development; changing demographic patterns and early retirement possibilities; and better health status of people and increase of life expectancy are some other factors behind the phenomenal growth of international tourism. Globalization, liberalization and spread of international trade resulted in an increased level of business tourism. Favourable visa and other policies related to international travel; advancements in information and communication technology; escalating lure of tourism and related industries' marketing and promotion; and the emergence of new economic giants also influenced the growth of tourism worldwide.

Growth in air travel and air transport can be attributed to a wide variety of factors. The prime reasons revolve around the advancements in aviation technology, and the economic development occurred across the world. Economic factors remain an important factor. Level of income of people in almost all societies in the world had substantial progress over the years. Increasing income resulted in an increased rate of disposable income that directly and indirectly influenced air travel for various purposes. Air travel products became increasingly accessible for people. There has been a consistent progress in economic situations of countries during the last half of a century. Currency rate variations also affected air travel as many countries could gain benefits from it. Higher economic standards drive the growth in air traffic for emerging economies as their propensity to spend has been growing at a higher pace, and it is still a fact that the aviation markets in such economies, particularly the Asian emerging economies, have not reached the maturity. Growing employment rates too accelerate the growth of air transport.

Technological advancements propelled the growth in air travel tremendously. At every regular interval, newer technologies came up to advance air transport. Many such incidents are cited below in the section that deals with the history of air transport. At every stage of advancements, speed, comfort, capacity and safety got improved substantially. Efficiency of aircraft engines multiplied many times over a few decades in the history of aviation. Increasing efficiency is directly correlated with the speed, capacity, range and safety of aircraft. Emergence of wide body jet aircrafts in the 1950s marked an important milestone that caused the popularization of air transport in a significant manner. A consistent increase in safety also resulted in an increase in travel propensity of people. Air travel

Table 2.2 Growth in Air Transport (Scheduled Services)

Year	International Passengers (Million)	Passengers-International and Domestic (millions)	Freight Tonnes (millions)	Mail Tonne-km (millions)
2007	890	2 462	41.4	4 418
2008	920	2 500	39.9	4 894
2009	932	2 490	39.6	4 620
2010	1 031	2 707	47.2	4 855
2011	1 119	2 872	48.2	5 006
2012	1 186	3 006	47.5	5 195
2013	1 247	3 140	48.6	5 586
2014	1 327	3 319	50.2	6 076
2015	1 430	3 558	50.5	6 549
2016	1 539	3 797	52.3	6 681
2017	1 660	4 071	56.1	7 449
2018	1 764	4 322	58.0	7 393

Source: ICAO Air Transport Reporting Form A and A-S plus ICAO estimates, data available online at https://www.icao.int/annual-report-2018/Documents/Annual.Report.2018_Air%20Transport%20 Statistics.pdf

became the fastest mode of commercial transport by the tremendous increase in speed of aircraft. Regularity and reliability of air transport also registered a significant growth. Advancements in aviation technology has an inverse relationship with cost of air travel; as technology advanced, the cost of air travel got reduced. As the efficiency of air transport increased, air travel became more economic and affordable. More sections of the societies across the world could access air transport greatly. Use of wide-bodied aircraft also contributed to it since the passenger and cargo carrying capacities of aircraft increased tremendously. An increase in the passenger capacity helped in the reduction in air travel cost, and subsequently, air travel fares reduced. In the last few decades, the unit cost per trip has been on a downtrend, due to improvements in aviation efficiency. Other factor also involved in the reduction in cost of travel is rise in competition.

Changes in demographic factors too have a significant contribution in the evolution of air transport and in the growth in air travel. Increase in population, increase in urbanization, reduction in household size, etc. have a significant share in the growth in air travel. The rate of urbanization is high in the recent decades, which has social and economic determinants that can stimulate air travel. Populous countries such as China, India, Indonesia, etc. have remarkable demographic changes in the last few decades, all of which prompt air travel propensity greatly. In fact, as per the latest statistics, these countries, commonly referred to as emerging economies, have the fastest growth rate in air transport.

One of the most important milestones in the history of commercial air transport is the deregulation initiated by the United States in the second half of the 1970s. The dynamic changes emerged in the post-deregulated air transport economy in the United States and, later, in other developed countries resulted in dramatic changes in the air transport industry. Competition increased greatly and the efficiency of air services too increased along with the emergence of private airlines. Air fares dropped significantly. New airline model like low-cost carriers (LCCs) became a norm in the industry. All such factors enabled the growth of air transport and increased share of the populations could afford to travel by air. Increase in leisure tourism is another major contributor in the growth of air transport all over the world. Emergence of globalization and expansion of international trade augmented air travel remarkably. Cook and Billig (2017) identified that the four factors in the growth of air transport – namely globalization that includes trade, international expansion of business, capital movement, human resource mobility and migration; demographic factors such as population growth, urbanization, diaspora and per-capita income; liberalization and privatization in the air transport sector; and the factors of production, which includes fuel and labour cost – can either hinder or amplify the growth of air transport. Infrastructure too has to be there for the expansion of air transport (Cook & Billig, 2017). To sum up, the following are the major contributing factors in the growth of air travel.

- Consistent global economic progress
- Globalization and increasing international trade
- Increase in income level of people and the rising disposable income
- Growth in population and the changes in demographic patterns
- Fast rate of urbanization
- Changes in social lifestyle
- Consistent advancements in aviation technology
- Reducing cost of air travel
- Industry factors, such as increased regularity, reliability, frequency and comfort
- Deregulation and privatization in air transport
- Emergence of new business models such as LCCs and hybrid airlines
- Increasing rate of competition
- Better marketing, management strategies and practices by commercial air service providers
- Emergence of new economic giants
- Most modern aircraft types with ultra-long-haul capacity (can afford non-stop flying time more than 18 hours)
- Most modernized airports

Air travel, as seen today, is made possible by the evolution of aviation. Let's have a look into the concept of aviation in detail.

2.3 Aviation

Air travel is possible with combined efforts of a number of players, all of which are interrelated and interdependent. Aviation is an umbrella term used to represent the combination of all such players. It's now a huge sector with varied socio-economic significance. It is considered as "one of the most 'global' industries: connecting people, cultures and businesses across continents" (IHLG, 2017a). Even before the revolutionary flight of Wright Brothers in 1903, some have ventured air travel with the help of gliders, kites, balloons, etc. Use of mechanized heavier-than-air flight became a reality by early decades of 20th century that paved the way for the beginning of modern aviation, which enables people to travel at a speed of almost 1,000 kmph from one place to another. Aerospace industry is another term used in a similar context. According to Wensveen (2007), this sector consists of

> those firms engaged in research, development, and manufacture of all of the following: aerospace systems, including manned and unmanned aircraft; missiles, space-launch vehicles, and spacecraft; propulsion, guidance, and control units for all of the foregoing; and a variety of airborne and ground-based equipment essential to the testing, operation, and maintenance of flight vehicles.

It mainly involved in the developing and production of defence, space and other government-required systems. The focus of aerospace industry is different from aviation, technically. "While the aerospace industry also designs and manufactures various forms of aircraft, the industry, as a whole, extends beyond operations within the earth's atmosphere and conducts aircraft operations in space" (Crystal Vogt, smallbusiness.chron.com). In aerospace sector, the consumer base mainly involves military and industrial clientele with an eye toward space travel or space communications. The design, development and production of aircrafts; use and operation of aircrafts, especially heavier-than-air, for various purposes, including that for military; and maintenance of them are the essential components of aviation.

As an economic sector, aviation involves a number of varied sectors and those together enable the movement of people and cargo from place to place via air mode of transport service. According to Bieger and Wittmer (2011), the industries involved in the value chain of aviation are:

- Aircraft manufacturers
- Lessors who buy aircraft and lease them to the airlines
- Airport ground services
- Airlines
- Computer reservation systems (CRS)/Global distribution systems (GDS)
- Travel agents and similar agencies
- Freight forwarders to the customers in the airfreight sector

Though aviation industry is primarily a service industry providing transport services (Pompl, 2006), it consists of other sector like aircraft manufacturers who supply physical goods for conducting the transport services. This sector is featured with consistent advancements and corresponding changes in the nature and characteristics of operations and functioning. Being a multi-stakeholder sector, the influences on the nature of changes in this sector are not just by the rigorous changes in the external environments, but from various factors and players as well.

> The fact that there are various fields of development indicates that the industry development is not only influenced by the industry actors themselves, but also by its structures and institutional surroundings. In turn, the development of the industry shapes its actors and competition structures.
>
> (Bieger & Wittmer, 2011)

Table 2.3 Federal Aviation Administration: Types of Aeronautical Functions (General Aviation)

Emergency Preparedness and Response Functions

Aeronautical flights
Law enforcement/national security/border security
Emergency response
Aerial fire-fighting support
Emergency diversionary airport
Disaster relief and search and rescue
Critical federal functions

Critical Community Access

Remote population/island access
Air taxi/charter services
Essential scheduled air service cargo

Other Aviation Specific Functions

Self-piloted business flights
Corporate aviation
Flight instruction
Personal flying
Charter passenger services
Aircraft/avionics maintenance/manufacturing
Aircraft storage
Aerospace engineering and research

Commercial Industrial and Economic Activities

Agricultural support
Aerial surveying and observation
Low-orbit space launch and landing
Oil and mineral exploration and survey
Utility/pipeline control and inspection
Business executive flight service
Manufacturing and distribution
Express delivery service
Air cargo

Destination and Special Events

Tourism access to special events
Intermodal connections
Special aeronautical

FAA, 2012, General Aviation Airports: A National Asset, Federal Aviation-US Department of Transportation. https://www.faa.gov/airports/planning_capacity/ga_study/media/2012AssetReport.pdf

Prior to the 1950s, irregular transformation was seen in the aviation sector. Since the 1950s, a consistent progress was registered. Introduction of jet-powered supersonic military airplane brought dramatic changes, such as new types of engines, totally different airframes, different on board equipment and new tooling and facilities (Wensveen, 2007). The challenges thus emerged resulted in greater emphasis on research and development. This sector is poised for further development in a great manner as rigorous research and development activities are being pursued at various levels, in addition to the growing needs of the change that are emanated from various stakeholders.

2.4 Types of aviation

Aviation is primarily classified into civil aviation and military aviation. Commercial air transportation and general aviation (GA) are part of civil aviation; i.e., all types of air transportation other than military aviation are included in civil aviation.

2.4.1 Civil aviation

Civil aviation is the largest component in aviation. Over the last several years, it has turned to be the most significant transport system in the world. According to International Labour Organization (ILO),

> Civil aviation has become a major industry in our time. Without air travel, mass international tourism would not exist, nor could global supply chains function. Some 40% of high-tech sales depend on good quality air transport, and there is no alternative mode of transport for perishable commodities such as fresh food or cut flowers.
>
> (ILO, 2013)

This industry is described as consisting of scheduled air transport, non-scheduled air transport and other supporting air transport activities such as airport infrastructure, air traffic control, baggage handling and technical maintenance (Eurofound, 2010). To be more specific, this includes commercial carriage by air transport; non-commercial flying, like private flying; commercial non-transport, like aerial crop dusting; air transport infrastructure, like airports and air navigation facilities; and aircraft manufacturing sector. Civil aviation also includes the Regulatory and Advisory Services regulating the operations. Such agencies can regulate the air transport for smooth and safe operations. Moreover, there are some other organizations that enable the operations from a technical perspective, like navigation services. GA includes all other civil flights, private or commercial. Although scheduled air transport is the larger in terms of passenger numbers, GA is the larger in terms of the number of flights and the number of airports used.

Commercial air transportation, which is all about the transport of passengers, cargo or mail in a professional manner, is the most prominent one. Scheduled services (e.g. major airlines) and non-scheduled services (e.g. charter airlines) are the two major components of commercial air transportation. Major airlines, regional airlines, LCCs and charter airlines are all components of commercial air transportation. This has turned to be the most important form of transport, particularly in

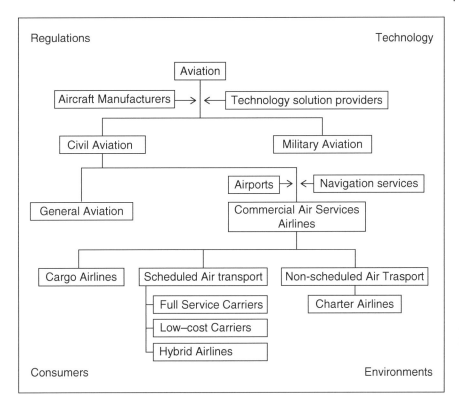

Figure 2.1 Aviation: elements

the international sector, in the post Second World War era. Furthermore, this sector contributes the largest share of socio-economic benefits of air transportation. A country with a dynamic, strong and fast-growing commercial air transport sector is often considered as an indicator of the economic growth and development. Civil aviation industry is characterized by a range of distinct features. It is certainly a transnational industry, though it is firmly anchored to countries. Moreover, it's highly regulated internationally and nationally mainly for safety and security purposes and for economic and political reasons (Figure 2.1).

2.4.1.1 *General aviation*

In addition to scheduled and non-scheduled commercial air transport operations, there are a number of other commercial applications such as air taxi services, business aviation services and aerial applications. They primarily focus on more specialized services that scheduled airline services cannot provide, and they come under the GA category. GA, including air taxi operators, is the largest segment (63% of all towered operations in 2011) of civil aviation in the United States (Shetty & Hansman, 2012). ICAO defines it as "all civil aviation operations other than scheduled air services and non-scheduled air transport operations for remuneration or hire" (ICAO, 2009).

Air transport

This sector involves a wide variety of services. According to Aircraft Owners and Pilots Association,

> General aviation includes flying as diverse as overnight package delivery and a weekend visit back home; as different as emergency medical evacuation and inspection trips to remote construction sites; as complimentary as aerial application to keep crops healthy and airborne law enforcement to keep the peace.
>
> (AOPA, www.aopa.org)

A wide variety of services are included in this category. The flights in GA include aerial application planes, land survey flights, air ambulances, holiday vacation flights, air taxi services and special mission flights. Business aviation, which includes the use of aircrafts and helicopters for business purposes, is a dominant category in this type of services. Business people travel for the purpose of attending work related meetings, visiting clients or expanding and supporting the financial objectives of the businesses concerned. ICAO (2009) identifies six categories in this aviation, namely instructional flying, pleasure flying, business flying, aerial work, agricultural flying and other flying. Details of them are as follows:

- Instructional flying: Instructional flights are used for learning how to fly an aircraft.
- Pleasure flying: Use of flights for personal or recreational purposes.
- Business flying: Use of an aircraft to carry personnel and/or property to meet the transport needs of officials of a business, firm, company or corporation.
- Aerial work: Use of aircraft for specialized services such as agriculture, construction, photography, surveying, observation and patrol, search and rescue, aerial advertisement, etc.
- Agricultural flying: Use of aircraft to apply crop protection products, fertilizer and even seed to grow and protect crops.
- Other flying: A few others are also there, like all GA flights other than glider and free balloon flights that cannot be included in the above five categories.

2.4.1.2 Air taxi service

Air taxi service is common in many of the developed countries. These services are usually small commercial flights holding an air taxi operating certificate, for hire. These services make short flights on demand, and the distance covered is relatively less. Usually, these services are done for short distances. Flights are with a limited capacity, 20 or less. Speed is also relatively less. From a technical point of view, air taxi system attempts to bridge the gap between scheduled flights and expensive jet charters. Air taxis service has many advantages, some of which are as follows:

- No formalities: the passengers need not to wait in queues for check-in, boarding, and security check.
- Quick and convenient: It is up to the passengers to decide when to fly and to return.

> **Table 2.4** Reasons and Benefits of Business Aviation

The reasons and the benefits of business aviation, according to National Business Aviation Association (NBAA), are as follows:

- Saving employee time.
- Enhancing productivity enroute.
- Reducing non-business hours away from home.
- Safeguarding company employees and the business information.
- Maximizing safety and peace of mind for travellers.
- Ensuring management control over efficient and reliable scheduling.
- Projecting a positive corporate image.
- Attracting and retaining key stakeholders.
- Reducing post-trip fatigue and increasing post-trip productivity.
- Optimizing payroll.
- Truncating cycle times.
- Charging the entrepreneurial spirit.

Source: NBAA (1997), reported in Sheehan, J.J., (2003), *Business and Corporate Aviation Management: On-Demand Air Transportation*, New York: McGraw Hill.

- Time efficiency: Usual delays of commercial transportation are not there in this service, and the passengers can be closer to the final destination.
- Personalization: The service is more personalized considering the specific requirements of the passengers.

Aircrafts of single-engine turbo propeller to the business jets are offered in the category of air taxis now. Flights are also used for research purposes, marketing purposes and many other purposes that come under the GA.

2.4.2 Military aviation

Military aviation is a separate aviation sector that is featured with more regular advancements and involving unique aircrafts meant exclusively for military purposes. Unlike commercial transportation aircrafts, some of them are meant for destroying enemy aircrafts and some others are used for attacking with bombs or missiles. Military aviation involves this section of aviation meant primarily for military purposes. It is usually part of the defence systems of the sovereign nations. Countries with advanced military aviation systems are considered strong in terms of defence. Military aviation too has a long history. The first military airplane, the 1909 Wright Military Flyer developed by Wright Brothers, was bought by the US Army for $30,000. Even before that, aerial vehicles were used for military purposes. For instance, hot-air hydrogen balloons were used for military purposes in the late 18th century. But the modern military aviation began only with the invention of Wright Brother's aircrafts. Now a range of aircrafts are used in military aviation. Usually, they are different

---

Table 2.5 General Aviation: Some Factors

- It accounts for more than 416,000 general aviation aircraft flying worldwide today, ranging from two-seat training aircraft and utility helicopters to intercontinental business jets, of which over 210,000 aircraft are based in the United States and over 140,000 aircraft are based in Europe.
- It supports $219 billion in total economic output and 1.1 million total jobs in the United States.
- It flies over 24 million flight hours, of which two-thirds are for business purposes in the United States.
- It flies to more than 5,000 US public airports, while scheduled airlines serve less than 400 airports. The European general aviation fleet can access over 4,200 airports.
- It's the primary training ground for most commercial airline pilots.

Source: GAMA 2017, 2016 General Aviation Statistical Data Book and 2017 Industry Outlook, General Aviation Manufacturer's Association, data available online at https://gama.aero/wp-content/uploads/2016-GAMA-Databook_forWeb.pdf

from those aircrafts used in civil aviation. The major types of them include the following:

- Fighter aircrafts: These aircrafts are primarily used to destroy other aircrafts and can secure the control of essential airspaces by driving off or destroying enemy aircraft (e.g. MiG-29).
- Ground support, or attack aircrafts: These aircrafts are used against tactical earthbound targets and operate at lower altitudes than bombers and air superiority fighters. Tanks, troop formations and the similar are their usual targets (e.g. A-10).
- Reconnaissance/surveillance aircrafts like U-2 and MiG-25R have special capabilities used for reconnaissance.
- Bombers: These are generally used against more strategic targets and are larger, heavier and less-manoeuvrable craft designed to attack surface targets with bombs or missiles (e.g. Zeppelin, B-29 and the B-52).
- Helicopters, the rotary-winged aircraft, that are used for ground support, for carrying assault troops and for short-distance transport and surveillance.
- Unarmed aerial vehicles that are remotely controlled or autonomously guided aircraft that carry sensors, target designators, and for the similar purposes.
- Common transport and cargo aircrafts for carrying troops and arms and ammunition.

For a country, usually exclusive defence division called air force will be there. Their primary purpose is to involve in aerial warfare. Along with defence activities, air force, using different types of military aircraft, engages in strategic bombing, interdiction, close air support, intelligence gathering, battle space management and some sort of transport functions. They also take part in some other duties like rescue operations and providing services to civil government agencies as per the requirements. However, other divisions of the defence system, like Army as well as Navy, also use military aircrafts of different types. The advancements emerged in the military aviation as a result of rigorous research and development helped the civil aviation also to get advanced. During the World Wars, aircrafts were extensively used for the transportation of arms and ammunition, mainly. Developed countries of those times engaged in developing military aviation for gaining the competitive advantage in the wars. The experimental use of aircrafts and associated technologies had taken place immensely and those, later, brought in rapid growth, greater operational capabilities and status as a reliable transport mode. Larger aircrafts, mostly single-engine or twin-engine bombers used in the First World War, were modified later for civil aviation. This trend continued in the Second World War as well, and eventually, all enabled the air transport to evolve as a major transport mode.

2.5 Air transportation system

Air transportation system has a complex structure, and the smooth, safe and efficient transportation necessitates coordinated efforts of all the components involved in it. A wide range of complex tasks and activities are involved in it, which are performed by a range of physical as well as intangible elements ranging from human elements to the most advanced technological instruments. All of the elements do have interdependencies and have a symbiotic relationship among them. According to Air Transport Action Group (ATAG), the elements are air transport, airports and services, aviation services, freight handlers, governments, passengers and manufacturers. Each element of air transportation system is introduced below.

2.5.1 Airlines

Airlines represent the commercial organizations that undertake the passenger as well as cargo air transport services. Different types of airline services are there now. Airlines are classified in different ways. Scheduled and non-scheduled services constitute a major classification. Scheduled services represent the airline that follow a pre-set schedule of operations which are published in advance. The following are the categories in it now.

- Full-service carriers (FSCs): These are the airlines that provide all services as part of commercial passenger transportation.
- Low-cost carriers (LCCs): This type includes a category of airlines that follow a business model that can reduce the cost of operations substantially and subsequently provide air transport services at much lower cost comparatively. Unlike full-service airlines, these carriers provide limited services on board, along with certain other business strategies, to minimize the cost of operation.
- Hybrid airlines: These airlines are the recent addition in the realm of scheduled airlines and their model operation stands in between the FSCs and LCCs.
- Cargo carriers: Some airlines focus on cargo transportation services alone.

There are some airlines that follow service on ad hoc service basis. Charter airlines are of this kind. Leisure tourism, particularly the package holidays, is the primary market base for this kind of air transport services.

2.5.2 Airport

Airport, like a terminal in a transportation system, constitutes a set of essential facilities and services for the conduct of regular air transport services by airlines. It's like a hub of air transportation from where passengers can board and disembark flights, airlines can process passengers for travel, aircrafts can be controlled for smooth landing and take-off, and freight forwarders can process cargo/consignments for shipments. In an airport, a range of associating organizations and businesses are also there for the smooth conduct of the air transportation. Various aspects of airlines and airports are discussed in detail in separate chapters later in this book.

2.5.3 Air navigation services

Air travel needs a fine-tuned support system for the safe and smooth operation. A range of complexities are involved in air transportation. An aircraft while flying cannot stop and wait for information. It flies very fast, and a sudden change in direction or altitude is something very difficult. Air navigation services is the system that makes the air transportation a smooth and safe affair. It involves facilities and services that provide a pilot with information to enable him/her to reach the destination smoothly, safely and in time.

2.5.4 Freight forwarder

Freight forwarder is an agent

> who act for shippers as forwarding agents (though some may also operate their own aircraft) and often consolidate shipments from more than one shipper into larger units which are tendered to airlines, benefiting from reduced freight rates for bulk shipments.
>
> (ICAO, 2004)

They act on behalf of airlines, and according to William O'Conoor (2001), air freight forwarder is an "indirect carrier" and the forwarder is responsible for the consignee for the safe delivery of the cargo into the hands of the recipient and charges the consignee in accordance with its own set of rates. They are responsible for the movement of cargo from the shipper to the consignee by using the services of airlines to carry the consignments.

2.5.5 Governments

In order to ensure a safe and smooth air transportation, governments have a significant role to play. Authorities at different levels, mainly at the national level, are primarily responsible for ensuring the safety, security and smooth services; engaging in bilateral agreements; ensuring the standards and qualities; expanding air transport infrastructure, etc. Under the government, there may be different agencies vested with the specific authority in each area of aviation services.

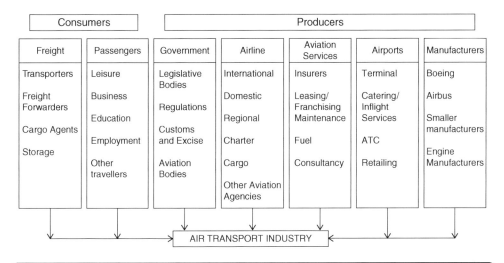

Figure 2.2 Structure of the air transport sector
Source: Adapted form ATAG, 2000. The Eonomic Benefits of Airports; shown in page, 2007

2.5.6 Passengers and shippers

They are the prime consumers of air transport services. Passengers make use of the services of airlines and airports directly and get transported from one place to another. Tourists is a major passenger category, and passengers consume the air transport services to have a good tourist experience. Shippers get the services of freight forwarders or cargo services to transport their consignments or similar items to a different place (Figure 2.2).

2.5.7 Aircrafts and aircraft manufacturers

Airlines are undertaking air transport services using aircraft. Any transport service providers need a vehicle that can carry passengers or any other items from one place to another. Aircraft serves the same purpose. It comes in different size, shape, purpose, capacity, weight, speed and configuration; it is simply the device used to carry passengers and cargo from one place to another. Aircraft is defined as "all airborne vehicles supported either by buoyancy or by dynamic action. Used in this text in a restricted sense to mean an airplane – any winged aircraft, including helicopters but excluding gliders and guided missiles" (Wensveen, 2009). Details of aircrafts and their use in the parlance of tourism are given in Chapter 11.

2.6 Conclusion

Currently, air travel can connect more people and places than ever before. Both passenger and cargo transportation sectors are recording a tremendous growth.

It has a remarkable significance in the world's socio-economic impacts. Being the fastest mode of transport, it is the most suitable mean where time is an important factor. The global economic downturn, the spread of infectious diseases, wars, safety and security issues have affected the growth of aviation at regular intervals over the past several years. Nevertheless, aviation continued to grow exponentially and expand significantly. The constant advancement in aviation technology and the corresponding increase in comfort, speed and aviation safety are leading to the further development of tourism.

Aviation is an umbrella term that represents the combined, interconnected and interdependent efforts of different players. It is divided into civil aviation and military aviation. Civil aviation consists of all commercial, business and personal transportation using aircrafts, which is the largest component in aviation. GA is also a part of civil aviation, which consists of instructional flying, pleasure flying, business flying, aerial work, agricultural flying, air taxi services etc. Major airlines, regional airlines, LCCs and charter airlines are all components of commercial air transportation. FSCs, LCCs, hybrid airlines and cargo carriers are the categories of airlines. Charter airlines follow service on ad hoc service basis. Other components of the air transport system include airports and navigation services, aviation services, cargo handlers, governments, passengers and aircraft manufacturers.

Sample questions

Short/medium answer-type questions

- Define aviation.
- Describe the elements of air transportation
- Distinguish between the terms "aviation" and "air transportation"
- What are the different types of GA categories?
- Define instructional flying
- Differentiate between GA and civil aviation
- What do you mean by pleasure flying?
- What is business flying?
- Write a brief account on aircraft manufacturers
- What are the aerial applications of GA?

Essay type questions

- Write an essay on the growth of air travel and the factors contributed to it
- Discuss about the structure of air transportation system and the interrelationships among the elements within it.

Suggested readings

Cook, Gerald N., & Billig, Bruce. (2017). *Airline Operations and Management: A Management Textbook*. London: Routledge.
Doganis R. (2006). *The Airline Business in the Twenty First Century*. London: Routledge.

Harvey, G. (2007). *Management in the Airline Industry*. London: Routledge.

Rhoades, Dawna L. (2014). *Evolution of International Aviation: Phoenix Rising*. London: Routledge.

Schmitt, D., & Gollnick, V. (2016). *The Air Transport System. In: Air Transport System*. Vienna: Springer.

Wensveen, J. (2009) *Air Transportation: A Management Perspective*, 6th Edn. Aldershot: Ashgate.

Wittmer, Andreas, Bieger, Thomas, & Muller, Roland. (2013). *Aviation Systems: Management of the Integrated Aviation Value Chain*. New York: Springer.

Chapter 3

Tourism: an introduction

Learning outcomes

By the end of this chapter, you would be able to:

- Describe the concept of tourism.
- Distinguish between leisure and business tourisms.
- Analyse tourism demand.
- Identify the components of tourism industry.
- Explain the intricate relationship among the elements of tourism industry.

3.1 Introduction

Tourism, one of the most significant economic sectors in the world, has become the fastest growing industry as well, with remarkable socio-economic contributions. Its history spans over several centuries and, though not been recognized as tourism, similar recreational trips existed since the ancient times. It, along with the evolution of transport, got transformed to become modern tourism that turned to be part and parcel of the modern society as well. It is often cited that tourism is a "major force in the global economy", an "engine of economic growth", a "determinant of development" and a "key driver for socio-economic progress". Countries across the world would like to develop tourism, and it could become a priority sector in the developmental paradigms. Despite having immense socio-economic benefits, this multi-faceted and multi-dimensional activity has been criticized severely for its impacts as well. Ranges of impacts are created on society, culture, nature and economy. The modern form of tourism got evolved since the end of the Second World War, and then onwards, it could register consistent enhancement taking the advantages in the air transport as well. Zurab Pololikashvili

 DOI: 10.4324/9781003136927-3

(UNWTO Secretary-General) has highlighted the growth of international tourism and its significance in the following way:

> Driven by a relatively strong global economy, a growing middle class in emerging economies, technological advances, new business models, affordable travel costs and visa facilitation, international tourist arrivals grew 5% in 2018 to reach the 1.4 billion mark. … export earnings generated by tourism have grown to USD 1.7 trillion. This makes the sector a true global force for economic growth and development, driving the creation of more and better jobs and serving as catalyst for innovation and entrepreneurship…. Growth in international tourist arrivals and receipts continues to outpace the world economy and both emerging and advanced economies are benefiting from rising tourism income. For the seventh year in a row, tourism exports grew faster than merchandise exports, reducing trade deficits in many countries.
>
> (UNWTO International Tourism highlights, 2019)

This book explores the relationship between air transport and tourism. Before going into the nuances of the relationship between both the sectors, an introduction to tourism is given in this chapter in order to have a clarity on the concept of it and its various aspects.

3.2 What is tourism?

Multiple approaches can be seen in the literature of tourism in conceptualizing it. Technically, it has been viewed as a social process emanating from the movement of people from their usual place of work and residence to a distant place for a non-remunerative purpose and engaging in touristic activities for a period less than 24 hours. The UNWTO specifies,

> Tourism is a social, cultural and economic phenomenon which entails the movement of people to countries or places outside their usual environment for personal or business/professional purposes. These people are called visitors (which may be either tourists or excursionists; residents or non-residents) and tourism has to do with their activities, some of which involve tourism expenditure.
>
> (UNWTO/Glossary of Tourism Terms)

The travel in tourism is specified to be from the place of 'usual environment' to a different place. The "usual environment" essentially includes the place of residence and/or work where the usual day-to-day life takes place. The distance to the place travelling to may vary, and the minimum duration of stay in the destination has to be one day. The maximum duration of stay in the destination visited is stipulated to be one year at a single trip.

The tourist visiting a place has to take part in certain activities, which are of touristic characteristics, like sightseeing. Furthermore, the tourist, during the entire process of travel, should not take part in any activity that would enable him or her to earn money as remuneration directly. There can be certain physical or

Table 3.1 Growth of Tourism: Factors Contributed

- Increased political stability and peace among sovereign nations after the Second World War
- Increased dynamism in attractions and product development
- Consistent advancement in aviation technology and corresponding increase in comfort, speed and safety of air transport
- Changing attitude of local population towards tourism
- Increase in accessibility and affordability of transport
- Increased government involvement for tourism development
- Changing demographic patterns and early retirement possibilities
- Better health status of people and increase of life expectancy
- Spread of economic development to many more countries
- Rising income opportunities and increase in discretionary income
- Increasing rate of urbanization
- Rising social status of tourism
- Globalization, liberalization and spread of international trade resulted in an increased level of business tourism
- Phenomenal rise of tourism as a leading recreational activity
- Increasing amount of leisure time
- Favourable visa and other policies related to international travel
- Advancements in information and communication technology
- Escalating lure of tourism and related industries' marketing and promotion
- Emergence new economic giants

Source: Dileep (2018).

psychological reasons, or both in visiting a destination. A variety of physical or psychological reasons can be identified in the whole lot of tourism. These reasons are usually referred to as travel motivators. The common purposes for the visit are diverse, and UNWTO has identified a list of general purposes to engage in tourism, which are given in Table 3.2.

In the parlance of tourism, the person who engages in travel is identified as tourist. In order to identify and distinguish tourist in the whole ambit of travelling, travellers need to be classified into two groups: those for who travel for visiting and those for non-visiting purposes. The distinction elaborated by the UN and WTO (1994) in the document titled "Recommendations on Tourism Statistics" is indeed sufficient enough to decipher the needed differences. According to it, travellers consist of "visitors" and "other travellers". Visitors are those who make a trip for tourism purposes. A visitor is "any person travelling to a place other than that of his/her usual environment for less than 12 months and whose main purpose of trip is other than the exercise of an activity remunerated from within the place visited".

The visitors are classified further into two categories: "tourists" and "same-day visitors". This distinction is based on the duration of stay in the destination visited. A visitor is called a tourist if the traveller stays in the destination visited

---

Table 3.2 UN & WTO Classified List of Purposes Associated with Tourism

---

Leisure, recreation and holidays:
Sightseeing, shopping, attending sporting and cultural events, recreation and cultural activities, use of beaches, cruises, gambling, non-professional active sports, trekking and mountaineering, rest and recreation for armed forces, summer camp, honeymooning, etc.

Visiting friends and relatives:
Visits to relatives or friends, home leave, attending funerals, etc.

Business and professional:
Installing equipment, inspection, purchases, sales for foreign enterprises; attending meetings, conferences or congresses, trade fairs and exhibitions; employer incentive tours; giving lectures or concerts; participation in professional sports activities; government missions, including diplomatic, military or international organization personnel, except when stationed on duty in the country visited; programming tourist travel, contracting of accommodation and transport, working as guides and other tourism professionals; paid study, education and research, such as university sabbatical leave; language, professional or other special courses in connection with and supported by visitor's business or profession.

Health treatment:
Spas, fitness, thalassotherapy, health resorts and other treatments and cures.

Religion/pilgrimages:
Attending religious events and pilgrimages.

Other:
Aircraft and ship crews on public carriers, transit and other or unknown activities.

Source: UN & WTO (1994).

for a period of minimum 24 hours. If the duration is less than 24 hours, the visitor is referred to as "same-day visitor". Tourist can be inferred as any person who travels to a place other than that in which she/he has his/her usual residence, but outside his/her usual environment for a period of minimum 24 hours, not exceeding 12 months and whose main purpose of visit is other than the exercise of an activity remunerated from the place visited. Tourists are defined separately as international tourist and domestic tourist depending upon the country of visit. If the visit is to a foreign country, the tourist is an international tourist, whereas the domestic tourist travels to a place within the country of residence, but outside his/her usual environment. Same-day visitor is also referred to as "excursionist".

Dileep (2019) after analysing various definitions of tourism sums up the concept of it in the following manner:

> ...., tourism is a social process that involves short term movement of people from a place of usual environment to a distant one, staying there for at least 24 hours, and engaging in certain activities that are non-remunerative in

nature. During the course of the stay, the traveller interacts with a variety of host communities and consumes a range of services and products offered by different businesses and facilities that generates an economic activity with positive as well as negative social, cultural and environmental ramifications.

Table 3.3 Categories of Travellers/Trips Not Included in Tourist Statistics, as Per UN and WTO (1994)

Travellers should not be included in international visitor arrivals and departures:

- Persons entering or leaving a country as migrants, including dependents accompanying or joining them;
- Persons, known as border workers, residing near the border in one country and working in another;
- Diplomats, consular officers and members of the armed forces when travelling from their country of origin to the country of their assignment or vice versa, including household servants and dependents accompanying or joining them;
- Persons travelling as refugees or nomads;
- Persons in transit who do not formally enter the country through passport control, such as air transit passengers who remain for a short period in a designated area of the air terminal or ship passengers who are not permitted to disembark. This category includes passengers transferred directly between airports or other terminals. Other passengers in transit through a country are classified as visitors.

Trips should not be included in domestic visitor arrivals and departures:

- Residents travelling to another place within the country with the intention of setting up their usual residence in that place;
- Persons who travel to another place within the country to exercise an activity remunerated from within the place visited;
- Persons who travel to work temporarily in institutions within the country;
- Persons who travel regularly or frequently between neighbouring localities to work or study;
- Nomads and persons without fixed residence;
- Armed forces on manoeuvre.

Source: UN & WTO (1994).

Table 3.4 UNWTO Definitions of Basic Tourism Types

Domestic tourism, which comprises the activities of a resident visitor within the country of reference either as part of a domestic tourism trip or as part of an outbound tourism trip.

Inbound tourism, which comprises the activities of a non-resident visitor within the country of reference on an inbound tourism trip.

Outbound tourism, which comprises the activities of a resident visitor outside the country of reference, either as part of an outbound tourism trip or as part of a domestic tourism trip.

Internal tourism, which comprises domestic tourism and inbound tourism, that is the activities of resident and non-resident visitors within the country of reference as part of domestic or international tourism trips.

National tourism, which comprises domestic tourism and outbound tourism, that is the activities of resident visitors within and outside the country of reference, either as part of domestic trips or as part of outbound tourism trips.

International tourism, which comprises inbound tourism and outbound tourism, that is the activities of resident visitors outside the country of reference, either as part of domestic trips or as part of outbound tourism trips, and the activities of non-resident visitors within the country of reference on inbound tourism trips.

Source: UN and UNWTO, International Recommendations for Tourism Statistics 2008, Department of Economic and Social Affairs: Statistics Division, United Nations Publications.

3.3 Leisure and business tourism

International tourism, from a broad perspective, involves leisure tourism and business tourism. The former refers to the tourism that takes place due to the movement of people for the purpose of pleasure, in one way or other, and to spend their free time. Leisure and recreation are connected to each other. Recreation is all about the activities people engage in leisure, and both the terms are often used interchangeably. In fact, an increase in leisure time itself is a major reason for the growth of tourism worldwide. Business tourism is all about the travel with a business or a profession-related purpose or reason that does not directly result in earning money. Though the main purpose is for a business-related reason, the leisure aspect also forms an inevitable part of it with a varying degree. In a broader concept, business tourism covers off-site face-to-face meetings with business partners, incentive trips as part of rewarding and motivating employees or as part of sales promotion, and the travel for participating in large-scale conferences, conventions, exhibitions and trade shows (UNWTO, 2013). Davidson (1994) opined that business tourism could involve a substantial leisure element. For instance, even the conference delegates, visitors to trade fairs and individual business travellers may partake in trips to local attractions and/or places of entertainment, and experience local cuisine as a way of relaxing at the end of the day after the busy hours. In many cases, business tourist may bring their families along for vacation. In such cases, the stay in the destination may extend for some more days after the business part of the trip is over. The industrial elements that cater to the needs of the business travellers are also the same as those of leisure tourism. They also need accommodation services, transport system, entertainment options, shopping sector and the like (Table 3.5).

MICE tourism is the core of business tourism. The term "MICE" represents meetings, incentives, conventions and exhibitions. In tourism literature, it is also expanded as meetings, incentives, conferences and events. At times, both the terms are used interchangeably also in tourism literature. This broad term is used to embrace MICE (meeting, incentive, convention and exhibition) markets, as well sports, concerts and festivals, among others (Getz, 2008).

Table 3.5 Differences between Business Tourism and Leisure Tourism

---

Business Tourism	Leisure Tourism
Destination choice is not in the hands of the traveller; it depends upon the venue of the event	Traveller has upper hand in destination choice.
Primary purpose of travel is for business, profession or related activities	Leisure and recreation form the prime purpose.
Less price sensitive and higher level of spending power	Price-sensitive travellers. Spending capacity depends upon travellers' discretionary income
The travel decision depends upon official reasons.	Decision to travel is more of personal, with or without influence of family/peer groups
Traveller is the ultimate consumer, need not be the customer always	Leisure is usually the customer as well as the consumer
Lead time after decision is relatively less	Lead time after travel decision is high.
Accommodation preferences are different, primarily oriented to have good accessibility with nearness to the location of the event.	Leisure tourists' accommodation preferences are varied and may prefer that enhances tourist experience.
Travel may take place more on working days	Travel may take place more on holidays
Usually frequent and more experienced travellers	Frequency and experience base of leisure tourists are widely varied
Travel and stay for a few days	Trip duration varies from short breaks of two or three days to a number of months.
Business tourism is less seasonal	Seasonal fluctuation in demand is high
Destinations are generally urban centres	Along with urban centres, non-urban centres/rural regions too have substantial share

Source: Dileep, (2018)

3.4 Tourism demand

Tourism demand, in general, indicates the magnitude of tourism. Though the definition of demand varies according to the subject perspectives, it can be considered as the desire of people for particular goods or services. One aspect of tourism demand, which is more in use, denotes the quantity of people who travel, or wish to travel, for the purpose of visit. Another aspect is that demand represents the relationship between individuals' motivation to travel and their ability to do so (Pearce, 1995). Mathieson and Wall (1982) define tourism demand as the "total number of persons who travel, or wish to travel, to use tourist facilities and services at places away from their place of work and residence". Page (2009) is of the opinion that tourism demand is about using tourism as a form of consumption to achieve a level of satisfaction for an individual, and involves understanding their behaviour and actions, and what shape these human characteristics. According to Goeldner and Ritchie (2011), the demand for travel to a particular destination will be a function of the propensity of individual to travel and the reciprocal of the resistance of the link between origin and destination areas.

There can be energizers of demand, which constitute the factors that motivate people to take part in tourism. Effecters of demand may enhance or suppress the energizers that promote decision to take a tour. Filterers of demand can be there, which consist of social, economic and psychological factors that determine the choice of particular destination. Some of such factors can hinder the demand, although there exists a wish to go for a tour; i.e., they have the ability to filter out the inappropriate. In the general perspective, tourism demand is represented by using the number of tourists. From that perspective, it can be suggested that there are three basic components, which constitute the demand for tourism (Page, 2003; Cooper et al., 2008). Effective or actual demand is the first one, which tells about the actual number of participants in tourism or the number of people who are travelling. Suppressed demand is another category and comprises category of people who do not travel due to circumstances from his/her personal side or from the industry side in general. *Potential demand* category, the first type of suppressed demand, represents the factors associated with the person's circumstances, like health problem, which hinder him/her in taking part in tourism. *Deferred demand* is the second type of the suppressed demand and consists of people whose demand has been postponed because of the problem in the supply or the industry environment. No demand category refers to the section

Table 3.6 Determinants of Tourism Demand

Economic Determinants	Social–psychological Determinants	Exogenous Determinants (Business Environment)
Discretionary income	Demographic factors	Available of supply of
GNP per-capita income	Travel preferences	resources
Cost of living	Motivation	Economic growth and
Tourism prices	Attitudes about	stability
Exchange rate differentials	destinations	Natural disasters
Promotional expenditures	Cognitive destinations	Epidemics
Marketing effectiveness	Amount of travel time	War and terrorism
Private consumption	Amount of leisure time	Social and cultural
Transportation cost	Benefits sought	attractiveness
Cost of living in relation to	Perception of destination	Technological advancement
destination	Images of destination	Accessibility
Physical distance	Awareness of opportunities	Political and sociological
Relative prices among	Paid vacation	environment
competitive destinations	Past experience	Levels of development
	Life span	Degree of urbanization
	Physical capacity, health,	Special factors
	wellness	Restriction, rules, laws
	Cultural similarities	Barriers and obstacles
	Affiliation	

Source: Uysal (1998).

of population who do not like to take part in travel or are unable to take part in travel due to some reasons (Page, 2003; Cooper et al., 2008).

Travel propensity, which refers to the penetration of tourism trips in a population, is considered as an effective indicator of effective or actual demand (Cooper et al., 2010). It is a person's predisposition to travel, which deals with the willingness of an individual to travel, the type of travel experiences traveller prefers and the types of destinations preferred. Net travel propensity (NTP) is a type of travel propensity that refers to the percentage of the population that takes at least one tourism trip in a given period of time. The number of trips a person is undertaking is not considered. Gross travel propensity (GTP) considers the total number of trips taken by the travelling population, instead of the number of people who take part in tourism. Travel frequency can be found out from these, by dividing GTP by NTP. Due to suppressed demand and no demand categories, NTP can never be 100%, but in societies with high travel tendency, the GTP can go beyond 100%, even two to three times of it. There can be various factors that can influence the tourism demand. A list of such factors is given in Table 3.6.

3.5 Tourism industry: the structure and components

Though there is a strong argument to consider tourism as an economic sector instead of an industry, it has increasingly been represented as an industry. It is conceptualized from varied perspectives. Some of the definitions focus on the range of businesses involved in it. For instance, Leiper (1990) suggests that tourism industry is defined as the range of businesses and organizations involved in delivering tourism products. Riley et.al., opine that tourism industry, in general, can include a number of industries, like hotels and resorts; transport; tour operators; travel agencies; tourist attractions; conference business; tour guides; tourist information services; souvenir shops; beach vendors; relevant government offices; NGOs; and educational establishments (Riley et al., 2002). There exists strong and complex interrelationship among the elements. Goeldner and Ritchie (2011) opined that tourism represents "....the sum of those industrial and commercial activities producing goods and services wholly or mainly consumed by foreign visitors or by domestic tourists". Tourism industry involves diverse sectors, which are as follows:

- Destinations and attractions
- Government organizations
- Intermediaries
- Transportation
  - Air transport
  - Land transport
    - Road transport
    - Rail transport
  - Water transport
- Accommodation/hospitality
- Entertainment and recreation
- Shopping
- Hospitality
- Infrastructure

3.5.1 Destination and attractions

Destination involves attractions that have the capacity to "pull" tourists to visit. Generally, it is viewed from a geographical perspective, and according to it, destinations are specific areas, which travellers choose to visit and spend a significant amount of time. A good share of other tourism industries is situated within destination. Transport primarily links destination with tourist-generating regions. Attractions, the vital elements of destination mix, come in many forms, and all such can be classified mainly under two headings, namely natural and man-made. Natural attraction comprises a variety of attractions, and in this world of modern tourism, natural attractions have much importance. Beaches, lakes, mountains, wildlife, forests, valleys, rivers, landscape, spas, etc. are some of the natural attractions. Each destination will have different attractions or will have a combination of many attractions. Man-made attractions are usually the facilities, events or constructions, which are artificial, built/organized either solely for the tourism purpose or for some other purposes, but being used as an attraction for the tourism purposes. Sport facilities, museums, forts, theme

Table 3.7 Basic Classification of Attractions

Natural Attractions

Climate	Rivers
Beaches	Mountains
Landscapes	Forests
Spas	Wildlife
Lakes	Valleys, etc

Man-made Attractions

Artistic and cultural heritage	**Entertainment**
Historic buildings	Cinemas
Archaeological sites	Night clubs
Museums	Zoos
Paintings/art forms	Race course
Art/music festivals	Theme parks
Monuments, etc.	Casinos, etc.
Sport facilities	**Rides and transport**
Ski stapes	Coaches
Tennis courts	Camel/elephant rides
Swimming pools	Railways
Water-based sports centres	Cruises
Polo centres	House boats
Adventure sport facilities	**Shopping**
	Duty-free shopping
	Handicrafts markets
	Hypermarkets, etc.

parks, zoos, etc. can be considered as man-made tourism attractions. Destination management organization (DMO) is there in many destinations. They primarily look after the managing, promotion and sustainability aspects of tourism in destinations.

3.5.1.1 Elements of a destination

A destination involves certain elements that are primarily required for tourism. A number of basic elements can be identified, and they are categorized into a framework of 7A's, namely attractions, accessibility, accommodation, amenities, ancillary services, activities and awareness. In addition to attractions, accessibility is critical in the success of destinations. Accessibility refers to "how to reach" and the easiness in reaching a destination. Efficient transportation system has to be there to the destination and also within the destination. An airport, railway station, bus stand, etc. near to the destination will increase accessibility. The distance from the tourism markets; the availability of various modes of transport; frequency of transport; time taken for reaching, safety and security; and smoothness and comfort of travel are the factors associated with accessibility that contributes in making a destination successful.

Amenities are those essential services catering to the requirements of the tourists. In some cases, amenities are represented as infrastructure required for tourism. They include the facilities such as food services, local transport, information centres, and the necessary infrastructure to support tourism such as roads, public utility services and parking facilities. In certain cases, amenities themselves will act as attractions. Ancillary services refer to the auxiliary or the supplementary services offered at the destination. While some are in the public sector, some others may be voluntary support bodies. There are some private organizations as well. Local organizations are the best examples, which usually offer various services to the tourists. Successful destinations are now making possible activities as well along with the attractions. Engaging in activities is considered important among the modern tourists. Experiential tourism, which is a trend nowadays, demands activities as well. Information forms the core in awareness, and it has to be disseminated efficiently and effectively. The awareness about the attractions should be there in the tourist markets. The local should have a positive awareness on tourism. Destinations should have an efficient information dissemination system to generate awareness about it.

3.5.2 Government organizations

Government plays multiple roles in tourism. Being a facilitator for tourism development and growth, government has other responsibilities as well, like immigration activities, negotiating aviation rights, visa regulations and so on. Such responsibilities are usually done by different departments functioning under the government, not by the tourism authorities directly. Government's direct involvement in tourism has to be for developing tourism by acting as a facilitator and promoter. On the other hand, government also has to give attention in tourism development to minimize environmental damage, cultural erosion and social "impacts". Government takes up a number of functions in the parlance of tourism, and the following constitute the major of them:

- Planning, policymaking and development of tourism
- Infrastructure creation and development
- Marketing, destination image building and promotion of tourism
- Initiate research and generate research data/measure tourism
- Ensuring regular flow of tourists by minimizing seasonality
- Engage in instilling dynamism in tourism, and ensure product diversity
- Human resource development
- Raise standards of tourism services and facilities
- Develop indigenous entrepreneurship
- Promote social tourism
- Ensure visitor facilities are accessible
- Attain and maintain regional and international recognition
- Contribute intellectual leadership to tourism development.
- Information provision
- Engage in sustainable development of tourism through multiple ways
- Ensure visitor management measures in destinations

As part of its functional duties, government also takes up the responsibility to encourage and facilitate the industry by the provision of financial and other aids. Furthermore, policies are periodically formed by the authorities to give direction to tourism development. National Tourism Organization/National Tourist Office (NTOs) are established for the promotion and development of tourism at the national level. NTOs usually have a statutory obligation to promote tourism. NTOs have a position within the framework of tourism authority at the national level, which may be inside or outside the ministry of tourism of a country.

3.5.3 Intermediaries

Tourism is featured with high level of intermediary involvement. Traditionally, this aspect has been there in the realm of tourism. Intermediaries are the persons or agencies that are there in between the producers/suppliers and the final consumers. Intermediaries provide a range of benefits for all the stakeholders in the tourism sector. According to Cooper et al. (2008), the benefits of the presence of intermediaries for major tourism stakeholders are given in the following section.

Principals
- Selling product in bulk and through it, transferring the risk of selling to the tour operator.
- Reducing the marketing and promotion cost by focusing on travel trade, instead of consumer promotion.

Consumers
- Minimize search and transaction costs (by purchasing package holidays).
- Reduce uncertainties of travel by getting reliable information and advices.
- Price advantages by buying inclusive package holidays.

Destinations
- Reduction in marketing and promotion costs, along with the scope for a regular flow of tourists (Cooper et al., 2008).

Intermediaries have a range of roles in the tourism sector. They are not just distributors of products of the principals. In fact, they perform a variety of value-added functions, and of them, the major functions are as follows:

- Providing information on types and availability of service offerings
- Contacting current and potential consumers
- Preparing tickets and/or providing confirmation
- Arranging extensive marketing data to tourism suppliers through databases containing targeted consumer behaviour information
- Minimizing costs of acquiring new customers
- Arranging reservation and other travel facilitators
- Assembling services to meet travellers' needs
- Initiating a repeated use of supplier channels
- Marketing excess inventories
- Risk taking by buying or booking large quantities of services in advance and then reselling them to the individuals and groups (Cook et al., 2007)

Online intermediation is a new trend, which is called as "reintermediation". A range of online intermeddles are there now. Online travel agents like Expedia are having a significant share in the distribution of travel products. Almost all the tourism products are now sold online.

Travel agent is defined as an intermediary selling the wholesome travel products or parts of products or a combination of the parts to the consumer (Goeldner & Ritchie, 2003). A travel agent can be viewed from marketing perspective as well as from legal perspective. In the former case, it is an agent middleman, acting on behalf of the clients, making arrangement with suppliers of travel products and receiving commission from the clients. On the other hand, on legal terms, it is an agent of the principals, like airlines, cruise companies, etc., to sell their products. According to Page (2003), the tasks performed by travel agencies include the following:

- Making reservation
- Calculating fares and charges
- Producing tickets
- Provision of travel information
- Planning itineraries
- Advising clients on destinations and industries
- Communicating and negotiating with other clients
- Arranging travel facilitators
- Taking up the role of middleman when costumer complaints occur
- Maintaining accurate records on reservation

A **tour operator** basically puts together the tour components and sells the package tour through his or her own company, retail outlets and/or through approved retail travel agents (Goeldner & Ritchie, 2003). Another definition, as suggested by Yale, involves more details. It says that tour operator is

> a person or a company who purchases the different items that make up an inclusive holiday in bulk, combines them together to produce package holidays and then sells the final products to the public either directly or through travel agencies.
>
> (Yale, 2001)

Though it fulfils a number of roles, the basic role is to organize, package different elements of the tourism experiences, offer them for sale to the public through different channels and operate the tour as per the preset itinerary (Page, 2003). These definitions reiterate the significance of intermediaries in the realm of tourism.

3.5.4 Transportation

Indeed, provision of adequate, safe, comfortable, fast, convenient and cheaper public transport is a prerequisite for mass-market tourism. In most cases, tourism has been developed in areas where extensive transportation networks were in place and the potential for further development was available. Tourism demand has stimulated the rapid development of transportation, and vice versa. The development in technology has been helping the transport sector to develop and expand. Transportation encompasses different modes of transport. Transport provides the means of travel to the destination from the tourist's place of origin, and back again. In addition, it provides the means of travelling in and around the destination after reaching there. Moreover, tourist can travel from one destination to another using various transport modes. In addition, transport can be a main feature of a tourist trip when the form of transport itself is one of the main reasons for taking the trip.

3.5.5 Accommodation/hospitality

Hospitality industry is a part of larger enterprise known as travel and tourism industry. The travel and tourism industry is a vast group of business with one goal in common providing necessary and desired products and services to customers and travellers. Destinations have to make sure that adequate stay facilities, commonly called as accommodation, are there for the visiting population. Accommodation facilities constitute a vital and fundamental part of tourism supply. The hospitality industry mix consists of a wide range of elements. Hotels, resorts, motels, bed and breakfast (B&B), lodges and home stays constitute some of the common hospitality elements seen in destination. Being a service sector, the quality of the services delivered influences the satisfaction level of tourists. Destinations should also have to ensure a variety in the hospitality sector as per the needs of the tourists. Some of the tourists prefer up market hotels, whereas some backpackers may prefer small-scale non-serviced accommodation units. Accommodation is also considered a part of amenities, yet the increasing relevance of it makes to treat it separately.

Food and beverage, commonly represented as F&B, is part of the hospitality sector. It consists of the following distinct market segments:

- Restaurant market: This consists of restaurant, café, fast-food establishments, pubs, etc.
- Travel and lodging market: Restaurants and other food units within the accommodation industries. For example, hotels and resorts have multiple restaurants and cafes within them.
- Contract feeding market: This includes food vendors and catering services attached to large establishments. Food services under this category are usually subsidized or for welfare purposes.

3.5.6 Other elements

Ensuring **entertainment and recreation** is a major concern for destinations. Leisure tourism primarily depends on the entertainment and recreation options available within the destinations as well. Depending on the nature of the destinations, the recreational options can vary. An entertainment centre itself will be an attraction for tourism, and the best example of it is the Disney world. Cinemas, fairgrounds, nightclubs, zoos, racecourses, theme parks, etc. come under the category of entertainment-related attractions. **Shopping** is getting increasing significance in tourism. It has multiple aspects. Timothy (2005) is of the opinion that shopping tourists "are consumers who enjoy shopping as a leisure-time activity". "Hedonistic shopping" is a trend visible in the parlance of tourism. Shopping is not restricted to the shops in the home city alone, as curious shoppers fly across the borders and travel to far away cities with the ambition of joyous shopping. Souvenir shopping is an inevitable part of tourist sites. Apart from it, large-scale shopping centres are also gaining an increased importance, particularly in the city-based tourism. Shopping malls, boutique shopping centres and exclusive shopping avenues are important in tourism in the cities that attract tourists with the primary intention of shopping. Moreover, shopping festivals have so much of tourism significance. Furthermore, tourism needs a range of infrastructure, particularly associated with the destination. These shopping centres are used both by the tourists and by the local people together.

3.6 Conclusion

Tourism is a dynamic and competitive industry that requires the ability to adapt to the changing needs and desires of consumers, as safety, enjoyment and customer satisfaction are at the heart of the tourism business. With the evolution of transport, tourism has also transformed into modern tourism, which has become an indispensable part of modern society. A tourist is a person who is engaged in tourism and travel for recreational, medical, leisure or business purposes. From a broader perspective, tourism can be divided into leisure tourism and business tourism. In the general perspective, tourism demand is represented by using the number of tourists, and it indicates the magnitude of tourism.

Travel propensity is the willingness of a person to be a tourist, which is deeply rooted into the core of tourism demand. The tourism industry is defined by the range of businesses and organizations involved in the delivery of tourism products. The attractions in the destinations can be classified into natural and man-made. The basic elements of tourism can be identified and categorized as a framework of 7A's, i.e. attractions, accessibility, accommodation, amenities, ancillary services, activities and awareness. The National Tourism Organization/NTOs are established for the promotion and development of tourism in a country, and they are responsible for promoting and facilitating the industry by providing financial and other aids. NTOs are keen in formulating the policies periodically to give direction to tourism development. Intermediaries play a major role in the tourism sector. Online intermediation is a new trend and called "reintermediation". Nowadays, almost all tourism products are sold online. Travel agents and tour operators are the major intermediaries in the travel and tourism sector. The hospitality industry is a part of the travel and tourism industry, which includes hotels, resorts, motels, lodges, home stays, etc. Food and beverage, commonly represented as F&B, is the crucial part of the hospitality sector. Entertainment, recreation, shopping, etc. are the other major elements to attract the tourist to a destination.

Sample questions

Short/medium answer-type questions

- Define tourism
- Write the parameters to consider a traveller a tourist
- "All the travellers are not tourists". Comment upon the statement
- Write a brief account on tourism industry
- Explain the major common characteristics of tourism industry
- Discuss the role of attractions in tourism
- Explain the role and responsibilities of government in tourism development
- What is an NTO? What are its functions?
- Explain why intermediaries are so important in the tourism process
- Explain the functions of a tour operator
- Explain the significance of accommodation industry in tourism
- Give a brief account on tourism infrastructure

Essay type questions

- Write an essay on tourism industry. Discuss the role and relevance of each component of industry in tourism
- Explain the concept of tourism. Discuss how to identify tourists from other group of travellers

Suggested readings

Cooper, Chris, & Michael Hall, C. (2007). *Contemporary Tourism: An International Approach*. London: Routledge.

Cooper, Chris, Fletcher, John, Fyall, Allan, Gilbert, David, & Wanhill, Stephen. (2008). *Tourism: Principles and Practice*. London: Financial Times/ Prentice Hall.

Goeldner, R.C., & Ritchie, J.R.B. (2003). *Tourism Principles, Policies and Practices*. New Jersey: John Wiley & Sons.

Holloway, J.C. (2006). *The Business of Tourism*, 2nd Edn. England: Pearson Education.

Page, Stephen J. (2019). *Tourism Management*. London: Routledge.

Chapter 4

Trends in air transport and the influence on tourism

Learning outcomes

After reading this chapter, you would be able to:

*   Comprehend the economic significance of airline as a global industry.
*   Describe the transformations in air transport.
*   Correlate the changes and advancements in air transport with the growth of tourism.
*   Analyse the impact of IT in enhancing traveller experience.
*   Assess the rising significance of new business models in airline industry.

4.1 Introduction

The evolution of aviation as the fastest and safest mode of transport in less than a century's time transformed the global transportation scenario. Twentieth century is often marked with the incredible evolution of a new mode of transportation that made astonishing progress in the mobility of people globally. Until then, the prevailed transportation modes were evolved over a number of centuries' time. Though myriad reasons stimulated in the remarkable progress of aviation as the most significant mode of transport, the technological advancements that took place at regular intervals constituted the prime reason. Indeed, the transformation of aviation occurred not on a single aspect; a number of transformation scenarios can be identified in the realm of air transport. Once upon a time, flight journey was so luxurious with wider seat for a comfortable sitting experience with lavish food and beverage services. Even smoking was permitted with exclusive designated space on board for smokers. Passengers were permitted at times to move into the cockpit. All these are not happening now. Then, the world has seen many safety and security issues including hijacking of flights and bomb blasts, along with the rise of air transport. Technological advancements at regular

DOI: 10.4324/9781003136927-4

intervals enhanced the speed, range and comfort of air travel remarkably. The advent of information technology contributed remarkably in the evolution of modern aviation. In the meanwhile, deregulation process started from the west which laid down the foundation for dynamic growth of the sector. Air transportation, in terms of affordability, became dearer to the people and more sections of the society started to travel via air. New airline business model, in the name of LCCs, slowly crept into the market of flag carriers and other network carriers. Slowly, the new model got established as a trend setter in the industry which forced the rest of the players in industry to be dynamic so as to modify their strategies to cope with the mounting pressure of the LCCs. All these eventually complemented tourism as well in its progress. The transformations in the global air transportation that have some impact on tourism worldwide are discussed in detail in the following sections.

4.2 Air transport: a global industry with immense economic potentials

Air transportation has become a global industry, which can connect almost all parts of the globe and can generate immense socio-economic benefits. Though there was an attempt to have commercial passenger transportation just more than a century ago, it took many more years to shape it into a proper form of transportation. However, within the past one hundred years, the way that sector has progressed is in an amazing manner. Currently, it is the most important mode of transport with widest connectivity. If the first attempt of an airline was for transporting a single person, of late, millions depend on air transport for their most comfortable movement. Let us go through the socio-economic aspects of air transportation in the year 2017 by the facts given by Air Transport Action Group (ATAG).

- More 1,300 airlines using the services of 3,759 commercial airports carried 4.1 billion passengers.
- There were 45,091 routes globally.
- Air transportation generated a global economic impact (including direct, indirect, induced and tourism catalytic) worth $2.7 trillion.
- Share of air transportation in the global GDP is 3.6%.
- It being a mega business sector, air transport sector generated 65.5 million jobs worldwide.
- Every day, air transport sector supports 12 million passengers to move to their desired location in the most comfortable and fastest manner.
- Nearly 62 million tonnes of freight were carried by air.
- The total value of goods transported by air is $6 trillion, which amounts to 35% of all international trade (ATAG, 2018).

Coronavirus disease 2019 (COVID-19) pandemic has put a dramatic stop in the air transportation's consistent progress. This is a major destabilizing threat to the global economy. Tourism has been hit hardest by the travel ban, the closure of public places, including travel attractions, and government advice against travel.

Table 4.1 Drivers of Change in Air Transportation in the Evolution of Air Transport in the Coming Years

Society	Technology	Environment	Economy	Politics
• Terrorism	• Cyber security	• Regulations on emissions and noise pollution	• Global income inequality	• Bribery and corruption
• Urbanization, rise of megacities	• Increasing human potential	• Resource nationalism	• Strength and volatility of global economy	• Geopolitical (in)stability
• "Passenger identity and fraud"	• Robotics and automation	• Personal carbon quotas	• Price of oil	• Government ownership of airspace and critical infrastructure
• Global ageing	• 3D printing and new manufacturing techniques	• Water and food security	• Level of integration along air industry supply chain	• Strength of governance
• Middle-class growth in the Asia-Pacific region	• Virtual and augmented reality	• Environmental activism	• Shift to knowledge-based economy	• Anti-competitive decisions
• Emerging consumption modes	• Internet of Things	• Extreme weather events	• Infrastructure investment	• Defence priorities dominate civilian needs
• Conflicts between data privacy and surveillance	• Alternative fuels and energy sources	• Rising sea levels and reclaimed habitats	• Concentration of wealth	• Shifting borders, boundaries and sovereignty
• Global population growth led by Asia and Africa	• New aircraft designs	• Human-controlled weather	• Unionization of labour and regional independence	• Growing influence of alternative regional and global institutions
• Shifting ethnic, political and religious identities	• Alternative modes of rapid transit	• Circular economy	• Open data and radical transparency	• Trade protection and open borders
• Disability, fitness, wellness and health	• Geospatial technology	• Infectious disease and pandemics	• Changing nature of work and competition for talent	• Rise of populist movements

Source: IATA, 2018, https://www.iata.org/contentassets/690df4ddf39b47b5a075bb5dff30e1d8/iata-future-airline-industry-pdf.pdf

Several airlines cancelled flights due to low demand. The cruise line industry was badly affected, and many train stations and ferry ports were closed. The sector may progress further once the situation comes to normal.

IATA has identified a number of factors that can act as drivers of change in the air transportation in the years to come. They are listed in Table 4.1.

Tourism has evolved into another global economic sector taking the advantages of the astonishing growth of air transportation as well. In the post-Second World War history, during the late 1970s also the rising air transport spurred the tourism growth. The World Tourism Organization (WTO) (1981) indicated that air transport remained fundamental in the growth of tourism in the America region. Though fare increase was there, the air transport demand in tourism has increased on a year-to-year basis. Developing regions also had similar effect. In the Asia-Pacific region, the air transport remained the principal means for international tourism and the following features are evident:

- Certain routes experienced hike in the frequency of services.
- Some of the carriers could expand the route network.
- Service and scheduling of flights enhanced.
- Wide-body aircrafts became prevalent, replacing the narrow body aircrafts.
- Package tours increased, and low fares and excursion fares are introduced into the market. (WTO, 1981).

The advancements and the dynamism experienced in the aviation sector have directly influenced the tourism to become a global sector. This chapter discusses in detail the major evolutions in the air transport sector, which directly or indirectly influenced the tourism sector to emerge as one of the largest economic sectors in the world.

4.3 Passenger traffic flow: Asia gaining strength

Air transport remains strong in the developed regions of the world, particularly in the north-western region as North America and Europe combined have a large chunk of air transportation globally. Though this scenario is there, the Asian region, which includes the developing countries within it, has come up as a strong contender in the international and domestic air traffic scenario. Traffic flow is strong within Europe; between Europe and North America; and between Asia and developed regions. This can be understood from the following discussion based on a latest statistics. An analysis of air transport statistics is undertaken to get an idea about the trends in traffic flow based on the statistics published by International Air Transport Association (IATA). The following is an analysis of the international traffic flow in a year (2018) using the aviation performance measure of Revenue Passenger-Kilometres (RPK) based on the data published by IATA (IATA-WATS, 2019). The percentage of RPK is taken for the discussion. The largest share of international passenger transportation takes place within Europe. 18.9% of international travel using commercial air transpiration happens among countries within Europe. This shows strong air travel demand among the countries in Europe and that can be seen in the case of international tourism as well, that

Europe has the largest share in international tourism, including in the case of intra-regional tourism.

Europe is followed by Asia, which has a share of 13.9%. The trend reveals that the transportation within Asia has grown significantly over the years, which was not the case a few decades ago. Akin to international air traffic flow, tourist flow among countries like China, Thailand, India, Japan, Indonesia, Malaysia, and South Korea is also grown substantially over the years. Currently, China is the number one outbound tourist market in the world, pushing the US down to the second position. Among intercontinental air transportation, the largest share is between the North America and Europe (12.1%). It is followed by the transport between Asia and Europe, with a share of 10.4%. Traffic flow between the North America and Asia is also high (7.8%), and between the Middle East and Asia is just below that which accounts for 7.7%. Other traffic flow patterns, which have considerable shares, are the following: between Asia and the South West Pacific including Africa (3.7%), Europe and the Middle East (5.4%), Europe and Africa (3.6%), North America and the Middle east (2%), Europe and the Central America (3.2%), North America and South America (2.4%), North America and Central America (3%), and Europe and South America (2%). Figure 4.1 furnishes the air passenger growth since 1970 until 2018.

Regarding domestic air transportation, the US still remains on top of the list with 587 million passengers in the year 2018. Having 515 million domestic passengers, China follows the US. The following countries in the list of top ten domestic air transport markets are as follows: India (116 million), Indonesia (103 million), Japan (94 million), Brazil (72 million), Australia (57 million), Russia (50 million), Mexico (43 million), Spain-UK (International country pairing, 42 million), Turkey (40 million) and Spain (34 million).

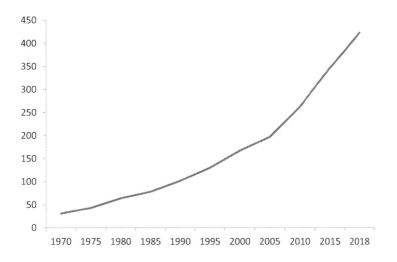

Figure 4.1 Air traffic growth since 1970 to 2018
Source: ICAO, as reported in World Bank Data Bank https://data.worldbank.org/indicator/IS.AIR.PSGR?end=2018&start=1970.

The forecast by ICAO predicts that all route groups involving Central Southwest Asia are among the top ten fastest growing ones, and the North Asia-Central Southwest Asia route may have the highest growth rate at in the years to come. The traffic between Africa, Central America/Caribbean and the Middle East may have growth rate matching with the global expected rate (4.3%). However, the growth rates can be lower in mature regions like Europe, North America and North Asia (www.icao.int).

4.4 "Emerging Markets and Developing Economies" (EMDE) records higher prospects

The so-called emerging and developing economies have been experiencing rise in the living standards, populations and demographics, and overall growth, which are some of the major drivers of passenger growth as well. All those contributed in the growth of aviation as well. New market leaders emerged due to the rising dynamism in the air transport sector coupled with the socio-economic transformations. Countries like India and Indonesia have been facing remarkable urbanization process which directly influenced the growth of air transportation in those regions. Having huge population base, the scope for rise in air travel propensity is immense. This can promote tourism as well, as the rising dynamism in the air transport sectors in those economies can make the air travel economically dearer for the people.

According to Airports Council International (ACI), the mature markets of North America and Europe are registering modest growth levels only and the major emerging economies, such as the BRICS (Brazil, Russia, India, China and South Africa) group of nations, posted significantly higher gains in recent years (Lucas, 2019). Turkey is another potential candidate in the rise in air transport. IATA predicted an eastward shift in air passenger traffic in the years to come. The report of IATA reveals that in the following way:

> The biggest driver of demand will be the Asia-Pacific region. The region will be the source of more than half the new passengers over the next two decades. The point at which China will displace the United States as the world's largest aviation market (defined as traffic to, from and within the country) has moved two years closer since last year's forecast. We now anticipate this will occur around 2022, through a combination of slightly faster Chinese growth and slightly reduced growth in the US. The UK will fall to fifth place, surpassed by India in 2025, and Indonesia in 2030. Thailand and Turkey will enter the top ten largest markets, while France and Italy will fall in the rankings to 11th and 12th respectively.
>
> (IATA, 2017)

From Asia, China, India and Indonesia are in the top positions in the forecast of air traffic until 2036. IATA also predicted that the Asia-Pacific region will have the largest share in passenger transportation in the world by then. Also, Africa (5.9%) and the Middle East (5%) may have the highest growth rates followed by Asia-Pacific (4.6%) and the Latin America (4.2%) (IATA, 2017). Along with the rise in socio-economic standards of the people in the emerging economies, the possibility of expansion of air transportation is very high and that, in turn, can drive the tourism over there, both inbound and outbound, immensely. The current trends already revealed that phenomenon. China has become the number one country in outbound tourism and one among the top five in the list of international tourist arrivals. The position of India has advanced much over the years. Other emerging economies like Brazil and Indonesia are also recording significant tourism growth, matching with the growth in air transportation.

4.5 Technology revolutionizes traveller experience

Information and Communication Technology (ICT) is deeply immersed into the system of air transportation, and as of now, air transport sector cannot function even for seconds without the support of ICT tools. Most of the functions are fully or partially integrated with information technology applications. The ICTs

> facilitate and enable airport operations to take place at different geographical places, to become knowledge based and to be managed in real-time and to be streamlined, whilst also providing self-service possibilities to passengers who are simultaneously provided with additional value added personalized services and information. For airport management, ICT fosters and enables major reengineering efforts and the reorganization of processes which manage passenger flows and airport assets.
>
> (Sigala, 2008)

The beneficiaries of this ICT integration certainly include passengers. The air transport sector is nowadays using a wide range of ICT tools in order to make the operations efficient and to provide increased passenger experience. SABRE opines that

> Today, it is estimated that as many as 70 individual systems are required for airlines to operate every day – that's not only a lot of data, but it's a lot of opportunity for data to become out of sync and inaccurate. With industry standards such as New Distribution Capability (NDC) becoming more widespread, airlines must create an integrated system where knowledge and data can easily be shared across the business. Only then can airlines create a more personalized experience for their customers.
>
> (SABRE, 2018)

The use of biometrics, artificial intelligence, machine learning, robotics and blockchain is transforming the passengers' handling. Artificial intelligence can provide valuable insights to the airlines and provide new ways of working. The use of digital technologies is enhancing customer service, operations and efficiency, and passengers can experience increased ease of travel. According to UNWTO International Tourism highlights 2019, " Artificial Intelligence is transforming tourism, from virtual assistants to companies being able to offer hyper-personalized customer experiences and improve business performance" and "increasing number of destinations are measuring tourism in real time for a better management of visitor flows" (UNWTO International Tourism highlights, 2019).

Intelligent tools are there so that airlines can automate schedule changes between airlines and their codeshare partners, which can be intimated to the passengers without delay using the latest measures. Baggage handling process is being enhanced with the use of latest tools with data science and machine learning application, which can provide better passenger experience. Airlines are now using one-way message to communicate with passengers over text messages, smartphone, or email, or use a two-way feedback messaging system. Moreover, GPS system helps to keep track the passengers as well. Biometrics are increasingly being integrated with portable check-in and bag drop kiosks, security checkpoints and e-gates, which can enhance the smoothness of travel flow and the travel experience. Airline apps suitable for smartphones are already in place, which benefits the passengers greatly. Physical check-in hurdle can be minimized. The passenger identity can be easily recognized at the airports using latest artificial intelligent tools, and hence, the passenger processing mechanism is improved greatly.

Digitization in product distribution has completely transformed the product distribution. The shopping experience is changed. The purchase of airline product is much easier and accessible for the traveller now. The entire service options are now accessible for the passengers to choose from as per their requirement. Even, passengers have increased options for sharing their experience with others which can be beneficial for the potential travellers.

> Development of information and communication technologies has provided passengers more opportunities to share their flight experience on social networks and on-line platforms. Through electronic word-of-mouth, they can exchange their feedback and opinion on the quality of the service and their flight experience. Not only is this information fruitful for future passengers, but it is considered an invaluable resource in the airline industry to assess the airline performance from the passenger's point of view.
>
> (Punel et al., 2019)

The digitization of air transportation provides the following benefits for the travellers.

- Easier product accessibility
- Good airline shopping experience
- Easy sharing of travel experience
- Vast range of information sources for a better decision-making
- Digital check-in
- Smooth flow within terminal
- Better travel experience
- Easy retrieval of baggage
- Wider options for inflight entertainment
- Value-added personalized services and information
- Comfortable passenger handling experience
- Real-time access about flight information through smartphones
- Increased safety and security, including for baggage.

4.6 From regulated pricing to dynamic and unbundled pricing

Airline pricing has been digitized greatly. Once upon a time, when copybook kind of fare preparation was in practice, pricing happened under regulated environments. Things have changed recently. Now, the pricing practice is more or less digitized. The buyer can have a shopping experience while booking a seat to travel from one place to another. The seat can be chosen according to his/her interest. Food and snacks can be purchased as per liking. Priority entertainments can also be chosen. Boarding priority is also possible. Duty-free shopping item can also be preferred. These are some examples. In the inflight services itself, airlines now go for unbundled pricing system. In "A la Carte Pricing", the customer can choose the services needed. It is also called "Menu Pricing" and in which separate charges may be there for reservation, inflight meals, beverages, seat selection/preferences, etc. This enables airlines to increase profitability as well.

Moreover, airlines follow dynamic pricing backed with revenue management systems. Even in a day's duration, the demand fluctuations with regard to ticket bookings are there and the price may be adjusted according to the situations. In airline sector, revenue management is practiced for achieving

> the higher revenue possible through a combination of price discrimination and seat inventory management. Several prices within the same class of service are available, but the number of seats available at each price is limited by estimated demand, thereby exploiting the passengers willingness to pay.
>
> (Cook & Billig, 2017)

Details of revenue management and unbundled pricing are given in Chapter 16.

4.7 Travellers have wider options for product access

As technology advances, travel product distribution system is also experiencing changes and is poised to face dramatic changes in the near future. According to Harteveldt (2016), airline distribution is facing a phenomenal change from the current passive, rigid and technology-centric state to active distribution mode, which is more flexible, dynamic and passenger-centric environment. Artificial intelligence and virtual reality will have role in airline distribution through mobile platforms. Speech and voice recognition technologies may be integrated with mobile-based booking systems. With unbundled pricing strategy, and having different items to choose from, airline websites are now turned to be shopping space that can provide enhanced airline seat booking experience.

Sales agents sold airline tickets once upon a time when commercial air transportation was in its infancy. Travel agents entered into the scene later, and then, they became the prime channel for the retailing of the airline products. By 1960s and 1970s, computer reservation systems got established as inevitable channel in the distribution of airline products. Later, through integration and expansion of services, the computer reservation systems got modified into global distribution systems (GDSs) and their role in the global distribution of travel products became essential. By 2000s, alternative channels emerged like GDS New Entrants (GNEs), and sooner, direct selling trend also began. Online agencies of diverse nature got established as inevitable players in the travel distribution by the beginning of the new millennium.

IATA's initiative of New Distribution Capability (NDC) has already raised challenges for the GDSs and aims to revolutionize the airline distribution mechanism into a modern one. Customers will get enhanced shopping experience by availing product purchase through NDC. Online travel agents (OTAs) are well established now. Metasearch engines too have a role in the distribution of travel and tourism products. They primarily enable the customer to search, compare and to choose the best option, and then lead them to the respective sites where booking can be done. Travel aggregators, affiliates, opaque sites, etc. too have a role in airline distribution. Disintermediation is going on, and on the other hand,

---

Table 4.2 Airports in the 21st Century: Tourists Can Have More Choices Now

---

Airports Council International (ACI) listed the following passenger choices travellers can enjoy in the contemporary airport sector

- Travellers can have increased choices along with the rapid development in new routes, and most of them have a choice between two and more airports.
- In some regions, a large geographic overlap by having a high concentration of airports is seen. For example, In Europe, majority of the people over there is accessible to at least two airports within two hours' drive, and hence, airports may face competition to attract passengers.
- Local departing travellers have more choice due to the hike in the number of routes served by airlines, and hence, increasing number of travellers (on an average, around half of the local travellers on intra-European routes) can have a comparable service at a nearby airport.
- Transfer passengers have increased choices, and between 2002 and 2011, the share of such travellers with a realistic transfer alternative increased from 57 per cent to 63 per cent, along with increased share of the population having the choice of at least one direct alternative.
- Travellers are becoming more price sensitive and better informed, and the number of leisure tourists, who are highly price sensitive, has grown considerably, which makes the market increasingly price sensitive than a few years ago.
- Along with the increase in the leisure travel segment, which has the scope for destination switching, airlines are also willing to switch one destination for another.
- Considering the above, it can be argued that travellers have both a significant and increasing degree of choice over which airport to fly from, and this scope of choice poses a competitive constraint on airports, which increasingly have to make themselves attractive to travellers.

Source: ACI/ICAO, 2013, Airport Competition, Airport Council International-International Civil Aviation Organization, data available online at https://www.icao.int/Meetings/atconf6/Documents/WorkingPapers/ATConf.6.WP.090.en.pdf

"reintermediation" is gaining increasing significance. Currently, mobile apps are gaining importance for booking of airline tickets. In many countries, mobile is rapidly becoming the primary means of booking, and hence, airlines and travel agents are moving to provide mobile booking options.

4.8 LCCs rule the skies

Major carriers, more technically full-service carriers (FSCs), are in the race to cope with the emerging challenges created by LCCs. As LCCs have started getting increased market share, FSCs are also initiating compromises on fares by suggesting competitive fares (Dresner, 2006). The situation of competition between LCCs and network carriers within Europe is described by Fageda et al. (2017) in the following manner.

> In Europe, low-cost airlines have developed an extensive network of routes and they operate in different types of airports including large and small airports and airports located in big cities or tourist destinations. In contrast, network airlines have increasingly concentrated their services in their hub airports. Hence, they run short-haul flights simply to feed the hubs where they offer a wide range of non-stop long-haul flights. To date, low-cost airlines have become dominant on short-haul flights while network airlines are still competitive on long-haul flights.
>
> (Fageda et al., 2017)

Though the LCC airline business model started before deregulation, since deregulation, there was a sudden rise in the demand for LCCs. "Some studies have suggested that low cost carriers (hereafter LCC) stimulate new demand, while others have found that they encroach on the turf of full-service or legacy carriers with negligible impact on total demand" (Chung & Whang, 2011). LCCs caused the phenomenal expansion in air transportation and its market. A wide range of reasons contributes into it, yet the increasing affordability of air travel was the prime reason, which was more or less a contribution of LCCs during those days, just after the deregulation. Along with the demand rise in air travel, LCCs started encroaching the market share of FSCs, and currently, they have a significant share in the overall air transport market. Schlumberger and Weisskop (2014) pointed out that

> Since 2000, the LCC market has virtually exploded, covering dense networks across international markets. Presently, around 128 airlines are defined as LCCs, representing over 26% of all globally available seats in May 2012. Initially bound to the air transport markets of developed countries, a significant push in LCC capacity growth has resulted from the entrance of LCCs in developing countries, particularly in Asia and Latin America.

LCCs focused on point-to-point route network structure, though many focus on operation from base cities, and regional routes initially to undertake flights to compete with FSCs which follow the complex hub-and-spoke route system.

4.9 Upholding hypermobility

The world seems shrinking spatially as a consequence of increased transport featured with speed and connectivity. Locations in any corner of the world are easier to access and closer to reach due to the speed of transportation and expansion of transport infrastructure globally. In this phenomenon, air transport has the greatest role. Even in the history, there has been a small share of a population, who are highly prone to frequent travel. It is continuing, and the advancements in aviation keep on contributing into this tendency of hypermobility. Hypermobility denotes the mobility that is frequent and often long haul due to the growing network of airports, perceived cheap fares and higher levels of education, income and leisure (Becken & Hay, 2007). In some societies, a small share of the population over there may engage in frequent travel extraordinarily. Passion to explore, business-related reasons, etc. can be some of the reasons for such a kind of travel propensity. These highly mobile travellers have a great role in the increasing rate of air transportation, and similarly, the increasing air transport infrastructure "push" the potential hypermobile travellers to engage in more frequent travel.

The enhanced speed and comfort, decline in travel cost and hassles in international travel, etc. augment not only the travel propensity but also to travel more distant places. Globalization and liberalization do have remarkable contribution in the evolution of modern-day hypermobility as transnational corporations and enhanced cross-border trade too intensified the excessive travel tendency of a small share of international travellers. Furthermore, the phenomenal development of tourism globally became another major factor in the remarkable rise in hypermobility. The following are the contribution of modern aviation in the hypermobility of travellers.

- Relative decline in travel cost
- Enhanced comfort in long haul travel
- Remarkable hike in speed of air transport
- Increased travel options in the wake of the entry of new business models
- Remarkable rise in frequency in air transport
- Growth in regional air connectivity within destinations/countries
- Enhanced global connectivity due to alliances, code shares, interline agreements and hub-and-spoke arrangements
- Global expansion of air transport infrastructure
- Upsurge in accessibility, irrespective of regions
- Easy access of flight booking and tickets
- Better travel experience due to the application of latest ICT tools by air transport sector
- Liberal international air transport regulation
- Favourable national policies and easier emigration processes in airports
- Attractiveness, comfort and luxuriousness provided by the modern airports

This discussion reveals that air transportation caused in the increase of hypermobility, which eventually led to the rise of international and domestic tourist arrivals as well. Hypermobility greatly influence both leisure as well as business tourism demand. Tourism is thus a beneficiary of the hypermobility phenomenon induced by the air transport growth as well.

4.10 From monopoly to oligopoly

Until deregulation, monopoly prevailed in the air transport sector. Government-owned and government-operated airlines using the services of government-owned and government-operated airports undertook air transport services. The flag bearers could control the air transportation. Competition was nullified, and dynamism was restricted due to the high-level regulated environment. Deregulation instilled a range of transformations in the sector, and soon, a number of airlines entered into the scene, which could generate competition as well. Some of the airlines could survive the competition and remained competitive. In the meanwhile, in most of the economies, the airline industry experienced consolidation, with a number of carriers merging to form the top carriers that dominate market share, and that situation limited the scope of competition. Still, the situation is better than the previous state. Thus, oligopoly started to be seen in the international air transport sector almost all regions in the world. For instance, "The United States airline industry today is arguably an oligopoly. An oligopoly exists when a market is controlled by a small group of firms, often because the barriers to entry are significant enough to discourage potential competitors" (Segal, 2020). Airline industry is featured with oligopoly. In most of the markets, just a few airlines survive in the long run. The main reason of oligopoly is the high level of entry barriers, which limit the entry of new competitors.

Airline being a high capital-intensive sector with the need to acquire a range of certificates and licenses, it is not easy for a new airline to enter into a market. Similar to other tourism industries like hotels, airlines are also highly labour intensive. A wide range of human resource requirements with extremely varied qualifications and skills are required to man the business. As many of the job positions necessitate high qualifications and skills, the salary/wage to be offered is also high. Too much of labour expense is thus obvious in airline sector. Moreover, fuel expenses are also high. For flying, large quantity of fuel is required. Airport industry, on the other hand, predominantly has regional monopoly, yet larger cities do have more of oligopolistic character. Traditionally, airports are featured with monopoly (ICAO, 2013). Before deregulation and liberalization of the air transport industry, airports are operated in an environment where, with few exceptions, national and state-owned airlines were strictly regulated, with limited freedom to compete across borders. Much has changed in the last 20 years, with the progressive liberalization of aviation markets worldwide. As oligopoly is seen widely in the parlance of air transportation, compared to monopoly prevailed earlier, it is better for tourism since possible oligopoly within the aviation industry offers competitive pricing options, better customer service and the like.

4.11 Profit enhancement through yield/revenue management

Airline is widely considered as an industry with low profit margin. Due to the hypercompetition prevailing in the air transport sector, among the airlines, they have to be tactful in offering the price of each seat of a particular flight. Competitive price has to be provided, yet profitability needs to be taken care of. Air transport is featured with high elasticity of demand. Yet there are groups of customers who are able to make higher rates and willing to pay higher rates depending upon their travel circumstances. Therefore, as discussed above in dynamic pricing concept, airlines follow the revenue management concept. Understanding the demand variation and customer willingness, followed by offering the right price, is that what is undertaken by airlines to cope with the challenges related to competitive pricing. As described by Benckendroff et al. (2014), airlines can optimize revenue and load factors by providing the most suitable product to the right group of customers at the right price at the most appropriate time. By this, airlines can sell the same type of seat at different rates and higher rates can be charged when demand increases. As the lower rated tickets are sold early with highest restrictions, airlines then adjust the prices according to market response. The concept of revenue management, yield management and revenue optimization is discussed well in Chapter 15.

Leisure tourists are benefited more by this as they go for advance ticket purchase compared to business travellers. Business travellers generally get less time in deciding trips, whereas leisure tourists may take decisions much in advance, even months earlier. Yet, business travellers are benefited since there will be some tickets left out for last minute sale though the ticket rates will be high.

4.12 Tickets vanished

Handwritten tickets, that too a rectangular booklet type with multiple leaves, were used until recently for air travel. That booklet had different coupons, including for the agent's purpose, for carrier's use and for travel for each sector in a multi-sector itinerary. Later, a small printout was used when e-ticketing became a norm. Currently, the text message in a smartphone of confirmation of the booking that contains the PNR or a ticket number would be sufficient for a travel. Now, travellers have the freedom of not carrying any ticket and the fear of misplacing or losing of ticket is not there.

It was 1994 when e-ticket got introduced. United Airlines is the first airline started issuing e-ticket instead of the traditional booklet type of ticket with multiple coupons. E-ticket is basically the electronic version of the conventional paper ticket, which contains the electronic record kept in the airline's reservations system. By 2004, IATA has taken the initiative to urge airlines to have e-ticket, and by 2008, all IATA airlines, travel agents, airports, system providers and GDSs have moved an entire industry from the paper age into the full electronic era (IATA/www.iata.org). For some years since then, the passengers had to carry printed version of the e-ticket while they reach airport for travelling. From then, it moved further that now there is no need to have any paper record to produce, instead the digital data only to be provided for check-in to get the boarding pass.

4.13 Highest safety and security standards

Aviation safety has recorded phenomenal progress over the last several decades. Currently, it is considered one of the safest modes of transports in the world.

Table 4.3 Air Transport Safety Statistics

	2018	2019	Five Year Average from 2014 to 2018
All accident rate, per 1 million flights	1.36 accident every 733,000 flights	1.13 accident every 884,000 flights	1.56 accident every 640,000 flights
Total accidents	62	53	63.2
Fatal accidents	11 accidents, 523 casualties	8 accidents (4 jet and 4 turboprop aircrafts). 240 casualties	8.2 accidents per year. 303.4 fatalities each year
Fatality risk	0.17	0.09	0.17

Source: Adapted from IATA 2019 Safety Report, data available online at https://www.iata.org/en/pressroom/pr/2020-04-06-01/

Decades ago, security screening was more of a formality. Indeed, the scenario got drastically changed since the Sep.11 attacks in the US.

> The safety performance of the world's commercial aviation industry continues to improve, with an accident rate of 1.35 accidents per million sectors in 2018, compared to 1.79 for the five-year period average from 2013 to 2017. The safety levels that global air transport enjoys today represent an achievement built on the determination and efforts of the entire aviation community.
>
> (IHLG, 2019)

ICAO acts as an apex agency for ensuring the safe air transport globally. It promulgates Standards and Recommended Practices (SARPs) to facilitate harmonized regulations in aviation safety, security, efficiency and environmental protection on a global basis.

Being the hub of aviation security, a wide variety of measures is taken in the airports to avoid safety and security issues. ICAO (2005) defines security as "Safeguarding civil aviation against acts of unlawful interference. This objective is achieved by a combination of measures and human and material resources". Safety and security remain a prime priority on air transportation now, particularly since the Sep. 11 terrorist attacks in the US. Strict measures are taken to ensure security for passengers, passengers, crews, ground personnel, aircraft, airports and navigation facilities. There were many security-related incidents in the history of aviation of varied kinds, including plane hijacking and bombings. Since the commercial air transportation started to enhance the hard security measures at a uniform level across the world, the rate of such incidents is drastically declined. After Sep. 11 incident, airport security checks made stringent, with efficient multilevel passenger and baggage screening, and changing the inflight security measures like fortifying the cockpit doors, and cooperation between airlines and security officials. Currently, latest ICTs are utilized effectively for ensuring the safety and security in air transportation.

Improved safety and security in air transportation have certainly impacted on the growth of air transportation and on the subsequent rise in international tourism. Transport safety and security remain as essential aspects of the tourism industry. Image of it as a safe mode of transport always prompted people to make use of commercial air transport services to engage in leisure as well as business travel. A small security issue can dampen tourism in a destination. Currently, the hard security measures may make the passengers bit annoyed, yet there is a common understanding among the travellers about the need of stringent measures.

4.14 Hybridization of airline business models

Along with the growth of LCCs, in the new millennium, it was seen that some of the LCCs were increasing the services offered to travellers, more than those expected in ideal LCCs. According to Schlumberger and Weisskopf (2014) "Particularly in the United States, but also in Europe, many LCCs have been 'hybridizing' their models as more mature LCC competition, higher fuel prices, and powerful network alliances have shifted the focus to higher yield opportunities". This kind of airlines which stand in between the LCC and FSC airlines is referred to as hybrid airlines, and the number of such airlines is increasing. A study by Klophaus et al. (2012) on LCCs in Europe revealed that, as LCCs had been facing increasing challenge from FSCs with competitive pricing strategies, they are forced to change or enhance their business strategies, which led to the adoption of a hybrid market strategy modifying the fundamental elements of their basic business model. Currently, hybrid airline is there, which is a blend of LCC and FSC types of airlines. Hybrid airlines is, at times, considered as an evolved group of LCCs which offer higher standard of services to the passengers though many business strategies remain same as those of LCCs. This trend began by the new millennium and got quick market acceptability.

The attributes of hybrid airlines may include "international routes, use of the global distribution system (GDS), codeshare agreements, connecting services, multiple fares available at any time, advanced ticketing procedures, multiple aircraft types, multiple classes of service, interline agreements and long-haul destinations" (Sabre, 2008). In the evolution of hybrid models of airline businesses, the blending happened at most of the areas of business practices like in airline operation, on-board services, distribution channels, customer retention and fleet diversity.

There are many reasons why LCCs go for hybridization of their business strategies. Among them, the major are as follows:

- To expand the market share, by adding business traveller segment.
- The objective of route network expansion into longer distant destinations as well, which needs better services on board, diverse fleet, etc.
- The need of overcoming the challenge of increasing price competition from the FSCs.

Nevertheless, the latest trends show that, along with LCCs, even some of the FSCs are also involved in the hybridization process. Stoenescu and Gheorghe (2017) opine that "f[F]or the moment, 'hybrid' airlines represent either LCCs with traditional characteristics or FSCs with low-cost features, but there is no clear line determining the moment an airline becomes 'hybrid'". Hybridization is still in the evolution stage only, and hence, more specifications in business aspects can be seen in the coming years as well.

4.15 Air transport turned to be the largest contributor in climate change

Though sustainability has been a buzzword in the parlance of tourism as well as air transport, both these sectors have been criticized widely for unsustainability. Over the years, along with the growth of air transportation globally, the emission rates from the sector also got increased exponentially. As of now, aviation is one of the largest contributors of greenhouse gas (CHG) emissions, which have a considerable share in the global climate change. Among different contributors of carbon emissions in the tourism industry, aviation stands out with its largest share (Peeters et al., 2006). Since air transport has been growing, and poised to grow further at a good rate, the chances of having drastic reduction in CHG emissions are less. As the air transport demand is forecasted to continue in the coming decades as well, the concern on environmental consequences of aviation tends to increase (Adler et al., 2013). According to the Committee on Climate Change (2008), if the aviation continues to grow at a high rate, the carbon dioxide emissions by 2050 shall be 7–8 times the levels of 1990 (reported in Adler et al., 2013). It has been opined that the air traffic demand growth is predicted to exceed the scope of carbon emission rate due to combined effects in aircraft technology and similar efforts (Hares et al., 2010).

Certainly, the industry has been taking utmost efforts to change the scenario. Aircraft and engine technology improvement, operational improvements, attempts to have alternative fuels and futuristic policies and strategies are being undertaken to mitigate aviation emissions. According to ICAO, the amount of CO_2 emissions from aviation may grow at an average rate of 3% to 4% and the medium-term mitigation for CO_2 emissions from this sector is expected to be from improved fuel efficiency. ICAO also opined that the so-called efficiency improvement could only partially offset the growth of CO_2 aviation emissions (ICAO, 2010). In the parlance of tourism transportation, particularly air transportation has the largest share in its effect on climate change. A multi-pronged strategy, with utmost dedication and diligence, is inevitable in the considerable mitigation of environmental impacts of tourism.

4.16 Consolidation continuing

Airline industry, the inevitable, yet financially fragile economic sector, often witnesses the consolidation of different kinds. At times, bankruptcy calls for acquisition. In certain cases, competition urges the mergers. Once deregulation started, air transport sector started showing dynamism and number of airlines increased. However, at regular intervals, mergers and acquisitions took place. The first two decades in the 21st century have witnessed sharp decline in the number of major airlines in the US by half. As consolidation progresses, though the number of passengers rise steadily, number of airlines decline, and at times, new entrants are seen, which may or may not survive in the long run.

The need of consolidation in the European region has been presented by Oliver Wyman in the following way

> While the situation is nowhere near the crisis that enveloped carriers in the United States a decade ago when they underwent a major consolidation, the option to consolidate for European airlines today has become not only necessary but also inevitable. Facing rising operating costs and labour shortages for pilots and mechanics, European carriers — including some of the larger ones — find themselves unable to generate sufficient profitability to invest, innovate, and grow at a rate that keeps pace with international rivals.
>
> (Maul & Spear/Oliver Wyman, 2018)

Now, consolidation in the airline sector has turned more common, not only in developed regions, but in other regions as well, particularly in the developing and emerging nations. Consolidation through mergers and acquisition is expected in airline industry at any point of time. The COVID-19 crisis and the consolidation aspects are yet to be seen only. The following are the common reasons behind the rising state of consolidation in airline industry.

- Hypercompetition at national and international levels
- Rising operating costs
- Insufficient highly skilled and trained personnel
- Price war among airlines
- Challenge of raising profit
- Financial problems and bankruptcy
- Technology challenges, including the advanced ICT
- Challenge of fleet expansion
- Marketing challenges
- Emerging industry norms and practices
- Airport-related issues, like the slot availability.

Consolidation is rather attributed more with the impacts on tourism as the consumer benefits of consolidations are less reported. On the negative side, consolidation can reduce competition, which can dampen the scope of decline in travel cost and limiting the services offered. In some regions, it encourages monopoly on airports by a particular airline and may prevent the entry of smaller airlines (Nguyen, 2017). On one side, airline consolidation strengthens the oligopoly in airline industry which itself can have some impacts. "Consolidation and alliances reduce the number of independent airline competitors which can lead to higher fares and restricted supply" (GRA Inc., 2017). There is another argument that the average consumer has benefited from the airline consolidation and the average airfares have not increased (Eno Centre for Transportation, 2017). Economy of scale can reduce the cost of airline services and that can be reflected in the prices. Due to consolidation, frequency of flights to long-haul destination increased. This benefits long-haul leisure tourism as well. There are increasing number of

> **Table 4.4** Consolidation History of Four Mega Airlines in the US since Deregulation

American Airlines

Current American Airlines has become a mega airline by the merger with two major airlines such as Trans World Airlines and US Airways in its recent history. Before that, a series of mergers and acquisitions were held before. The milestones in the history of American Airlines, its merged airlines such as Trans World and US airways are listed below:

- 1986: Trans World airlines took over Ozark, US Airways acquired Empire Airlines, and American Airlines acquired Air California.
- 1987: AirCal was acquired by American Airlines.
- 1987: Pacific Southwest merged with the US Airways.
- 1989: Piedmont merged with the US Airways.
- 1990: American Airlines acquired Eastern Airlines Latin routes.
- 1998: US Airways purchased Shuttle Inc.
- 1999: American Airlines acquired Reno Air.
- 2001: Trans World was acquired by American Airlines.
- 2005: US Airways merged with America West.
- 2013: US Airways merged with American Airlines.

Delta Airlines

In 1987, Western Airlines merged with Delta, and thus, it became the fourth-largest U.S. carrier and a leading airline in the world. By 2008, it acquires Northwest Airlines to become a global airline with major operations in every region of the world. The major milestones in their consolidation history are the following:

- 1979: North Central Airlines and Southern Airways merged to form Republic Airlines.
- 1986: Republic Airlines merged with Northwest Airlines.
- 1987: Western Airlines merged with Delta Airlines.
- 1991: Purchased Pan Am transatlantic routes and Shuttle.
- 2000: Delta Airlines expanded by the purchase of Atlantic Southeast Airlines (ASA) and Comair.
- 2008: Delta acquires Northwest Airlines.

United Airlines

Among the consolidation history of United Airlines, the merger of it with Continental Airlines in 2010 was a landmark one. Since deregulation, it has experienced different types of consolidation with People Express, New York Air, Frontier and Texas International.

Southwest Airlines

Southwest Airlines has been acquiring a few small airlines such as Muse, Morris and ValuJet, and by 2010, it acquired AirTran Airways. Currently, Southwest has a significant market share in the US air transport sector.

Source: Author collected data from various sources.

non-stop flights between hub cities and long-haul destinations. This can cause lessening of travel time and rising of convenience. There is an argument from the side of airline industry that consolidation can achieve improved consumer benefits such as "seamless service, fare combinability, integrated frequent flyer plans and some customised offers"(GRA Inc., 2017). Tourism industry can expect some benefits from it as well.

4.17 Alliances strengthening network carriers

In the post-deregulation era, airlines faced the harsh competition and the expansion, and for the growth of the airline business, they had to adopt various strategies. Alliances were formed "to cover as wide an area as possible, align products and services, networks, and so forth, in order to provide 'seamless' global coverage to all member-carrier passengers as if they were travelling on their own home country's airline" (Williams, 2018). The areas of cooperation may vary from one alliance to another. Code sharing, marketing cooperation, pricing, inventory control and frequent flyer programmes, coordination in scheduling and sharing of offices and airport facilities are the major focus areas of cooperation in alliances. Benefits through economy of scale and scope are also there for airlines involved in alliances. Large-scale alliances at global level enable extended global network for airlines to offer to the costumers. Moreover, alliances help airlines to overcome regulatory restrictions as well to some extent. Airlines become part of alliances due to a range of reasons, including economic gain, like productivity gains; better customer service and subsequent scope for competitive advantage; cost reductions by sharing stipulated facilities and services like airport lounge facilities, terminal facilities, code sharing and pooling; economic benefit through joint purchasing; able to offer service in a much wider network and into more destinations; scope for wider market access; and economies of scale and scope in marketing (Morley, 2006).

Table 4.5 Commercial Alliance and Strategic Alliance: Differences in Agreements, Terms and Conditions

Commercial Alliance	Strategic Alliance
Interline/Pro-rate[a]	Franchising
Mutual Ground Handling	Common Branding
Frequent Flyer Programmes	Joint Cargo and Passenger Service
Code Share	Ventures
Block Space	Full Merger
Common Sales/Ticketing Outlets	
Schedule/Capacity Coordination	
Joint Engineering	
Joint Flights	

Source: Doganis (2005).
[a] Pro-rate is the price or tariff airlines agree to charge for carrying each other's passengers on their own aircrafts.

According to ICAO (2004),

> Modern alliances differ from traditional airline cooperation (such as pooling) in that the latter usually involves an inter-airline agreement on tariffs and/ or sharing of capacity, cost and revenue, which usually covers duopoly routes and provides little incentive for competition or efficiency; whereas modern alliances are normally built around possible synergies and complementary route structures and services.

The following are the focus areas of some of the modern alliances in general:

* Sharing of ICT facilities for the purpose of reservations, scheduling, fleet and crew planning.
* Pooling of air services between two of more airlines, which can help to have a wider choice of frequencies and to maximize load factors.
* Pooling of aircraft spare equipment.
* Purchasing of aircraft and equipment.
* Developing of regional airline training centres.
* Agreements for aircraft and engine overhaul and maintenance.
* Establishment of independent fuel service companies to maintain stable fuel supplies (IATA, 2006).

Alliances bring in a range of benefits. All the stakeholders can enjoy the benefits. Passengers, the consumers of airline industry, can enjoy benefits like lower price, access to the round-the-world tickets at better prices and the mileage rewards on a single account from different carriers. The four general prepositions alliances offer to the passengers are as follows:

* global access through code share and schedule harmonization;
* seamless travel through coordinated schedules, simplified pricing, interline e-ticketing; through-check of baggage and seating, terminal co-location and one point of service contact;
* recognition through FFPs, lounge access and priority handling and boarding; and
* Value through lower fares, simplified round-the-world fares and possible discounts. (Williams, 2018)

Airlines can be benefited by improved efficiency; increasing of market share; increased customer service; and decreased cost through sharing of sales offices, maintenance facilities, operational facilities, operational staff, technology infrastructure, investments and purchases. Types of alliances are as follows:

* Global alliances,
* Regional alliances,
* Domestic alliances.

Global alliances are the airline alliances formed at the world level. This is a network of airlines from different geographical areas. Airlines from different parts of the world will be part of the global alliances. This is formed mainly with the intention to achieve all the market benefits of scope and cost economies from any synergies by linking two or more large airlines. Though many airlines are members in global alliances, some have separate memberships with regional alliances or bilateral alliances. The following are the major global alliances in the world now.

- Star Alliance is a leading global airline alliance started way back in 1997. Currently, it is a 28-member alliance with a vast global network with services to 1,317 destinations.
- SkyTeam Airline Alliance is currently a 19-member airline alliance covering 1,150 destinations worldwide.
- Oneworld was started in 1999 and currently consists of 13 airlines from world over and covers 1,000 destinations around the globe.

Regional alliance is formed at a particular region. These are geographically specific, and the scope of alliance is restricted to the region in which the alliance is formed. Two types can be seen in this category, such as (Doganis, 2005)

- Regional Commercial Agreement
  This includes many routes that are to and from a particular geographic region or country. Code share, joint marketing and sales, capacity coordination, use of other's business lounges, etc. can be the terms within these agreements.
- Regional Franchise Agreement
  This is between a larger carrier and a regional or commuter operator. The regional or commuter/feeder airline adopts the different standards of the franchiser along with flight code.

Domestic alliances are also there in some large countries where a number of domestic airlines are there. ICAO (2004) identified a range of impacts of global

---

Table 4.6 Benefits of Global Alliance

- Airlines can expand their existing markets with little extra cost.
- Expand and develop new markets that were previously inaccessible to them.
- Better marketing possibilities in a wider area.
- Cost reduction through:
  a. Increased market power will result in higher traffic volumes
  b. The synergy of alliance members to share some costs or reduce costs through route rationalization. Partner airlines can share many facilities, like sales office and airport facilities.
  c. Major airlines can benefit from smaller partners' lower operating costs.
  d. Scope for cost reduction through joint purchasing in many areas.
- Reduction in effective competition.
- Helps in bypassing some regulatory barriers, while operate internationally.

Source: Based on Doganis (2005).

alliance in the airline industry. Those impacts are following. Some of the alliances enable partner airlines to dominate in hubs. Small and medium-sized airlines concerned about their survival, which has prompted them to either develop a particular segment of a market or compete as low-cost point-to-point airlines. Some small airlines also moved to form regional alliances to enter into franchise agreements with major airlines. Regulatory authorities' attention has been there due to the potential impact on market access, competition and consumer interests. In some cases, certain regulatory measures were introduced to ameliorate the anti-competitive aspects of the arrangements, like the surrender of a certain number of slots to facilitate other airlines' entry into the market.

4.17.1 Benefits of alliances for the travellers

As discussed above, diverse kinds of alliances are there. Irrespective of the nature of alliance, there are some common benefits for the travellers as well.

- Travellers can enjoy improved services.
- Lowering of operating cost may help in improving the airline services and lowering of costs.
- Easy to travel on more complicated itineraries.
- Easier and more convenient connections.
- Possibility of increased frequency.
- Single/convenient booking and ticketing on a round trip.
- Single fare for multi-sector trips.
- Frequent flyer status is considered.
- Miles earnings can be there, though travelling on different carriers.
- Get access to extra services in airports, like extended longue access.
- Get the benefit of wider network of the alliance.
- May have better chance for travel via more convenient/better airports.
- Transferable priority status, like priority check-in and baggage handling
- Single check-in for onward and return journeys.
- Through baggage checking and convenient baggage retrieval.
- Possibility of having stopover breaks, etc., though it is a single booking.

Tourists, both leisure and business travellers, are benefited by all of the above. Business travellers can enjoy some of the benefits more, like airport longue access, during a tight scheduled trip. While travelling in the flights of alliance members also, both leisure as well as business travellers get the advantage of mile points associated with the frequent flyer schemes. On a complicated itinerary, having a single check-in and through luggage checking are of great support. Stopover benefits stimulate tourism in many cities as some of the travellers destined to move to some other destinations may take a short break over there.

4.18 Conclusion

The air transport is considered as the fastest and safest mode of transport. Taking advantage of the phenomenal growth of air transport, tourism has evolved into another global economic sector. Advances and dynamics in the aviation sector have influenced tourism to become a global sector. With the rising socio-economic status of the people in the growing economy, the potential for expansion of air transport is very high, which in turn helps to take tourism in and out of the country.

The air transport sector is nowadays using a wide range of ICT equipment to streamline operations and enhance the passenger experience. The use of biometrics, artificial intelligence, machine learning, robotics and block chain handles passengers. Passenger identification at airports can be easily identified using the latest artificial intelligence devices, so the passenger processing system has been greatly improved. Airline pricing has been greatly digitized. Moreover, airlines follow dynamic pricing with the support of revenue management systems. With unbundled pricing strategy and different item selection, airline websites have now become a shopping destination that can offer a better airline seat booking experience. Airlines and travel agents are moving to offer mobile booking options.

Low-cost carriers (LCCs) caused the phenomenal expansion in air transportation and its market. Tourism is the beneficiary of the hypermobility phenomenon that also stimulates the growth of air transport. Airlines can sell the same type of seat at different rates and charge higher rates as demand increases, which in turn boosted the airline revenue management. Currently, all airlines use e-tickets to replace old paper booklet tickets. Safety and security remain a prime priority on air transportation. It is currently considered one of the safest modes of transportation in the world, with significant improvements in aviation safety over the past several decades. Improved safety and security in air transportation have certainly influenced the growth of air transportation and subsequent rise in international tourism. Currently, there are hybrid airlines, which are a combination of LCC- and FSC-type airlines. This trend started in the new millennium and quickly gained market acceptance. A multifaceted strategy with utmost dedication and enthusiasm is essential in significantly mitigating the environmental impact of travel and tourism. As the airline industry is a fragile economic sector, the consolidation through mergers and acquisitions is expected at any time. Airline alliances have sprung up so that passengers and customers in the airline industry can enjoy benefits such as lower prices, better access to tickets around the world, and mileage rewards in a single account from different carriers.

Sample questions

Short/medium-answer-type questions

- Write the economic significance of air transport.
- Airline is a global industry: comment upon the statement.
- Identify the changes in the air traffic movement patterns.
- Emerging Markets and Developing Economies.
- Discuss the role of ICT in enhancing the passenger experience.
- Differentiate between dynamic pricing and unbundled pricing.
- Write how air transport influences the increase of hypermobility.
- How does now business models in airline industry influence on the growth of tourism?
- What do you mean by hybridization of airline business models?

- Find out the role of air transport in climate change.
- Discuss the reasons in the continuing consolidation in airline sector.
- What are the benefits for airline in joining an alliances?
- Discuss how tourists are benefited by airline alliances.

Essay type questions

- Describe the trends in air transport sector.
- Explain the transformations in air transport sector and the impact on tourism.

Suggested readings

Bieger, T., Do¨ ring, T., & Laesser, C. (2002a). Transformation of business models in the airline industry—Impact on tourism. In Peter Keller, Thomas Bieger (Eds.) *Air Transport and Tourism*. St. Gallen: AIEST.

Cristina, S., & Monica, C.G. (2017). "Hybrid" airlines – Generating value between low-cost and traditional. *Proceedings of the International Conference on Business Excellence, Sciendo*, 11(1), 577–587, July.

Dileep, M.R. (2019). *Tourism, Transport and Travel Management*. London: Routledge.

O'Connell, John F., & Williams, George. (2016). *Air Transport in the 21st Century: Key Strategic Developments*. London: Routledge.

Spasojevic, B., Lohmann, G., & Scott, N. (2017). Air transport and tourism – A systematic literature review (2000–2014). *Current Issues in Tourism*, 21, doi:10.1080/13683 500.2017.1334762.

Chapter 5

COVID-19: impacts on tourism and air transport

Learning outcomes

After studying this chapter, you would be able to:

- Elucidate the vulnerability of air transport and tourism to crises.
- Identify the impacts of COVID-19 on air transportation and tourism.
- Analyse the measures and strategies taken by both the sectors to overcome the impact.
- Discuss the scope of revival of air transport and tourism sectors.

5.1 Introduction

The world has experienced a worst crisis led by the coronavirus (COVID-19) pandemic that spread so fast across the world. Pandemics occurred many a time in the millennia-old history of human beings. They always led to crises of diverse magnitudes, and tourism sector too faced harsh repercussions of them. Though tourism was affected by crises of varied kinds throughout its history, it could demonstrate extreme resilience to recover to normalcy. It is the case with air transport as well. Despite facing hindrances at different occasions due to myriad reasons, the quest for travel has been growing since time immemorial. Human beings have overcome the difficulties, and the urge for it is there ever. The global corona pandemic shattered the scope and hope of tourism sector for some months, and then, it started reviving and anticipating a complete recovery, though may be by taking a few years of time. We have neither imagined nor heard that the demand of a particular business sector would be declined by more than 90%. However, it happened in 2020. No tourist destination, tourism market or airline is left untouched by the COVID-19 pandemic. Air passenger traffic was declined by 98% in April 2020 due to the pandemic (Abou-Ragheb, 2020). Air transport and tourism were the hardest hit sectors. Destinations were closed for months. Air transport sector was paralysed, except some cargo

   DOI: 10.4324/9781003136927-5

operations. Airports were deserted. Borders of the countries were closed for months. Most of the countries in the world went into lockdown, and movement of people was restricted for some weeks. The world started reeling under the financial implications that are being left by the pandemic. The financial impacts may have increased pressure on the air transport and tourism sectors over a couple of years to come as well. It is important to have a look into various aspects of the crisis led by COVID-19 pandemic. Therefore, this chapter has been structured in a way to include a discussion on the impacts created on the tourism and air transport sectors, the strategies and practices undertaken by the sectors to survive, the emerging trends in the wake of the pandemic, and the possibilities in the near future.

5.2 Air transport, tourism and crisis

Tourism is certainly one of the most vulnerable sectors that are being affected severely by the external occurrences. Air transport is no different to it. Many authors have pointed out the vulnerability of the tourism sector. For instance, Pforr and Hosie (2008) stated "Tourism is an industry which is highly susceptible to negative events and, since there is always a crisis somewhere in the world, the sector appears to be under an almost permanent threat of yet another crisis looming". Evans et al. (2003) are of the opinion that

> ... the inherent characteristics of this service based industry (such as the perishability of the product and the interdependence of elements of the product) make the risks potentially very difficult to manage, because supply often cannot quickly be matched to rapid declines in demand.

Every element in the tourism industry amalgam faces immediate effects of crises of varied sorts. Crisis exerts excessive pressure on travel sector particularly. Due to some of the inherent characteristics of travel sector and tourism, at large, crisis may occur more often than in other sectors. According to Evans and Elphick (2005), "As the travel industry is unpredictable and many external factors can create a crisis, it is almost certain that a crisis of some sort will occur at some point in time. Air transport too has high vulnerability rate in terms of crisis. Air traffic, the most important aspect that determines air transport demand, is vulnerable to external factors, which may include oil crises, natural disasters, armed conflicts, terrorist attacks, economic recessions and disease outbreaks" (Suau-Sanchez et al., 2020). The effect of such factors is quicker and severe in air transport which immediately faces flight cancellations, aircraft groundings, travel bans and border closures, decline in load factors and yields and loss of non-aeronautical revenues (Voltes-Dorta & Pagliari, 2012).

Different authors define crisis in different ways. According to Santana (2004, p. 307), "the literature provides no generally accepted definition of crisis and attempts to categorize types or forms of crises have been sparse". Faulkner states that a crisis, simply, is a "sudden challenges which might test the organisation's ability to cope" (Faulkner, 2001, p. 136). Earlier, Booth (1993) argued that crisis can be classified into three such as gradual threat, periodic threat and sudden threat. According to Santana (2004), based on a Framework of Generic Causes of Crises in Tourism, the crises that affect tourism can be classified into eight categories such as:

- Psychopath behaviour (terrorism, crime, kidnapping, sabotage and robbery).
- Conflicts (wars, guerrilla, civil unrest, disturbance and threat).
- Natural disasters (floods, earthquakes, hurricanes, drought, etc.).
- Infrastructure (over-development and saturation).
- Health (contamination, pest and epidemics).
- Communication (false advertising, Public Relations (PR) disasters, over-reaction and ambush interviews).
- Market (competition, strikes and image/reputation).
- System failures (major industrial accidents, aircraft disasters and transport disasters).

Crisis and disaster are viewed differently; a disaster is a sort of crisis, and it leads to crisis as well. Faulkner distinguishes crisis and disaster in the following way. Crisis occurs in a situation in which "...the root cause of an event is, to some extent, self-inflicted through such problems as inept management structures and practices or a failure to adapt to change". On the other hand, a disaster is defined as "situations where an enterprise (or collection of enterprises in the case of a tourist destination) is confronted with sudden unpredictable catastrophic changes over which it has little control" (Faulkner, 2001). Here, we face a health-related disaster which generated a grave crisis having wide varied dimensions. It is imperative to have efficient management to overcome the consequences of crises of all sorts.

Dealing with crisis is not an easy task. "When a crisis occurs, it usually arrives as a barrage of urgent, unexpected and unpleasant events, allowing little time to organize or plan appropriate responses" (Nathan, 2000, p. 12). Managing a crisis needs anticipation, plans and strategies. It is not easy to prevent a crisis. Rather precautions can be taken effectively. Certainly, crisis management aims to minimize the impacts and to take initiatives for recovery. Santana (2004, p. 308) defines crisis management as

> an ongoing integrated and comprehensive effort that organizations effectively put into place in an attempt to first and foremost understand and prevent crisis, and to effectively manage those that occur, taking into account in each and every step of their planning and training activities, the interest of their stakeholders.

When an extraordinary crisis occurs, there may not be adequate time to respond even with traditional strategies (Wenzel et al., 2020). This is what happened with COVID-19 crisis as well. Things turned out of hands within days as the virus could spread so fast. The world has surpassed different stages of the pandemic-induced crisis now, and the recovery process began. COVID-19 crisis, impacts and strategies are discussed below in air transport and tourism separately.

5.3 Air transport sector

Air transport sector was clueless in the beginning. Initial steps were to take measures to prevent the spread of the disease through air travel. Travel restrictions were imposed, as suggested by World Health Organization in the beginning.

Social distancing measures, touch-free passenger processing, use of masks and gloves, regular cleaning and disinfecting, etc., were introduced on urgent basis. Airlines and airports had to adapt quickly to the emerging situation in the wake of corona. Sooner, the industry started to face the pinch of the crisis. Flights remained landed, and passenger movement was stopped almost completely. Very soon, financial crises loomed large over the sector. Day-to-day survival went into crisis. Airlines and airports had to survive somehow. In order to ensure health protocols to prevent the spread of the virus, airports particularly had to find out source to meet additional costs like that for cleaning, ensuring social distance, etc. According to Albers and Rundshagen (2020), airlines engaged in one or more of the typical response strategies, which consist of entering into any "response path" through a sequential order; engaging a hybrid strategy; and availing financial assistance from the government.

- The "response paths" are as follows: immediately engage in retrenchment by drastic cost reduction before embarking into other directions; move from retrenchment to exit; and enter into a sequence of proceeding from short- and long-term cost-cutting to persevering.
- Hybrid strategies: airlines engaged in different strategies simultaneously, like engaging in cost reduction measures, amassing financial persevering and engaging in innovation like converting passenger aircraft into freight carriers.
- Role by national governments: governments attempted in backing up some of the airlines and supported them their efforts in undertaking persevering and innovating strategies.

According to Serrano and Kazda (2020), the essential aspects being followed by airports with regard to financial sustainability include deferring non-essential expenditure, avoiding non-critical recruitment, managing with suppliers to ensure cost-saving solutions in place, minimizing non-essential contracts, closing or scaling down non-operational areas and entertaining outsourcing on possible non-core services. Other aspects to take care of include integration of biometric and self-service process, capabilities to minimize human-to-human interactions and enhanced coordination with stakeholders in envisaging vision and strategies. From a long-term perspective, let the airports be increasingly capable to handle crises of varied sorts.

5.4 Impacts of COVID-19 crisis

Wide ranges of impacts were there in the air transport sector. Sudden decline in demand led to acute financial crisis in the sector. Increasing rate of job loss became a major concern as the number is being estimated in millions. Stark decline in revenue turned to be another major concern. These aspects are discussed further below.

5.4.1 Plummeting demand

The primary issues airports faced due to the pandemic are lowest demand levels, costly health regulations and airlines and tenants failing to pay their bills on time (Serrano & Kazda, 2020). International Civil Aviation Association (ICAO) estimated that the impact on global scheduled passenger traffic based on the anticipated figures reveals that there could be an overall reduction ranging from 50% to 52% of airline seats, reduction of 2,875 to 2,978 million passengers and loss of gross passenger operating revenues by approximately $386 to 399 billion in the year 2020 (ICAO, 2020). The impact of the pandemic on air transport demand, based on International Air Transport Association's (IATA) reports from the beginning of 2020 until the end of the first three quarters of the year, is summarized as follows. In January, the demand for air transport rose by 2.5% compared to January 2019, down from 3.7% growth the previous month. In February, IATA predicted a potential 13% full-year loss of passenger demand for carriers in the Asia-Pacific region. In the same month, the global passenger traffic data measured in total revenue passenger kilometres fell 14.1% compared to the same month in the previous year (IATA Press Releases, 2020).

By March, the demand recorded the lowest level till that era, and it declined by 52.9% compared to the year-ago period. By April, the demand plunged 94.3%, an unprecedented fall since 1990. Still, a ray of hope was there in domestic travel as it slightly progressed towards the end of April and the daily flight totals rose 30% by then. Further decline was there later in international passenger demand, which fell 98.3% in the month of May. Domestic market in China started rising. The trend continued, though with slight change as the demand fell by 79.8% compared to the same month in the previous year. By this time, domestic market has registered slight improvement mainly in China and Russia. Market reopening in

Figure 5.1 Impact of COVID-19. Deserted North Terminal of Gatwick Airport in the month of July 2020
Source: Wikipedia Commons.

the Schengen Area caused an increase in international demand in Europe alone. Passenger demand in August continued to be at low level, registering a fall of 75.3% compared to August 2019. Domestic markets have shown a comparative progress in terms of recovery in passenger demand. By this time, the traffic forecast for 2020 was downgraded by IATA due to the experience of weaker-than-expected recovery; the full-year traffic was reported to be down 66% compared to 2019 (IATA Press Releases, 2020).

5.4.2 Loss of jobs

As pandemic erupted and the operations faced a standstill, air transport sector had little choice than to reduce the workforce. As far as the sector is concerned, labour cost is a major share in the overall cost in this sector. Airport Council International (ACI), citing the Air Transport Action Group (ATAG), revealed that by the end of the third quarter of 2020, the downward trend in traffic resulted in a loss of up to 46 million jobs normally supported by aviation around the globe. It also predicted that the recovery of air transport sector to the pre-COVID levels will not take place until around 2024 (www.aci.aero). In the month of April 2020, IATA came out with a job loss estimate, showing some 25 million jobs were at risk of disappearing due to the plummeting demand for air travel. It also suggested that the second quarter would be the most critical with demand falling 70% at its worst point, and airlines burning through $61 billion in cash. The break-up of the employment loss scenario is listed as follows (IATA Press Releases, 2020):

- 11.2 million jobs in Asia-Pacific.
- 5.6 million jobs in Europe.
- 2.9 million jobs in Latin America.
- 2.0 million jobs in North America.
- 2.0 million jobs in Africa.
- 0.9 million jobs in the Middle East.

5.4.3 Revenue decline

In February 2020, IATA reported that carriers outside Asia-Pacific are forecast to bear a revenue loss of $1.5 billion, and the total global loss of revenue could be $29.3 billion. In the next month, it is reported that the losses from passenger business could range between $63 billion (in a scenario where COVID-19 is contained in current markets with over 100 cases as of 2 March) and $113 billion (in a scenario with a broader spreading of COVID-19). Later, in the same month, it was estimated that the passenger revenues could plummet $252 billion or 44% below the previous year's figure. By 14 April, IATA reported a revenue drop by $314 billion in 2020, a 55% decline compared to 2019. Later, on 9 June, it released a financial outlook for the global air transport industry which revealed that airlines are expected to lose $84.3 billion in 2020 for a net profit margin of -20.1%. Moreover, revenues are expected to fall by 50% to $419 billion from $838 billion in 2019. In addition, it estimated that in 2021, losses are expected to be cut to $15.8 billion as revenues rise to $598 billion (IATA Press Releases, 2020).

5.4.4 Financial support

As air transport sector faced the worst crisis ever, many of the governments offered financial support as a lending hand to the air transport sector, particularly to the airlines. The financial support by the government is seen in diverse ways. In the air transport sector, akin to other industrial sectors, airlines are approaching the governments for financial support as bailout packages, loans at preferred conditions/state guarantees, subsidies (Albers & Rundshagen, 2020), moratorium for repayment of bank loans, financial assistance, tax evasions, etc. A summary of the financial supports given by various governments during the initial stages of COVID-19 crisis, as reported by IATA (IATA Press Releases, 2020), is as follows:

- Brazil had ensured a number of supporting measures which include postponing of the payment of air navigation fees by airlines by half a year, deferment of airport concession fee payments by private airport operators until the end of the year, permission for more flexibility in the time frame of refunding tickets for cancelled flights, attempt for a special credit line to support airlines' financial liquidity and attempt for waiving the minimum 80% slot usage rule for airlines for a period of time.
- Australia announced an A$715 million (US$430 million) aid package comprising refunds and forward waivers on fuel taxes, and domestic air navigation and regional aviation security charges.
- China initiated a number of measures, including reductions in landing, parking and air navigation charges as well as subsidies for airlines that continued to mount flights to the country.
- Hong Kong provided a total relief package valued at HK$2.6 billion (US$335 million) for the airport community including waivers on airport charges and certain licensing fees; rent reductions for aviation services providers, etc.
- New Zealand intended to open a NZ$900 million (US$580 million) loan facility to the national carrier along with an additional NZ$600 million relief package for the aviation sector.
- Norway provided a conditional state loan guarantee for its aviation industry totalling US$533 million.
- Qatar provided support to its national carrier.
- Singapore undertook relief measures valued at S$112 million (US$82 million) that consists of rebates on airport charges, assistance to ground handling agents and rental rebates at Changi Airport.
- Sweden and Denmark announced $300m in state loan guarantees for their airlines.
- Colombia provided significant share of tax relief for airline tickets, jet fuel and tourism to their already comprehensive package of relief measures.
- Senegal initiated US$128 million in relief for the tourism and air transport sectors.
- Seychelles waived all landing and parking fees for a short period of time.
- The 41 Eurocontrol states and their air navigation service providers (ANSPs) deferred air navigation service charges worth EUR1.1 billion and terminal charges valuing more than EUR190 million, for a similar period.

5.5 "New normal" in air transport: trends and strategies

COVID-19 induced changes in almost all spheres of life. Businesses have to adapt themselves to face the new normal in the wake of COVID-19 repercussions. The new normal is defined by the urbandictionary.com as "The current state of being after some dramatic change has transpired. What replaces the expected, usual, typical state after an event occurs. The new normal encourages one to deal with current situations rather than lamenting what could have been". Indeed, travel and tourism sectors have to modify their business processes to accommodate the patterns of new normal and a range of new practices and solutions are put in place to get adapted to the new situations in the post-COVID era. Crisis response strategies were different for different airlines, though there were common approaches. Four types of strategic crisis response categories are identified, which involve retrenchment, persevering, innovating and exit (Albers & Rundshagen, 2020; Wenzel et al., 2020), that are briefly introduced below.

- Retrenchment: cost, overhead and/or asset reductions in order to survive in short run.
- Persevering: this is more of a medium-run response strategy, and efforts like debt financing are taken to preserve pre-crisis situation of the firm and its activities.
- Innovating: strategic renewal through various measures that may lead to irrevocable changes in the business.
- Exit: it can be forced exit due to lack of scope of recovery or to discontinue as a strategic response to the ongoing crisis.

Air transport sector is forced to use maximum the latest information and communication technology-based solutions in passenger handling, security checks and smooth operations in order to ensure contactless services and acceleration of latest biometric technologies (Serrano & Kazda, 2020) including facial recognition in airports. Moreover, airports also focus on increasing non-traffic revenue (Serrano & Kazda, 2020). According to Albers and Rundshagen (2020), as part of strategic innovation, airlines attempted to ensure a series of measures, which includes converting passenger aircraft into freight carriers, engages in strategic moves like preparations for joint ventures, entering new markets, or establishing joint ventures, which can ensure improvements in strategic position in the long term. Expanding into new markets after crisis, sell out or retire a section of the fleet (fleet cut), engage in price competition, engage in cost reduction strategies and minimizing cash-burn tactics, innovative moves like converting passenger aircraft into cargo carries, etc., are visible in the airline industry. Some of the airlines could involve in the transporting medical supplies when pandemic started to spread. There was severe shortage of medical supplies including medicines, equipment like ventilators, personal protective equipment (PPE) for the medical staff, etc. As the airline industry turned to the national governments for financial supports, many of them responded positively by offering bailout packages, loans, tax waiving periods, loan repayment moratoriums, etc. Some of the governments laid out clear-cut conditions in lending financial support which was accepted by the most, but some were reluctant to adhere to those conditions.

In the pandemic period, it has been visible that carriers become open to bypassing major hubs, thus moving away from the traditional route and network structure, and instead focused on city pairs that could yield well (Bauer et al., 2020; Bloch, 2020). **Ultra long-haul (ULH)** services are gaining increasing significance in the emerging situation of pandemic and are highly preferable for corporate travellers (Bauer et al., 2020). ULH services "seek to directly connect cities in far reaching corners of the earth, leveraging the enhanced capabilities of new-age aircraft, thereby saving time-sensitive passengers hours of total travel-time when compared to a traditional one-stop, Hub & Spoke itinerary" (Bloch, 2020, p. 8). According to Bauer et al. (2020), the advantages of ULH include the following:

- It is an ideal option for the time-sensitive traveller.
- It simplifies operations, removing the need to stop over in foreign countries.
- It eliminates the financial and environmental burden of an additional take-off and landing.
- It provides a scope to generate product differentiation from competitors.
- Heightened level of efficiency.
- More premium and exclusive on-board product.
- Improved levels of privacy and safety.
- Shorter total travel time.
- Overall higher product quality level.
- Premium economy class of it offers affordable upgraded service option.
- Passengers can bypass busy international hub airports.

IATA urged the governments to take adequate measures in ensuring speedy transportation of vaccines for COVID-19 to be transported to the nook and corner of the world as and when it is ready. A well-established global time- and temperature-sensitive distribution system is inevitable for the same, and airlines have been engaging in the similar activity for several decades. However, this time, the requirement is extremely high.

Digital revolution is taking place in passenger handling. Technology enhancement can help airlines to cope with the new normal. Paperless process and advanced biometric technology solutions can be integrated in ensuring minimum passenger contact. A range of new initiatives are done to ensure minimum contact with passengers during service delivery. Biometrics is used for faster check-in process, self-service biometric-enabled baggage drop and facial recognition. Virtual reality (VR) and immersive experiences are integrated in in-flight entertainment systems. Voice recognition technology is being utilized by airlines as well, for voice check-in, etc. Airlines are planning to have in-flight Internet connectivity as well. Experiments are in place to integrate blockchain technology for enhancing operational efficiency, security and passenger experience. Artificial intelligence (AI) is used for voice-activated digital assistance and predictive analysis and is used as a recognition tool. Robotics is also being used for varied activities. Airlines also make use of chatbots and AI-powered chat platforms to interact with passengers. Internet of things and big data and analytics are also having applications in airline sector. Mobile applications are effectively used by airlines to have real-time information, and airlines can be in touch with passengers in order to make their travel more enjoyable.

Countries are engaged to form **travel bubbles** to have a safer air traffic flow between those countries. Two or more countries engage into agreements in order to have restricted flow of passengers among them during the COVID-19 period. According to the Ministry of Civil Aviation, Government of India, the travel bubble represents "temporary arrangements between two countries aimed at restarting commercial passenger services when regular international flights are suspended as a result of the COVID-19 pandemic. They are reciprocal in nature, meaning airlines from both countries enjoy similar benefits" (MOCA, 2020). This was formed with the intention to have regular flow of passengers between those countries when the international borders were closed for air transportation to other countries.

Airports too faced severe consequences of the pandemic. "The financial impact on airports is massive and it will take several years to regain what was lost during the COVID-19 standstill period" (Serrano & Kazda, 2020). ACI has summarized the estimated impacts in the ACI Advisory Bulletin (August 2020) with the following highlights. Airport sector anticipates a 59.6% reduction in passenger volumes in the year 2020 compared to the pre-COVID-19 forecast for 2020 and a 58.4% reduction in passengers as compared to 2019. In total, the reduction in passengers may be around 5.6 billion for the year. Revenue decline may be up to 60% and $10.3 and $39.5 billion in Q1 and Q2 of 2020, respectively, compared to the projected baseline. In terms of revenue shortfall, $104.5 billion reduction in revenue for 2020 is estimated (ACI, 2020). Airports have to integrate digital technology, sense the emerging situations, reposition in the global aviation sector, improve airline connectivity with more cities, engage in customer retention practices, engage in strategies at expanding market share, be proactive, etc. When passenger demand faced worst crisis, airports had little choice than to maintain their operations to facilitate important movement such as repatriation and cargo flights, as well as to support airlines by providing certain area to use as new aircraft parking positions (Serrano & Kazda, 2020). Many airports closed some sections of operations and engaged in revaluating the airport capital expenditure to reduce the cost to a minimum (Serrano & Kazda, 2020). Another strategy is to resize the available infrastructure at landside, terminal as well as airside, matching the new demand situations. Some airports reduced operations to a part of the terminal or in one terminal alone where multiple terminals are in service. According to Abou-Ragheb (2020), the following are the changes happening in airports:

- Rapid adoption of better design and technology features.
- Biometric technology, including facial recognition, is rapidly being adopted by airports, and it not only enhances speedier and smoother passenger handling, but also ensures minimum passenger interaction and human touching.
- COVID-19 is likely to prompt long-term changes to airport design.
- Automated screening systems that can screen the hand luggage without human touch and the check-in duration can be reduced greatly.
- Airports turned increasingly cleaner and follow new hygiene habits.

Table 5.1 Airports: Strategies and Measures for Post-COVID-19

According to Serrano and Kazda (2020), the following are some of the major strategies and measures that can be undertaken by the airport sector to face the pandemic-induced challenges to strive ahead.

Financial decisions

- Defer or avoid infrastructural investment and optimize existing infrastructure.
- Review the budgets to reduce operational cost.
- Engage in planning and improved process aimed at future operations when normalcy starts gaining.

Revenue increase measures

Take measures to increase aeronautical and non-aeronautical revenue options. Strategies:

- Increase market share and increase aeronautical revenue.
- Ensure non-aeronautical revenue through rent from commercial services and concessionaries.
- Enhance the quality of services, sanitized environment, customer loyalty and passenger experience.

Financial support

- Liaison for economic, financial and fiscal relief measures with authorities and government.

Diversify

- Diversify the business options in airports and more commercial airline services including cargo movements.
- Create common funds for government incentives and public agencies.
- Ensure airlines are having increased support from local stakeholders in participating in the development of continuous demand in the possible manner.

Review the debt profile to ensure the business continuity.

- If needed, go for refinancing and readjusting the original terms of the debt to facilitate repayment.
- Review concessionary contracts and agreements in the wake of the crisis.
- Carry out cost-benefit studies of the entire impact of an airport, both directly and induced in the region.
- Go for cost optimization plans.

Optimize commercial contracts in terminal – food and beverage and airport retail in order to have increased sales potential for them and in ensuring accountability and transparency.

Table 5.1 (Continued)

Automate – digitalize process

- Have latest technology for digital identity using biometrics, business, sustainability, customer support, security, environmental integration and smart service management initiatives.
- Use technology for smart operations and maintenance management, using video analytics, the Internet of things and autonomous vehicles and handling.

Review service levels with providers of services, ensure quality services with the outsourced service providers within airports, renegotiate payments to the government regarding concession fees and space rent, attempt airport concessionaire joint ventures, outsource some of the non-core activities

Manpower preparedness post-COVID-19 operations

- Due to possibilities of spread of disease, either ensure alternative suppliers who can take over the duties of the critical functions or reduce the number of required staff to skeleton mode.
- Ensure proper training for staff to handle the situation in the new normal.

Source: Adapted from Serrano and Kazda (2020).

Now, robots are increasingly used in airports, and their significance increased since the pandemic started spreading globally. One innovative use of robot now is for disinfecting the airport parts. It was reported that the Gerald R. Ford International Airport (Michigan, USA) was used as a test site for a new autonomous robot that disinfects using ultraviolet (UV) technology (Security Magazine, 2020). That UVD Robot, which is to be implemented in areas such as baggage claim and the security checkpoint, is a novel mobile platform for UV technology that can destroy effectively the bacteria, viruses and fungi or pathogens by emitting concentrated UVC light onto all touch services. Ultraviolet Footwear Sanitizing Station; Pod for sanitizing wheelchairs and luggage trolleys and Chamber that will allow guests to disinfect their phones, tablets, keys, etc. are also there nowadays. Hong Kong International Airport (HKIA) has introduced an Intelligent Sterilization Robot which is kitted with UV sterilizer and air sterilizer and maintains the public toilets, as well as crucial operating areas within airport (Hardingham-Gill, 2020). It, according to the above report, has also established a full-body disinfection booth that contains antimicrobial coating, which can remotely kill any viruses and/ or bacteria found on clothing, as well as the body, by using photocatalyst advances along with "nano-needles".

In the meanwhile, airports are urged to use automated software, termed crowd monitoring software, to ensure health precautions and enhance efficiency, profitability and passenger experience. Some of the available software can process live video from commercial off-the-shelf (COTS) cameras and simultaneously analyse passenger flows with the help of advanced AI techniques (Airport Technology/

www.airporttechnology.com). They can analyse passengers "retail habits within airports, continuous and comprehensive monitoring of traffic flows. According to Black (2020), Honeywell International Inc. has introduced a range of technology solutions to face the health challenges faced by the airline and airport industry and it includes infrared camera that can automatically measures the temperature level of passengers while entering airport and can ensure that they wear masks; robots to disinfect the aisle of aircrafts during turnaround time; sensors to assess the purity of the air inside; etc. ACI urged the airports to ensure 11 different mitigation measures to physical distancing to keep passengers and staff safe, and it essentially includes the use of face masks, pre-travel testing, continuous tray or UVC cleaning and high touchpoint cleaning, installation of Plexiglas and crowd monitoring software (www.aci.aero/news).

5.6 Tourism demand slump and recovery

The effect of the pandemic in tourism was so harsh as the industry got into standstill for months. According to the UN, the global tourism industry has been devastated by the coronavirus pandemic and lost $320 billion in exports in the first five months of the year 2020, along with causing troubles for 120 million jobs (Lederer, 2020). The COVID-19 induced lockdown that caused continued physical, material and mental health challenges which altogether led to widespread dissatisfaction among the common people in the USA and that led to protests as well, over there (www.washingtonpost.org). The pandemic has created a bag of severe emotional consequences among people, which include "the presence of extreme fear, confusion and volatile sentiments, mixed along with trust and anticipation" (Samuel et al., 2020). The global community is facing a dramatic effect due to the pandemic, and the effect will be the same in the long term as well (Chang et al., 2020). UNWTO World Tourism Barometer (2020) reveals that the first half of 2020 recorded a slump in international tourist arrivals, which was a decline of 65% compared to the same period of the previous year. Of the decline, the largest contribution was from the second quarter, which witnessed an unprecedented plummeting demand by 95%. The above slump in international tourism demand in the first half of 2020 resulted in the loss of about $ 460 billion in export revenues. While looking at region-wise, the Asia and the Pacific registered a decrease of 72% in arrivals, followed by Europe (66%), Americas (55%) and Africa and the Middle East recorded 57% decrease. Travellers are being affected by a range of factors for being averse to travel, and media-related aspects are also impacting the travel propensity, as Zheng et al. (2020) pointed out that the exaggerated and distorted media coverage affects the travellers negatively.

After a standstill for a few months, destinations started to rejuvenate the tourism sector slowly. Some of the European destinations paved the way for that. Spain is one of the countries that took a lead role in the beginning though the pandemic was still being spread. By September beginning, according to UNWTO's report on travel restrictions released on 10 September 2020, a total of 115 destinations (53% of all destinations worldwide) have eased travel restrictions, either partially or fully. The trend of opening destinations continued. Many of the destinations depended on domestic tourism to uphold tourism. For instance, China, the number one tourist market in the world, made outstanding efforts to instil confidence among the tourism industry by initiating strategies to spur domestic tourism. By April 2020 itself, China eased domestic travel restrictions, and sooner, there was rush into some of the famous tourist attractions over there, and by October, there was heavy rush in many destinations including the Great Wall of China (Elliott, 2020).

5.7 Transformation and innovations

Unlike in the previous crises in the recent history of tourism, the impact of COVID-19 in tourism is predicted to be long term. Though the COVID-19 pandemic is around, the world is gearing up to manage the new normal. The societies across the world are in the process of taking consequential decisions in order to balance the requirement to mitigate the risks of COVID-19 with other social, economic and health priorities (Lappan et al., 2020). People are now being adapted to the emerging situations. Amidst crisis and severe economic consequences in the wake of corona crisis, Qiu et al. (2020), based on an empirical study on social costs of tourism during the current pandemic, revealed that the residents are ready to bear the brunt of the pandemic crisis in order to contribute in risk reduction and action in responding to the crisis. Moreover, they pointed out that the influx of tourists in this current crisis period affected most of the local people and augmented the pressure on the local healthcare system. Along with recovery attempts, tourism sector is poised for transformation on different aspects.

Table 5.2 WTTC Recommendations for Recovery

World Travel and Tourism Council (WTTC) suggested the following for the recovery in travel and tourism

Make through the crisis

Reduce the guesswork

- Coordinate border openings and ensure repatriation.
- Define common health and safety standards.
- Prioritize destination readiness.
- Expand testing availability.

Give business a boost

- Implement enabling policies for business.
- Promote destinations in need.

Support our people

- Facilitate short-term workforce mobility.
- Strengthen worker support schemes.

(Continued)

Table 5.2 (Continued)

Adapt to the "new normal"

A new beginning

- Co-create with the private sector.
- Incentivize travel.

Leap into digital

- Facilitate seamless coordination.
- Integrate digital identities.
- Spotlight cybersecurity.
- Extend digital infrastructure to rural destinations.

Re-imagine work

- Sponsor mental health.
- Rethink the workplace.
- Forge partnerships for upskilling.

Cultivate resilience

Protect people, wildlife and the environment

- Establish sustainability guidelines.
- Ban wildlife trafficking.
- Eradicate human trafficking.
- Stimulate sustainability practices.

Nurture the community

- Amplify local voices.
- Showcase lesser-known destinations.
- Protect the traveller.

Protect the workforce

- Hire remotely.
- Be diverse and inclusive.
- Strike a balance in labour regulations.

Source: WTTC, The Recovery and Beyond, September 2020, data available online at https://wttc.org/Research/To-Recovery-Beyond.

According to Higgins-Desbiolles (2020), the COVID-19 crisis poses the potentials of transforming the tourism industry and it offers a golden opportunity to rethink and reset the sector in leading it in a better pathway for the future, particularly by adopting "community-centred tourism framework", which can cause more "socialized" tourism through benefiting the public well. Changes are visible in the elements of tourism industrial system.

In the hospitality sector, post-COVID strategies are of varied kinds. Hao et al. (2020) summarized that post-COVID strategies will affect the aspects of the hospitality sector such as "multi-business and multi-channels, product design and investment prefer-ence, digital and intelligent transformation, and market reshuffle". Social distancing is now being made possible in the hospitality industry by using latest technologies. According to Shin and Kang (2020), hospitality sector, as part of reducing the staff direct interaction with the guests, is now increasingly depending on mobile check-in systems, self-service kiosks and robot cleaning systems. Advanced cleaning technolo-gies for enhanced disinfection (e.g. electrostatic sprayers and UV light technology) are also being used (Garcia, 2020). AI-based technology solutions are in place mainly for check-in and customer identification. Biosafety certification that proclaims the depth of safety measures taken by the hotels in preventing the spread of coronavirus is in-troduced by some destinations, like Columbia (Moss, 2020). Hotels, like that of Hilton, are also attempting to use electrostatic sprayers with hospital-grade disinfectants, frequent cleaning of "high-touch" surfaces, supplementing paper amenities with digital amenities, contact over phone for all communications, placing room seal to intimate the freshness of room, etc. (Garcia, 2020). The pandemic-induced psychologi-cal problems and the need to overcome it became a base for suggesting an innovative wellness tourism product, called "healing tourism". It primarily consists of psycholog-ical intervention and counselling methods to provide mental support to tourists (Ma et al., 2020). "Staycation" (spending time more on hotels than on sightseeing), "niche tourism", solo travel tours (using private vehicles), wellness tours and virtual tourism are emerging trends in the realm of tourism currently (Yuswohady, 2020).

5.7.1 Virtual tours and immersive tours

The scope of virtual tourism multiplied during the pandemic period. It has been defined as "the use of technology to artificially enhance or create a tourism ex-perience" (Stainton, 2020). The pandemic-induced movement restrictions created interest among the exploring enthusiasts to adhere to virtual tourism options. Destinations started to promote virtual tourism greatly, with a prime intention to generate and/or retain interest and appeal of their tourist attractions. Tradi-tionally, Web-based virtual tours are considered as an effective marketing tool for tourism marketers in order to promote the destination since they have the ability to lead the potential consumers to evaluate a destination in a unique and personal way based on the spatial, factual and experiential information; equip them to obtain information represented by way of experiential aspects of the destination at less cost; facilitate them to evaluate memorable experience more accurately, elevate the related memories; and to generate a personal story of the destination (Cho et al., 2002). Virtual tourism, in fact, encompasses a range of

> virtual experiences available in the tourism sector; from watching a promo-tional video through to an interactive museum experience to experiencing an entire holiday through virtual means in a style similar to the computer pro-gramme Second Life or the film Avatar.
>
> (Stainton, 2020)

Similar to virtual tours, immersive tours are also there, that, using the advanced technology solutions, enable the tourists to explore the tourism features in a better way. Augmented reality-based immersive tours are having increased significance in order to gain better experience. Immersive tour experience which gives the tourist the lively experiences like that in the actual tourist attraction provides an experience that is close to the real situation (Park et al., 2006). Destinations, hospitality industry, cultural sites and museums, etc., have been utilizing VR tours and immersive tours well during the corona period. In fact, the scope for these types of tours got increased manifold in the pandemic era.

5.7.2 Staycation

Staycation became a buzzword throughout the pandemic period. Lexico.com defines staycation as "A holiday spent in one's home country rather than abroad, or one spent at home and involving day trips to local attractions". It was anticipated from the beginning of the year itself that staycation may increase during the period of the pandemic (Suau-Sanchez et al., 2020). Many countries have started urging people to engage in staycation as it is important for each individual country particularly since the borders were closed and the scope for inbound tourism was nil along with the attempt to support the tourism industry elements within the country. According to Google Trends, popularity of the concept of staycation had a sudden upsurge since May 2020 and the rate of growth in it was dramatic throughout the year, at least up to the end of October 2020 (Google Trends). Due to rise in it, tourism establishments started attracting local guests as well to get some business instead of closing the business for a long term.

5.7.3 Border miles loyalty programme

This is an innovative idea put in practice by some destinations. The idea is well used by Maldives, and it is like a customer relationship management practice that is ideal for destinations. The programme initiated by Maldives ensures the tourists who enrol in the programme points based on the number of visits and duration of stays, along with additional points awarded for visits to celebrate special occasions (Maker, 2020). It's a three-tiered loyalty programme, by which the traveller

---

Table 5.3 World Economic Forum: Suggested Strategies to Help Tourism Recover in Latin America

---

Target Millennial travellers

As Millennials are outnumbering Baby Boomers recently, it is better to focus on them and emphasis can be given to increased personalization and technology incorporation. Moreover, ensuring better authenticity, unique experiences and adventurous options can be more useful.

Strengthens small businesses

Strengthening the Small and Medium Enterprises (SMEs) using different strategies including offering financial support would be vital to tourism's stability.

Table 5.3 (Continued)

Stay competitive

Utilize effectively the rich cultural and natural resources for tourism and ensure competitive prices. Focus on devising creative ways to improve competitiveness and for differentiation. Moreover, engage in marketing communication to appraise the various tourist opportunities.

Highlight health and hygiene efforts

Adhere to latest suggestions from respective national and international health agencies like WHO. Make sure health and hygiene and safety aspects are taken care of well and adequate facilities and services are in place for the same. Certifications, etc., can be beneficial for accommodation units, etc.

Embrace digitalization

Undertake increased investments in digitalization, and enhance the utility of online intermediaries like online travel aggregators, meta-search engines and travel service platforms. Moreover, it is important to ensure digital experiences and latest digital tools that can be applied in the diverse industrial elements of tourism in getting better tourist experience.

Focus on conversions

As there exists an opportunity for conversion in the independent and private sector of hospitality, the high proportion of products from this sector can be made use for more distribution power. Greater distribution and access scope for local industries to provide unique experiences.

Source: Fenton, D. (2020), These six strategies can help tourism recover in Latin America. *World Economic Forum*, https://www.weforum.org/agenda/2020/10/these-6-strategies-can-help-tourism-recover-in-latin-america-df689974cd.

earns points when he/she visit Maldives or crossing the border of the country. A set variety of rewards, services or benefits are offered to those who could gain the points required to get into each of the tier.

5.7.4 Domestic tourism push

UNWTO urged the destinations across the world to encourage domestic tourism considering its significance and the possible way out to begin tourism after the unprecedented slump in demand. Its third Tourism and Covid-19 Briefing Notes pointed out that nine billion domestic tourism trips, which is six times the tourist arrival figure of international tourist arrivals, were made worldwide in 2018 and argued that domestic tourism got the potential to recover faster and stronger than international travel, as the latter involves increased complications due to the issues associated with inbound and outbound travel in the COVID era (UNWTO News Sep 20). It also pointed out that the domestic tourism has increased economic significance than inbound tourism in many destinations. UNWTO, in the above cited document, identified a few examples to highlight the steps taken by some countries in encouraging domestic tourism first to recover from the devastated state of tourism in their respective regions.

- Italy: offer of EUR 500 for families with limited income to spend on domestic tourism accommodation under the "Bonus Vacanze" initiative.
- Malaysia: personal tax relief (up to $227) for expenditure related to domestic tourism and earmarked $113 million worth of travel discount vouchers.
- Costa Rica: it moved all holidays of 2020 and 2021 to Mondays for its citizens to enjoy long weekends to travel domestically and to extend their stays.
- France: initiated a campaign titled "This Summer, I visit France" to encourage the people to visit their home country by highlighting the diversity of destinations across the country.
- Argentina: an observatory is being created for domestic tourism to provide a better profile of domestic tourists.
- Thailand: ventured to subsidize 5 million nights of hotel rates at 40% of normal rates for up to five nights.

5.8 Conclusion

There have been many pandemics in human history, and the travel and tourism sectors have been severely affected by them. They have high vulnerability rate in terms of crisis. We are facing a health-related catastrophe that has created a crisis of varying degrees that is COVID-19 pandemic. Things happened within days as the virus spread very quickly. It is essential to have effective management to overcome the consequences of all kinds of crises. Crisis management aims to mitigate the effects and take the initiative for recovery. The drop in demand led to a severe financial crisis in the aviation sector. The rate of job losses and a significant decline in income became a major concern.

When the aviation sector faced the worst crisis ever, many governments provided financial assistance by lending to the air transport sector, especially the airlines. Businesses need to adapt themselves to face the new normal in the wake of the COVID-19 repercussions. In fact, the travel and tourism sectors need to innovate new common practices in their business processes and introduce new methods and solutions to adapt to the new conditions of the post-COVID period. To overcome this crisis, four types of strategic crisis response units are identified and implemented worldwide including retrenchment, persistence, innovation and exit. Improvements in technology will help airlines cope with the new normal. Biometrics is used for faster check-in process, self-service biometric-enabled baggage drop and facial recognition. More cleanliness and new hygiene practices are followed by the airports. To keep passengers and staff safe, airports take steps to maintain physical distance, which includes face masks, pre-flight inspection, UVC cleaning, high touchpoint cleaning, Plexiglas installation and crowd monitoring software.

The impact of the pandemic on tourism was severe as the industry stagnated for months. After being halted for a few months, the destinations began to slowly revive the tourism sector. The scope of virtual tourism increased during the pandemic period. Augmented reality-based immersive tours are more important for a better experience. Destinations, hospitality industry, cultural sites and museums make good use of VR tours and immersive tours during the corona era. In fact, the probability of such tours multiplied during the pandemic period. In the wake of the unprecedented decline in demand, the UNWTO has called for the promotion of destinations around the world in view of the importance of domestic tourism and the possible way to start tourism.

Sample questions

Short/medium answer type questions

- "Tourism is highly vulnerable to external occurrences": Comment upon the statement.
- Discuss how the pandemic affected tourism and air transport demand.
- Discuss the scope of the support from government to manage the financial crisis in tourism and air transport.
- Discuss ultra long-haul airline business model.
- What are the possible strategic crisis response categories in air transport sector?
- What are the transformations taking place in airport sector in the wake of pandemic?
- Give a brief account on innovations taking place in tourism currently.
- Discuss the scope of virtual tours in tourism.
- What do you mean by "staycation"?

Essay type questions

- Explain the impacts of pandemic in air transport sector.
- Write an essay on the measures and strategies being undertaken by the air transport and tourism sectors to overcome the pandemic-induced crisis.

Suggested readings

Faulkner, B. (2001). Towards a framework for tourism disaster management. *Tourism Management*, 22(2), 135–147.

Nhamo, G., Dube, K., & Chikodzi, D. (2020). *Counting the Cost of COVID-19 on the Global Tourism Industry*. New York: Springer.

Pforr, C., & Hosie. J.P. (2008). Crisis management in tourism. *Journal of Travel & Tourism Marketing*, 23(2–4), 249–264.

Serrano, F., & Kazda, A. (2020). The future of airport post COVID-19. *Journal of Air Transport Management*, 89, 101900.

Taneja, N.K. (2021). *Airlines in a Post-Pandemic World: Preparing for Constant Turbulence Ahead*. London: Routledge.

Chapter 6

Role of air transport in tourism

Learning outcomes

By the end of this lesson, you will be able to:

- Describe how the growth in air transport contributes in the evolution of tourism.
- Explain the intricate relationship between air transport and tourism.
- Understand the role of different airline business models in tourism.
- Assess the benefits of tourists by the increasing dynamism in air transport.

6.1 Introduction

This chapter discusses in length the way air transport influences and impacts tourism. We have already discussed that there is a strong reciprocal and symbiotic relationship between tourism and air transport (Bieger & Wittmer 2006; Forsyth, 2010). Their mutual dependence makes the tourism system more complex and the various industrial elements require the smooth air transport services in order to perform their functions. The increasing dependency on air transport by the industrial elements like accommodation sector is making the relationship between tourism and air transport more complex. Lohmann and Duval (2014) identify three parallels between tourism and transport, which are more relevant in the case of air transport and tourism. They are regulatory synergies, objective function and shared emphasis on sustainability. There can be "regulatory synergies" that can emerge between transport and tourism which denotes that the regulation in one sector can have a meaningful and direct effect on the other; for example, tourism marketing can boost air transport and, on the other hand, new airline business models can enhance tourist arrivals. In the case of objective function, this means

DOI: 10.4324/9781003136927-6

that similar things are involved in both of them, though the nature of them may be different. For instance, personal mobility is part of both, but the end results vary. In addition, both make attempts at sustainability efforts.

Air transport is considered an ideal transport mode in international tourism and travellers benefit from better transportation and accessibility as their trips become easier and more comfortable (Gunn & Var, 2002). Furthermore, a good transportation system to and at destination can reduce travel costs, making the destination even more accessible due to overall cost savings (Prideaux, 2000a; Masson & Petiot, 2009). International tourist destinations now increasingly depend on air transport for tourism flows. A fluctuation in air transport demand directly affects the tourist flow into the destinations. According to Bieger and Wittmer (2006), air transport is the prime transport mode in many destinations, and up to 100% in some of the destinations; and cheap air services constitute a driving force in tourism growth. Airlines are instrumental in channelizing tourism demand, and they perform the task of transporting tourists from the city of origin to the destination and in return utilizing the services of airports, another major segment in the air transport sector. "Without airlines some continents, many countries, regions, and islands would have remained inaccessible for most of us and even established destinations would have had far fewer tourists" (James, 2008). Airlines do have diverse business models, and their impact on tourist traffic flow is also different. According to Bieger et al. (2002), the business models of airlines and their impact on tourism flows, in short, are as follows. Network/hub airlines do have only a small group of tourists, and tourist flows are just a secondary product to get market share and size. For regional airlines, since regional tourism flow (in the upscale segment) is an important part of the business, close cooperation with regional incoming tour operators and marketing organizations is undertaken. Tourism is just a part of the general traffic flows for low-cost carriers (LCCs). For them, there may be blocked space for marketing through tour operators in the long run. For charter airlines, relation or integration with tour operation sector is important and tourist traffic forms the main product. These aspects will be clearer as we proceed further in this book.

6.2 Rise of new international destinations due to air transport

In the history of modern tourism, many of the destinations evolved into status of major international tourist destinations with the support of air transport. According to Papatheodorou and Zenelis (2013),

> Technological advancements in the air transport sector, the size of the airline networks and the routes operated in conjunction with the appropriate pricing and promotional strategies are some of the factors that played an important role in the establishment and growth of new destinations and attractions.

Air transport, thus, takes up a key role in the emergence of destinations and shaping it into a competitive international tourism destination. Once the wide-body aircraft began to be used in commercial air transportation widely, the accessibility coupled with affordability to long-haul destinations enhanced, which enabled those destinations to rise to the international tourism scenario. According to Bieger and Wittmer (2006), "... air transport opened new destinations and tourism forms such as long-haul excursions". Far eastern Asian destinations got the fillip during the 1970s and 1980s to rise to the level of competitive destinations when long-haul travel scope increased by the introduction of wide-body aircraft. Currently, countries like Thailand, Indonesia, Vietnam and Philippines are receiving tourists from everywhere and the access is primarily through air mode of transport. The scenario is the same in the case of island destinations like Mauritius and Seychelles. Kaspar (1993) noted that the increasing use of long-haul charter flights for tourism caused the evolution of "exotic" destinations such as the Caribbean Islands, the Maldives and Seychelles (Kaspar, 1993).

Destinations could get access to distant markets by way of getting connectivity through air transport and that made them the confidence to market their offerings in those markets. "New aviation technology has made it possible to develop distant markets for tourism, and tourism between the continents is flourishing" (Keller, 2000). Maldives is now depending much on air transport to remain an international destination, and their economy has a strong dependence on tourism. Though Caribbean tourism has a considerable share of cruise visitors as well, the destinations over there became prominent ones with the support of air transport. LCCs also influenced greatly the emergence of destinations into major ones. According to Vojvodić (2006), LCCs have enabled access to otherwise inaccessible destinations, which directly influenced the development of tourism in those areas. This phenomenon has been continuing, and now hybrid airlines too add to the phenomenon. Middle East destinations, like Dubai, have risen suddenly as leading international destinations along with the rise of air accessibility. Dubai has turned as a major international air transport hub.

6.3 Improvised air transport supply

The expansion, growth, quality enhancement and improvisation of air transport supply invigorate tourism potentials of destinations. Airline network expansion, connecting the destinations to more cities, certainly gives the destination an opportunity to expand its market share. Certainly, destinations will attempt to coax the airlines to expand their services to more areas. Moreover, destinations prefer to attract more airlines to conduct operations in the destination airports. The way the access to the destination will be changed by the introduction of airport is great. It gives the destination the needed strength to compete in the international market. Khadaroo and Seetanah (2008) argue that "Provision of suitable transport has transformed dead centres of tourist interest into active and prosperous places attracting multitudes of people". International airport turns to be a major element in the destination's competitiveness spectrum. "Access to international airports is a vital component in the development of international markets" (Prideaux, 2000). Even the location of the airport is significant in the success of destinations. Airports need to be located strategically accessible from the destination and other places of importance.

Quality of the transport infrastructure and services is also important. For instance, it is argued that the travellers from places with quality modern transport infrastructure may prefer similar quality/comfort levels in the transport infrastructure in the places visited as well (Mo et al., 1993). If the case is the opposite, there are chances that such tourists may opt for alternative destinations. Certainly, tourism became a factor in making the airports to enhance the quality of services and facilities, along with adding the features. Airports have an important role in tourism since tourists would like to have a pleasant and exciting environment within the airport. For them, it is a point of both first impression and lasting impressions. They may go for some shopping within airports and prefer good options for refreshments as well. Moreover, tourists may be more tired after a long visit to the destination and would like to relax within airport until being boarded into the flight. Smooth emigration services, quality concierge services, good shopping options, quality refreshment options, hassle-free passenger processing services, etc., in airports can give a better feel for the tourist. Many of the mass tourist destinations are expanding their services, facilities, space and features along with enhancing quality in order to attract more travellers. Destinations too are keen to pursue the air transport authorities to invigorate the success attributes of airports.

6.4 Air transport causes new forms of tourism

Throughout the history of modern tourism, air transport enabled the tourism sectors to be dynamic to either innovate or strengthen some of the existing forms of tourism along with changing the patterns of tourism. Nilsson (2009) pointed out that along with the dynamism and evolution in the air transport with the introduction of new models of airlines, new patterns of travel and tourism are emerging (Nilsson, 2009). The air transport flow within Europe was a prime reason for the intra-European tourism's surge, and it remains as a leading tourism region in the world with remarkable air transport network. As the transport network gets expanded into newer horizons, the international tourism spectrum also got expanded. This is applicable in the case of domestic tourism, and regional tourism gets strengthened further with the rise of some new forms of tourism over there. The following are some examples to substantiate the above.

6.4.1 Short-haul city tourism

City tourism got a momentum due to the rise in LCCs. Short-haul city tourism is relatively a new segment in the international tourism sector. According to Olipra (2011), LCCs supported the growth of new forms of tourism, like short-haul city tourism. LCCs usually operate services to short-haul destinations. The cost of travel also gets reduced. This tempts the travel enthusiasts to engage on short trips to nearby cities, for a short visit, shopping, relaxation and meeting friends as well as relatives. Bieger and Wittmer (2006), citing Bieger and Laesser (2001), also opine that the tourism forms in trend like short vacations and visit friends and relatives caused greater requirement for greater flexibility in the transport system. Urban tourism and city tourism have been there in the parlance of tourism for long, but the trend of short-haul city tours has relatively short history. Shopping tourism is a major segment now in this category. Besides, weekend holidays too are complementary to this. International tourism and domestic tourism have now this kind of tourism with much significance.

6.4.2 Stopover tourism

The term stopover is more often associated with air travel. Airlines offer the provision of having stopovers in destinations for a few days. This provision has been on offer for some decades. However, it led to the rise of stopover tourism nowadays. Considering the significance of air transport services in the customer satisfaction, Cristina (2017) argues

> airlines, airports and tourism organizations started to collaborate, focusing on enhancing the passenger experience. "Stopover" programs were developed by airlines in partnership with airports and tourism organizations, offering passengers the possibility to experience the destination while being in transit for a few hours or a few days. This led to the emergence of a new form of tourism: "stopover tourism".

Stopover comes in the midst of a continuous journey to another destination from the origin city, and it comes as an option for a connection flight to the final destination. The traveller, before joining the connecting flight, can avail some hours to a few days as stopover in the hub city through which the itinerary is routed. Before joining the flight to the final destination, the traveller can be free to visit the hub city. Usually, choosing the stopover time will not take extra charge. Many cities now promote stopover tourism as well with the support of their flag carriers as well as other airlines that undertake services into the destinations. Specific visa services are also offered. The traveller has many advantages by using this. Without taking extra travel expenditure, he/she can visit the destination city for a couple of days' time and thus can save the travel cost. Moreover, getting visa has become easier.

6.4.3 VFR

Visiting friends and relatives (VFR) is an important segment of tourism. Emergence of LCCs has given an impetus to this segment, and now, it has increased significance as many prefer to travel to meet their kith and kin taking the advantage of air travel with cheaper rates. Bieger and Wittmer (2006) also pointed out that the emergence of LCCs stimulated the VFR travel. Though in-flight services are limited in the LCCs, VFR category of tourists is less impacted by them, and they are more interested in reaching the destinations to meet the friends and relatives. Other factors that influence travellers in making travel decisions are less significant in the case of VFR. LCCs now offer wider network and increased frequency. This makes their travel more convenient, easier and matching their schedules. Flexibility in the operations of LCCs is an advantage for VFR tourists.

6.4.4 Long-haul tourism

Long-haul tourism emerged as major segment by the introduction of wide-body aircraft in the 1970s. This is an ideal example of how a form of tourism gets elevated to a major tourism segment. Once long-haul flight became more common using wide-body aircraft and the consequent decline in air travel cost, long-haul tourism gained increased significance. Tourists use aviation as the principal means of travelling to their destinations, particularly for long-haul destination as well as for trips between countries separated by sea (Duval, 2012). As of now, long-haul tourism is a major segment in the international tourism with the advancements in air transport in terms of efficiency, cost, comfort, smoothness as well as convenience. As tourism was concentrated in the western developed regions once, the emergence of long-haul flight paved the way for the expansion of tourism into other regions as well.

6.5 Distance and air transport correlation

The significance of air transport increases with the distance to cover between origin point and destination. The more the distance between origin and the destination, the greater the significance for air transport in tourism. For instance, Papatheodorou and Zenelis (2013) specify that the prominence of air transport for tourism is proportional to the distance between the origin place and the destination city as majority of other forms of transport cannot support a long-haul transfer service in a comfortable and time-saving way. Though the significance of air transport is gaining increasing importance in short-haul tourism as well, still distance remains a major determinant in the demand for air transport in tourism. When distance is more, speed, convenience, time factor, comfort and safety are relatively more favourable for air transport compared to road and water transport forms. Many regions in the world are rich in cultural and natural resources. Yet, those countries struggled to get wealthy tourists from other regions when air transport access was limited in the history. Distance to cover was much higher compared to many other destinations. Since the distance was high, the cost of travel was also high.

Distance and air travel cost are directly linked. Travel cost poses challenge for destinations located far away from major tourism markets. The evolution of air transport and the decline in relative air travel cost enable destinations to overcome that difficulty. Nowadays, destinations that are more distant are taking the advantage of advancements in air transportation. Europe and North American regions have been the major tourism market regions for several centuries. They had intensive tourism activities, particularly the intra-regional tourism, due to the well-networked air transport connectivity. Europe has many major tourism markets, and those nations are located nearby, and thus, the distance to cover to reach destinations is also less. There were many reasons in the hegemony of Europe and America together holding the largest share in international tourism, and of which, accessibility and proximity of tourism markets constituted some of the major reasons. Things got a shift recently as other regions are also well-connected and intra-regional travel too got strengthened in many regions like within Asia, and between Asia and the Middle East. Now, China is the number one country in the world in terms of producing international tourists and there are a number of leading destinations within Asia itself. Besides, though the distance is greater, air transport became more affordable for people and frequency and connectivity are much higher. These make faraway destinations also take the advantages of tourism.

Furthermore, distance makes other modes of transport less convenient for tourism. Water-based transportation, though cheaper, is highly time-consuming and less comfortable. Moreover, it is less convenient. Accessing water transport services, like ship services, is also less inconvenient. Using road transportation has limitations in covering longer routes to destinations. Many regions have intra-regional tourism still depending on road transportation as the distance to cover is less. Having an automobile to reach the destination is a nice option to venture into the destination. But this option may not be easy when the destinations are located far away from the market regions. When the destination and tourism markets are separated by water bodies, using road transport services is also not that feasible. The case is the same with rail transport as well. Rail services are a safer and comfortable option to reach destinations. Unfortunately, it is not a major mode of transport in most of the regions in the world. Moreover, the distance to cover by railways has also got limitations and presence of the sea, etc., can make rail transport less significant. While looking at these limitations, distance is the main factor that makes air transport highly significant in tourism, particularly in international tourism. Now, long-haul tourism, tourism in the islands and remote regions, etc., is depending greatly on air transport, primarily due to the distance factor.

6.6 Direct air link and tourism

Air transport has increased significance when direct air connectivity is there between origin and destination. Direct connectivity increases along with the progress in tourism in the destination and the economic significance of the region. Cities with more direct links with other regions in the world are getting increasing traffic and gaining increased international reputation. From the tourism perspective, the following benefits can be there when the destination has direct connectivity with tourism origin cities.

- Direct connectivity can reduce the distance (compared to flights through hub and spoke system, etc.).
- Tourists can avoid waiting for connection flights.
- Direct link can eliminate hassles of changing flights.
- Tourists can be free from the worry of missing flights.
- Direct connectivity can save total time of travel to reach the destination.
- Baggage, both hand baggage and checked-in baggage, handling is easier.
- Comfort and convenience are better in direct trips, compared to others.
- Avoid troubles of repeat security checks.
- Direct connectivity leads to less travel fatigue.
- Duty-free shopping and carrying of items are less difficult.
- Chances of missing luggage are less.
- Single boarding pass flight is more convenient.
- Less expenditure in airports as scope for increased spending is higher in connection airports.

6.7 Evolution of tourism with the growth of air transport

Modern tourism, since the end of the Second World War, was evolved together with the growth of aviation. The major aviation-related events that spurred the growth of tourism are described in the first chapter. Different phases can be seen in the history of modern tourism when we look at it from air transport evolution perspective as well. Bieger and Wittmer (2006) identified four phases, rather overlapping, of evolution of tourism together with air transport. The phases identified are as follows: tourism as neglected business, tourism as a secondary activity, specialization in tourism, and tourism and business traffic combined. In the first phase, just after the First World War, tourism had limited significance, and air transport has grown with postal services and services for business travellers. Tourism-related traffic slowly began part of it during the 1930s, when bigger planes were introduced into services. Later, after the Second World War, larger planes entered into the scene, and thus, the second phase began. Larger air carriers started to rely on passenger revenue from tourists as well. Charter services are also gaining momentum. Sooner, the specialization in tourism era started when the capacity increased along with the use of wide-body aircraft and the consequent result of economy of scale and cheaper fares. Long-haul tourism trips increased, while the newer fares, such as Apex and Super Apex fares, were introduced. The next phase began since the deregulation in the USA in the late 1970s and later in Europe. The tourist traffic gained momentum when the LCC model of airline business began to gain significant market share, and short-stay city tourism, second-home tourism and VFR got increased. One significant change that happened was the replacing of the charter tourism from the short-haul routes.

The above is a summary of the occurrences that took place related to air transport growth and tourism evolution. In the new millennium, the progress continued. We could see tremendous progress in tourism and air transport, and the expansion of air transport had contributed greatly in the last two decades until the pandemic era. COVID-19 pandemic completely paralysed both the sectors. Until then, expansion continued. Airport expansion was a major trend in the recent history. Runways had to be expanded to accommodate increasing number of flights as well as to receive larger aircraft. The entry of Airbus A380 was phenomenal as many major airports had to expand runways in length and width. Moreover, number of runways also increased over the last two decades to cater to the increasing number of flight operations.

The emergence of LCCs as major air transport service providers suddenly spurred the growth of passenger traffic. More services added. These caused airports to expand their airside. Entry of more airlines led the airports to create more slots within them. All these led to the dramatic expansion in airport sector world over. Moreover, new airports were constructed in many parts of the world and a number of domestic airports were upgraded to international status to cater to the increasing demand and operations. Moreover, airports started to face increasing challenge to attract passengers and tourists and that led them to increase their appeal by adding facilities, services and features. All these directly and indirectly contributed in stimulating tourist traffic as well. Along with the rise of LCCs, entry of hybrid airlines further invigorated the progress of tourism. Medium- and long-haul tourism got a fillip by this. Moreover, policy changes were in many origin and destination countries favouring air transport, which too added the scope for tourism. Open sky policy regulations and regional agreements got increased in the last a few decades which resulted in the increased tourist traffic. Thus, the last two decades, in addition to the phenomenal evolution of commercial air transport since the 1950s, have recorded dramatic expansion in air transport and that directly contributed in the progress of tourism as well.

6.8 Affordability stimulates tourism demand

Affordability of air transport has a direct impact on air travel and tourism demand, as the better the affordability the greater the travel and tourism demand. The increasing rate of affordability of air transport among more sections of the society has been contributing well in the rising tourism demand world over. Travel is fundamental in the process of tourism, and international tourism involves covering more distances along with crossing borders. Air transport is the preferred mode of transport in the arena of international tourism; this trend has been increasing for several decades. While we analyse the tourism demand trend and the cost factors involved, one comes to notice that travel cost, particularly the international travel cost, is one of the largest. For many destinations, travel cost is still acting as a major bottleneck in the progress of tourism. The affordability of air transport, especially in the case of leisure tourism, is a determinant in tourism demand, as leisure tourists are price-sensitive.

Affordability of air transport got enhanced at regular intervals of the progress of air transport. When wide-body aircraft were introduced into commercial aviation, there was steep decline in the air travel cost, which, as discussed elsewhere, enhances travel and tourism propensity. Deregulation process began in the USA and later spread to other parts of the world instilled too much of competition in the airline sector, which encouraged price war which could eventually lead to the hike in affordability of air transport. Long-haul international tourism got stimulated during then. With regard to the reduction of cost of air travel, James (2012) cited an example, as follows:

> It is sobering to reflect back to the 1960s when the cost of a return ticket from Europe to Australia was equivalent to 10 months of an average income. In 2012 the fare is closer to the wages of a few weeks' work.

LCCs caused the lowering of travel cost and enhanced the affordability of air transport greatly. Moreover, this posed challenges for full-service carriers (FSCs) as well in considering their pricing strategies to be cautious.

Although affordability is associated greatly with the relative cost of travel, other determinants too have considerable significance in it. "…, mass tourism and aviation development led to higher competition and reduced prices, which further enabled other people to afford air travel" (Ivanova, 2017). The rising economic standards of the more sections of the society are another significant factor supporting affordability. Economic standards of people of almost all nations have recorded substantial increase since the end of the Second World War. Employment rates increased manifold. It is the case with income levels as well. People are better educated and better aware of the scope of air transport. Air travel became dearer for middle-class population in the recent history due to varied reasons like rise in their economic standards and availability of cheaper air travel options. The rise in travel propensity among the middle-class population became a prime reason for the dramatic rise of air travel demand in emerging markets like India, China, Indonesia and Brazil. Air travel was a luxury once upon a time, but the same is now a more common mode of transport in many societies. This has an increasing role in tourism as well. More sections of the society can now make use of air transport for their international as well as domestic and leisure as well as business trips. The penetration of air travel propensity is deeply connected to the increasing rate of affordability. Information technology impacted in the easier accessibility of air transport products and in enhancing the affordability of air transport.

6.9 The travel cost advantage

Travel cost, as already discussed, is a major determinant in tourism. It simply represents the cost of round-trip travel between the origin and destination, i.e. to reach the destination from the origin point and to return to the intended place after the trip. Travel cost affects tourism in varied manner, but primarily by enhancing the demand. Li (2008) states that "Travel cost can be major determinant of leisure travel". It is a major part of the overall holiday cost of a tour and does have a key role in the choice of a tourism destination (Seetaram et al., 2016). In choosing a destination, a tourist may have the concern of cost of reaching it as well. Alderighi and Gaggero (2018) pointed out "The link between airline supply and international tourism is tied to the travel costs, which are an important component of the destination choice". Since travel cost has so much of significance, destinations having lesser travel cost by way of affordable accessibility with major tourism markets can enjoy it as a destination attribute in attracting tourists. Similar opinion is given by Divisekera (2003) who argues that lower travel cost is usually a determinant in the relative competitiveness of a destination, with an increased desirability.

Cost of air travel reduction is due to myriad of factors. Frequency and reliability of flights along with advancements in aircraft design and technology have contributed to bringing down the cost of air travel in real terms (James, 2008). Efficiency of aircraft enhanced substantially and that leads to less consumption of fuel for flying. This is another factor contributed in the reduction in travel cost. Use of larger flights too has a role in the reduction of the cost of flying. Technology integration significantly affected upon the lessening of flight operations. Use of advanced technology solutions helps in cost reduction by minimizing the human resource requirements and by enhancing the efficiency. Commission provided to intermediaries, like travel agents and tour operators for selling flight tickets, too has drastically declined. Many a time, it has been pointed out that zero commission policy is followed by airline sector.

The above discussion points out different aspects of the effect of reduction in travel cost. Destinations can effectively make use of reduced travel cost for their marketing advantage as well. It can be considered as a factor in the competitiveness spectrum of the destinations. While travel cost is a determinant in the leisure tourism demand particularly, it can be noted that the same influences in the decision-making by leisure tourists in choosing the destination. Furthermore, reduced travel cost can encourage the tourist in spending more on various items while on tour within the destination. The following aspects can be identified in association with reduction in travel cost and tourism. Travel cost is as follows:

- A determinant in leisure tourism demand.
- A marketing proposition.
- A destination competition attribute.
- A determinant in the travel decision-making (mainly in leisure tourism).
- A motivator in better destination spending.

6.10 LCCs, travel propensity and addition of tourism demand

LCC is a perfect example of how a new business model can make dramatic changes in the demand. Though began in the early 1970s, LCCs became a major player only after the Deregulation process started by the USA. Soon after the entry of LCC into the mainstream air transport scenario, it created waves among the societies to get attracted to air transport. It could enable the air transportation as a common mode of transport accessible for more sections of the society. LCCs increase travel propensity by making air travel affordable for people in the tourism markets. According to Schlumberger and Weisskopf (2014),

> the entrance of LCCs has not only brought lower fares to the air transport market, but has also made a substantial contribution to countries' economies. Tourism, for example, has been a key beneficiary of the emergence of LCCs, particularly for isolated island states, many of which are developing countries.

The rising travel propensity of people across the world, augmented by the lure of cheaper fares of the LCCs, instilled cascading effect in the local economy and played a catalytic role in generating mass tourism in the destinations.

The experience from the history reveals that the LCCs have become a key driver of tourism development (Chung & Whang, 2011; Dobruszkes & Mondou, 2013). Moreover, there is ample proof to state that there exists a strong effect that low-cost airlines have on tourist outcomes (Chung & Whang, 2011; Rey et al., 2011). The effect is not only into domestic tourism since LCCs initially focused services on short-haul routes. Later, LCCs ventured into international routes as well and could create profound impacts on the air transport demand rise. Alderighi and Gaggero (2018) undertook an analysis on the effect of flight supply on international tourism flows between 20 Italian regions and 24 European countries and found out that the LCCs have a prominent role in attracting international tourism flows.

Table 6.1 Benefits of LCCs for Tourism

Benefits for Destinations	Benefits for Travellers
• Accessibility	• Affordability
• Marketing preposition	• Enhanced mobility
• Competitive prices and choices for tourists	• Increased opportunities for taking part in leisure travel
• Enhanced connectivity	• Scope for business travel
• Airport development	• Increased convenience
• Improved transport network	• Accessibility to nearer locations
• Industry expansion and growth	• Take part in circuit tourism
• Socio-economic transformation	• Cost saving
• Lessening of season	• Scope for more spending for other
• Increased tourism flow	tourism activities/shopping

An important factor to point out as part of the impact of LCCs in tourism is that as LCCs became a choice for transport between origin and tourist destination cities, the destinations used experience an addition in the overall tourism demand into them. It is reported based on a study by Chung and Whang (2011), who reveals that LCCs have induced additional tourism demand to the study destination area and also have contributed towards improving local economies over there. Another notable impact of LCCs on tourism is that it has given a stimulus to independent travel. Traditionally, mass leisure tourism, with the support of charter airline sector, thrived mainly due to package holidays. Nevertheless, as LCC became predominant, independent travel has been increased. Leisure tourism is a big gainer due to the establishment of LCCs, on both international and domestic routes. Rey et al. (2011), after an analysis on the effect of low-cost airlines on tourism in Spain, revealed that LCCs have significant impact on tourist arrivals to Spain from EU-15 countries. The following effects in tourism are visible due to LCCs:

- Addition of demand in leisure tourism category.
- Business tourists also started using LCC services conveniently.
- Regional tourism strengthened.
- Domestic tourism got a fillip.
- Convenience of travel enhanced.
- Better frequency of services and consequent rise in new forms of tourism.
- Accessibility of destinations multiplied.
- Short-haul international tourism gained strength.
- Decline in travel cost led to the rise in travel propensity.
- Price competition among airlines.
- Increase in expenditure by the tourists in the destination.
- Offsetting seasonality.

Some of the important aspects mentioned above which need further elaboration are dealt in detail below.

6.10.1 Domestic tourism in destinations

LCCs have directly affected the remarkable progress of domestic tourism across the world. This is more relevant in countries with vast area. Large countries by size like China, India and Brazil have been gaining the advantage of LCCs in the development of domestic tourism over there. Domestic tourism is also benefited greatly by the presence of air transport services as it can play an important role in linking domestic destinations (Prideaux & Whyte, 2014). A study by Tsui's (2017) on the correlation of LCCs with domestic tourism demand and growth of it in New Zealand revealed a significant effect of LCCs on domestic tourism demand. It could increase and boost tourism demand greatly. LCCs enable air transport sector to expand the route network to wider areas within the country. More destinations become air accessible. This results in reduced time in accessing those destinations. Along with giving impetus for the lesser rich category of populations within the country, LCCs strengthen the air travel propensity greatly in the populations. Many of the natural and cultural tourism destinations may be situated at distance from the major cities, and LCC services can connect them with the main cities.

Domestic tourism benefit is primarily due to the factors like decline of travel cost, increase in air service frequency, reduced time taken for travel, convenience and comfort in reaching the destinations, increase in the air connectivity to smaller cities and the scope of having increased options to choose the right one for the traveller. Moreover, people from smaller cities and rural markets can access air services, which complement the overall domestic tourism demand.

6.10.2 Regional tourism growth

Regional tourism has been greatly benefited by LCCs. By principle, LCCs often focus on regional or secondary airports that are sidelined by network carriers (Halpern et al., 2016) which benefited in the growth of tourism in rural regions as well. Intra-regional tourism is a major beneficiary of LCC growth. According to Fageda et al. (2017), the dominance of LCCs in "intra-European routes may have helped to promote tourism within Europe as low-cost airlines are able to offer services at lower prices than network airlines". Growth in regional air markets spurred tourism in remote locations, and regional markets for air travel became more prevalent. The air connectivity dramatically increases when LCCs start regular operations between cities of neighbouring countries. Inside Europe, this phenomenon is predominantly seen. The same is the case with Asia as well. Many of the LCCs within Asia are conducting international services, and tourism is benefited by this.

6.10.3 Increased expenditure in destination

As discussed earlier, travel cost is a major component in the overall tourism expenditure (Dileep, 2019). Spending less on travel enables the tourist to spend more in the destination as well. This may not be true in all the cases, but the tendency of spending more amount when the tourist gains travel cost advantage is seen in international tourism. A tourist spends money on a wide variety of items within the destination while on a holiday, and as far as a destination is concerned, increased expenditure by the tourist is a welcome one. Many a time, tourists are restricted to spend much on various items within the destination, as the amount spent for international air travel is high. LCCs give an opportunity for tourists to engage in expenditure on a wide variety of items. The tourist may prefer better quality accommodation and costlier food items and buy more souvenir items, etc.

6.10.4 Addition of tourism demand

Generally, decline in price of any component of tourism like accommodation and transport can cause increase in tourist flow there. LCCs certainly add tourism demand in a destination. Since LCCs give opportunities for more sections of the society to use air travel, destinations that are connected by LCCs can bring in more number of people to visit. A study by Chung and Whang (2011) shows that LCCs have induced additional tourism demand to the study destination area and also have contributed to improving local economies over there. Donzelli (2010), based on a study in Southern Italy, stated that LCCs not only generate the additional demand diverting existing demand from FSCs, but also contribute in employment generation, increasing in tourism revenue in the region and in spreading tourism demand more evenly across the months of the year. Travel cost advantage, frequency of services and wider connectivity contribute greatly in the addition of tourism demand in domestic and regional tourism destinations.

6.10.5 Globalization of tourism

It is already discussed how the air transport and tourism evolved hand in hand. Both have contributed in the growth of each other. In fact, the spread of international tourism to the nook and corner of the world is greatly attributed to air transport sector as well. Many new entrants in the parlance of international tourism would not have gained the status they enjoy currently without the support of air transport expansion into those regions. Keller (2000) argued that air transport has also contributed greatly to the globalization of tourism. Tourism globalization was complimented by the emergence of new destinations and increasing the competition. As travel and communication became easier, tourism could enjoy a quick expansion globally. Eliminating trade barriers is key in the globalization process. "In fact, by offering point-to-point services and using secondary airports, the LCCs have managed to redefine the geography of air transport dramatically improving accessibility to a number of previously remote destinations in Europe and the USA" (Papatheodorou, 2008). International tourism too could eliminate a range of barriers, and of them, accessibility barrier was a major one which could easily be overcome by the smart evolution of aviation. Countries started developing air transport infrastructure tremendously. Developing and undeveloped regions also gave emphasis on air transport expansion. Number of airports increased remarkably. Along with the rise in economic standards, affordability of air transport also increased. Simultaneous development was also seen in tourism sector in those regions. Tourism has thus grown with the support of tourism, and the spread of tourism faced a globalization effect.

6.10.6 Air transport sector to attract tourists

Certainly, a new dimension seen in the modern air transport is the attempt by the sector in attracting passengers increasingly. Airports, for instance, have transformed themselves to increase attractiveness rather than being idle sector offering just passenger and cargo handling and serving airlines. The competition erupted into the airport sector recently in attracting passengers; particularly, the tourists cause them to enhance the quality, increase facilities and services and upgrade quality along with increase in appeal.

> The nature of network, charter and low cost carriers, and the way that they each serve the leisure market is changing, as is the distribution channels that are used. In addition, airports are becoming much more proactive and experienced in trying to attract leisure demand and in providing a level of service which is appealing to leisure travelers.
>
> (Graham et al., 2008)

Airports are not only trying to attract leisure tourists more, but the same intensity is given in attracting business tourists as well. There are a number of services ensured within airports that are focusing mainly on business tourists. Car rental services are of this type, which is nowadays offered from the premises of airports itself. Connectivity with the cities nearby is being ensured well. High-quality refreshment options, entertainment options and shopping options are there being arranged nowadays targeting the tourist category primarily. Airlines also offer hotel booking services, arranging car rental services, etc., and encouraging stopovers is a welcome sign from the international airlines as it can complement tourism well in cities. These are offered in addition to the common facilities and services to ensure the air transportation smooth, comfortable and safe. Overall, the air transport sector is giving increased interest in attracting tourists which eventually contribute in the growth of tourism.

6.10.7 Air transport policy and liberalization

Air transport policy has a significant role in the expansion of tourism globally. It has varied dimensions. Liberal approach in bilateral agreements and multilateral agreements supports tourism positively.

> The country's political situation and its legal regulation of air transport will directly impact the tourism development of any of its destinations. Availability of bilateral or multilateral agreements affects the possibilities of flights operating, and a lack of flights will of course hurt the tourism industry at the destination.
>
> (Ivanova, 2017)

Countries that intend to develop tourism usually go for liberal policies in terms of international air transportation. These are discussed well in Chapter 7. Policy changes are key in other aspects as well. For instance, Alderighi and Gaggero (2018) argued that favourable policy interventions are required for the expansion of air transport within the destination nations and ensuring all sections of the air transport sector the scope for expansion is important. For instance, governments have to ensure airports designed to meet the specific needs of LCCs in order to increase the tourist influx into the destination.

Liberalization is key in air transportation. The effects and the way dynamism is being introduced into the air transport sector are discussed well while discussing deregulation. According to Papatheodorou (2008), "…… the liberalization of the market has resulted in a dramatic reduction of fares, especially on routes where LCC operate, with an undoubtedly positive effect on leisure tourism". Though leisure tourism is specified in many cases, business travel also got impetus by privatization and the dramatic rise of business travel as part of globalization in the world is partly due to the increasing affordability of air transport as well. Privatization and public–private partnerships are now gaining increased importance in the airport sector. Liberalization in this sector too can have significance in the growth of tourism, as witnessed on some regions at least. Singapore is an ideal example of liberalization, and using it, it could become a major aviation hub in the region, and it could foster the growth of short-stay stopover tourism (Forsyth, 2008).

6.10.8 Offsetting seasonality

Seasonality is a feature of not only tourism, but also air transport. The air traffic flow has fluctuations often. Though air transport sector has seasonality, a segment of it has the ability to reduce seasonality of tourism and ensure tourist influx into the destinations in low seasons as well. Charter flights are known for this. Tour operators usually depend on charter fight services to conduct tours to destinations. Low season-based tours are also offered taking charter flights. Tourism is a seasonal economic sector as it sees peaks and lows in tourism demand at regular intervals often. This affects the industries within the destinations, and the income and employment opportunities are severely impacted if the seasonal fluctuations are more. According to Keller (2000), charter flights help to offset the seasonal nature of tourism demand. Availability of air services at affordable cost tempts travel enthusiasts to explore destinations during off-seasons as well. Nowadays, LCCs are also considered for package tours. During low seasons, the price level of LCCs will be further lower and this advantage is utilized by the tour operators in offering tours to destinations in low seasons. By this, the cost and price of tours will be much lower and tour operators get a price advantage.

6.10.9 Determinant in tourist buying behaviour

A potential tourist passes through a series of stages in taking a decision in choosing the destination to visit. "The variety and convenience of transport connections are estimated to be among the most important factors in choosing a destination" (Ivanova, 2017). As travel is fundamental in tourism and the travel cost is very significant in the overall expenditure, a section of the tourists will choose the alternative option available at lower cost and with convenient connectivity. In this matter, LCCs have an advantage and increased relevance in the short-haul tourism. Leisure tourists are particularly price-sensitive customers. The advantage of having lower cost enables them to make use of LCCs to engage in tourism.

6.11 Dependence of tourism industry over air transport

In the tourism system, air transport plays a crucial role by which other sectors within it are directly or indirectly depending on it for making available the customers. Tourism sector is featured with inseparability, geographic fragmentation of the industries and perishability. Due to inseparability, production takes place in the presence of the consumers. The industries are located far away from the place of the consumers. It is inevitable for the consumers, tourists, to reach the location of the industry to consume the products of tourism. Moreover, due to perishability, these products cannot be stored for future sale. All these make the role of air transport so important. Air transport, being the fastest mode of transport, smartly enables the consumers to access the products that are present far away. It can ensure better comfort, travel experience and speed in accessing the location. An impact of this is that other key players in the tourism industry have a dependence on transport sector in getting the customers at the right time. This aspect is highlighted by Keller (2000) that "…, suppliers of tourism products and services are dependent on air transport to an extent that depends on their geographical situation and their source markets".

Role of air transport in tourism

Dependence on air transport is crucial in international tourism. Due to it, a crisis in transport sector can directly or indirectly affect the rest of the industry players in tourism. In the recent history, the 9/11 terrorist attack on world trade centre in the USA was more of an air transport industry-based crisis, but the global tourism sector faced slump in demand for a few months. Different partnerships between airlines and components of tourism like hotels, tour operators, restaurants and rental cars have been there in the parlance of international tourism (Lohman and Duval, 2011). Hotels, attractions, restaurants, etc., are situated in the destination, which is geographically separated from the source markets, and they have to depend on air transport to ensure availability of their customers. Some other key players in the industry like tour operators and travel agents have increased dependence on air transport. Travel agency sector primarily depends on air transport for their survival. Traditionally, travel agents are the intermediaries of air transport sector and still the dependence continues, though they have been doing diversification in their business focuses.

Table 6.2 Linking Tourism Industry Elements: Additional Services of Lufthansa

Lufthansa Car Rental Partner

Lufthansa offers exclusive benefits for using car rental services of it. It partners with car rental firms and arranges an option for booking rental cars through their sites. Currently, Lufthansa partners with leading car rental firms like Europcar, Hertz and SIXT. They have a mileage plan as well linked to car rental service. Those passengers earn 500 miles with a particular car usage, as part of their customer retention strategies, and can earn rewards, and the rate of rewards increases with the mile points accrued.

Booking Accommodation

Lufthansa partners with Booking.com to ensure accommodation arrangements of its passengers. Here also, mile points are provided. The members of their miles scheme can earn valuable mile points with every stay. Mile point is accrued in every euro spent in accommodation units.

City break, relaxation trip or entertainment holidays

As part of stopover promotion, Lufthansa provides options for booking a city break in major cities like New York, Paris and Tokyo. It enables passengers to engage in shopping in exclusive showrooms, go for culinary varieties, short trip within cities, etc. Through Booking.com, a short relaxation holiday can also be enjoyed, like a yoga holiday, relaxation in a thermal bath or a temple visit. Similar options are there in taking part in entertainment events as well.

Source: www.lufthansa.com, data available online at https://www.lufthansa.com/in/en/homepage

6.12 Business travel versus leisure travel

Leisure travel forms the core of tourism and has been growing at a significant rate until the global tourism hit harshly by the global pandemic. "Leisure travel demand can be defined as the quantity of leisure travel products (such as air transport) that a tourist is willing and able to purchase" (Li, 2008). On the other hand, business tourism segment is also growing fast and the role of air transport is increasingly relevant for its dramatic growth for the last a few decades. Though dependence is there, slight difference can be there in the demand patterns. Leisure tourists are more price-sensitive which makes travel cost more important. Cost factor is considered a determinant in the leisure tourism segment. On the other hand, business tourism is less price-sensitive. Distance factor is also thus related to leisure tourism, and demand depends on the function of demand and cost of travel. For a business traveller, time is an important factor and the increased frequency of transport services does have significance. Establishment of LCCs has significantly contributed in the leisure tourism segment. Some of the studies have pointed out that business tourism is also getting influenced by LCCs. Yet, the impact remains less comparatively. Nilsson (2009) noted that though some business travellers use LCCs, the inflexible ticket systems, prolonged check-in times and more time-consuming connections cause this group rather small. Along with demand addition, cheaper rate-based air transport helps in diversification on the air transport industry as well. The role played by travel cost and low-cost airlines is described well above.

6.13 Alliances to support tourism growth

Airline alliances have a role in tourism as well. Alliances are based primarily on cooperation on certain areas in order to gain competitive advantages by way of synergistic effects and economies of scale, among other things (Gross & Klemmer, 2014). According to Gross and Klemmer (2014)

> Such relationships can be of a horizontal nature (collaboration between companies providing the same product or operating within the same market), vertical nature (collaboration with companies along different stages of the value chain-suppliers, intermediaries, distributors or buyers) or diagonal nature (collaboration with companies from different industries).

They can enable international travel smoother and make the journeys having complicated travel itineraries easy. Airline alliances can have a role in tourism as well by involving in the mechanism of fares and total travel time, connectivity, and cooperative promotion (Morley, 2003). Both leisure and business travellers gain the benefits of airline alliances. The prime targets of airline alliances in terms of tourism are as follows:

- Those who fly on transatlantic and transpacific routes.
- Business travellers combining business with leisure.
- Some other upmarket passengers (Iatrou & Tsitsiragou, 2008).

While in alliances, airlines engage in cooperation and mutual support among themselves in a number of crucial areas. All these make the journey of passenger smooth. This is more relevant for international tourism as tourists may travel to more destinations in a single trip and thus the tour itinerary can be more complicated than that of other type of passengers. Airline alliances made it possible for the airline industry to provide tourists the increased frequency, integrated route network and lower-priced service around the world (Iatrou & Tsitsiragou, 2008). Getting connectivity to different regions is easy for tourists when airlines are in some alliance. Codeshare agreements and technology sharing enable tourists to get booking done easily. In addition to the provision of global network for travelling to multiple destinations, lounge access in airports and loyalty scheme benefits; airline alliance membership can ensure a 'seamless' travel experience by providing convenient departure timings and minimum waiting time in the transit points (Iatrou & Oretti, 2007). Hence, alliances, directly or indirectly, facilitate the process of tourism more smooth.

6.14 Air transport to enhance tourist experience

Transport is usually part of the composite tourism product. Certainly, transport experience is an important element of the tourist experience.

> The nature of tourism transport experience is defined either by a single mode or a combination of transport modes, it still involves movement from one location to another, and a degree of attraction or more precisely a satisfaction of wants associated with the actual process of traveling. The key distinction in transport for tourism tends to offer low intrinsic values within the overall experience and the tourism transport experience a higher intrinsic value.
>
> (Lumsdon & Page, 2004)

Tourism, being a service product, aims at providing an experience, which enables the tourists to have fond memories of the visit and in making positive recommendations and future visits. Tourist satisfaction and tourist experience are closely interconnected. Being a composite product, the tourist expects high satisfaction levels from all the services and products consumed from the beginning of the journey till reaches back to his/her place after the tour. The satisfaction, the impressions generated and the feel gained from each service are combined to form the overall tourist experience. A pleasurable experience adds to the sweet memories of the trip later on. Quality transport makes tourists comfortable and can enhance the scope for repeat visit to the same destination. A poor transport experience can lead to dissatisfaction and consequently affect the overall tourist experience.

Air transport, being integral elements in the tourism system, has to provide quality services. The facilities and services offered have to be matching with international standards as tourists are coming from different regions in the world who are mostly aware of the quality standards in air transport. Thompson and Schofield (2007) pointed out that the quality of transport infrastructure and the services offered by the elements in it do have a role in the overall tourist experience. Therefore, airlines and airports usually make efforts to offer the most possible

---

Table 6.3 Holiday Options Offered By Emirates

Emirates is a leading and global airline offering air transportation services in a wide network from Dubai, UAE. It is actively involved in holiday promotion as well.

All-Inclusive Holidays

A range of all-inclusive holiday packages to major destinations are provided by Emirates, and additional offers are also provided for those who use these holidays like guaranteed savings and upgrades.

Business Class Trips

Luxurious holiday packages with business class seat travel, chauffeur-driven transfers and stay in high-class hotels are a specialty of Emirates. Comfort, priority check-in, 40kg baggage allowance and comfortable lounge access are part of the features of this type of holidays.

Dubai Holiday Offers

Dubai's man-made wonders and beaches can be enjoyed through Emirate's Dubai holiday package. Accommodation in famous resorts is also part of the package. Guaranteed savings, upgrades and some extras can make the holiday rememberable. The diversity of packages includes beach holidays, luxury holidays, city breaks, family holidays and honeymoon trips. Canada packages, European packages, Historical Jordan package, Kenya Safari package, South Africa packages, Splendours of the Nile and US packages are provided as packaged holidays. Group holiday package is also offered for which the airline has to be contacted directly.

Source: www.emiratesholidays.com

facilities and quality services to the tourists. Airport's efficiency in ensuring quality passenger handling services is key in the tourist experience. The digitalization within airport in smooth airport functioning, quality of the personnel involved in delivering the service, the options for availing ancillary services, availability of shopping and refreshment options, etc., do matter in contributing tourist experience. Airline delay, poor in-flight services, unfavourable weather conditions, etc., can dampen tourist experience.

6.15 Airlines take part in packaging

Airlines increasingly offer package holidays and market those through their channels of distribution. Holiday packages are offered now into the destinations where the airline has services. Group tour booking option is also provided. Usually, many of the airlines provide high-quality package holiday services. At times, airlines provide only accommodation and transport arrangement alone, whereas in some other cases, they provide all-inclusive packages. This is directly promoting tourism and adds tourism demand. Airline holiday packages are rated as good ones by a good share of the tourist population.

6.16 Conclusion

In this chapter, we discussed in detail how aviation affects and influences tourism. The three parallels between tourism and transportation are regulatory synergies, objective function and shared sustainability. Airlines have a wide variety of business models, which affect tourism considerably. The expansion, growth, quality improvement and improvement of the airline supply chain will strengthen the tourism potential of the destinations. As the transportation network expands to new horizons, so does the international tourism spectrum. Due to the increase in LCCs, short-haul city tourism becomes popular among different income groups and inspires the tourism sector for visiting friends and relatives. Many cities are now promoting stopover tourism and their flag carriers and with the support of other airlines. Long-haul tourism has now become more popular as long-haul travel has become more common with the use of wide-body aircraft, resulting in lower air travel costs.

Distance and air travel are directly linked, making it more difficult to reach destinations that are far away from major tourist market areas. However, major airlines opened routes to these destinations. Direct connectivity by air to the destination enhances the development of tourism and the economic importance of the area. With the growing demand for tourism around the world, there is a growing rate of air travel among more and more sections of society. Air travel has become a favourite of middle-class people in recent history for a variety of reasons, including the rise in economic status and the availability of cheaper air travel options. The infiltration of the air travel trend is deeply linked to the increasing affordability rate. Travel cost is a major determinant in tourism, which has been reduced considerably due to various reasons. LCCs are increasing the travel propensity, so that people in the tourism market can afford air travel. Larger countries are benefiting from the LCCs in the development of domestic tourism. Intra-regional tourism is a major beneficiary of LCC growth. LCC is definitely increasing the demand for tourism in a destination. The air transport sector is becoming more and more interested in attracting leisure tourists and business tourists, which is leading to the growth of tourism. The liberal approach to bilateral agreements and the multifaceted agreements in the air transport industry positively supports tourism. Through alliances, airlines engage in cooperation, support in a number of critical areas and facilitate passenger travel. Airlines and airports usually make efforts to offer the most possible facilities and quality services to the tourists. Airlines also started to provide all-inclusive tours, which directly promote tourism on a larger scale. Of late, airports also started offering package tours that can promote tourism further.

Sample questions

Short/medium answer type questions

- Discuss the role of air transport in the rise of new destinations and new forms of tourism.
- Distinguish between short-haul city tourism and stopover tourism.
- Explain how distance is connected to air transport.

- Describe the way the growth of air transport stimulates tourism.
- Summarize the way air transport impacts the growth of tourism.
- Elucidate the relationship between distance and air transport correlation.
- Identify the benefits that can be there when the destination has direct connectivity with tourism origin cities.
- Write how travel cost and affordability influence tourism.
- Write a brief note on the dependability of tourism on air transport.
- Outline the role of air transport in enhancing tourist experience.

Essay type questions

- Discuss the significance of LCCs in the progress of tourism.
- Describe how the growth in air transport contributes in the evolution of tourism.
- Explain the intricate relationship between air transport and tourism.

Suggested readings

Bieger, T., & Wittmer, A. (2006). Air transport and tourism – Perspectives and challenges for destinations, airlines and governments. *Journal of Air Transport Management*, 12(1), 40–46.

Cristina, S. (2017). New perspectives of the tourism and air transport relationship. *Cactus Tourism Journal*, 15(2), 24–32.

Duval, D.T. (2013). Critical issues in air transport and tourism. *Tourism Geographies*, 15(3), 494–510.

Dileep, M.R. (2019). *Tourism, Transport and Travel Management*. London: Routledge.

Graham, A., & Dobruszkes, F. (Eds.) (2019). *Air Transport – A Tourism Perspective*. Oxford: Elsevier.

Ivanova, M. (2017). *Air Transport – Tourism Nexus: A Destination Management Perspective*. Varna: Zangador.

Papatheodorou, A., & Forsyth, P. (Eds.) (2008). *Aviation and Tourism: Implications for Leisure Travel*. Hampshire: Ashgate.

Spasojevic, B., Lohmann, G., & Scott, N. (2017). Air transport and tourism – a systematic literature review (2000–2014). *Current Issues in Tourism*, 21, 975–997.

Chapter 7

Air transport regulations and tourism

Learning outcomes

After reading this chapter, you will be able to:

- Define international air transport regulations.
- Analyse the role of regulations in the growth of tourism.
- Understand the nuances of national regulations.
- Comprehend the bilateral regulations.
- Learn the "freedoms of the air".
- Narrate the evolution of bilateral regulations.
- Explain multilateral regulations.

7.1 Introduction

Akin to other modes of transport, air transport is also born with fewer regulations. Yet, unlike other modes, it became imminent to have strict regulations very soon. The need for crossing the borders and fly in airspace over the territories of other sovereign countries created the inevitability for regulations. Moreover, the need for protecting the rights and responsibilities of service providers and consumers also caused the requirement for regulations. Safety and security contributed to the need for regulations at multiple levels. The smoothness in air transportation that we enjoy in this 21st century is also due to the result of regulations and agreements that were evolved through several decades and with the help of various conventions, conferences and discussions that happened at the international level. In fact, the attempts to frame regulations began in the first decade of invention of the aircrafts heavier than air. So far, aviation is the most strictly and highly regulated industry (Milde, 2008). The political and regulatory environment of aviation is shaped by different bodies functioning at national, regional as well as global levels. Most of the regulations, particularly the technical

 DOI: 10.4324/9781003136927-7

and operational, are based upon international regulations that are imposed by respective agencies, like International Civil Aviation Organization (ICAO). Among various attempts, Chicago Convention is the most important one that could pave the way for a smooth international air service operations and the base for negotiations and agreements between countries. The history of the evolution of air transport regulations, the nature and types of regulations and the influence of such regulations in the growth of tourism are discussed in detail in this chapter.

7.2 Air transport policies and tourism

International tourism has been growing at a tremendous pace during the last half a century with the immense support of air transportation. This aspect has been discussed at length in different chapters in this book. Air transport-related policies and regulations have a significant impact on the flourishing of international air transportation and in the corresponding rise of tourism worldwide. At the destination level also, this past has much relevance. Papatheodorou and Zenelis (2013) opine, "Aviation policies and government decisions concerning the smooth cooperation of tourism and aviation can make a big difference in the prosperity of a leisure destination". Furthermore, a country's

> political situation and its legal regulation of air transport will directly impact its tourism development. Availability of bilateral or multilateral agreements affects the possibilities of flights operating, and a lack of flights will of course hurt the tourism industry at the destination.
>
> (Ivanova, 2017)

Regulations that restrict air transport can have detrimental effects on tourism, and at the same time, easing regulations has the capacity to stimulate the tourism demand as well. With regard to air transport and tourism, Duval (2012) identified a number of aspects that restrict tourist flow into destinations. The major of them are as follows: restriction through air service agreements (ASAs) by limiting seats, restricting the frequency of service by setting a capacity limit; by specifying ownership criteria in agreements; and by limiting the airports/destination cities the airlines of other states can undertake services to. There can be restrictions in tourist flow as well through ASAs by way of limiting the number of seats, frequency or aircraft size. Another scope of the restriction is through the specification of ownership and control parameters, like those in the case of flag carriers. Restricting the access to specific destination/airport is another way of imposing limitation using traffic rights. By having such specifications in the agreement, countries can reduce points to be served by designated airlines of other countries.

On the other hand, Duval (2012) also specified that market access policies constitute another aspect that can influence tourism and tourist flow, and it is particularly relevant when there is a move towards less regulated international air transport. Open sky policy is an example which can stimulate the tourist flow. Since 1978, a watershed year in the history of international air transport that marked the beginning of privatization due to the initiation of deregulation in the USA, air transport sector has been experiencing increasing rate of liberalization and efforts for smoothening of air transportation among countries. Tourism could progress in the circumstance that emerged after the deregulation. The recent history of tourism includes the instances of initiating favourable air transport policies by the national authorities. For instance, Forsyth (2006) stated that though much consideration was not there in the history of air transport negotiations, the importance of international aviation for tourism and the issue of restrictive aviation policies in curtailing tourism are being increasingly recognized now. That made many countries to revise their international aviation policies to have explicit recognition of tourism benefits. Of late, having the intention to promote tourism further, more number of nations is interested in engaging in bilateral and multilateral air transport agreements that aim at easing restrictions. Moreover, the trend of engaging in open sky policies is also on the increase. Further, favourable air transport policies by the nations boost domestic air transport as well.

7.3 Air transport regulation: concept and types

Civil aviation is certainly the most comprehensively and strictly regulated mode of transport in the world (Milde, 2008). Regulation in air transport has varied dimensions. It involves aviation-related policy-making, agreements for granting rights to fly and undertake commercial air transportation nationally and internationally, ensuring standardization in equipment used and operations, licensing of air service providers, regulating tariffs and prices, controlling various aspects of operations, to advance the growth and safety of air travel and the like. Thus, regulation is fundamental and important to the industry and provides the required authority, responsibility and sanctions (Bartsch, 2018). Different types of regulations are applicable for international commercial air transportation since the transportation happens in and out from other sovereign countries. Hence, regulations can be seen at different levels, and a broad classification of air transport regulations is as follows:

- National regulations.
- Bilateral regulations.
- Multilateral regulations.

7.4 National regulations

National regulations involve all regulatory measures that are to be followed, within the territory of a country/state. These are usually established in adherence to the international mandatory regulations. Moreover, the nation's multilateral and bilateral agreements with other countries are also to be considered while developing regulations at the national level. All air transport activities, including domestic and international, within the country have to follow the regulations stipulated by the national authorities. Countries will be having specific aviation laws to regulate air transport services. According to ICAO (2004), the following are three distinct focus areas that come under national regulations:

- Legislating. This involves the following major activities:
  - Law-making: it is a long-time process and done least often.

- o   Policy-making: this is done considering the prevailing aviation environments.
  - o   Writing rules and regulations: this is done more frequently and more detailed.
- Licensing. This involves the following major activities:
  - o   Granting or conditioning of licences to conduct air transport services, cargo services, intermediary services, etc., on a continuous or long-term basis.
  - o   Denying or withholding permission to conduct air transport services, tariffs, cargo services, intermediary services, etc., under certain necessary circumstances
- Ad hoc authorization
  - o   It is done for granting, denying or withholding permission for single flight or a series of non-scheduled flights, tariffs, schedule filing, etc. This is primarily related to day-to-day decisions on specific matters.

The structure of the organization of national authorities may vary from country to country. There can be a single organization that handles all aspects of regulations of air transport in the country or can be more than one organization with separate tasks vested upon each of them. National authorities are often called as Civil Aviation Authority (CAA). The CAA or National Aviation Authority of a country regulates all the airports within the country to ensure they comply with all international and national safety standards. Though CAAs are statutory authorities, in some countries, CAAs are quasi-judicial organizations.

7.5 National regulations and tourism

In this era of liberalization also, many aspects are included in the national regulations that may be contradicting the liberalization agendas. Tourism can flourish when fewer regulations are there. Certain aspects are mandatory, particularly those in meeting the safety and security standards, etc. In fact, the attempts to frame regulations began in the first decade of invention of the aircrafts heavier than air. The following are highlighted by Hindley (2004) as the current national regulation practices and that are inconsistent with liberalization movements.

- Restrictions on foreign ownership of domestic carriers.
- Restrictions on the nationality of crew members on internal routes.
- Restrictions on access of foreign carriers to internal routes within a country.
- Prohibitions on wet leasing (renting of aircraft and crews) from foreigners.
- Requirements that government travellers use domestic carriers.
- Methods of allocating take-off and landing slots at airports.

All the above are restricting factors for domestic tourism as well as international tourism. However, General Agreement on Trade in Service (GATS) agreement of World Trade Association, which aims at liberalized global trade, does not prohibit any such, for the flourishing of air transport in both domestic and international routes, and liberalized national policies can be of increasing advantage.

7.6 Bilateral regulations, Air Service Agreement (ASA) and tourism

Bilateral regulations are initiated between two countries/states for the smooth conduct of air transport between them, and those can ensure the smooth, comfortable and convenient movement of tourist traffic between those countries. If an airline of a country would like to operate international services to another country, the respective government should have undertaken efforts to negotiate a treaty-level agreement with the government of the destination country. Bilateral regulations seen today are a result of a number of efforts in the form of conventions, meetings, summits and discussion that were there in different stages of aviation history. According to ICAO (2004), "a significant amount of intergovernmental bilateral regulatory activities involves formal consultation undertaken to conclude, interpret, expand or amend, or resolve a dispute under an intergovernmental agreement, or arrangement or understanding concerning international air services". According to Haanappel (1980), bilateral agreements are "international trade agreements, in which governmental authorities of two sovereign States attempt to regulate the performance of air services between their respective territories and beyond, in some cases".

The term used for international agreements is **air service agreement (ASA)**, and bilateral ASAs have been evolved as a tool for originating, modifying and regulating international transportation services (Odoni, 2009). Bilateral air transport agreement or ASA is the "basic document most often used by States to jointly regulate their international air services relationships" (ICAO, 2004). According to Piermartini and Rousova (2008), air service agreement "...establishes the conditions under which air companies operate in each country. These rules define, for instance, whether airlines can freely set prices, how many airlines can operate a service and their capacity. Clearly, the degree of liberalization of air transport services between two countries is determined by the specific design of each ASA".

According to the Department of Infrastructure, Regional Development and Cities of Australian Government (www.gov.au), the following are the elements in bilateral agreements in international air transportation.

- Traffic rights: the routes, including the cities that can be served within, airlines can fly; between and beyond the bilateral partners.
- Designation, ownership and control: the number of airlines that can be nominated to operate services and the required ownership criteria of airlines. Foreign ownership restrictions are also part of this, sometimes.
- Capacity: the number of flights that can be operated or passengers that can be carried.
- Tariffs: i.e. prices. Some agreements necessitate airlines to submit ticket prices to aeronautical authorities for approval.
- Many other clauses addressing airline competition policy, safety and security.

Doganis (2005) identified "hard rights" and "soft rights" that are part of the ASAs. Hard rights deal with economic aspects, the number of designated airlines and the regulation of tariffs and capacity traffic rights. Soft rights facilitate the operation of air services, like those cover taxation issues, exemption from customs duties on imports of aircraft parts, airport charges, transfer abroad of airline funds and so on. Joint bilateral regulations (between one state and two or more other states) are possible. A common organization of different states can also perform bilateral negotiation with a state. Other types are also seen. Plurilateral agreements are also possible. Such would be initially bilateral; later, it may be expanded to include more parties.

Bilateral agreements are fundamental in international air transport. Liberal approaches and increased bilateral agreements with fewer restrictions enable smoother, strengthened and increased international air transport, which paves the way for increasing the tourism demand between those countries.

7.7 Market access right

Market access is important for commercial air transport service providers to access the market and to get the passengers/cargo to be transported. Market access right is the term used in this context, and it represents a group of rights that are negotiated, exchanged or traded under a plethora of bilateral and multilateral arrangements as "air traffic rights", and includes rights such as capacity, frequency and routes. In scheduled international air transport, different market access rights are discussed. According to ICAO (2004), market access has varied forms, such as basic market access rights, route rights, operational rights and traffic rights. A basic right is pertaining to access in foreign countries with specification of routes, etc. Route rights are all about accessing route/routes with authorized places to serve. Operational rights deal with number of carriers to undertake services, nature and type of aircraft used for air service, etc. Traffic rights are all about the right to transport passengers, cargo and mail. Traffic rights start from third "freedom of the air" onwards. Bilateral agreements through some of their elements ensure the market access as well. Getting the right to market access is important for airlines to operate services. Country-to-country negotiations will specify the terms for market access rights as well.

7.8 Tariffs

Earlier regulations were applicable more on tariffs to ensure fair opportunity for price-wise competition, to encourage related sectors like trade and tourism and to restrict unfair practices by the air service providers. Regulations on tariff vary widely. In this era of deregulation, limited regulations are prevailing, though some aspects of tariff are still under the purview of regulations. Tariff is basically associated with the price charged for the transportation of passengers, bag and cargo. The conditions governing its availability and use are also part of the tariff domestically and internationally. Tariffs have certain general rules to follow. Examples include fare construction rules, currency conversion rules, and baggage allowances and excess baggage charges. Specific rules are also there which are associated with each fare. Examples may include rules associated with stopovers, transfers, fare combination and re-booking/re-routing. These tariffs are considered subject to international tariff regimes and/or national tariff regulatory regimes. The conditions in international tariff regime may vary. In some cases, both the countries have to approve the tariff (double approval system). Flexible pricing zones and free pricing zones are also there in international tariff regimes. Traditionally, double approval system was followed along with the international rate fixing mechanism (usually IATA's standard system) wherever possible. However, nowadays, things are more liberalized, though a standard mechanism is followed. Of late, hybrid approaches are also seen that are a combination of different approaches.

Most bilateral air transport agreements deal only with scheduled international air services. Of late, non-scheduled or charter air services have increasingly been included in bilateral agreements. While some of the agreements for charter airlines are clubbed with that of scheduled airlines, some others are exclusive bilateral agreements for charter airlines alone. National authorities issue the necessary licence/permit or an ad hoc authorization for undertaking non-scheduled services. Some of the bilateral agreements may have consideration for non-scheduled transportation as well. A few of the multilateral agreements have separate provisions for non-scheduled international transportation, and most of them have a liberalized approach for international non-scheduled transportation among the signatory countries.

7.9 Freedoms of the air

Freedoms of the air provide traffic rights; that is, they refer to "the rights that an airline of any state may enjoy with respect to another state or states" (Belobaba & Odoni, 2009). This market access right grants a country's airline the privilege to enter and land in another country's airspace. It denotes the right to transport passengers, cargo and mail, separately or in any combination, and is expressed as "freedom of the air". These traffic rights/market access rights are negotiated not by the world's airlines but between their home states. The first five freedoms are the most common and the rest are called 'so-called freedoms'. Among the five freedoms, the first and second freedom rights are granted essentially automatically when countries gave consent to International Air Services Transit Agreement. Most of the nations exchange these two. The rest three become valid when countries engage in bilateral/multilateral agreements and sign the necessary agreements. Of them, third and fourth are granted together. The cabotage freedoms (eighth and ninth) are granted in limited instances. The freedoms of the air (Boeing-. www.boeing.com and ICAO/Chicago Convention) are introduced below.

7.9.1 First freedom of the air

This provides the negotiated right of a scheduled international airline of one country to fly over the territory of another country, i.e. the right or privilege granted by one state/nation to another state/nation or states/nations to fly across its territory without landing (Figure 7.1).

7.9.2 Second freedom of the air

The right or privilege granted by one state/nation to another state/nation or states/nations to land in its territory for non-traffic purposes; that is, the flight of

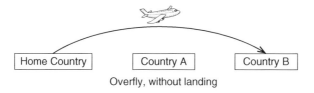

Overfly, without landing

Figure 7.1 First freedom of the air

Landing for Technical reasons

Figure 7.2 Second freedom of the air

an international airline of a country can make an intermediate landing in another state/nation for technical reasons like refuelling or maintenance (Figure 7.2).

7.9.3 Third freedom of the air

This provides the negotiated right for an international scheduled airline of one country to deliver revenue passengers in another country, i.e. the right or privilege granted by one state/nation to another state/nation to put down, in the territory of the first state/nation, traffic coming from the home state/nation of the carrier. Simply, it is the right to transport passengers, cargo and mail from the home country of the airline to another country (Figure 7.3).

7.9.4 Fourth freedom of the air

This provides the negotiated right for an international scheduled airline of one country to carry revenue passengers from another country, i.e. the right or

Carry revenue traffic
from home country to another country

Figure 7.3 Third freedom of the air

Carry revenue traffic
from another county to Home country

Figure 7.4 Fourth freedom of the air

privilege granted by one state/nation to another state/nation to take on, in the territory of the first state/nation, traffic destined for the home state/nation of the carrier. Simply, it is the right to transport passengers, cargo and mail to the home country of the airline from another country (Figure 7.4).

7.9.5 Fifth freedom of the air

The right or privilege granted by one state/nation to another state/nation to put down and to take on, in the territory of the first state/nation, traffic coming from or destined to a third state. It provides the right for an international airline of a country to take revenue passengers from its home country, deposit them in another country, and then pick up and carry passengers to another destination in a third country. Simply, by this negotiated right, the international airline of one country can transport passengers, cargo and mail to the partner country and from there to another country (Figure 7.5).

7.9.6 Sixth freedom of the air

This provides the negotiated right or privilege of transporting, via the home state/nation of the carrier, traffic moving between two other states/nations. By this, an international airline of one country can transport passengers, cargo and mail between two foreign countries via the home country. Simple, an airline can undertake commercial transportation from one partner country to another country via the home country (Figure 7.6).

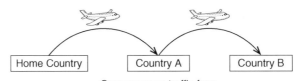

Carry revenue traffic from
home country and then drop-off and pick-up
traffic from that country to a third country

Figure 7.5 Fifth freedom of the air

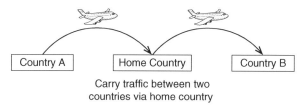

Carry traffic between two
countries via home country

Figure 7.6 Sixth freedom of the air

7.9.7 Seventh freedom of the air

This provides the right to undertake commercial air transportation between two foreign countries without landing in the home country of the airline. The international airline gets the right or privilege granted by one state/nation to another state/nation for transporting traffic between the territory of the granting state/nation and any third state/nation with no requirement to include on such operation any point in the territory of the recipient state/nation. While doing international air transport service between two foreign countries, the airline need not connect to or be an extension of any service to/from the home state/nation of the carrier (Figure 7.7).

7.9.8 Eighth freedom of the air

This is also known as cabotage right (consecutive cabotage), and it gives the right or privilege, in respect of scheduled international air services, of transporting cabotage traffic between two points in the territory of the granting state/nation on a service which originates or terminates in the home country. By this, the international airline of one country can undertake transport services between two points within a foreign country and the services begin or end in the home country of the airline. Simply, the airlines can transport passengers, cargo or mail within the partner state/country on a flight commencing or ending in the home state/country (Figure 7.8).

Carry revenue traffic
between two other countries

Figure 7.7 Seventh freedom of the air

Carry revenue traffic between
two points within another country, covering
from or destined to home country

Figure 7.8 Eighth freedom of the air

Carry revenue traffic within another country,
without continuing to home country

Figure 7.9 Ninth freedom of the air

7.9.9 Ninth freedom of the air

This is also called stand-alone cabotage, and it provides the right or privilege of transporting cabotage traffic of the granting state/nation on a service performed entirely within the territory of the granting state. By this, an international airline of one country can undertake passenger, cargo or mail transportation between points situated within a foreign country, without commencing or ending services in the home country (Figure 7.9).

7.10 History of bilateral regulations

Only a few agreements were there before the Second World War. The need of having international regulations and agreements became imminent. In 1910, the Government of France initiated 21 European countries for being part of the International Conference of Air Navigation in Paris. It could not give a convincing outcome, yet the sovereignty aspect of airspace over countries became a factor/matter in international air transport. The beginning of the formation of bilateral regulations took place in the 1920s. The major events are briefed below.

7.10.1 Paris Conference (1919)

The 1910 conference paved the way for a 1919 diplomatic conference during which an Aeronautical Commission of the Peace Conference drafted the Paris

Convention for the Regulation of Aerial Navigation, also called Paris Convention. This specified and confirmed the sovereignty of airspace over countries. Representatives from allied nations and associated nations participated in Paris Convention, and ultimately, 38 states became parties to that accord. It became the first international multilateral convention on the Regulation of Aerial Navigation. This convention recognized the principle of airspace sovereignty, until then customarily enforced by states. Apart from the reservation of the sovereignty of airspace by the contracting nations, the issuance of certificate of airworthiness, each nation's registry of aircraft, the flight of aircraft over air above the other countries territories, international air navigation rules, prohibition of carriage of arms and ammunition and establishment and maintenance of a permanent commission for air navigation were finalised in Paris conference. Moreover, the convention also produced the International Commission on Air Navigation (ICAN), a permanent Paris-based organization with a full-time secretariat. This commission was vested with the responsibility of execution, administration and updating of the Paris Convention.

7.10.2 Madrid Convention

In 1926, an attempt was there to create Ibero-American Convention Relating to Air Navigation (Madrid Convention). It was virtually identical to the Paris Convention but with equality for states rather than weighted voting. However, this did not come into force.

7.10.3 Havana Convention (1928)

The **Fifth Pan-American Conference** was also held in Santiago in 1923, and it resolved that an Inter-American Commission on Commercial Aviation be established, consisting of not more than three delegates of each State Member of the Pan-American Union. It was mooted to formulate a code of laws and regulations. They dealt with commercial aviation, the determination of air routes, the establishment of special customs procedures for aviation, the determination of adequate landing policies and recommendations with respect to the places at which landing facilities should be established (Wells, 1988).

In the meanwhile, an attempt was made at Madrid, Spain, in 1926, to create an Ibero-American Convention Relating to Air Navigation, also known as the Madrid Convention, but the same did not enter into effect. The Inter-American Commission met for the first time in Washington in May of 1927 and prepared a draft code, which was revised by the Director General of Union. The same was submitted to the 6th Pan-American Conference, held in Havana, Cuba, in 1928 and got ratified by the participating states. It was similar to Paris Convention in content, without provision for a governing body. Sixteen states in the Americas ratified it. Similar regional conventions were held in the 1930s, like in Latin America, Buenos Aires Convention (1935), and in Europe, Bucharest Convention (1936) and the Zemun Agreement (1937).

7.10.4 Warsaw Convention (1929)

Before Warsaw Convention, there were no uniform rules of law related to international carriage by air. The Government of France made an attempt in 1923 to adopt national laws relating to liability in the carriage by air, but sooner realized the need for a unified law at an international level to prevent the unforeseeable conflicts of law and conflicts of jurisdiction. The 1923 event adopted a resolution calling the attention of the public to the need for the establishment of a uniform code. The French Government took initiative to have further discussion on the above, and representatives of 43 nations met in Paris in 1925. The conference established the International Committee of Technical Experts of Air Jurisprudence (Comité International Technique d'Experts Juridiques Aériens – CITEJA) with headquarters in Paris. The draft prepared by the Committee was submitted for consideration at the Second International Conference on Private Air Law held in the Royal Castle at Warsaw, Poland, in 1929. This convention "adopted a uniform set of rules governing international carriage by air, and deals with the rights of passengers and owners or consignors of cargo and provides for internationally accepted limits on carrier's liability for death, injury or damage" (Bartsch, 2018). Thus, the Warsaw Convention, formally entitled "Convention for the Unification of Certain Rules Relating to International Carriage by Air", came into effect. According to Warsaw Convention, an airline is liable for damages in the event of:

- Death or injury to the passengers.
- Destruction, loss or damage to baggage or goods.
- Loss resulting from delay in transportation of passengers, baggage or merchandise.

A few other efforts were also held in between though those could not make much progress in regulating the international air transportation.

7.10.5 Chicago Convention (1944)

Based on the invitation of the US government, representatives of 52 nations assembled in Chicago in November 1944. It was organized with the intention to foster the development of international civil aviation in a safe and orderly manner and to promote international air transport services on the basis of equality of opportunity and sound and economic operation. The general objectives of the gathering are as follows:

- Economic
  - Promotion of freedom of airspace to nations and airlines.
  - Procedures for determining airfares, frequencies, schedules and capacities.
  - Arrangements for simplifying customs procedures.
  - Standardizing visas and other documentation.
- Technical: To establish international standards related to:
  - Licensing of pilots and mechanics.
  - Registering and certifying the airworthiness of aircraft.
  - Planning and development of navigational aids (Bartsch, 2018).

This convention on international civil aviation reaffirmed the air sovereignty of nations. It is often remarked as the "Magna Carta for the post-war development of international civil aviation" (Wober, 2003). The Chicago Convention could establish the rules under which international aviation operates. Also,

> under the Chicago Convention 1944, all scheduled international air services (that either pass through airspace of more than one state; carry passengers, mail or cargo or service two or more destinations in accordance with a published timetable) must acquire prior permission before flying into or over foreign territories.
>
> (Bartsch, 2018)

The conference also produced the International Air Services Transit Agreement, the International Air Transport Agreement, drafts of 12 technical Annexes to the Chicago Convention and a Standard Form of Bilateral Agreement. In addition to the agreements, the Chicago Conference provided recommendations to foster smooth flow of international air transport, through intergovernmental agreements. Chicago standard form, an outcome of the convention, has been adopted by many countries as a basis for arrangements.

Chicago Convention raised for the first time the issues concerning exchange of commercial rights in international civil aviation. It decided to simply create a framework within which the rules regarding international air transportation could be established for regularity of air transport services between pairs of countries. The convention established bilateral agreements that can regulate international air transport. Bilateral ASAs thus emerged as the instrument for initiating or modifying international transportation and for regularity of those services (Odoni, 2009). The convention made it mandatory to follow the international standards and practices to the highest degree of uniformity by all contracting states in terms of the following.

- Characteristics of airports and landing areas.
- Communication systems and air navigation aids, including ground markings.
- Licensing of operational and mechanical personnel.
- Registration and identification of aircraft.
- Aircraft flying rules and air traffic control (ATC) practices.
- Airworthiness of aircraft.
- Aeronautical maps and charts.
- Gathering and exchange of meteorological information.
- Matter concerning the safety, regularity and efficiency of air navigation.
- Customs and immigration procedures.
- Aircraft in distress and investigation of accidents of all types.
- Logbooks (Wells, 1988; Wensveen, 2007).

7.10.6 International Civil Aviation Organization (ICAO)

ICAO, established by the states in 1944 to manage the administration and governance of the Chicago Convention on international civil aviation, is the apex body of regulations, policies and guidelines pertaining to various aspects of civil aviation. ICAO came into being on 4 April 1947, and in October of the same year, it became a specialized agency of the United Nations (UN) linked to Economic and Social Council (ECOSOC). ICAO was established with the objective to foster the planning and development of international air transport in accordance with certain enumerated principles. Currently, ICAO works with the convention's 192 member states and industry groups to reach a consensus on international civil aviation Standards and Recommended Practices (SARPs) and policies in support of a safe, efficient, secure, economically sustainable and environmentally responsible civil aviation sector. Through its various efforts, it enhances the benchmarks for optimum safety and security; the continued progressive, worldwide liberalization of air transport; a globally interoperable, harmonized and seamless air traffic management system; maximum compatibility between the safe and orderly development of civil aviation and the quality of the environment; and further development of a unified global legal framework (ICAO, 2007). Moreover, it:

- Coordinates assistance and capacity building for nations in support of numerous aviation development objectives.
- Produces global plans to coordinate multilateral strategic progress for safety and air navigation.
- Monitors and reports on numerous air transport sector performance metrics.
- Audits states' civil aviation oversight capabilities in the areas of safety and security.

Ensuring safety is one of the prime concerns of ICAO. It takes utmost efforts to implement practical and achievable measures to improve safety and efficiency in all sectors of the air transportation system. The Air Navigation Bureau manages the Safety and Air Navigation Capacity and Efficiency strategies of ICAO in collaboration with aviation stakeholders. Efforts are also there to foster the development of an economically viable civil aviation system and enhance its economic efficiency and transparency while facilitating access to funding for aviation infrastructure and other investment needs, technology transfer and capacity building to support the growth of air transport and for the benefit of all stakeholders. A major challenge taken up by ICAO is enhancing the environmental performance of aviation, and for the same, it develops a range of standards, policies and guidance materials for the application of integrated measures to address aircraft noise and emissions embracing technological improvements, operating procedures, proper organization of air traffic, appropriate airport and land-use planning, and the use of market-based options. Moreover, ICAO has launched the Next Generation of Aviation Professionals (NGAP) initiative to ensure adequate qualified and competent aviation professionals available to operate, manage and maintain the future international air transport system. Its Global Aviation Training (GAT) Office seeks to lead Human Resources Development strategies established by member states and industry to ensure the availability of sufficient number of qualified and competent personnel. The Technical Co-operation Programme of ICAO provides advice and assistance in the development and implementation of projects across the full spectrum of civil aviation aimed at the safety, security, environmental protection and sustainable development of national and international civil aviation (ICAO, www.icao.int).

7.10.7 Bermuda Convention

After 1944 event, the next most important development was the 1946 agree-ment between the UK and the USA, which is known as Bermuda I Agreement. This event helped to incorporate Chicago standard clauses and stipulated that disputes that could not be settled through bilateral consultations have to be put before ICAO for advisory opinion. The Bermuda Agreement gave a satisfactory reconciliation of the differences that existed on international air policy between the USA and the UK after the Chicago Conference. After the discussion, a com-promise emerged regarding tariffs and routes. Routes were specified, and tar-iffs were agreed to be established by the airlines through the International Air Transport Association (IATA), subject to the approval of both parties. Capacity was decided to be determined by airlines based on agreed terms and conditions. This, known as Bermuda I Agreement, became the most successful bilateral agreement after Chicago Convention period, the success of this became an inspiration for other countries, and Bermuda Agreement became a model.

In the second half of the 1970s, the USA came up with **deregulation policy** in air transport which became a milestone in the history of air transport. Under this policy of "deregulation", the role of government in the economic regulation of air transport became minimum, as economic decisions and policies are left to the determination of individual airlines and to the free forces of the marketplace. Air transport sector experienced dynamism. Still, bilateral regulation efforts continued. Many countries adopted more policies for the regulation of interna-tional air transport. For instance, eleven new bilateral air transport agreements or amendments to the existing agreements have been entered into by the USA in the period 1978–1980 (Haanappel, 1980). Bermuda II Agreement replaced the original Bermuda Agreement (1946) and came into effect on 23 July 1977. This is more complex and detailed. Sooner, open sky policies got increased significance as more and more countries wanted to have less hindrance to undertake interna-tional air transport operations between countries. During the 1990s, the changes in civil aviation, according to ICAO (2004), are as follows:

- Rapid changes in the regulatory environments and evolution of liberal policies worldwide.
- Rapid changes in operation environment of international air transport.
- Widespread liberalization.
- Open skies policies began spreading.
- Growing regionalism in international air transport regulations.
- Conversion of some bilateral regulations and regional or subregional multina-tional regulations.

7.10.8 Montreal Convention (1999) (MC99)

Montreal Convention has been organized with the specific objective to replace the patchwork of regimes that developed since the Warsaw Convention in 1929. This enabled unification of certain rules for international carriage by air. One hun-dred twenty-eight states and the EU have ratified this convention. This came into effect in 2003. The convention governs airline liability for passengers, baggage and cargo in cases of death, injury or delay to passengers; delay, loss or damage to baggage; and delay, loss or damage to cargo (IATA/Colehan).

7.11 Multilateral regulations

As the aviation sector progressed, bilateral ASAs became inadequate to cope up with the dynamism being created in the arena of international air transportation. Deregulation in the USA in the late 1970s and later embracing of liberalization in the European air transport market necessitated the increasing use of multilateral agreements along with the increasing acceptance of open skies. ICAO (2004) defines multilateral regulation as follows:

> "... regulation undertaken jointly by three or more States, within the framework of an international organization and/or a multilateral treaty or agreement, or as a separate specific activity, and may be broadly construed to include relevant regulatory processes and structures, outcomes or output written as treaties or other agreements, resolutions, decisions, directives, or regulations, as well as the observations, conclusions, guidance and discussions of multinational bodies, both intergovernmental and non-governmental".

Multilateral agreements became a practice even before Deregulation in the US. The circumstances or benefits that support multilateral agreements, according to John Kiser (2003) include the following.

- The quick expansion of international air transportation and the continuing requirements for air carriers to obtain government approval for changes to routes, schedules and prices inhibit further development of trade and tourism.
- The experience under bilateral open skies agreements has registered significant growth in traffic between the parties involved to the benefit of airlines, airports, consumers, communities, the tourism industry and national economies.
- These agreements build on the progress made under bilateral open skies regimes and provide a coherent, streamlined mechanism for expanding commercial aviation relations.
- The enhanced access of airlines based in economies with small capital markets to broader sources of investment.
- The ability to achieve open access to multiple markets in one agreement at one time (particularly beneficial for countries with limited negotiating resources).
- These agreements allow nations to gain market access more readily than could be achieved through individual bilateral agreements.
- Prospects for air services providers to operate more freely across the globe, meeting the requirements of the world's traders, travellers and shippers.

7.12 "Open skies" to stimulate tourism

"Open skies" agreements were begun on the US-European and intra-European route regions in the beginning and later spread to other parts across the world (Doganis, 2006). Open skies policies led to lower the fares, increased access and surge in regional market demand, and all these in turn promoted international tourism further. These agreements are giving ample rights for airlines of two or more countries to have frequent and less restricted flights in foreign countries. It is referred to as either a bilateral or a multilateral transport agreement between countries, which liberalizes the rules for international aviation markets and minimizes government intervention. Mostly, open sky is multilateral agreement. Under this, airlines of both countries can fly any route they wish between the countries and can continue those flights into third countries (Wensveen, 2007). Open skies agreement is

> a type of agreement which, while not uniformly defined by its various advocates, would create a regulatory regime that relies chiefly on sustained market competition for the achievement of its air services goals and is largely or entirely devoid of a priori governmental management of access rights, capacity and pricing, while having safeguards appropriate to maintaining the minimum regulation necessary to achieve the goals of the agreement.
>
> (ICAO, 2004)

Dezhbankhan and Dezhbankhan (2014) summarized the features of open skies in the following way:

- Multiple designations with or without route restrictions.
- Unrestricted capacity and frequencies on all routes.
- Liberal charter arrangements.
- Development of airline alliances, code-sharing opportunities and facilitation of other commercial agreements.
- Open route access.
- Expanded air freedom rights (third, fourth and fifth freedom rights).
- More competitive air cargo services.
- Full market access without restrictions.
- No-tariff controls.
- Gauge break permission (Doganis, 2006).
- Traffic growth of international routes associated with open skies and alliances (Brueckner & Pels, 2007).
- A "double disapproval" (a fare can be disallowed only if both governments agree) and "free pricing" provision.
- Facilitation of computer reservation system (CRS) facilities.
- Widened criteria of airline ownership and control.
- Leasing of aircraft and intermodal transport rights (Fu et al., 2010).

As discussed above, open sky policy has varied dimension which directly or indirectly promotes tourism. Having fewer route restrictions will enable the destination to expand its accessibility with increased number of destinations. While capacity and frequency increase, tourists face enhanced convenience in reaching the destination and these directly influence in the buying behaviour of them as well. As discussed in another chapter, when airlines have alliance partnership and more code-sharing practices, tourists have better convenience and comfort in travelling. Complete market access for foreign airlines is a boon for international tourism sector. This can increase competition, enhance efficiency in operations and reduce travel cost. The absence of tariff control is also a facilitating factor. Dynamism emerges out of open skies augment the tourist traffic to the destination.

Table 7.1 Features of ASAs: Comparison of Bilateral and Open Skies Agreements

Traditional	Open Skies
Limited number of city-pair markets is allowed, only the two states have access to markets	More than two states are involved in contracts
The number of airlines that can operate within such markets is specified	Provide access to other cities and states without any limitation
Usually, non-scheduled services are not considered, and if included, it is only granted on the flight-by-flight basis	Charter/non-scheduled services are also considered
Each country is allowed to assign only one of its airlines to operate between specific pair of cities unless there will be major markets with a high demand	Multiple designations are possible. That is, do not provide a limitation on the number of airlines that are designated by countries.
The frequency of flights and the number of seats offered are strictly limited	There are no capacity restrictions. Changing aircraft gauge on fifth freedom flights and code-sharing are allowed
All airfares or tariffs are to be approved by governments involved on a basis of "cost plus profit" formula	Airfares are not required to be agreed upon by the government, except in a few necessary situations

Source: Dezhbankhan and Dezhbankhan (2014).

7.13 IATA and its role in international air transport

International Air Transport Association (IATA), which consists of 290 member airlines, is one of the largest trade associations in the global air travel industry. IATA is the trade association of the global airline industry. This is also formed after the Second World War, in 1945, when modern commercial air transport began its great strides to the future. It has been playing a crucial role in the air transportation by ensuring standardization in all its commercial aspects. According to IATA, it has supported the development of the commercial standards upon which the global air transport industry is built. Since its inception, efforts have been there to simplify the processes and increase the passenger convenience while reducing costs and improving efficiency. Another significant role played by IATA is its intervention in the standardized and efficient distribution of air travel products. It has a mechanism to accredit travel agents who have been traditionally the mainstay in the distribution of airline tickets. Moreover, it ensures an easy and convenient payment mechanism for travel agents to make payments of tickets sold, with airlines.

Enhancing the quality of services, IATA has been in the forefront to initiate the airlines. Moreover, stern actions were taken at different points of time to enable airlines to adopt latest practices for their advantages. For example, IATA was instrumental in ensuring e-ticketing practice in airline sector. In addition, it initiated the zero commission agenda on behalf of airlines with regard to distribution of airline tickets. The recent intervention in the distribution of airline product is revolutionary; IATA has established New Distribution Capability (NDC), which can distribute airline products more easily and efficiently using latest technologies and features. IATA undertakes training and development programmes as well in the area of travel and tourism to cater to the specific manpower requirements of the sector. The following critical initiatives of IATA have been so significant in the smooth, efficient and sustainable air transportation (IATA 2007).

Simplifying the Business

This helps in improving the efficiency, enhancing the passengers' convenience and reducing the cost of operations. The following are key initiatives IATA has persuaded:

- E-ticketing (ET): the aim was to eliminate traditional booklet type of tickets and to achieve 100% e-ticketing by 2007.
- IATA e-freight: this enables easy processing, eliminating the use of paper and to improve efficiency in cargo handling.
- Bar-coded boarding passes (BCBP): passengers can bypass airport queues and can check in and print their boarding passes online at home or at the office.
- Common-use self-services (CUSSs) check-in: this allows passengers to check in at their leisure, cut check-in time and make decisions on the spot.
- Radio-frequency identification (RFID) for baggage: it can reduce the number of mishandled bags and associated delays.

Safety and Security

In order to complement world air transport sector's efforts to enhance safety and security, IATA undertakes the following measures.

- The IATA Operational Safety Audit (IOSA), to assess the operational management and control systems of an airline.
- Integrated airline management system (integrated AMS), which coordinates the functions of safety management systems (SMSs) throughout an airline.
- Airport design, airspace and air traffic management (ATM) systems all have an effect on safety.
- For cargo safety, IATA develops IOSA for dedicated cargo operations and seminars on safety issues.
- Safety data management and analysis: this includes confidential reporting systems; flight data analysis; and STEADES, a global repository of occurrence reports coming directly from aircrews.
- Flying operations programme: it covers safety issues relating to flight operations, ground and cabin operations, maintenance, dispatch, and emergency response planning (ERP).
- For ensuring security measures also, IATA supports international agencies like ICAO to implement the latest practices.

Government Regulations and Environmental Considerations

- IATA has been urging governments and respective authorities to ensure liberalization in air transport, in protecting the consumer rights, and to consider the social concerns.
- Also, IATA implements an industry-wide strategy to address climate change that consists of a four-point strategy involving focuses on technology, infrastructure enhancements, opposition to fuel taxes and a preference for emissions trading instead of taxes.

7.13.1 Other efforts of ICAO

A few of the other measures of ICAO to standardize the activities, procedures and certification of various industries in the air transport sector are briefed below.

Standards and Recommended Practices (SARPs)

ICAO developed stipulates the required standards and other provisions in the following forms:

- Standards and Recommended Practices (SARPs).
- Procedures for Air Navigation Services (PANS).
- Regional Supplementary Procedures (SUPPS).
- Guidance material in several formats.

In order to ensure uniform application for the safety or for the regularity of international air navigation, recommended standards involve various specifications for physical characteristics, configuration, materials, performance, procedure and personnel. Recommended Practices are mandatory, and the uniform applications are only desirable. These are published as Annexes of Chicago Convention. Procedures for Air Navigation Services (PANS) detail the various procedures to be applied by air traffic services units as part of their services. Basically, these specify the operating practices and material too detailed for Standards or Recommended Practices. Regional Supplementary Procedures (SUPPS) are similar to the Procedures for Air Navigation Services and specify details of all such aspects in the respective regional contexts. Guidance materials, given with the scope of providing guidance with or without binding effects, consist of the regulations or directions issued as Attachments to Annexes, policies, manuals and circulars.

"Rules of the Air"

ICAO stipulated the rules of the air, which has to be followed by the aircraft while flying. Aircraft have to adhere to either the visual flight rules or the instrument flight rules.

- Visual flight rules (VFRs): Aircraft have to maintain separation from other aircraft on a "see and avoid" basis. This needs clear vision for flying. Minimum flying altitude and limits of visibility based on the visual meteorological conditions (VMCs) as specified by the authority concerned have to be there for applying this rule.

- Instrument flight rules (IFRs). Commercial operations, mostly, apply this rule, and the flying is depending on the instructions provided by the authorities concerned. The pilot should follow the instructions received through the instruments to fly and from take-off.

7.14 Conclusion

Aviation is one of the most strict and highly regulated industries. Regulations restricting air traffic adversely affect tourism, while easing restrictions has the potential to stimulate tourism demand. Many countries have been forced to revise their international aviation policies in order to gain clear recognition of tourism benefits. There are different levels of control over air transportation, because of transportation in and out to other sovereign countries. The comprehensive classification of air transport regulations is national regulations, bilateral regulations and multilateral regulations. The national authorities are called the CAA or National Aviation Authority. The structure of the organization of national authorities will be different for each country. Some aspects are mandatory, especially security, safety and compliance with safety standards. Bilateral restrictions are introduced to facilitate smoother air traffic between the two countries or states. Liberal approaches and bilateral agreements with less restrictions result in the strengthening and enhancement of international aviation, which in turn increases the demand for tourism between those countries. It is important for airlines to have the right to market access in order to operate services.

The nine "freedoms of the air" are the rights of the airlines to enter another country's airspace and land there and refer to the rights to carry luggage and mail separately or in combination. The Warsaw Convention enacted certain laws governing international carriage by air. The Chicago Convention in 1944 was the first to raise issues related to the exchange of commercial rights in international civil aviation and considered as the Magna Carta for the post-war development of international civil aviation. This convention established the ICAO, a specialized agency of the UN charged with coordinating international air travel. The convention establishes rules of airspace, aircraft registration and safety, security and sustainability and details the rights of the signatories in relation to air travel. The convention also contains provisions pertaining to taxation. The deregulations and the open sky policy stimulated the flow of tourists to a large extent across the globe. The International Air Transport Association – IATA – formed in 1945 – is a voluntary non-political industry association, which serves as a forum for airlines to develop common programmes for the smooth running of the international air transport system, representing 290 airlines in 120 countries.

Sample questions

Short/medium answer type questions

- What are the areas in which regulations are there in air transportation now?
- Give a brief account on regulations that existed in the history of air transportation till deregulation.

- Classify the regulations in air transport.
- What do you mean by freedoms of the air?
- What is air service agreement (ASA)?
- Elucidate the components of an air service agreement (ASA).
- Explain the types of bilateral regulations.
- Describe the term market access right.
- What are cabotage rights?
- What are the objectives of the Chicago Convention?
- What are the results of the Chicago Convention?
- What are the results of Bermuda Convention?
- What do you mean by deregulation?
- Define open sky policy.
- What are the principles agreed as per Montreal Convention?
- Define multilateral regulations.
- Distinguish between bilateral agreements and multilateral agreements.
- Discuss the role of IATA in international air transportation.

Essay type questions

- Write an essay on bilateral agreements in international air transportation.
- Discuss in detail the role of bilateral regulations in the growth of tourism.

Suggested readings

Abeyratne, R. (2016). *Regulation of Air Transport: The Slumbering Sentinels.* New York: Springer.

Duval, D.T. (2013). Critical issues in air transport and tourism. *Tourism Geographies*, 15(3), 494–510.

Fu, X., Oum, H.T., & Zhang, A. (2010). Air transport liberalization and its impacts on airline competition and air passenger traffic. *Transportation Journal*, 49(4), 24–41.

ICAO (2004). Manual on the Regulation of International Air Transport, International Civil Aviation Organization, Doc 9626, data available online at https://www.icao.int/Meetings/atconf6/Documents/Doc%209626_en.pdf

Airlines: a key service provider in tourism

After reading this chapter, you will be able to:

- Understand the concept of airline, its products and consumers.
- Describe the characteristics of airline industry.
- Analyse the role of airlines in tourism.
- Discuss the types of airlines.

8.1 Introduction

Airlines, the most important element and the most visible player in the aviation sector, are involved in the commercial transport services for the public. Began sometime in the second decade of 20th century, this sector has grown and evolved to become one of the largest industries in the world. The airline industry (scheduled) completed a century of its evolution. The year 2014 became a landmark year in the history of airline industry. It had its hundredth centenary celebration in January 2014. Moreover, by the time, scheduled air transport carried more than 3 billion passengers in a year. The first fixed winged airline service, in 1914, carried only one passenger as the flight was a single capacity carrier. A hundred years ago, on the New Year day, the first service of the first airline started off a new form of commercial transportation, scheduled passenger air transport, from St. Petersburg in Florida in the USA. St. Petersburg–Tampa Airboat Line, the first scheduled passenger airline service in the world, organized it. Even before that, passenger air transport service was there. There was a passenger airline called DELAG (Deutsche Luftschiffahrts-Aktiengesellschaft, or German Airship Transportation Corporation Ltd) which began its operation in 1909. However, it was not providing regular scheduled air services then and the focus in the early periods was on holiday purposes. As years went by, commercial air transport expanded,

DOI: 10.4324/9781003136927-8

grown and became a huge industry and the most prominent mode of transport in the world.

The growth was a result mainly of the consistent advancements that took place in the aviation technology along with the transformation occurred in the socio-economic scenario across the world. According to Air Transport Action Group's (ATAG) report, more than 4 billion passengers are transported annually by this sector now. Around 1,300 airlines operate services, using a total fleet of over 31,000 aircraft. Almost 4,000 airports through a route network of several million kilometres managed by 170 air navigation service providers are served by these airlines (ATAG, 2018). Airlines, by transporting over 4 billion passengers annually, generated nearly 8 trillion revenue passenger kilometres in 2017. Every country enjoys remarkable social and economic benefits from the airline sector. For instance, in the USA, according to the Airlines of America, this sector helps drive $1.5 trillion economic activity. Being one of the safest forms of intercity transportation in the USA, airlines transport more than 2.4 million passengers and more than 58,000 tons of cargo every day. Having 27,000 daily flights, US passenger and cargo airlines employ more than 700,000 people worldwide and help drive more than 10 million American jobs. Commercial aviation drives 5% of the US gross domestic product, and the airline sector stimulates the commercial aviation industry, as well as the broader economy through increased connectivity, trade and enhanced mobility of people, cultures, goods and ideas (Airlines of America, www.airlines.org). In the air transport system, airlines constitute the key sector, which is the ultimate service provider that provides services for the public. The rest of the sectors have the primary objective of serving the airlines to perform the transport operations (Figure 8.1).

Figure 8.1 An aircraft of British Airways
Source: Wikipedia Commons.

8.2 Airlines: a key service provider in tourism

Airline is a crucial sector in the tourism industrial spectrum.

> Airlines are the most powerful players from the air transport industry that actually perform the core service, which is transportation from one point to another. In this regard, airlines, being an external player, would impose a certain amount of influence over the destination, and also would experience a similar impact from the destination.
>
> (Ivanova, 2017)

Its services are vital in ensuring the tourist flow into the destinations. The advancements in airline sector constitute a prime reason for the rise of international tourism as one of the largest economic sectors in the world. Over the last a few decades, airlines became the primary transport provider that could ensure access for the tourists to more destinations located world over.

With regard to tourism, airlines basically provide the service of transporting tourists from the origin city of the tourist to the destination which is located far away. As part of this process, airlines provide comfortable, fastest and convenient journey and a memorable experience for the tourist. In order to make the journey more interesting, airlines ensure in-flight entertainment options including videos and music varieties. Reading materials are also provided. Food and beverage offered within flights are of high quality to generate interest among the travellers. Within the limitations, airlines try to provide comfortable seats as well. Airlines make use of the services of airports to undertake the transportation. While in airports as part of departure and arrival procedures also, tourists can have a pleasant experience, particularly when the airports are equipped well to handle and amuse international tourists well. Airlines with the assistance of airports also make utmost efforts to ensure safety, security and good experience for the travellers.

A number of determinants can be identified that contribute in the significance of airlines in the promotion of tourism. Affordability of air services is a prime factor that stimulated air travel propensity and eventually spurs the tourism demand. Over the years, air travel became increasingly accessible for more sections of the society. Privatization, hyper-competition within the airline sector, better fuel efficiency of aircraft, economy of scale, lowering of fuel cost, use of advanced aircraft, etc., contributed in this phenomenon. The air travel experience, to a large extent, is depending on the service provided by airlines. Tourist experience includes air travel experience as well, and therefore, airlines have to ensure quality services. Destination connectivity is depending upon the networks the serving airlines follow, and better network ensures increased connectivity for the destinations. Frequency of services, type of aircraft used, type of network followed by airlines, etc., too have much significance with regard to tourism. As air transport gains increased efficiency, international tourism gains from it. Both the sectors complement each other in their progress.

8.3 Airline industry

Airlines form a global industry that has the capacity to serve virtually every corner of the globe, with a significant role in the socio-economic spectrum in those places, be it anywhere. The term airline represents a commercial organization that undertakes transportation of people, cargo and mail from one place to another. As an air transport system, airline includes its equipment, routes, operating personnel and management systems (Spisto, 2018). Airlines, also called airways, form a system or organization that provides typically scheduled flights for passengers or cargo among specified points.

Air carrier is another term used to denote an airline. According to Wensveen (2007), air carriers are "the commercial system of air transportation, consisting of domestic and international certificated and charter carriers". An industry is something, which consists of a number of competing firms having similar products. Airlines too form an industry that provides services for people who intend to travel or send consignments from one place to another in air mode of transport in an efficient manner. The presence of the industry in different regions may vary. Yet, they serve almost all locations globally wherever adequate human population is there. Though competing firms are there, the number of airlines present in an economy is usually small. This makes the airline sector with oligopoly as a feature. This industry, though the number of firms is limited, itself is a major economic force, in terms of both its own operations and its impacts on related industries.

Though this industry exists as a major one, it functions as a part of a larger industry of air transportation. Many other sectors, as stated before, depend on airline industry for their survival. According to Alexander Wells, airline industry is "an industry which consists of a vast network of routes that connect cities in different parts of a country/world, and over the network a large number of airlines carry passengers and cargo on scheduled services" (Wells, 1988). Another definition says "airline industry, the business of transporting paying passengers and freight by air along regularly scheduled routes, typically by airplanes but also by helicopter" (The Free Dictionary-,www.encyclopedia2.thefreedictionary.com). Though the number of airlines is small, the way it serves the transportation requirements across the world is amazing. Just with less than 1,500 scheduled airlines, this industry caters to the air travel requirements of 4 billion consumers (passengers) every year. Apart from passengers, there are other customers as well those who use the services of airlines for freight as well as mail transportation. In fact, the first airline in the world, just more than a century ago, carried only one passenger. Now, a single flight can carry more than 800 passengers. Moreover, the service provision spans over the whole globe, which is made possible by extensive route network system and with the help of strategies like hub and spoke system and code-sharing. While an airline forms its own network of operation, airline industry makes a larger network and the global airline industry integrates all the smaller networks into a global one with all the cities and towns with airports connected together.

Currently, this industry provides the fastest commercial transportation services in the world. Emergence of it as the fastest mode of transport happened along with the advancements in the aviation technology. Every now and then, newer technologies emerged. Safety too increased along with the evolution of air transportation. Fastest services are provided by airline industry with the help of latest aircraft, which can cruise more than thousand kilometres per hour. This industry too consists of different types of airlines. While some operate within the boundaries of a country, some others cross the borders for international air transportation.

Table 8.1 Airline Industry: Features

Intangibility: Airlines provide the service of transporting people and goods, and the product is experienced than having possession of a physical good. Airline journey experience is the outcome of the consumption of the product.

Perishability: Extreme perishability is a feature as each seat represents a product to be sold for a specific flight in passenger transportation and the same cannot be stored for a future sale. Balancing the demand and supply is crucial for airlines to survive competitively.

Inseparability: Passenger has to reach for travelling, and thus, the product is consumed at the same time when it is produced and it is difficult to separate the customer from the production.

Variability: Due to a range of external as well as internal factors, the airline service provided may vary in standard, quality or performance from one provider to the next as well as from one occasion to the next.

Global industry: Its operations and services span across the world.

Crisis-vulnerable sector: Airline is highly vulnerable to a wide range of external factors.

High interdependency: All the elements within air transportation system have close interrelationships.

High barriers to entry and exit: High capital requirements, too many legal aspects to follow, etc., make it difficult for new entrants. In addition, due to legal and financial complications, leaving the business is also not easy.

Capital-intensive and high fixed costs: Capital requirement for starting the airline business is extremely high, and it has large proportion of fixed cost in comparison with the total cost.

Rigidity of supply: Though demand varies often, the supply may remain the same in the short run. Even if demand is more, a flight on a particular trip scheduled earlier cannot increase number of seats.

Dynamic pricing: Airlines, based on revenue management and yield management principles, follow dynamic pricing matching with the demand variations.

Dominant role of intermediaries: Traditionally, intermediaries have been playing an important role in air transport sector. Now, online intermediaries too have significant role.

Oligopolistic and non-price competition: A small number of firms dominate in the market, and the sector is also known for non-price competition.

Highly regulated: Particularly due to high safety and security concerns as well as due to the reason of crossing of borders for international travel, air transport is the most regulated transport mode.

Labour-intensive: Airlines need a large amount of labour to produce and serve the travellers.

(Continued)

Table 8.1 (Continued)

Immovability: The industry and the products cannot be moved to the location where consumers are there; rather, the consumers have to travel to the location of airline to access its service.

Thin profit margin and poor financial performance: Break-even is very long, and the sector is featured with low profit margin, all of which eventually make it highly vulnerable for financial crisis more often than many other sectors.

Seasonality and fluctuating demand: Airline sector has more seasonality variations, with varied magnitude. This affects the demand, pricing strategies as well as profit levels.

Elasticity of demand: Airline industry is featured with price elasticity of demand. Fluctuations in price affect the demand directly.

Source: Dileep (2019).

Table 8.2 Economic Significance of Airline Industry (2017)

- 2.7 million jobs are created directly by airlines in the form of flight and cabin crews, executives, ground services, check-in, training and maintenance staff. (525,000 jobs in airport operation, 5.6 million jobs in airport-related areas, 1.2 million jobs in civil aerospace and 233,000 jobs are created by air navigation service providers.)
- 45,091 routes served globally, and this includes 20,032 unique city pairs.
- Airlines undertook 41.9 million scheduled commercial flights worldwide.
- Air transport carries around 35% of world trade by value and less than 1% by volume.
- 57 percentage of international tourists who travel by air.
- 61.9 million tonnes of freight handled by airlines.
- $6 trillion value of cargo handled by air.

Source: ATAG (2018).

Some are large business organizations with large number of employees, and some others are smaller organizations with small fleet size. In fact, airline industry is responsible for the quick evolution of long-haul travel in the world. In addition, it is responsible for the quick movement of freight of varied kinds.

8.4 Airline demand

Airlines provide an intangible product for consumption. It is "inseparable" in nature and highly "perishable". According to Barnes (2012), "airline sells air transportation service between two or more cities at a certain price with specified purchase requirements and restrictions". Here, as in the case of service products, the selling of air ticket leads to the transaction of invisible, rather intangible, products between the airline its customers. Airline, eventually, provide the service of transportation of passengers and cargo from one place to another, as per the needs of the customer. Scheduled flights fly from one place to another and transport passengers and cargo as per a published timetable (Wensveen, 2009). Consignors or shippers form another major customer group in airlines. Consumers in this category include those who send the consignments from one place to another via air mode of transport. People can send cargo directly with airline as well, without using the service of freight forwarders.

Simply, demand can be considered as the desire of people for particular goods or services. The definition of demand varies according to the subject perspectives. Economists consider demand to be the schedule of the amount of any product or service that people are willing and able to buy at each specific price in a set of possible prices during a specified period of time. Psychologists' view on demand is different. They look demand from the perspective of motivation and behaviour. In marketing, demand is generated when there is a need to have a product and the need is being supplemented by a desire to buy and it is supported by the capacity and willingness to buy. Ultimately, the willingness and the ability to purchase are important while considering demand. When it comes to air transportation, the demand is generated when there is a need to travel, and it is being complemented by the desire to travel by air mode of transport. The willingness to travel and the ability to afford the ticket are crucial in determining the demand. Airline provides services to people who wish to travel from one place to another for varied reasons or who wish to send freight/goods, consignments or mail. The demand for airline is derived from that group of people. It is particularly defined for an origin–destination market, i.e. from where the traveller intends to start journey and where he/she would like to reach.

A large number of factors are influencing airline demand. Factors that may affect traffic demand of a scheduled airline, according to ICAO (2004), are as follows:

- Price (while high tariff may discourage use, a low tariff may result in a higher load factor but generates lower yields).
- Frequency (though more choices, that can attract more customers, can be provided by a high-frequency service, it may not be economically viable on a route with a low volume of traffic.
- Route structure (a multiple-stop service is not as attractive as a non-stop service that serves the same two cities).
- Service via a hub (the required en route change of aircraft lessens the attraction even though the increased frequency typically adds to the attraction).
- Type of aircraft (passengers may opt a wide-body aircraft to a narrow-body aircraft, or a jet to a propeller aircraft).
- Season (summer may see more people travelling than winter, and warm destinations are more popular in winter; a pre-holiday period may produce more freight, and a holiday period may produce more passengers).
- Economic circumstances in the states involved and/or the regional or global economy (demand will be less during an economic recession).
- The security situation in the destination state can affect the demand.
- Concerns about flight security in general.

The recent spur in airline demand world over is due to a number of macro-economic factors as well. Economic standards of people are increasing that amplify the growth in airline demand. Airline is becoming increasingly affordable for more societies across the world. Increasing urbanization is another factor that

> **Table 8.3** Airline Demand – Why Is Demand So Fickle?

According to Paul Stephen Dempsey, the reasons are as follows:

- Demand is highly cyclical (depends on time of day, day of week and season).
- Demand can be adversely affected with broader changes in the economy.
- In mature markets, air travel growth slows.
- Globalization caused decline in domestic growth, as production has moved offshore.
- Information and communications technology advancements have eroded market share for air travel.
- The inability to cover costs led carriers to cut costs by reducing service, thereby reducing product differentiation.
- The commoditization of air travel left airlines with little opportunities for product differentiation other than price; service has deteriorated industry-wide (air travel is credence good, an intermediate good and, for many travellers, a fungible commodity, particularly for short flights).
- Demand can be dampened by recession, war, terrorism or health concerns.
- Price elasticities of demand are segmented along leisure and business traveller lines.
- Business travellers tend to be less price-sensitive, and business travel is paid for with pre-tax dollars, which may end up in tangible benefits. On the other hand, leisure travel is paid for in post-tax dollars, results in intangible benefits, and can be postponed if times are not favourable. The market also is segmented according to distance, with surface modes of transport competing for short-distance trips.

Source: Paul Stephen Dempsey, 2017, Introduction to AIRLINE ECONOMICS, McGill University Institute of Air & Space Lawhttps://www.mcgill.ca/iasl/files/iasl/airline_economics_psd.pdf

determines the airline demand. Certainly, population growth too leads to increased air travel. Air travel safety and security have increased manifold over the last several years and that instilled confidence among the people to use airlines for their travel purposes. Air transport infrastructure is also increasing in every country and that propels air travel demand. As route networks are also getting expanded, even smaller cities are getting connected by air transport service. This enables more societies to access airline services. Availability of more alternative transportation can reduce the air travel demand.

Though oligopoly is there, more airlines are entering into service nowadays and that enhances the competition. This can help in increasing quality of services and lowering of price. Travel hindrances are getting reduced, and liberal policies are being adopted by countries in permitting international air transport services. As speed increases, total transportation time decreases. Such factors that are associated with the quality of services too enhance the airline demand world over. Increased service frequency, more choices, more networks, easy connections, convenient timings, etc., always enhance airline demand greatly. Internationally, the opening up of new markets helped to grow the global air travel demand greatly. Emerging economies like India, China and Indonesia could register substantial growth in air transportation, and airline demand in those regions is growing at remarkable pace.

Table 8.4 Airline Business Environments

Airline is highly vulnerable to external and internal factors. The major influencing factors are as follows:

Economic

Macro-economic factors, including the national economic policies, economic growth in the country/region and overall economic circumstances, have much significance in airline business. International economic situation too affects airline business. Economic recession, rise in oil price, fluctuations in interest and exchange rates, inflation, etc., have affected airlines in the recent history.

Political and legal factors

National policies have a great role in international air transport. Engaging in bilateral, multilateral and open sky policies depends on national interests as well. Political stability in the country, political risks, national security, corporate influence in politics and influence of foreign political factors are some other factors. Political views on liberalization too have significant impact. International and national political circumstances, terrorism, etc., always affect upon the scope of airline business.

Sociocultural factors

Rate of urbanization, changes in lifestyle, changes in consumer attitudes and buying patterns, educational progress, level of living conditions, rate of unemployment, health parameters have a significant role in the business of airlines. Airlines are yet to recover from a severe pandemic that shattered the global airline business.

Technological factors

Airlines highly depend on information and communication technologies for their functioning as well as in remaining competitive. It has to be responsive to the advancements in technology.

Environmental factors

Airlines have to accept new regulations and guidelines that aim to conserve and preserve the nature and its features. Sustainability parameters always challenge airlines. Climatic factors like rain, snowfall and fog can affect the daily routines of airline operations. Other natural calamities like earthquakes, flood and volcano eruption can have severe impacts.

International factors

These factors exist at the global level or at least in two or more countries. Global recession, regional wars, international rules, laws, human rights issues, regionalism, etc., can pose challenges for air transportation as well.

8.5 Types of airlines

Airlines can be classified on different perspectives. The following are the major classification and types of airlines seen in the domestic and international air transport sectors.

8.5.1 Scheduled airlines

Commercial air transportation is dominated by scheduled airlines. They are regular service providers and operate services based on a pre-fixed and published schedule. Over the years, scheduled air transportation has grown and expanded and different models got emerged in between. Once upon a time, scheduled air transportation was controlled by the governments and was highly regulated, including the tariff. Many changes happened since deregulation in the USA in 1978 regarding regulations, and airlines are having increased commercial freedom, of late.

> Scheduled airlines are scheduled to fly a particular route a particular time on a regular basis, daily, weekly, etc.....A published schedule is the base for operating services regularly between the departing airports to the transit and/or the final ports as per the itinerary. General public can travel on these by availing the services as they are open to direct booking by members of the public.
>
> (Dileep, 2019)

The same aspect is highlighted in the definition given by Wensveen (2007), which says that

> A scheduled airline will fly to different destinations using a published time schedule......Depending on the country of registration, the airline will operate under a particular flight certificate authorizing scheduled service. This certificate is issued by the government (civil aviation authority) of that country.

ICAO (2009) defines scheduled services (revenue) as

> ....flights scheduled and performed for remuneration according to a published timetable or as regular or frequent as to constitute a recognizably systematic series, which are open to direct booking by members of the public; and extra section flights occasioned by overflow traffic from scheduled flights.

Scheduled airlines constitute the backbone of air transportation, and their share in the socio-economic contribution of air transportation is the maximum. Scheduled air transportation itself has become one of the leading industries in the world. Though scheduled passenger transportation generates more economic benefits, now passenger transportation, which consists of cargo and mail, has been growing tremendously to become an important component of air transportation. When jet engines entered into commercial transportation, scheduled air transport gained increased significance. The use of wide-body aircraft for passenger transportation gave a fillip to scheduled passenger transportation. Recently, cargo transportation is gaining increased importance. Airlines provide scheduled domestic air services as well as international air services. Some of the airlines provide both the types together. Now, increased competition is there which instilled dynamism and innovation along with increased affordability for air travel. Different types of scheduled airlines can be seen, and some of them are introduced below.

8.5.2 International and domestic airlines

International airlines are the scheduled airlines that operate services to foreign countries from the home country and vice versa. These are required to link major cities in a country with major cities in other parts of the world. Every country has certain restrictions and regulations to permit one airline to undertake international air services. Airline alliances, hub and spoke system, interline agreements, code-sharing, etc. (all are discussed in detail later in this book), facilitate the smooth and efficient international air services by the airlines. According to International Air Transportation Association (IATA), international passenger traffic in 2018 climbed 6.3% compared to 2017, down from 8.6% annual growth the year before. Capacity rose 5.7%, and load factor climbed by 0.4 percentage point to 81.2% (IATA, 2018b). All regions recorded year-over-year increases in traffic, led by Asia-Pacific. Domestic services will be limited within the borders of a country. They are also significant for a country to have an integrated transport system. Domestic air travel is growing at a remarkable rate recently. The trend in domestic air travel has been advanced in emerging economies as well and that contributes significantly in the growth of air transport in the world.

8.5.3 Cargo airlines

As stated before, cargo/freight transportation has been increasing remarkably over the years. The recent trends lead to further improvement in cargo transportation in the years to come as well. There are some dedicated airlines focusing on

Table 8.5 Some Other Types of Airlines

Major airlines: They undertake services on long-haul routes and between major cities. Larger aircraft are used for services. In hub and spoke system, these airlines focus services between hub cities or from a hub city to another major city.

Comprehensive network carriers: These are the airlines with services to large number of destinations, using hub and spoke route system on international routes, for example, Emirates, British Airways and Delta. They have a multi-channel distribution system and have different classes of service on-board along with frequent flyer programme options. In addition, such airlines have a large and heterogeneous fleet. The network carrier is the traditional and the fundamental airline business model with a wide range of differentiated product/service offers and multiple classes of services (Gross & Klemmer, 2014).

(Continued)

Table 8.5 (Continued)

Trunk carriers: Trunk carriers undertake service between hub cities or between a hub city and another major city. Major airlines are also called trunk carriers. Usually, they focus on long-haul routes with extensive route system.

Regional airlines: Regional airlines also operate within a region in a country and enable enhanced access between smaller cities and big cities. While some of them are part of comprehensive network carriers, some operate services only to feed large airlines. They may have a lower cost structure, and when it is a part or in contract with a comprehensive network carrier, it benefits from brand recognition, marketing and distribution coverage, pricing advantages, purchasing power, network efficiencies and loyalty programmes (Cook & Billig, 2017). When they operate flight using small aircraft on short-haul routes, they are also called **commuter airlines** in some regions.

Shuttle airline: This is another type of airline operating on domestic routes. "A shuttle airline caters mainly to business travellers seeking movement between two major cities. The shuttle concept is similar to a conventional bus service offering a reasonable airfare with no reservation. High frequency and easily remembered times are typical attributes of a shuttle" (Wensveen, 2007).

All business class airlines: These are the airlines operated with business class alone, aiming at business and other upmarket passengers. These are very limited in number and are seen primarily in busy business routes.

National airlines: National airlines usually operate services within the boundaries of a country. Yet some undertake international services as well. Having flights with seats ranges from 100 and above up to 150, and these include airlines between major and regional carriers.

Flag carrier: Flag carrier denotes the official airlines of a country. These were the airlines that dominated in the air transportation in the world for a long time, until privatization became a norm in the industry. Owned by the government, these operate services mainly on international routes, though they may operate on domestic routes as well.

Supplement carriers: These are operated by charter airlines to supplement the air service when demand is very high in scheduled services (Cook & Billing, 2017).

---

cargo transportation. Passenger airlines also undertake cargo transportation services. Unlike passenger airlines, cargo airlines may change routing due to demand variations. Combination carriers (scheduled airlines that provide freighter services as well), integrated cargo airline (express carriers) and all-cargo airlines are the different types of cargo airlines.

8.5.4 Full-Service Carriers (FSCs) and Low-Cost Carriers (LCCs)

The current air transport market has significant presence of LCCs as well, which was not the same scenario a few decades back. The air transportation sector has been registering dramatic growth of LCCs since the 1980s. FSCs are also called

---

Table 8.6 Low-Cost Service Model, The South West Airlines

Product/Operating Features	Strategies
Fares	Low
	Simple
	Point-to-point
	No interlining
In-flight services	Single-class, high-density
	No seat assignment
	No meals
	Snacks and light beverages
Frequency of operations	High
Punctuality	Very good
Product distribution	Direct sales, travel agents, ticketless, e-ticket
Aircraft	Single type
	High utilization
Sectors	Short or average
Airports	Secondary or un-congested
	15–20-minute turnaround
Staff	Competitive
	Wages
	Profit sharing since 1973
	High productivity

Source: Doganis (2005).

full-service airlines (FSAs) as well as legacy airlines. They are the traditional airlines that can be called complete airlines. FSCs provide meals, beverages, airport lounges, entertainment and the like. Moreover, they have different classes of service, and seat configuration is different from that of LCCs. Minimum business class and economy classes are offered in FSCs. In many airlines, more than two classes of services are there. The services offered in higher classes are more and are of better quality. The number of staff for in-flight services is also more in FSCs. The coverage of service is on a wider area, and hub and spoke system, etc., are well utilized by these airlines. The fleet of FSCs will have different types of aircraft.

8.5.4.1 Low-Cost Carriers (LCCs)

LCCs also called "no-frills" airlines and possess a unique business model in air transportation. They have been emerged as an innovative model to cater to the growing requirement of the people who have high air travel propensity, yet with little affordability for FSCs. But this section of the air travel market expanded significantly, and LCCs got wider acceptance sooner. It is not just the low price that attracts, they offer simple model of air transportation which is adequate for a journey, that too a short-haul journey. In fact, passengers consume airline's product mainly to reach the destination and to engage in certain activities based on their motivation to travel. Travel and the consumption of airline's ancillary service, like on-board food services, are usually not the primary purposes of using the services of airlines. Moreover, when the fare is low on a short-haul route and when the passenger can reach in lesser time, many of those who had been using substitutes to air transport may easily be attracted to LCCs.

Though LCCs are also referred to as "no-frills", differences can be noted between them as well. According to Wensveen (2007),

> In terms of cost structure, a low-cost airline offers a reasonable airfare resulting from low-cost management strategies. A no-frills airline also offers reasonable or cheap airfare resulting from what might be considered extreme low-cost management strategies. Basically, a no-frills airline offers a seat from point A to point B with no in-flight service. In the United States, Southwest Airlines is considered the leading low-cost no-frills air carrier.

Hence, the difference is there in terms of the price management strategies. No-frills go for the lowest fares with nil in-flight services. The above reveals one thing that the base of considering one airline as low cost or no-frill is the fare charged and the services offered.

LCCs may go for least number of services on-board. Yet, a number of other management strategies can be identified about LCCs. They usually operate point-to-point services. By this, maximum aircraft utilization can be ensured and delays can be minimized. LCCs usually do not offer connection flights. The fleet of LCCs consists mostly of the same type of aircraft, that too smaller ones. This helps them to have less number of specialized engineers, and other technical staff to repair and for maintenance. Moreover, by having the same type

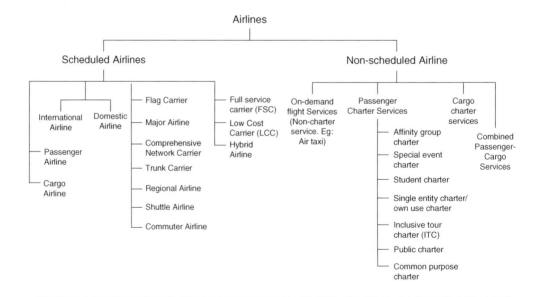

Figure 8.2 Airline classification

of fleet, they can save some cost for spare parts as well. Smaller aircraft utilization helps them by reducing turnaround time. The focus of service for LCCs is primarily on less congested and second-tier city airports. That too helps in faster turnaround. Less turnaround time helps in increased aircraft utilization. On-board services are minimum. Some snacks are provided on-board for sale. At the time of booking also, orders can be given for availing on-board food and beverage services. It is seen that they sell limited food and beverage items at a relatively higher price. "A la Carte" pricing strategy is used in such cases. Also, when they do not serve food and beverage, they can save time from not loading and unloading food items. Due to this also, turnaround time can be reduced.

As part of product distribution, LCCs avoid intermediaries and sell seats primarily through own websites, own offices and call centers. Nowadays, other online intermediaries are also being used for product distribution.

Staff size is made small by using different strategies. Using single aircraft can reduce the number of maintenance staff, etc. By having single class, separate crew is not required on-board to take care of the higher class passengers. Moreover, since in-flight services are minimum, the cabin crew requirement is also minimum. The less employee utilization saves immensely for the LCCs. For instance, Ryanair "transports 9,738 passengers annually per staff member versus only 1,000 passenger per employee for British Airways and cites unit costs 13% less than Spirit Airlines, the US low cost leader" (Cook & Billig, 2017). Besides, some companies recruit employees on contract. In addition, they cross-utilize their employees (Barret, 2008).

Different types of money saving strategies are used. Leaner crew results in lower labour charges. No-frills save significant amount in each flight. Savings are there in technical areas as well by having the same and smaller aircraft, and maximum

---

Table 8.7 Features of LCCs and FSCs

LCC	FSC
• Simple brand	• Complex brand
• Low fare	• Service classes and fare classes
• Simpler fare structure	• Complex fare structure
• Focus on secondary airports and multiple bases	• Hubs at major airports
• High aircraft utilization	• Lower utilization of aircraft
• No or little interlining	• Interlining, possible bilateral and multilateral alliances
• Offer is basic transportation, all else is ancillary.	• Complex, integrated/bundled products
• Short-haul focus for transportation	• Short-haul, long-haul and possible multi-sector routes.
• Single aircraft fleet	• Complex fleet, route type structures.
• Airline and call centre booking	• Multi-intermediary and direct product distribution system
• Simple network for operation	• Complex network for operation

Source: King (2018).

utilization of aircraft, etc. Saving from product distribution is also important. Some airlines carry advertisements of other companies in flight. On-board sale is a revenue source for LCCs now. A variety of items, like pen, jewellery and books, are sold under the title of duty-free shopping on-board. Free baggage allowance is less for such airlines, and by reducing leg space, the number of seats is increased. For extra baggage, etc., they charge. The availability of more seats helps to sell more. Demand and supply constitute the base for pricing. They attract customers by notifying the lowest fare months in advance. As demand increases, price levels increase tremendously. Last-minute sales may happen at the highest rates. The use of revenue management practices in pricing is of much use for airlines recently.

To sum up, the following are the strategies used by LCCs to manage the business profitably.

- Usually, they fly at off-peak times.
- Point-to-point, short-haul route services are undertaken to get higher aircraft as well as crew utilization.
- More focus on less congested airports so as to get low landing charges and quick turnaround time.
- Operate at a higher seat density with less legroom. So more seats will be available and will lead to higher load factor.
- Provide only basic service, with no in-flight catering.
- Operate with minimum staff.
- Selling tickets more online and avoiding travel agents.
- Operate with only one type of aircraft. This helps to save training costs, also cost saving of spare parts, maintenance equipment, etc. (Harvey, 2007).
- Some LCCs take fee for checked baggage.
- Other ancillary fees may be charged for additional baggage fee, overweight fee, snacks, drinks, pets in cabin, fee for unaccompanied minor, insurance, duty-free sale, etc.

Though LCCs are primarily meant for short-haul services, the recent trends reveal that medium- and long-haul LCCs are also there in the market. Such LCCs usually provide in-flight meals with or without charging extra amount.

8.5.5 Hybrid airlines

As the competition among the LCCs increased and since airlines want to expand operations into long-haul routes as well, some of the low-cost airlines and new airlines have tried to have more features and to adopt some of the characteristics of FSCs. This trend has been growing, and thus, a new breed of airline generated, called hybrid airlines. The hybrid model is a competition-induced one and a blend of LCC business model and FSC business model. Cristina and Gheorghe (2017) illustrated this evolution in the following way:

> As traditional airlines developed strategies to become competitive in this new environment, low-cost airlines started focusing on new ways of enhancing passenger experience and attracting new market segments. As a result, the fragmentation of the market segments addressed by low cost carriers and

Table 8.8 Characteristics of Hybrid LCCs

- Single type or mix fleet.
- Narrow body and wide body for long-haul routes.
- Code-sharing may be used.
- Transfer between flights is possible.
- Can be member in airline alliances.
- Can serve long-haul destinations.
- Fare bundling can be seen, by having different fare bundles offering different levels of service.
- Product distribution primarily through online platforms, along with GDS.
- Loyalty schemes may be used.
- Frills, like in-flight food service and free baggage allowance, are given depending on fare bundle offered.

Source: Modified from Fageda et al. (2015), based on m Mason and Morrison (2008), Klophaus et al. (2012) and Doganis (2013).

traditional airlines became less obvious and the characteristics of both business models started to blend at all levels (airline operation, distribution channels, loyalty programs, fleet selection). Thus, this new competition became the foundation of the development of a new "hybrid" carrier, between the low-cost and the traditional models.

(Stoenescu & Gheorghe, 2017)

These are the airlines that cannot be classified as either comprehensive network carrier (CNC) or LCC (Cook & Billig, 2017). Differences can be seen in in-flight services, product distribution, network routes, etc. The following example of Southwest Airlines gives a hint about the evolution of hybrid airlines. "Southwest is, however, in the process of reinventing itself: It appears to be reaching the limits of growth as an LCC and is moving towards a hybrid model" (King, 2018). A study by Sabre (2008), a leading global distribution system (GDS) and airline technology solution providers, illustrates the new phenomenon in the following way.

" The study shows that full-service carrier attributes being introduced by LCCs include: international routes, use of the global distribution system (GDS), codeshare agreements, connecting services, multiple fares available at any time, advanced ticketing procedures, multiple aircraft types, multiple classes of service, interline agreements and long-haul destinations". The study also reveals that, of the 540 airlines studied, 123 are self-nominated as LCCs. Among those self-nominated LCCs, 59 percent have added enough complexity to their business model. 7 percent have turned into full-service airlines. The remaining (52%) have become "hybrid" carriers, which blend low-cost carrier traits with that of full-service carriers" (Sabre, 2008). Thus, hybrid airline can be considered as an airline business model that operates with a low-cost business model but provides more services and business practices that are similar to those of full service carriers.

8.5.6 Scheduled airlines and tourism

In fact, scheduled airlines got a significant role in international tourism bit later than non-scheduled airlines. While Europe was surging ahead with tourism after the end of the Second World War, charter airlines played a crucial role in enhancing the tourism demand in many destinations over there. On the other hand, scheduled airlines started to play a major role in tourist traffic by the 1970s and the far-reaching effects of deregulation and the process of liberalization transformed the role played by scheduled airlines. It got stimulus by the entry of wide-body aircraft as well. The use of scheduled airlines got a fillip by the dynamism occurred when the airline industry started experiencing much dynamism in the 1970s and 1980s. Long-haul tourism became a buzzword during then, when scheduled airline began using wide-body aircraft. The increased comfort and decline in travel cost paved the way for the rise of long-haul tourism, particularly from the west to the east. Later, the liberalization and increase in the adoption of open sky policies by more countries led to scheduled airlines to increase their role in international as well as domestic tourism.

Charter airlines still remained as a strong contender in international tourism, particularly in the leisure tourism segment. While globalization process marched across the world, the business travel sector recorded a dramatic rise. Scheduled airlines could gain much from this phenomenon. Business travel segment depended on scheduled sector for both domestic and international travel. As liberalization process continued, scheduled airlines began dominating the tourist traffic flow. The rise of LCCs as a major segment in the scheduled sector and their role in tourism also got enhanced greatly. Business travel segment still depended on scheduled airlines, particularly the FSCs for their journeys. Recently, hybrid airlines began to have a share in the international tourist traffic. Currently, scheduled airlines have a predominant role in the air transport connected to international tourism and the trend is expected to continue in the years as well.

While LCCs were gaining increasing significance in leisure tourism, FSCs also attempted to tap the tourism potentials by adapting their services and strategies. FSCs, in order to compete with LCCs, used a range of commercial strategies, like measures to reduce labour costs, increase productivity in operations, setting up of LCCs, transferring of services to regional partners, and reducing distribution costs (Dennis, 2009). Certainly, network carriers have much role in the international tourism. In medium-, long-haul and complicated itineraries, it is more beneficial to have network carriers and to make use of alliance partner benefits. With regard to leisure tourists, in order to overcome the issue of competitive pricing by LCCs, etc., network carriers could adopt strategies by taking the advantages of more codeshare and interline agreements and better tailor-made travel packages (Papatheodorou & Iatrou, 2007). This practice is still continuing. Longer distance air transport is more comfortable with network carriers due to the advantages particularly due to comfort, quality in-flight services and entertainment, convenience and other benefits associated with alliances. The impact of LCCs in tourism is described further in Chapter 6.

Hybrid airlines provide a new ray of hope for tourism. It can bridge the gap existed between LCCs and FSCs in terms of a combination of factors consisting of affordability, variety of in-flight services, distance covering in accessing longer haul destinations, etc. A study by Stoenescu and Gheorghe (2017) pointed out that though price remains an important determinant, airline buying behaviour, quality and variety of the services too are much demanded, which give increasing significance for hybridization of airline business models. From a tourism perspective, this aspect has much relevance. Price, quality of service and diverse services are important determinants. Indeed, hybrid airlines are becoming increasingly significant due to this. Moreover, hybrid airlines can offer lower price compared to FSCs, offer variety of quality services compared to LCCs and offer services into longer haul destinations, and these aspects make hybrid airline very relevant in the international tourism lately.

8.5.7 Non-scheduled air services

Non-scheduled air services, the commercial air services that do not operate services based on a pre-fixed and published schedule, are also having comparable significance with scheduled transportation in some regions, like in Europe, particularly for the development of package tourism. ICAO (2009) defines it as ".... a commercial air transport service performed as other than a scheduled air service". "A non-scheduled airline will offer services to different destinations but will not fly according to a published time schedule. Again, depending on the country of registration, the airline will be issued a specific flight certificate authorizing non-scheduled service" (Wensveen, 2007). Usually, they conduct operations on point-to-point basis and have no botheration for operating flights on a pre-fixed schedule. Non-scheduled airlines have low risk of selling seats as that responsibility is vested with the agency that makes contract with the charter airline. Permission has to be obtained from the origin country as well as the destination country for undertaking the service, for each flight or for a series of flights. Demand is the criterion for operation instead of regularity and fixed schedule. Non-scheduled services are operated based on national authorization to do so. There are some provisions included in the bilateral/multilateral agreements signed by countries which permit non-scheduled airlines to provide international services as well. The following constitute a classification of non-scheduled air services.

- Passenger charter services.
- On-demand flight services.
- Cargo charter services.
- Combined passenger–cargo services.

8.5.7.1 Charter airlines

Charter air services are a prominent category in air transportation, particularly in international tourism. Charter flight is simply a one-time flight and not part of a regular schedule. This is a good example of non-scheduled air transportation. Some of the charter airlines are subsidiaries of major carriers. ICAO (2009) defines charter service as

> a non-scheduled operation using a chartered aircraft. Though the terms non-scheduled and charter (i.e. a contractual arrangement between an air carrier and an entity hiring or leasing its aircraft) have come to be used interchangeably, it should be noted that not all commercial non-scheduled operations are charter flights.

> **Table 8.9** Differences Between Scheduled Flights and Charter Flights: A Tour Operator's Perspective

Scheduled Flights	Charter Flights
The cost of flight is high	Cheaper than scheduled flights
Flexibility is very less as tour operator has to follow the schedules of airline	Very flexible, even destinations can be altered as per the need.
Suitable for multi-destination tours	Suitable more for single-destination tours
In-flight services are more and less boring	Relatively, in-flight services are less and more boring
More suitable for long-hauls as well.	Usually for short-haul, and used for long-haul also.
Different classes of services are available	Such distinction is rarely seen
Used by all types of tour operators	Mainly used by mass operators as well as specialist operators

Source: Dileep (2019).

Though charter airlines undertake air transportation services, the task of selling the seats is vested with the entity that makes contract with the charter airline.

> A charter airline offers services to destinations based on demand without using a published time schedule. In other words, the aircraft might be rented one time or multiple times to transport people or goods to specific destinations. This type of service is referred to as an ad-hoc charter. The more common type of charter caters to passengers seeking leisure-oriented destinations. Most airlines in the charter market operate by a non-published time schedule to specific destinations on a seasonal basis.
>
> (Wensveen, 2007)

International tour operators have much dependence on charter services. They find many advantages of using charter flights for tour operation. The departure and arrival time of flights can be done according to the convenience of the tour operators. Charter services are much cheaper compared to scheduled airlines. Tour operators usually make contracts with charter airlines in advance for conducting overseas tours. Three types of contracting are seen commonly in the international tourism sector, such as time series chartering, part chartering and ad hoc chartering (Yale, 2001). In time series contract, a charter aircraft is fully contracted for a specific period, usually a season. Back-to-back operations are undertaken using this chartered flight by the tour operator. Among the contracting types, this is the cheapest though the risk is high since the tour operator is vested with the responsibility to sell or utilize all the seats. In the second category, a section of the capacity can be booked. The risk is less, but the rates may be higher than the first category. Ad hoc chartering enables tour operator to contract specific number of seats for specific dates, not for a period, and as and when required. This has the lowest risk, though the rates may be the highest.

ICAO (2004) has identified different types of passenger charter services such as non-affinity group charter, inclusive tour charter (ITC), public charter, affinity group charter, common purpose charter, special event charter, student charter and single entity charter or own-use charter. **Non-affinity group charter** is being used by a charter or travel organizer to resell the seats to the public. The passengers do not belong to an affinity group. The **inclusive tour charter (ITC)** is being carried out by a tour operator for the conduct of its package tour. It includes charter flights in use for all-inclusive holidays. **Public charter** is meant for public's transportation, which is managed with the help of an intermediary. The **affinity group charter** is meant for members of an affinity group for travelling for specific purpose, like holiday. The **common purpose charter** is being arranged for persons who travel for a common purpose, like **attending** a particular event. The **special event charter** is arranged exclusively for those who would like to participate in a special event, like religious and sports events. The **student charter** is meant for students of a recognized establishment of higher education. The **single entity charter** or **own-use charter** is being chartered by one entity (e.g. an individual, corporation, government) solely for its own use for the carriage of passengers and/or freight.

On-demand flight services include all other non-scheduled non-charter services and transport individually ticketed or individually way billed traffic. Air taxi revenue flight is defined as

> on-demand, non-scheduled flights on short notice for the carriage by air of passengers, freight or mail, or any combination thereof for remuneration usually performed with smaller aircraft including helicopters (typically no more than 30 seats). This definition includes any positioning flights required for the provision of the service.
>
> (ICAO, 2009)

Cargo charter services are also there. These are chartered for the purposes of freight forwarders and other players in cargo transportation. Cargo, mail, courier, other freight items, express/small packages, etc., are the items that are transported by this section of charter flight. Combined passenger–cargo charter carries both passengers and cargo together in the same flight. Different one-time flights can also be seen, like inaugural flights.

8.5.7.2 Charter tourism

The development of charter flights is indeed an essentially European phenomenon, which principally concerns the Mediterranean countries, and certain intra-European links are touristic in nature (WTO, 2000). Evolution of charter airlines and tourism were complementary to each other. Tourism certainly stimulated the development of charter airlines (Bieger &Wittmer, 2006). On the other hand, charter airlines could augment tourism's growth after the Second World War. They had significant share, particularly in the leisure sector, in European tourism until the late 1980s, particularly by offering a low-cost service as part of a bundled holiday package (Papatheodorou & Zenelis, 2013). It is at times referred to as leisure carrier, tourist carrier or holiday airline as well (Gross & Klemmer, 2014). Packaged holiday tourism segment was dominated by charter air transport for the up and down travel of tourists. The ad hoc nature of the charter flight service offers direct connection to tourist destinations avoiding transit flights, while the high load factors achieved result in substantial unit cost reductions (Papatheodorou & Zenelis, 2013). Charter airlines can operate with lower costs per passenger than that of scheduled airlines when they utilize a combination of larger aircraft, longer flight sectors, greater aircraft and crew utilization, efficient seating configurations and higher load factors (Williams et al., 2003). All these factors contribute in the growth of charter tourism. Gross and Klemmer (2014), based on various sources, listed the following tourism-related characteristics of charter airlines:

- Heavy dependence on tour operators as the prime target group is leisure tourist.
- Single class seat configuration, usually, though exemptions can be seen.
- Destinations of service can be mainly on the same continent.
- Route structure is predominantly point-to-point (usually with high seat load factor due to a consistent length of stay).
- Fleet consists usually of single type aircraft that can carry between 150 and 250 seats.
- Though tour operator and direct sales still constitute the main mode of product distribution, other channels are also being dependent on sales.

Charter tourism still retains a good share in international tourism, particularly in the leisure tourism segment. Leisure travellers got affinity to charter services due to the following factors:

- Cheaper rates and rate at bundle price level.
- Quality services.
- Convenient services.
- Safety and security.
- Freedom of being with an interested group (for package holidays).
- Longer lead time possibility.

Due to liberalization, charter airlines could sell openly on a "seat only" basis (Shaw, 2008). Earlier, charter airlines, instead of selling seats directly to passengers, included seats in the package tours offered by tour operators (Gross & Klemmer, 2014). Due to tourism pressure, some countries had to open up air transport markets earlier than deregulation in 1978 in the USA, and Spain is an example for it, which experienced air charter boom in the 1960s, and liberalized policies to accommodate increased charter services to facilitate tourism (Forsyth, 2008). Spain succeeded in gaining tourist inflow from Northern European countries by opening up routes to charter airlines in the 1960s and 1970s. However, later, as LCCs started getting much progress, the scenario changed and charter airlines started losing the importance they had before. The charter tourism phenomenon had much prominence in the European region for a longer era. Papatheodorou (2008) pointed out that

> ....charter airlines were the engine behind leisure tourism traffic in Europe (at least until the emergence of low cost carriers) as they ensured cheap flights

to a multitude of tourism destinations during the peak seasons (especially in the summer) as part of a holiday package offered by a tour operator at an inclusive price.

In fact, charter tourism gained much popularity in the Scandinavian counties. People over there preferred to travel to the warmer southern region of Europe in the winter seasons in order to avoid long, cold and dark winters.

8.6 Conclusion

The airline sector has grown and developed into one of the largest industries in the world. Every country enjoys significant social and economic benefits from the airline sector. The airline product is intangible, perishable and inseparable. In air transport, the readiness to travel and the ability to afford tickets are crucial in determining the demand. The growth in airline demand increases as the economic status of the people increases. The factors greatly upsurge the airline demand are increased service frequency, more choices, more networks, easier connections, more convenient time, etc. Airlines can be classified on different perspectives. Scheduled airlines are regular service providers, operating services based on a pre-arranged and published timetable. International airlines, domestic airlines and cargo airlines are the different types of scheduled airlines. The current air transport market has the presence of LCCs along with the FSCs or legacy carriers. The LCC air travel market expanded considerably and soon gained wide acceptance. They are also called "no-frills" airlines and have a business model that specializes in air travel. Nowadays, on LCC flights, you can see limited food and beverages being sold at relatively high prices. They use different types of cost saving strategies. The hybrid model is a combination of the LCC business model and the FSC business model, and one can see the difference in in-flight services, product delivery, network routes, etc.

The growth of the airline sector is one of the main reasons for the rise of international tourism, one of the largest economic sectors in the world. Over time, air travel has become more and more accessible to more and more sections of society. Travel and tourism complement each other in their progress. Charter air services are an important segment in aviation, especially in international tourism. International tour operators rely heavily on charter services, as they are much cheaper considering scheduled services. The ad hoc nature of the charter flight service offers a direct connection to tourist destinations that avoid transit flights, which contribute to the growth of charter tourism, and they maintain a good share of international tourism, especially in the field of recreational tourism.

Sample questions

Short/medium answer type questions

- Describe the concept of airline industry.
- Describe the economic benefits of airline industry.
- Elucidate the role of airline industry in tourism.

- What are the characteristics of airline industry?
- Discuss the feature of perishability in airline industry.
- Discuss how airlines have high barriers of entry and exit.
- Describe an airline's product.
- Who are the consumers of airlines?
- What are the factors that influence airline demand?
- What do you mean by scheduled airlines?
- What is a combination carrier?
- What are the features of regional carriers?
- Discuss in detail the business model of LCCs.
- What are hybrid airlines?
- What are the different non-scheduled airlines?

Essay type questions

- Compare the business models of FSC, LCC and hybrid airlines.
- Discuss in detail the features and business environments of airline industry.

Suggested readings

Belobaba, P, Odoni, A., & Barnhart, C. (2009). *The Global Airline Industry.* West Sussex: John Wiley & Sons.

Belobaba, P., Odoni, A., & Barnhart, C. (2015). *The Global Airline Industry.* West Sussex: John Wiley & Sons.

Budd, L., & Ison, S. (2019). *Air Transport Management: An International Perspective.* London: Routledge.

Bruce, P., Gao, Y., & King, J.M.C. (Eds.) (2017). *Airline Operations: A Practical Guide.* London: Routledge.

Cook, G.N., & Billig, B. (2017). *Airline Operations and Management: A Management Textbook.* London: Routledge.

Dunleavy, H., & Philips, G. (2009). The future of airline management. *Journal of Revenue and Pricing Management*, 8(4), 388–395.

Vasigh, B., Fleming, K., & Thomas, T. (2018). *Tacker Introduction to Air Transport Economics: From Theory to Applications.* London: Routledge.

Chapter 9

Airport

Learning outcomes

After reading this chapter, you will be able to:

- Understand the concept of airport.
- Categorize airports on a different basis.
- Assess the role of airports in tourism.
- Identify the facilities and services needed by tourists.
- Discuss the ownership and privatization in airlines.
- Understand the certification, standardization, etc., in airport sector.

9.1 Introduction

The transformation of airports from a space for aircraft landing and take-off to a huge physical site with necessary air transport infrastructure along with diverse facilities and services matching those of a city is incredible. Moreover, emerging demand and supply challenges keep on necessitating airports to expand and enhance facilities and services. Currently, airports are not just viewed from a point of transportation; rather they are also viewed as "powerful engines of economic growth and possibility for local communities" (ACI, 2018). The consistent growth in air travel propensity not only demands expansion of existing airports, but also causing the construction of greenfield airports the world over. Though there are a large number of airports, the majority are in the general aviation category. The number of airports in commercial aviation is much less. According to a recent report of the International Civil Aviation Organization (ICAO) (2015), there are more than 4,000 commercial airports, but the number is going to increase significantly, as the global commercial air transportation is poised for tremendous growth in the coming years. As stated in a previous chapter based on the International Air Transport Association (2018) report, by 2037, the number of air travellers may

DOI: 10.4324/9781003136927-9

double to 8.2 billion compared to the status of demand in 2016 (4.1 billion passengers on scheduled services). According to the Airports Council International (ACI), in 2017, the commercial airports in the world served more than 8.3 billion air passengers and enabled the transportation of 118.6 million metric tonnes of cargo. Moreover, there were 95 million aircraft movements through the commercial airports in the world in 2017. ACI also predicts a global average annual growth rate of 4.1% in passenger traffic through these airports, 2.4% in the air cargo and 2% in aircraft movements from 2018 to 2040 (ACI, 2018).

9.2 Airport and air transport

Terminal is a key element in any transport system. It is where the transportation commences/ends and gives access to the way for the users. Terminals can also act as interchanges in which travellers may transfer between modes. Many of the coordinating activities for the smooth conduct of the transport are done in terminals. Air transport also needs a terminal, a dedicated space that consists of facilities and services for aircraft landing and take-off, aircraft ground handling activities, passenger and cargo processing, and the required technical and technological services to enable smooth and safe transport services. All those are provided in one location and it is referred to as an airport. Thus, it is one of the integral elements in the air transport system. While we discuss airport as a system, the term terminal is used to indicate the construction, a component of it, which encompasses the needed services and facilities for passenger and cargo processing for enabling them to change the mode of transport either from land to air mode of transport or vice versa. There are other components in an airport, which all together enable air transport service providers to undertake air services. Airport, as the inevitable component of the air transport system, provides the entire infrastructure needed to enable passengers and freight to transfer from surface modes of transport to air modes of transport and to allow airlines to take off and land (Graham, 2003). According to Ashford et al. (2013), airport acts as the point of interaction of the following three major components of the air transport system:

- The airport
- The airline
- The user.

All the above elements have significant roles in the air transportation. Moreover, they are inextricably linked and interdependent. Having a key role, planning and meticulous operation is of extreme significance for the successful functioning of airports in the air transportation system. Apart from playing a crucial role within the air transport sector, airports are of strategic importance to the regions they serve. In a number of countries, they are increasingly becoming integrated within the overall transport system by establishing links to high-speed rail and key road networks. Airports can bring greater wealth, provide substantial employment opportunities and encourage economic development. However, they do have a very significant effect, both on the environment in which they are located and on the quality of life of the residents living nearby. A growing awareness of general environmental issues has heightened the environmental concerns about airports.

Table 9.1 Top 20 Airports in the World

Rank	City (Airport)	Passengers	Rank	City (Airport)	Passengers
1	ATLANTA GA, US (ATL)	104,171,935	11	DALLAS/FORT WORTH TX, US (DFW)	65,670,697
2	BEIJING, CN (PEK)	94,393,454	12	AMSTERDAM, NL (AMS)	63,625,534
3	DUBAI, AE (DXB)	83,654,250	13	FRANKFURT, DE (FRA)	60,786,937
4	LOS ANGELES CA, US (LAX)	80,921,527	14	ISTANBUL, TR (IST)	60,422,847
5	TOKYO, JP (HND)	79,699,762	15	GUANGZHOU, CN (CAN)	59,732,147
6	CHICAGO IL, US (ORD)	77,960,588	16	NEW YORK NY, US (JFK)	59,105,513
7	LONDON, GB (LHR)	75,715,474	17	SINGAPORE, SG (SIN)	58,698,000
8	HONG KONG, HK (HKG)	70,305,857	18	DENVER CO, US (DEN)	58,266,515
9	SHANGHAI, CN (PVG)	66,002,414	19	JAKARTA, ID (CGK)	58,195,484
10	PARIS, FR (CDG)	65,933,145	20	INCHEON, KR (ICN)	57,849,814

Source: Airports Council International (ACI), based on 2016 statistics, data available online at https://aci.aero/data-centre/annual-traffic-data/passengers/2016-final-summary/

Airports are recognized for their ability to multiply business activity in their proximity and stimulate further development. Furthermore, an airport is a matter of pride and economic advancement of a state.

9.3 Concept of airport

The airport, being a physical site, essentially consists of runways for the take-off and landing, and the other needed space with facilities for loading and offloading of passengers and cargo, buildings with facilities for passenger and cargo processing and for the maintenance of civil aircraft. Generally, it is viewed as an aerodrome with added facilities for the commercial air transport. Airports often have facilities to store and maintain aircraft and a control tower. Airport provides "all the infrastructure needed to enable passengers and freight to transfer from surface to air modes of transport and to allow airlines to take off and land" (Page, 2009). An airport consists of a landing area, which comprises an aerially accessible open space including at least one operationally active surface such as a runway for a plane to take off or a helipad, and often includes adjacent utility buildings such as control towers, hangars and terminals. Larger airports may have fixed-base operator services, airport aprons, taxiway bridges, air traffic control centres, passenger facilities such as restaurants and lounges, and emergency services.

In many a case, the term aerodrome is used for referring to an airport. According to ICAO, aerodrome is a defined area on land or water (including any buildings, installations and equipment) intended to be used either wholly or in part for the arrival, departure and surface movement of aircraft (ICAO Annex 14, Volume 1, Chapter I, Page 1-2). This is a broader definition encompasses all sort of airports and airstrips. Further, ICAO defines an international airport as any airport designated by the contracting state in whose territory it is situated as an airport of entry and departure for international air traffic, where the formalities incident to customs, immigration, public health, agricultural quarantine and similar procedures are carried out (ICAO 1994 Statistics Manual).

In simple functional terms, the airport must be designed to enable an aircraft to land and take off. In between these two operations, the aircraft may, if required, unload and load payload and crew and to be serviced. The functions of airport terminals are following (Ashford et al., 2013).

- *Change of mode* from surface to air.
- *Processing and provision* of necessary facilities for ticketing, documentation and control of passengers and freight.
- *Change of movement type* of passengers, baggage, freight, mail, etc., to a pre-planned schedule.

Undertaking the above functions requires a wide range of services and facilities. In fact, an airport is a large organization in which a wide range of activities takes place. Airport offers all the facilities and services required for smooth and efficient air transport operations. According to Ashford et al. (2013), the following facilities are either provided or administered by an airport of modern times:

- Passenger handling;
- Servicing, maintaining, repairing and engineering of aircraft;
- Airline operations, including the various crew and terminal and office staff;
- Various businesses that offer services and products to passengers, like concessionaries and leasing companies;
- Aviation support facilities, like Air Traffic Control (ATC) and meteorological services;
- Government functions, like customs and immigration.

The following aspects, suggested as the dimensions of an airport by Graham (2003), too specify the services and facilities provided or supplied by airports for the smooth conduct of air transport. An airport:

- brings together a wide range of facilities and services so as to fulfil its role within the air transport industry.
- offers a wide range of commercial facilities, ranging from shops and restaurants to conference facilities.

It also specifies that an airport:

- ensures strategic importance in the region where it is located by integrating within the overall transport system by establishing links with rail and road networks.

- brings greater economic development, provides substantial employment opportunities and can be a lifeline to isolated communities.

Therefore, though an airport is a physical space for coordination of activities for the smooth and efficient air transportation, it has increased dimensions with economic, social and strategic perspectives. For instance, Wells and Young (2004) introduce the increasing dimensions of a modern airport in the following way.

> Similar to a city, an airport is comprised of a huge variety of facilities, systems, users, workers, rules, and regulations. Also, just as cities thrive on trade and commerce with other cities, airports are successful in part by their ability to successfully be the location where passengers and cargo travel to and from other airports. Furthermore, just as cities find their place as part of its county's, state's, and country's economy, airports, too, must operate successfully as part of the nation's system of airports

The above attempt is to compare the diversity of operations and other aspects of a modern airport with those of a city. Though city is a large area, airport too has so varied operations and functions along with socio-economic significance. All happen in a much smaller area. The trend of expanding airports and increasing facilities and services in airports is going on and newer airports can have added services and facilities not only to cater to the needs of passengers, but also to attract more customers to the airports. While reading the rest of this chapter, more clarity will be there on the significance of airport on various counts.

9.4 Importance of airport for tourism

Airport, as a key element in the destination transport infrastructure, possesses a significant role in tourism in a destination. Certainly, airport enhances the accessibility of the destination. In general, airport is a fundamental element in the destination system. Mass tourism destinations find airports as crucial in their competitive survival. Airports are needed for ensuring the inflow of tourists from outside and airlines can serve the destination in ensuring the movement of tourists only with the help of airports. Papatheodorou and Zenelis (2013) opined "… airports and tourism are structurally interdependent as the former exist because the airlines use their facilities to offer transport services to passengers the majority of which travel for tourism purposes". Either airports are expanded or new airports are developed when a destination is growing at a remarkable rate. World over, this phenomenon can be seen. Moreover, international tourism is depending on air transport more than ever before, and hence, airports have an increasing role in the growth of tourism. They also have evolved greatly from a space for changing the mode of transport from land to air to a modern infrastructure with almost all the facilities and services of a small city. Long-haul tourists do find airports more important for their relaxation and refreshments.

The airport and its facilities and services are an inseparable part of the tourism industry and act as a major service provider to tourists. Being a service provider, the service of it has a considerable contribution in the tourist experience. For an inbound tourist, airport is the first point of encounter and the experience gained from there builds up the first impression about the destination as well. It offers the tourist a range of services so that the journey of him or her is comfortable and the travellers can have the necessary rest and relaxation over there. Many of the tourists purchase souvenir and gift items from airports while returning to his or her origin place. As an airport offers space for some of the tourism businesses to have outlets within the terminal and in the landside of an airport, tourists can easily access the products of elements of the tourism industry in the destination. Moreover, tourists search for information about varied aspects of the destination and most of them can be obtained from the airport itself. An airport has a marketing and promotion role as well. Destination marketing communication can be done through airports. Airports can host advertisements, banners, posters, etc., as part of destination promotion. Some of the airports in the world have significant touristic appeal. The features, facilities and services may have the ability to prompt tourists to choose those airports and to contribute a share in the overall attractiveness of the destination in which the airport is situated. Many a times, tourists make use of airports also for shopping purposes as well. Leisure tourists do have more inclination for shopping from airports. A detailed discussion on the relationship between airport and tourist destination is given in Chapter 10.

9.5 Airport classification

Airports are classified in different ways. According to Wells and Young (2004), the major measures used to indicate the level of airport are as follows.

- Number of passengers handled (enplanements or deplaning)
- Cargo activity (for airports that are dedicated to freight and mail)
- Aircraft operations (mainly in general aviation airports)
- Number of based aircraft (Based aircraft: those aircraft registered as a resident of the airport. This measure is also used more in small, private general aviation airports.)

The primary classification is based on the categories of aviation, which is following.

- Civil aviation airports
  - General aviation airports
  - Commercial service airports
- Military airports

Among the above categories, the most visible are the commercial service airports. Yet, the number of general aviation airports is much more than the other in some countries. Our focus is more on the commercial service airports.

9.5.1 Civil aviation airports

Civil aviation airport denotes all the airports other than military airports. The large number of civil aviation airports is there in the world. Of them, some are general aviation airports, which are used for specific purposes, including private airports. Commercial airports constitute the other category, which handles commercial passenger and cargo transportation.

9.5.2 General aviation airports

These are the airports, which are meant for general aviation purposes. Generally, they are smaller airports. According to the Federal Aviation Administration (FAA), these are "civilian airports that do not serve scheduled passenger service are typically known as general aviation airports. These airports usually serve private aircraft and small aircraft charter operations" (www.faa.gov). It means they are public-use airports that do not have scheduled service. FAA (2015) also specifies that there are different categories in it, such as national, regional, local, basic and unclassified. National represents those general aviation airports that support the national and state system by providing communities with access to national and international markets in multiple states and throughout the United States. On the contrary, the second category, regional airport, facilitates the regional economies by connecting communities statewide and interstate markets. Local category supplements communities by providing access to primarily intrastate and some interstate markets. Basic links the community with the national airport system and supports general aviation activities (e.g. emergency services). The last category enables access to the aviation system.

9.5.3 Commercial airports

Commercial ones are the most prominent category. These are the common airports that we see while travelling to different places. It is used by the general public, and the services are offered for passengers and cargo movement. Commercial airports mainly undertake scheduled services. Yet, many of them have space for other services like helicopter services and charter services also. Moreover, aircraft maintenance services are also provided within commercial airports. The number of commercial airports is on the increase, along with the rigorous expansion of existing airports to accommodate the growing needs from the supply as well as demand sides. Airline operations are from commercial airports.

9.5.4 Military airports

Military airports are basically the exclusive aerodrome set-ups for the operation of military aircraft. The size, facilities and services vary depending upon the requirements connected to the nature of operations and the aircraft used. Different terminologies are seen in this category like military airbase, military airfield, military airport, air-force station or air-force base. Some of the military airports permit civil aviation activities as well. Ownership of these airports is with the national authorities concerned with defence activities.

9.5.5 Private airports

While commercial airport provides services for the general public, a private airport serves a limited population. These are smaller airports and meant for operation for small privately owned aircraft, flying clubs, etc. This can vary from a private strip for specific purposes to an aerodrome with basic facilities for general aviation purposes.

9.5.6 Heliports

These are rather smaller aerodromes with basic facilities for the landing, take-off or surface movement of helicopters. The main facility is the helipad, which is the landing and take-off area for helicopters.

9.5.7 Stolports

The term STOL represents "short take-off and landing" and stolports are small aerodromes designed for STOL aircraft services. The STOL aircraft are usually the small ones, probably the smaller propeller aircraft, and often with limits on the amount of fuel that can be taken. The airstrips are also relatively small.

9.5.8 International airports

Some of the commercial airports are international airports, classified on the basis of destinations to which services are offered to. According to ICAO, "an international airport is a designated airport of entry and departure for international air services, where formalities such as customs, immigration, public health, animal and plant quarantine and similar procedures are carried out" (ICAO Doc 9626. Manual on the Regulation of International Air Transport). Though the focus of these airports is international operations, domestic services may also be there from some of the international airports.

9.5.9 Gateway airports

These are international airports that are the first point of arrival while arriving from a foreign country or the last point of departure when moving to a foreign country.

9.5.10 Domestic airports

From a domestic airport, services will be to a destination within the boundaries of a country. International services will not be there from domestic airports. In many cities, separate international and domestic airports are there.

9.5.11 Primary airports

These are the category of airports seen in the United States, and the classification of these, according to FAA (2015), is based on the number of passenger boarding annually. According to them, these are the commercial airports that have more than 10,000 passenger boarding each year.

9.5.12 Cargo airports

These are the airports dedicated to cargo services. According to FAA (2015), cargo service airports are the airports that, in addition to any other air transportation services that may be available, are served by aircraft providing air transportation of only cargo with a total annual landed weight (the weight of aircraft transporting only cargo in domestic and international routes) of more than 100 million pounds. ICAO identifies "cargo hub" as an airport in which facilities are provided for easy and fast connections and transhipment of air cargo traffic.

9.5.13 Regional airports

Regional airports primarily host the air transport services to short-haul routes in a region. Usually, they are medium or small airports with domestic services, and hence, there may not have customs and immigration facilities to process traffic between countries. In addition, these are not based in a capital city or the metro/large cities in a country. Most of them are natural counterparts of big and medium-sized hubs, and hence, they complement the larger air transportation network in a country. Apart from ensuring accessibility to smaller cities, these have great social, economic and development significance in tier-2 lower level cities.

9.5.14 Congested airports

This classification is based on the capacity of the airport and the demand. ICAO defines that it as an airport "whose capacity for handling traffic (air or ground) is inadequate to accommodate demand" (ICAO Doc 9626. Manual on the Regulation of International Air Transport). Congestion is an issue in many airports as the air travel propensity is on a steady increase. Generally, two types of airports are seen intended to relieve the congestion in large airports. They are reliever airports and supplemental airports.

9.5.15 Reliever airports

Some airports are designated as reliever airports that are built with the intention to divert traffic from major commercial airports. In the United States, these are the airports designated by the FAA to relieve congestion at commercial service airports and to provide improved general aviation access to the overall community. These may be publicly or privately owned (FAA, 2015). These can also be the existing airports that are designated to handle a specific class of aircraft such as general aviation or these can also be general aviation airports with a designated purpose of relieving congestion at commercial airports.

9.5.16 Supplemental airports

These are the airports that primarily focus on general aviation and placed away from commercial busy airports, thus relieving congestion in particular markets. Charter services are also there from these airports.

9.5.17 Hub airports

Hub airports are the large commercial airports from where air services are there to many other cities. From hub airport, people can travel to many cities and people can arrive from one city to the hub and move to another city from here. Airlines find it easy for operations through a "hub-and-spoke" route system (explained in chapter 13). In fact, theoretically, hub-based operation is basically pooling the demand of travel to various cities in one city. Undertaking direct flights between all the cities may not be possible, and hence, they route the demand via hubs. ICAO specifies it as

> any airport having numerous inbound and outbound flights and a high percentage of connecting traffic; while in the context of scheduling and marketing from a hub operating air carrier's perspective, it denotes an airport where many of its inbound and outbound schedules are coordinated with the aim of producing the most convenient connections and/or transhipment for passengers, freight and/or mail.
>
> (ICAO Doc 9626. Manual on the Regulation of International Air Transport)

In hub airports, one or more airlines concentrate passenger traffic and flight operations and use such airport as transfer points to get passengers to their final destination. Only thing is that people have to change the aircraft at the hub for boarding to travel to the next city. In fact, different types of hub airports can be there. ICAO identifies the following types.

- Major hub
- regional hub
- interline hub
- online hub
- Mini-hub
- Mega-hub/super-hub
- second country hub
- cargo hub
- postal/mail hub
- Intermodal hub/multimodal hub (ICAO, ICAO Doc 9626. Manual on the Regulation of International Air Transport).

A major hub may be used by more than one airline as the hub for long-haul operations. Such airports may handle a large volume of passengers. Further, these are centrally situated, in major cities. On the contrary, a regional hub entertains services within a region and the volume of passenger transportation may be lesser than that of major hubs. The next one, interline hub, is a hub from where connections or transferring of traffic is chiefly made between flights of different carriers. In online hubs, connections or transferring of traffic is mostly undertaken between different flights of the same airline. A mini-hub is a secondary hub set up by an airline and a mega-hub or a super-hub is a very large hub. Second country hub represents an airlines' hub airport in a foreign country for connecting various cities in the home country to numerous third countries. There are hub airports for handling cargo transportation as well. A cargo hub is meant for easy and fast connections and transhipment of air cargo traffic. Postal hub or mail hub serves as a transit centre for postal or mail shipments. Intermodal hub or multimodal hub ensures convenient connections or transhipment of traffic from one mode of transport to another (e.g. surface to air on a sea–air routing).

9.6 Airport customers and tourists

Airport, a business management and marketing perspective, is an organization that offers a variety of services, all of which eventually aims to ensure a comfortable, safe and convenient air transport. A diverse group of people/businesses consumes those services. Though varieties of services are offered, it is conceptually considered as a composite product. The core product of it, with regard to an airline, a category of its customers, is the ability to land and take off an aircraft smoothly and efficiently, along with the ability for smooth, efficient and quick passenger and cargo handling. Airline is only one type of customer. According to Graham (2003), in addition to passengers and travel and tourism sector industry elements such as airlines, tour operators, freight forwarders and other elements in the civil aviation sector, the customers of airport also include a number of groups such as tenants and concessionaires, host community members, employees and other businesses that have business relation with the airport. Services consumed by other types of customers can be different. Let us see the major categories of customers of an airport. Brilha (2008) illustrates this aspect in the following manner.

> Airports serve a range of different passengers with diverse motivations and needs, from leisure to business, and from transfer to charter or low-cost. Since most airports process more than one of these passenger segments, the non-aeronautical choice of products and services should be adapted to each segment's individual value or share. Moreover, in addition to passenger profiles, the scale and diversity of non-aeronautical activities also derives from the total volume of traffic processed and the airport's strategic positioning as a hub, a feeder or a destination airport.

Herrmann and Hazel (2012) attempt to categorize the airport customers into five such as:

- Airlines
- Passengers
- Non-travellers (employees, visitors and retail customers, meet and greeters, and neighbours),
- Tenants/service providers (retail, car park, ground handling, advertisers)
- Potential development partners (real estate developers, hospitality, transportation service providers and the government)

Furthermore, airport provides services to the commercial agents/firms like duty-free markets, currency exchange dealers, catering establishments, and car parking agents. In addition, airport provides services and facilities for the freight forwarders. Cargo may be sorted, stored, loaded, and unloaded in the airport. Among the customers, airline is the major customer of airport services. In fact, airlines use the services of the airports to serve their customers, who are the passengers, mainly. These passengers are the users of various services of airport as well. Cargo transportation is another function of airlines and they use the services of airports too for the same. Airline's consumption of services of airports includes

Table 9.2 Revenue Opportunities for Airports

Aircraft landing fee	Airport ATC charges
Aircraft parking fee	Passenger charges
Freight charges	Aircraft handling services
Rent or lease income for airport tenants	Concession income for duty free, etc.
Direct sales in shops operated by airports	Vehicle parking fee
Advertisements	Cargo handling

the services for landing and taking off flights, space for parking, loading and unloading of the flights, baggage handling, check-in services along with emigration and security check-in, and other services necessary for operating the flight services. Cargo agents too avail services of airports, directly or indirectly.

Tourists constitute a major category of consumers of airports. In mass tourism destinations, tourists may be the prime consumer group compared to the rest of the passengers. Tourists, with regard to airports, are usually classified into two segments such as leisure tourists and business tourists. Though both have some common behaviour patterns, some differences can also be identified. Leisure tourists may spend more time in airports and engage in more shopping activities, along with increased spending for different items from the airport. Business tourists prefer rather quicker services and have better quality expectations. Yet, for a tourist, airport is an important space for rest and relaxation as well and the contribution of the experience they get from the airport has a share in the overall tourist experience. While departing for a tour abroad, a tourist may desire:

- Speed check-in process
- Smooth and fast emigration clearance
- Hassle-free security check
- Easy access to gates
- Quality refreshment options
- Good duty-free shopping facility
- Enthusing interior
- Sufficient and comfortable space for waiting
- Quality customer service
- Promptness in departure information provision
- Smooth boarding process

On the contrary, an arriving tourist expects the following in the airport.

- Easy access to the arrival area
- Efficient transit services
- Quick and efficient passport control/emigration services
- Quick and efficient baggage claim/retrieval
- Smart customs activities
- Diverse concessionaries and other commercial centres
- Good duty-free shopping facility

Airport

- Availability of some of the centres of tourism industries
- Commercial services in the arrival hall
- Facilities for visitors
- Sufficient taxi and other transport services
- Attractive interior and pleasing premises
- Quality information services

In order to increase the chances of securing cost-effective levels of business activity, airports have to offer better quality services than the expected levels of the passengers and tourists (Graham, 2008). Concessionaries within airports depend much on tourists for increasing their profit levels. For infrequent leisure travellers, the commercial shops within airports do have some attractions and they may spend some amount on purchase of different items, therefore be induced to spend considerable amounts of money on shopping (Papatheodorou, 2008). Leisure tourists also consume food and beverages relatively more from the airport. Many of the Low Cost Carrier (LCC) travellers also consume food and beverages in the airport refreshment centres as LCCs do not offer complimentary inflight catering services (Papatheodorou & Lei, 2006). An airport will have a range of facilities and services targeted at tourists. All of them have a share in the airport's contribution in the overall tourist experience. The following are the major of those facilities and services, of which some are common ones for all types of passengers.

Check-in counters
Baggage screening
Baggage measuring gauge
Baggage packing and wrapping service
Baggage porter service
Baggage storage
Self-baggage drop service
Self-check-in services
SIM cards and pocket Wi-Fi
Wi-Fi and Internet services
Security check
Concessionaries and retail counters
Restaurants and coffee shops
Passenger lounges
Drinking water facilities
Washrooms and toilets
Electric vehicles
Baggage claim
National Tourism Organization/Destination Management Organization Office
Duty-free shops
Gift shops, souvenir shops and bookstalls
Money exchange centres
Banks and ATMs
Medical clinics

Airport courier service and postal services
Meet and Assist Service
Wheelchairs and mobility services
Police assistance services
Prayer rooms
Smoking corners
Public phones
Parking
Tourist information centres
Special assistance services
Ground transportation services
National immigration services
Hotel and travel agent counters
Trolleys, infant strollers and baby strollers
Fire and safety services
Waiting areas
Battery recharge services and mobile charging services
Relaxations centres, shower facilities, yoga rooms, spas
Caring corner for disabled tourists
Kid's entertainment corners
Reprographic services
Communication centres, including facsimile

Special passenger assistance corner
Customer service centres
Customs services
Baggage claim areas
Baggage delivery service
Immediate assistance counters
Lost and found assistance
Hotel coaches/transfers.

Conference centres
Automated people mover between
    terminals
Art, entertainment and cultural events
    and services
Multimodal transport network and
    mainland connectivity services

9.7 Airport business and its socio-economic impact

Airport, in addition to providing the required facilities and services for the trans-portation of passenger and cargo, has many other dimensions coupled with socio-economic significance. According to Graham (2014), there are basically two types of economic impacts on airports. First one is the direct economic benefits, in terms of income, employment, capital investment and tax revenues, which airport operations can bring by nature of the fact that they are significant generators of economic activity. The second aspect is the wider catalytic or spin-off benefits, such as inward investment or the development of tourism that can occur as the result of the presence of the airport. This can contribute to the economic de-velopment of the area surrounding the airport. Airport is considered an agent of economic progress of a region as well. Direct, indirect and induced economic benefits are there due to the establishment of airports in a region. Employment opportunities are provided directly and indirectly: on and off the airport.

    The direct impact of an airport on the local economy reflects the jobs, payroll, and sales directly related to airport operations. This includes the management and operation of the airport, commercial airlines, air terminal vendors, airport national authorities, transportation security administration, as well as businesses providing aircraft maintenance, fuelling, storage, rental and leasing activities. In an airport, there is a wide variety of employment opportunities, like in the ar-eas associated with aircraft operations and maintenance, passenger and freight

Table 9.3 Revenue Generated By Airports (in 2017)

Global airport sector revenue	$ 151.8 billion
Aeronautical revenue	56%
Non-aeronautical revenue	39.8%
Non-operating revenue	4.2%
Global aeronautical revenue per passenger	$ 11.23
Global non-aeronautical revenue per passenger	$ 7.97
Total cost per passenger	$ 15.58
Industry net profit margin	17.2%
Global return on invested capital	6.4%

Source: ACI, data available online at https://aci.aero/Media/7b66fe0e-23b7-4935-b2b8-a99a25495226/lb1pdA/Statistics%20and%20Data/Infographics/KPI_Aiport_economics_at-a-glance_2016_5x10.pdf

handling, air traffic control and safety, transport and logistics, airport management, planning and construction, and various retail and commercial services inside the airport. Allied businesses also offer a diverse range of employment in and around the city in which the airport is located. The passengers who are coming into the region also spend on a wide variety of items that will have a multiplier effect on the economy. The arriving passengers' spending, or the direct impact of airport users, is the amount of money flowing into the local economy. They spend money on accommodation, meals, ground transportation and retail purchases within the county. The multiplier effect also occurs as part of the extra expenditure made by the incoming passengers. Public revenue will also be generated from airport- and aviation-related fees. Income is generated and value addition takes place, in terms of wages, salaries, interest and profits. It directly helps to have more investments in the economy.

Along with regional development, increased productivity, both directly and indirectly, can occur. The role of the airport is connecting communities, people and markets and enhancing the mobility of the population. Airports can enable remote regions to have access to essential services such as hospitals and higher education. They can also make the communities more attractive places to work and can contribute to attracting and retaining skilled labour in the area. Moreover, it helps in having strengthened link between different countries and cultures, which altogether can help in cultural exchange as well. Increased mobility and access to places is something the community can be enjoyed by the establishment of an airport. Furthermore, airport is crucial in the tourism development and growth. For both inbound and outbound tourism, air connectivity has tremendous significance. More than half of the international tourists depend on air transportation for reaching the destination and for returning. The socio-economic benefits derived from the airport can be summarized as follows.

- Enhancement to accessibility and global connectivity
- Population can enjoy better mobility
- Speedier, safer and more comfortable mode of transportation
- Acceleration in trade due to faster means of transportation
- Increased scope for imports and exports
- Stimulation in the tourism sector
- Increased scope for income and employment opportunities
- Scope for cultural exchange
- Increased communication and information inflow and outflow across the globe.

9.8 Airport ownership

Airports traditionally formed part of the public sector, being originally built either by national, regional or local governments. In the very early stages of evolution of air transport, airports were privately owned, and sooner governments initiated to take the control of airport along with the increasing significance of air transportation. Some were managed and operated by semi-autonomous bodies. Some others were operated by agencies like companies with public shareholdings, on a concession basis for long periods from national governments (Dileep, 2019).

After world wars, air transport surged and quick changes were visible in the air-port environments. During the 1980s and 90s, after the deregulation, the major developments that took place in the air transport sector were airport privatiza-tion, commercialization and globalization (Graham, 2008). Through corporati-zation, airport management moved from state-run administrations towards the more typical commercial corporate structures often found in the private sector, such as a limited company or public corporation with shareholders. Ownership of such corporatized airports could, however, remain with the state, for example, through the state being the owner of 100% of the airport corporation's shares. However, such corporatization facilitated the introduction of a more commercial style of management, with a focus on increasing revenues and reducing costs (and in some cases, the removal of staff's civil service-type employment privileges).

Private sector involvement in airport ownership and management is now in-creasing. While privatization deals with the transfer of management and/ or ownership, fully or partially to the private sector using different practices, airport commercialization is all about the metamorphosis of an airport from a public utility to a commercial enterprise incorporating modern management principles, practices and philosophies (Dileep, 2019). "Airport privatization, in particular, typically involves the lease of airport property and/or facilities to a private company to build, operate and/or manage commercial services offered at the airport" (Wells & Young, 2004). In addition to fully private investors, many of the major "corporatized" airport groups with significant or majority public sector in their home country act as entirely private sector investors in foreign markets, often in partnership with financial institutions or investment funds. Aéroports de Paris (owner of the Paris Airports) and Fraport (owner of Frankfurt Airport) are good examples of this. In some cases, corporatization also facili-tated the involvement of the private sector, through sales of the airport corpo-ration to investors via trade sales or public offerings. Private sector involvement has been introduced at a growing number of airports over the last few decades, motivated by the:

- Opportunity to raise funds for the public sector through the sale of the asset;
- Increased efficiency of operation assumed to be achieved in the private sector; and
- Opportunity to support investment in airport infrastructure: adding terminals, runways and other airport facilities, thereby improving the transport assets of the country concerned without recourse to public funds.

Private sector involvement can take a number of different forms, ranging from

- Outright sale of the airport asset to the private sector or a partial sale of shares in the airport company with some control by the state;
- Build-operate-transfer (BOT);
- Time-limited operating concession;
- Concessions for a part of the airport, such as a terminal;
- Management contracts;
- Project finance; and
- Private sector investment (like by way of purchase of a minority share).

Table 9.4 Airport Privatization: Prospects and Concerns

Prospects

- Helps to reduce government expenditure in the air transport sector
- Airports can be operated and managed in the same way as privately growth-oriented enterprises, which may be beneficial in a way to have increased customer orientation that eventually may lead to lower prices or other customer benefits
- Enables to open up new sources of income and taking advantage of new growth opportunities
- Increased diversification of opportunities for the airport, like the opportunities to set up a range of different pillars
- Greater incentives for both management and employees to operate the airport in an increasingly efficient and profitable manner

Concerns

- Possible that a private monopoly with inflated prices
- Insufficient investment plans due to commercially responsible private investments
- Can lower service standards
- Airport can have the opportunity of acting as a natural monopoly due to their size and indivisibility
- Insufficient concerns for ecological and social aspects
- Being dependent on investors and their short- to long-term objectives, which, in the context of airports as national or regional assets and in the context of economy, society, and environment, is a matter of controversial debate
- Less importance could be attached to regional requirements, due to the commercial orientations.

Source: Adapted from Urfer and Weinert (2011)

9.8.1 Public–Private Partnership (PPP) airport project

Public–private partnership is gaining increasing significance in air transport sector. According to ICAO (https://www.icao.int/sustainability/Pages/im-ppp.aspx):

> A Public-Private Partnership (PPP) is a partnership between the public sector and the private sector for the purpose of delivering a project or a service traditionally provided by the public sector. The advantage of a PPP is that the management skills and financial acumen of private businesses could create better value for money for taxpayers when proper cooperative arrangements between the public and private sectors are used.

The PPP model of airport development and management is on the increase. For instance, five major airports in India are run as PPPs – Delhi (operated by GMR and Fraport), Mumbai (GVK), Hyderabad (GMR), Bangalore (GVK, Siemens and Zurich Airport) and Cochin (Non-Resident Indians (NRIs)); all have minority public

Table 9.5 Public–Private Partnership (PPP) – Case Study

Airport: Cochin International Airport (ICAO: VOCI, IATA: COK)

Cochin International Airport is operated by Cochin International Airport Ltd. (CIAL), a unique entity founded in 1994. It is the first greenfield airport in the country, build from scratch, with private participation, and is thus a pioneer of the Indian airport PPP model. Shareholders, with around 18,000 from more than 25 countries, mainly include the state government (Kerala), financial institutions, NRIs, airport service providers and public sector agencies, like Bharat Petroleum and Air India. The Kochi International Airport Society (KIAS) was founded by the Government of Kerala in 1993 in order to plan the international airport and to mobilize and manage financial resources under the PPP project. The novel financing scheme proposed included government funding, interest-free loans and donations from NRIs, airport users, foreign countries, financial institutions and airport service providers. Contributors were entitled to certain facilities such as a special lounge and a separate check-in counter after the opening of the airport.

Source: PPP (2018).

sector ownership. The benefits of PPP can be the quality enhancement, increase in efficiency and improvement in the competitiveness of public services. Another advantage is that the finance required for the investment can be shared by the private sector, which can be a great relief for the governments. Moreover, the effective use of private sector operational efficiencies can increase quality to the public and the ability to speed up infrastructure development.

When considering the commercialization or privatization of airports and air navigation services providers (ANSPs), states should bear in mind that they are ultimately responsible for safety, security and economic oversight of these entities (Doc 9082 – ICAO's Policies on Charges for Airports and Air Navigation Services – Section I, para. 6 refers).

Privatization should not in any way diminish the state's requirement to fulfil its international obligations, notably those contained in the Chicago Convention, its Annexes and air services agreements, and to observe ICAO's policies on charges in Doc 9082 (Doc 9562 – Airport Economics Manual – para. 2.27 refers and Doc 9161 – Manual on Air Navigation Services Economics – para. 2.27 refers).

9.9 Modern airports

Modern airport terminals are in a position to provide a good experience for the passengers while being within the airports. The use of advanced technology makes the passenger processing easy and less time-consuming. Now, electronic emigration services are also there which make the smooth passage of passengers from the entry point until the departure gates. Of late, there have been quite a few airport terminals constructed and remodelled that incorporate stylish aesthetics as well as features that allow travellers to get things done easily. Passengers are impressed by the great use of natural light, smart and sustainable building, top-notch amenities, and high-end useful features. These modern airport terminals are visually stunning and they give flyers a taste of the best in what new design and technology bring (SeatMaestro, www.seamaestro.com).

The concept of Smart Airports is gaining significance. The Smart Airports are connected, immersive, personalized, and multisensory. It puts the customer experience at the centre of the entire operation and is supported by collaborative technology and a partner ecosystem. The below, according to Doshi (2017), are the main features of a customer-centric Smart Airport

- Customer's needs at the heart of the operation
- Safety and security
- Networked
- Adaptable
- Flexibility
- Virtualization
- Sustainable.

Airports across the world are increasingly examining the airport-processing experience. Passenger experience enhancement is an important matter of consideration for airport owners. A range of new and emerging technology-based solutions promise improved operational efficiency and new approaches to engaging customers, and which hold the potential for new revenues. Additionally, airports are driven to find new ways to process and interact with a new generation of tech-savvy travellers. They expect instant interaction, engaging customer service and memorable experiences. Furthermore, many of these enabling technologies can also lower operational costs and enhance customer service.

During the next ten years or so, airports are likely to leverage and extend the efficiencies outlined in **IATA's Fast Travel initiative**. This program aims to deliver self-service options in **six areas** of a passenger's day of travel journey: **check-in, bags ready-to-go, document check, flight rebooking, self-boarding and bag recovery**. IATA estimates that these initiatives will save the industry approximately US$2.1 billion while providing passengers with options for more control over their airport journey. IATA's vision is that "by 2020, 80 per cent of global passengers will be offered a complete relevant self-service suite throughout their journey to provide better convenience and reduce queues" (IATA Program Strategy, 2016). By implementing many of these solutions and extending into additional areas of the traveller's experience, airlines and airports are poised to continue realizing incremental gains in the efficiency. Moreover, these solutions will make the traveller's experience less stressful and intrusive, and return a degree of control to the traveller, especially during times of irregular operations where the customer's journey is disrupted.

9.10 Airport standards and certification

Airports are subject to a number of different regulations at both international and national levels. Many of these are technical regulations related to the operational, safety and security aspects of managing an airport. Airports are also increasingly becoming subject to environmental regulations, which may, for example, restrict aircraft movements due to noise considerations or limit airport infrastructure development. Then, there is economic regulation with the main focus being on charge or tariff control. Other economic aspects of operation such as handling activities and slot allocation are also regulated in some areas of the world. Overall, the economic regulatory interest in airports seems to be increasing at a time when, ironically, the airlines business is being progressively deregulated.

Safety is the principal requirement in aviation. Standardization is one of the means to achieve it. In the case of airports, it has standardization of facilities, ground equipment and procedures. The only justification for differences is to match the types of aircraft that may be expected to use the airports. It is, obviously, fundamental for the norms to be fitting and to be concurred by the aviation community.

In the Chicago Convention, in compliance with Article 37 of the Convention on International Civil Aviation in Chicago in 1944, the ICAO adopted **Annex 14-Aerodromes to the Convention on 29th May 1951.** Annex 14 provides the required set of standards for aerodromes used by international air transport. The Annex contains information for planning, designing and operating airports. With the developments in aircraft technology, together with the consequent changes to airports, Annex 14 has been regularly amended and supplemented. Each of the ICAO member states may propose a supplement or amendment to an Annex through its aviation authority. The proposal is usually assessed or further examined by a panel of experts. Each of the member states may nominate its experts to the panel. Within ICAO, there are panels that have been dedicated to several specific issues for a long time. A few of them are:

Some of the major ICAO Air Navigation Commission (ANC) panels are following.

- Aerodrome Design and Operations Panel
- Accident Investigation Panel
- Airworthiness Panel
- Air Traffic Management Operations Panel
- ATM Requirements & Performance Panel
- Safety Management Panel
- Flight Operations Panel
- Instrument Flight Procedures Panel

The conclusions reached by the panels are reported in the form of working papers that are sent to the states for comments. Each of the ICAO member states is obliged to issue a national set of Standards and Recommended Practices (SARPs) regulating the points in question for their international airports, and amplifying them as necessary. This can give rise to problems of language. The options for an ICAO member state are either to adopt one of the official ICAO languages (English, French, Spanish or Russian) or to translate it into its own language and notify ICAO accordingly. If there is a need, the member state may adapt some of the provisions in its national SARPs if it files the differences with ICAO. The provisions in the Annex have two different levels of obligation and relevance:

Standards contain specifications for some physical characteristics, configuration, materials, performance, personnel or procedures. Their uniform acceptance is unconditional in order to ensure safety or regularity of international air navigation. In the event that a member state cannot accept the standard, it is compulsory to notify the ICAO Council of a difference between the national standard and the binding provision.

Recommendations include specifications referring to other physical characteristics; configuration; and interest of safety, regularity or economy of international air navigation. The member states should endeavour, in compliance with the convention, to incorporate them into national regulations. The member states are not obliged to notify the differences between recommendations in the Annex and the national SARPs. However, it is considered helpful to do so, provided such a provision is important to the safety of air transport.

Furthermore, the member states are invited to inform ICAO of any other changes that may occur. In addition, the states should publish the differences between their national regulation and the Annex by the means of the Flight Information Service. At present Annex 14 has two volumes, Volume I Aerodrome Design and Operations and Volume II Heliports. Besides the Annexes, ICAO issues other publications.

ICAO's International Standards and Recommended Practices (SARPs), detailed in Annex 14 and Doc 9774, state that all aerodromes should be certified by the state and licensed for use. This explains the certification process applied to state regulators and what aerodromes must do to not only become "certified" but to remain certified as traffic grows and the aerodrome expands to accommodate future traffic demand. Airport Certificate is an official document issued by the regulatory authority supported by technical documentation demonstrating that the aerodrome for which it was issued meets specific Air Safety-Related Criteria.

All signatory countries to ICAO are obliged to apply the ICAO standards to their international airports. It would be uneconomic to apply them fully to their more numerous domestic airports, though it is sensible to take note of the principles embodied in the ICAO documents. Therefore, every state has a possibility of making its own national SARPs dealing with specific problems of domestic airports and airfields exclusively within the territory of the particular state for aerial works in agriculture, general aviation airports as well as for limited commercial operations. Besides the various types of civilian airports, there are also military airports. Their physical characteristics, marking and equipment may be different from the characteristics recommended for civil aerodromes. In creating a national set of SARPs that do not derive directly from Annex 14 or another ICAO publication, the aviation authority usually puts an expert in charge of elaborating a draft of the document.

9.10.1 Aerodrome operator

An aerodrome/airport operator is vested with a range of duties and responsibilities. The holder of an airport certificate shall:

- comply with all conditions and limitations prescribed in the certificate;
- maintain the standards, conditions, airside services and facilities
- immediately notify the Director General, Civil Aviation Authority, of intention to change any specifications contained in the Aerodrome Manual;

- conduct regular scheduled safety inspections of the airport and special inspections as required, such as after an accident or incident;
- arrange for the issuance of a Notice to Airmen (NOTAM) in accordance with the appropriate NOTAM procedures when obstructions or hazards appear or changes in the level of service occur. When possible, for programmed construction or maintenance, a Class II NOTAM shall be issued giving advance notification at least 10 days before the proposed movement area restrictions. In cases where 10 is not possible, the maximum possible notice shall be provided by Class I NOTAM. If the proposed restrictions are delayed, the NOTAM shall be cancelled and revised information provided if necessary;
  - o A **NOTAM** is a notice filed with an aviation authority to alert aircraft pilots of potential hazards along a flight route or at a location that could affect the safety of the flight.
- ensure that information appearing in aeronautical information publications with respect to the airport is current and correct; and
- submit a Plan of Construction Operations to the Director General, Civil Aviation Authority, to obtain approval prior to carrying out any construction activities while continuing the operational use of runways, taxiways or other manoeuvring surfaces at the airport. All details of the construction activities, precautions, signage to be used, etc., are to be included in the plan.

9.10.2 Aerodrome manual

The Aerodrome Manual (AM) compiles the obligations undertaken by the airport operator to maintain standards and to provide specified airside services at an agreed-upon level. The drafting of an AM is the responsibility of the applicant aerodrome operator. Where necessary, an Aerodrome Standards Civil Aviation Inspector will assist the applicant in drafting the AM. An AM is a requirement for certifying an aerodrome as an airport. The AM provides a reference document for certification inspections. During an airport certification inspection, the AM is used by an Aerodrome Standards Civil Aviation Inspector as a checklist of the airport certification standards to be maintained and of the level of airside services being provided. AM is used as:

- a legal reference between the airport operator and the regulatory authority, with respect to the standards, conditions and levels of service to be maintained for certification;
- a reference document for airport inspections;
- A reference document for airport users and tenants; and
- A legal instrument to record any approved changes of the airport's standards, conditions or levels of service.

9.11 Airport names and IATA codes

The IATA codes are an integral part of the travel industry, and essential for the identification of an airline, its destinations and its traffic documents. They are also fundamental to the smooth running of hundreds of electronic applications that have been built around these coding systems for passenger and cargo traffic purposes.

An IATA airport code, also known as an IATA location identifier, IATA station code or simply a location identifier is a three-letter code designating many airports around the world, defined by IATA. The characters prominently displayed on baggage tags attached at airport check-in desks are an example of a way these codes are used.

The assignment of these codes is governed by IATA Resolution 763, and it is administered by IATA headquarters in Montreal. The codes are published semi-annually in the IATA Airline Coding Directory. City and airport codes may remain the same in many cases, particularly when a city has only one airport. When more than one airport is there, separate airport codes are provided.

For example, the London city code is LON. Airport codes over there are as follows.

- Heathrow: LHR
- Gatwick: LGW
- London city: LCY
- Luton: LTN
- Southwest: SEN
- Stansted: STN

9.12 ICAO airport codes

The ICAO airport code or location indicator is a four-letter code designating airports around the world. These codes are defined by the ICAO and published in ICAO Document 7910. **ICAO codes** are used for "official" purposes such as Air Traffic Control; for example, flight plans use **ICAO codes** for airports and airline flight identification.

ICAO codes are separate and different from IATA codes, which are generally used for airline timetables, reservations and baggage tags. For example, the IATA code for London's Heathrow Airport is LHR and its ICAO code is EGLL. ICAO codes are commonly seen by passengers and the general public on flight-tracking services such as Flight Aware, though passengers will more often see the IATA codes, on their tickets and their luggage tags. In general, IATA codes are usually derived from the name of the airport or the city it serves, while ICAO codes are distributed by region and country.

9.13 Conclusion

Airports are now seen as powerful engines of "economic growth" and the potential of local communities. An airport is the pride and economic advancement of a state. In general, the airport is a basic component of the destination system. Mass tourism destinations see airports as crucial in their competitive existence.

Airports are classified in different ways. The primary classification of airports is based on the categories of aviation, which is civil aviation airports and military airports. Civil aviation airports can be further classified into general aviation and commercial service airports. The most important category is commercial airports, which are the most common airports we see while travelling to different places. Airlines find it easy for operations through a "hub-and-spoke" route system. Hub airports are large commercial airports, used by multiple airlines as a hub for long-haul operations.

Airport is a company that offers a wide range of services, with a business management and marketing perspective, all of which ultimately aims to ensure comfortable, safe and convenient air travel. Tourists, both leisure and business tourists, are the main segment of customers at airports. There are direct, indirect and induced economic benefits due to the setting up airports in a region. The direct impact of an airport on the local economy is reflected in the jobs, salaries and sales directly related to airport operations. Airports have traditionally been part of the public sector, built by national, local or regional governments. Private sector involvement in airport ownership and management is currently on the rise. The PPP model of airport development and management is growing. Modern airports with advanced technology make passenger processing easier and less time-consuming. Over the next ten years, airports have the potential to increase and expand the efficiency described in IATA's fast travel initiative, which aims to deliver self-service options in check-in, bags ready-to-go, document check, flight rebooking, self-boarding and bag recovery. Airports are subject to many different regulations, both internationally and nationally, which includes safety, security environmental and economic aspects of managing an airport. Safety and security are the principal requirements in aviation. ICAO Annexe14 provides the required standards for aerodromes used by international aviation. The Annex contains information on planning, designing and operation of airports. An aerodrome/airport operator has many responsibilities. The Aerodrome Manual summarizes the responsibilities of the airport operator to meet the standards and provide specific airside services at an approved level. The IATA Airport Code or Location Identifier is a three-letter code that defines the number of airports around the world as defined by IATA. The ICAO Airport Code, or Location Indicator, is a four-character code used by airports around the world for official purposes.

Sample questions

Short/Medium Answer-type Questions

- "Airports have a major role in promoting social inclusion for remote and island communities". Comment upon the statement.
- What are the types of airport ownership?
- What are the typical economic impact of airport business?
- What is PPP model of airport project? Explain the advantages of PPP.
- Write a brief account on the significance of airport in tourism

- Explain the difference between the Airport coding by IATA and ICAO.
- Bring out the role of airport operator?
- What are the requirements of an Airport Certificate?

Essay type questions

- Discuss the facilities and services that are arranged within airport targeting the tourists
- Describe the structure of an airport and the facilities and services offered within it.

Suggested readings

Ashford, J.N., Stanton, P.H., Moore, A.C., Coutu, P., & Beasley, R.J. (2013). *Airport Operations*. New York: McGraw Hill.
Graham, A. (2018). *Managing Airports: An International Perspective*. London: Routledge.
Wells, T.A., & Young, S. (2004). *Airport: Planning and Management*, 5th ed. New York: McGraw-Hill.
Young, S., & Wells, A. (2019). *Airport Planning & Management*, 7th ed. New York: McGraw-Hill.

Chapter 10

Destination, airport and airline nexus

Learning outcomes

After studying this chapter, you would be able to:

- Describe the role of air transport in ensuring the accessibility and link for destinations.
- Comprehend the nuances of airline, airport and destination collaboration.
- Analyse the role of policies in making a destination competitive.
- Elaborate the role of air transport in generating tourist appeal.
- Evaluate various aspects of dependency of destinations on air transport.

10.1 Introduction

Transport is indeed a crucial element of a destination and plays a critical role in the success of it in remaining competitive in this hypercompetitive global tourism environment. "Indeed, transportation acts as one of the main determinants of a tourist destination as it improves accessibility to a particular location" (Fageda et al., 2017). Hall (1999) identified four roles assigned to the transport concerning tourism and they include linking the source market with the host destination, provisioning mobility and access within the destination area, provisioning mobility and access within an actual tourism attraction and facilitating travel along a recreational route. There can be more aspects as well. Air transport is the predominant mode of transport form that links the origin place of the tourism and the destination and vice versa. Air transport plays a significant role in the destination travel, within the destination connecting different attractions and sites situated at different locations. In some cases, general aviation services can also be used for reaching remote locations, etc. For instance, helicopter services are used for linking some tourist attractions that are remotely located. Air transport, of

DOI: 10.4324/9781003136927-10

late, could get establish the status of a catalyst in the evolution, growth and promotion of tourism in destinations. Further to the significant role it plays in enhancing the accessibility of the destination, air transport ensures smooth, comfortable and convenient mobility within destinations as well. The presence of an international airport becomes inevitable for destinations to compete in the international tourism market. Moreover, from a destination marketing perspective also, air transport plays a significant role. To some extent, air transport becomes a marketing preposition as well for the destination. Airport, particularly, is a key component in the composite destination product, and therefore, the same has to perform effectively and efficiently in ensuring tourist satisfaction and in generating a good tourist experience. Destinations can make use of some elements of aviation to enhance the touristic attractiveness as well as in ensuring recreational options suiting the visitor. Being a vital component in the destination's competitiveness, air transport infrastructure takes up a key role in enhancing the level of destination to find a place in the global tourism map. Moreover, air transport is a great socio-economic contributor in a destination, directly and indirectly. Its benefits do not limit to tourism, rather it has immense socio-economic potentials in generating revenue, employment opportunities and stimulating the scope of business and trade in the region in which the tourist destination is situated.

10.2 Destination: the concept

In the realm of tourism, the destination is used to refer to a specific area in which travellers choose to visit and engage in certain activities other than non-remunerative and spend a certain amount of time. Gunn (1994) points out that the destination zone is the geographic area containing a critical mass of development that satisfies travellers' objectives. Of late, this view of destination is also not relevant since the aspect of space is also missing in a few cases, like in cruise tourism in which the prime objective of travel is not to visit a specific geographical location; rather, the focus of it is basically the recreational experience while on the cruise. In space tourism, the location is not on earth, but it takes place in the outer space. Still, the concept of destination in tourism has much emphasis on a geographical location with certain inevitable elements as the vital components of it. Though the destination is often associated with the geographical region, the specification of boundary, shape and size cannot be stipulated when we refer to a destination. While a country can be called a destination, the same can be used for a continent as well. There is no dispute in calling a region within a country also a destination. Any place with potential can become a destination once the destination-oriented development takes place. According to Howie (2003), the following are some of the essential actions to be done as part of it.

- Make use of resources with potential for attractions
- Provide an appropriate transport to, from and within the destination
- Provide an appropriate range of tourist accommodation
- Ensure the successful integration of the tourist-related developments into the changing activity patterns of the place on a long-term sustainable basis.

A destination and its attractions must have "pull" capacity to induce travellers to visit there. In the concept of destination itself, transport provisions are considered fundamental. As stated above, there are inevitable elements associated with a destination concept and those elements are included in a destination framework of 7As (Dileep, 2018). Attractions, Accessibility, Accommodation, Amenities, Ancillary Services, Activities and Awareness are those elements, and, of them, accessibility is associated with transport service provisions and infrastructure. Having quality transport provisions become key in the success of destinations and those have a significant role in the "pull" capacity of the destinations. Air transport thus becomes crucial for destinations in their competitive survival.

10.3 Air transport to ensure accessibility and link

Accessibility is a prime factor that a destination is dependent upon. While it is an advantage for several destinations, it is a concern for some others. A destination surrounded by rich tourism source markets has an extremely high accessibility advantage, whereas another one with similar or better amount of attractions without source markets nearby got a disadvantage in terms of accessibility. Many of the European destinations are having this advantage as a number of source markets are nearby which can provide a regular flow of tourists. Accessibility is all about "how to reach" along with the convenience and easiness of reaching a destination (Dileep, 2019). Accessibility is multifaceted having diverse dimensions, and usually, it consists of distance to reach from source markets, availability of transport services, quality of transport services, convenience and frequency of services, level of tourist infrastructure and types of air transport services. Tóth and David (2010) point out that good accessibility itself can be of high importance and a source of destination competitiveness when customers have to choose between destinations with similar attributes.

   In the history of modern tourism, destinations have always enjoyed the rise in tourist arrivals and consequent tourist receipts due to the increased accessibility as part of surge in air transport (Duval, 2013). Accessibility is a factor that people consider greatly while choosing a destination. Celata (2007) is of the opinion that customers, after their selection of the most suitable destination based on the preferred attractions, compare the accessibility of it with others. The travel cost, the time to reach and the distance to travel are some critical factors associated with accessibility that have a strong influence on destination selection (Prideaux 2000). "Customers' evaluation of destination accessibility depends on both available transport connections and distance, but also it depends largely on personal preferences and specific characteristics of the modes of transport" (Ivanova, 2017). The concept of destination accessibility is being changed. While the opinion that travel is something that needs to be promoted in order to let the people travel freely is getting increased attention, and the argument indicating that access to tourism is a right is also getting increased significance (UNEP-IE, 1993; Dubois & Ceron, 2000). The socio-economic changes across the world contributed greatly in the remarkable progress in the accessibility. World over, destinations are trying to enhance their accessibility. Sometimes, it is part of the general and business-related upgradation as well. Certainly, the scope of business transactions too has a share in the rise of accessibility. Page (2009) argued that the increased globalization process also resulted in improved accessibility for destinations. By looking at various aspects of accessibility of tourist destinations, the following specific dimensions can be identified.

*   A determinant in destination competitiveness
*   A factor contributing towards destination success
*   Value preposition for destination marketing
*   Factor influencer of tourist buying behaviour
*   An element in the travel cost.

As mentioned above, accessibility has a significant marketing dimension as well. The role of air transport in the destination accessibility is well stated. For instance, Ivanova (2017) states that

> .... higher accessibility closely correlates with increased visibility of the destination, thus including an element of marketing to the complex nature of this attribute. That is especially valid for air transport where the establishment of a new route directly places the destination on the airline's route map and includes it in the airline and/or air alliance network.

Air transport has the potential to enhance accessibility greatly by enabling the destination to get connected to a geographically wider area and facilitate the destination to claim good accessibility that can be marketed. Increased connectivity by having a wider air transport network is usually considered as a vital factor in the success of the destination, in attracting more tourists and to remain a successful destination with regular tourist flows. Nilsson (2009) is of the opinion that "Increased demand for travel combined with improved connectivity, resulting in rapidly rising numbers of passengers, has had a substantial impact on (tourist) destinations". A wide range of factors affects tourist buying behaviour. While searching for information, tourists may seek information on convenient air connectivity as well. Well-connected air transport accessibility can enable the potential tourist to consider the destination in choosing for a visit. This is more relevant in the case of mass tourist destinations. Accessibility is an element in the travel cost as well. Compared to other destinations with equal distance, those with better accessibility may have lesser travel cost. Though a few other factors are also important, we can observe that travel cost has an inverse relationship with accessibility as when air transport accessibility is higher, the air travel cost seems lesser.

The above discussion reveals that, for destinations, accessibility featured with good air transport connectivity is a value proposition, inevitable element, a determinant in destination success and a factor of competitiveness. Generally, air transport is an integral element in the tourism system of the destinations, and shortage of it in terms of adequacy and sufficiency can be a deterrent in the success of the destinations as well.

10.4 Airline, airport and destination collaboration

Undeniably, air transport is part and parcel of a destination. "The importance of airports for the local economies, especially of those located near leisure destinations, is so high that their operations are often supported or even subsidized by local authorities and tourism associations either directly or indirectly" (Papatheodorou & Zenelis, 2013). Having tremendous significance of air transport for destinations, it is important to work together and to have a collaboration between destination authorities and air transport stakeholders to stimulate tourism demand and capacity growth and to lower the operating risks for airlines along with ensuring the long-term viability of routes that are set up (Everis/UNWTO, 2012). Any destination that aims at progressing well and to have an increased inflow of tourists requires to have close collaboration with the air transport sector as well while formulating policies, making plans for expansion, to ensure mutual support and in promoting their products. Effective communication and an efficient interaction mechanism are inevitable in order to proceed with stakeholder participation for tourism success in destinations. According to Ivanova (2017), as airports and airlines have twofold role in tourism, such as that of the suppliers as well as external stakeholders, "they are entitled to closely communicate and collaborate with the other tourist service providers and destination governance organizations, and therefore, the most obvious impacts take place exactly within those interactions". Indeed, being key stakeholders, air transport and destination authorities together have to devise strategies and make decisions so as to attract more inbound passengers, particularly tourists: utilize air transport accessibility as a marketing value point, expand the air transport network, formulate strategies for tourism development and generate policies favouring tourism, etc.

Having the objective of tourism promotion as well as increased tourist traffic into the destination, airport authorities usually engage in initiating efforts to attract more airlines. Airports, lately, have more interest in attracting low-cost carriers (LCCs) as well as hybrid carriers in order to augment leisure tourist inflow. Some of those measures may include offering low airport charges, convenient gates/ramp areas for extra payment, etc. (Fageda et al., 2017). Developing each of the sectors may also be a priority for those stakeholders. While airports wish to have more tourism development, the destination prefers to have an expanded airport. In tandem with the surge in tourism demand, existing airports may face space limitations in expanding, and the respective authorities may plan for constructing a new airport. As pointed out by Lohmann and Vianna (2016), airports may get the opportunity in the planning and development of destinations and destinations may invest in airports over there or in the development of new routes. There can be joint ventures or alliances between destinations and airlines in order to enhance the tourist inflow particularly when the demand is neither stable nor sufficient, or when the destination is with limited international accessibility, and that can make to have underwrites between destinations and airlines (Nolan et al., 2005; Duval, 2013).

10.5 Policies to make destination competitive

Policies have a great role in the development of tourism in a destination and in enhancing the accessibility, particularly that related to air transport. Though liberalization is still progressing in the arena of air transport, it is remaining one of the most regulated economic sectors in the world. Being a global industry, air transport is flourishing with the support of bilateral and multilateral regulations that make the smooth conduct of international operations and serious intervention is there in ensuring the safety and security of air transport. The prevailing political environment needs to be conducive for air transport development, which can eventually enable increased tourist traffic. The various aspects related to regulations and aviation policies are well discussed in Chapter 7. Destinations, in order to be successful in international tourism markets, need favourable policy interventions in the air transport sector. Policy can be there to have a liberal approach in permitting airlines to operate to and from the destination. Regulations can influence the rate of increase of airline routes, which can enhance competition and can affect the spatial patterns associated with tourist traffic (Forsyth, 2008).

More countries are now involved in participating in open sky policies. It can result in a better frequency of operations, particularly. According to Zhang and Findlay (2014), open skies have a definite role in the inflow of tourists to a destination. In special circumstances, the authorities may go for more favourable and encouraging actions in order to stimulate air-based tourism demand. For instance, in the case of remote destinations and of the destinations with "thin-markets", the national or the state authorities may go for exceptional deals with air transport service providers to amplify air connectivity (Halpern, 2010; Matisziw et al., 2011). Remote destinations certainly need air connectivity and more frequent services from source markets or hub cities. Therefore, authorities can take a role in bettering the scenario. At times, some relaxations are given to inspire the air transport service providers to offer favourable air services to those destinations. Some of the relaxations can be there in terms of waiving airport charges, subsidies for regular operations, etc. As noted by Duval (2013), direct or indirect air subsidization of air services by authorities concerned are seen in certain cases. During the time of COVID-19 pandemic, critical role was taken up by the government in protecting the air transport sector as well as the tourism sector.

Tourism-favoured visa regulation is a common initiative from the government nowadays. Visa-on-arrival (VOA) service is having increased acceptance among the destination countries, and by this, airports become the hub for getting visa directly once landing in the destination airport. Immigration-related policies are also relevant in this context. Likewise, the government's role is critical in expanding airport and in attracting more airlines into the destination. Airport expansion involved so many environmental issues, along with huge investment requirement and land-related complications. Together with the growth of tourism in the destination, the authorities have to be propitious in expanding the airport and in ensuring good connectivity of the airport with the other cities within the destination. More land may have to be acquired and displacement of residents may require which is a matter of concern for any government. Raising the capital for the expansion is also a cause of concern for many governments. In addition, effective collaboration with air transport stakeholders is also a matter that has to be dealt with by the governmental authorities. Therefore, government, with regard to tourism development, has a crucial role in expanding and supporting air transport.

10.6 Destination marketing and airlines

Usually, there exists a close cooperation in promoting the destination by the airlines and airports with National Tourism Organizations (NTOs)/Destination

Management Organizations (DMOs) for mutual benefits. Airports, as part of the efforts to enhance the touristic potentials of the destination in which it is situated, attempt to provide high quality facilities and services, competitive rates for services and good air connectivity with the assistance of serving airlines. As part of pricing, airport rates too have a role in the air travel cost, and having competitive rates can add to the attractiveness of the destination. All the airport product elements have to be favourable for enhancing the competitiveness of the destination. With regard to regional development and tourism in destinations, there is an argument in favour of marketing measures that can be undertaken by both airports and airlines (Schano, 2008; Halpern, 2010). Airlines usually include attractive features of tourism attractions of their destination cities in their inflight magazine. These magazines are kept to be accessible for each passenger to read, and these are widely used by the passengers while flying. The feature stories are given in stylish and flowery language depicting the cultural and natural varieties of the destination. Flag carriers of the countries usually undertake different types of destination marketing strategies. They may use symbols representing the destination as a part of their branding, positioning and image building measures. In addition, advertisements of different types are given in online media, through their website and the like. Moreover, holiday packages combining major tourist attractions of the destination are also offered by the airlines. Though, traditionally, joint marketing relationships between airlines and destinations are not uncommon, there can be considerable variation in it from case to case (Duval, 2013). Recently, airline collaboration with DMOs is getting increased importance. According to Castillo-Manzano et al. (2011), more and more airlines join with DMOs as marketing vehicles. Some of the promotional efforts are sponsored by the DMOs whereas some others are done on a mutually agreed basis.

10.7 Tourist appeal and pull factor

As already stated, the airport has a significant role in attracting tourists to the destination. It can emanate an appeal to tourists. The appeal can ignite the visitor to use it again and the contribution of it along with the overall transport infrastructure can be a part in the "pull factor" of the destination. Air transport infrastructure and accessibility can constitute a major element in the destination's pull factor. Truong and Shimizu (2017) are of the opinion that

> On the supply side, transportation, as well as the attractions, services, information, and promotions available at the destination, are the driving forces behind the supply side of the tourism industry. Every element plays its own role, and harmonic interactions among these five supply side components may strengthen the "pull factor". As a result of healthy supply side elements, a destination may see increases in the number of arrivals.

Tourists are induced by "push factors" from the demand side and "pull factors" from the supply side. Both function together in the successful and sustainable tourism progress in destinations. Transport in general and air transport in particular become an element in the "pull factors" present in the destination, which is a combination of varied factors. There are thousands of suitable destinations across

Figure 10.1 Entrance to the shopping area at Birmingham Airport, England
Source: Wikipedia Commons.

the world and as far as a tourist is concerned, choosing the right destination for a visit is being influenced by the "pull factors" of the destination as well. Range of tourist attractions, quality and diversity of accommodation facilities, etc., are some other major elements in the destination "pull factor" (Figure 10.1).

Realizing the significance of airports in the tourism value chain, airports are increasingly interested in exciting the travellers by creating a "sense of place and unique identity which is represented in the design, services and overall ambience of the facilities" (Brilha, 2008). An exciting airport is always an advantage for international tourism. In order to have increased traffic flow into the destination, the airports have to be designed in such a way to accommodate larger flights, etc., at the planning stage itself. In addition to the enhancement of capacity, space and airside facilities, airports are now increasing passenger convenience within terminals particularly. The access to the boarding gates is a key in increasing the appeal of the airport. Easiness in access, hassle-free security checks as well as emigration clearance, etc., add to the appeal. Some destination airports may go for theme-based artistic designs matching with the touristic attractions of the destination, within the passenger terminals. This trend is growing. Major mass tourism destinations are now interested in including attractive posters, banners, displays, virtual tours, digital displays, etc., to enhance the attractiveness. A variety of refreshment centres is always an attraction. Airports attempt to ensure food outlets of different types. Also vending machines for tea, coffee, water bottles, soft drinks, etc., are ensured. Popular culinary varieties, like Chinese, Thai, Indian, South Indian, Arabic, Continental, French, etc., add to the appeal. Good duty-free shopping centre is a basic requirement and the level of it can enhance the attractiveness of the airport. Shopping options other than duty free also are a necessity nowadays. Souvenir shops have so much importance in destination-based airports.

Provision of taxi services, car rentals, etc., is another basic requirement. The better the transport provisions from the airport to other parts of the destination, the greater the appeal for the airport. Airport connectivity with the city and tourist sites is a crucial aspect. The aesthetic aspects within the airport give an eye-catching and soothing experience. The behaviour of the staff and security personnel too has a lot of significance in the appeal of the airport. Good ambience of refreshment centres, other service outlets and the concourse can excite the travellers. Of late, technology integration is a key aspect. During the pandemic period, advanced cleaning system and disinfecting mechanism, etc., gave increasing appeal. Touch-free passenger handling became inevitable for the airports. Artificial intelligence (AI)-based systems and mechanisms are used for better passenger handling. Robots are now becoming part of the service delivery within airports. Biometric technology-based passenger handling is gaining increasing importance. Advanced versions of all these surely excite the travellers.

10.8 Airport and destinations

From a tourism perspective, airport can play some crucial roles directly affecting the tourists. These roles certainly complement the overall tourism service provision of the destination. The major ones are introduced below.

10.8.1 Airport: a key element of destination mix

From a tourism perspective, airports, in addition to having the primary role of acting as a connecting node between land and air mode of transportation, do have a key position in the aviation system by forming the first and the last impression on the visitors of a tourist resort (Paraschi et al., 2019). As stated by Papatheodorou and Zenelis (2013), the airport environment and facilities are considered to be inseparable components of the tourism industry. Airport forms a key element in the destination mix. A destination involves diverse elements. Infrastructure, attractions, people, packages and all intangible services are part of the destination mix. Among those vital elements, airport is an inevitable part of tourism infrastructure and a crucial element in the quality tourism accessibility.

10.8.2 Airports as gateways to tourism destinations

Indeed, airports are gateways into the destinations. Amiable entry and exit of tourists through an airport can enthuse tourists further in exploring. A pleasant experience at an entry point certainly augments the tourist experience. Papatheodorou and Zenelis (2013) pointed out the significance of airport as the first impression point of a destination and last impression point after a trip. The first impression generated would certainly complement the rest of the journey of tourist. Even the last impression at the airport will surely complement the tourist experience and have a lasting influence on the post-tour behaviour of the tourists. Moreover, the entry and exit formalities for foreign tourists are done at the airports for those tourists who travel by flights.

10.8.3 Information centre

Acting as a concierge is important for an airport. Travellers land at an airport with diverse queries. Information centre has to be there at an easily accessible location within an airport. The Centre needs efficient and resourceful staff to handle the information requirements of the incoming passengers. Inbound tourists will be curious to know about various aspects of the destination. Along with the provision of information, the staff may have to promote the touristic features of the destination as well and create increased interest among the tourists to visit and explore. Moreover, the quality of information provision can add to the tourist satisfaction.

10.8.4 Airport is a marketing space

The marketing role of airport is already introduced. Airport has a significant role in destination marketing. They usually collaborate with DMO in marketing the local attractions. Airport provides the space for showcasing the natural and cultural varieties of the destination. Displays, banners, etc., can be displayed within terminals of an airport. Moreover, there are sculptors of varied size depicting symbolically the nuances of the destination, features of the tourist attractions. Touristic information provision is already discussed above. Moreover, some of the hotels, tour operators, etc., may have own marketing efforts within the airports to attract tourists as well as to pursue them to consume their products. Besides, ensuring touristic appeal by the airport itself is advantageous for the destination. All these efforts are in addition to the basic support provided as part of ensuring accessibility for the destination.

10.8.5 Single space for tourists to access tourism industry

Tourism industries try to have their own outlets within the terminals or in the airport premises. Moreover, destination enables the tourism industry to distribute their products through outlets located within the airports. Some of the leading industries may open outlets in the arrival area. Having such options is an advantage for getting access for the inbound tourists directly. Moreover, tourists may feel better comfort in getting the scope of services confirmed from the landing airport itself. Car rental companies constitute a common presence in the arrival area of the airports. Same is the case with accommodation sector as well. Contact centres for major attractions of the destination as well as events are also provided within the terminal of many airports that aggressively promote tourism (Figure 10.2).

10.8.6 Airport is an attraction

This aspect has been introduced in other chapters as well. Airports are now increasingly trying to become a minicity with almost all the facilities and services that are provided within them. Large international airports do have a wide variety of services and features that can attract people to spend time within the airport without feeling bored. Supplementary services like spa can enhance the attractiveness of the airport. Ash (2020) cites the following examples that can substantiate the above argument. Hong Kong Airport hosts a four-month cultural

Figure 10.2 EVA Air Infinity Lounge at Taiwan Taoyuan International Airport
Source: Wikipedia Commons.

festival, showcasing music and art along with a workshop where passengers can make personalized gifts and enjoy Virtual Reality (VR) experiences. Amsterdam Schiphol Airport engenders Dutch heritage to the departure area with two of the museums, such as NEMO and Rijksmuseum located within the airport and got a library too. Vancouver International Airport encompasses a spa, dental service and an aquarium with a gift centre. Munich Airport has an Audi showroom (Ash, 2020). These are more possible with hub airports when large-scale passenger movement is taking place. Hub airports and large airports can go for the provision of very diverse non-aeronautical services, including the fitness centres and casinos matching the needs of different customer groups. A good share of the passengers may get more time for consuming the exciting services offered by those airports. Each of the extra facilities offered can be revenue-generating options for airports.

10.8.7 Shopping

Corollary to the above, airports can be a suitable space for shopping as well. It does not mean that people will travel to airport and flock in for purchasing things. There is a scope for it, particularly among the leisure tourists. Shopping within the airport too adds value to the touristic significance of the destination. Non-aviation features and services within airports have significance for the travellers (Fasone et al., 2016). For infrequent leisure travellers, the commercial shops within airports do have some attractions and they may spend some amount on purchase of different items, therefore be induced to spend considerable amounts of money on shopping (Papatheodorou, 2008). Leisure tourists are reported to make more purchase from airports. They, due to limited time to spend in the destination for shopping, etc., and since they prefer to have items bought from the destinations, can be some of the "highest spenders at the airport although this additionally depends on factors such as country of origin and party size" (Brilha, 2008). The time the tourists get after clearing the check-in process is utilized for some simple purchases, buying souvenirs as well as for buying some luxury products that have some sort of specialty connected to the destination city. Many of the LCC travellers, particularly, may also consume food and drinks in the airport refreshment centres that LCC do not offer complimentary inflight catering (Papatheodorou & Lei, 2006).

London Heathrow (LHR), Paris Charles de Gaulle (CDG), Hong Kong International Airport (HKG), Singapore Changi Airport (SIN), Dubai International Airport (DXB), Hamad International Airport, Qatar (DOH), Istanbul Airport (IST), Sydney Airport (SYD), Denver International Airport (DEN), Vancouver International Airport (YVR), Incheon International Airport in South Korea, etc., are some good examples of airports that offer quality shopping experience within terminals. Echevarne (2008), citing the reports of Pragma Consulting/ARC Retail Consultants,

---

Table 10.1 Singapore's Jewel: A Unique Airport with Immense Tourist Potentials

---

Singapore revolutionized the airport concept with magnificent artificial attractions, eye-catching amenities and unique features within it. Jewel, the new shopping and airport facilities complex set among the previously existed terminals, has an artificial waterfall within the terminal complex as well! Jewel Changi Airport, an addition to the Changi Airport Complex, is a mixed-use development aimed at creating a public hub at an airport facility and also functions as a central connector between the existing airport terminals.

The travellers as well as the local community can enjoy a unique experience within a massive dome-shaped structure having five floors above the ground and 5 basement levels. It encompasses indoor gardens, 300 retail and dining facilities, recreational centres and a hotel. A multilevel retail space with an integrated natural surroundings and Forest Valley. The hotel, located at the fourth level, can accommodate 130 rooms. Bus services and skytrain/inter-terminal train journeys through the indoor gardens are there to connect the terminals for the passengers. Rainwater gushes inside the terminal through a well-designed system and the same serves the purpose of passive cooling. Light and sound show is arranged at the Rain Vortex in the night. The Forest Valley, a lush and abundant stepped indoor garden, offers an impressive and wide-ranging selection of more than 200 plant species and has walkways and adequate seating. A Canopy Park is arranged at the fifth level which includes Sky Nets (Bouncing Net and a Walking Net), Canopy Mazes (Hedge Maze and a Mirror Maze), a partly glass-panelled Canopy Bridge (a 50-metre-long one 23 metres above the ground), a Topiary Walk and Petal Garden, event plaza (capacity of up to 1,000 people), etc. All these make Changi Airport one of the finest in the world and the touristic potentials of it are lauded by one and all.

Source: Raut, A. (2019). Singapore's Jewel Changi Airport is home to the world's tallest indoor waterfall, data available online at https://www.architecturaldigest.in/content/singapore-changi-airport-worlds-tallest-indoor-waterfall-safdie-architects/

reports the major items that are bought by passengers in the airport such as travel emergency/necessity items (forgotten, medical emergency, things to consume during travel, etc.); destination/souvenirs items (local art and craft items, etc.); gift for those at the home/destination (for spouse, children and friends); personal self-treat items (as part of self-indulgence like jewellery, accessories, designer dress items); convenience items (for normal use, but can be bought conveniently from the airport, like a tie for executives); exclusive opportunity to buy/price-driven items (e.g. duty-free items); and trip enhancement stuff (e.g. sunglasses).

10.8.8 Catalyst in destination development

While the destination evolves from the introduction stage to grow further, the airport becomes part and parcel of the destination mix. If an airport is there already within an accessible distance, then the need for expansion of airport services and facilities may be felt. On the contrary, if there is not any airport at a comfortable distance, destination may feel the need of having a new one. According to Khan et al. (2017), constructing or extending airports and airport services enhance international tourism flows. A rise of a destination at an international level necessitates expansion or addition of airport infrastructure. Spasojevic et al., (2017) argue that air transport has an important influence on destination development. Bieger and Wittmer (2006) point out that

> Destinations in reasonable proximity of an airport with high-quality infra-structure—e.g., runway of more than 3000 m, comfortable departure and arrival services, etc.—tend, for economic reasons, to attract bigger airplanes at lower frequencies. The smaller airports, and those with lower quality services, tend to offer feeder services by the major carriers and point-to-point services from LCC and charters—smaller aircraft are the norm.

However, the need for a new airport usually arises at a later stage of the evolution of a destination, particularly when the tourist arrival as well and the passenger traffic gets multiplied. Many of the mass tourism destinations have constructed new airports when the existing ones faced challenges in expanding them. Expansion of airport and air transport, in general, assumes a great role in the destination development as well. Certainly, it acts as a catalyst as the scope for destination development is directly linked to the growth and expansion in airport as well. As the airport expands, it induces air traffic demand and consequently gives better scope for tourism over there. Moreover, the industries within the destination too get better scope for growth and prosperity.

10.8.9 Airport as a determinant in tourist decision-making

As discussed above, airport has multiple roles in tourism and all of them together can be a determinant in the decision-making of the tourist in choosing the destination. According to Brilha (2008), the factors influencing airport choice for different airport customers are summarized as follows:

- Airlines: market potential – volume and mix of passengers; availability of slots; availability of facilities – air bridges and CIP lounges; total visiting costs – landing

charges, handling, refuelling; and reliability and quality of service – quick turna-round and baggage handling.
- Business passengers: network – destinations, frequencies, day return flights; quality of facilities and services offered; speed of process – fast track; and access – road access and parking facilities.
- Leisure passengers: destination attractiveness; leisure package components; package price; and price of facilities and services at the airport.

While leisure tourists and business tourists have different set of influencing fac-tors, airports need to focus on a wide variety of aspects to get tourists' prefer-ence. For a leisure tourist, cost is an important factor and airports need to take care of the prices of the services and facilities offered by them and the agencies functioning within them. On the contrary, business tourist focuses more onto the efficiency and quality aspects of airports' functions and operations.

10.8.10 Airport: a security checkpoint

Being an entry point, airports have a prominent role in the safety and security of the destination. Usually, the safety and security aspects are handled based on in-ternational and national rules and regulations. Nevertheless, the manner in which these tasks are handled by the airport is also important. Terrorism is a major threat for both tourism and aviation sectors. Every now and then, the safety and security norms are updated by the air transport sector. Probably, air transport is the only mode of transport that takes the maximum efforts in ensuring safe and secure travel. Airport is the hub of safety and security measures in air transportation.

10.8.11 Airports to focus on customer needs

In any commercial activity, customer needs form the fundamental aspect to look into and the same aspect has increased significance in service sectors, including tourism. Tourists are certainly a heterogenic group, coming from diverse sociocul-tural backgrounds. Airport is a key sector in the destination product bundle and along with the efforts to attract tourists; airports too have to pursue the custom-ers to increase the tourist traffic. Focusing on customer needs become important and airports have to get equipped to satisfy the customer needs most possibly. The airports catering to the tourism markets primarily need to assess the airport requirements of the tourist community and their demand patterns. In addition, the estimate of tourist flow and airline's future plans of expansion need to be aware of. This can be useful for arranging the facilities and services targeting the tourists and to arrange the infrastructure, like the runways needed, slot requirements, ramp requirements, for the airlines to conduct the air transport operations.

10.9 Dependency of destinations

As air transport is the most preferred mode of transport in international tour-ism, there is no ambiguity in explaining the dependency of destinations in air transport. But, in certain cases, air transport dependency is near to cent percent-age. According to Bieger and Wittmer (2006), air transport is the prime transport mode in many destinations, and up to 100% in some of the destinations, and cheap air services constitute a driving force in tourism growth. That dependency is usually connected to the geographical location of the destination. For examples, the dependency of tourism in islands and remote destinations on air transport is very high (Lohman & Duval, 2011). Destinations depend on airport not just as a transport infrastructure in order to provide access to the travellers. Rather, it is a matter of pride for the destination, an economically significant infrastructure, etc. When the airport is an attractive one, tourism industry considers it strategically and for marketing and promotion as well. From an economic perspective also, airports have increased significance nowadays, as it can contribute greatly in the socio-economic spectrum of the destination as well. Moreover, having air transport options can bring the destination in the global air transport network and ensure a place in the international tourism map.

10.10 LCCs and destinations

Regional tourism, domestic tourism and short-haul tourism are strongly influenced by LCCs. They have been proven instrumental in maintaining or enhancing tourist arrivals (Castillo-Manzano et al., 2011). The benefits for tourism due to the promotion of LCCs into a region have been summarized into three groups by the European Low Fares Airline Association (ELFAA), in the following manner:

- Increase in tourism activities, particularly due to the usage of secondary airports in destination,
- Reduction of seasonality effects by better distribution of traffic throughout the year,
- Mid-week holiday travel increased due to the low off-peak fares provided by the LCCs. (ELFAA, 2004).

The LCCs enable the destination countries in distributing tourism developments into wider areas as well as into less urban regions. International and domestic tourism are being spread into more regions. For instance, Whyte and Prideaux (2007) have revealed that the growth in Australian domestic air travel can be attributed to a couple of LCCs over there and they benefited the regional tourism in some of the destinations in Queensland. As LCCs focus their operations in secondary airports as well as regional airports, the scope for destinations in smaller cities and rural regions escalated greatly. Seasonality advantage of LCCs is already discussed. Destinations, due to the services provided by LCCs, get better tourist traffic in the low seasons as well; LCCs caused a shift in tourist traffic pattern (Donzelli, 2010). Smaller rural and island destinations have got benefited greatly by the LCCs (Schlumberger & Weisskopf, 2014). In fact, these destinations are depending more on air transport for tourist traffic, and due to the recent trends, dependence on LCCs may be higher for many of those destinations. Bieger and Witmer (2006) argued that the LCCs make an appeal to tourists by offering low fares, and they appealed to business travellers by offering high frequencies in selected city-pair markets.

There are some disadvantages also for tourist destinations. According to Nilsson (2009), "The downsides are of course a growing dependency on single LCCs and, depending on the mix of routes, a risk of large outflows of tourism, a decline in the tourism home market". Moreover, the tendency of having more outbound travellers can also be possible by having good air connectivity, particularly low cost. LCCs are more vulnerable to demand loss due to price hike. "It is estimated that a 10 per cent increase in the price of a ticket will result in a concomitant 15 per cent fall in the demand for air travel, which could hit LCCs harder than network carriers" (Flight International, 2007).

10.11 Quality enhances destination performance

Air transport quality does matter in the overall performance of the tourism sector in the destination. Thompson and Schofield (2007) state that quality of transport infrastructure and the services offered by the elements in it have a contribution in the overall performance of destination. The air transport-based tourism market is usually consisting of people from rich to average economic backgrounds, and the air transport infrastructure has to ensure the matching facilities and services in order to meet the expectations of their customer base. Therefore, airports face the challenges in arranging facilities and services at par with international standards. The quality levels in service delivery need to be of good standards. The staffs need to be well trained to serve the travelling population in the most possible way. Service delivery has a direct impact on customer satisfaction as well. These usually prompt the air transport sector in following the service quality standards in all its servicescapes. Airport is key sector and the quality of the services offered in an airport can influence the perception of incoming tourist on the destination (Tang et al., 2017). Airport is the first impression point of a destination and the point for getting lasting impression as well. Increased frequency, lower airport turnaround time and lower fare are the major factors that pursue different types of travellers to visit other destinations (Chang & Hung, 2013; Budd et al., 2014). Good-quality infrastructure and service can contribute in the overall tourist satisfaction as well as in the tourist experience.

10.12 Economic perspectives

Air transport, particularly airport, is a major contributor in the socio-economic development of the region in which it is located. Halpern and Brathen (2011) argue that airports can play a critical role in regional development and, as a continuation, tourism as well. Along with contributing greatly towards tourism development, airport and other air transport elements cause in the overall development of the destination. Airports of all types have a significant role in developing the destination. For instance, based on a study in the UK, Papatheodorou and Lei (2006, p. 51) argue that "no matter whether a regional airport operates as an origin or destination gateway, notable improvements in accessibility can play a significant role in economic and/or tourism development". Moreover, air transport has a significant share in the employment generation within the destination in connection with tourism. Airlines and airport generate a variety of job opportunities directly. In addition, they cause more job opportunities in associated sectors as well. Other benefits of having international air transport connections are there like the scope for export and import and enhancing the scope for trade and commerce. Therefore, an air transport has significant influence in enhancing the destination, its tourism, trade and socio-economic standards.

10.13 Charter flights, facilitator of destinations

Charter flights have contributed much to the tourism development in many destinations (Keller, 2000). In fact, the role of charter airlines is not just limited to contributing in destination development. It has multiple roles. Primarily, it facilitates regular flow of tourists into the destination. Tour operators use charter flights in organizing package holidays. Usually, they plan tours for the following years, and it can help the destinations to forecast capacity needs in advance. Moreover, tour operators plan holidays during off seasons as well using charter flights. By this, charter flights become part in the destination efforts in offsetting the seasonality impacts. Charter flights have an increased significance in the tourism in destinations that have a lower level of accessibility. Some of the naturally and culturally rich destinations may not have sufficient scheduled air transport services. In such locations, the tourism industry may depend more on charter flights. Long-haul destinations also get regular charter tourism package services.

10.14 Recreational role of aviation

Destinations utilize some elements of aviation for offering recreational services and as attractions. Aviation-based recreational activities can instil enthusiasm and provide scope for adventure tourism in the possible locations. Lighter-than-air aircraft-based recreational sports are offered in many destinations. Similarly, destinations that have suitable geographical features make use of heavier-than-air aircraft-based tourism activities as well. Helicopter-based recreational trips are common across the world. Seaplane is another good example of aircraft that is used in the parlance of tourism for making the visit of tourists pleasurable. Recreational aspect of air transport in the parlance of tourism is the focus of the next chapter.

10.15 Conclusion

Air transport is the main mode of transport that connects the place of origin and destination of tourism. It is also considered as a stimulus in the evolution, growth and promotion of tourism in destinations. The presence of international airports is essential to compete for destinations in the international tourism market. The essential elements related to the destination concept are attractions, accessibility, accommodation, ancillary services, activities and awareness, among which accessibility is related to transportation service conditions and infrastructure. Air transport becomes crucial to their competitive existence of destinations. Destinations need favourable policy interventions in the aviation sector to succeed in international tourism markets. Tourism-friendly visa restrictions are great initiatives from the governments. Airport connectivity with the city and tourist sites is a crucial factor.

Airports are the gateways to destinations. The airport plays a significant role in destination marketing. Destination enables the tourism industry to distribute their products through their outlets located at airports. Some large international airports have a variety of services and features that attract people to spend time inside the airport without feeling bored. Duty-free shopping inside the airport also adds value to the tourist significance of the destination. As the airport expands, it increases the need for air traffic and thus offers better potential for tourism there. Although there are different factors of influence for leisure tourists and business tourists, airports need to focus on a variety of factors in order to get the tourist preference. The airports are the hub for safety and security measures. Airports need to be set up to meet the needs of customers. While the airport is an attractive one, the tourism industry uses it strategically for marketing and promotion. The LCCs promote regional tourism, domestic tourism and short-term tourism strongly. Air transport, especially the airport, is an important contributor to the socio-economic development of the region in which it is located. Moreover, air transport plays a significant role in the employment opportunities within the destination in relation to tourism. Tour operators use charter flights to organize package tours and facilitate the regular arrival of tourists to their destinations. Aviation-based recreational activities can create excitement and make adventure tourism possible in certain destinations.

Sample questions

Short/Medium answer type questions

- Comprehend the significance of accessibility for a destination.
- Elucidate the role of air transport in a destination's accessibility.
- Discuss the benefits of collaboration between air transport and destination.
- How do policies ensure competitiveness for a destination?
- "Air transport has a role in enhancing tourist appeal of destinations". Comment upon the statement.
- "Lately, airports have an increasing significance for shopping". Discuss it.
- Identify the role of LCC with regard to a tourist destination in its growth and survival.

Essay type questions

- Discuss in detail the roles played by airport in tourist destination's success.
- Describe the advantages of having quality air transport system for tourist destinations.

Suggested readings

Bieger, T., & Wittmer, A. (2006). Air transport and tourism – Perspectives and challenges for destinations, airlines and governments. *Journal of Air Transport Management*, 12(1), 40–46.

Cristina, S. (2017). New perspectives of the tourism and air transport relationship. *Cactus Tourism Journal*, 15(2), 24–32.

Graham A., & Dobruszkes, F. (Eds.) (2019). *Air Transport – A Tourism Perspective*. Oxford: Elsevier.

Ivanova, M. (2017). *Air Transport – Tourism Nexus: A Destination Management Perspective*. Varna: Zangador.

Papatheodorou, A., & Forsyth, P. (Eds.) (2008). *Aviation and Tourism: Implications for Leisure Travel*. Hampshire: Ashgate.

Chapter 11

Aircraft, spacecraft and tourism

Learning outcomes

At the end of this chapter, you will be able to:

- Describe the concept, parts and types of aircraft.
- Understand the way different types of aircraft contribute in tourism.
- Elaborate the recreational use of aircraft in the realm of tourism.
- Discuss the scope of spacecraft in tourism.

11.1 Introduction

In fact, the history of aviation is greatly associated with the evolution of aircraft as well. Every stage of aircraft's evolution has subsequently transformed aviation and stimulated the progress of air transport. Indubitably, modern tourism's progress coincided with the advancements in air transport and complemented each other in their progress. While we analyse the history of aviation, a number of milestones can be identified that had remarkable contribution in the progress of aviation. Of them, the most noteworthy is the introduction of jet engines and wide-body aircraft. At every stage of advancement in aircraft, air transport turned speedier, smoother, more comfortable, safer and increasingly attractive. This chapter is an exploration into a new area of tourism, aircraft- and spacecraft-based tourism, by elaborating the role played by aircraft and spacecraft in leisure and business trips. Certainly, aircraft, both lighter-than-air and heavier-than-air, have diverse roles in tourism. Some enable tourists to move from their place of origin to the destination and to return and offer significant contribution by ensuring economical, comfortable and safe travel. Some others have recreational significance in the spectrum of leisure tourism. Aircraft thus turns into tourist attractions and contributes in the tourist experience. Spacecraft, still in its early stages of evolution, offers the scope for amazing tourism opportunities in the years to come. Let us

DOI: 10.4324/9781003136927-11

have a journey through the way aircraft and spacecraft contribute in the increasing phenomenon of tourism, one of the largest economic sectors in the world.

11.2 Aircraft

In air transportation system, aircraft is one of the primary elements that enable the air transport service providers to undertake the operation to carry people and goods from one place to another and is considered as the vehicle used for transportation via air. Basically, it represents only a machine with necessary equipment and features to fly. According to ICAO (2003), aircraft is "Any machine that can derive support in the atmosphere from the reactions of the air other than the reactions of the air against the earth's surface". It is also defined as "…a heavier-than-air-machine that depends on the movement of air, either by the engine(s) or through the influence of the aircraft's shape, and most significantly by the wing, to attain and sustain normal flight" (Ashford et al., 2013b). Modern air transportation encompasses a wide range of aircraft. They vary in size, performance, capacity, etc. Some of the aircraft move beyond the speed of sound even. Some can carry more than 800 passengers. Innovation is a regular phenomenon in aircraft design and it is continuing. The current focus is to increase the efficiency of flying with maximum fuel efficiency and minimum pollution. An aircraft can have the following major components.

* Fuselage
* Engine
* Wings
* Tail structure
* Landing gear.

The fuselage is the main body of an aircraft, which is cylindrical in shape and all other components are attached to it. The divisions in it include the cockpit or flight deck, passenger compartment and cargo compartment. In order to keep it lightweight, very thin metal has been used to make it. In a passenger aircraft, passenger compartment is considered the main deck and cargo section is the lower deck. The passenger section is fitted with seats, temperature control devices, bathrooms, galleys, etc. The engine is also the propulsion unit, and they enable the aircraft to move ahead by pushing air backward with the objective of causing a thrust in the forward direction. The wings, aerofoils attached to each side of the fuselage, provide the required push to lift to the aircraft. Tail structure, also known as the empennage, consists of two parts: the vertical part (fin) and the horizontal part (stabilizer). Both are with movable parts, which enable movement of the aircraft nose. The horizontal part is with elevator, which enables the aircraft nose to move up and vice versa. This phenomenon is called pitching. The vertical part, the fin, is with rudder, which causes yawing. It takes place when rudder side moved to the left will cause the aircraft nose to move to the left and vice versa. Landing gear or undercarriage is the part by which the aircraft touches down on the runway. The main function of it is to ensure smooth landing and cushion and absorb the shock waves resulting from the impact. When a flight is flying, the following four forces are acting.

- Lift
- Weight
- Thrust
- Drag.

Lift is the upward force. It helps in opposing the downward force of weight. It is generated mainly by the dynamic effect of the air acting on the wing. Weight, try to pull the aeroplane down, is due to gravitational force, and it is the combined load of the aeroplane itself, the crew, the fuel, passenger, and the cargo or baggage. Thrust is produced by the engine of the aircraft. This enables the aircraft to overcome the force of drag for the aircraft to move forward. Drag opposes thrust, and it is a rearward or air resistance force occurs when the aircraft move ahead. When more thrust is there, the aircraft will accelerate. When the aircraft is climbing, more lift is there on it. The lift is generated when the aircraft is in forward motion and the wings are created that way to generate lift. A wing has the following parts:

- Ailerons
- Slats
- Flaps.

The ailerons, located at the trailing edge of the wing, help in the turning of the aircraft from left to right (rolling/banking). Slats, seen at the leading edge of the wings, support the movement of air from the bottom to the top of the wing to accelerate the speed of airflow at the top of the wing. Flaps are found at the

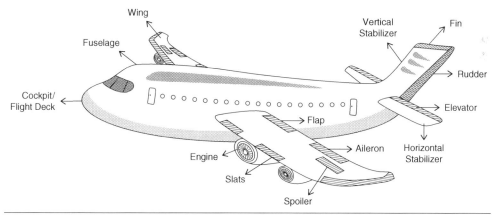

Cockpit : Compartment for pilots to aviate, navigate and communicate
Fuselage : The main body of the aircraft
Wing : The appendages attached to fuselage that enable lift of aircraft
Slat : On the leading edge of wings, to increase lift during low speed operations
Flap : To increase lift during take off.
Aileron : To control the aircraft's rolling
Spoiler : To reduse lift and increase drag
Vertical stabilizer : Stabilizes arround vertical axis
Horizontal stabilizer : Stabilizes the aircraft around lateral axis
Elevator : To control aircraft's pitch
Rudder : To change yaw

Figure 11.1 Parts of aircraft

trailing edge of the wing and work together with the slats to increase lift. Due to the actions of the components, the following movements take place.

- Yawing
- Pitching
- Rolling.

Rudder enables the yawing by which the aircraft nose can move from side to side. Pitching is the movement of the aircraft nose up and down. The elevator causes this function and its moving up enables the aircraft nose to move upwards and vice versa. The ailerons facilitate rolling. If the right aileron is raised, and the left aileron is lowered, the plane will roll to the right and vice versa.

11.3 Types of aircraft

Aircraft are classified on a diverse basis. One type of classification is based on the nature of the aircraft in association with the heaviness related to the density of it with that of air.

11.3.1 Heavier-than-air aircraft

This category consists of "Any aircraft deriving its lift in flight chiefly from aerodynamic forces" (ICAO, 2003). These are fitted with source to provide power to fly, with the help of lift primarily. Ranges of air-based vehicles are there included in this category, which include autogyros, helicopters and gyrocopters, and conventional fixed-wing aircraft (aeroplanes). Fixed-wing aircraft takes the advantage of wings to generate lift due to the peculiar shape of them and the internal-combustion engine (except in gliders) in the form of a piston engine that can generate 'thrust' to move forward. Aerodyne is a terminology used interchangeably for representing these types of aircraft. The term aerodyne is considered rather as a technical term to represent heavier-than-air aircraft that derive lift in flight primarily from aerodynamic forces. There are powered as well as non-powered aerodynes. Examples for unpowered manned heavier-than-air vehicles include hang gliders, gliders and sailplanes, which also can fly. Aircraft we see usually, which are used in commercial air transportation as well as in military aviation, are included in this category. Powered aerodynes (with engines) are classified as follows:

- Aeroplane
- Rotorcraft
- Ornithopter.

Aeroplanes are power driven with engine that achieves lift from the dynamic action of air against fixed wings. The required lift in flight is achieved mainly from aerodynamic reactions on surfaces, which remain fixed under given conditions of flight. The following are the two types.

- Seaplane
- Landplane.

A seaplane is an aeroplane that can take off and land upon the water. The float-plane and flying boat are the categories in this. **Floatplanes (pontoon planes)** are the seaplanes with separate pontoons or floats. Slender pontoons are mounted beneath the fuselage in floatplanes. It is supported on water by a pair of floats instead of a hull. Seaplanes with boat like hulls are called **flying boats**. Hull acts as its main body and it also supports the aircraft on water. Landplane can land and take off on land surface. **Amphibian floats** are also there.

Rotorcraft represents rotary-wing aircraft, which gain the lift through the dynamic action of air against rotating wings. The flight of this is supported by the reactions of the air on one or more rotors. This consists of the following categories:

* Helicopter
* Gyroplane.

In the case of helicopter, the lift is provided by the reactions of the air on one or more power-driven rotors. The horizontally spanning propellers or rotors enable the helicopters to take off and land vertically, to remain stationary in the air and even to move in any direction. Rotating rotors provide the lift and thrust. Helicopters with single main rotor with tail rotor, side-by-side non-intermeshing rotors, torque less single rotor, tandem rotors, coaxial rotors, etc., can be seen. Land helicopter, sea helicopter and amphibian helicopter are there in use. Land helicopters are used more in the realm of tourism. Gyroplane, also known as autogyro, is another type of heavier-than-air aircraft that obtains thrust from a conventional engine and lift from a rotor freely rotating in the horizontal plane, on a vertical axis. It "is a type of rotorcraft that uses an unpowered rotor in autorotation to develop lift, and an engine-powered propeller, similar to that of a fixed-wing aircraft, to provide thrust" (www.casa.gov.au). Ornithopter is "supported in flight chiefly by the reactions of the air on planes to which a flapping motion is imparted" (ICAO, 2003). The flapping wings, like a bird, generate the lift for this type of aircraft. The types in this may include land ornithopter, sea ornithopter and amphibian ornithopter.

Non-powered/non-power-driven (aerodynes without engines) aerodynes consists mainly of the following categories.

* Glider
* Sailplane
* Kite.

Glider is heavier than air which is a non-power-driven vehicle and flies without any applied power. It obtains the required lift from aerodynamic reactions on surfaces. Lift is derived mainly from its wings and initial thrust is given by some launching mechanism. This vehicle, without an engine, is used for gliding from a higher to a lower and vice versa and can sustain flight for certain duration with the actions of air currents. According to the Federal Aviation Administration (FAA), a glider is "as a heavier-than-air aircraft that is supported in flight by the dynamic reaction of the air against its lifting surfaces, and whose free flight does not depend principally on an engine" (FAA Handbook). Sailplanes have standard aircraft parts, design and systems, which are high-performance ones that can fly higher and for an extended duration covering a longer distance. FAA defines it

Table 11.1 Aircraft Typology

Based on Engines	Based on Mach Number
Propeller: thrust for flight from a rotating propeller, supported by an engine inside, that can convert rotational energy into propulsive force	(Mach number represents the ratio of the speed of an object to the speed of sound. If an aircraft has Mach speed means, it moves at a speed of sound, under certain conditions)
Turboprop: This also has propeller, and the gas-turbine engines that turn the propeller(s)	**Subsonic**: Aircraft with maximum speed much less than that of sound (M < 1). Majority of the civil aviation aircraft as subsonic
Turbofan: This has engine, which is the modern version of gas-turbine engine. The engine is a sort of air-breathing jet engine, and the mechanical energy is from combustion	**Transonic**: Transonic aircraft fly at a speed matching with that of sound (M ~ 1)
Turbojet: This has a jet engine, which emits a high-energy gas stream through exhaust nozzle to derive the needed thrust	**Supersonic**: Aircraft that moves faster than the speed of sound. Concorde flights are examples of this (M > 1)
Ramjet: This aircraft, which can move very fast, has another type of air-breathing jet engine, which operates with no major moving parts	**Hypersonic** (M >> 1): Hypersonic represents much higher Mach speed. The scope of it is mainly for defence purposes

Based on Range	Based on Number of Wings
(Range: the maximum distance an aircraft can fly at a stretch, from take-off to landing)	Aircraft can also be classified based on the number of wings
Short range: flights with a range up to 500 kms (e.g. some of the general aviation aircraft come in this category)	**Monoplane**: Flight with a single pair of wings. Commercial air transport is dominated by this category of flights
Medium range: flights with range around 3000kms (e.g. Dornier 328, Embraer 135)	**Biplane**: Two wings are there, one above other
Long range: flights of range well above 3000kms (e.g. Boeing 777-200LR: range 17,395km. Airbus A340–500: range 16,670km)	**Triplanes** and **quad planes**: though rarely these are also there

Source: Author collected data from various sources.

as "a glider (heavier-than-air fixed-wing aircraft) designed to fly efficiently and gain altitude solely from natural forces, such as thermals and ridge waves" (FAA Handbook). There are powered sailplanes also in use with certain specific purposes. Kite is a simple form used for flight that can be anchored from the earth and obtains lift from aerodynamic forces.

11.3.2 Lighter-than-air aircraft/aerostats

These vehicles, when filled with gas which is lighter than air, displace the surrounding ambient air and floats. Such aircraft, known as aerostat, are kept aloft by using buoyant gas. They are used mainly for recreational purposes. These vehicles can contain a sufficient volume of gas lighter than air, like heated air, hydrogen or helium; and hence, it can displace the surrounding ambient air so as to float in the air. In this also, powered as well as non-powered categories are there. The following are the types of lighter-than-air aircraft.

- Powered lighter-than-air aircraft
  - Airship (rigid, semi-rigid and non-rigid airships/blimps)
- Non-powered lighter-than-air aircraft
  - Free balloon (spherical and non-spherical free balloons)
  - Captive balloon (spherical and kite/non-spherical free balloons).

Airships have a simple power-deriving mechanism within it. It is used for both propulsion and steering the craft. This can navigate through the air under its own power and can gain lift and float with the assistance of the less dense gas filled within. Non-rigid airships are often called "blimps", which depend mainly on internal pressure to maintain their shape. Semi-rigid airships have a supporting structure to maintain shape and the rigid ones consist of outer structural framework in order to maintain the shape.

Free balloons are not anchored ones, having the freedom to move with the wind. These are not engine driven, yet can sustain flight by using gas buoyancy or an airborne heater. The captive balloons are with lighter-than-air gas filled within and remain connected to the ground with a cord. In order to maintain stability

Table 11.2 Classification of Aircraft

Aircraft

	Heavier-than-air Aircraft				*Lighter-than-air Aircraft*		
	Power Driven			*Non-power Driven*	*Power Driven*	*Non-power Driven*	
Ornithopter	Rotorcraft		Aeroplane	Glider, Kite	Airship	Captive Balloon	Free Balloon
Land ornithopter, sea ornithopter, amphibian ornithopter	Helicopter: land helicopter, sea helicopter, amphibian helicopter	Gyroplane: land gyroplane, sea gyroplane, amphibian gyroplane	Landplane, seaplane, amphibian	Land glider, sea glider	Rigid airship, semi-rigid airship, non-rigid airship	Spherical captive balloon, non-spherical captive balloon	Spherical free balloon, non-spherical free balloon

Source: ICAO (2003).

from wind, kite balloon is shaped and trimmed and combines a lifting gas with active lift structures like wings to fly in all aerial conditions.

11.3.3 Aircraft classification based on purpose

Another classification of the aircraft is based on the purpose of flying. The following are the categories:

- Civil aircraft
  - General aviation aircraft
    - Private aircraft
    - Business planes
  - Commercial aircraft
  - Passenger aircraft
  - Freighter
  - Combi-aircraft
- Military aircraft.

Table 11.3 Aircraft Used for General Aviation and State's Purposes

Aircraft used for	Aircraft used for aerial operations	Aircraft used for State's purposes (non-general aviation category)
• Corporate aviation (corporate's own use) • Fractional ownership operations (aircraft operated by a specialized company on behalf of multiple co-owners) • Business travel (self-flown for business purposes) • Personal/ private travel • Travel for personal reasons/personal transport • Air tourism (self-flown inbound/outbound tours) • Recreational flying (powered/ non-powered leisure flying activities) • Air sports (e.g. aerobatics, air races, competitions)	• Aerial crane operations • Aerial survey • Agricultural flights • Banner towing/ Advertising flights • Environment surveillance and enforcement • Ferry flights/delivery flights • Flight demonstrations (air shows) • Fire fighting • Glider towing • Medical evacuations • Nostalgic flights using vintage aircraft • Pilot training • R&D flights • Search and rescue • Sightseeing flights • Skydiver hoisting • Supplies dropping • Traffic surveillance • Transplant organ transports • TV-live reporting • Weather research	• State VIP transports • Police/customs aircraft • General air traffic (military) • Operational air traffic (military) Surveillance/ identification, air superiority defence, tactical intelligence/ photography, ground troops support, training for the above, etc.

Source: Adapted from International Council of Aircraft Owner and Pilot Associations (IAOPA). https://www.iaopa.eu/what-is-general-aviation

Civil aircraft include all the non-military aircraft. Among the civil aviation aircraft, those used for general aviation constitute the majority. It "includes over 416,000 general aviation aircraft flying worldwide today, ranging from two-seat training aircraft and utility helicopters to intercontinental business jets...." (GAMA, 2016). The range of aircraft widely varies, from small, single-seater as well as non-powered recreational aircraft to modern business jets. Private aircraft are personal planes used for pleasure flying, often single-engine monoplanes. Business aircraft can be small single-engine aircraft used for pilot training or to transport small packages over short distances to four-engine executive jets that can fly across continents and oceans. Different types of planes are used for varied purposes like traffic reporting, forest-fire fighting, medical evacuation, pipeline surveillance, freight hauling and many other applications.

The most visible category is the aircraft used for commercial aviation. Small aircraft to large aircraft like A 380, which can carry more than 800 passengers, are there. Commercial aircraft have advanced greatly by having high standards of comfort, efficiency, fuel efficiency, value to customers, versatility and in providing a flying experience. Single-aisle and twin-aisle to double-decker aircraft are there in use. There are smaller aircraft also in service.

Table 11.4 Wide-Body Aircraft

Wide-body aircraft transport began in the 1970s, by the use of Boeing 747, McDonnell Douglas DC-10, Lockheed L-1011, Airbus 300, etc.

Wide-body aircraft has a wider fuselage so that it can have more seats in each row. The forward section may have first and/or business class. The economy compartment will have two aisles, and the seats are arranged on the sides of both the aisles. Basically, it will have seven seats. Depending on the size of the aircraft, ten seats can also be there in a row. Narrow-body aircraft having a small first or business class compartment with four-abreast seating and a longer economy class compartment with six-abreast seating, along with a single aisle by which the seats are arranged on either side of the aisle

Boeing 747 became the pioneer in the wide-body aircraft revolution. It was introduced by the beginning of the 1970s. The first version of B747 had four efficient high-bypass turbofan engines and could carry up to 400 passengers. Lockheed L-1011 and the McDonnell Douglas DC-10 the other wide-body aircraft were in use during the 1970s. McDonnell Douglas DC-10 had the capacity of 250–360 seats. A300 was initially designed as 300 seater

Currently, a number of wide-body aircraft are in use. Airbus A380 is the widest with a width 7.14 metres. Boeing 747 currently has a width of 6.5 metres. Boeing 777/777X, Ilyushin 86/96, and Lockheed L-1011 TriStar are some of the other major wide-body aircraft in wide use nowadays. They are used mainly in long-haul and medium-haul routes. They can carry passengers from 200 to 850 passengers and typically have twin-aisle cabins

---

Source: Author collected data from various sources.

One more general classification of aircraft can be seen based on the volume/width of them. The following are the categories:

- Narrow-body aircraft and
- Wide-body aircraft.

Narrow-body aircraft are smaller and have a single aisle through the passenger cabin. It may have a fuselage diameter of 3 to 4 m, e.g. Embraer E-Jet E2, Airbus 320, Boeing737. Wide-body aircraft may typically have two aisles that divide the seating into three groups, and with a fuselage diameter varying from 5 to 6 m, e.g. Boeing 747, McDonnell Douglas DC-10, Lockheed L-1011 TriStar, Airbus A300, Airbus 380. Jumbo jets are there depending upon the size. They are usually of very large size, e.g. Boeing 747, Airbus A380 (superjumbo jet).

11.4 Aircraft manufacturers

Manufacturers include a variety of firms, such as airframe manufacturers, engine manufacturers, manufactures of mechanical systems, creators of computer hardware and software, and producers of materials and chemicals required for various air transport operations. Aircraft manufacturing is one of the most concentrated industries in the world with extreme oligopoly. A few players are dominated in the international market. Airbus, Boeing and Tupolev focus on the wide-body and narrow-body jet airliners. Bombardier, ATR and Embraer concentrate on smaller aircraft useful for the regional airlines. Though they are the major aircraft manufacturers, the engines required for the aircraft are manufactured by other companies. A brief about major of them are given below.

11.4.1 Airbus

Airbus design, manufacture and deliver industry-leading commercial aircraft, helicopters, military transports, satellites and launch vehicles, as well as providing data services, navigation, secure communications, urban mobility and other solutions for customers on a global scale. In commercial aviation sector, Airbus' diverse product line includes everything from passenger jetliners to freighters and private jets. The product range in this category ranges in size from 100-seat jetliners to the double-deck A380 that is capable of transporting more than 850 passengers. Airbus is based in Europe with its headquarters in Toulouse, France, and has 12 sites in Europe located in France, Germany, Spain and UK. Airbus also has three subsidiaries in the USA, Japan and China. The major commercial aircraft in service are A 300, A301, A318, A319, A 320, A320neo, A 321, A 330, A330neo, A350 and Airbus Beluga XL (www.airbus.com).

11.4.2 Boeing

Boeing is one of the largest aerospace companies and a leading manufacturer of commercial jetliners, defence, space and security systems and service provider of aftermarket support. With corporate offices in Chicago, it employs more than 153,000 people across the United States and in more than 65 countries (www.

boeing.com). Currently, Boeing manufactures the 737, 747, 767, 777 and 787 families of aeroplanes and the Boeing Business Jet range. New product development efforts include the Boeing 787-10 Dreamliner, the 737 MAX, and the 777X. As of now, more than 10,000 Boeing-built commercial jetliners are in service across the world. It also offers the most complete family of freighters, and, according to it, a vast majority of world's cargo is carried onboard Boeing planes.

11.4.3 Bombardier

Bombardier focuses on aerospace and rail transportation. Bombardier Aerospace are leading civil aircraft manufacturers and are leaders in the design and manufacture of innovative aviation products and services for the business, regional and amphibious aircraft markets. It is headquartered in Montréal, Canada, and its aircraft and services are seen in a number of different markets including business aircraft, commercial aircraft and amphibious aircraft. Its Canadair Regional Jet (CRJ) is one of the most successful families of regional jets. This company has already sold more than 1,900 aircraft, flying people in more than 90 countries (www.bombardier.com).

11.4.4 Embraer

Embraer has become one of the main aircraft manufacturers in the world by focusing on specific market segments with high growth potential in commercial, defence and executive aviation. Embraer is based in São José dos Campos, Brazil. It is considered the 3rd largest commercial jets manufacturer that has delivered more than 8.000 aeroplanes. Over the years, it has established factories, offices and centres of distribution for parts and services in the Americas, Africa, Asia and Europe. E-JETS E2 is its latest jet aircraft with advanced technologies. This company has set a standard in manufacturing smaller aircraft in the series of E-Jets having a capacity of 70–130-seats. ERJs are another major aircraft family of Embraer with a capacity of 37–50-seats. Today, some 70 operators fly the Embraer model, ERJ 145.

11.4.5 Tupolev

Tupolev is a Russian aerospace and defence company, headquartered in Moscow, Russia, and is officially known as Public Stock Company (PSC), Tupolev. It is the head enterprise of the strategic and long-range aviation division of the United Aircraft Corporation (UAC). Built since 1923, about 1,000 of them delivered to 20 countries. Tu-214 and Tu-204 are the major commercial aircraft in service now (www.tupolev.ru).

11.4.6 ATR (Avions de transport Regional)

ATR is a Toulouse, Southern France-based turboprop aircraft manufacturer, who is currently a leader in the market for regional aircraft up to 90 seats. Established in November 1981, it is a joint partnership between two major European aeronautics players, Airbus and Leonardo. As of now, it has sold nearly 1,700 aircraft and has over 200 operators in more than 100 countries (www.atraircraft.com). It manufactures two sizes of turboprop aircraft, the 70-seat ATR 72 and the 50-seat ATR 42.

These are ideal for airlines servicing smaller markets and to have regular services between regional airports and to main airports and hubs.

11.4.7 McDonnell Douglas Corporation

This was a major American aircraft manufacturing company and was taken over by Boeing. They produced jet fighters, commercial aircraft and space vehicles. They were having a range of propeller as well as jet aircraft. McDonnell Douglass DC-9 and DC-10 are some of the major aircraft of them in service.

Aircraft manufacturers make use of the engines that are manufactured by other companies. The major aircraft engine manufacturers are as follows:

*   Rolls-Royce plc. (UK),
*   Pratt & Whitney (P&W) (USA),
*   General Electric (GE Aircraft Engines) (USA),
*   IAE (International Aero Engines-AG) (Switzerland and USA),
*   Rolls Smiths Engine Controls Ltd. (UK).

11.5 Jet engines and tourism growth

It has been well stated that modern tourism started growing since the end of the Second World War. In fact, one of the major reasons for the growth of international tourism in the post-Second World War era is the evolution and advancements in aviation as well. It was during then jet engines were used in commercial air transportation widely, which had immense influence on the increase in cross-border travel. Jet engines were found to be more reliable, safer, and with operational economy. Moreover, aircraft with jet engines had much more range and with larger size so that more passengers could be accommodated. Commercial air transportation has seen jet engine aircraft use in the second half of the 1950s. Boeing 707 and Douglas DC-8 were used for the same in the beginning. British de Havilland D.H. 106 Comets and Soviet Tupolev Tu-104s were also in use during then.

Jet engines were experimentally used in aviation before the Second World War and used during the war and commercial application took more time, towards the end of the 1950s. Jet engine is a marvellous innovation in the aircraft technology, a breakthrough which could revolutionize the people's travel by air, and the concept of it is simply illustrated by NASA in the following way.

> The engine sucks air in at the front with a fan. A compressor raises the pressure of the air. The compressor is made with many blades attached to a shaft. The blades spin at high speed and compress or squeeze the air. The compressed air is then sprayed with fuel and an electric spark lights the mixture. The burning gases expand and blast out through the nozzle, at the back of the engine. As the jets of gas shoot backward, the engine and the aircraft are thrust forward. As the hot air is going to the nozzle, it passes through another group of blades called the turbine. The turbine is attached to the same shaft as the compressor. Spinning the turbine causes the compressor to spin.
>
> (NASA/www.grc.nasa.gov)

By the second half of the last century, the relationship between air transport and tourism became evident, particularly since the introduction of jet aircraft in commercial air transportation (May & Hill, 2002). Thus, aircraft with jet engines propelled the aviation to newer heights and subsequently contributed greatly in the evolution of modern tourism. Due to the introduction of jet engines, there were dramatic changes in the aviation sector. Speed of travel increased tremendously.

11.6 Wide-body aircraft and tourism

Wide-body aircraft is a trendsetter in international tourism by triggering long-haul mass tourism in the 1970s. It caused due to the scope of carrying more people in one flight that can fly larger distance at a stretch and other benefits of increased comfort and engine efficiency. Many of the destinations in Asia got increased influx of tourists from the West primarily due to the air connectivity augmented by the introduction of wide-body aircraft during the 1970s and 80s. Due to the availability of more seats, airline could provide seats at a lower price and that initiated competition within the industry in providing a competitive price. Air travel cost is certainly a major determinant in tourism. Moreover, there were changes in the entire air transport system due to the arrival of wide-body aircraft. Air transport experienced expansion greatly to accommodate increasing influx of passengers and to receive more wide-body aircraft of that era.

Wide-body aircraft has a wider fuselage so that it can have more seats in each row. The forward section may have first and/or business class four-abreast compartment. The economy compartment will have two aisles, and the seats are arranged on the sides of both the aisles. Basically, it will have seven seats. Depending on the size of the aircraft, ten seats can also be there in a row. Wide-body aircraft transport began in the 1970s, by the use of Boeing 747, the McDonnell Douglas DC-10, Lockheed L-1011, Airbus 300, etc. Boeing 747 became the pioneer in the wide-body aircraft revolution. It was introduced at the beginning of the 1970s. The first version of B747 had four efficient high-bypass turbofan engines and could carry up to 400 passengers. Lockheed L-1011 and the McDonnell Douglas DC-10 the other wide-body aircraft were in use during the 1970s. McDonnell Douglas DC-10 had the capacity of 250–360 seats. A300 was initially designed as a 300 seater. Currently, a number of wide-body aircraft are in use. Airbus A380 is the widest with a width of 7.14 metres. Boeing 747 currently has a width of 6.5 metres. Boeing 777/777X, Ilyushin 86/96, and Lockheed L-1011 TriStar are some of the other major wide-body aircraft in wide use nowadays. They are used mainly in long-haul and medium-haul routes. They can carry passengers from 200 to 850 passengers and typically have twin-aisle cabins.

Indeed, wide-body aircraft have transformed tourism greatly. By the 1970s, when such aircraft were introduced, there was a dramatic change in long-haul travel. Wide-body aircraft could carry a large number of passengers and travel became a more comfortable option on long-distance routes. The transformation happened in air travel due to the use of Boeing 747, the pioneer commercially

> **Table 11.5** Will Supersonic Aircraft Make Waves in Tourism?

The rise of supersonic commercial flights again into realm of passenger transportation on a large scale may invigorate the scope of international tourism further in the coming decades. Certainly, MICE tourism will be the lone beneficiary in the beginning. As per the latest reports, the 2020s are going to be the era of supersonic air transport that will be featured with a staggering reduction in the time taken for travel. Such a flight from New York to London may take only three hours. It can fly from Los Angeles to Tokyo in six hours. One firm that is in the making of more advanced flights claims that their jet flight will be capable of reaching Mach 4 (about 2,600 mph, or almost twice the speed of the Concorde). Though it sounds amazing, within a few years of time it will become a reality. One of the prime bottlenecks of tourism is indeed the amount of time needed for travel. By and large, travel duration retains an inverse relation with travel propensity. The lesser the time taken for travel, the higher the chance of choosing this leisure activity. This is the reason why the new supersonic mode of transport becomes more relevant in the realm of tourism. Currently, flights are moving at a pace in between 600 and 900 kmph or bit higher. But the supersonic flights can make up to 2000 kmph and even much above

As per the reports regarding the new invention, Airbus is teaming up with US-based aerospace firm Aerion to create a supersonic jet that can fly from London to New York in three hours and from Los Angeles to Tokyo in six. The Aerion AS2 aircraft is currently being developed which is hope to have experimental flights soon. The Aerion AS2 business jet will fly at 1,217 mph, using proprietary supersonic laminar flow technology – almost as fast as Concorde, which flew at 1,350 mph. Regular commercial airliners typically fly from between 480–560 mph. AS2's 30-foot-long cabin is designed to carry 12 passengers and will have seats that will berth for overnight flights. The new design will help to reduce drag on wings and fuselage by 20%

Boston-based Spike Aerospace, another firm in the same path is in the making of S-512 Supersonic Jet that is designed to fly at Mach 1.6, while seating 12–18 passengers. UK-based HyperMach is aiming at a higher level. Their ambitious SonicStar claims to be capable of reaching Mach 4 (about 2,600 mph, or almost twice the speed of the Concorde)

British Airways used Concorde jet flight, a supersonic flight, which had a cruising speed of 1,350 mph, more than twice the speed of sound. On 24 October 2003, they withdrew it, bringing to a close the world's only supersonic passenger service. But now, the ongoing experiments are much hopeful to the air transport sector. Already there is a competition among the supersonic aircraft manufacturers which will make things better for the air transport industry in order to get increased efficient flights and to get the cost cheaper. Moreover, the size of the flights has to be improved so as to use for the regular transport services which may take place without much delay. Tourism sector is waiting to welcome this as they constitute the largest beneficiary of the new development in the air transport

Source: Dileep, 2014, Supersonic Jets to hasten tourism's surge, Destination Mice Magazine, Nov. 2014.

used wide-body aircraft, has been described in the following manner. The introduction of 747 into service led to

> the growth in air travel, tourism, and connections between people around the world. In its first year, a fully-loaded 747 cut the cost of flying a passenger by half. Flying became instantly more accessible. But may be the award for the biggest change in air travel should go to the 747's older sibling, the 707. That smooth-flying, jet-powered pioneer was a quantum leap from the "piston-pounders" that preceded it. It connected continents in mere hours and showed the world the power of jet travel.
>
> (Slutsken, 2020)

According to Peterson (2018), the introduction of B747 "literally it launched the era of mass tourism across the Atlantic". Similarly, long-haul tourism to the Far East from the West started growing since then as the travel cost on long-haul routes started to reduce. Moreover, according to Slutsken (2020), due to the arrival of wide-body aircraft, airports have to adapt to the situation. Boarding lounges, emigration counters, check-in counters, customs facilities and terminals were getting expanded. Ground handling equipment, including refuelling tankers, had to grow. Moreover, engines became more advanced with less sound, increased fuel efficiency and more power. All of the above led caused a stride in international tourism. Thus, wide-body aircraft were instrumental in the rise in international tourism at a remarkable rate since 1970.

11.7 Helicopters and tourism

Helicopters, though got little attention in the tourism literature, have increasing importance in tourism nowadays. Helicopters are used as a means for transport as part of a tourism as well as a tool to gain a mesmerizing touristic experience. Use of helicopter as a vehicle for movement has less significance from a tourism point of view compared to helicopter-based tourism, which is at times referred to as helicopter tourism. Heli-tourism is also a term used to represent a similar concept, yet there, the same covers short trips using helicopter to experience aerial view. Heli-tourism covers diverse types of tourism as well. For instance, according to Hudson and Miller (2005), under the term of heli-tourism, "several subcategories have evolved, offering the public a diverse range of activities encompassing everything from heli-fly fishing to heli-picnicking. But the most popular are winter heli-skiing and summer heli-hiking". Yet, both the terms are used interchangeably on the literature as well as in the industry.

Helicopter tourism, which involves a significant contribution of helicopters in the overall tourist experience, is gaining increasing significance in many regions of the world. According to Torrez and Kozak (2019), helicopters are found in niche markets that are highly specialized like aerial tourism, news reporting, etc. Helicopter tourism has been growing and anticipated to reach USD 941.6 million by 2023 at a compound annual growth rate (CAGR) of 4.17% during the forecast period (Market Research Future, 2017). According to another market research group, The Insight Partners, "The helicopter tourism market was valued at US$

851.9 million in 2018 and is expected to grow at a CAGR of 4.7% from 2019 to 2027 to reach US$ 1,253.9 million by 2027" (The Insight Partners, 2002). In the post-COVID-19 era, this growth rate will certainly change; yet, the future of helicopter tourism seems bright. Panoramic flights have amazing feel, particularly when it is on sites with natural attractions. The following are the major sites on which helicopter recreational flights are common.

- Mountain ranges
- Forests and woods
- Valleys
- Glaciers
- Beaches
- Volcanoes
- Waterfalls
- Lakes and rivers.

Ride over large cities and heritage sites are also gaining significance. There are popular helicopter trips over mega cities in the world like New York. The primary reason for the surge in helicopter tourism, in addition to the industrial causes, is the convenience and viewing experience it provides to the tourists. Aerial view of scenic attractions is always enthralling for the people. According to Market Research Future, Americas

> … is expected to dominate the helicopter tourism market due to rising helicopter tourism in major markets such as U.S., Argentina, Canada, Brazil, Mexico, and Peru. The Americas include a number of tourist destinations, ranging from Florida Keys in the US to Niagara Falls in Canada, the Iguaçu Falls in Brazil to Barbados in the Caribbean, and from Los Roques in Venezuela to Cartagena in Colombia. Such places are a treat to view from the top, due to their natural exquisiteness.
> (Market Research Future/www.marketresearchfuture.com)

Helicopter tours are famous in Hawaii by which tourists can enjoy the spectacular view of the terrain much closer and to have a better experience (Haaland et al., 2009). The reasons for the growth of helicopter tourism are following:

- Traffic congestion and crowding in urban destinations
- Lure of aerial view of scenic sites
- Interest in aerial photography
- Scope for customized enthusing trips
- Ideal for physically challenged and aged travellers as well
- Thrilling experience
- Ideal experience in shorter holidays
- Suitability to access remote sites
- Time saving in reaching sites.

Helicopter-based recreational tourism trips are of varied kinds. Advanced helicopters are used in heli-tours nowadays. Moreover, facilities like microphones, noise-reducing headphones and inside cameras are equipped within

Table 11.6 Helicopter Tourism Market Segments

	Segments			
Type	Customized (market share-62% in 2016) Helicopter service providers and resorts provide a lead in offering customized helicopter tours		General (market share-37%) General package helicopter tours	
Ownership	Fractional ownership (largest market share)	Charter service (tours using charter helicopters)	Joint ownership (with two or more co-owners)	
Regions	Americas Largest market share	Europe Second largest	Asia Pacific	Rest of the world

Source: Market Research Future (2017).

helicopters to make the trip pleasurable for the passengers. Moreover, in adventurous heli-activities, tour operators ensure that the equipment required to undertake recreational activities can be carried by the helicopters. According to Heli USA, the following featured heli-tours are possible.

- Along with other visits/activities, they offer quick 20-minute flyover tours over scenic attractions/cities
- Extensive package tours that include lunch, activities and long in-depth flights with informative narration.
- Trips on helicopters, either as part of an extensive package or short-duration trips, arranging landing in enchanting and remote protected location that are otherwise difficult to reach, and arrange scope for interaction with the local indigenous people. (www.heliusa.com)

Among the above, the second and third categories have more significance from a tourism point of view. In the first category, helicopters are just used only for a few hours for a ride and the rest of the time, in the whole visit, the tourists are neither associated with helicopters nor getting benefit of helicopters to enjoy tourism in the destination. The second category can have elongated holidays using helicopter services, and in the third category, the tourists are benefited greatly from the use of helicopters and helicopters do have a substantial role in the overall tourist experience generated. In the city helicopter tourism markets, ride over New York City and Chicago from the USA has gained global attention. Similar attention is there on helicopter rides over Hong Kong city as well. Many other urbanscapes have helicopter tourism potentials that lure tourists from far and wide. Glaciers offer a mesmerizing experience for the aerial trip enthusiasts. Some of the glaciers have already helicopter tourism taking place at a grand level. For instance, an aerial visit over Glacier Country (New Zealand) and Mendenhall Glacier (Alaska) are some examples of global helicopter-based glacier tourist destinations. Victoria Falls (Zambia and Zimbabwe), Niagara Falls (USA), Iguazu Falls (Brazil–Argentine border), etc., have been world-renowned helicopter tourism options in the waterfall regions. Himalayan mountain ranges, Columbia Mountains (Canada), Alps mountain ranges in Switzerland, etc., have helicopter tourism potentials greatly. Grand Canyon in the USA is a major helicopter tourism attraction. Some of the Hawaii islands are very popular for such tourism. Varied tourist sites that have helicopter tourism happening at an international level include Great Barrier Reef (Australia), Amalfi Coast (Italy) and Laikipia Plateau (Kenya). The above are few examples only. Helicopter tourism is taking place at a large number of sites across the world.

Table 11.7 Aircraft Used in Helicopter Tourism

A-Star

A-Star is an Airbus helicopter (AS350 series, currently H125) and is a single-engine category with good performance standards. While it can accommodate five or six passengers, this has very good manoeuvrability and can fly at higher altitudes

Eco Star

The Eco Star (Eurocopter/Airbus EC130) is rather a comfortable and quieter helicopter with Fenestron Tail Rotor engine. The outside view is better and has a larger cabin that can accommodate seven passengers

Bell 206

The Bell 206 is a highly capable helicopter with a twin-bladed rotor system. It offers a comfortable trip, can carry seven passengers, and provides very good photo opportunities and Vista View windows

Bell 407 (and Bell 427)

This, having a Rolls-Royce turbine engine, featured with high-level efficiency in terms of operations. Also, it offers low skids for entry and exit and has Vista View windows which are ideal for photo opportunities. While Bell 407 can accommodate five passengers, the other has a capacity to carry up to eight

Robinson R44

This is a lighter helicopter with fewer seats featured with smooth handling, reliability, safety and comfort. Due to the open design feature, tourists can enjoy unobstructed views

Hughes MD500

This is another small and lightweight helicopter that has high manoeuvring capability and can hover and land anywhere so that it can be used for reaching remote terrains

Source: Heli USA, data available online at https://www.heliusa.com/types-of-helicopters/

11.7.1 Heli-fly fishing

It is a niche/special interest tourism category. Those who have a specific desire to venture fishing in remote locations, helicopter-based trips can be made use of. Fishing tourism itself is a special interested tourism category. When it is clubbed with aerial trip using helicopters, there will be value addition and enhancement of tourist experience. Moreover, the experience is augmented when fishing location is otherwise inaccessible and on remote locations. There are multiple benefits for tourists who engage in this type of tourism activity. Tourists can have a panoramic view while flying in the helicopter, which adds value to the overall experience. Helicopters enable the special interest tourists to access remote rivers, lakes and streams so as to engage in their desired fishing activity. They can save a lot of time by moving fast compared to other forms of transport to reach such kinds of locations.

11.7.2 Heli-picnicking

This is an exciting trip to natural attractions where a picnic kind of seeing is ensured as well. Food services are arranged at the sites where the helicopter can land. For instance, as part of enjoyment of panoramic view of a mountain, a gourmet picnic meal can be served in an ideal location as well. Heli-picnic usually involves lunch and helicopter-based ride over naturally beautiful remote locations. Customized heli-picnicking as well as group packages are there. Some of the heli-picnic operators use two or three helicopters for a group heli-picnic tour. Night camps are also organized in a similar manner.

11.7.3 Heli-wine tours

The idea of clubbing wine tour experience with heli-tourism is mesmerizing and is being explored by many tour operators in those regions that are famous for wine yards and wineries. Wine tours themselves are enthralling. In this category, a scenic helicopter tour is combined with trips to wineries to relax and enjoy the beverage. Extended wine tourism packages can also be possible. Wine tourism is a growing segment of tourism. Wine tourism involves visits to wine yards as well as to the wineries.

11.7.4 Heli-skiing

Skiing has been an important motivation for recreation-seekers to engage in tourism for a long. Heli-skiing, a sport with unique and special attributes and requirements, is a kind of mountain-based skiing that utilizes helicopters to reach mountain ranges with significant vertical drops of untracked powder snow (Williams & Hunter, 2002). It is an adventurous skiing type on the mountains and the skiers can enjoy the thrill of accessing untapped terrain in the wilderness with the assistance of helicopters. It is an off-trail downhill skiing or snowboarding with the specific assistance of helicopters in accessing the tall mountains. Skiing tourism is one of the early special interest tourism categories and even in the 19th century, specialized tour operation started focussing on skiing holidays. Accessing remote mountains on helicopters themselves is a thrilling experience.

11.7.5 Heli-biking

Heli-biking is a thrilling one for the bike riding lovers who can travel aboard helicopters along with the bikes up to the location from where biking can be done. Use of the helicopters helps the riders to experience endless panoramic vistas of the mountain ranges and similar terrains. Biking is a kind of outdoor sport, off-road, even on rough terrains, including mountain ranges, using specially designed bikes/bicycles. The tour packages offer professional guide services and other assistance required to enable the bikers to enjoy the ride on the countrysides and mountainsides. The bikes are attached to the helicopters. Some operators provide all the equipment required for the heli-biking experience.

11.7.6 Heli-hiking

Heli-hiking stands for helicopter-assisted hiking. Hiking, according to *collinsdictionary.com*, is a "sporting or leisure activity of going for long, often strenuous, walks in the country". In the case of heli-hiking, the recreational tourists are transported by helicopter up through a mountain valley and dropped off onto an ideal location in order to enjoy the hiking experience. The tour operators will ensure all the required equipment and accessories to have a smooth trek over there. The scenic view that can be enjoyed while flying on helicopter adds to the tourist experience.

11.7.7 Heli-mountaineering

Helicopter-assisted mountaineering is gaining importance. Hiking, climbing and simple walking on hilly or mountainous surfaces, with the help of technical equipment and support, are part of mountaineering depending upon the locations. It is different from rock climbing and more strenuous than trekking and hiking. In the case of helicopter-assisted mountaineering, the visitors can reach the different peaks of mountain ranges on helicopters and can engage in mountaineering and associated activities to gain tourist experience. It has been considered as one of the most exquisite ways to experience the remote untouched wilderness and mountain regions. Due to the use of helicopters to access the remote locations, mountaineers can maximize their time in the mountains. The activity in it can be thrilling by engaging in more adventurous movement on cutting-edge rock and mountain routes as well.

11.8 Seaplanes

Seaplanes can land, float and take off on water surface and have the capability to fly low and fast. Water-alone and amphibious seaplanes are there under this category. Amphibious aircraft, equipped with wheels as well, can land and take off at both land and water. Flying boats are also seaplanes, but with boat like hulls, and use fuselage for buoyancy. Floatplanes are also there which are with separate floats/pontoons mounted under the fuselage to provide buoyancy. Seaplanes have become a popular tourism and transportation means due to the ability of them to take off and land on water (Xia et al., 2020). In fact, seaplane services got a fillip when tourism potentials were realized and tourism destinations started promoting seaplane tourism as well to diversify the attractions to attract tourists. There are two aspects seaplanes have much significance in the realm of tourism. One is that some of the natural, aesthetic and enchanting tourist attractions are located remotely, which cannot be accessed by land transport as well as by land planes. In such cases, particularly when water bodies are surrounded, seaplanes have much tourist importance. Seaplanes are also used for a ride over some water bodies as well as beautiful landscapes and to reach some ideal location, which gives a great tourist experience. Such trips can provide a bird's-eye view of the picturesque landscape to have a memorable experience. Some of the beach tourism locations are accessed well by seaplanes. Many tourist destinations added exciting seaplane tours as well in their spectrum of tourist attractions. Seaplanes are used for city tours as well. In most of the short tours, seaplane provides water take-off and landing to give a breath-taking experience. Usually, comfortable window seats are offered.

11.9 Hot-air ballooning tourism

Hot-air ballooning tourism is a popular tourism activity in many parts of the world. Tourists who engage in this activity often enjoy the quiet ride and the bird's-eye view of the world below. Hot-air ballooning tours are organized widely in many locations. In many cases, these, which can provide exciting feeling, are part of the bundle of tourism activities in destinations. Having a 360-degree view of beautiful sites, hovering high and low on a thrilling hot-air balloon ride constitutes the exciting experience for the tourists. While on balloons, tourists can enjoy a romantic getaway in the skies, fly over scenic attractions and urbanscapes. This segment has been growing at a steady rate in some regions particularly. For instance, "hot-air balloon tourism, which is constantly growing and increasingly demanded since the beginning of the 1990s in Turkey, has become an important attraction among the tourism activities carried out especially in the Cappadocia Region" (Acar & Altas, 2017). Rides are organized on a wide variety of landscapes, including deserts, mountain ranges, valleys, cities, historical sites and protected forest areas.

According to Bertan (2020), hot-air ballooning provides an unforgettable tourism experience, particularly the factors associated with happiness, satisfaction, and spending level that are positively impacted by the support given for the improvement of hot-air balloon activities by the authorities and operators in the destination. Destinations usually keep this as an ideal recreational option for those visiting the destination. Balloon rides are organized at ideal locations. The duration for it may vary, from 30 to 90 minutes or even more. There are tailored rides for special occasions as well. Customized packages are offered to suit the specific needs of groups as well. Destinations with hot-air ballooning are marketed by highlighting ballooning experience as well. It is promoted as the best way to experience the sites, by floating on balloons to see the incredible landscape from the air. Buffet breakfast/lunch with a glass of champagne/coffee/tea, memorable souvenirs, etc., are offered as part of hot-air ballooning ride packages to increase attractiveness. Guide services are also arranged when the ride is over the heritage destinations and urban location in order to interpret the features. At times, hot-air ballooning rides are part of the tours into historic sites and heritage destinations as well. Therefore, the tourist can experience the visit both from land as well as air and the experience will be multiplied by the clubbing of both.

11.10 Paragliding, hand gliding and paramotoring

Paragliding has been promoted as part of recreational tourism activities and some regions integrate it into their marketing mix strategies aimed at pursuing the potential tourists to visit (Costa & Chalip, 2005). "Paragliding is an exciting form of air adventure that satisfies the tourists' need, thereby explaining why it has become a popular adventure activity" (Ayazlar, 2015). Paragliding is a parachute-based sport. No fixed rigid framework is there. The rectangular parachute used by the glider is inflated as the user runs down a hill and the required lift is produced by baffles that are sewn into the leading edge, along with steering possibilities using hands with the toggles attached to the parachute's lines (Costa & Chalip, 2005). Paragliding

> can range from simple rides from the top of a hill, or a trek to the top of a mountain from which one can glide down the valley. For the daring that seek something more, paragliding also offers aerobatic manoeuvres, cross-country flights and official competitions. Its appeal to all thrill-seekers throughout the world lies in its ease of use and the affordable price and it is now promoted in almost all countries around the globe.
>
> (Mekinc & Music, 2015)

Paragliding gives an experience with a feel of weightlessness while floating through the air. Some of the operators arrange guide services as well, and they drive the gliders up to certain high on mountains, etc., and the gliding starts from there. Some operators provide complimentary like beverage coupons to have it after the flight.

Hang gliding has a slight difference with paragliding. The difference is associated with structure, equipment and weight. Hang gliding equipment has a metal rigid frame with a triangular shape and the parachute canopy acts as a wing and is more rigid. Moreover, managing a hang gliding is bit more difficult than paraglide.

Paramotoring is powered paragliding. A fixed frame is there that combines the motor, propeller, harness (with integrated seats) and cage. The participant sits in the cage (trike) along with the pilot. It has an engine, which is needed only for gaining altitude, and then, the parachute will provide the needed support to float. It is one of the easiest and most convenient kinds of motorized flying. In addition, it is considered very safe particularly due to its low speed during launching and landing and high stability. This has been gaining increasing significance in tourism.

11.10.1 Parasailing in tourism

Parasailing is a common recreational activity in many of the coastal tourist sites across the world. It takes place when someone is towed by a boat while connected to a parachute that is specially designed for this purpose. While the boat moves ahead fast, the sail gets the lift to reach a certain altitude, and then, the partici- pant can sail through the air. The fun in the activity is associated with soaring high effortlessly attached to a gorgeously designed parachute. In many beach tourist centres, parasailing is a major activity that attracts visitors. Usually, parasailing is done for a single person, but depending upon the power of the boat, two or three people can parasail in a single trip.

11.11 Skydiving

Certainly, flying in a plane itself is a nice experience and when it is over a land- scape with beautiful scenery around, the experience gets enhanced. In addition, once you fly, if you get an opportunity to jump out of it, the experience would be thrilling and adrenaline high. Skydiving gives an opportunity for the same. It is all about the descent of an adventure seeker from an aircraft while in flight and uses a parachute to land. It is a free fall for some moments and then descending down with the help of the parachute. The descend starts from thousands of me- tres above the earth surface. According to United States Parachutes Association (USPA), skydive represents "The descent of a person to the surface from an air- craft in flight when he or she uses or intends to use a parachute during all or part of that descent" (USPA, 2018). The nature of the aircraft may vary from lighter- than-air to small heavier-than-air aircraft. The height of fall is usually more than 2,000 metres above the earth's surface. Skydiving-related trips constitute a niche sector, and packages are offered across the world to experience skydiving by the enthusiasts. Though this activity has been there since the 1700s, it emerged as a recreational option recently only. Necessary training and precautions have to be undertaken prior to take part in this adventurous sport. Tour operators and travel agents arrange trips for the enthusiasts to take part in this sport. Group skydiving has increased significance nowadays.

Table 11.8 Skydiving Styles

United States Parachutes Association (USPA) identifies the following skydiving types to conduct competitions

Canopy Formation	Canopy Piloting
In this, the divers open their parachutes soon after exiting the aeroplane and then proceed to make different formations by linking them together using feet in flight. Types include 2-Way Team Sequential, 4-Way Team Rotation, and 4-Way Team Sequential	Divers fly their parachutes through a prescribed course over water and land. Speed, distance and accuracy are the parameters used for measuring performance

(*Continued*)

Table **11.8** (Continued)

Artistic Events (Freestyle and Freefly)	Wingsuit Flying (Acrobatic and Performance)
In the freestyle, the flyers perform a sequence of moves, like fluid and ballet-like movements, for compulsory and creative points during freefall In the other category, vertical free fall, either head-down, stand-up or a sit position, as well as all the movements in between are entertained. Two performers are needed for this and the performance includes fluid movement in every axis and intricate choreography	Wingsuit flying performance consists of a single flyer passing through a 1,000-metre vertical course. Maximum distance, speed or time of flight, one jump of each per round is the tasks, which are assessed using GPS mounted on the helmet. Acrobatic type accommodates two flyers performing manoeuvres in formation flight, and the number of formations and the quality of transitions are the performance parameters
Freefall Style	Accuracy Landing
This category includes the performance in a prescribed sequence of manoeuvres in freefall as correctly and as quickly as possible	The performers fly their parachutes down to land on the centre of a target, which is a very small one, of 2 cm diameter
Formation Skydiving	Mixed Formation and Vertical Formation Skydivings
This is basically a freefall jump and it is needed to perform a designated formation or a sequential series of formations with precise intermediate manoeuvres drawn from a "dive pool". Different types are there like 4-Way, 8-Way, 10-Way and 16-Way.	In the mixed freefall type, a sequence of formations is performed while flying in three different orientations, such as vertical head-down, vertical upright and belly-to-earth (flat). In the other category, they perform a sequence of formations in a head-down or upright, vertical axis

Source: Modified from United States Parachutes Association (USPA), data available online at https://uspa.org/Competition/Disciplines

11.12 Air safari

Air safari, simply, denotes exploring the scenic attractions and wildlife from the sky with the help of either a lighter-than-air aircraft or small heavier-than-air aircraft suitable in specific locations. Powered parachutes, paramotors, small single- or double-engine aircraft, helicopters, trikes, paragliders and powered parachutes are used in this context. Air safaris in Africa are popular, dragging tourists from all over the world. Some of the heavier-than-air aircraft used in African safaris include Cessna Caravan, Cessna 206, 208 and 210, and King Airs and Islanders (twin engine). Such lightweight aircraft have seating capacity vary from 4 to 20.

Using lightweight aircraft has some specific advantages than just seeing scenic places from the air. Aircraft can land inside the parks, and thus, safari can be started immediately and increased time can be there to have expeditions inside the forestlands. These safaris usually opt weight restrictions as big luggage can be uncomfortable in lightweight aircraft. Some of the air safaris into African destinations have stay in tents and forest lodges along with safari on automobiles suitable for venturing inside the forests.

11.13 Kite boarding/kite surfing

This is another adventurous recreational activity, which is also promoted in tourist destinations in order to attract tourists and to diversify the product range over there. According to International Kite Boarding Association, kite boarding is

> a surface water (also snow and land) sport combining aspects of sailing, wakeboarding, windsurfing, surfing and paragliding, into one extreme sport. A kite boarder harnesses the power of the wind with a large controllable power kite to be propelled across the water on a kite board similar to a wakeboard or a small surfboard, with or without foot straps or bindings.
>
> (IKA, International Kite boarding Association)

Of late, kite surfing has increased significance in tourism, particularly in the coastal tourism areas, since the popularity of the sport is increasing remarkably. On water surfaces, kite boarder makes use of a board to surf over water and the kite is connected to his or her harness, which is worn around boarder's body. Minimum wind speed is required to undertake this sport. Inflatable kites (C-Kite, Bow Kite, Delta Kite, Hybrid Kite) and foil kites are commonly used in kite surfing across the world (www.surftoday.com). This is an adrenalin high water sport, though it is done on other surfaces as well.

Table 11.9 Kite Boarding Types

Kite Skiing (snow kiting or kite snow skiing)	Kite Buggying (buggy kiting or power kiting)
The kite pulls the boarder over the snow	Instead of a board in which the broader stands, kite buggy, a 3-wheeled vehicle, is used
Kite Skate boarding	Kite land boarding
This is done on land using a trainer kite and a skateboard	Boarding on open land using a land board
Kite Skim Boarding	Wakestyle kiteboarding
This is just a variation of kite boarding, in which the board used is skimboard	This is also similar to freestyle, but it includes features like kickers, rails or even natural obstacles

Source: Modified from Air Parade, http://www.airpadrekiteboarding.com/what-is-kiteboarding.html

Some other aircraft-related recreational activities are also there which need a high level of experience and expertise. **Aerobatics (aerial acrobatics)** involves the performance of flying manoeuvres using aircraft. Powered as well as glider aircraft are used. It is basically a skilful display of flying as well. **Drone racing** is another recreational activity, which has caught the growth momentum recently. First-person view (FPV) systems are used now in drone racing. It denotes a

> sport where drone pilots strive to build extremely fast and agile multi-rotors (otherwise known as drones) to fly around a set course as fast as possible....FPV is a type of drone flying where pilots use cameras to fly drones as if they were sitting in the cockpit. Some pilots fly using FPV monitors, whereas others use specialized FPV goggles to give them a more immersive experience.
>
> (Smith, 2015)

Cross-country **air racing** is also in vogue in some locations.

11.14 Spacecraft and tourism

Spacecraft simply represents a specially designed vehicle for flying in space. It is more of a generic term used to denote a vehicle meant for space travel. Usually, it carries small rocket engines in order to manoeuvre and orient in space (www.britania.com). They are used for varied purposes, like meteorological purposes, earth mission and communication. Spaceship, another term used in the parlance of space movements, is "designed to travel in space and may be launched from Earth by a launch vehicle. It may carry a payload to accomplish a mission with or without people and return to Earth" (NASA, 1996). The term space shuttle denotes a reusable spacecraft designed to transport into space and back again, carrying people, cargo and at times satellites or other equipment into orbit. Rocket is another term used, in the space mission, which represents a vehicle that launches into space as well as a type of engine meant for space missions (NASA, 2010). Robotic spacecraft are there, and according to NASA, they are specially designed and developed systems, which can function in specific hostile environments; the following are the different types of such spacecraft (NASA, 2003).

- Flyby spacecraft
- Orbiter spacecraft
- Atmospheric spacecraft
- Lander spacecraft
- Rover spacecraft
- Penetrator spacecraft
- Observatory spacecraft
- Communications spacecraft.

In the parlance of space tourism, a wide variety of such vehicles is used, like winged vehicles, vertical rockets with capsules and high-altitude balloons. Some of the advanced spacecraft that are experimentally used for space tourism are given in the following section.

11.15 Space tourism

When the new millennium began, another landmark was marked in the history of tourism. Space tourism, another futuristic tourism type, was begun by an incredible sojourn of a tourist into space. Even before that, terrestrial space tourism has been underway for some years, and leisure trip to outer space has been anticipated for years (Ashford, 1990). It was in 2001, Dennis Tito, an American businessman and former JPL scientist, had a recreational trip to space with a reported cost of USD 20 million. This event got much attention from many space travel enthusiasts. Sooner, the next tourist had a recreational journey onto the space. Mark Shuttleworth, the second space tourist, had a journey in the very next year and wandered in the space for eleven days, at almost the same cost. Yet, the same could not become a commercial activity though many are in the queue, waiting for getting an opportunity to visit space.

Recently, two billionaires, marking another milestone in the history of space tourism, had space tour ventures. Richard Branson reached the edge of space on board Virgin Galactic rocket plane and Jeff Bezos made a suborbital flight into space on Blue Origin's New Shepard launch vehicle.

Space tourism is envisaged as a commercial activity, which can involve the temporary movement of people from the earth using a spacecraft or aircraft to experience the space travel. It also represents "an industry where customers pay for travel to space" (Livingston, 2010). According to European Space Agency (ESA) (2008), space tourism represents "suborbital flights by privately funded and/or privately operated vehicles and the associated technology development driven by the space tourism market". Next, orbital space tourism is also being ventured. It is "another niche segment of the aviation industry that seeks to give tourists the ability to become astronauts and experience space travel for recreational, leisure, or business purposes" (Henderson & Tsui, 2019). Another definition by Revfine makes the concept of space tourism easy to understand. According to it, space tourism is all about the "activity of travelling into space for recreational purposes. It is sometimes referred to as citizen space exploration, personal spaceflight, or commercial human spaceflight, and it covers spaceflights which are suborbital, orbital, and even beyond the earth orbit" (www.revfine.com).

Certainly, space tourism is a niche tourism category, and it cannot be a mass tourism type in the immediate future also. Even terming it as niche tourism is difficult since the scope of the market size is very small in the immediate future. Moreover, strong desire and willingness to experience space travel are inevitable to be part of this. "'Space tourism' activities may thus include the use of an aircraft and/or spacecraft" (Hobe, 2007). Space tourism activities may range from long-term stays in orbital facilities to short-term orbital or suborbital flights, along with parabolic flights that provide short periods of weightlessness to passengers (Hobe & Cloppenburg, 2004). Space tourism contributes a share in the rapid commercialization of outer space (Spector & Higham, 2019). When space tourism begins on a commercial basis, it is predicted to grow vigorously up to and including large-scale lunar tourism, particularly since the scope for enormous pent-up demand and advancements in engineering (Collins, 2006).

According to Crouch (2001), the evolution and development of space tourism have been facing a number of hurdles. Travelling to space is a costly affair and many reports say that in the short run, space tourism will gain important status due to the use of short suborbital flight. Attempts for orbital space tourism were began with the ambition of having larger numbers of tourists into space to generate sufficient economies of scale and learning effects, which will result in a reduction in the cost per passenger soon (Commercial Space Transportation Study 1994, reported in Crouch, 2001). Space tourism has to include the market for the product and the means of transport along with the destination. Page (2007) opines that in the long run, enhanced space tourism possibilities will be there due to the availabilities of short earth orbital flights using reusable spacecraft and the making of space hotels located around earth's orbit. It is forecast that in the future space tourism options will not only include the ability to travel to destinations in space, but also activities such as orbital flight or the ability to stay in space-based hotels or stations (Cooper et al. 2008).

NASA opened the International Space Station (ISS) for tourists, which can accommodate a dozen tourists each year for a maximum of thirty days. Another space hotel called "Aurora Station", which can accommodate four paying guests and two crewmembers, is being built by a firm called Orion Span. Different types of space tourism are there now. Suborbital and orbital space tourism are two prominent categories. According to Livingston (2010), while suborbital space tourism let the tourist to go to space and come back down without entering orbit, the orbital space tourism ensures at least one full orbit of the Earth before returning to Earth. Moreover, point-to-point space tourism is also there, which offers less than a full-orbit trip and the launch and landing sites are different. Crouch et al. (2009) classified the following types of space tourism trips:

- High-altitude jet fighter flights
- Atmospheric zero-gravity flights
- Short-duration suborbital flights
- Longer-duration orbital trips into space.

The travel motivation in space tourism is yet to be studied well. Yet Reddy et al. (2012) identified the following motivational factors behind space tourism (in order of importance).

- Vision of earth from space
- Weightlessness
- High-speed experience
- Unusual experience
- Scientific contribution.

Table 11.10 Space Tourism Activities

Acceleration G force	Participate in science, research and academic projects
View or Earth	View both day and night
Earth observation	Reentry G's, etc.
Freely floating in weightlessness	

Source: Adapted from Livingston (2010).

Space tourism is expected to grow since a share of the population has "allo-centric" characteristics of the tourists, who want to experience the variety and something unusual. Similar opinion is given by Reddy et al. (2012), which says that the tourism market will include "tourists who are interested in doing something new and unusual from the adventure tourism sphere as well as the established space-related interests such as viewing Earth from the space (rather than for scientific purposes)". There are early attempts to mention the space tourism markets. For instance, according to the National Space Society, the potential space tourism markets include the existing markets consisting of extreme sports enthusiasts who seek the excitement of experiencing a new sensation of high acceleration and zero gravity and the very rich leisure travellers (NSS, 2009).

As indicated earlier, a number of space travel enthusiasts are waiting for the chance to fly into the space to have a different experience. Yet, the same is not adequate enough to be accounted as a commercial activity that can define the demand and its determinants clearly. Demand for space tourism is yet to define well as the sector is still in the pre-infant stage. Varied assumptions are there, though there are a number of people, particularly with higher income levels, who have intimated their willingness to be part of space sojourns. The demand description can be done once the scope of space tourism is realized in a commercial manner, which may take place a few more years. There are many references that a large number of enthusiasts who are willing to pay high rates to experience space trips, and once space accommodation is fully realized, the demand for short space travel may grow many-fold (Collins et al., 1994). Difference in opinion is also there, like Spector and Higham (2019) argued. According to them,

> While space tourism developments are motivated by a very small cadre of individuals, companies, and governments, the concomitant impacts extend throughout human societies, across the planet, and even into the cosmos. Despite the claims of pro-space narratives, a tiny fraction of humankind – the 'space billionaires,' the investors backing them, and a select number of extremely wealthy tourists – rather than the entire species, is not only driving forward ambitious space tourism programmes but is also primed to attain most of the benefits available in outer space.
>
> (Spector and Higham, 2019)

Astro-tourism is also with similar intent but with a different concept. Fayos-Solà and Marín (2009) define astro-tourism as the "tourism using the natural resource of unpolluted night skies for astronomical, cultural or environmental activities". SPACE India opines that astro-tourism offers travellers the unique opportunity to satisfy their curiosity and learn truths about the mysterious skies (space-india.com). Space Camps to NASA, Archeo-Astronomy, Star Parties, Astrophotography, etc., are some of their astro-tourism programmes (Table 11.11).

The following are some of the major companies, along with their major designated spacecraft, involved in the space tourism ventures currently.

Table 11.11 Case: Space Tourism Competition

Though only a handful of companies are competing neck and neck to be leaders in the emerging market of space tourism, the type of the products that they may offer vary from one firm to another. The major difference lies in the fact that whether the passenger reaches suborbital and orbital space. That difference makes notable distinctions in the cost, experience and even risk of what it means to be a space tourist. According to a report, with both suborbital and orbital together, it has a potential market value of $3 billion by 2030. Virgin Galactic and Blue Origin compete in the sector of suborbital tourism. Suborbital tourism reaches an altitude of about 100 kilometres (or 330,000 feet) and gives passengers a few minutes in space

Orbital tourism too has strong contenders. This category involves cruising at an altitude of over 400 kilometres (or 1.3 million feet) and spends days or even more than a week in space. This type of space tourism, up till now, has been limited to a few flights to the ISS that used the Russian Soyuz spacecraft. SpaceX, with its Falcon 9 rocket and Crew Dragon capsule, has recently entered the orbital tourism arena. Along with Crew Dragon, Boeing's Starliner capsule is also designed to carry as many as seven passengers. As per reports, Boeing's contract with NASA to fly four astronauts at a time, the company is allowed to sell the fifth seat to prospective space tourists. While SpaceX is working on its next-generation Starship rocket, Crew Dragon and Starliner may remain the two best options for orbital tourists

There are orbital brokers and services in the space tourism arena. They are helped find interested passengers and get them ready to launch. Space Adventures, Axiom Space and Virgin Galactic are examples of this category. The US-based Space Adventures has flown seven tourists using Russian spacecraft. Space Adventures, in collaboration with SpaceX, using Crew Dragon capsule, plans to enable four tourists on a "free-flyer" mission to orbit. Houston-based start-up Axiom Space is also on a similar 10-day mission. Axiom acts to provide varied services to the space tourism aspirants, from training to management and more. Virgin Galactic also plans to be a player in the provision of the orbital tourism service

---

Source: Michael Sheetz (2020), How SpaceX, Virgin Galactic, Blue Origin and others compete in the growing space tourism market, www.cnbc.com, data available online at https://www.cnbc.com/2020/09/26/space-tourism-how-spacex-virgin-galactic-blue-origin-axiom-compete.html

- Virgin Galactic
    It is a major spaceflight company involved in the making and use of the next generation of reusable space vehicles. The following spacecraft are built for space tourism.
    o   White Knight Two: It, with four engines and two fuselages, can fly high at an altitude of 50,000 feet above the earth.
    o   SpaceShipTwo: It, powered by a hybrid rocket motor, can carry eight passengers and is reusable as well.
- Blue Origin
    Blue Origin Federation is a privately funded firm involved in aerospace manufacturing and suborbital spaceflight services. The following are their spacecraft of relevance now.

- New Shepard (NS-12): A reusable suborbital rocket system that can carry people and research payloads past the Kármán line (space boundary). With speed up to Mach 3, the space enthusiasts can return to Earth in the capsule's parachutes.
- SpaceX
  This, another major aerospace manufacturer and space transportation service company, also offers commercial flights for people to both Earth and lunar orbits. The following are their major spacecraft intended for space tourism:
  - Dragon: It can carry seven passengers to earth orbit and beyond and its pressurized section of the capsule can carry both people and environmentally sensitive cargo.
  - Tarship: it is a reusable one that can carry passengers and cargo to earth's orbit, the Moon, Mars and beyond.
- Boeing
  Boeing, one of the largest aircraft manufacturing companies in the world, is involved in spacecraft technology as well. The following is an example of one of its spacecraft.
  - CST-100 Starliner: Crew Space Transportation (CST)-100 Starliner, a reusable one up to ten times, can carry seven passengers, for a low-earth orbit mission.

11.16 Conclusion

The introduction of jet engines and wide-body aircraft is the milestone that had remarkable contribution in the history of aviation. Nowadays, the most modern aircraft enhances the travel experience and contribute in the overall tourist experience. Innovation is a regular phenomenon in aircraft design, and the current focus is on increasing efficiency in flying with maximum fuel efficiency and low emissions. Aircraft are powered by an engine that lifts from the dynamic action of air against fixed wings. The complex structure of the aircraft includes fuselage, engine, wings, tail structure and landing gear. The four forces acting on a flight are lift, weight, thrust and drag. The movements of an aircraft include yawing, pitching and rolling due to the action of the aircraft components. Aircraft are heavier-than-air and lighter-than-air categories. The former receives lifts from aerodynamic forces while the latter is lighter than air, gas filled and used for recreational purposes. Aircraft are classified on a diverse basis of engines, range, Mach number and number of wings. Another classification of aircraft is based on the purpose of flight, which is civil aircraft and military aircraft. Yet another classification of the aircraft is based on the volume/width of them which is narrow-body and wide-body aircraft. Airbus, Boeing, Tupolev, Bombardier, ATR, Embraer and McDonnell Douglas Corporation are the world's leading aircraft manufacturers. Aircraft manufacturers use engines manufactured by other companies like Rolls-Royce plc. (UK), Pratt & Whitney (P&W) (USA) and General Electric (GE Aircraft Engines) (USA).

Aircraft with jet engines took aviation to new heights and later greatly contributed to the development of modern tourism. Wide-body aircraft is a trendsetter in international tourism by triggering long-haul mass tourism in the 1970s. Helicopter tourism is gaining importance in many parts of the world and is of varied kinds like heli-fly fishing, heli-picnicking and heli-wine tours, heli-skiing, heli-biking, heli-hiking and heli-mountaineering. Seaplane services got a fillip when tourism destinations started promoting seaplane tourism to diversify the attractions to attract tourists. Hot-air ballooning is very popular in many parts of the world and includes rides in a variety of landscapes, including deserts, mountains, valleys, cities, historical sites, protected forest areas and vineyards. Paragliding, hang gliding, paramotoring, parasailing, air safari, kite boarding and skydiving are other forms of recreational activities that are widely accepted around the world. Space tourism is the incredible voyage of a tourist into space, started by another type of futuristic tourism. Space tourism is a niche tourism sector that will not be a mass tourism sector in the near future and it is still in the infancy stage.

Sample questions

Short/medium answer-type questions

- Identify the parts of an aircraft.
- Distinguish between heavier-than-air and lighter-than-air aircraft.
- Give a brief account of wide-body aircraft.
- Identify major aircraft manufacturers.
- Explain how jet engines and wide-body aircraft contributed in the evolution of tourism.
- Give a brief account of the use of seaplane in tourism.
- What is hot-air ballooning?
- Differentiate between paragliding and paramotoring.
- Write about the use of kites and balloons in tourism.
- Identify the scope of space tourism.
- What are the different types of space tourism activities?

Essay type questions

- Write an essay on the use of helicopters in the realm of tourism.
- Explain the contribution of aircraft in the evolution of tourism.
- Elaborate the recreational use of aircraft in destinations.

Suggested readings

Avery, P. (2018). Aircraft load planning and control. In Bruce, P., Gao, Y., & King, J. M. (Eds.), *Airline Operations: A Practical Guide*. London: Routledge, pp. 220–238.
Cole, S. (2015). Space tourism: Prospects, positioning, and planning. *Journal of Tourism Futures*, 1(2), 131–140. https://doi.org/10.1108/JTF-12-2014-0014.
Encyclopedia of Aircraft (2014). *Bath*. UK: North Parade Publishing.
O'Connell, J. F., & Williams, G. (2016). *Air Transport in the 21st Century: Key Strategic Developments*. London: Routledge.
Rhoades, D. L. (2014). *Evolution of International Aviation: Phoenix Rising*. London: Routledge.

Role of tourism in air transport

12.1 Introduction

The incredible growth of tourism created profound impacts on air transportation in multiple ways. Air transport industry depends on diverse sectors to generate demand, and of those sectors, tourism is a major one having varying effects. In addition to the inducement in the air travel demand, tourism progress could alter the global geographical spread of aviation sector, changes in the industry structure, shifts in traffic flows, industry expansion and quality and efficiency enhancement. In some regions, the effect on air transport demand is high, like in the case of remote and island international tourist destinations. In fact, the role of tourism in air transport is a less studied area and needs further empirical researches in order to explore further the nuances of tourism, both domestic and international, on air transport. The tourism and air transport literature elaborates the role of air transport in tourism reasonably well, though quite often points out that both the sectors are mutually dependent. Certainly, there exists a strong reciprocal and symbiotic relationship between tourism and air transport (Bieger &

Wittmer, 2006; Forsyth, 2010). The growth of tourism since the end of the Second World War depends greatly on the advancements in air transport. Similarly, the widespread development and global promotion of tourism could give rise to ripples in the air transport sector across the world. Air transport became a global business sector with the help of tourism as well. Some remote regions became part of the air transport network due to tourism development.

The developments in tourism sector reflect on air transport sector as well. Certainly, the phenomenal expansion of tourism industry at the global level has critical effect on the air transport geography. Growth rate in air traffic is also pegged with rising figures in international tourist arrivals for the last seven decades or so. From an economic perspective, in addition to the revenue potentials, tourism contributes a share in generating employment opportunities of varied kinds within air transport sector. Air transport-related seasonality patterns have shifts in some regions in the wake of tourism demand. Tourism sector demands efficient transport infrastructure, and the recent incidents indicate the increasing pressure among destinations to insist on enhancing air transport infrastructure. This directly leads in air transport development over there. Lohmann and Duval (2014) identified three parallels between tourism and transport, which are more relevant in the case of air transport and tourism. They are regulatory synergies, objective function and shared emphasis on sustainability. There can be "Regulatory synergies" that can emerge between transport and tourism which denotes that the regulation in one sector can have a meaningful and direct effect on the other; for example, tourism marketing can boost air transport and, on the other hand, new airline business models can enhance tourist arrivals. In the case of objective function, this means that similar things are involved in both of them, though the nature of them may be different. For instance, personal mobility is part of both, but the end results vary. While both the sectors complement each other, tourism and air transport evolved into the modern form taking the support mutually. This chapter explores various aspects associated with the effect of tourism on air transportation.

12.2 Increasing tourist arrivals and shifts in travel pattern

The history of tourism dates back to several centuries. Yet, the modern form of tourism has a beginning sometime after the end of the Second World War. The international tourist arrival figures since 1950 have recorded a consistent growth, though there were some setbacks in between for short durations. Those setbacks were primarily due to crises of diverse kinds. But, whenever decline in tourist arrivals occurred, the tourism sector had shown extreme resilience to bounce back to the growth trajectory.

Let us have an analysis of international tourist arrivals to get an idea about the changes in tourist traffic since 1950. A change in international tourist arrivals can be seen which reveals that the scope for international tourism in the eastern hemisphere of the globe is increasing whereas that in the west is observed to have consolidation in terms of growth in tourist arrivals. The data considered for analysis are from the published data of WTO at different points of time. In 1950, when

Table 12.1 International Tourist Arrivals (Million)

Regions	1990	1995	2000	2005	2010	2015	2016	2017	2018
Europe	264.8	309.3	384.1	452.7	487.7	605.1	619.5	673.3	710.0
Asia and the Pacific	57.7	85.0	114.9	154.1	208.2	284.1	306.0	324.0	347.7
Americas	92.8	109.0	128.2	133.3	150.4	194.1	201.3	210.8	215.7
Africa	15.2	20.4	28.2	34.8	50.4	53.6	57.7	62.7	67.1
Middle East	10.0	14.3	25.2	33.7	55.4	58.1	55.6	57.7	60.5
Advanced economies		342	430	469	515	655	686	730	762
Emerging economies		189	250	339	437	540	554	598	639
World	441	538	681	809	952	1195	1240	1329	1401

Source: Data collected from international tourism statistics published by UNWTO at different periods.

the modern tourism was taken off as a significant economic force, the number of international tourist arrivals was merely 25.3 million (UNWTO, 2000). Of them, the vast majority travelled to European countries and the American continent, particularly to the USA. Europe received 16.8 million, and Americas received 7.5 million tourists, and that constitute 96% of the total tourist arrivals. Africa, Asia and the Pacific, and the Middle East received only marginal share during then. When it turned 2,000, tourist arrivals were raised to 687 million, of which Europe received 395 million and Americas got 128 million (UNWTO, 2002). The share of Americas and Europe together constitutes 76%, a drop from 96% in 1950.

In 2018, Europe received 710 million arrivals and the American continent received 215.7 million, which altogether makes 925.7 million, which is around 66% of the total arrivals. In a span of 68 years, the share of the Europe and Americas together declined from 96% to 66%. This means that the rest of the world increased their share. In the same, remarkable progress has been done by Asia-Pacific and Middle East regions together. In 1990, they had a share of 15 percentage of the total arrivals. But, in 2018, it has increased to 29 percentage. Furthermore, the emerging economies have progressed remarkably over the years. Their share in the world's arrivals was 35% in 1995, and it has turned to 45% in 2015. All the above state that the developed countries, particularly that belong to the west, face a sluggish growth in terms of tourist arrivals and the rest of the world has advanced well. Asia-Pacific region and the Middle East have progressed commendably over the same era.

The regions such as Asia and the Pacific, Africa and the Middle East have been growing at a good rate, and Table 12.2 reveals that the Asia-Pacific region has significantly grown over the four decades. Europe's share has decreased from 71% in 1979 to 59% in 1999 and further down to 51% by 2019. To sum up, the rest of the regions have crept into the global market shares of the US and Europe, though they were also growing, which was outpaced by the growth of other regions. This trend was visible in the air transport growth as well, as discussed in Chapter 3. Therefore, it can be stated that the shifts in tourist arrival patterns at a

Role of tourism in air transport

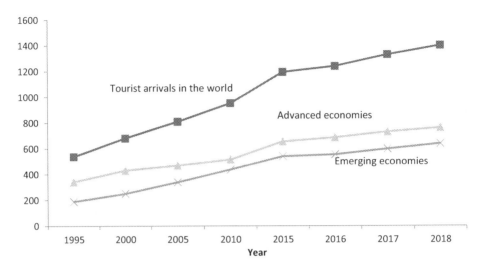

Figure 12.1 International tourist arrivals

Table 12.2 Comparison of International Tourist Arrivals in Regions

	Percentage of Total Arrivals		
Region	1979	1999	2019
Africa	2	4	5
Americas	19	19	15
Asia-Pacific	6	16	25
Europe	71	59	51
Middle East	2	3	4

Source: Tourism Highlights of the World Tourism Organization (UNWTO) of 1981 and 2000 and UNWTO Tourism Barometer January 2020.

macro-level globally are matching with the shifts in air passenger traffic patterns as well.

Regarding the purpose of travel, according to the latest statistics, leisure tourists dominate in international tourism. This has been the trend for several decades, though the business travel had a better share a couple of decades ago. When leisure tourism is more, it means low-cost carriers (LCCs) also have a correlation with it.

UNWTO summarizes the trends in tourism, as per 2018 status, in the following manner (UNWTO, 2019). Asia and the Pacific recorded the highest growth in tourism arrivals, closely followed by Africa. Europe still leads in international tourism with half of the world's international arrivals, followed by Asia and the Pacific

Table 12.3 Mode of Transport Used in International Tourism: Comparison between 1988 and 2018

Mode of Transport	1988	2018	Change in 2 Decades of Time
Air	43.7%	58%	Phenomenal increase
Road	41.4%	37%	Marginal decrease
Rail	7.0%	2%	Significant decrease
Water/Sea	7.8%	4%	Considerable decrease

Source: UNWTO tourism highlights 2000 and 2019. https://www.e-unwto.org/doi/pdf/10.18111/9789284421152

International tourist arrivals: Purposes of visit

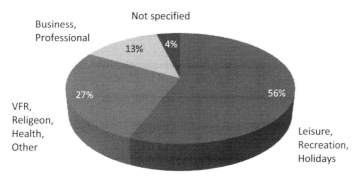

Figure 12.2 International tourist arrivals: purpose of visit

with 1 in 4 arrivals. Leisure travel has been growing as the main purpose of visit in international tourism, except in the Middle East, where visiting friends and relatives (VFR), or for health or religious purposes have a dominant share. Also, the share of travel by tourists using air transport services has increased from 46% in 2000 to 58% in 2018, while land transport (including rail and road) has decreased from 49% to 39% in the same period (UNWTO, 2019). Table 12.3 shows that the decline is much more in rail transport than road transport which has a marginal decline only.

12.3 Catalytic role of tourism development in air transport

Tourism has enormous economic significance, and the development of tourism necessitates the development of transport infrastructure as well. Developing airports, creating multimodal transport system, enhancing interconnectivity, negotiating for international connectivity through air service agreements, etc. become inevitable for the host country/region as part of tourism development. All those can help the air transport sector to flourish further. Moreover, the scope for intra-destination/domestic air transport will also grow. For instance, Fernández et al. (2018) state that, in addition to other factors, commercial air transport is to a large extent determined by tourism, including the "low-cost" passenger model and the "charter" passenger model.

Airports and air transport accessibility is a prime concern in the tourism development agendas. This has been visible over the last several decades. The post-world war era is marked with the increasing urge among nations, particularly the former colonies of European countries, to embrace tourism for quick economic benefits. Considering the socio-economic significance of tourism, the UN has declared 1967 as "International Tourist Year". As part of it, the UN stated the significance of tourism as a basic and most desirable human activity to be considered by all governments. It also emphasises that tourism is an invisible export, which necessitates promotion particularly in developing economies; a tool for understanding, peace and cultural exchange; etc. (www.un.org). This became a stimulator for many economies across the world to move ahead with the tourism development agendas. In the tourism development programmes and plans of countries and regions, transport infrastructure occasioned to be a major component and countries attempt to enhance international transport accessibility.

As mentioned above, the analysis of tourism growth over the years since 1950s reveals the rise of air transportation along with the evolution of modern tourism. Surge in leisure tourism in European countries, particularly, stimulated charter airline sector to innovate and develop. For instance, Bieger and Wittmer (2006) stated that the

> Developments in tourism, especially new forms of tourism and new destinations, also affected air transport by influencing demand. The emergence of attractions such as theme parks or the requirements of second home owners for flexible travels to their secondary property have been important in creating large and regular traffic streams that in Europe are now supporting some low-cost carriers.

In Asian countries, increasing rate of tourism, to a significant extent, is backed by the growth in aviation and, simultaneously, air transport sector over there had to be dynamic and go for adopting newer models in air transportation. Hybridization of airline business models in airline sector is visible in Asian region, and intra-regional tourism has a significant role in the quick evolution of hybrid airlines over there. In the past also, due to the growing tourism demand, there was pressure on air transport infrastructure to expand. For instance, in 1980, Europe experienced the need to expand airport infrastructure greatly. According to the tourism statistics of that era, WTO intimated that airports increased dramatically within Europe and "question arose as to what extent airports, both international and domestic, would be capable of accommodating significant increase in passenger traffic" (WTO, 1980). Along with the dynamic involvement of the authorities in developing tourism and the favourable shifts in the micro- as well as macro-socio-economic environments, tourism industries in those countries emerged as major economic sectors and that stirred the developments and growth of air transport over there substantially. Therefore, tourism assumes a catalytic role in the evolution of air transport.

12.4 Destination evolution and subsequent developments in air transport

Conceptually, tourism expands in a destination in a progressive manner, though the rate of progression may vary from destination to destination. According to Tourism Area Life Cycle (TALC) concept propounded by Butler (1980), a destination passes through various stages in its evolution from a normal place having visit by just a few enthusiasts to a mass tourist destination. Later, it reaches up to a maximum limit, before start declining in terms of tourist arrivals and appeal. He pointed out that there are six or seven distinguishable stages in the life cycle of a destination such as exploration, involvement, development, consolidation, stagnation, decline and rejuvenation. Lohman and Duval (2011) are of the opinion, as there is a symbiotic relationship between air travel and tourism existing, transport sector is being influenced by the attractiveness and the viability of tourist destinations. Here, the same concept is utilized to discuss the nature of air transport evolution through the stages of tourism progress in a destination.

12.4.1 Exploration stage

Exploration stage is marked by the visit of only a few tourists in the destination, which may not have adequate level of accessibility from a tourism perspective. The possible type of tourists who visit over there in this stage consists predominantly of explorers, who tend to shun institutionalized travel, and hence, air transport development is not a matter of concern in the destination.

12.4.2 Involvement

The destination slowly gets to have touristic activities as increased number of outsiders starts to visit over there. Later, there may be some tourists reaching from faraway markets as publicity efforts will begin gradually. As the number of arrivals progresses, local people involvement takes place in a minimum level through the provision of tourist facilities and services in a possible manner. Soon, the pressure will mount on the government to expand infrastructure, which will include air transport accessibility concerns as well.

12.4.3 Development

Furtherance of touristic activities and the progress in influx of tourists, the development stage begins which leads to making of infrastructure development plans and execution of marketing activities at different levels. Air transport development plans become a key component in the respective tourism development plans. There may be regional/national planning initiatives as well which have the link with the respective destination development plans. Airport requirements will be a prominent aspect to address, which will aim at increasing accessibility to airport by increased network of land transport system, to start planning for a new airport if there is no airport at a comfortable distance, or to expand the existing airport to cater to the forecasted increase in traffic flow in the wake of escalating tourism potentials. Development of a destination at international level essentially requires airport expansion matching with the growth rate of tourism. The airports catering to the tourism markets primarily need to assess the airport requirements of the tourist community visiting and the demand patterns. As airport accessibility provisions are set up, steps are taken to attract airlines to start operation connecting the destination with possible cities. At this stage, it is important to work together and to have collaboration between destination authorities and air transport stakeholders to increase tourism demand and capacity growth, and to lower the operating risks for airlines and in ensuring the long-term viability of routes that are set up (Everis/UNWTO, 2012).

A number of tourist arrivals progress at a rapid pace later, along with increased marketing efforts and accessibility. The destination becomes part of itineraries of holiday packages of tour operators.

> Destinations offering important natural or man-made attractions (such as historic cities) are traditionally served by network carriers that find them a suitable base for their mixed traffic streams. On the other hand, destinations with large number of decentralized managed second homes, and thus a need for flexible traffic connections, provide a good market for LCCs. Traditional hotel destinations provide a good basis for charter services, and especially in exclusive segments, for network carriers and regional airlines.
>
> (Bieger & Wittmer, 2006)

As tourism progresses well, airports add non-aeronautical services to provide better shopping and touristic experience. Leisure tourists, due to limited time to spend in the destination for shopping, etc., and prefer to have items bought from the destinations while returning home, can be some of the "highest spenders at the airport although this additionally depends on factors such as country of origin and party size" (Brilha, 2008). Furthering of air transport provisions into the destination, destination authorities need to focus on estimates of tourist flow in the years to come and airline's future plans of expansion. This can be useful for ensuring greater facilities and services in the airports and to extend the infrastructural provisions, like the runways needed, slot requirements and ramp requirements, for the airlines to conduct the increased air transport operations. At this stage, accompanied by the rise in tourist traffic, there may be significant rise in passenger numbers who travel for other reasons due to the possibility of enhancement in the socio-economic and industrial developments in the destination.

12.4.4 Consolidation

Later, though the visitor arrivals increase, there can be a considerable decline in the growth rate of arrivals. By this stage of consolidation, the destination would have reached a full-fledged mass tourism site, having tourism as a major economic sector. Marketing efforts is usually strengthened aiming at extending tourist seasons and markets. At this stage, air transport would still escalate since there is a scope for the evolution of other industries with the scope for inducing passenger as well as cargo transportation. The economic standards of the population will be better with greater socio-economic standards. All such developments can stimulate the growth of air transport as well. Many of the established destinations in the world are now in this stage. Air transport sector will still rise due to the increased opportunities in other sectors as well.

Airports may further expand, and more routes may be there from other cities or by new airlines. Bieger and Wittmer (2006) pointed out that the development of tourism in a destination can contribute in the improvement of the airport over there, attracting new airlines and, over time, enhancing the airport into a hub. According to Cristina (2017), a number of airports diversified the facilities offered, creating tourist attractions in their own right (e.g. Tropical Garden in Changi Airport Singapore, brewery at Munich International Airport and IMAX Cinema at Hong Kong International Airport). In order to increase appeal of the destinations, airports also attempt to enhance the services and facilities. Some destination airports may go for theme-based artistic designs matching with the touristic attractions of the destination, within the passenger terminals.

The destination would have increased business opportunities due to "accelerator effect" emanating from tourism investments. Hence, rise in the traffic inflow may be higher. Tourism traffic will remain the major market for air transport. There can be price war, and hybridization of airline business models can take place. LCC market will be dominated by short-haul leisure tourists. Hybridized and network carriers focus more onto long-haul and hub-to-hub (trunk) routes. Airlines can enjoy the economies of scale. As the destination-based airport has already been elevated into the status of a hub airport, feeder services will get strengthened. Domestic air transport may see increased growth rate, and regional air transport will have much more dynamism. Policy interventions may be there to ease international air transport by engaging in bilateral agreements, and the like, which are detailed in another section below.

While the destination flourishes in terms of tourism and trade, the major airline of that region may have started to use that airport as a hub, and a separate terminal would have been dedicated for its operations. There may be a need for another airport arises due to the limitations of the existing one in accommodating the increasing rate of passengers. Constructing or extending airports and airport services enhance international tourism flows (Khan et al., 2017). For instance, Dubai has become a global destination for trade and tourism activities recently. Though the existing airport could handle several millions of passengers annually, due to rise in both business and leisure travel, along with air traffic for a few other reasons including employment-related mobility, the authorities took strides to establish a new airport that has almost double capacity. Currently, Dubai International Airport is handling almost 90 million passengers per annum (www.khaleej-times.com), but the new airport, Dubai World Central (Al Maktoum International Airport), is expected to have a capacity of handling more than 160 million passengers per year. It will also serve as a multimodal logistics hub for 12 million tonnes of freight (www.dubaiairports.ae). Dubai is still growing at an average rate of more or less 5% (www.dubai-online.com). Its growth rate has not declined which means that it is still in the development stage as the diversification of attractions and increasing business tourism significance making the growth rate sustain for some years to come as well. This is an example in the mid of the evolution of a destination in which remarkable airport expansion and construction of a new airport can be possible and airline network expansion can be phenomenal.

12.4.5 Stagnation

By this stage, the lure of the destination starts waning and the tourist capacity either reached or exceeded. Now, we see a number of incidents of local opposition in well-established destinations against the "over tourism" and related issue for the local people (https://www.e-unwto.org/doi/pdf/10.18111/9789284420070). Many cities with large-scale tourism activities in the major destination countries in the world have been facing the issue of over tourism for a couple of years. Primary focus of air transport services may slowly shift from tourists to other types of passengers. In order to attract the leisure travellers more, airlines may offer cheaper fares increasingly. Leisure tourists are attracted more using pricing strategies by airlines. Unless and until other economic sectors do not cause rise in passenger influx, newer airlines may not have this destination in their priority list for route and network expansion. Charter airlines may still be involved in tourist transport through package holidays organized by tour operators from medium and longer distant markets mainly (Figure 12.3).

12.4.6 Decline and rejuvenation

The decline stage is a challenge for destinations. As visitors start losing for other destination, the negative impacts may rise. The authorities of the destination, at this stage, have to decide to rejuvenate/ relaunch the destination by looking

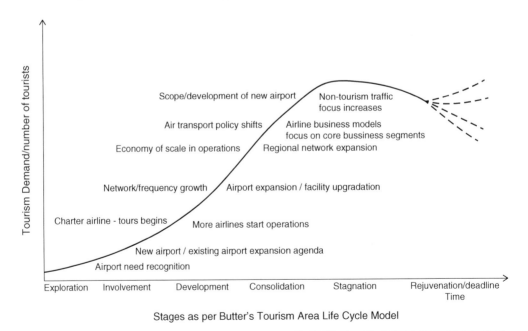

Figure 12.3 Destination evolution and growth of air transport [based on Butler's (1980) Tourism Area Life Cycle model]

at new markets/product diversification. Adding attractions, satellite destinations, etc. are some common strategies to revive tourism. Airport authorities may be involved into the realm of strategy making. Airlines may not find any interest in adding routes, etc. unless and until other reasons are there. Tourism-related air transport will also start weakening.

Hence, the evolution of a mass tourism destination spurs growth and instils dynamism in air transport, and both are mutually dependent while sharing a symbiotic relationship. The following changes and developments can be identified in the realm of air transportation along with the evolution of an international-level mass tourism destination.

1 Air transport, particularly airport, becomes a key element in the destination development plans.
2 The scope of an airport, in the absence of one at a comfortable distance, will be explored.
3 As tourist influx into the destination begins, airlines begin services, and later, more routes will be added.
4 If there is a scope for a new airport, plans and steps will be taken to make it.
5 Charter airlines, by the involvement of tour operators, get trips to the destination.
6 More airlines begin to add the destination in their future expansion plans.
7 As development gathers momentum, airports are forced to expand.
8 Airport service and facility upgradation become compelling.
9 As tourism progresses, airlines may go for bigger aircrafts for services.
10 Increase in long-haul flights
11 Economies of scale in operation.
12 Shopping options within airports get expanded.
13 Airports may add non-aeronautical services.
14 Enhanced regional air transport network.
15 Domestic air transport services are complimented.
16 Increased feeder services for the network carriers/major carriers.
17 Scope for air transport policy shifts, like initiating open skies.
18 Overall quality enhancement in air transport services.
19 Full-service carriers (FSCs) may shift to long haul.
20 LCCs may get lead role in short haul particularly.
21 Possibility of hybridization in airline sector.
22 If needed, plans for a new airport get momentum and may materialize soon.
23 Airline sector witnesses shift towards oligopoly.
24 Non-touristic transport also increases.
25 Cargo transportation increases due to possible export and imports.
26 On the later stages, airlines target non-tourist markets more.

12.5 Tourism and air transport efficiency

It may be interesting to note that tourism can have a role in increasing the efficiency in air transport components. For instance, tourism turned out to be a reason for enhancing airports' efficiency, though contradictory views are also there in the case of LCCs. Fernández et al. (2018), based on an empirical study on 35 airports in Spain, one of the topmost leisure tourist destinations in the world, state

> ... tourist-orientated airports are more efficient than non-tourist-oriented ones. Airports located in eminently tourist areas, such as the major cities in the Balearic and Canary Islands, Alicante and the Costa del Sol, were, on average, 7.2 per cent more efficient than the rest of Spanish airports during the research period.

They further argue, "It appears that the development of LCCs in Spain has transformed tourism and improved airport efficiency. By comparison, we found that the airports with a higher share of charter passengers relative to total airport passengers are less efficient" (Fernández et al., 2018). As tourism grows, airports have the need to make them more attractive for the travelling community who are arriving from various corners of the world.

Airports nowadays attempt to ensure touristic appeal, at times matching with the indigenous themes as well, as part of their efforts to promote both the airport and the destination. Destinations have the increasing pressure to have airports as international gateways into the destinations, which can provide high-quality services. Airport is the first point in an inbound tourism, which can create first impression about the destination. Moreover, airports have the challenge of attracting maximum passengers in this hypercompetitive air transport environment. Ensuring high quality may be a priority of destinations that have immense international tourism potential. The major aspects that air travellers associate airports with a destination, according to Wattanacharoensil et al. (2016), are the following. An airport:

- is a representative of a tourist destination,
- demonstrates the positive characteristics of a destination, and
- is perceived as an inherent element of tourism experience.

These three aspects have extreme significance from a tourism perspective, and, hence, airports have to enhance the quality of services provided to the passengers. Another study by Kirk et al. (2014) points out that a negative airport experience can potentially influence future travel decisions of a traveller to a destination. Akin to airports, airlines may also have to beef up services to attract more and more passengers into tourist destinations. FSCs may have the challenge more to attract more leisure and business travellers, whereas service expectations of passengers in LCCs may not be that much of challenging for them. As stated earlier, air transport has a significant role in the tourist experience, and therefore, it becomes a priority for the components of the air transport system to perform efficiently and to provide quality services. Avoiding delay is another significant aspect for airlines that undertake services to tourist destinations. A holiday travel is for a short term, and hence, a longer flight delay can dampen the leisure expectations of a tourist. The overall efficiency thus covers a number of aspects of air transport, and international tourism in a destination may stimulate the quality, efficiency and attractiveness of air transport linked to the destination.

12.6 Tourism stimulates changes and innovation in air transport

The scope of tourism and the emergence of new destinations stimulate air transport components to get adapted to the emerging requirements thereof. "Tourism is a driving factor for and, in some cases, a stimulator of change in air transport..." (Bieger & Wittmer, 2006). There exists an important stimulating factor from the side of tourism in initiating changes and innovation in air transport. Fernández et al. (2018) states "Tourism is a stimulator of change in air transport, as exemplified by the development of the low-cost and charter passenger models". Mass destinations may prompt all types of airlines, like LCCs, FSCs and hybrid airlines to cater to the increasing travel demand consisting people from all walks of life. Quick expansion of tourism in Asia demanded modified versions of airline services catering to longer haul travel. There arises the scope of hybridization of business model, and hybrid airline now plays a key role. LCCs are particularly significant in leisure tourism. Leisure tourists are relatively more price sensitive, and the rise in short-haul tourism in many regions intensified the LCC sector to expand services and new ones to enter into service. Airport is a good example, which attempt innovations and changes according to the emerging demands in tourism in the region. Airports are key in serving inbound tourists and creating impressions that lasts longer. Moreover, they have a significant role, as stated above, in the tourist experience. As indicated by Wattanacharoensil et al. (2016) in the case of leisure tourist experience, the aspects of functional experience and service personnel of airports are critical in ensuring tourist satisfaction and high-level tourist experience, and other complementary aspects will have a role only when the tourist is happy with the basic aspects. Modernization of the airports to a great extent furthers the appeal of it.

Quality/level of in-flight services and ground handling activities do have a significant role in air transport experience of tourists. This prompts air transport sector to provide the most possible quality service. Punctuality, frequency, features of airports, image of the airport and airline, quality of inflight services, etc. too add to the spectrum of air transport experience. There exists a challenge for airports to add services and facilities to attract more tourists, as there can be financial burdens and limitations in adding and expanding facilities. The concerned people may have to think out of the box to bring in innovation in enhancing touristic appeal of airports. Technological changes have been incorporated into the airports, and the advancements in those are challenging, yet beneficial in smoothening in the operations in imparting greater tourist satisfaction. Tourists are now an increasingly sophisticated segment of passengers, and hence, airports have the challenge to incorporate latest technologies to compete with similar destinations. Large airports nowadays go for artificial intelligence and virtual reality-based solutions to ensure smooth and comfortable flow of travellers within the airports. Having advanced technology for passenger handling within airport can complement the attractiveness of the airports and the overall image of the destination, at large.

12.7 Global marketing

Tourism marketing and promotion activities at local, regional, national and international level certainly result in enhanced demand for air services, and there can be some favourable changes in the policy and regulatory aspects which could supplement the growth in air transport into the destinations. When the customer base is from multiple countries, international tourist destinations, through implementing effective marketing strategies, can induce changes in the structure and nature of air transport from those origin markets to the destinations. For an international tourism destination, markets are foreign countries. Marketing of tourism has heightened complexity due to locational disadvantages as the potential tourists are not the residents of that destination. Travel is fundamental in the tourism process, and its customers/consumers have to travel from the origin place to engage in tourism activities in the destination and to return to the origin place after the visit. Hence, destination marketers need to communicate to an audience situated far away from the destination. In addition, these audiences do not belong to a single place since the tourists emerge from different countries.

Marketers have to be tactful in efficiently communicating to these diverse audiences belonging to different regions in the world. Therefore, marketing communication targets people from different regions and the communication passes to all those regions using a wide variety of media. Organizations undertake marketing mix, a set of diverse marketing strategies undertaken in order to persuade the targeted group of customers to buy the product (Kotler et al., 2013). Among the marketing mix strategies, promotion is the one, which destinations depend more onto reach the target group of customers located far away from them. As part of the process, destinations essentially execute integrated marketing communications (IMC) which involves a combination of tools like advertising, interactive marketing, publicity and public relations to inform, create awareness, stimulate interest and persuade them to visit the destination. In this marketing communication process, destinations get increased awareness and the touristic potentials can entice many from tourism markets to travel and visit the destination. By creating interest and inducing them to travel, the marketing process generates demand for transport sector, predominantly air transport in the case international tourism. The air travel demand generation is from a much wider area, and the established mass tourism destinations can evoke significant and sustainable demand from most of the regions in the world. Together with the increase in tourist flow, airlines may expand network to those destination and hike the frequency of services. Eventually, destination marketing directly affects air transport by accelerating the travel demand, which in turn may lead to changes in the nature and structure of air transport industry associated with the destination. Furthermore, every tourist destination has the potential to supplement into the air travel demand in varying degrees from almost all the tourism markets.

12.8 Network expansion due to the dramatic rise of tourism in emerging markets

While consolidation and stagnation looming large over the destinations in the developed regions, particularly in the west, many new destinations are emerging.

Emerging markets in the tourism paradigm has so much of relevance in international tourism now. Of them, many are fastest growing tourism regions in the world. Some of the Asian countries have been witnessing incredible economic progress and consequent changes in the lifestyle, education and health conditions, for some decades, and for them, tourism development is a priority. Countries like China, Malaysia, Thailand, Singapore, Turkey, UAE, India and Indonesia have become major international destinations within some decades. As discussed before Asia and the Pacific, Africa and the Middle East have advanced remarkably in tourism and add a significant share in international tourism. China is now the number one outbound tourist destination and one among the top five inbound tourism destinations. This phenomenal rise of touristic potentials stirred the need of expanding air transport infrastructure in all those countries. The Asia-Pacific region is achieving an unprecedented growth rate in aviation. With regard to the rise in commercial air transport, according to a report of IATA, "This high growth rate is expected to continue in the coming decades, an observation backed up by the large number of aircraft scheduled for future delivery to carriers in the region. By 2030, it is estimated that air travel in Asia will be greater than Europe and North America combined… However, there is concern that the development of aviation infrastructure in the region is not keeping pace with growth in demand, putting some of the potential future economic benefits of aviation at risk" (InterVistas, 2015). This denotes that there is scope for further expansion of air transport infrastructure as well. Moreover the increasing number of tourist arrivals has effected in the rise of air transport in this region.

To a large extent, the development of transport to stimulate inbound tourism is motivated by the desire of the authorities, particularly the government, to increase tourism revenue, especially in less developed countries seeking to modernize their post-colonial economies (Scheyvens, 2002). As tourism development became mandatory in the emerging destination belonging to developing regions due to the economic reasons, primarily, parallel expansion was taking place in air transport infrastructure development as well as in air transport network expansion. All major tourist destinations in the region, particularly China, Japan, Thailand, Malaysia, Philippines, Indonesia, South Korea, India, GCC countries, Turkey, Mexico, Brazil, etc., are some of the fast-growing emerging air transport destinations (IATA, 2019), and they are the fast-growing tourism regions as well. The unique attractions, rich cultural and natural heritage, growing diversification in product range, etc. are attracting tourists from across the world to these emerging markets and that instil dynamism in the air transport to surge ahead. Certainly, increasing lure of the attractions in the emerging markets is one of the major reasons in attracting people from all over the world to visit.

12.9 Tourism policies to augment inbound air traffic

Certainly, countries are in tough competition so as to enhance tourist influx into their destinations. Liberal approach towards permitting international air transport operations is fundamental in increasing air transport services. "Other than market forces, government policy has been one of the most crucial components in shaping the operation and development of scheduled passenger air services" (Schlumberger & Weisskopf, 2014). Realizing the escalating need for enhancing international air transport, countries prefer to engage in bilateral agreements and open sky agreements. "Quite often, tourism is constrained by restrictive international aviation regulation. There has been a gradual trend towards liberalisation and this has stimulated tourism, but this regulation still acts as a constraint" (Forsyth, 2008). Usually, tourism turns to be a prime factor in the positive approaches towards liberalizing air transportation. In order to enable the airlines to fly other countries, to carry passengers from those countries to their cities and to promote inbound tourism, governments engage in negotiation with others to grant certain "freedoms" (these freedoms are discussed well in Chapter 7). It has been a known fact that open sky policy is crucial in stimulating international tourism further in destinations. Open skies policies led to lower the fares, increased access, and surge in regional market demand.

Increasingly tourism turns to be a critical factor in policy decisions regarding air transport expansion and promotion. According to Forsyth (2006) "...... it should be recognised that tourism benefits have been an important driver of aviation policies even where policy makers have not attempted to take a quantitative approach to assess how large the benefits and costs might be". In order to enhance international tourism further, authorities make favourable policy decisions and engage in bilateral agreements with potential tourism markets. Those decisions favouring international traffic flow have certain impacts on tourism and economy of the regions. "Aviation policies and government decisions concerning the smooth cooperation of tourism and aviation can make a big difference in the prosperity of a leisure destination" (Papatheodorou & Zenelis, 2013).

Furthermore, countries are forced to liberalize the visa rules and regulations to attract more tourists. E-Visa and visa on arrival policies are now widely put into practice by countries. Many of the recently emerged tourism destinations in the world have adopted liberalized visa regulations and norms, and the trend is on the increase. These constitute a category of determinants in the demand for tourism and consequently stimulate international air transport possibilities into the countries. Thus, tourism acts as a factor in the liberalization of air transport policies, determinant in the easing of visa policies and regulations, and reason in the expansion of aviation infrastructure in the destination region, and these factors altogether contribute greatly in the surge in air transport at international level.

12.10 Tourism in remote locations and islands

Remote regions, rural areas, islands, etc. with ample natural and cultural features form a category of ideal tourist destinations. Since 1950s, the trend of developing tourism in such kind of locations has been increasing and leisure tourism thrives many of those areas. Earlier, accessibility was a major bottleneck in many of such destinations, but the developments in regional transport networks and the expansion of air transport networks led these destinations to tap the tourism potentials. In many a case, air transportation is, usually, the only viable means of mobility in remote regions (Fageda et al., 2019) that have immense touristic potentials. The development of tourism over there created increased demand for air transport. A study by Doerr et al. (2020) on airport infrastructure promoting tourism found out that additional tourist inflows are particularly pronounced and robust in the county, particularly in the regional and rural area where the airport is located, and are driven by guest arrivals from abroad. Many of the leading island destinations are thriving due to air transport, and on the other hand, without tourism, the scope of air transport into these destinations would be meagre. The Seychelles is a popular holiday destination in the Indian Ocean. In some ways, it has become too popular, with several major international carriers introducing services to the archipelago in recent months (www.africanaerospace.aero). Many of the similar remote and island tourist destinations depend much on air transport services for the forward and backward movements. On the other hand, tourism is the primary reason for the increased air transport network and frequency in those island destinations.

12.11 Increasing dynamism and diversification of tourism

Modern tourism is featured with increasing rate of dynamism. Countries and destinations are competing internationally to remain successful and that too leads in increased dynamism in ensuring innovative tourism products and services to attract more tourists. Along with innovation, product diversification takes place at a large scale. Bieger and Wittmer (2006) based on another source opine that the tourism forms in trend like short vacations, visit friends and relatives caused greater requirement for greater flexibility in the transport system. The significance of this category, including health-related travel, has a significant share in the international tourism now. In 2017, VFR, religion, health and other similar types together account for 27% in international tourist arrivals (UNWTO, 2018b). Wellness tourism has expanded significantly and the same, particularly the medical tourism necessitates air travel. For a medical treatment, a patient prefers to have smoother and faster transport mode.

Shopping tourism is another one, which has been gaining greater significance in the recent years. Paris, Madrid, London, Los Angeles, Singapore, Kaulalumpur, Dubai, etc. are some of the examples where shopping tourists flock to choose the items of interest. Air transport seems a priority for shopping tourists as they club holidays with shopping experience. Business tourism is certainly a significant contributor in international tourism and globalization spurred to the growth of it dramatically. Certainly, business travellers have less time to spend for travel purpose and air transport is always their preferred mode of transport, irrespective of financial implications. Dubai is an example. Travel for trade-related reasons along with leisure tourist flow made this destination a global air transport hub. It is located ideally between the east and the west, and hence, the destination is using the advantages of the same for both the promotion of air transport and tourism. Experiential tourism, along with special interest tourism, is another trend in the realm of international tourism. Short-break tourism is also on the rise, and due to the increasing presence of LCCs, air transport-based short breaks are in vogue. One trend that inspired air transportation is the long-haul holidays that has been rising since 1970s when wide-bodied aircrafts were started to use widely by airlines. Both complimented each other, and due to tourism, long-haul air transport scope enhanced and tourists were enthused to move to destinations located far away. The favourable effects of air transport due to the after effects of using wide-bodied aircrafts, like decline in travel cost, increased smoothness on travel and speed contributed greatly.

12.12 Tour operator's role in air transport

Tour operators, being inevitable part in the tourism system, contribute in the regular flow of tourists to destinations globally. Charter airline sector is surviving mainly due to the package holidays, the prime product of tour operators. Since 1950s, charter airlines' dependence on tour operation industry is profound and the same is continuing. Of late, tour operators are using the services of scheduled airlines as well. Even, LCCs' services are utilized by the tour operators in arranging transportation for reaching destination and for returning. Role of tour operator in maintaining demand into many of the destinations is important. Speciality tour operators too contribute, though a small share, in the evolution of tourism and air transport. With regard to speciality tour operation, many a times, their operations may be to remote regions as well and hence that can strengthen the air transport operations into those regions. Tourism regions are now interested in arranging niche tourism attractions. Operators specialized in niche tourism can add air travel demand into those destinations with unique attractions.

12.13 Conclusion

The growth of tourism since the end of World War II has largely depended on the development of aviation. Due to the development of tourism, many remote areas have become part of the air transport network. The three most relevant parallels to aviation and tourism are regulatory synergies, objective function and shared emphasis on sustainability. The tourism growth over the years since 1950s reveals the rise of air transportation along with it. Tourism develops progressively at a destination, and there are different stages in the life cycle of the destination, such as exploration, involvement, development, consolidation, stagnation, decline and rejuvenation. Tourism has been a factor in increasing the efficiency of airports. The airport is the first point of inbound tourism, which creates the first impression of the destination.

A vacation trip is short-lived, so a long flight delay can dampen a tourist's leisure expectations. Overall efficiency covers many aspects of aviation and may enhance the quality, efficiency and attractiveness of a destination linked to an international tourism destination. The quality and level of in-flight services play an important role in the air travel experience of tourists. Punctuality, frequency, amenities at airports, image of airport and airline, and quality of services also enhance the spectrum of air travel experience. Adding services and facilities to attract more tourists is a challenge for airports because of financial constraints and limitations in increasing and expanding facilities. Many airports now provide artificial intelligence and virtual reality-based solutions to ensure a smooth and comfortable flow of passengers at airports. Tourism marketing and promotion activities at the local, regional, national and international levels will certainly increase the demand for air services, and the positive changes in policy and regulation will facilitate the growth of air transport to destinations. Emerging markets on tourism are now very relevant in international tourism, and the increase in tourist arrivals has led to an increase in air traffic in the region. The liberal approach to allowing international air traffic operations and reducing visa or travel restrictions is crucial to the development of international air transport services. Tourism is the main reason for the increase in the network and frequency of air transport to island destinations. Travel for trade-related reasons along with leisure tourist flow made certain destination a global air transport hub. Tour operators with special expertise in niche tourism add the need for air travel to destinations with special attractions.

Sample questions

Short/Medium-answer-type questions

- Discuss about the changes in international tourist arrival patterns.
- Explain the role of tourism in the development of air transport.
- What is TALC?
- Write how does tourism help in increasing efficiency in air transport.
- "Tourism contributes in the globalization of air transport". Comment upon the statement.
- Elucidate the role of tourism in network expansion.
- Analyse the role of tourism policies in air transportation.
- How does dynamism in tourism contribute in air transport growth?
- Write the role of tour operators in air transportation.

Essay type questions

- Discuss the development in air transport sector along with the evolution of a mass tourism destination.
- Explain the contribution of tourism in the expansion and growth of air transport sector.

Suggested readings

Bieger, T., & Wittmer, A. (2006). Air transport and tourism – Perspectives and challenges for destinations, airlines and governments. *Journal of Air Transport Management*, 12(1), 40–46.

Duval, D.T. (2013). Critical issues in air transport and tourism. *Tourism Geographies*, 15(3), 494–510.

Fernández, L.X., Coto-Millán, P., & Díaz-Medina, B. (2018). The impact of tourism on airport efficiency: The Spanish case. *Utilities Policy*, 55, 52–58. https://doi.org/10.1016/j.jup.2018.09.002.

Graham, A., Papatheodorou, A., & Forsyth, P. (Ed.). (2008). *Aviation and Tourism: Implications for Leisure Travel*. Hampshire: Ashgate.

Spasojevic, B., Lohmann, G., & Scott, N. (2017). Air transport and tourism – a systematic literature review (2000–2014). *Current Issues in Tourism*, 21(9), 975–997.

Wittmer, A., Bieger, T., & Muller, R. (2013) *Aviation Systems: Management of the Integrated Aviation Value Chain*. New York: Springer.

Chapter 13

Airline planning

Learning outcomes

After reading this chapter, you will be able to:

- Comprehend planning in airlines.
- Analyse the importance of airline operations from a tourism perspective.
- Describe the following:
  - Fleet planning
  - Network/route planning
  - Schedule planning and development
  - Crew planning and scheduling

13.1 Introduction

Airline is a commercial organization demanding efficient planning and management. An organization consists of diverse resources, which range from men to materials, and the proper and effective utilization of them can enable an organization to achieve the organizational objectives and goals. Decision-making is key in the performance of various activities, performed by personnel and/or machines that are needed for the effective utilization of those resources. Effective and efficient coordination and controlling of them is required. Koontz and Weihrich (1990) define management as "the process of designing and maintaining an environment in which individuals, working together in groups, efficiently accomplish selected aims". It applies to any kind of organization and to managers at all organizational levels and involves different interrelated managerial functions of planning, organizing, staffing, leading and controlling. As a process, managing an organization is primarily the efficient execution of various activities associated with forecasting and planning, organizing, commanding, coordinating and controlling. Certainly, planning is fundamental to all management functions.

DOI: 10.4324/9781003136927-13

Planning is simply defined as the determination of a future course of action to achieve the desired result. It is a kind of future picture and a framework for future activities. Organizational objectives can be accomplished by utilizing different kinds of resources like human resources, financial resources, material resources, etc. Proper and effective planning aims at optimization of resources. It involves deciding in advance what to do, when to do, where to do, how to do and who will do and how the results are to be evaluated. Planning implies making choices, committing resources and time horizon, and it involves selecting missions, objectives and actions to achieve them. Here, decision-making is relevant which is pertaining to choosing the future course of action among the alternatives. The outcome of this are plans which are of different types.

> A plan … enables us to identify where we are going and how to get there (emphasis added) – in other words it should clarify the path that is to be taken and the outcomes or end results. It also draws attention to the stages on the way and … helps to set and establish priorities that can assist in the scheduling of activities.
>
> (McCabe et al., 2000)

There are long-range and short-range plans. Along with the organizational goal, departments within the organization too have separate plans. Strategic and operational plans are another classification, which is based on the nature of plans. A strategic plan will be future-oriented whereas operational will be merely activity-oriented. Other kinds of plans are also there. The planning stage requires different kinds of information and the accuracy, relevance and quality of the information matter in planning. The above discussion reveals the importance of planning in an organization and in airlines, planning has utmost importance. The nuances of planning in airline organizations are discussed below.

13.2 Significance of airline planning in tourist experience

Airlines are the most important service provider in the international tourism transport system. The experience with airline services certainly matters in the travel experience and contributes to the overall tourist experience. Price, safety, timelines, baggage handling, quality of in-flight food and beverage services, seat comfort, check-in process, and in-flight service are some of the key service quality attributes for airline passengers (Gourdin, 1988). A study by Punel et al. (2019) which explored the interdependence between passenger travel experience and service quality in the airlines in different regions found out that the local influence is there in having travel experience, perception and evaluation of airline services. Among various attributes, seat comfort is considered the most important factor to evaluate the value for money of the flight and cabin staff service as the cardinal feature to rate the overall flight experience. The study found out that though seat comfort, food and beverages and in-flight entertainment are significant factors, they are more significant for upper-class passengers than the economy class of travellers. On the other hand, economy-class passengers are concerned about the value of money, more. Another study reveals that overall satisfaction, loyalty and advocacy for airline journey of passengers are correlated with cabin features (satisfaction) and in-flight food and drink (for loyalty and advocacy) (Laming & Mason, 2014).

One of the most important aspects airlines have to take into consideration is the flight delay. Delay and cancellation constitute a serious concern within the airline industry. These are not just due to internal factors; rather several external factors too can cause those. Still, some delays are manageable and can be avoided. How efficiently airlines manage services without causing delays is a success factor for them. Airline punctuality is a critical factor in passengers' airline selection and in satisfaction. This aspect is more important for the tourists. A tourist's movement is for the short term, and a long flight delay can dampen the scope of the holiday. When a flight delay occurs, if connection flights are there in the journey, there is a chance of missing those as well. Efficient planning is vital in all these. Airline planning is rather a complex process and it involves planning at different operational areas as well. Fleet planning, fleet assignment, route planning, etc. are fundamental in ensuring smooth operations in the future. Truitt and Haynes (1994) argued that aircraft type is another important quality attribute. Fleet assignment process of airlines has to ensure to have the right type of aircraft for the right route. Crew scheduling is also crucial. The quality delivery of in-flight services demands the right combination of staff on board which can be ensured by the crew scheduling process.

The crew has an important role in the delivery of service while on the flight. Quality of service delivery takes part in customer satisfaction. Both leisure as well as business travellers do consider quality attributes in airline service while making the decision to travel by an airline. According to Gursoy et al. (2003), airline service quality is an important critical factor that is likely to influence travellers' airline selection decision and there exists a significant relationship between reputation, service and retained preference. In-flight staff, particularly the cabin crew, can perform quality service while the tourists are on the way to the destination. Safety, timelines, luggage transportation, quality of food and beverage, seat comfort, smoothness in check-in process, quality of on board services, etc. have a critical role in traveller satisfaction. The experience the tourists get from their service influences tourist satisfaction. The crew has to be of high-quality level to offer internal level service to the tourists. It is stated that for delivering consistent service excellence in an efficient manner and achieving sustainable competitive advantage for airlines, it is important to maintain "stringent selection and recruitment processes, extensive training and retraining, successful service delivery teams, empowerment of front-line staff to control service quality, and motivating staff through rewards and recognition" (Wirtz, et al., 2008). A smooth take-off, landing and flight en route can increase the comfort level of the traveller. Getting right foods while on the flight would enhance the journey more pleasurable. Some others may prefer to have varieties and the diversity of food and beverage offering can enthuse them. Quality of the food too matters. A longer journey would require good entertainment options within flights. Airlines started to provide apps to enjoy free in-flight movies and on-demand content for an enjoyable journey. Airline entertainment options are usually free of cost and multicultural varieties are offered. Seat comfort, leg space, etc. are a matter of concern for travellers on long international routes.

Airline planning

A passenger expects a smooth check-in process and the completion of airport formalities. Nowadays, airlines provide the opportunity for online check-in many hours
before the flight itself. Airline mobile applications can also help the passenger to
have a timely online check-in process. This can avoid the stress and difficulties associated with the airport check-in process within terminals. Moreover, self-tagging
baggage facility is also there, offered by airlines to avoid waiting in line for it, to
be done by the airline staff. Baggage handling is another important task to be
taken care of efficiently. A missed baggage can severely affect a traveller. Delay and

Table 13.1 Airline Service Quality: Influencing Factors

De Jager et al. (2012) utilized a wide range of factors for finding out their significance
in service quality assessment of airline passengers. The major common factors, with
varied significance, used for the study in two different samples were classified into
different sets, as follows:

- Cabin servicescape (food & films)

    o Variety of food served during flight
    o Quality of the food served
    o Amount of the food served during flight
    o Films and broadcasts during flight
    o Continuous innovation and improvements in services

- Convenience of booking

    o Online booking
    o Availability of airline website on the internet
    o Convenience in making reservation/booking
    o Attractive ticket fares
    o Special offers for frequent fliers

- Cabin servicescape (cabin & cabin crew)

    o Physical appearance of a cabin crew
    o Cabin cleanliness
    o Speed of check-in
    o Cabin crew's ability to speak foreign languages

- Timeliness of flights

    o Frequent flights to destination
    o Direct service to destination
    o On-time departures and arrivals
    o Comforts of seats

- Country of origin of airlines

    o Country of origin of airlines
    o Being my national airline

Source: De Jager, W.J., Van Zyl, D., & Toriola, L.A. (2012). Airline service quality in South Africa and
Italy. *Journal of Air Transport Management*, 25, 19–21.

difficulties encountered while inside the airport can also dissatisfy a traveller. This can negatively affect the tourist experience. Airlines need to ensure smooth passenger handling within airports. The boarding process also needs to be hassle-free and smooth. Airline pricing is at times confusing and baffling for passengers. Those who paid higher rates may bother more about the quality of service.

The above discussion reveals that efficient planning, diligent execution of the plans and technology integrated operations would enable the airline to provide quality services as well as in ensuring customer satisfaction that can lead to a good share in the tourist experience. We will discuss in detail various types of planning in airlines in this chapter and the operations are detailed in the following chapter.

13.3 Planning in airlines

Planning is all pervasive and the organization as a whole and every functional department in it necessitate planning. As in other organizations, in airlines also planning is there at strategic as well as operational levels. Airline planning is more complicated due to the specific characteristics of the sector, as discussed in the previous chapter. "An airline is dependent for its very existence on the ability of its top planners. Failure to forecast the demand for air travel and to plan how to meet a rising or shrinking demand spells the difference between success and failure" (Wensveen, 2009). Operational planning has so much significance in airlines particularly since most of the activities are time-bound. While planning, aiming at the optimization of each and every operational activity is of extreme significance in order to generate revenue and to gain profit, especially since the sector is marred with a thin profit margin. Resource requirement for executing plans is high and needs a large number of people for service delivery.

Strategic planning is inevitable for any organization that aims at growth and competitive survival. Strategic planning, basically long-term planning ranging from 5 to 20 years, aligns with corporate vision and mission. It is defined as "a process of looking into the future and identifying trends and issues against which to align organizational priorities…" (UN, www.hr.un.org). It is usually a continual process for improving organizational performance by developing strategies to produce results. The focus is to look at the future where the airline would like to reach, assessing its current situation and developing and implementing approaches for moving forward. Airline is surrounded by unpredictable business environments and faces varying external factors often that can challenge the business harshly. Market conditions keep on change and competition is severe most of the time. Economic circumstances pertaining to airlines vary more often. In order to respond to these kinds of challenges and to tap the opportunities to grow, airlines certainly need strategic plans.

Here, in this chapter, specific function-related planning is described. These functions are the crucial activities in an airline, all of which together form the base for future actions and strategic growth. Air transportation service by each airline is undertaken based on different plans that are created months in advance. Some of such plans are more strategic in nature, whereas some others are more operational. For instance, fleet planning is more of strategic planning in nature, as it is done for the long term. The following are different planning types undertaken in airlines.

- Fleet planning
- Network/route planning
- Schedule planning and development
  o Airline schedules
  o Fleet assignment
  o Aircraft routing
- Crew planning and scheduling
  o Crew pairing
  o Crew rostering

Each of the above is discussed in detail below.

13.4 Fleet planning

One of the most crucial strategic planning activities in an airline organization is certainly fleet planning. The fleet of an airline represents the group or collection of aircraft, which they can use for flight operations as part of air transportation services. Simply, the term fleet encompasses the types of aircraft in possession of airlines. The fleet size quantifies the number of aircraft available. Aircraft vary, and subsequently, their capacity, range, size, load factor, etc. also vary. Larger airlines will certainly have a larger fleet size. It is an important decision for an airline whether to buy a new aircraft or get an aircraft on lease, etc. as it involves both huge financial investments and risks. Of the major factors that contribute to the success of an airline, fleet optimization is an important one. The fleet available should match the current and potential demand. In addition, the decision to purchase/lease aircraft has to be based on the demand forecasts and future network expansion plans. The type of aircraft to purchase is also a strategic decision because some of the airlines would like to have specific types of aircraft. As discussed in the previous chapter, low-cost carriers (LCCs) usually try to have the same type of aircraft.

Table 13.2 Fleet Selection Process: Elements Considered

Category	Elements Considered in Fleet Selection Process
Finance and contractual cost	Purchase v/s lease of aircraft, residual value, buy-back possibilities, insurance, price escalation, guarantees, price of spare parts, etc.
Markets and routes	Market size, mix and growth; schedule forecast; airport compatibility, performance and economics, etc.
Engineering	Inventory of spares, pooling, maintenance facilities, commonality, availability of technical skills, etc.
Operations	Crewing, aircraft mix, extended-range twin-engine operational performance standards, performance of aircraft, etc.
Regulatory and environmental	Certification rules, standards, environmental aspects, etc.

Source: Adapted from Clerk (2007).

Fleet planning deals with determining the number and type of aircraft required to implement the corporate strategy in the coming years (Wensveen, 2007). It is also called the aircraft selection process. The two key factors, which determine the fleet planning, are the right aircraft type and the right time of acquisition. Based on the future demand factor, an airline plans to select, buy or lease the right type of aircraft at the right time.

> An airline's fleet plan therefore reflects a strategy for multiple periods into the future, including the number of aircraft required by aircraft type, the timing of future deliveries, and retirement of existing fleet, as well as contingency plans to allow for flexibility in the fleet plan given the tremendous uncertainty about future market conditions.
>
> (Belobaba, 2009)

Fleet planning has much significance in the financial position of airlines. Airline is a capital-intensive industry. Buying an aircraft is a costly affair as the acquisition cost of aircraft is so high.

Fleet expansion necessitates acquiring the required number of aircraft in the future. A huge amount of money has to be earmarked for fleet expansion. Furthermore, airlines may have to consider whether it makes better financial sense to replace old aircraft with new or modernize available old aircraft. Leasing aircraft is another possible option, which also has to be weighed using diverse aspects of profitability. Moreover, operating costs of flight operations also need to be considered. Plans of airlines, market expansion potentials, financial position and forecasts, external environmental factors and the abilities of aircraft are some of the factors that need to be considered in fleet planning. Detailed, systematic and in-depth knowledge and understanding of aircraft performance, as well as aircraft economics are essential for a fleet planning decision. It necessitates a blend of engineering and commercial know-how, the ability to predict the future, and a good deal of intuition, along with luck as well (Clerk, 2007). Although larger aircraft have better unit cost, demand changes, particularly a slump, can affect the profit level badly. On the other hand, smaller flights can also be beneficial in certain cases. The decision regarding fleet acquisition in the future requires forecasts

---

Table 13.3 Constraints of Airline Expansion

- Limited capacity of airports
- Bilateral air service agreements between countries
- Limited air traffic services
- Fluctuating market demands
- Extreme competition
- Huge investment requirements
- Airline regulations in the country
- Marginal profit level
- Recurring crisis of different types

Source: Adapted from Wu (2010).

of traffic demand, and average load factor and available seat kilometres that are to be generated to meet the traffic demand, the productivity of the aircraft and revenue estimates. Next to be considered is the air transport industry forecast within the overall economy, including such items as revenue passengers and cargo tonnage, revenue passenger miles, cargo ton miles, revenue block hours and so forth. There are a large number of factors that need to be taken care of while doing fleet planning. Some of such major factors are listed below:

- Number and type aircraft needed
- Technical performance of aircraft
- Operational performance
- Safety records
- Price of new aircraft
- Cabin comfort
- Relative revenue driven by seat count
- Crew requirements
- Demand forecast
- Fuel efficiency
- Maintenance requirements
- Environmental performance
- Type of existing aircraft and their performance
- Optimum number of fleet types
- Fleet commonality
- Certification rules and standards
- Aircraft payload range capability
- Aircraft take-off performance
- Maintenance cost and support capability
- Cargo capacity
- Old versus new trade-offs
- Aircraft pricing/lease rates
- Aircraft buy versus lease trade-offs
- Financing issues

The drivers that assist fleet expansion decisions can include traffic forecasts, yield forecasts, operating cost estimation and the estimated aircraft productivity (ICAO, 2017). As pointed out before, fleet planning is a critical activity. A wrong decision can cause irreversible financial consequences for an airline. Certainly, decisions have to be made meticulously after the due evaluation process to assess the impact of the new aircraft on an airline's financial performance.

13.5 Network planning

The airline industry is a network-based industry, which provides services in routes within the network formed by a number of airlines. In fact, this network system helps the industry to operate services across the world and that makes the industry a truly global industry. A network of an airline consists of routes on which it operates services. These routes are served by flights and needed facilities and resources are available to facilitate the delivery of transport services on those routes. Franke (2018) describes it as to offer their air transport service to clients, airlines need to define a certain number of flights on specific routes they intend to operate, hopefully meeting demand for airborne mobility. The entirety of these flights and routes, complemented by the assets and resources required to physically deliver the offered services, is usually referred to as a network.

(Franke, 2018)

Network planning, also called route planning, is a crucial activity in airline planning and management. It is simply a "process of designing, creating, and publishing the network plan" (HCL, 2013).

Network planning is closely associated with **product planning**. Product planning is important to determine the markets to expand the business. Here, it is connected to the new routes and destinations to serve. While doing network planning, demand from-and-to origin and destination (O&D) points have to be assessed. In hub-and-spoke system, it is not always possible to select only high-demand routes. In order to remain competitive, airlines may go for wider coverage. Expanding the existing network needs meticulous planning. According to Franke (2018), "the primary goal of designing an air transport network is to capture as much demand as possible in a profitable way". For network planning, it is important to have the stock of a sufficient number of aircraft, airport slots and crews as resources for the operations. Network planning is one of the most important panning activities in airlines. It is done to explore the potential markets and forecast market demands of specific market segments. It may consist of demand modelling, market forecasting and initial schedule establishment (Wu, 2010). It has different dimensions. The success of network carriers depends on some key performance indicators, such as:

- Connectivity: ability to connect inbound and outbound traffic flow conveniently
- Productivity: of aircraft and other resources
- Operational stability
- Profitability of offered connections (Franke, 2018)

While doing network planning, it is important to consider the above. It ultimately focusses on the optimization of how airlines serve markets, how to best deploy their fleets and how decisions are taken to open up new routes and services. Obviously, it forms the base for the expansion and growth of an airline. Moreover, the revenue earning and profit potentials constitute the most important aspect of network planning. This can enable airlines to enter into new destinations as well. New destinations can be linked to other parts of the world by the expansion of networks of airlines. Airline's network planning sequence has the following patterns:

- Long-term strategic planning: three to ten years prior to departure
- Mid-term planning and scheduling: six months to three years in advance of a flight departure
- Short-term operational planning and resource steering (a few weeks before the departure) (Franke, 2018).

Multiple route evaluations, in order to know whether a route will be profitable in the long term or not, are undertaken when airlines plan new routes. During the process of network planning, airlines have to see the scope of demand in the prospective routes that intend to operate. Demand forecasting can be a prerequisite for this. Airport access is another aspect. Airport slots, that are allocated for particular airlines for landing and take-off in the airport, in the destination and origin cities have to be considered. Some of the airports are crowded and getting slots can be arduous. Fleet strength is another issue to look into. Availability of aircraft for an expansion of service must be considered while doing network planning. The scope of sharing crew is also important while thinking of expanding the network. Both cabin crew, as well as cockpit crew availabilities, are to be thought of. Existing and the scope of future competition is another aspect to look into. Entering into a new market with the extreme competition will be challenging. Executing the most apt marketing mix strategies will become inevitable for beating the completion in such situations. According to HCL Technology Solution providers, the utility solutions (use cases) of networking planning technology solutions for the short and long terms are the following:

- Short-term
  - Plane switching use case, where planes need to be substituted by another aircraft due to mechanical problems, delayed flights and oversold or undersold situations.
  - Crew recovery use case, where the flight crew for the plane is incomplete due to illness, missing connecting flights, flight delays, etc.
- Long-term
  - Opening new flight routes
  - Decreasing or increasing flight frequency on an existing route due to variations in demand and/or profitability
  - Closing existing routes due to the change in demand/profitability (HCL, 2013).

13.5.1 Types of network

Different types of networks can be seen in air transportation. Franke (2018) identified three types of networks, such as hub and spoke network, point-to-point network and gateway network for express cargo. Linear network is another common network seen in air transportation, particularly in domestic sectors. Hybrid network structure has been followed by some airlines now. Thus, the types of networks can be summarized as below:

- Linear
- Point-to-point
- Hub and spoke
- Hybrid
- Gateway network

13.5.2 Linear network

Akin to a train service, linear route structure involves flight operation from one city to the next and on to the next (Cook and Billing, 2018). Instead of returning to the origin city, the flight continues service to the next destination. This can

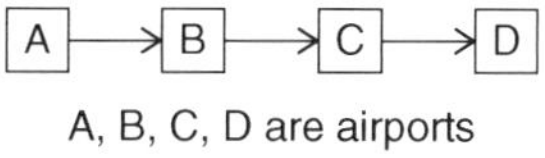

A ——→ B ——→ C ——→ D

A, B, C, D are airports

Figure 13.1 Linear network

continue to other cities as well. Long-distance travellers will see the stopping of flights in a number of intermediate stops. This is like a chain, connecting services linearly from one point to another through a number of intermediate stops. The following are the features of a linear structure:

- Simplified scheduling and operational control
- Disruption on one route does not affect the other
- High frequency of services
- High asset utilization
- Service to smaller cities can be done with adequate capacity
- Utilization by combined demand from different intermediate points
- Delay may be there in reaching final destination due to intermediate stops
- The same flight can be used for operations
- Destinations are linked one to the next and on.

13.5.3 Point-to-point network

This is the simplest among all route structures. In this, the interdependency of resources is very less. No hubs and, thus, no transfer of passengers. No waiting for incoming flights. Non-stop flights are operated between origin and destination (O&D) cities. Features of point-to-point route structure are:

- The simplest system with the highest operational control
- Geographical coverage of operations is very less
- Operation to a smaller number of cities
- Possible only to between cities where there is sufficient demand
- High frequency of operations can be possible
- Service to destinations with minimum possible disruptions
- No connection flights are there
- No change of flight in between
- Highly stable in high-demand routes
- Fastest to reach the destination

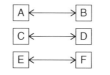

A, B, C, D, E & F are airports

Figure 13.2 Point-to-point network

- Shortest flight duration
- Independent flight operation, without the link with other airlines
- Very useful for business travellers
- Irregular flight operations may not affect other services
- High utilization of human resource and airport infrastructure
- Seasonality is a factor in the demand and nature of service can be altered accordingly
- Type of aircraft used can be different for different cities, e.g. smaller cities need smaller aircraft
- Dispersed routes can be possible.

13.5.4 Hub-and-spoke system

This is another predominant route structure, which is being followed by major airlines in the world, particularly in the international air transportation. Certainly, major airlines prefer to have "hub" cities to focus transport services to other cities located at different directions. This is different from point-to-point network. This system

> connects many cities using fewer aircraft than a linear or point to point route system, and provides an airline with a better opportunity to keep its passengers all the way to their final destination rather than handling them off to other countries.
>
> (Cook and Billig, 2018)

Hub-and-spoke system consists of a set of "spoke" routes flying to and from minor airports to a major city, called "hub", i.e. a hub is a central airport where flights are routed through, and spokes represent routes from the hub airport to other cities in different directions. Services from these hubs are usually operated in smaller cities, other than the long-haul flight. Several points of departure are fed into the hub airport from which connecting flights operate services to their various destinations along the "spokes".

Hub-and-spoke system consists of at least one hub airport that plays the role of collecting and distributing passenger traffic among flights at an airport (Wu, 2010).

> The system is optimized when providing air service to a wide geographic area and many destinations. Passengers departing from any non-hub (spoke) city bound to another spoke in the network are first flown to the hub where they connect to a second flight to the destination. Thus, passengers can travel between any two cities in the route system with one connecting stop at the hub.
>
> (Cook & Goodwin, 2008)

According to Markus Franke (2018), "network carriers operate hubs to accumulate demand in one spot and leverage that scale effect to offer more routes, capture more revenue potentials and deploy large aircraft than carriers with a focus on P2P services" (Franke, 2018). P2P stands for "point-to-point" service. Passenger movement from one spoke city to another is routed via hub. From the hub, the passenger has to board another flight. The baggage and cargo to that destination are also shifted to the new flight. This system can ensure convenient connections to a number of destinations from the hub. Large airlines may have more than one hub, even up to five, whereas smaller ones may have one hub. Airlines usually use large capacity aircraft, with non-stop service between hub cities.

One major motive of airlines while moving for "hub-and-spoke" system is to increase the average number of passengers on its flights. Due to this system, higher revenue can be earned with better efficiency of operations using a smaller number of aircraft. In other words, "In hub-and-spoke systems, several points of departure are fed into a single airport (the 'hub'), from which connecting flights transport passengers to their various destinations (along the 'spokes')" (Wensveen, 2007). Many times, services to smaller airports are undertaken by different smaller airlines. These smaller airlines and the major ones operate on the basis of agreements between them, and this helps the major airlines to operate on longer routes with better load and smaller airlines to benefit greatly. Airlines could serve far more markets using the same-size fleet. In the hub-and-spoke system, ensuring minimum connecting time is very important. An inbound passenger has to pass through a series of procedures, mainly immigration requirements, which may take time. Scheduling of flight has to consider it. Also, a domestic passenger moving abroad, coming from a spoke city too, has to pass through such procedures. From spoke city, passengers to many destinations can be transported to the hub city in one flight. For an airline, choosing a hub depends on a variety of factors, like location, the centrality of the airport, quality of services, availability of facilities, accessibility of the airport, etc.

13.5.5 Benefits of hub-and-spoke system

Demand from each spoke city may not be adequate enough to all other spoke cities.

> In a hub and spoke network, the number of economically viable destinations is boosted by accumulating demand in one or more central airports and feeding/de-feeding flights that would otherwise have too little demand for a decent service quality (i.e. frequency of flights per day/per week).
>
> (Franke, 2018)

These are designed as a result of economic and commercial viability. By the use of hub-and-spoke system, it is easy for the airlines to consolidate demand from varied spoke cities and to operate services. Usually, airlines get a good share of revenue from smaller cities. This is more important in the case of international operations. A domestic spoke city demand can be conveniently consolidated for an international operation. Passengers do not have to shift to other airlines. As the frequency of flight services between major cities is increased, passengers get the necessary convenience for travel. Aircraft seat capacity utilization can be maximum. The benefits of hub-and-spoke system are summarized as follows:

- Easy management of varying demands from and between different smaller and bigger cities
- More economical since lesser demand routes are operated by smaller flights and the demand for longer routes are consolidated through hubs

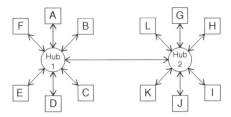

A, B, C, D, E, F, G, H, I, J, K & L are different smaller airports

Figure 13.3 "Hub-and-spoke" network (bi-hub)

- Highest/widest geographical coverage of operation
- Convenient consolidation of domestic demand into international routes
- Airlines can dominate in the hubs
- Lowest number of aircraft required
- Getting airport slot/space and facilities is easier
- Easy and less expensive to expand the network by adding spoke destinations
- Airlines can consolidate the demand from multiple cities
- Frequency of flight service between major cities can be enhanced
- Different types of aircraft are needed
- Passengers can travel from origin to the final destination in a single airline
- Loyalty programme advantage is also there for airlines when larger and wider network is there
- Convenient use of aircraft in the trunk routes
- Marketing advantage is there to cover a larger area
- High-load factors can be ensured
- Increased flight frequency can be possible
- Product distribution via traditional intermediaries is possible in a wider area.

Though many advantages are there, a few disadvantages can also be identified. This system is functioning through connection flights, and flight delays can disrupt the whole operation. In case of any issue in one route, it can affect the connected routes as well. The need for an increased labour force is there. Moreover, a flight service between two spoke points becomes more expensive as the same involves a stop and change of flight at the hub. It is more complicated due to the need for interlinking of resources.

13.5.6 Types of hub-and-spoke networks

- Single hub network
- Bi-hub network
- Multi-hub network
- Rolling hub network
- Tailored complexes
- Directional hub network

Usually, hub-and-spoke system is with one hub city which is referred to as a single hub network. Bi-hub network involves two hubs and corresponding spoke routes from both the hubs. For instance, from one spoke to a distant spoke city, we can have two hubs depending upon the size, etc. of the airlines. Circuitous routing and airport congestion in a hub can be reduced due to this. Rarely, multiple hubs can be seen when there are more than two hubs for operation. In directional hub,

> only flights from spoke cities in one geographical side of the hub airport are scheduled to arrive for a complex. After the transfers, baggage, and cargo are complete, flights then depart for spoke cities on the opposite geographical side of the hub.
>
> (Cook & Billig, 2018)

Rolling hub (depeaking) is practised in routes with high congestion. To reduce congestion, etc., inbound and outbound flights (including domestic) are spread throughout the day. It can lead to a long waiting time for passengers to some destinations. Airlines with a large number of connections may opt for this, but preference for immediate connections may be given to high-demand routes with more profitability. Tailored complexes are envisaged to meet the specific objectives, and hub operations are adjusted according to the profitability and demand. For instance, one specific route may be focussed at one time, and the next route may be focussed at a different time.

13.5.7 Hybrid network

Some airlines do not stick to one type of network for their operations; rather they may operate flights in a network which is a combination of two or more of the above route structures. Large airlines can have the freedom of having hybrid network–based operation since they are required to have the operation in a wider geographical area with adequate fleet and crew size. On some routes, they may have to operate point-to-point services. Hub-and-spoke system may be the base for all other operations for major airlines.

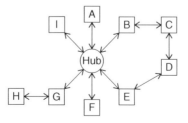

Figure 13.4 Hybrid network

13.5.8 Gateway network

This is also a hub-and-spoke system–based route network. It

> is the typical operational model of global express delivery companies (integrators) such as FedEx, UPS, or DHL. It is based on regional/continental networks with a very high density for time-definite parcel delivery, connected on a global level through long-haul flights between gateway hubs.
>
> (Franke, 2018)

For the speed transportation of cargo and other consignments, the regional route network is connected to the international long-range trunk routes.

13.6 Code-sharing

Code-sharing is a very common practice among airlines to enable more choices for passengers, and this is made possible through commercial contracts between the marketing and operating airlines. A definition by the US Department of Transportation specifies it as "a marketing arrangement in which an airline places its designator code on a flight operated by another airline and sells tickets for that flight" (US DOT – www.transportation.gov). By this, airlines can offer its passengers a greatly enhanced network by utilizing the actual network of another carrier" (Williams, 2018). A major carrier shares a code with a smaller carrier or it can be an arrangement between the two. In some cases, three or more international airlines share a code for an international flight operated in cooperation or for a connecting service that uses the same code (ICAO, 2004). The same description has been given by Wensveen. According to him, it

> refers to two airlines, usually a major and a regional carrier, that share the same identification codes on airline schedules. By code sharing with a regional airline, a major can advertise flights to a much larger market area and expand its market at relatively low cost.
>
> (Wensveen, 2007)

Air India, the flag carrier of India illustrates the concept well in the following way.

> a code share flight is a flight that is marketed by one carrier and operated by another. Code share flights come about as a result of agreements between airlines to sell seats on each other's flights in order to provide passengers with a wider choice of destinations. The ticket would be booked on the flight number of the airline that you have booked your travel, however it may be operated by another carrier.
>
> (Air India, www.airindia.in)

Certainly, the motive and scope of code-sharing are more than providing more choices for passengers. This can be undertaken to sell seats on each other's flights in order to provide passengers with a wider choice of destinations. The ticket would be booked on the flight code of an airline but the service may be by another carrier. A seat can be purchased from an airline on a flight that is actually operated by another airline having a different code. Still, the passenger is given the code of the airline of which he/she booked the seat. The following illustration by Rodney Williams can help in understanding the concept better

> ...Qantas does not fly the domestic sector Tokyo to Sapporo. Assuming Qantas has the bilateral traffic rights to do so, then Qantas could enter into an agreement with Japan Airlines and code share on this sector. The actual flight would be operated by Japan Airlines' Flight JL456, together with Qantas' marketing code of QF5678. Both carriers could then sell the same service under two flight numbers.
>
> (Williams, 2018)

By this, the airlines can broaden the offer of what they can make to customers in terms of the number of destinations and, in some cases, the flight timings that they can offer to potential customers, without the costs and difficulties involved in additional investment in equipment or in mergers with other airlines (Szakal, 2013). The smaller communities are being linked to the large air transport network at the national and international level. According to ICAO, the reasons for code-sharing are:

- To achieve a better display position in computer reservation systems/global distribution systems in cases where the flight is treated as an online service with a higher priority in listing than an interline service
- To form some kind of cooperative links with other airlines to maintain, protect and improve their positions in the wake of growing competition
- To achieve better presence using a relatively inexpensive marketing tool on routes they do not fly
- To enable two carriers to operate a viable joint service where traffic volumes are not sufficient for separate operations by two airlines
- To obtain traffic from feeder routes
- To remain competitive or to enhance competitive position by obtaining traffic within the ambit of code-sharing partners
- To gain increased market access to points that were restricted by capacity provisions in bilateral air service agreements (ICAO, 2004).

13.6.1 Types of code-shares

According to Williams (2018), there are two types, such as "free sale" and "hard block" code-shares.

- Free sale code-share
  The marketing airline is free to sell as many numbers of seats as per the need on the operator's flight. This is less price competing. The marketing carrier gets the freedom of accessing the inventory of the other airline. Also, it can market and sell the seats independently of the operating airline.

- Hard block code-share

  The marketing carrier purchases a specific number of seats by paying the price for all those seats. The marketing carrier has the freedom only on that number or percentage of reserved seats that are provided by the operating carrier. In this, price competition tendency is high since the marketing carrier has to sell all the seats blocked. Both the airlines have equal responsibility in selling the seats.

13.7 Interline agreements

No airlines can provide air travel services to all parts of the world. Only a few pair of destinations can be provided direct services by airlines. The rest of the connections are made through certain common commercial agreements by which airlines can provide services to different parts of the world. Globally, for a large proportion of journeys, the services of two or more airlines are necessary for a passenger to complete a single air trip with multiple destinations. Interline agreement is one of that kind which is undertaken between two airlines in order to allow connecting flights between them to be placed on the same ticket. This enables passengers to travel on multiple airlines on the same itinerary. Moreover, this allows passengers to check their bags through and check-in all the way to the final destination. By this, airlines can handle passengers travelling on itineraries consisting of multiple destinations on multiple airlines.

Through the provision of air travel between two or more airlines, the respective airlines can extend their route network so as to provide services to passengers to more destinations. Interline agreement can be differentiated from code-share agreements. It is explained by Michael Strauss in the following way

> Interlining agreements differ from code-share agreements where a flight is numbered with the airline's code although it is operated by another airline. If you fly for instance from Dubai to New York on Emirates and then carry on to Miami on American, this requires an interline agreement between Emirates and American for you to not have to check-in again....
>
> (Strauss, 2017)

According to ICAO (2004), two types of interline methods can be seen in international air transportation. They are:

- IATA interlining
- Non-IATA interlining

The first category is based on IATA fares in order to make the process of interchangeability of tickets easy and simple. Non-IATA interlining, also called club interlining or bilateral interlining, takes place based on airline fares even without any pre-agreements about fare levels, conditions and the scope of transporting airlines and available routing options. Usually, issuing airlines will determine the routing and the transporting carrier accepts tickets which receive the revenue for it as well. This gives more flexibility.

13.8 Network carriers, hub-and-spoke and the benefits for tourists

Major carriers, also called network carriers, form the backbone of international tourism transportation. Although LCCs are getting increasing relevance in tourism, international tourism is still depending much on network carriers. Business tourists, particularly, depend more on network carriers for their trips. By using hub-and-spoke system, tourists can have easy access to many destinations while on their holidays. Travel on a complex itinerary can be managed only with the help of network carriers. While code-sharing is followed by network carriers, travel becomes hassle-free from depending on multiple airlines and baggage handling difficulties in different airports. Single booking is adequate for the tourists to travel throughout the complex itinerary. Airlines can help the tourists in this aspect by having a code-share with other airlines and by being part in airline alliances. Network carriers offer services on a wider network and that helps the tourists in fixing their itineraries as well. Frequency of flight and convenient timing are possible by using the services of network carriers. International travel becomes smoother for the tourists who wish to engage in multicentre holidays. Moreover, due to airline alliances, airlines can provide tourists the increased frequency, integrated route networks and lower-priced services around the world (Iatrou & Tsitsiragou, 2008). Moreover, these alliances enable tourists to use lounges in other airports than the hubs of the booked airline and increase loyalty points.

By having hubs, network airlines can ensure global connectivity for the tourists. Moreover, in certain cases, a hub is significant for a tourist to have a better travel experience as well. When the journey duration is more, having a stop in a hub can rejuvenate the tourist to have the next leg of the journey more relaxed. Moreover, hubs offer good shopping options, leisure and relaxation options, recreational options and rest. Some of the hub airports are akin to cities and this can help business tourists more in engaging in meetings and taking part in conferences using the meeting facilities within the hubs. Hub airports usually have better tourist appeal and services and facilities catering to the needs of tourists. Multicultural entertainment, refreshment and cultural varieties are available in hub airports. This can enthuse tourists further and enhance their tourist experience. When connecting flights are there, the issues of baggage handling in the hub airports are not there, until and unless required by the traveller. The waiting period during then can be effectively utilized by the tourists by engaging in recreation, refreshment and shopping. All these certainly can have a share in their experience.

In addition to the above benefits, tourists can have a better experience with network carriers by having better in-flight services. These airlines are full-service carriers and provide almost all the services that are supposed to be provided for international air transport service providers as per the industry standards. A variety of food and beverage options is there. In-flight entertainment system of network carriers is usually with more options and the tourists can enjoy the journey better by these as well. Seat comfort is also better in many cases. Overall, network carriers can offer a better travel experience compared to other airline types.

13.9 Schedule planning and development

Commercial air transportation is dominated by scheduled air transportation and the base of classifying air transportation into scheduled types is the prefixed and published schedules of operation. Specific schedules enable the airlines to undertake marketing as well as to conduct air transportation services mainly for passengers. Airlines' commercial interests are driven by the desire to maximize revenue. Therefore, airline scheduling is of utmost importance to utilize the resources effectively and to the "perishability" of the product. The schedules that the airlines use are not just developed on a fine morning. Nevertheless, they have been designed after a meticulous process and by considering a wide range of factors. A process called schedule planning precedes the finalization and publishing of schedules. Schedule planning will reveal where and when the airline will fly. According to Wells (1988), it is "the art of designing system-wide flight patterns that provide optimum public service, in both quantity and quality, consistent with the financial health of the carriers". Schedule design describes which markets to serve and with what frequency, and how to schedule flights to meet these frequencies.

Flight schedule provides the routes served, flight frequency and times, and aircraft types assigned. It's like a timetable involving the cities to fly and the timings. It can reveal its competitive position, routes served, flight frequency and times and aircraft types assigned. Schedules include origin, destination, days of operation, flight number, types of aircraft, classes of service, transfer points and departure and arrival times. Uses of flight schedules include the following as well:

- For assigning fleet and aircraft routing
- For marketing of airline products
- For product distribution through various channels
- For selling of seats in advance
- For recruiting and staffing
- For crew planning and scheduling
- For periodical maintenance purposes
- For arranging ground handling services
- For flight operations.

The base of airline scheduling may consist of market demand forecast, available human resources, available aircraft, operating characteristics, regulations and competitors. Schedule development is mostly done as part of marketing activities. Still exclusive schedule planning section or department can be there in some airlines. In many cases, flight scheduling is a revision of existing schedules. Yet, developing new schedules becomes important for new airlines, route expansion and for strategic growth and diversification. The flight schedule is stored electronically in the passenger service system/reservation system.

Systematic and efficient flight scheduling is not only of crucial importance for long-term planning, but also for the operative airport business. It is a critical part of any airline for revenue optimization, operation planning and passenger loyalty. Eventually, optimizing the deployment of the airline's resources in order to meet demands and maximize profits is the prime objective of this process. The schedule that meets supply and demand efficiently is the key to airline profitability. General market conditions, costs of capital, fuel and labour, along with the level

Table 13.4 Flight Scheduling and Decisions Made at Different Stages

Time Period	60 Months or Above	36 to 12 Months	12 to 3 Months	4 to 1 Months
Nature	Long-range planning	Market evaluations	Schedule optimization	Schedule issues
Decisions	Fleet diversity. Manpower planning. Protecting hubs. Adding or changing hubs. Adequate facilities at airports.	Pricing policies. Predicting competitors' behaviours. Code-sharing agreements and alliances.	Developing initial schedule based on available fleets. Assigning aircraft to flights. Evaluating facilities and manpower capabilities.	Crew issues. Arrival–departure times. Maintenance issues.

Source: Modified from Bazargau (2010).

and nature of competition are the aspects that should be anticipated to deliver a profitable solution. According to Benckendroff et al. (2014), the output of flight scheduling consists of "flight schedules that maximize load factors and revenue per available seat mile and minimize costs per available seat miles". Objectives of flight scheduling include the following:

- Optimization of revenue
- Minimize the cost of operations
- Optimization of demand with supply using available and potential capacity
- Gaining marketing advantage
- Increasing market share
- Competitive and attractive flight schedules
- Convenient schedule for passengers
- Maximization of aircraft utilization
- Effective utilization of crew
- Effective utilization of airport slot and other facilities
- Contributing to strategic growth
- Capable to absorb delays and other disruptions

Usually, cyclical patterns covering a day or week are constructed to minimize the complexity of scheduling. The same can be repeated for the rest of the period. The real scheduling follows the identification of origin–destination city pairs. It is important to assign the number of flights to each origin–destination pair. Estimated departure and arrival times need to be finalized. Forecasting is the basis for most of the planning activities in airlines. With regard to schedule planning, route-based forecasts as well as sales and yield forecasts are also prepared. The revenue and cost associated with each schedule are based on different views of the same information. Individual flight legs between two cities are essential elements in the schedule. Airlines create the possible number of O&D markets to meet the requirements of a wide variety of customers.

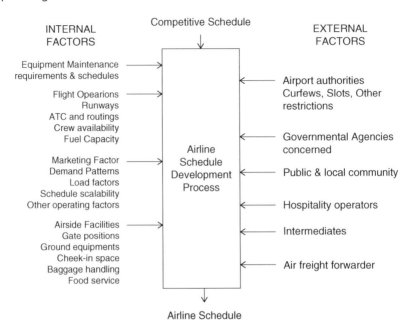

Figure 13.5 Airline scheduling and associated factors: a conceptual framework
Source: Adapted from Wensveen, (2007).

Flight scheduling takes place as a process. Different stages can be identified in different approaches to flight scheduling. Ashford et al. (2013) identified the stages of schedule planning in the following way. According to them, the first state is a market research and it provides input for the commercial economist and he/she, with the support of route divisions, advises in schedule planning. The factors influencing commercial economists can include the historical nature of the route; existing route capacity; aircraft type; fare structure; the social need for route and substitutes; political factors; competition; and requirements for special events. While the schedule is being generated by the schedule planning department, a number of factors will be affecting it, such as length of the route; airport's acceptability of service schedule; availability of crew; availability of aircraft; and legal clearances for operating services into foreign airports. The planned schedule is examined and, once satisfied, it moves in for current planning for the implementation of the schedule. The final implementation is done under operations control. Another approach suggested by Mathaisel (1997), the following four stages can be identified:

- Planning a schedule of services
- Generation of an operationally feasible schedule
- Assignment of specific resources
- Execution of rescheduling (operations control).

Table 13.5 Airline Scheduling: Some of the Factors to Consider

---

- Crews: crew routings, rest time, experience, etc.
- Marketing factors: market size, trip length, time zones involved, traffic flow, customer preferences.
- Facilities: Accessibility, check-in point gate, space and location, baggage handling areas, airport capacity, etc.
- Equipment maintenance: Maintenance requires time and the aircraft have to be transported to other stations, if needed.
- Climatic conditions: E.g. Wind, rain, snow fall, etc.
- Flight related: Airport runway length and width, fuel capacity, ATC and routings.
- Airport authority: E.g. Norms/conditions for getting slots, restrictions, etc.
- Political factors: E.g. Curfew, change in political conditions, etc.
- Local community: Various factors associated with it.

Source: Based on Wells (1998).

The output of the first phase is a generic service plan, which consists of a basic, feasible, set of services, with no specific aircraft or crew assignments, and with tentative service times of departure and arrival. In order to plan the initial schedule services, airlines need inputs like forecasts of available resources and market situations. Besides, the desired market initiatives like current schedules are also needed in this stage. Generation of an operationally feasible schedule is the next stage, which is also referred to as current scheduling. Focus of this stage is to create a feasible monthly schedule of operations for the airline, provided the expected resources are available. The basic service plan created by the marketing department, expected resources from maintenance and flight operations control, generic sets of cockpit and cabin crews, weekend and holiday service plans, hub-related constraints, etc. are the inputs needed. A detailed operational schedule suitable for publication in the Official Airline Guide and the airline's reservation system; optimal rotations for the aircraft and crews; airport gate assignments; station personnel requirements; etc. constitute the outcome of the second stage.

The third phase, which is resource assignment, focusses on finding optimal work assignments for the airline's specific resources: aircraft by tail number, crews by name, and gates by number. The inputs are an operational schedule (from phase 2), time and cycles on the aircraft and components (for maintenance), aircraft rotations and layovers, crew rotations and trips, gate loadings and station personnel loadings. The outcome of this phase includes the aircraft routings with scheduled maintenance, maintenance schedule of activities, crew bid lines and assignments (including reserves), gate schedules and station personnel assignments. The final phase referred to as system operations control or operations control centres or flight operations occurs on the day that the schedule plan is to be executed. The focus of this stage is to execute the operational schedule at least extra cost, which happens due to unplanned operational deviations, such as delays, diversions, or cancellations. The inputs are an operational schedule; work assignments; operational deviations; weather, breakdowns and sickness events;

Airline planning

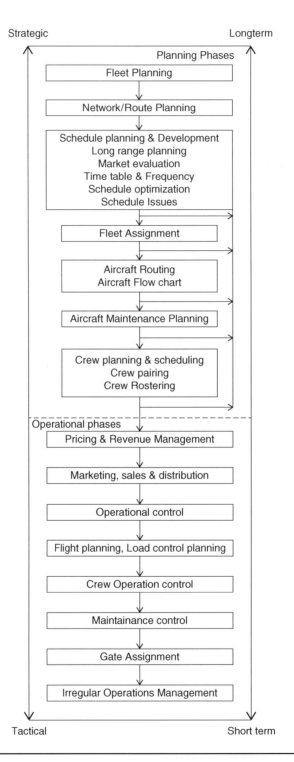

Figure 13.6 The hierarchy of airline planning
Source: Adapted from Barzagan, 2010

late arrivals; expected on-board traffic loads; and short-term operating costs. The outputs expected from this phase are a modified execution schedule; cancellations, delays, extra-stops and overfly; and reassignment of resources. Recent developments related to this are focussing on the dynamic rescheduling of schedule deviations.

The scheduling process is influenced by inputs of different kinds. Some of the major are listed below:

- Strategic goals, particularly about markets, competition, pricing, managerial resources, etc.
- Route network to ensure maximum aircraft utilization and convenient connections
- Passenger demand forecasts from revenue management modules
- Alliances: Partner airline schedules for convenient connections
- Aircraft types by considering the range, capacity, fuel efficiency, maintenance requirements, etc.
- Human resource: availability of various types of crews, their shift patterns, legal aspects, rest required, etc.
- Airport restrictions due to slot availability, congestion, safety, gate availability, etc.
- Contingency factors, like weather, ATC delays, etc.
- Environmental and safety regulations (Benckendroff et al., 2014).

The operating cost of the schedule depends on the flight legs, which determines the number and type of the aircraft used for the operation. The cost and availability of cabin crew and deck crew, the availability of aircraft after regular maintenance, the location and size of ground facilities and the number and location of crew and maintenance bases also affect the scheduling process. Large-scale combinatorial optimization techniques are used by airlines to address many scheduling issues such as assigning aircraft and crews to flights, routing aircraft to maintenance bases, etc. Some of the scheduled carriers fly with relatively low load factors but remain reasonably profitable due to the limited competition created by government regulation.

With regard to schedule planning and development, there have been several new methods introduced to improve the schedule efficiency and profitability. Integration of crew and scheduling processes to develop more efficient flying schedules and the implementation of demand-driven dispatch, where fleet assignment changes are made between crew-compatible aircraft close to the day of departure to better match passenger demand, are a few of such techniques.

13.10 Fleet assignment

Asset assignment is an important function. It is important to assign the required crew and facilities and services for implementing a schedule. Aircraft constitutes the most critical resource and asset in an airline organization. An airline will have different aircraft and determining which one is to assign for a particular flight sector or leg is a crucial task. Moreover, it is important to ensure that an aircraft is flying maximum every day instead of being parked. Fleet assignment is all about assigning the specific type of aircraft to the basic schedule. In other words, it specifies what type of airplane to assign each flight leg. Right type of fleet to each flight in the schedule has to be assigned. Based on the previous initial schedule, it explores the best possible way to execute the timetable by identifying available fleets with the lowest operating costs (Wu, 2010). Assigning fleet is part of aircraft assignment which defines the specific aircraft that will match the needs of each route scheduled. The best type of aircraft has to be assigned to each route, considering the economic aspects and maintenance aspects (Caetano & Fares Gualda, 2010). Different aircraft have different capacity, range and speed. The number of seats in economy class and other classes may also vary. The forecasted demand needs to match with the type of aircraft. Moreover, the distance to cover and the time needed are important determinants. Moreover, the required type of aircraft needs to be available for operation without a delay. The task of fleet assignment is a process of

> assigning aircraft types, each having a different capacity, to the scheduled flights, based on equipment capabilities and availabilities, operational costs, and potential revenues. An airline's fleeting decision highly impacts its revenues, and thus, constitutes an essential component of its overall scheduling process.
>
> (Sherali et al., 2006)

The focus of fleet assignment is to "solve the minimum cost assignment problem in order to assign the most suitable type of aircraft for individual flights in the timetable while meeting the maintenance requirements of aircraft" (Wu, 2010). This process is usually undertaken with the objective of assigning the most-suited aircraft, which is most cost-effective as well, to the flight legs in airline's network so as to meet passenger demand, while satisfying a variety of constraints. Fleet assignment optimization has been in wide use and it is attributed with generating solutions that lead to significant improvements in operating profit (Banhart,

Table 13.6 Difference between Four Major Airline Functions

Schedule Design	Fleet Assignment
Define which markets to serve and with what frequency, and how to schedule flights to meet these frequencies.	Specify what type of airplane to assign each flight leg.

Aircraft Routing	Crew Scheduling
Determining how to route airplanes to cover each flight leg with one and only airplane and to ensure maintenance requirements for airplanes.	Select which crews will cover each flight leg in order to minimize global crew costs.

Source: Parmentier (2013).

2009). Optimum utilization of aircraft, which deals with catering to the demand with the number of flights, is another focus of fleet assignment. Fleet assignment is done approximately three to four months before the scheduled time. Based on the previous initial schedule, it explores the best possible way to execute the timetable by identifying available fleets with the lowest operating costs. "An airline's fleeting decision highly impacts its revenues, and thus, constitutes an essential component of its overall scheduling process" (Sherali et al., 2006). Airline has to identify the type of fleet needed for each leg/sector considering both the technical aspects of the aircraft and the availability of them. The capacity of the available fleet in terms of demand is also crucial in fleet assignment. Moreover, fleet assignment should not result in a reduction in profit and has to help in maximizing revenue, while minimizing cost.

13.11 Aircraft routing

Once the fleet assignment is done, the next task is to determine routing (a sequence of flights covered by a single airplane) or rotations (a routing that starts and ends at the same location) for each airplane (Parmentier, 2013). Routing determines how to route airplanes to cover each flight leg with one and only airplane and to ensure maintenance requirements for airplanes. It is "the process of assigning each individual aircraft (referred to as tail number) within each fleet to flight legs. The aircraft routing is also referred to as aircraft rotation, aircraft assignment or tail assignment" (Bazargan, 2010). It is done with the intention to utilize available aircraft in each fleet to operate flights at the right time and between the right city pairs. By this, flights on the same route are operated by the same aircraft sequentially. This process usually starts one or two months prior to operation. Routing is also a difficult task, which needs to be managed meticulously. The chronological arrangement of flights on different routes in a profitable manner along with maintenance schedules is the integral part of aircraft routing (Wu, 2010). Yan and Kung (2015) suggested a robust aircraft routing mechanism in which the aircraft routing problem is as follows:

> given a set of aircraft of a specific fleet type and a set of flights that must be operated, determine how the fleet can be routed so that each flight leg is included in exactly one aircraft routing, and all aircraft are properly maintained. Among all feasible assignment of aircraft to routes, we seek the one that incurs the least amount of total propagated delay.

Regarding maintenance, it is important that all airports may not have adequate maintenance facilities. Maintenance of aircraft takes place at different periods and levels. Routine maintenance is inevitable. A lapse in it can lead to severe safety issues. This is an important consideration while routing is done. When a flight is in a route as per the schedule, the necessary maintenance has to be done. It means that airports with adequate facilities for doing routine maintenance that matching the maintenance needs of a particular aircraft also have to be there in the route (further details of aircraft maintenance are given in the following chapter). Demand is another concern while assigning an aircraft in a flight leg. The same aircraft has to be assigned in the route sequentially, and it should have the capacity to match with the demand in all flight legs. Scheduled arrival and departure times as well as that particular aircraft's turnaround time also need to be matched while doing aircraft routing. Simply, aircraft routing enables us to understand the chronological movement of a single aircraft in a route along with the maintenance schedule. **Aircraft flow chart** can be ready after this. An aircraft flow chart will be displayed soon. The following considerations (Clarke et al., 1997; Gopalan & Talluri, 1998; Papadakos, 2009; Bazargan, 2010) should be given:

- Flight coverage: single aircraft to cover each flight leg
- Aircraft load balance: balanced utilization loads should be there in the aircraft
- Maintenance requirements: there should be adequate facilities in the airports concerned to receive the required routine checks, at the right time and at the right base.

13.12 Crew planning and scheduling

After aircraft, personnel are the most important resource of an airline. Among airline personnel, crews have some special significance as they form part of product realization and consumption. Identifying the most efficient staff with quality personnel that suit the routes chosen is a critical financial consideration. Therefore, good planning is crucial for the effective utilization of the entire fleet and crews. Basically,

> Crew planning involves the creations of a time table that allocates a crew member to a specific duty. This may be a flight, a series of flights, or another assignment such as standby, training or ground duties, and these activities collectively form a duty roster.
>
> (Fennell, 2018)

Manpower scheduling is a broader term used in this context. It represents "the actual work plan including working, non-working days, times, shifts, locations and leave periods" (Barzagan, 2010). Crew planning is all about crew scheduling which is done to determine the sequences of flight legs and assigning both cockpit and cabin crews to these sequences. It takes place on a long-term as well as short-term basis. Rather, it's better to classify crew planning into two, such as strategic and tactical crew planning. A number of factors need to be taken into consideration for crew planning. These factors include legal, ICAO regulations, place of domicile, flight aspects, etc. Crew scheduling for both cabin as well as cockpit crew is a daunting task, and efficient crew scheduling can reduce cost. One of the major objectives of this stage is to minimize the total cost of crewing along with allocating suitable crew as per the requirements of both types of crews. The major inputs and considerations in crew scheduling involve crew requests for routes, seniority, base city of crew members, legal aspects, rest periods and compensation. In a crew scheduling system, a "computer programme called pairing optimizer assembles flight schedules for each crew member". (Benckendroff et al., 2014). Crew scheduling consists of two integral components, such as crew pairing and crew rostering.

13.12.1 Crew pairing

Individual crew members are assigned to crew pairings, usually on a monthly basis. Crew pairing is all about creating a number of crew pairings at the lowest cost. "The objective of crew pairing is to find a set of pairings that covers all flights and minimizes the total crew cost. The final crew pairing includes dates and times for each day" (Bazargan, 2010). Crew pairing is basically the generation of mini schedules, called pairings.

> A pairing is a sequence of flight segments, or sectors, connected to form a flight duty that starts and ends in the same crew base. It can span one day or several days, depending on the operation, and may or may not include one or more layovers.
>
> (Fennell, 2018)

Short-haul pairing is easy. Long-haul needs layover and legal rest is to be included. The working hours of the flight crew are also regulated as part of safety consideration and fatigue management. In addition, the location of the crew base is also a factor considered. Tour of duty (TOD) is the term used for showing it. According to Cheng Lung WU,

> A TOD may last for 1 to 2 days for a domestic crew, to a number of days for an international crew, depending on flight timetables and airline networks. If a TOD involves overnights at ports other than the base of a crew, airlines will incur other crewing expenses such as accommodation, grand transport and meal allowance.
>
> (Wu, 2010)

Crew pairing needs to be based on the length of the flight sequence from the beginning place and returning. Rest duration, place of domicile, time of flights, etc. need to be considered. Multiple days can also be there in each pairing. Usually, specialized pilots are there for each type of aircraft. For an airline, a large number of different pairings are required for a complete flight schedule.

13.12.2 Crew rostering

Crew rostering represents the process of building up detailed rosters for an individual crew within a particular period. This stage deals with how to utilize crew resources to execute the planned schedule/timetable at minimum cost (Wu, 2010). It involves pairings that are assembled into longer crew schedules in the form of "rosters" or "bidlines". Roster is basically a work schedule generated for each crew member according to his/her preferences, capabilities and requirements. Roster consists of all such pairings along with non-flying assignments, off-day training, etc.

> A roster describes a crew member's flight activity for some period (typically a month), and consists of sequences of flight duty and days off (e.g. three days

on, two days off). In some airlines, "bidlines" are made available based on the flying requirements for a given crew base, then awarded in order of seniority through a bidding process.

(Midkiff et al., 2009)

Elements of monthly crew roster consist of the following:

- Flight duties
- Reserve duties (airport and home)
- Ground duties (administration work and medical check)
- Training
- Rest periods
- Days off (mandatory and requested)
- Annual leave (Fennell, 2018).

13.12.3 Bidding

Bidding is the term used for representing bids from the crew. Crew members can bid for a preferred bidline/roster, and it is assigned based on various factors like position and seniority.

The process of requesting a particular schedule is called **bidding.** Generally, each crew member submits their bids monthly. The monthly work schedule allocated to a crew member is called a **line,** which consists of a series of **crew pairings**. A crew pairing is a sequence of flights or legs that start and end at the same base destination (i.e. round trip).

(Benckendroff et al., 2014)

Bidline is a generic schedule assigned to each crew member. Bidline represents a sequential listing of all trips that each crew member will be taking in a specific period of time. Roster/bidline schedules are usually fit into thirteen 28-day or 56-day roster/bid periods per year (Horswell, 2018). Reserve crew members are also to be identified. Pairing assignment follows three types of methods, such as line bidding, preferential bidding system (PBS) and fair assignment (Fennell, 2018).

- Line bidding
    Bidlines (pre-customized duty rosters) are released early for review and the bid is awarded as per seniority.
- PBS
    Preference of the staff will be taken to assign a bid.
- Fair assignment

Every staff gets an equal chance to be assigned duty, irrespective of seniority, etc. After it, a conflict resolution is done before publishing the roster.

Software is available to manage the tasks of pairing and lines/rosters. Advanced algorithms and mathematical models are used nowadays for pairing and rostering that can yield "full coverage of the flying programme with the smallest number of pairings and crew, at the lowest cost". (Fennell, 2018). According to Banhart

(2009), the following criteria are considered by crew planners while developing schedules in order to maximize crew satisfaction.

- Maximizing all the individual crew requests that are satisfied by the schedules or maximizing the minimum number of requests satisfied for any one individual.
- Maximizing the minimum number of flying hours in any one individual's schedule to achieve equity in the workloads of individuals.
- Optimizing the spacing between periods of work to keep the diurnal clocks consistent and to let the crew members take the advantage of extended time-off periods.

While crew scheduling, it is important to consider the rest period of the crew.

> air carriers have the responsibility to conduct their operations at the highest level of safety. That includes establishing appropriate scheduling practices that provide pilots with adequate rest. Preventing the degradation of alertness and performance caused by fatigue is a shared responsibility that brings shared benefits in terms of increased safety, better working conditions, and greater overall operational efficiencies.
>
> (Holt & Poyner, 2018)

Crew should get adequate and suggested level of rest before next duty. Pilots and staff should have proper rest time. Report time and release time for a crew have to be properly scheduled considering the regulations concerning the rest period. Again, there can be issues in broken duty schedules and the "maximum duty day" considerations.

13.13 Conclusion

The airline industry needs efficient planning and management. Airline punctuality is a crucial factor in airline selection and satisfaction for passengers. Airline planning is a complex process and fleet planning, fleet assignment and route planning are fundamental to ensure smooth operations. Quality airline services are definitely important for a better travel experience and contribute to the overall tourism experience. Some of the airlines' plans are more strategic, while others are more operational. Strategic planning is a long-term plan of 5 to 20 years that fits the corporate vision and mission. Operational planning is also very important in airlines, especially since most activities are time-bound.

The most crucial strategic planning activity of an airline organization is, of course, fleet planning, which is the aircraft selection process. Strategic decisions need to be made accurately after a thorough evaluation process to assess the impact of a new aircraft on the financial performance of an airline. A network of airlines contains routes on which they operate. Network planning, also known as route planning, is a critical activity in airline planning and management. Precise planning is required to expand the existing network. Different types of networks can be found in air transportation, such as linear, point-to-point, hub-and-spoke, gateway and hybrid. Code-sharing is a common practice on airlines to enable more choices for travellers and is made possible by commercial agreements between marketing and operating airlines. The interline agreement between the airlines allows passengers to travel on multiple airlines on the same itinerary. Moreover, it allows passengers to check their baggage all the way to the final destination. International tourism is more dependent on network carriers, and with hubs, network airlines can ensure global connectivity for tourists. Schedule planning and development are vital for commercial airlines, which will enable them to undertake marketing smoothly. Fleet assignment is for assigning specific types of aircraft to the basic schedule that will match the needs of each route scheduled. Aircraft routing refers to the sequence of flights covered by a single airplane, also referred to as aircraft rotation, aircraft assignment or tail assignment. When a flight is on a route according to the schedule, necessary maintenance needs to be done in regular intervals. Crew planning is about crew scheduling, which determines the order of flight legs and assigns the cockpit and cabin crew to these sequences. Crew scheduling consists of two integral components, such as crew pairing and crew rostering. Advanced software with algorithms and mathematical models is used nowadays to manage the tasks of crew pairing and rostering. Crew should get adequate and suggested level of rest before next duty as well.

Sample questions

Short/medium answer-type questions:

- Write the significance of planning in airlines
- Write the importance of strategic planning in airlines
- Elucidate different types of planning in airlines
- Describe fleet planning in airlines
- What do you mean by fleet assignment?
- What are the factors to consider on fleet planning?
- What are different types of networks?
- What are the advantages of point-to-point network?
- Describe hub-and-spoke system
- Elucidate the benefits of hub-and-spoke system for tourists
- Discuss why airlines enter into code-sharing
- What are the contents in a flight schedule?
- Explain the flight scheduling process
- What do you mean by fleet assignment?
- Describe aircraft routing
- What do you mean by crew pairing?
- Distinguish between crew rostering and bidding
- Explain the crew scheduling process

Essay type questions

- Discuss in detail about the importance of planning in airlines from a tourism perspective
- Write an essay on planning in airlines
- Discuss in detail about airline networks and network planning

Suggested readings

Bruce, P., Gao, Y., & King, J.M. (Eds.). (2017). *Airline Operations: A Practical Guide*. London: Routledge.

Cook, G.N., & Billing, G.B. (2018). *Airline Operations and Management: A Management Textbook*. London: Routledge.

Cook, N.G., & Goodwin, J., 2008, Airline networks: Comparison of hub and spoke and point to point systems. *Journal of Aviation/Aerosoace Education and Research JAAER*, 17(2), 51–60.

Wu, C.-L. (2010). *Airline Operations and Delay Management*. Surrey: Ashgate.

Chapter 14

Airline operations and management

14.1 Introduction

Airline operations involve complex tasks, and the smooth functioning of flight services needs diligent planning and careful and efficient execution. These operations are supposed to be on a planned schedule, though stochastic disrupting events may occur to any component of the airline systems. Time is a crucial factor in airline operations. A small deviation from a preset schedule can cause financial issues as well as managerial glitches to deliver services to the already sold items. A delay in a sector can delay the corresponding schedules, and passengers, airport operators and many others can be affected. The airline industry is featured with extreme punctiliousness and involvedness as Sabre opines

> Few industries generate the level of attention and notoriety as the aviation industry when it is at its best - or its worst. From the announcement of new

 DOI: 10.4324/9781003136927-14

aircraft to major irregular operations that cancel hundreds of flights and strand thousands of passengers, airlines are constantly in the spotlight.

(Sabre-www.sabreairlinesolutions.com)

It also states that

> Efficient operations don't just happen. Airlines face myriad operational challenges - schedule disruptions, limited resources such as aircraft, crew and maintenance personnel, and increasing customer expectations. And each day brings a new set of challenges that personnel must react to when accomplishing the safe and efficient movement of passengers and cargo.

Even if the planning is done well, execution of all the preset plans has to take place at the right time with extreme precision. Standard operating procedures are there to follow. Certainly, it is of extreme significance to reduce the risk of flight operation incidents and accidents, and in each and every step, all the necessary precautions have to be taken. A lapse in any one of the activities can cause severe consequences. Moreover, influences of external factors are also severe, and the operations can be adversely affected by them. Such can cause irregular operations that can lead to a large number of people being stranded in airports. Moreover, a wide variety of personnel are involved in the performances of airline operations, and all those personnel and operations need to be coordinated well for successful airline functioning. Let's go through the operations in an airline in detail.

14.2 Airline operations

Flight operation is the most crucial task in airline operations. All the planning done earlier is implemented in order to execute the flight operation to transport people and cargo from one place to another. Accurate and meticulous planning can help in efficient execution of flight operations, though the efficiency is linked to some external factors as well. Most of the planning discussed in the previous chapter is more strategic in nature. The tactical operations mainly focus on the execution of flight schedules and utilizing the resources thereof. Execution of pre-planned schedules is the prime task. During the process of execution, there may have been minor updates of the schedules as per the emerging circumstances. Minor changes are common and may not affect future operations in maintaining the forthcoming schedules set earlier. At times, due to various reasons, there can be major delays and irregular operations. These are to be handled carefully and quick actions are needed to make things right in order to avoid delays in future schedules. Traditionally, the following are the centres that handle all the activities that lead to the conduct of the flight operations in a smooth and safe manner.

- Airline Operations Control Centre (AOCC)/Integrated Operations Centre (IOC)/ Network Operations Centre (NOC)
- Station Operations Control Centre (SOCC)
- Maintenance Operations Control Centre (MOCC)

14.3 Airline operation control

Operational control is all about

> the exercise of authenticity over initiating, conducting or terminating a flight. In practice, an air carrier exercises operational control by making the necessary decisions and performing the required procedures to operate flight safely and in compliance with FARs and the air carrier's OP specs.
>
> (Holt & Poyner, 2006)

OP specs denote operations specifications. AOCC is the hub of airline's flight operations operational control centre, and the "operational nerve centre of the airline" (Kim, 2018). This is the space from where almost all crucial operational activities are being undertaken. Traditionally, all activities other than maintenance control and station operation activities are planned and implemented from here. Operations Control Centre (OCC) manages the daily activities of an airline and co-ordinates the operations, crew management and flight dispatch. Nowadays, this is more of an integrated centre with even maintenance activities also being controlled from here. Hence, the concept of this kind of AOCC has been advanced to IOC. According to Buchanan (2018 in Bruce, Gao & King), lately, traditional model of OCC is being transformed, and airlines are now turning into a new model called IOC and in some airlines, it is also called NOC. Cook and Billig (2017) also have come up with a similar opinion and according to them

> over the last few decades, airlines have moved daily operations managers and staff to a single operations centre in order to improve coordination, communication, and tactical decision-making. The development of the Airline Operations Control Centre (AOCC)-the name varies across airlines-is one of the major airline management evolutions ranking alongside network development and revenue management.

This IOC is now the space from where all the decision-making departments are located in one room. Moreover, the processes are integrated between the departments to bring together collaborative and dynamic decision-making processes (Buchanan, 2018). According to Ashford et al. (2013), the following functions are performed by AOCC to achieve its objectives:

- Supervision/coordination of all services that are associated with the processing of passengers, freight and aircraft.
- Coordination of fire, rescue, police, security and other emergency forces in accordance with the operational needs.
- Supervision of the control of access to the airside and the rest of restricted areas.
- Enforcement of all operational procedures, like emergency plan and snow control programme.
- Relay of information between terminal service units and dissemination of action directives to the operational employees.
- Updating of information status displays, obtaining seasonal flight schedules for pre-planning the assignment of airport facilities, supervision of assignment of common use facilities and flight and baggage display system monitoring.

- Ongoing analysis of the impact of current and anticipated passenger and flight activity levels on operational systems.
- Coordination of maintenance activities

AOCC traditionally consists of key personnel who are vested with the responsibility of managing and tracking the schedules and controlling the operations along with adjusting the schedules in the wake of irregular operations. The following, according to Barnhart (2009), are the key personnel in an AOCC.

- **Airline operations controllers**
   They are responsible for aircraft rerouting and decisions on flight cancellations, ground delays and diversions for aircraft.
- **Dispatchers**
   Dispatchers constitute another group of key personnel who provide flight plans and relevant information to pilots.
- **Crew planners**
   They find efficient recovery solutions for crews and coordinate with the airline operations controllers in order to make sure that considered operational decisions are feasible with respect to crews.
- **Customer service coordinators**
   They find efficient recovery solutions for passengers and coordinate with the airline operations controllers in order to contribute to an assessment of the impact of possible operational decisions on passengers.
- **Air traffic control group**
   This group collects and provides information pertaining to the flight of an aircraft to airline operations controllers.

As part of operational control, it is important to deal with three key factors: schedule integrity, disruptions and delays (Buchanan, 2018). The department will face many challenges, like weather variations, mechanical problems, airport-related issues, etc. Controlled and uncontrolled delays and disruptions can be there. Of late, maintenance controllers are also being accommodated within the AOCC, when there is no separate maintenance control centre over there.

14.4 Operations control

In an AOCC, operations controllers are there with adequate staff. Airline operation controllers maintain all operational versions of the schedules. They may revise the schedules as per the prevailing circumstances. If needed, new schedules are developed. Input from all sections of airlines will be available, and the personnel over there resolve issues that emerge as part of operations. Input sources for airline operations controllers include flight dispatchers, crew operators, station managers, ramp service managers, maintenance and engineering department, meteorology, route planners and ATC coordinator. Operational schedules are revised as per the need based on the emerging situations. If needed, new schedules bring the operations to normalcy. Dispatchers are there for flight planning and issuing the flight plan to pilots and observing the flight operation. Though dispatchers are vested with the responsibility of a successful release of a flight, when

Table 14.1 Elements of a Flight Plan, Based on Excerpts from a Sample Flight Plan

Header	Waypoints
• Flight plan summary • Fuel summary • Alternate destination routing • Aircraft type • Departure details • Cruise Mach • Cruise altitude • Filed routing • Destination • Estimated en route flight time • Destination alternate • Estimated flight times to ATC sector boundary crossings • Aircraft registration	• Waypoint IDs • Flight level • Forecast wind • Wind component relative to course • Latitude/longitude of waypoints • Magnetic course to waypoint • Magnetic heading (course adjusted for wind) • Terrain height • Mach • True airspeed (TAS) • Ground speed • Temperature deviation • Forecast turbulence index • Distances from and between waypoints • Total distance remaining • Total flight time to waypoints • Segment fuel burn • Total fuel used from departure to waypoints

Fuel	Take-off Planning
• Expected en route fuel/time/distance • En route reserves required for overwater operations • Regular reserves • Dispatch addition • Fuel to get to the destination alternate • Holding fuel • Buffer fuel • Take-off fuel • Taxi from gate to runway • Total fuel load at release	• Minimum TOW • Maximum TOW • Runway-limited weight • Structural weight limit of the airframe • Climb-limited weight • Maximum LDW • Planned TOW • Take-off decision speed • Rotation speed • Take-off safety speed • Fan rotation speed (N1) or engine pressure ratio (EPR)

Source: Modified from Midkiff et al. (2009).

irregular operations occur, dispatchers will inform the operations controller for further actions. Holt and Poyner (2006) identify most of the following duties of director of operations:

• Provides operational control of flight operations.
• Directs and supervises the chief pilot, directing in-flight and flight operation staff.

- Develops budget for flight operations.
- Ensures proper training for the required staff and quality.
- Ensures the quality of contract services along with ensuring proper ground handling services.
- Supervises collection and storage of key data, like flight/load manifest, weight and balance.
- Ensures the discipline and reward and employs/terminates employees.
- Ensures flight operations safety as per regulations.
- Communicates with authorities and maintains records
- Manages the minimum equipment list (MEL) programme.
- Schedules aircraft availability for operation and inspection.
- Coordinates with the maintenance director for timely repairs, etc.

Operations manuals are there for the standard operations. Flight operation manual, ground operation manual and management policy and procedures are the available manuals for the same. Airline flight manual (AFM) is provided by aircraft manufacturers. Operation manual is provided by the airline, which includes policies and procedures for the performance of duties smoothly and safely. Maintenance manual is also there provided by the manufacturers.

14.5 Flight planning and dispatch

Flight dispatch does not happen all of a sudden when the pilots arrive to take control of the flight. A range of procedures are to be followed and specific information has to be ready and provided to all those personnel who require that relevant information. Flight planning consists of diverse activities, like flight plan preparation, the estimate of fuel requirement, etc. Dispatch section is vested with the responsibility of flight dispatch mainly. A flight dispatcher undertakes certain operational control functions of a flight, which includes flight planning, maintaining communication with the flight crew about the weather, operational limitations, etc. (Holt & Poyner, 2006). A dispatcher is jointly responsible with the pilot in command for preflight planning, delay and dispatch release. Also, during the flight, he/she is responsible for monitoring the progress of the flight, issuing necessary information for the safety and cancelling or redispatching as per the circumstances, which do not permit to operate or continue to operate as planned/released (Holt & Poyner, 2006). Large airlines have a team to deal with flight operation with dispatchers assisted by aircraft routers, ATC coordinators, flight followers, load planners, maintenance controllers and maintenance meteorologists (Kim, 2018). The following stages are essentially passed through before a flight lands at the destination:

- Flight dispatcher gets familiarized with weather and airport conditions from the departure till the destination.
- Flight dispatcher plans the flight route and fuel load considering the payload, aircraft maintenance, restrictive aircraft MEL items, en route winds and possible delays and restrictions.

- Flight plan is prepared and it is filed with ATC to include proposed departure time, route, altitude, flying time and aircraft details.
- After the flight's dispatch, the flight's progress is monitored, and revised information according to changing conditions is issued. If a delay occurs, replanning may take place. (Kim, 2018)

In the flight planning stage, it is important to gather the weather conditions and airport conditions. A thorough check of the weather is needed. Flight planning process comprises

> selecting the best routing (in terms of time, fuel burn, ride conditions, etc.) given the available information, and generating a "flight plan" that can be programmed into the aircraft automation. This accounts for aircraft type, forecast weather conditions, aircraft performance, loads and operating weights, aircraft mechanical condition, marketing constraints, airport limitations/curfews and company priorities (e.g., minimum fuel versus minimum time trajectory).
>
> (Midkiff et al., 2009)

Current weather conditions (Meteorological Aerodrome Reports: METARs) and forecasts (Terminal Area Forecast: TAFs) for all airports involved in a flight are continuously monitored. The visibility at the airport as well as conditions at the destination airport and possible alternate airports need to be verified. Moreover, the airport's surface conditions are cross-checked to know water or ice deposits, etc. Considering the weather conditions, etc. routing can be finalized. The needed fuel requirements are also determined considering the regulatory and aircraft requirements. The weather conditions at the departure and arrival airports, along the route, and at the alternative airport are taken into account in this stage. The following are the factors considered in determining the final routing:

- Winds
- En route weather
- ATC costs
- Payload and fuel restrictions
- Regulatory requirements
- Notices to airmen (NOTAMs)
- Other route limitations from ATC, etc.
- Any aircraft restrictions (MEL) (Collier & Smith, 2017).

Load factors are also finalized. Flight plans can be ready by then. Currently, flight planning is done electronically (E.g. using Jespersen). According to Kim (2018), "..., Flight Dispatchers use computer-based flight planning systems to optimize routes, calculate performance, calculate fuel load, apply MEL restrictions and file flight plans with ATC". A flight plan is needed to ensure that the aircraft meets all of the operational regulations for a specific flight, give the flight crew information to help them conduct the flight safely, and coordinate with ATC (Altus, 2009). According to Altus (2009), the following are the various aspects of a flight plan. The route to fly, specifications of altitudes and speeds, the fuel needed for flying and additional fuel needs are the essential elements of a flight plan. Varying the route (i.e. ground track), altitudes, speeds and amount of departure fuel can help reduce the fuel costs, time-based costs, overflight costs, etc., subject to airplane performance, weather, allowed route and altitude structure, schedule constraints and operational constraints. Optimizing flight planning can provide the opportunity for cost optimization by enabling the airlines to determine the optimal route, altitudes, speeds and amount of fuel to load in an airplane. Route optimization is one aspect of flight optimization, and it is all about determining the best route to fly, which depends on the forecast of upper air winds and temperatures, the amount of payload and the time-based costs on that particular day. Fuel accuracy is also an aspect, which is relevant for flight plan optimization.

> Accurate, optimized flight plans can save airlines millions of gallons of fuel every year — without forcing the airlines to compromise their schedules or service. Airlines can realize their benefits by investing in a higher-end flight planning system with advanced optimization capabilities and then ensuring accuracy by comparing flight plan values to actual flight data, identifying the cause of discrepancies, and using this information to update the parameters used in the flight plan calculation.
>
> (Altus, 2009)

Air navigations service providers/ATC can be handed over the flight plan along with the dispatch release. A dispatch release document is usually issued before the departure, which may contain:

- Aircraft identification number
- Flight number (trip number)
- Type of operation (IFR/VFR)
- All airports concerned (departure airport, destination airport, intermediate stops and alternatives)
- Minimum required fuel supply
- Latest weather reports and forecasts at the time of departure
  (Holt & Poyner, 2006).

Once the flight begins its journey, the dispatcher has to monitor the progress of the flight continuously. Along with monitoring the progress of each flight, safety information needs to be updated regularly by the dispatcher, and in case of issues, he/she needs to instruct to cancel the flight. In flight plans, alternate destinations are identified. "Destination alternate requirements are driven by forecast weather conditions at the airport of intended landing, and in cases where weather conditions are good and not expected to be a factor, no alternate may be required" (Midkiff et al., 2009). While finalizing fuel and load control also, distant alternate destinations are clearly specified. The pilot in command has to be updated frequently about the weather conditions while on the flight. Alterations in flights can be done, like cancellation due to different reasons like unfavourable weather to continue operation, mechanical issues, security, reasons, etc.

A flight dispatcher's duty is continuous and personnel are assigned on a shift basis. With regard to flight control, a number of activities and functions have to be performed, which may include ensuring engine airworthiness before flight; conduct dispatch and release of concerned operations; find out solutions for disruptions of various kinds; verify the norms regarding assigned crew schedules, flight planning, release generation and flight following each flight (within its jurisdiction); maintain current summary list; authorize the departure of revenue flight; ensure suitable weather condition at origin and destination prior to release of aircraft; provide the captain with information on weather forecasts, relevant NOTAMs, all significant meteorological information, adversaries on possible weather changes, possible traffic delays, field condition reports and braking reports, etc. Safe and smooth flight from the origin airport to the destination airport is the joint responsibility of the pilot in command and the dispatcher.

14.6 Load control planning and load sheet preparation

Aircraft weight is also a major safety concern. It is extremely important for maintaining the balance of an aircraft. Knowing aircraft weight is inevitable in determining aircraft performance from take-off until landing, determining fuel requirements, and letting the aircraft remain compliant with the manufacturer's limitations (Avery, 2018). According to USDOT-FAA (2016),

> weight is a major factor in airplane construction and operation, and it demands respect from all pilots and particular diligence by all maintenance personnel. Excessive weight reduces the efficiency of an aircraft and the available safety margin if an emergency condition should arise.

Operating above the maximum weight limitation can lead to discrepancy in the structural integrity of an aircraft and can adversely affect its performance. Load planning is all about planning where each item is to be loaded in an aircraft. Aircraft loading needs precision with a basic understanding of the principles of centre of gravity and balance and that can enable the aircraft loading easy and quick. The balance is related to the centre of gravity along the longitudinal axis where all weight is concentrated or balanced in an aircraft. "Aircraft centre of gravity is the point at which the aircraft would balance if set upon a pivot" (Avery, 2018). Distribution of weight is the most important aspect. The important aspects of weight and balance system for aircraft are the following:

- Weighing of the aircraft
- Maintaining of the weight and balance records
- Proper loading of the aircraft (US DOT-FAA, 2016).

All of the above have to be properly and accurately measured or managed. A lapse can cause serious consequences. Load control takes information from the cargo section, baggage section, passenger section, catering, cabin services, fuelling, etc. In the load control planning stage, different types of weights are calculated. The following are the major types of weights in general:

- Manufacturer's empty weight (MEW)
- Basic weight (BW)
- Dry operating weight (DOW)
- Taxi/ramp weight (RWT)

- Zero fuel weight (ZFW)
- Take-off weight (TOW)
- Landing weight (LDW)

Manufacturer's empty weight (MEW) is referred to the weight of the structure and equipment, and BW is used to represent the weight of the aircraft without passengers, baggage and unusable fuel. BW is the basic empty weight, which includes aircraft structure, systems, engines, irremovable equipment, unusable liquids and standard loose equipment. The following types of weights are taken while preparing the load control plan:

- DOW
  BW with crew, pantry items and crew baggage
- ZFW
  DOW plus total traffic load
- Maximum Taxi Weight
  ZFW with block fuel
- Maximum ZFW
  Maximum weight before usable fuel
- Ramp weight
  TOW plus taxi fuel: the weight of loaded aircraft before starting the engines
- TOW
  Gross weight of aircraft at brake releases for take-off: the actual ZFW plus take-off fuel
- Maximum TOW
  Maximum weight, which is allowed to take-off
- LDW
  TOW minus trip fuel
- Maximum LDW
  Authorized for normal landing
- Actual ZFW
  DOW and final payload, and it is important to ensure that it does not exceed MZFW
- Maximum zero fuel weight (MZFW)
  The maximum weight allowed before usable fuel is loaded as per the structural limit
- Payload
  Includes passengers, baggage, cargo and mail
- Allowable payload (Under load)
  Payload that aircraft is able to carry with weight and balance limitation

DOW is the weight of the aircraft prior to the loading of passengers, baggage, cargo and fuel. BW denotes the weight of the aircraft without crew, catering and adjustments. After taking DOW, the weight of the fuel has to be considered. For flying an aircraft from departure airport to destination, enough fuel has to be there:

- to fly to the destination airport (destination fuel)
- to fly to the most distant alternative airport (alternate fuel)

- 10% to 15% of the fuel required at destination/alternate airport
- to fly for extra 30/45 minutes at normal cruising fuel consumption rates (holding fuel) (Holt & Poyner, 2018)

Load planning is an important task. A load planner's responsibility is to prepare a load plan by gathering data on items to be loaded on the aircraft in coordination with the flight crew, dispatchers, fuellers, cargo agents, check-in agents and ramp personnel (SABRE-White Paper on Load Planning), based on these basic operating empty weight or DOW. Weight of booked passengers, estimated bags and mail and cargo for a particular flight leg will provide the estimated ZFW.

Aircraft has a maximum acceptable load. Aircraft load planning and control involve a range of activities to ensure that the aircraft is loaded properly, safely and in an efficient manner. The safely loaded aircraft is what is expected from the load control process. In it, the principles of loading along with the accurate determination of different weights have to be taken care of well. Load control is done to perform aircraft weight and balance within limits and actual load is recorded. Weight and balance are all about the total mass of the loaded aircraft and the centre of gravity position. The distribution of weight will change as the flight progresses since the fuel is being consumed. Weight and balance have to be planned for take-off, during flight as well as for landing. Aircraft manufacturers usually provide weight limitations.

Load sheet is an outcome of the load control planning. Load control finally provides the calculated aircraft weight and centre of gravity. All will be entered onto load sheet/load and trim sheet for the use of a flight crew. Essential elements of a load manifest, another term used to refer to the same kind of document, is:

- weight of the loaded aircraft
- maximum allowable weight that must not exceed the least of:
  o maximum TOW for runway
  o maximum TOW that allows compliance with en route limitations
  o maxim TOW (considering fuel/oil consumption) that allows compliance with maximum LDW limitations
  o maximum TOW (considering fuel/oil consumptions) that allows compliance with landing distance limitations on arrival at the destination/alternative airports.
- total weight computed under an approved procedure
- evidence that the aircraft is loaded within the centre of gravity limits (Holt & Poyner, 2006).

Loading instruction report (LIR) is also provided. This is "the document used to transfer loading requirements to ramp staff" (Avery, 2018). It can show where the items can be loaded. Loading in an aircraft is done by the ground handling section. According to the pyramid method of loading, it is better to load the heaviest items in the centre of balance, at the optimum CG station of the aircraft. The next heaviest item can be loaded forwards of the first item and so on. There can be exceptions and other types of loading practices are also there (www.globalsecurity. org). Weight and balance records are generally retained for a period of six months in accordance with National Civil Aviation Authority requirements. The safety of a flight requires accurate planning, recording and reporting of all actual load

Table 14.2 Problems of Overloading in Aircraft

The common problems that can occur due to overloading in an aircraft.

- The aircraft needs a higher take-off speed, which causes longer take-off run
- Reduction in rate and angle of climb
- Service ceiling is lowered
- Reduced cruising speed
- Shortened cruising range
- Manoeuvrability is decreased
- A longer landing roll is required due to higher landing speed
- Excessive loads are imposed on the structure, especially the landing gear

Source: US DOT-FAA (2016).

boarded on an aircraft. The load and trim sheet, prepared in triplicate, are signed by the responsible officer and by the loading supervisor. It's a legal document, staff licencing required and has to be under investigation in case of any accidents/incidents. The commander of the aircraft has to approve it. Of the three copies, the first one goes to the captain, the second one to the senior cabin crew and the third one to the station trip file.

14.7 Crew operations control

Managing crew during the course of flight operations is another crucial task. It is imminent to have a timely arrangement in situations when a scheduled crew is unable to attend duty. The crew controlling section is vested with the responsibility for making suitable alternate arrangements in such situations of the absence of scheduled crews. It monitors the crew checks, check-ins and check-outs and updates and changes the crew roster according to the disruptions that might appear during the operation. There will be disruption and deviation from the preset schedules. There will be crew control staff to recover from the issues. Crew schedulers deal with the duty progress of each crew and maintain the latest status and make adjustments. Crew operation controllers' prime duties include crew scheduling, maintaining crew schedules, tracking of schedules, rescheduling if needed and calling resource crews when the need arises. In case of any crew being unable to attend, arranging crew from the reserve or exchanging crew members from other flights are among the possible actions used to solve crew problems.

14.8 Maintenance control

Aircraft maintenance is an important task to be performed by airlines. Different types of maintenance are mandatory for aircraft. While doing maintenance planning, it is important to have coordination between the maintenance department and operations control in order to ensure the availability of aircraft for the schedules. Payload limitation is a prime concern in operational planning. Usually, the maintenance planning document, which consists of the maintenance functions required at different intervals, is provided. Objectives of engineering and maintenance progress of an airline are to:

- ensure the airworthiness of aircraft
- restore the airworthiness periodically.

An aircraft is maintained as per the manufacture's guidelines approved by the aviation regulators. Scheduled maintenance and unscheduled maintenance are there in aircraft maintenance. Maintenance programme

> is a complicated set of processes and instructions aimed at restoring reliability of the aircraft as it deteriorates due to 'wear and tear' or exposure to its environment. The output of the programme will be either detailed instructions to rectify a fault (i.e. unscheduled maintenance), or detailed instructions for scheduled maintenance to prevent a fault from occurring.
>
> (Swann, 2018)

Aircraft rotations are monitored by MOCC. In case of delay or irregular operations, data will be sent to AOCC for decision. The line mechanic will update information on the aircraft in the repairing process. In addition, they send suggestions about which aircraft to be used and the availability status to airline operation controllers. Aircraft routers are there. They follow the aircraft and aircraft rotations. Rotations represent repeating patterns of flight legs assigned for aircraft. Maintenance controllers coordinate maintenance activities. As part of maintenance activities, aircraft have to undergo routine maintenance checks. Visual checks are the most common. Routine ramp check, departure check or preflight or postflight check are different terms used to refer to this type of check. This is a routine check happening during the ground time, on the ramp and before/after every flight. Routine ramp checks primarily involve the following:

- The mechanics verify the aircraft on the basis of a checklist. It includes:
  - walk-around check
  - battery, landing gear and air pressure checks
  - cockpit equipment diagnostic check
  - detailed check on engines, exterior or cabin interior
  - checking aircraft's logbook, recorded by the pilot

Periodic checks are another category of checks done at regular intervals. Service checks are done at the major or designated class 1 stations. The common types of routine checks (Swann, 2018) are A-check, C-check and D-check. They are introduced below.

14.8.1 The A-Check

This is undertaken mostly at every 400 flight hours or more depending upon the type of aircraft. These are of short-duration overnight check, usually. This is "an amplified preflight visual inspection of the fuselage exterior, power plant and

Figure 14.1 Aircraft maintenance Austrian Airlines Boeing 777 in a hangar
Source: Wikipedia Commons.

certain readily accessible subsystems, including avionics (aviation electronics) and accessories and is conducted to ascertain the general condition of the aircraft" (Wensveen, 2007). Filters will be changed, key systems will be lubricated and a detailed inspection of all the emergency equipment is completed. Earlier B-check was also there, which has been merged now with other checks.

14.8.2 The C-Check

At every 4,000 flying hours, C-checks are done. Here also, the need for the number of hours can vary as defined by the manufacturer. Different C-checks are there. 1C (one-C) is the basic, which is done at 4,000 flying hours. The next is the 2C-check, which is done at every 8,000 flying hours. A 3C-check is undertaken when an aircraft completes 12,000 flying hours. In all, 1C-check will be done. Also, lower C-checks are included depending upon the need, and the duration of the checks varies from 6 days to 19 days. During a C-check, in-depth system checks and in-spection for corrosion, cracks, structural defects, in-depth lube of all fittings and cables are carried out. A C-check is done approximately every 12–18 months at a hangar, usually. Till the completion of the check, the aircraft will not be used for service. This maintenance check is usually done at major stations.

14.8.3 The D-Check (Overhaul)

This is an overhaul check and undertakes at 32,000 flying hours. Overhaul mainte-nance is the most detailed and important one for aircraft. This can be done only in maintenance bases. Maintenance base is the largest maintenance station for aircraft. The aircraft is basically dismantled and put back together. Everything in the cabin is taken out, the engines are taken off, landing gears are removed and all parts are verified meticulously and repaired or replaced and reinstalled. The major overhaul helps rework the aircraft in a like-new condition.

Non-routine maintenance is also undertaken in airlines in the wake of unanticipated incidents or as deemed necessary after any of the routine checks. Others are also there, like cabin upgrades and aircraft modification/conversion activities. Maintenance is done on contract in many cases as it is capital-intensive and labour-intensive and requires much technology, experience and expertise. Some airlines have their own maintenance facilities, including maintenance bases.

According to Wensveen (2007), the maintenance stations are classified into four such as maintenance base, major stations, service stations and other stations.

14.8.4 Maintenance centres

The following are the facilities for undertaking maintenance activities of aircraft.

14.8.4.1 Maintenance base

It is the largest, most versatile, and best-equipped facility for aircraft maintenance. This can repair almost all parts of an aircraft, and it is considered the "overhaul and modification centre" for an airline's fleet for undertaking maintenance activities of the fleet of an airline.

14.8.4.2 Major stations

These may consist of an airline's hub city stations that have relatively large numbers of maintenance personnel and extensive facilities. They also will have sufficient numbers of spare parts. These stations have the capacity to provide complete line maintenance of specific types of equipment and the stock of a substantial inventory of spare parts that is mainly supplied by the maintenance base.

14.8.4.3 Service stations

These are relatively large stations that are not located in major hub cities and are well equipped, along with sufficient line maintenance personnel, but with lesser than the major stations.

14.8.4.4 Other stations

These are stations with only sufficient numbers of licenced people to assure maintenance coverage for each flight before departure and with minimal facilities and spare parts. There can be Class 1, Class 2 and Class 3 stations depending upon the rate of availability of service personnel, facilities and spare parts.

14.9 Station Operations Control

SOCC essentially consists of the following staff:

- Station manager
- Gate coordinator

- Ramp service manager
- Passenger service manager

Gate scheduling is a major task and the prime function is to implement schedules. In hubs, airlines have to manage many gates. Assigning arriving flights to airport gates is an important issue in the daily operations of an airline, particularly since they have a major impact on maintaining the efficiency of flight schedules and passenger satisfaction (Barzagan, 2010). Schedule execution is a daily-based activity and it involves executing and updating the schedules. If needed, the personnel concerned have to reschedule irregular operations. Baggage handlers, gate agents, security personnel, ramp handlers and other ground handling personnel need to be scheduled. Individual gates are assigned to each flight. Gate restrictions are there like varying sizes of gates, scheduled order of arrival and departures, passenger walking distances, occupancy of adjacent gates, ramp congestion, aircraft rotation and aircraft service requirements. If any discrepancies are found, gates are to be reassigned. Ground handling tasks involving fuel arrangements, catering, staff assigning at gates, baggage handling, cargo-related activities and ramp crew scheduling are key in the efficient turnaround of an aircraft. Passenger handling is another important task. The provision of good hospitality is also a major concern.

14.10 Passenger processing and flight operation

Passenger processing within airports needs to be handled efficiently. "The purpose of passenger processing is to facilitate the movement of passengers at airports, either departing or arriving" (Wu, 2010). It is a major determinant of customer satisfaction. Usually, passengers arrive in the terminal much in advance of the departure time. Details of passengers and the required number of check-in counters, etc. would be kept ready with the airlines prior to the commencement of the check-in time. Check-in is an important activity in passenger processing at airports. An adequate number of check-in counters is to be earmarked for a smooth check-in process. Initially, check-in can be commenced with a minimum number of counters, and later, when the number of passengers increases, more counters can be added. Online check-in options are there; hence, many passengers prefer this as it avoids queuing in for a long time. For such passengers, airlines offer special arrangements for baggage collection, etc. The personnel over there have to ensure that long queues are not there. Airlines use the term **"dwell time"** to refer to the time between the arrival time of a passenger at a check-in lounge and the scheduled departure time of the flight (Wu, 2010). Passengers prefer less dwell time.

Proper assistance has to be provided for passengers for smooth emigration clearance and security checks. Passengers should feel relaxed and have proper space and facilities for rest and refreshing before boarding. Flight delay can also be due to delay in check-in as well as delay in boarding/deplaning and loading/unloading. Therefore, it is important to ensure timely processing of all required activities. The following are the major activities that are to be undertaken by airlines at airports:

- Passenger check-in and issuing a boarding pass
- Baggage check-in

- Passenger/baggage processing
- Cargo and goods handling
- Catering service preparation
- Passenger boarding at gates
- Turnaround of flights
  - Disembarkation of passengers
  - Cabin cleaning
  - Crew changing
  - Routine visual maintenance check
  - Refuelling
  - Cargo loading/unloading
  - Unloading and loading of catering services
  - Embarkation of passengers (Wu, 2010).

Other activities include mishandled baggage handling, special handling, cargo and dangerous goods handling, engineering services, etc. Passenger check-in is done once the passengers enter the departure area. In some airports, check-in luggage will be verified before the collection of luggage. Check-in baggage can be screened over there through an X-ray scanning machine. "Baggage is almost everything and anything a passenger brings on their flights" (Movig, 2018). The following constitutes different types of baggage:

- Normal baggage: These are the luggage within the applicable dimensions as per the airlines' baggage restrictions.
- Hand baggage/carry-on baggage: These are the carry-on/cabin bags. Passengers can carry them in their hands while on the flight. Restrictions in terms of size and items are there.
- Checked-in baggage: This consists of passengers' luggage that are loaded in the bulk/belly of an aircraft. These are not carried as hand baggage. This can vary based on the fare paid, passenger category, routing, group status or class. Checked-in baggage is also referred to as hold baggage. The baggage tag attached is the document that can be used for identifying the luggage.
- Odd size and out-of-gauge baggage: These constitute the hold baggage that is too large to handle and load. Out-of-gauge baggage is the normal baggage above the stipulated dimensions.
- Free carry-on items: A laptop; an overcoat; a wrap or blanket; an umbrella or a walking stick; a small camera or handheld video equipment; a lady's handbag, vanity case or purse; etc. can be carried as free carry-on items.

In some airports, baggage screening process takes place later, after collecting them by the airlines. After the entry and luggage screening, passengers can move to the check-in counters. Nowadays, self-check-in kiosks are there. Some passengers can collect their boarding pass from the kiosks themselves. If they have luggage, they will move to the check-in area to hand over the luggage, which will move inside as check-in luggage/baggage for baggage handling activities. At check-in counters, staff will weigh the luggage/baggage as per the free baggage allowance (FBA) restrictions. Check-in/checked baggage is the luggage that cannot be carried by passengers in hand and that are loaded in the specific place for luggage (hold) in an aircraft.

Table 14.3 Checked-in Baggage Free Baggage Allowance

The amount of checked-in baggage that can carry in a journey is fixed based on two concepts, such as:

- Weight concept
- Piece concept.

In the weight concept, the total weight of the baggage is considered for free baggage allowance. The following constitutes an example of weights permitted as part of free baggage allowance in a flight.

- First class 40 kg (88 lbs)
- Business class 30 kg (66 lbs)
- Economy class 20 kg (50 lbs)
- Infant (all classes) 10 kg (22 lbs) + one baby push chair or 1 stroller or 1 baby basket

The next category, the piece concept denotes the free baggage allowance based on the number, size and weight of the checked baggage. The following is an example of this category:

- First class/business class: Two checked pieces, with the total of three dimensions not exceeding 158 cm (62 inches) for each piece (maximum weight has to be 32 kg/70 lbs per piece
- Economy class: Two checked pieces, with the total of three dimensions not exceeding 158 cm (62 inches) for each piece (maximum weight 23 kg/50 lbs per piece)

FBA is given for up to a specific weight and size as per airlines' conditions. A fare includes the free transportation of a certain amount of baggage. This certain amount of baggage is called free baggage allowance. The number of pieces and the weight for each piece or the total weight a passenger allowed carrying depend on the class of travel or the itinerary of the passenger. Nowadays, along with the evolution of low-cost carriers (LCCs) as a major airline type, no standard FBA is followed by many of the airlines. Most of the LCCs consider check-in baggage as a revenue source, and hence they limit FBA. Airlines usually charge an additional rate for extra weight. In addition to LCCs, full-service carriers also charge extra for excess weight, which is referred to as **excess baggage charge**. Once weighed, the luggage is tagged, registered, and moved onto a conveyor belt. In the tag attached, necessary information will be there for identification and sorting. The following are the information in a baggage tag:

- Barcode with license plate
- Arrival airport name/code
- Departure time
- Airline code and flight number
- Passenger's name, etc.

Bags are sorted according to the tag's information about the aircraft to be loaded and destination to be moved to. Passengers' baggage has to be handled efficiently. Misplacing of baggage can cause further complications and financial burdens to airlines. The baggage, after X-ray screening, will move via the conveyor belt and then, after sorting and identifying respective airlines to carry, it will be loaded into a container/cart, which is sometimes called "make-up". Usually, an early baggage storage area is there where containers/carts are ready for loading. Ramp officers may supervise the loading process. Location of loading, etc. need to be specific and loading principles have to be followed. Proper loading in terms of weight and location is important, particularly for take-off, flight and landing. Baggage for transfer points is loaded near the door. Usually, cargo is loaded first. The baggage loaded has to be in line with passengers boarded. If any passenger is not boarded, the baggage should not be transported.

Baggage handling needs increased care, particularly since the baggage cannot speak if they are misrouted or mishandled. In the case of passenger handling, passengers themselves move according to the directions provided. According to Bazargan (2010),

> The transportation of baggage poses many challenges to airlines, including scheduling the number of baggage handlers, baggage trailers, delays, lost baggage, and missed connections. In fact, for major airlines baggage handling for transit passengers seems to be the dominant factor in gate assignment in their major hubs.

> (Barzagan, 2010)

Baggage-related common issues, according to Movig (2018), are:

- Missing/misreading of labels
- Mishandled bags/lost baggage (E.g. human errors, fall off a cart/conveyor belts, etc.
- Damaged bags.

Ramp control is an important function, which is basically to execute the preparation activities for a departing flight. Personnel involved in this function hand over the final flight documents to the captain and they coordinate the activities that lead to the departure.

Earlier, flight engineers were there in the aircraft. Of late, only two key personnel are there inside the cockpit, called cockpit crew, which consists of captain and the first officer. The captain is the pilot in command, who is the pilot flying, and the first officer is the pilot monitoring. For the duty, pilots will be provided a company-supplied briefing material including flight standing orders, international notice to ALL pilots, MEL, weather, NOTAMs, and flight plans (Miller, 2018). The flight crew must be provided with notification to the captain (NOTOC), the notification concerning the location on the aircraft where dangerous goods or special items were loaded and the names of the personnel who prepared the NOTOC. The focus is on aircraft status, availability to fly and fuel quality. Flight plan needs to be checked again. The captain should have copies of:

- Flight plan
- Load manifest
- Dispatch release
- Load and trim sheet

Briefings and cabin preparation will take place in between. The crew has to follow the activities listed in the "before start checklist". The crew has to determine the airworthiness of the aircraft. It mainly includes interior and exterior inspection. Preflight inspection points are usually given in the checklist for the crew. The exterior workaround preflight check, which may vary from 8 to 20 minutes depending on the size and condition of the aircraft and the number of wheels/tyres, involves visual inspection in which the crew member checks the fuselage, engines, wings and flight control surfaces to determine whether any damage is there or not. Tyre wear and pressure, brake wear indicators, absence of leaks or fluid on the ramp, condition of antennas, probes and lights, the necessity for de-icing (during winter, to remove the ice deposits on aircraft body) and any other factors are also inspected. Interior checks are also done on the electric power and air availability. Cabin crew has to check the status of catering and cabin emergency equipment, along with the general cabin condition. Cockpit crew also verifies system conditions, checks the documents required, etc. The pilot also has to finalize flight parameters by obtaining an update on weather conditions and runway utilization. Flight routing confirmation has to be obtained from ATC. Cockpit has flight management system (FMS), the key system to manage the flying. It consists of a flight management computer, automatic flight control system or automatic flight guidance system, aircraft navigation system and an electronic flight instrument system (Miller, 2018). With the help of global positioning system and internal reference system, FMS will enable the pilot to guide the flying.

Flight operation from a crew perspective, particularly from that of the cockpit crew, is detailed by Midkiff et al. (2009), and they identified a number of stages. A gist of the same is given below.

14.10.1 Crew sign-in

The crew will be present and sign in approximately an hour before the flight for getting acquainted with the flight details and get prepared for flying. Soon after, the cockpit crew will go ahead with the flight planning activities.

14.10.2 Flight planning

By this time, the flight dispatchers might have prepared a flight plan, and the same will be handed over to the cockpit crew. It will have details of various aspects of the flight, like routing, weather, alternate airport options, fuel requirements, take-off performance and loads.

14.10.3 Preflight activities

The designated crew has to determine the airworthiness of the aircraft. Interior and exterior inspection of flight has to be performed. Simultaneously, needed turnaround activities also have to be performed. The cabin crew also has to check the status of catering and cabin emergency equipment. Besides, it is to be verified whether all required manuals and paperwork are on board and complete. Verification of aircraft mechanical logbook is also important. Once such activities are over, the cockpit crew initiates FMS and auto-flight initialization programming to allow their use during the flight. By that time, passenger and baggage, as well as cargo boarding, will be progressing. As the departure time approaches, the cockpit crew will receive the fuel slip from the fueller to corroborate the fuel quantity and distribution (between different fuel tanks) with the flight plan and on-board sensors. The captain conducts a briefing with the purser or lead flight attendant about the standard information, which may include en route flight time and the weather conditions of the destination, safety and security affairs, various aspects of landing, etc.

14.10.4 Pre-departure

Sooner, the captain, lead gate agent and ground crew chief jointly ensure that all pre-departure requirements are met. Based on the latest updates, the pilots will finalize the FMS and auto-flight parameters, and they get confirmation of the flight's routing from ATC. Now, it is ready to perform the "before starting engines" checklist and turn on the "fasten seat belt" sign in order to enable the cabin crew to make ready the cabin for departure and deliver the requisite public address announcements. Once boarding is over, the agent coordinates the closing of the aircraft doors with the captain and lead flight attendant, and by that time, the ground crew completes baggage and cargo loading and closes the cargo doors. Now, the needed activities are undertaken for pushback.

14.10.5 Gate departure

Once everything is ready and ATC clearance is got, pushback clearance is given and the aircraft is pushed out of the gate area. Engines will be started only when the pushback crew intimates that the area is clear. Once the tow bar is disconnected, the aircraft will be ready for taxi-out.

14.10.6 Taxi-out

Now, all the details are checked out for taxiing and the captain conducts a take-off briefing. The aircraft will roll on over the taxi-out to the runway.

14.10.7 Take-off

Once everything is clear, ATC will send clearance for take-off to the pilots and take-off will be led soon.

14.10.8 Terminal area departure, climb and cruise

ATC will intimate the climb flight profile and will let the aircraft climb up. The aircraft leaves the terminal area to increase speed and to maintain the altitude. Separation will also have to be maintained. When the cruise altitude is reached, the power settings/Mach targets are established.

14.10.9 Descent, terminal area arrival and final approach

While nearing towards the destination, the initial descent takes place within about 30–40 minutes prior to landing, and, simultaneously landing preparations will begin. Necessary instructions will be made available from the navigational/ATC personnel. Approximately 10,000 feet above the airport, terminal area manoeuvring will begin. Real-time landing information or instructions are given as soon as it approaches the airport. As the aircraft near the airport for landing, all weather conditions will be considered again for landing.

14.10.10 Landing and roll-out

Landing will be done as per the instructions given by the ATC and the aircraft will leave the runway (turn-off) without any delay.

14.10.11 Taxi-in and parking

Pilots will roll out of runways and use taxiways to move ahead to the arrival gate while the crew readies the cockpit and cabin for parking. Once the aircraft is parked, turnaround activities will begin quickly. Crew change may or may not be there as per the crew schedules.

All activities over there are time-bound and the turnaround time of an aircraft is very crucial in ensuring punctuality in operations. "Turnaround coordinator" ensures smooth performance of turnaround activities. According to Wu (2010), the **aircraft turnaround** operations denote various activities undertaken to prepare an inbound aircraft at an airport for a following scheduled outbound flight. The activities include both inbound and outbound exchange of passengers, crew, catering services, cargo and baggage handling along with technical activities like fuelling, routine engineering check and cabin cleaning. Delay in activity can lead to delay in operation, and it can have ripple effects in the forthcoming operations as well.

14.11 Boarding and arrival procedures

While departing, once the passenger collects the boarding pass from the check-in counters/kiosks/web check-in services, the passenger moves to the emigration centre or called as passport control centre, in the case of international air travel. Security check is the next procedure, and hand baggage, electronic devices and others with passengers are screened and checked separately if found anything suspicious. After security check, passengers enter a concourse with a wide variety of commercial facilities, including duty-free shops, refreshment centres, gift shops and book shops. From there, after finishing the shopping and/or refreshments, passengers can move to the departure area where the gate is located. When the aircraft is ready for boarding, passengers are led to aircraft by walk or in a transfer vehicle or through a passenger jet bridge.

The boarding process may vary from airline to airline. Some airlines prefer passengers to board based on seat numbers. Boarding is a time-consuming activity and can affect the turnaround time. Different types of boarding strategies are there. Back-to-front, window-middle-aisle, random and rotating zone are the commonly seen strategies (Barzagan, 2010). In the back-to-front, the first and business class will be boarded first. Other passengers start entering and occupying seats from the back. Passengers are called to board on the basis of seat row numbers, by groups or zones. In the second category, airlines board passengers in window seats first, then the middle seats and finally the aisle seats. Random-type strategy follows no specification, but all board in one zone randomly. In the rotating zone type, passengers are grouped into zones. Boarding starts from the front, then in the back, followed by from the front, etc. While entering the aircraft, the flight crew may greet and welcome the passengers and lead them to their respective seats. Once the flight is ready for boarding, passengers are boarded, and baggage and cargo are loaded simultaneously. Cabin crew has to sign out 60–75 minutes prior to flight departure for international departure. Soon, the flight attendant has to undergo a line readiness check. Preflight meeting will be there, and after that, they can move to the gate. Cockpit crew/captain brief senior cabin crew members about the flight and journey. In addition, senior cabin crew members provide flight details to the captain. They then interact with ground handling staff to know the details about the flight, etc. The briefing consists of ISTOP threat, which includes the following:

- I-Introduction
- S-Aircraft status and confirm whether the crew is "fit to fly"
- T-Turbulence/weather
- O-Operational consideration
- P-Passwords
- Threat: other possible threats along with mitigation strategies.

It is important that they check all the facilities and services, like safety materials, doors, etc. The cabin staff have to verify the flight inside (clean, etc.). Passenger boarding has to be monitored well. After gate checks, passengers move to the aircraft for boarding. Once boarding starts, the in-flight crew welcome the passengers into the aircraft and assist them in taking seats and in storing the hand baggage. Pre-departure checks also have to be followed. During the pre-departure time, the cabin crew has to check the following:

- Ensure that passengers are seated
- Fastening of seat belts
- Infant restraints are fitted
- Upright seat position
- Stowing of all hand baggage
- Closing overhead lockers

- Tray tables and others stowed
- Keeping window shades up
- Secure galleys
- Carts and galley load unit latchet and secured
- Cabin dividers, etc. refrained
- Ensure that electronic devices of passengers are in an appropriate mode
- Ensure that aisles, exits and crossover are clean and ready for door closure and subsequent pushback (Horswell, 2018).

If time is less, then the first officer may proceed to the aircraft for preflight duties and submit the flight plan well in advance from the departure time of the flight. The flight plan must be accepted by the pilot. Crew operations are done to keep track of the crew and in case of irregular operations, attempt to bring back operations to normalcy. A pilot in command is responsible for the control and authority of aircraft operations/safety of the passengers and cargo and aircraft and to determine whether the aircraft is airworthy. A captain can rely on the aircraft's logbook's airworthiness release and can have a "walk-around" inspection before each flight. (Holt & Poyner, 2006). The flight plan will be prepared, which will have details of various aspects of the flight, such as routing, weather, alternate airport options, fuel requirements, take-off performance and loads. Flight path plan includes estimated fuel consumption, path, engine numbers and emergency needs, weather forecast and estimated TOW.

Take-off planning is another task during the preparation of flight plan, which may be done by dispatchers or load managers, and if any adjustments to take-off plans are required, it will be done according to the latest conditions. Once all doors are closed, ground crew does "pushback". Then, pushback request by captain, pushback by ground staff from gate to taxiway, aircraft taxiing on taxiway, waiting in the departure queue, and take-off. In the case of landing, landing, taxiing on the taxiway, to parking at the arrival gate. It is followed by execution of airline flight as per the flight path plan. After pushbacks, communication to ATC/ramp control for push back clearance. When it reaches out of the gate area, the engines are started. Then, taxi clearance will be performed. Once permission is obtained, aircraft can taxi into position and hold on the departure runway. Once the pilot receives take-off clearance, the aircraft will be positioned and necessary measures will be taken. ATC provides all necessary instructions including a climb flight profile. The crew will check necessary flight details as per given information like altitude, etc. Once it reaches a certain altitude, in-flight services will begin. While the flight is in the air also, the dispatcher updates the pilot in command about all the information. During the cruise, the crew performs monitoring of aircraft flight path and system maintaining, lateral fuel balance within time, cabin temperature and control, etc. As it reaches near destination, descent has to be done. ATC gives instructions. All information on destination like the weather will be provided to the pilot. They take measures to descent. They prepare cockpit and cabin for landing. They conform to ATC restrictions and plan an approach for landing. After landing, they roll-out and take taxiways as per instructions from ATC.

Once the flight route is completed, the flight will be ready for landing. The process of landing is an important activity in terms of safety as the same has to be performed smoothly. Necessary instructions will be received by the captain from time to time that can lead him to perform a smooth landing. From there, the flight will move to the ramp through the taxiway. Usually, the first class and business class passengers have the chance to disembark first and, once that is over, the economy class passengers will be moved. All will be transported to the arrival gate and then enter into the arrival concourse. From the arrival area, they move to passport verification and visa counters. At entry, passengers' eligibility to enter the country of destination is assessed by government officials, and it may be verified in terms of visa, its validity and having sufficient resources to maintain themselves in the visiting country (Lucas, 2018). Quarantine or biosecurity controls are also undertaken by some countries to restrict the entry of pests and diseases. Some countries may ask for vaccination certificates in certain cases. Also, in the case of people coming from some regions where communicable diseases are widespread, they may be checked.

Arriving passengers have to move to the baggage claim area (after completing the immigration formalities, in the case of international passengers) for collecting their luggage. In large airports, there will be a number of conveyor belts and the passengers have to identify their respective belts. The passengers can collect their luggage and verify its tag with the counterfoil issued from the boarding point. Once baggage is collected, the passengers can move ahead to the customs area. Customs check is done for:

- Preventing smuggling of illicit drugs
- Blocking trade of restricted items
- Preventing transportation of weapons illegally
- Collecting due duty from the items that are dutiable (Lucas, 2018).

There are two ways, such as **green channel** and **red channel**. Usually, baggage is screened through scanning machines. If a passenger has nothing to declare, like dutiable goods, he/she can move through the green channel. If there is any item for which a duty needs to be paid, then the passenger has to move through the red channel and pay the fee accordingly. Incoming passengers are free to move out after the customs procedures.

14.12 Airline disruptions and irregular operations

Disruptions in airline schedules and irregular operations constitute an important issue in airline operations while delays are common and irregular operations are more problematic for the airline industry. According to Filson (2017),

> Airline disruptions can arise at any time, and each one is characteristically unique, requiring solutions on the fly. As ominous as flight delays and cancellations may be, the outcome can be smoother than anticipated and, at the same time, can be cost effective. To achieve the best results, airlines must prepare diligently for all potential scenarios. To reach a high state of readiness, it is important to take a structured approach, focusing on each stage of the irregular operations business cycle.
>
> (Filson, 2017)

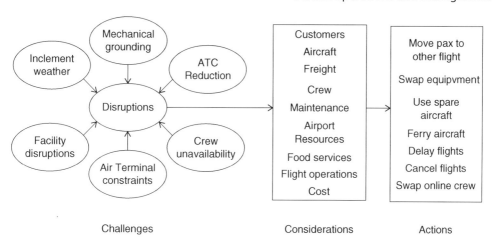

Figure 14.2 Airline operations: decision-making model
Source: Buchanan (2018).

The most appropriate decision has to be taken during delays. In this hypercompetitive business environment, ensuring on-time performance is extremely significant. Irregular operations mean any deviation that needs rerouting of the flight. Schedule revisions need to be undertaken timely whenever needed. Delays and disruptions cause a ripple effect in the hub-and-spoke system. Hub-and-spoke system is vulnerable to ripple effects due to a delay, particularly in hub. If any disruption or delay takes place in hub, the rest of the operation to the spokes will be affected. One delay causes delay in all connected routes. Similarly, a delay in spokes can also affect hub operations. The cost of airline disruption is a major concern for the airline industry. Disruptions certainly affect airlines monetarily as well and that erodes the profit potential of airlines. The following elucidation by Gershkof (2016) gives a hint on the overall cost of airline disruptions and irregular operations.

> The consensus estimate of the cost of these disruptions to the airlines is about 5% of airline revenue or about USD 35 billion worldwide. However, this is almost certainly not the whole story, as it does not include the cost of lost productivity to travellers and lost business for support industries such as hotels, business services, and tourism. The total value, including the value of all the lost productivity and downtime, is probably more like $60 billion.

14.12.1 Causes of delays and disruptions

Delays, disruptions and irregular operations can be due to a range of factors. According to Simillon (2017), there can be ten common causes of disruptions/irregular operations for airline operations. They are weather, strike action, third-party issues, crew logistics, natural disasters, civil unrest, local anomalies, mechanical and technical problems, operational issues and health. There can be more factors as well. The following are the major factors that cause delays:

- Weather
- Technical problems
- Aircraft repair/maintenance
- Political factors
- Civil unrest/terrorism
- Natural disasters
- Airport-related issues
- Crew-related issues
- Health
- Connectivity delays
- IT/computer failures
- Inefficient ground handling
- Safety and security *issues.*

Regional problems like for example animals obstructing runways; passenger-related obstructions like by expressing unruly; need for recheck of baggage; incidents affecting the airport or airline operation systems; crew violating rules; etc. too can lead to delays and disruptions to airline operations.

14.12.2 Managing disruptions

When disruptions occur, the prime priority is to return to the published schedule. There has to be a reserve crew always. Manning the aircraft for operation is so important wherever there is a need to replace staff. Spare aircraft may also be needed for meeting a situation. Delays may be managed by making attempts to reduce delay duration and still continuing service. Cancellation and rerouting are also undertaken depending upon the circumstances. AOCC usually undertakes efforts to recover from the disruptions and bring back the flight operations to the pre-scheduled status. Some of the following strategies, according to Barnhart (2009), are to adjust scheduled operations by:

- cancelling flight legs
- rerouting or *swapping aircraft,* which refers to reassigning aircraft among a subset of flight legs
- delaying flight departures until aircraft and/or crews are ready
- postponing the departure times of flight legs to prevent connecting passengers from missing their connections
- calling in new crews or reassigning existing crews
- reaccommodating disrupted passengers.

Airlines may use project evaluation and review technique (PERT) model with the intention to manage and model airline operations. Critical path method is also used/incorporated in this context. PERT is used with the following objectives:

- To evaluate and enhance the efficiency of airline operational procedures
- To enhance the efficiency of airline ground resource allocation (mainly HR) (Wu, 2010).

AOCC centrally manages operations of aircraft, crews and passengers and monitors flight irregularities. When irregularities occur, it implements recovery plans in order to return the schedule as early as possible.

14.13 Safety and security operations

Safety is a serious concern in airline operations. Every possible step is being taken to ensure maximum safety. Unlike other modes of transport, a negative reputation with regard to safety can dampen the scope of the industry as well. Safety in aviation has multiple areas and levels. Safety measures are taken not just alone by airlines, but usually, most of the safety operations are undertaken together by other elements in air transportation. In order to maximize safety in air transportation, each and every operation by an airline has to be performed based on standard practices accepted internationally. Together with the progress of aviation, safety and security threats too got compounded and posed critical challenges. There can be a number of factors that can affect the safety of the airside. Airports especially take utmost care to avoid safety issues due to such factors. The factors include the condition of runways, taxiways and aprons due to water logging, snow, ice and rubber deposits, obstacles locally around the airport, broken or damaged ground facilities like signs, approach lights, faded markings, presence of debris on the runways, taxiways or aprons, and bird or animal activity on and near the airport. Also, some airport facilities like passenger boarding bridge, catering tracks, to cargo belt loaders can also cause damage to aircraft. Usually, airports now have a safety management system (SMS) to look into this area. It is designed to manage any hazards that affect airline safety. Now, it is becoming mandatory for airports to have SMS in place; it is also now applicable to airlines and air navigation service providers. Ensuring ground and runway safety is critical in airline operations. Incursion can happen due to human factors, improper instructions and communication from ATC, climatic reasons like rain and poor visibility, inadequate markings and/or lightings and the like. Yet, all possible measures are taken to minimize safety issues. Aircraft may have issues due to bird strikes, etc. particularly near airports. Airports are nowadays careful about this to minimize such incidents. Aircraft manufacturers usually take adequate measures to save aircraft from damages and issues due to lightning. De-icing is a common strategy to remove ice and snow from aircraft bodies to save aircraft from various issues that occur during winter seasons. Strict maintenance checks and activities are done by airlines to avoid mechanical issues for aircraft. A lapse in such can be dangerous. Poor weather conditions are always an issue in air transportation. Advance systems are there to issue warnings and to take precautionary measures to avoid such.

All crews are properly trained to handle their respective tasks. Strict regulations are there regarding qualifications and experience to become a crew. One of the most important aspects of safety associated with a crew is the rest period.

air carriers have the responsibility to conduct their operations at the highest level of safety. That includes establishing appropriate scheduling practices that provide pilots with adequate rest. Preventing the degradation of alertness and performance caused by fatigue is a shared responsibility that brings shared benefits in terms of increased safety, better working conditions, and greater overall operational efficiencies.

(Holt & Poyner, 2006)

A poor decision, lack of carefulness, confusion, negligence, etc. can become fatal. Human error is a major reason for air safety issues. Human errors are of different kinds, like decision errors involving procedural errors, poor choices and problem-solving errors; errors associated with skills like inadvertent activation of controls and misordering of steps in procedures; perceptual errors; and violations of rules and guidelines of different kinds (FAA, 2005). Advanced systems are there now to alert aircraft while in the air to avoid any kind of accidents or collision. Security threats are also increasing. Though more and more measures are being imposed, newer threats are emerging. Terrorism is a serious concern and, in order to minimize such issues, strict security checks and screening of luggage, etc. are undertaken before the boarding of passengers and loading of baggage. The major components of aviation security include intelligence gathering, controlling access to secure air operation areas, screening of passengers and carry-on luggage, screening of checked baggage and cargo and aircraft protection (like cockpit protection) (Seidenstat, 2004).

In order to avoid the repetition of safety and security issues, a diligent investigation will be done. For instance, immediately after aircraft accidents, multilevel investigations will be undertaken to identify the root cause of it. Sooner, solutions will be determined to avoid such in future. Safety recommendation is the end product given out as an accident prevention measure, mainly. It will be issued as early as possible. A separate section may be there to look after the safety aspects of airline operations. An airline's director of safety is vested with the following tasks to perform:

- Conducts safety review whenever required
- Undertakes annual internal safety audits and investigations as per requirements
- Attends safety meeting/seminars of national authorities and industry associations
- Overseas communication between the company and national authorities regarding inspection results, safety review and enforcement actions
- Participates in the use of flight data recorder/engine monitoring information in order to design and recommend safety programmes and improvement actions.
- Undertakes routine surveillance and inspections in all route systems of the company
- Organizes regulatory and safety training for the managers and supervisors concerned (Holt & Poyner, 2006).

14.14 Airline key personnel and organization

An airline is not a small organization. Personnel are so important in the efficient functioning of airlines. The size, complexity of the organization and the number of positions may vary from airline to airline. Many airlines are huge organizations employing many thousands of people (Wensveen, 2007). Airlines usually have a board of directors at the helm. It is the cardinal policymaking body and strategic decisions are made at this level. They have the power to appoint top-level officials. Top-level management which gives recommendations to the board is ultimately responsible for the performance of the organization. President, executive vice president, general managers and vice presidents are members in the top-level management. Middle-level management is the second level and responsible for developing operations plans and procedures to implement the strategic objective set by the top-level management. It may include vice presidents, directors, superintendents and/or heads of departments/divisions. Operational level, which is the lowest level, includes managers, assistant managers, section chiefs, general supervisors and supervisors. The staff administration departments in a large airline can be finance and property, information services, HR, corporate communications, economic planning, legal and medical, etc. Line administration departments may consist of flight operations, engineering and maintenance and marketing. According to Dileep (2019), airline personnel are broadly classified into three areas such as:

- Flight operations
- Ground operations
- Commercial operations.

14.14.1 Flight operations personnel

Flight operations are a crucial task in airline's functioning. Employees in this category are responsible for safe and efficient operations of an airline's fleet, including training of their performance. Varied types of personnel are involved in this. In fact, some of them are functioning in airline's operational offices and some are performing their duties to fly the aircraft by being within the aircraft in the flight. The following types of staff are directly involved in flight operations:

- Personnel within OCCs
- Flight operations crew
  - Flight/cockpit crew
  - Cabin crew

Flight operations department is part of the line departments in an airline organization, and John Wensveen (2007) identified four-line departments in an airline organization, such as flight operations, engineering and maintenance, and marketing and services. Personnel in flight office/OCCs are varied. An OCC primarily functions to manage the operation of the airline schedule as planned, minimizes the impact of schedule disruptions on the airline, provides quality service to the maximum number of passengers, maximizes revenue retention and directs most cost-effective plan to return to the planned schedule (IATA, 2014). They are responsible for developing flight operations policies, procedures, techniques to promote safe, efficient and progressive operation of aircraft and the implementation of schedules developed. Administrative staff can develop schedules and procedures for economic utilization of flight equipment and personnel and direct an operations analysis and planning service, which effectively plans and exercises continuous control over flight operations activities. Air traffic and safety personnel develop and recommend ways to promote safe, economic and expeditious flow of air traffic, develop programmes for aircraft interior cabin safety and ensure safe aircraft operations, navigation aids and ground communications. The head of flight procedures and training develops operating policies, procedures, and techniques for the entire fleet; recommends the equipment; and directs the flight operations training department and the flight standards department. While the head of flying develops and directs pilot training programmes, the head of flight crew scheduling is vested with the task of developing crew schedules. At the division level, the director of flight dispatch may be there with the required staff for flight dispatch activities, including coordinating the regional flight managers. Flight managers are responsible to the regional managers of flight operations for all activities involving flight operations in their area. The director of meteorology may be there at the centralized weather service. The director of flight training is responsible for the training of flight crews on the airline. The director of flight procedures and standards is responsible for conducting proficiency checks on all flight officers. Key personnel in airline operation control offices include airline operations controllers, flight dispatchers, crew planners, maintenance controllers and air traffic control group.

Flight operation crew primarily involves the flight crew and cabin crew. Flight crew, also called the cockpit crew, is responsible for the operation and safety of the aircraft and passengers while flying. The following are the chief cockpit crew in modern commercial aviation.

14.14.1.1 Pilot in command/Captain

In commercial aviation, a flight usually has a pilot in command (captain) and a flight operation officer (first officer). Previously, flight engineer was also there, but nowadays, since the cockpit is highly automated, the need for flight engineer is not there. The captain, usually a senior pilot, is in command of the aircraft and may take any action deemed necessary to preserve and maintain the safety of the flight. He/she has to be legally certified to operate the aircraft for the specific flight and flight conditions. Due to the advancements in aviation, the tasks are simplified due to the regular updates and instructions that are given throughout the flight. Pilot and the flight dispatch officers together are responsible for the smooth and safe flying of a flight from the origin to the destinations. Captain takes a seat in the left cockpit seat and the first officer in the right cockpit seat. He/she is responsible for leading the flight while the flight is in emergencies.

The first officer, who is the second in command, is responsible to the captain for conduct and attention to duty during the flight. He has almost the same responsibilities as a captain. Almost the same experience and level of training are needed to become a first officer. While in the case of incapacitation of the captain, the first officer will assume command of the aircraft. Although the first officer is the flying pilot, eventually the captain is responsible for the aircraft, its passengers and the crew. Flight engineers may also be a trained pilot, but do not fly the plane; but their prime duty is to monitor the airplane's instruments and calculate figures like ideal take-off and landing speed, power settings, fuel management, etc.

Cabin crew constitutes the next important category of crew in airline operations. Their duty is within the cabin of an aircraft in which passengers are seated and the in-flight services are offered. Though they provide services to the passengers on board, their prime duty is to ensure safety in the cabin while flying. The following are the different cabin crew personnel:

- Fight service director
  Also called the chief purser, in-flight service manager, flight service manager, cabin service manager or cabin service director. Flight service director is the ultimate responsible personnel for cabin services.
- Purser
  Also called cabin manager or chief flight attendant. Purser supervises flight attendants in delivering the services and in ensuring the safety of the aircraft and passengers.
- Flight attendants/stewards/air hostesses
  Flight attendants can be stewards or air hostesses who are also responsible for providing customer service options like meals, entertainments and assistance while boarding. They are sufficiently trained in the area of aircraft emergencies, evacuation procedure, medical issues and health hazards, care of special needs passenger, flight regulations and meal service.

14.14.2 Ground and commercial operations staff

Ground operations staff consists of those personnel who are responsible for operation on land for passenger processing, baggage handling, aircraft handling and the support functions necessary for those operations. Some of them include:

- Reservation agents
- Check-in staff
- Gate personnel
- Ramp personnel
- Aircraft maintenance staff
- Passenger care/support staff
- Engineering staff, etc.

Commercial operations are a wider area and a wide range of staff positions are there. Commercial departments look after important focussed areas like revenue, sales, promotion, publicity, public relations, etc. Almost all types of managerial positions are there in airline organizations. From a managerial perspective, the following departments can be seen in airline organizations, and each of them has personnel of varied kinds:

- Marketing and products
- Sales and distributions
- Planning
- Government and legal affairs

- Human resources/employee relations
- Customer service and reservations
- Financial planning and analysis
- Corporate communications/public relations
- Properties and facilities/airport affairs
- Purchasing
- IT and systems management

Many of the ground handling–related jobs are usually outsourced by airlines. Some of them include cleaning, fuelling, de-icing and catering. Airline planning involves different planning activities, ranging from network planning to crew scheduling. All were discussed in the previous chapter. Experienced and qualified personnel at various levels are needed in each of those activities. Network planning, route planning, fleet planning, schedule development, crew scheduling, etc. are handled by experts in each of them. Air traffic and safety department develop and recommend ways and means to improve safe, economic and speedy transportation. Programmes for aircraft cabin safety, safe aircraft operations, navigation aids and ground communications are also developed by them. Customer affairs and services audit is another important department, especially since customer service quality is a serious affair in the air transport industry. Finance department has so much importance as the organization's financial survival depends on the efficiency of this department. Revenue optimization section too has significant contribution to airline profitability and competitive survival. Cargo operations are another important area of operation for airlines. Engineering and maintenance too plays an important role, particularly in ensuring the safety of flying.

14.15 Conclusion

Airline operations involve complex tasks that require careful planning and efficient management. Time is a crucial factor in airline operations. AOCC manages day-to-day operations of an airline and coordinates operations, crew management and flight dispatch. It is important to manage schedule integrity, interruptions and delays as part of operational control. Nowadays, it has been advanced to IOC, and in some airlines, it is also called NOC. Operational schedules are revised as per the need based on the emerging situations. Manuals available for normal operations are AFM, flight operation manual, ground operation manual, maintenance manual and policy and procedures manual. Flight dispatchers undertake certain operational control functions of a flight, including communicating with the flight crew about flight planning, weather and operational limitations.

Aircraft weight and balance to be within certain permissible limits to acquire maximum safety of the aircraft. The load planner plans the load to make it possible with precision. Aircraft load planning and control are a number of activities to ensure that the aircraft is loaded correctly, safely and efficiently. Weight and balance have to be planned for take-off, during flight and for landing. Aircraft manufacturers usually provide weight limitations. LIR is the document used to transfer aircraft loading requirements to ramp staff and load sheet is the outcome of load planning. Load sheet is a statement of weight and centre of gravity of the aircraft prepared by the licenced load control staff and must be approved by the flight commander before take-off. The main tasks of crew operation controllers are crew scheduling, maintenance of crew schedules, tracking of schedules, rescheduling if necessary and calling the resource crew when needed. Aircraft maintenance includes scheduled maintenance and non-scheduled maintenance, which has to be done as per the manufacturer's guidelines approved by the aviation regulators.

Passenger and baggage processing needs to be handled efficiently to facilitate departures or arrivals at airports. Ramp handling functions to be conducted in a safe and secure manner. The flight deck crew has to determine the airworthiness of the aircraft by following the checklists and has to perform the walkaround checks before the flight. All activities in ramp operations are time-bound and the turnaround time of an aircraft is very crucial in ensuring punctuality in operations. The boarding and arrival procedures are also to be streamlined to facilitate the passenger flow without any hassle. Delays, disruptions and irregular operations constitute important issues in airline operations; however, there should be clear procedures to implement recovery plans to return the schedule as early as possible. Safety and security are the prime concerns in airline operations and every step is being taken to ensure a maximum of these. Airline employees are diverse, varying in size and complex and the number of positions is different from airline to airline, which employs a large number of population across the globe.

Sample questions

Short/medium answer-type questions

- What are the centres that handle airline operations?
- Describe the functions in an airline OCC
- Who are the key personnel in an AOCC?
- Describe the process of flight planning
- What are the contents of a dispatch release document?
- Describe load control process in airlines
- Discuss how to prepare load sheet
- What are different types of weight applicable in airline loading?
- What are the considerations needed in loading in aircraft?
- List the contents in a load manifest
- Elucidate the types of routine maintenance types for aircraft
- What are the activities there in a station control office?
- Describe the passenger processing activities in an airport terminal
- Discuss the process of baggage handling
- What are the documents needed for the captain of a flight?
- Discuss the activities undertaken by cabin crew prior to the take-off of a flight
- Distinguish between cabin crew and cockpit crew
- Elucidate the causes of delays and disruptions in airline operations
- Explain how to manage delays and disruptions
- Describe the organization structure of airlines

Essay type questions

- Explain the activities prior to the flight dispatch.
- Describe the process of cargo and baggage loading and the preparation of load sheet.

Suggested readings

Bruce, P., Gao, Y., & King, J.M. (Eds.). (2017). *Airline Operations: A Practical Guide*. London: Routledge.
Cook, N.G., & Billing, G.B. (2017). *Airline Operations and Management: A Management Textbook*. London: Routledge.
Holt, J.M., & Poyner, J.P. (2006). *Air Carrier Operations*. New Castle: Aviation Suppliers and Academics.
Wu, C.-L. (2010). *Airline Operations and Delay Management*. Surrey: Ashgate.

Chapter 15

Traveller-oriented strategies and practices of the airlines

Learning outcomes

After reading this chapter, you will be able to:

- Describe the application of marketing concepts in the airline industry.
- Learn the application of marketing mix in the airlines.
- Understand the relationship management strategies of the airlines.
- Comprehend the concept of pricing and its application in the airlines.
- Analyze the way airline makes use of marketing tools to attract travellers and to ensure good travel experience.

15.1 Introduction

Although the airlines form a fast-growing industry, they always face economic challenges, and remaining strong in the hypercompetitive business environment is rather an arduous task for them. Financial stress always looms large over the sector. On the one side, consolidation continues through mergers and acquisitions, and on the other side, the airlines prevail as an enormously demanding industry. Although soft brand equity is a feature generally seen in the airline sector, its customers usually have high expectations and possess changing travel behaviour. Owing to the service characteristics of the airlines, they have to engage dynamically in attracting the customers and in selling the products at the right time. All the service sector characteristics make marketing very difficult for the airlines. Demand fluctuations are common in this sector, and when demand is high, they are not in a position to enhance the supply as well. On the other hand, low-demand inserts increased financial issues. Retaining the customers and ensuring repeat purchases is a tough task. Marketing for an airline is always a challenging activity owing to a range of reasons. The airlines offer highly perishable products,

DOI: 10.4324/9781003136927-15

and hence, the sale has to take place at the right time. Intangibility makes it hard for the airlines to convince the customer, and inseparability causes the airlines to focus on moments of the truth, although the success of an air trip is based on many of the external factors, such as climate. Service performance can, hence, be highly variable as well particularly as the service delivery involves people who are the personnel involved in ground handling as well as in-flight services. Moreover, the airlines have to use the services and facilities of other entities also to enable the transportation service. Furthermore, it is important for the airline to ensure customer satisfaction. A heterogeneous customer base makes it difficult for the airlines to ensure passenger satisfaction at a uniform rate. A wide range of external factors too have significant impacts on the performance of the airlines and ensuring customer satisfaction. The above are some reasons why airlines face difficulty to attract customers and maintain a balance in demand. In fact, they have to adopt a range of strategies and practices to attract the customers and to pursue them to consume their products. This chapter introduces the major marketing strategies used by the airlines to persuade potential customers and the practices adopted by them to remain competitive and to manage the business profitably.

15.2 Traveller buying behaviour

Purchase decision-making is considered as a process with a series of sequential stages. Marketers need to understand how a consumer makes a judgment while choosing a product and the influences. Leon Schiffman and Leslie Kanuk consider buying behaviour as "the process of making purchase decisions based on cognitive and emotional influences such as impulse, family, friends, advertisers, role models, moods, and situations that influence purchase" (Schiffman & Kanuk, 2009). Engel et al. (1995) are of the opinion that it is a process by which a consumer chooses to purchase or use a product or service. Other perspectives also can be seen in the literature. Details and the number of stages are given differently by different authors. Lovelock and Wirtz (2007) have identified the buying behaviour process into three stages such as the pre-purchase stage, service-encounter stage and post-encounter stage. The first stage is all about decision-making, which involves awareness of need, information search, evaluation of alternatives and making choices. It is followed by "moments of truth" and most importantly the service delivery. The postencounter stage includes the evaluation of service performed during service delivery and further intention formation. On the other hand, another viewpoint is that buying behaviour is a process of sequential stages such as need recognition, search for information on various products based on these needs, formation of alternative choices and evaluation of alternatives, act of purchase and consumption and postpurchase behaviour (Foxall & Goldsmith, 1994; Kotler et al., 2003; Horner & Swarbrooke, 2007).

Every purchase decision can be affected by a number of factors that are intrinsic as well as extrinsic. Theoretically, there are four distinct factors such as cultural, social, personal as well as psychological that can influence buying behaviour. There is a range of social influences on a consumer's purchasing behaviour, and according to Drummond et al. (2001), the factors can be classified under four areas such as social, personal, psychological and situational. The following are the factors in each category:

- Social factors are varied which are related to culture, subculture, social class, reference groups and family
- Personal influences such as age, self-concept, occupation and financial situation, their personality, their family life cycle stage and their lifestyle,
- Psychological factors include motivation, perception, learning, beliefs and attitudes
- Situational factors consist of self-image, perceived risk, social factors and hedonic factors.

In addition to many of the above general factors, in the airline sector, the factors influencing the buying behaviour and the purchase decision-making can be some other varied types as well owing to the peculiar characteristics of the airline industry and the products. The additional factors influencing the passenger's buying behaviour can be the following as well:

- Airport
- In-flight services and facilities
- Ground handling factors
- Airline schedules
- Airfare and associated factors
- Loyalty
- Product accessibility
- Route network
- Partnerships

> The traveller's choice of air transport services is influenced by a number of factors, and according to Nenem et al. (2020), it is affected by the following: … fare, scheduling convenience and other influences such as airline reputation, reliability, safety, in-flight services, seat availability, airline competition and frequent flyer programmes. Business passengers, being generally more journey time sensitive and less price sensitive than leisure passengers, are usually assumed to be particularly influenced by schedule factors and the design of airline networks.

The airport is also a factor in the passenger's decision-making. While choosing an airline, the airport location may become a matter of concern. It is better for an airline to choose the airport with good connectivity to the destination/city. Passengers often face a difficulty associated with the walking distance between the check-in location and boarding gates and vice versa within the terminals. Some prefer to have shopping within airports as well, and hence, having good commercial centres within airports can also influence travellers. Lately, airports are interested in creating appealing ambience and premises to attract travellers. Many of the airports have beautiful interiors and furnishings to give an appeal for passengers. Convenient security check facilities, comfortable emigration and customs services, comfortable waiting areas and ease in boarding, etc., are also some significant factors. Having convenient and easy boarding mechanisms can be of interest to the travellers. Such factors may be influencing a passenger more when the city has more than one airport.

In-flight services and facilities constitute a major influencer. The "moment of truth" associated with flying commences from the check-in time and ends once the journey completes. The passenger should feel comfort and smoothness in the entire process and can enjoy the flight. The cabin, its attractiveness, comfort for sitting, baggage storing facilities, entertainment systems, seat features such as width and legroom, catering services, etc., can be decisive factors in the traveller's buying behaviour. Ground handling factors constitute another influencing factor set and that consists of those factors connected to the passenger processing within the airport. Ease and convenience in check-in are very important. Having long queues is really irking for passengers while check-in as well as in boarding. Some airlines make the boarding process very convenient by making necessary measures. Providing airport lounge services can attract some passengers to opt for specific airlines.

One of the most important factors that influence a passenger while making buying decisions is certainly the flight schedules and timings. Passengers prefer air transport primarily for easier access to the destination. While speed is a factor, timing also has almost equal importance. A passenger usually looks for convenient timings. Similarly, the schedule frequency is also important because the passenger should get the freedom to select the right service from an array of options. Moreover, direct flights are more preferred as multiple stops in between the origin city and destination can be very tiring for passengers.

Another significant factor is "price" in the passenger's buying decision-making. The airline industry is featured with elasticity of demand as well. Leisure travellers are reported to possess price sensitiveness. Socio-economic profiles of travellers also influence their choice of air services (Milioti et al., 2015), along with income (Gallet & Doucouliagos, 2014) and trip purpose (Nenem et al., 2020). The airlines apply revenue management principles to enhance the profit level, and flexible pricing strategies are practised by them to tackle the demand. Purchase conditions, cancellation conditions, free baggage allowance, extra baggage fee, etc., have become so complicated after the dominance of low-cost carriers (LCCs) in the air transport sectors. Experienced travellers are careful in selecting a flight, considering the above factors as well. Loyalty factors are also important for the passengers. A passenger will be more interested in choosing a flight of an airline that has high punctuality history. Product accessibility denotes easiness and convenience in getting the tickets or the airlines. The cost of access is also a matter of concern while choosing a specific flight of a specific airline.

The network structure of an airline is significant for a passenger for travelling different places. Major carriers follow hub and spoke system, and hence, services to wider areas can be covered. Also, codeshare agreements help the passenger to book tickets of a single airline to travel to multiple cities. Transit points, connection timings, etc., also have much significance for a passenger while choosing a flight. The airlines with alliance and similar agreements can provide more options for the passengers to choose.

15.3 Segmentation, targeting and positioning

Market segmentation is the division of markets into various groups of customers with similar characteristics, yet, each of them reacting differently to promotion, communication, pricing and other variables of the marketing mix. "The aim of segmentation was to identify a group of people who have a need or needs that can be met by a single product, in order to concentrate the marketing firm's efforts most effectively and economically" (Blythe, 2005). It is not easy for making a product suitable for everyone in a market. Moreover, making products without targeting a group that is most suitable for their products is also wastage of resources. Theoretically, the buyers included in an identified market should have similar needs and interests. The segment identified is to be as follows:

- Measurable
- Accessible
- Relevant to the product
- Valid
- Distinguishable or differentiable
- Congruous
- Actionable or feasible
- With growth potential
- Profitable
- Less risk prone
- Less competition

According to Drummond et al. (2005), segmentation can be performed using different variables depending upon the market conditions and characteristics. For instance, they state as the below:

> The air travel market could be segmented according to the benefits sought (value or status), or usage occasion (business or holiday), or stage in the family lifecycle (young and single or middle aged, married with kids). On occasion it may be relevant to use a single variable to segment a market, more often than not they will be used in combination. For instance, a potential market segment in the air travel market could be middle-aged consumers with children who seek status benefits for business travel.
>
> (Drummond et al., 2005)

The following are the common bases used for market segmentation.

- Geographic
- Psychographic
- Socio-economic
- Behavioural
- Demographic

Geographic segmentations help in effective implementation of marketing strategies. Geographic bases can include countries, states, regions, districts, cities, localities, urban/rural and sales or distribution territories. The demographic segmentation is also widely used by tour operators (Horner & Swarbrooke, 2005). The bases of the demographic segmentation include the age and life-cycle stage, gender and sexual orientation, marital or co-habitational status, family size, occupation, etc. The psychographic segmentation bases include the dividing of markets based on lifestyle, personality, values, beliefs, attitudes, etc. The socio-economic segmentation is also performed commonly, and in this, buyers are divided into different groups on the basis of social class and income. Occupation, educational background and the place of residence are also factors in it. The income level of the buyers and the price of the airline seats have much correlation. At times, the behavioural segmentation is also performed in the airline sector, and the most common variables used are benefits, usage and purchase occasion. The travel purpose–based segmentation is very common. The main two variables can be leisure and business travel.

The market segment/s identified finally turns into the target market in which the marketing efforts can be concentrated. Once the segmentation is over, then the next step is to select the segment most suitable to target. This process, of selecting the right segment to aim at, is called targeting. Targeting involves evaluating market segments based on the objectives of the company, comparing them and choosing the most suitable one based on the segment's overall attractiveness in terms of size, growth, profitability, less competition, scale economics and low risk. Market positioning is all about designing the company's offering and image to occupy a distinctive place in the target market's mind. "The place a product occupies in a given market, as perceived by the relevant group of customers; that group of customers is known as the target segment of the market" (Wind, 1984). The position of a product is the sum of those attributes normally ascribed to it by the consumers – its standing, its quality, the type of people who use it, its strengths, its weaknesses, any other unusual or memorable characteristics it may possess, its price and the value it represents.

15.4 Marketing mix strategies

The core of airline marketing is primarily the application of "marketing mix" elements as the tools for creating, persuading and distributing airline services that fulfil the customer needs. Differentiating the products and services from others in the market for capturing the opportunity to earn a profit is important and helps in enhancing the quality of services as well. Organizing a systematic process by adopting an appropriate strategy for implementing marketing mix will help the organization in influencing the demand for that product or service (Bakhshi, 2007). The marketing mix was coined decades ago as the product, price, place and promotion (4Ps), and later, it got redefined by adding more Ps. "P" represents an element in the marketing mix in which each element consists of a range of tools that are developed and used to achieve marketing as well as business objectives at large and to remain competitive in this hypercompetitive business environment. Kotler et al. (2014) defined marketing mix as "The set of tactical marketing tools – product, price, place and promotion – that the firm blends to produce the response it wants in the target market". Mc Carthy (1987) described marketing mix as 4Ps of marketing as follows.

- Product
- Price
- Promotion
- Place

Later, Booms and Bitner (1981) have identified three more Ps into it, and in total, according to them, marketing mix is seven Ps of marketing.

- People
- Process
- Physical Evidence

The marketing mix elements must be chosen with greater care especially with services design, attachment to pieces of physical evidence and product delivery/distribution. Those firms that provide higher quality service levels than their competitors are likely to be successful in gaining a large number of customers. The following introduces the major marketing mix strategies used by the airlines.

15.5 Airline product management

An airline product is certainly a service product (Wensveen, 2007). A "product" is defined as a consistent "bundle of services" (Parker, 2018). Bateson (1979) argued that it is only from the idea of a consumer benefit that the service concept can be defined, and the consumer benefit is a bundle of functional, effectual and psychological attributes. According to Wensveen (2007), the airline product consists of the following:

> ... services that consumers find useful. Safety, on-time reliability, convenience in terms of airport proximity or seat availability, frequency of departures, in-flight cabin services, ground services including ticketing and baggage handling, aircraft type, and even the carrier's image are part of the airline product.

According to Barnes (2012), "airline sells air transportation service between two or more cities at a certain price with specified purchase requirements and restrictions". Connor (2001) opines that air transport is an intermediate product as most people use it as a means to achieve some other purposes. For example, when a tourist flies to a destination, he/she may have an objective of a happy vacation that he/she spends in the destination. The air trip is largely or entirely a means to accomplish that objective. Regarding the airline product strategy, decisions on seat quality such as seat pitch/legroom and width; meal service such as quality, variety and quality of beverage; entertainment to be provided such as visual systems, channels and periodicals to be kept; and service quality offered on board, like in terms of communication, interactions by crew, etc., are crucial in attracting customers. An airline product primarily comprises intangible elements that are offered in the market for the passenger's interest, purchase, use, or consumption that fulfils the consumer needs and provides satisfaction. Airline services have two important subsections:

- On the ground services.
- In-flight services

The "moments of truth" in the airline product consumption actually starts from the moment the passenger turns into an airport for travelling. Within the airport,

> **Table 15.1** Unique Characteristics of Airline Products

- Due to extreme "perishability", the product cannot be stored for future sale to match with demand hike, and the revenue lost due to the lack of timely sale of the seats is lost forever.
- Perception of service is more personalized. The passengers who travelled in the same flight may come away with diverse opinions about the service, depending on their individual experiences.
- There is no scope for replacement of a bad product.
- Prior checking of the quality of the service, before the final sale/consumption of the product, is difficult. The product/service is difficult to demonstrate for testing.
- Uncertainty with regard to the delivery of the product exists, since the service schedule can be disturbed by mechanical problems or the weather changes.
- The service can be produced only in batches, as against to individual units.

Source: Adapted from Wensveen (2007).

a range of services are rendered to the passenger, which altogether are referred to as passenger processing. The ease, comfort and quality of service received in the airport until boarding the flight constitute a major element in the airline customer satisfaction. The next session takes place within the flight while flying from the boarding time until the passenger disembarks at the destination airport. The quality of on-board catering, entertainment services, beverage services, cabin crew and service delivery, etc. do matter greatly in the customer satisfaction in the airline industry. In the arrival airport also, the passenger should feel the ease and comfort in moving through the mandatory procedures that are required to move out of the airport.

Although the passengers primarily buy the transportation service, it will include some tangibles as well, such as food and beverage. In the modern marketing concept, a product denotes customer value, which means the perceived benefits provided to meet the needs and wants, quality of service received and the value for money delivered assessed against the competition (Kotler & Armstrong, 2012). It involves the quality and performance level that the consumer receives, but in services, quality and higher standard of delivery assure the advantage over the competitor. The product offered to the marketplace by the firm must be designed to ensure segmentation fit and the quality to achieve customer satisfaction.

Different components can be identified in the airline product. Kotler and Armstrong (2013) identified the following levels in a product.

- The core customer value: This deals with what the consumer seeks from that specific product. In an airline, the need of the passenger particularly is to get transported from one place to another via the air mode of transportation. The passenger expects a range of services from the moment of purchase of ticket until the completion of the service when the passenger/cargo reaches the final destination. This expectation can include diverse services such as in-flight services and arrival in destination at the right time.

- Actual product: The product that is being developed to deliver the core customer value to the customer. It is developed by combining all the required benefits, services, quality level, features, etc., to enable the customer to consume the product to satisfy his/her needs and wants. In the airline industry, the airline will provide the actual product to the consumer by bundling a range of services on board as well as on the ground and with other features required for making the travel possible.
- Augmented product: Additional consumer services and benefits are provided along with the actual product so that it becomes more attractive than competitors' offers to their intended customers. Providing such can exceed customer expectations and that can bring customer delight as well. The airline product can be augmented with enhanced services such as personalized food provision and the provision of a large variety of in-flight entertainment (IFE) options.

They finally state as below:

> Consumers see products as complex bundles of benefits that satisfy their needs. When developing products, marketers first must identify the *core customer value* that consumers seek from the product. They must then design the *actual* product and find ways to *augment* it to create this customer value and the most satisfying customer experience.
>
> (Kotler and Armstrong, 2012)

The core product of scheduled flights is all about transporting passengers based on a published schedule or cargo from one place to another (Dileep, 2019). The core product includes the fundamental services or benefits that the customer is

Table 15.2 Ancillary Services in the Airline Sector

Air Extras	Travel Extra Services
Mobile phone access	Check-in at convenient locations
Blanket, inflatable neck support, eye shadow, etc.	Airport check-in at a staffed counter
	On-time airport lounge access
On-board pillow and blanket	Priority boarding and check-in
Seat-back entertainments	Fast-track security screening
Handheld entertainments devices and programmes	Premium meal services
	Seat assignment in front/forward rows, exit rows

Ticket Transaction Fees
Online booking charges
Receive itinerary via mobile phones
Online payment with credit/debit cards
Protection from booking change fees
Fare lock before purchase

Source: Parker (2018).

341

really buying. Nowadays, the airlines are giving an increasing significance for ancillary products. The transportation services involve a range of ancillary services, which make the air transportation possible as well as smooth, safe and comfortable for the consumers. Ancillary elements are undertaken to increase the level of performance and enhance the value of the core product. Nowadays, the airlines, particularly LCCs, find ancillary services as revenue-earning opportunities. Hybrid airlines also make use of some of the ancillary services as revenue sources. According to Parker (2018), there are three types of ancillary services in the airline industry, and they are as follows:

- Air extras: The services on board, such as IFE, Internet services, baggage services, meals, etc.
- Travel extras: The services offered whether before or after the flight, such as airport parking, lounge access, Etc.
- Ticket transaction fees: Different types of fee/charge that can be accrued along with ticket transaction fee.

Indeed, the modern air transport service consists of increased complementary services, and product differentiation is focusing more on it. While differentiating

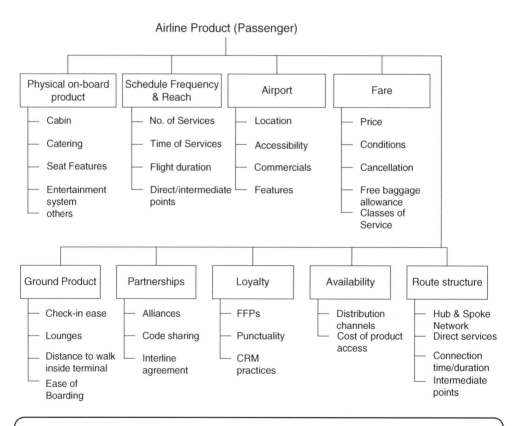

Figure 15.1 Airline product (passenger): elements

the product, the airlines may focus on the city pairs where they wanted to operate services, the frequency of operations, the type of aircraft used, classes of service offered, features of in-flight services and facilities, etc. Many airlines prefer the quality and variety of in-flight services and the features of seats and other facilities within the flight along with the punctuality of services for differentiating their products.

The LCC's product has some differences from that of the full-service carrier (FSC). LCCs may charge for many of the in-flight services. The following are some inevitable components of airline products:

- Quality of in-flight cabin services
- Efficient ground handling services
- Punctuality in operations
- Diversity and frequency of services
- Variety of IFE options
- Comfortable seats with good legroom
- Convenient departing and arrival airports
- Airport features and accessibility
- Efficient ticket reservation system
- Efficient and speedy baggage delivery
- Quality landside services and facilities at airports
- Necessary services, commercials and facilities in departing and arrival airports
- Efficient passenger handling
- Good safety and security provisions

15.6 In-flight services and classes of services

Traditional airline pricing is based on classes of service. Each class is based on the seating configuration, and there will be differences in services and product features offered in different classes. In the international airlines, there may be two or three classes of service seen, such as the first class, business class and economy class. Some airlines offer other classes also, such as the premium economy class. The services offered are not just limited to in-flight services, rather, a number of more advantageous services are offered as part of ground services as well as in booking terms and conditions.

15.6.1 In-flight services

In-flight services are extra offerings, both free and paid in advance or on board, provided by the airlines to improve their passengers' flying experience. This includes food, beverages and duty-free shopping, yet additionally the provision of entertainment services and Internet access through Wi-fi on board of the aircraft. This is making an open door for the airlines to generate ancillary revenue. Although there are variations in the in-flight services between the airlines, the two factors that typically have the biggest impact on what kind of service a passenger will receive on board the flight are the flight's distance and the booked class of service.

15.6.1.1 Airline travel classes

The airlines conventionally have three travel classes, the first class, business class and economy class. The aircraft cabin configuration will determine how many classes of service are offered. Here is a breakdown of the classes of service:

- **First class**: It is generally the most expensive and most comfortable spaces available on board.
- **Business class:** This is the high-quality class, also called executive class, traditionally purchased by business travellers.
- **Premium economy:** Certain airlines offer this slightly better economy-class seating having a greater distance between rows of seats and the seats themselves, wider than the regular economy class.
- **Economy class:** This is the basic travel class, commonly purchased by leisure and budget travellers. The fares are comparatively cheap and offer standard seats and limited meal service mainly dependent on the flight's length. Economy class is the largest section in a flight, also called the coach class. Seats are arranged closer with less seat pitch. Although all in-flight services are given in the economy class also, the variety offered may be less. In and around the seat, there will be an airsickness bag, in-flight magazine, duty-free catalogue and safety and evacuation card. Also, extras, such as blankets, amenity bags and headphones, are given based on the circumstances. A visual display mounted to the aircraft bulkhead is present, or individual screens for each seat may be present.

15.6.1.2 First-class services

First class is the most expensive one. First-class passengers usually have special check-in and security zones at the airport. Other services include airport lounge access, early boarding service, etc. They do not have to wait in long queues to check-in, board and disembark. Having the widest seats, this class is the most comfortable with heavier padding in each seat. Seating in this class is also featured with maximum legroom, and in some of the flights, the seats in the first class can turn into sleeper seats (mainly in long-haul routes). Best IFE is offered, and more personalized service is provided with the assistance of more attendants per passenger. With the introduction of the most modern fleet by the major aircraft manufacturers, the entire setup of the luxury journey in an aircraft has raised to a different level. Major FSCs in the world offer competing services to please their customers. The services offered by them include the below:

- Chaffer driven luxury car pickup and drop facility from the airport
- Staff-assisted check-in at the airport
- Access to the first-class lounge
  - Cigar lounge
  - Spa
  - In-lounge duty-free
  - Fine dining
  - Board directly from lounge in some airport terminals

- Private suite in some airlines with an automatic sliding door
    - Minibar and snacks bar
    - Standard brand amenity kit
    - Widescreen TV
    - Wide range of on-demand channels, music and movies selection
    - Live sports channels
    - Free Wi-fi throughout the flight
- A la carte menu with regionally inspired dishes servings on board
- On-board lounge in some most modern aircraft type (e.g., A380)
- Shower facility on board of A380
- Cabin can be converted to a bedroom with a fully flatbed

15.6.1.3 Business-class services

It was differentiated from the economy-class travel by the quality of seating, food, drinks, ground service and other amenities. Business-class consumers are more of time sensitive than price sensitive. The seats in this category are usually located behind the first class. The business class is distinguished from other lower travel classes by the quality of seating, food, drinks, ground service and other amenities. The seats are wider than the economy, and a wide choice of meals is offered. Akin to the first class, business-class passengers do have separate check-in counters and lounge facilities. Speedier check-in, boarding and disembarkation services are offered. Seats are less expensive than those in the first class, but certainly costlier than those in the economy class. The number of seats also will be limited. The business class is a much more considerable upgrade from the economy class.

Business-class facilities include the following:

- Additional inches of the seat width.
- More legroom.
- Extra degrees of recline of the seats.
- Electric seat controls for the leg-rest and lumbar support.
- Larger personal IFE screens.
- Laptop power ports.
- Premium food and beverage service.
- Additional cabin crew members to the passenger ratio.
- Premium eye masks and toiletries.

15.6.1.4 New trends in seating comfort

Apart from the above conventional classes of services, below are the new trends in seating comfort by the leading premium carriers in the world.

15.6.1.5 Cradle seats

Cradle seats are popular in the business class on shorter route flights for many airlines. These seats are with around 150–160 degrees of recline and with considerably more legroom. Cradle seats do not offer the significant recline as for the flat-bed seats but still offer superb space and comfort.

15.6.1.6 Angled lie-flat seats

These seats have 180 degrees of recline and offer a flat sleeping surface but are not parallel to the level of the aircraft. These seats are making them less comfortable in comparison with flat-bed seats

15.6.1.7 Flat-bed seats

Fully flat-bed seats recline into a flat sleeping surface, which is parallel to the floor of the aircraft. These seats always receive high comfort both as seats and beds.

15.6.1.8 Suites

This is one of the ultimate comforts of the travel experience offered by certain airlines. Suites offer the most privacy and comfort with its minicabin which includes a fully flat bed, workstation and many other personal amenities.

15.6.1.9 On-board Internet

As the demand for in-flight connectivity rises, satellites empower the airlines and in-flight connectivity players to boost passenger services and improve operational proficiency. Increasing the brand engagement with a seamless online in-flight experience, passengers can check the email, surf the Web and stream live content on their mobile devices. Enhanced in-flight connectivity also facilitates communications between the cabin crew and the ground staff. The airlines are fully incorporating these opportunities. Over the next decade, the number of commercial aircraft fitted out with a mobile Wi-fi service is projected to grow up nearly ten-fold as more airlines provide satellite-based Wi-fi connectivity to both the cabin and cockpit. Satellites are the key technology to unlock this market potential, with multiple spot beam architecture and high-frequency reuse of high-throughput satellites and payloads.

Each class is given separate codes in booking records. For instance, F is the code given for the first class; C, for the business class; and Y, for the economy class. Other codes are also given by some airlines.

Table 15.3 Common In-flight Services

- Meal services
- Beverages and liquors
- IFE services (movies, songs, etc.)
- Periodicals and dailies
- In-flight magazine

- Safety and security briefings and assistance
- Duty-free shopping
- Kids and baby-care services
- Flight information provision
- Welcoming and assistance for seating

15.7 Airline economics and pricing strategy

Survival and profitability of any business are closely related to pricing as well. The airlines have a bad name for profitability as the sector has been attributed to a thin profit margin. Every year, we hear stories of the airlines stopping operations due to financial crunch. According to Cook and Billig (2017), "by several measures, the airline industry has historically been low-margin, low-profit business". Pricing in the airline sector is so crucial owing to the special characteristics of the sector. The airline industry is featured with a high level of pricing instability. Maintaining a sustained profit margin itself is difficult for the airlines throughout the year, and hence, the peak-season pricing becomes so important for maintaining it. The airlines even follow a concept of "peak-load pricing", which is a pricing mechanism in which the pricing is performed to smooth the demand fluctuation on peak hours or days. The features that are crucial in airline profitability are unit costs, unit revenue (yield) and the LFs (Williams, 2018). To get an increased profit, one option is to increase the price. However, because of this, the LF can come down. Another method is to increase LFs. Giving discounts is an option to attract more passengers. However, this can reduce the yield as well. Flying an aircraft maximum and increasing the revenue is another option. Yet, a number of external factors can dampen the scope of increasing the revenue and profit whenever there is an adverse effect from those factors. A sudden climate change itself can cause delays and cancellations. Ensuring profitability is an arduous task for the airlines. Moreover, owing to frequent demand fluctuations, ensuring consistent performance is also a matter of concern for the airlines. The following are the various measures used to identify the profitability as well as the performance of airline business operations.

- **Net profit margin**
    It is the percentage of the total revenue that remains after paying all expenses. The measurement reveals the amount of profit that a business can extract from its total sales.
- **Return on invested capital (ROIC)**
    It is one of the best ways to analyze the profitability of the core business of a company. It determines the efficiency of the management in using its capital to work in profitable investments. Basically, this "compares profit to all invested capital, equity as well as debt-financed capital…" (Cook & Billig, 2017). ROIC is equal to the net profit divided by total assets.
- **Available seat mile (ASM)/Available Seat kilometre (ASK)**
    It gives an indication of the capacity available. ASK is the "Total capacity supply produced in a network" (Franke, 2018) and denotes the annual airline capacity/supply of seats. This is calculated by multiplying the number of seats available in a flight segment by the number of kilometres flown during that particular flight leg.
- **Revenue per available seat mile (RASM) (unit revenue)**
    RASM quantifies the amount an airline earns from a unit of production and represents how much an airline made across all available seats that were supplied. It is equal to the total revenue divided by ASMs.

- *Passenger revenue per available seat mile (PRASM)*
  Similar to RASM, PRASM measures the passenger service alone. It is obtained by dividing the operating income by ASMs. Higher values usually represent an increased profit.
- *Cost per available seat mile (CASM)/cost per available seat kilometre (CASK) (unit cost)*
  It determines the average cost of flying one seat for a mile/kilometre. In other words, it determines the operating cost to fly one aircraft seat per kilometre. It is obtained by dividing the total cost by ASMs. It is a measure of the cost, not revenue.
- *Revenue passenger mile (RPM)/revenue passenger kilometre (RPK)*
  It is a measure of the ability in selling seats. It is also considered as a measure of passenger traffic. It can be obtained by multiplying total miles/kilometres by total seats sold/passengers travelled on board. In other words, it is found out by multiplying the number of passengers (paying) by the number of kilometres flown during a segment of a flight (flight leg). It also indicates the sales volume of passenger traffic and represents the total number of kilometres travelled by all passengers.
- *Load factor (LF)*
  This is a measure of how well an airline is balancing the capacity it makes available with the traffic it could attract, i.e., this measure compares the actual passenger traffic to the capacity available. It is the percentage of seats occupied or the number of passengers on board divided by the total number of seats. It is also equal to RPMs divided by ASMs. It is a critical indicator of the airline business performance. Wensveen (2007) illustrates the significance of the LF in the following way:

  > Load factor has a critical impact on the cost and quality of air transportation services offered. Approximately, 65 percentage of airline's costs are directly related to the operations of aircraft and are independent of the number of passengers on aircraft. Therefore, a high load factor will allow the allocation of these costs over a large number of passengers, resulting in lower costs per passenger, which allows for lower fares.

  For the airlines to increase the profitability, the LF has to be increased, against the decrease of the cost factor. The airline has to maximize the yield, decrease seat costs and enhance the LF. A higher LF indicates fewer empty seats in flights.
- *Yield/average unit revenue*
  It is all about the price a passenger pays for per mile flown. This is the average revenue created while carrying one passenger per kilometre. It is equal to total passenger revenue divided by RPMs. The following dimensions are there for this.
  a. How much an airline earns per passenger mile/kilometre.
  b. How much an airline makes per mile/kilometre each seat sold.
  c. The average revenue created while carrying one passenger per kilometre.
  d. A measure of the average fare paid by all passengers per kilometres or mile flown in a market.
  e. Using this, it is easy to assess changes in fares over time.

- *Profit*

    Profit is equal to the total revenue minus the total cost. It is also equal to (Yield x LF x ASM) – (ASM x CASM).
- *Freight ton kilometre (FTK)*

    In the cargo sector, FTK is an indicator used to show the demand. It is calculated by multiplying the number of tons of freight by the number of kilometres flown during a certain period.
- *Aircraft utilization*

    This is a measure of aircraft productivity. It is measured as the period during which an aircraft is in use including the ground taxi type as well as flight times.

In the airline cost structure, fuel and labour are the predominant categories. In many a case, labour is the largest category. As this sector has relatively more unionized workforce, managing the task of reducing the labour cost is a challenging task. The aircraft operation cost is a major item in the airline's cost structure. It includes direct cost, which is related to the cost when a flight is flying. Direct operating costs, indirect operating costs and non-operating cost categories are there. The first category consists of the costs associated with the operation of an aircraft, and it is dependent on the type of the aircraft (e.g., fuel cost, maintenance cost, etc.). Indirect operating costs include those costs that are not affected by the change of aircraft type (e.g., cost for marketing and promotion, general and administration, etc.). Non-operating costs are also there and those include the expenses not directly related to the operation of the airline's own air transportation services (e.g., losses due to different reasons, interest paid on loans, etc.). The following are the principal cost categories (O'Connor, 2001; Wensveen, 2007).

Table 15.4 Airline Profit Maximizing Strategies

Strategy	Intended Benefits	Strategy Pitfalls
Cutting Fares/Yields	Stimulate Demand	The price cut must generate a disproportional increase in total demand, "elastic demand"
Increasing Fares/Yields	Increase Revenue	The price increase can be revenue positive if demand is "inelastic"
Increase Flights (ASM)	Stimulate Demand	Increases Operational Costs
Decrease Flights (ASM)	Reduce Operational Costs	Lower Frequencies made lead to market share losses and lost demand
Improve Passenger Service Quality	Stimulate Demand	Increases Operational Costs

Source: Adapted from Peter Belobaba, Amedeo Odoni, Cynthia Barnhart, Airline Economics, Centre for Air Transportation Systems Research, George Masons University, data available online at https://catsr.vse.gmu.edu/SYST660/Chap3_Airline_Economics[2].pdf

- Flying operations
  - Flight crew expenses
  - Cost for fuel and oil
- Direct maintenance (the costs of labour and materials for the routine maintenance and repairing of aircraft)
- Maintenance burden ("indirect maintenance costs": overhead costs for the upkeep and repair of flight equipment and other property)
- Airport and en route charges (e.g., landing fee and passenger facility charges levied on the number of passengers boarded at that airport)
- Depreciation and amortization
- Passenger service (cost of food and providing cabin attendants)
- Aircraft servicing (routine servicing, such as washing the aircraft and cleaning the passenger cabin, etc.)
- Traffic servicing (including ticketing and baggage handling)
- Aircraft insurance costs
- Other flight operations expenses (crew training expenses, route development expenses, etc.)
- Reservations and sales
- Advertising and publicity
- General and administrative

Outsourcing is a norm in the air transport sector and that helps the airlines to reduce the cost, and information and communication technology (ICT) integration greatly helps the airlines to manage the cost. The indirect cost consists of the fixed costs, mainly the depreciation and insurance. Traditionally, the airlines had a single price system to generate revenue. Airline's profitability depended mainly on the revenue generated from the passenger ticket sales and from the cargo transportation. In the passenger air transportation, the following are the revenue sources for the airlines:

- Ticket sales
- Sale of cargo space
- Sale of ancillary services

Now, the airlines realized the scope of earning an increased revenue from selling ancillary services by unbundling the airline product and its price. In the in-flight services itself, the airlines now go for an unbundled pricing system. In "a la carte pricing", a customer can choose the services needed. It is also called "menu pricing" in which separate charges may be there for reservation, in-flight meals, beverages, seat selection/preferences, etc. This enables the airlines to increase profitability as well. The ancillary service price addition has been expended nowadays. Many of the airlines, particularly the LCCs and hybrid airlines, have identified the scope of sale for more items. The following are the items now charged separately by many airlines:

- On-board sale of food and beverages
- Baggage check
- Extra baggage services
- Seat preferences

- Insurance programmes
- Call centre support for reservations
- Fees charged for purchases using credit/debit cards
- Priority check-in and screening
- VIP lounge access
- Priority boarding
- IFEs
- Internet access
- Ground transportation upon arrival (Parker, 2018).

The airlines also sell frequent flier miles, which tells about the selling of frequent flier miles to companies that can provide incentives to passengers. Recently, the baggage fee has also been seen as an element separately charged. The fee for overweight bags and extra bags have been there in the airline sector for a long time. Also, the airlines offer booking of other travel products, such as hotel accommodation, car rentals and travel insurance on commission basis, as well. Tax is always part of the price of airline's price. The following are the tax varieties seen associated with air transportation nowadays.

- Environmental tax
- Fuel tax
- Air transport tax
- Some special-purpose taxes
- Value-added tax

15.8 Airline pricing

Pricing is a crucial activity because the existence of the business and the generation of profit are, to a large extent, based on the pricing strategies. Price is all about the amount of money charged by the organization from the consumer for the product or service they provide. Price can also be explained as the sum of the values that consumers lose in exchange for using the benefits of having a product item or a service (Kotler & Armstrong, 2013). Middleton and Clarke (2001) are of the opinion that price refers to the below:

> the published or negotiated terms of the exchange transaction for a product between a producer aiming to achieve predetermined sales volume and revenue objectives, and prospective customers seeking to maximize their perceptions of value for money in the choices they make between alternative products.

Organizations undertake different strategies in connection with pricing. Cost-based (or cost-plus or cost-driven) pricing, which includes mark-up pricing/cost-plus pricing; absorption-cost pricing/full-cost pricing; target pricing/rate of return pricing and marginal-cost pricing, is used often by many sectors depending on the characteristics of the product, etc. Product line–oriented pricing is a common strategy used. It is performed by setting prices for multiple products that a company offers in coordination with one another. Tender pricing and affordability-based pricing are also common among various industries. Pricing based on matching the demand and supply is a common strategy. If the demand is high and the supply is low, premium pricing can be charged or vice versa. Premium pricing must be based on the quality, brand and significance of delivery. Differentiated pricing is made by selling the same product to different customers at different prices. The airlines also use this pricing strategy quite often. Perceived-value pricing and value pricing are also common pricing strategies among companies.

Competition-oriented pricing is another predominant pricing strategy. Premium pricing, discount pricing and parity pricing/going rate pricing are the common types of competition-based pricing strategies in the business spectrum. Competition is a factor in airline pricing, still demand has more significance. Demand or market-based (or market-driven) pricing is a common strategy used by the airline sector. Skimming pricing is a high (or premium) price strategy, which enables to have high profit margins, particularly in the markets where shortage of supply is there. Penetration pricing is more relevant when the firm likes to enter into a new market. The airlines, particularly LCCs, may enter into new markets with the penetration strategy by offering much low price compared with that of competitors. It seeks rapid market growth through increasing volumes of sales. Prestige pricing and psychological pricing are also seen in the common business markets. Price discrimination is also a strategy adopted by the airlines, and they may charge each customer the maximum price they are willing to pay. The airlines may also go for discriminatory price particularly for an off-peak visitor and thus contribute to high fixed overheads costs. Although different pricing approaches are used by the airlines, they have to adopt dynamic pricing, a part of the revenue management and yield management, to cope with the unique characteristics of the sector.

15.8.1 Dynamic pricing

Certainly, the airlines intend to maximize the revenue to increase the profit, as the airline cost structure is more of fixed cost dominated, at least for a short term. FSCs have a discriminatory pricing tendency based on classes of services, particularly. According to Gerardi and Shapiro (2007), many of the airlines use differentiated pricing, which is considered as a form of price discrimination that aims at selling air services at varying prices simultaneously to different segments. "Carriers often accomplish this by dividing each cabin of the aircraft (first, business and economy) into a number of travel classes for pricing purposes called 'buckets' that sell at higher and higher prices closer to the flight date" Gupta and Ganesh (2017). The dynamic pricing mechanism was once upon a time predominantly used by the LCCs. Moreover, different price types have been traditionally used by FSCs. LCCs had established the dynamic pricing as a norm in the industry, and FSCs had little choice than adopting it. Dynamic pricing, particularly the revenue management and yield management enable the airlines to effective capacity utilization, along with reserving available capacity for higher paying segments. It is a sophisticated approach to managing demands by changing fares and supply by controlling availability under varying degrees of constraints. Dynamic pricing is undertaken with the objective of increasing the profit. Dynamic pricing, according to McAfee and Velde (2005), is practised when the following product characteristics coexist.

- Perishability: When the product expires at a point in time, like as in the airline
- Fixed capacity: Capacity is fixed well in advance and can be increased only at a relatively high marginal cost.

Other conditions that favour the revenue management, particularly the dynamic pricing, are as follows:

- Fixed cost structure: The airline does have a relatively high fixed cost structure, at least for a short term.
- Variable and uncertain demand: The airline demand faces fluctuation more often than many other business sectors, and seasonality is a feature of the airline industry.
- Varying customer price sensitivity: Airline is a price-sensitive sector. Yet, price sensitiveness too may differ. Leisure tourists are more price sensitive. Business travellers have less sensitiveness. Passengers have different needs for travel. In emergency travel situations, passengers may not be affected by price sensitiveness.

Owing to the above characteristics, there are chances for the following situations:

- The airlines have to sell the products in time. To ensure sale, particularly when the demand is low, the airline may have to reduce the price.
- When there is a high demand and shortage of supply, the airlines get the opportunity to increase the price sharply.

Nowadays, in the airline sector, the above situations occur often, and the revenue management systems have the capability to adjust prices in accordance with the situations. Even in a day's time, the demand fluctuations with regard to ticket bookings are there, and the price may be adjusted based on the situations. In airline dynamic pricing, the change in price can be based on the following bases:

- An increase or decrease in the demand
- The type of the target customer
- Competition
- Changes in economic circumstances
- Sector and route length (lesser variation in price can be seen in long routes than in short-haul travel)
- Route frequency
- Seasonality
- Shortage of supply
- Willingness of the customer to pay

The willingness of customers can be because of varied reasons. For example, a passenger otherwise may not have opted to travel at a high price may become willing to pay a higher price when faces an urgency to travel. According to Lisa Magloff, the following types of dynamic pricing types are followed by the airlines:

- Segmented pricing
- Peak-user Pricing

- Service time–based pricing
- Time of purchase pricing
- Changing conditions–based pricing

In segmented pricing, willingness to pay is the base for pricing. For instance, business travellers are less price sensitive and are seen more willing to pay for a given service or product if it is based on their need for convenience, comfort or status and prestige, etc. Better service, higher quality and added features are acceptable for such segments of customers. The airlines commonly follow the peak-user pricing strategy, and using this, the airlines often charge a higher price to travel during a rush hour on Monday through Friday than at other times and on weekends. Service time–based pricing is another common strategy among the airlines. As per this, the airlines may charge for a faster service. The service time required for first-class and business-class passengers is much less. Late check-in is possible for higher class passengers and early disembarking can also be enjoyed by them. Time of purchase–based pricing offers customers with different prices based on the time of their purchase. The price of economy-class seats on a particular flight may fluctuate over time. Lower prices are offered in the initial days of the start of the booking, and it increases as days approach the day of flying. Changing conditions–based pricing is also being practised by the airlines as the market conditions are mostly uncertain, particularly as the product has a short life span. Dynamic pricing is a strategy that comes under the revenue management. Let us look more into the concept of the revenue management in the airlines.

15.8.2 Revenue management

More than two decades ago, Cross (1997) described the concept of the revenue management as selling "the right product to the right customer at the right time to the right price". This has been the mantra of profitability of many sectors, and the airlines adopted this concept quicker than many other sectors. The fundamental aspect of the revenue management in an airline is that "Airlines can maximize revenue and load factors by selling the right seats, at the right price to the right people, at the right time" (Benckendroff et al., 2014). The revenue maximization is undertaken with the help of a systematic approach toward understanding the demand variation and customer willingness. Robert Cross further specifies the concept as it "is the art and science of predicting real-time customer demand at the micromarket level and optimizing the price and availability of products". The yield management is another concept used interchangeably with the revenue management in the airline sector. The International Civil Aviation Organization (ICAO) (2004) opines that, in addition to various measures related to flight operations, optimum operation results can also be attempted by using the yield management and overbooking. It is basically described as follows:

> an inventory control involving the allocation and frequent adjustment of seat availability for the booking of each of many booking classes (fare types, e.g. normal economy, various discount tickets, free frequent flyer, etc.) and origin/destination combinations, in ways calculated to produce the maximum revenue for each flight sector at the fares offered.
>
> (ICAO, 2004)

In fact, the yield management is a narrower term compared with the revenue management as it does not take into account the cost associated with the service and ancillary revenue. The focus is more on the selling price and the volume of sales to generate the largest possible revenue from a limited and perishable inventory. Flavio Pintarelli states as below:

> The yield management is primarily concerned with enhancing profits and that is how it gives the activity to the revenue management, focused on the optimization pulling the pricing lever. Eventually, the revenue management is a more comprehensive term and the yield management can be under circumstances seen as a part of it. They are interlinked and hardly to separate one from the other.
>
> (Pintarelli, 2017)

The airlines undertake different strategies to execute the revenue management effectively. For estimating the demand for the revenue management, historical data is very much important. An expected booking schedule is prepared which will have a hint about how many tickets in which category will be sold in different periods. If more are sold than expected, then some of the lower fare tickets may be moved to the higher fare category inventory. If the situation is opposite, some of the higher-level fares may be brought to the lower-level category to spur the sale. Overbooking is a common strategy used by the airlines. By this, the airlines will accept more reservations than the available capacity, expecting no-shows and late cancellation.

The sell-up tariff structure is a strategy of the airlines. This is part of the revenue management mechanism of the airlines to increase the profit. Different classes of fares are structured in such a way that the lowest fare type is with maximum restrictions and highest fare is with least restrictions. Restrictions may be more for more discounted fares. Restrictions are imposed to prevent customers with purchasing ability for buying discounted fares. On the other hand, discounted fares lure passengers who may choose other modes of transport instead of the airlines. Highest fares rarely have restrictions, and refund possibility is high. Even though the ticket is economy class, different codes may be used. For example, "Y" is given for full-fare economy, and "Q" is given for the most discounted fare. Demand and capacity are the primary concern. When the capacity is less and demand is high, passengers are offered only higher, less restrictive fares. "Selling-up" takes place with some customers. They are ready to purchase discounted fares due with all restrictions, but may purchase the non-discounted fare. It can happen when all discounted fares are sold out or by the marketing pressure.

The revenue management in the airlines is now managed with the assistance of the latest software. These systems "automatically update booking limits and forecasts at regular intervals leading up to flight departure. Historical data are combined with actual booking information to determine whether demand for different fare categories is consistent with forecasts" (Benckendroff et al., 2014). Revenue management systems are capable to provide the following:

- Historical data: For identifying patterns and trends
- Forecasting: Demand forecasting
- Modelling: For recommendations regarding booking levels

- Decision Support: With regard to booking and overbooking limits (Belobaba et al., 2009)

Belobaba et al. (2017) further elaborate that an ideal Revenue Management (RM) system may include the capabilities to collect and maintain historical booking data; forecast future demand; make use of mathematical models to optimize total expected flight revenues; provide an interactive decision support for revenue management analysts to review, accept, or reject the overbooking; and booking limit recommendations. In case of unexpected bookings, the system will re-forecast the demand and re-optimize booking limits, all of which will result in the opening or closure of fare classes. In addition to the incremental revenue benefits, this helps the airlines to better balance the demand and supply at a tactical level. Moreover, the low-fare demand can be channelled to empty flights.

15.8.3 Revenue optimization

Revenue optimization is a strategy in practice in many airlines. Because this is gaining increased significance along with dynamic pricing based on the inventory, the airlines are slowly embracing the unbundled pricing strategies to sell ancillary services separately, particularly by the LCCs and hybrid airlines. The trend of revenue enhancement has been started recently by the airline industry by changing the pricing strategies by introducing separate ancillary pricing strategies. According to Boin et al. (2017), there is a fundamental industry change in airline pricing. They opined that "…an increasing percentage of revenue now comes from

Table 15.5 Steps to Success in the Airline Service Revenue Management Programme

---

- Defining ancillary revenue brand
  Airlines have to take efforts to define and create a brand for ancillary service revenue activities.
- Equipping managers with resources
  It is challenging to unbundle the product and charge for all ancillary services separately. Adequate consideration and resources have to be allocated for the managers who are assigned with the task of boosting sales.
- Creating consumer clarity
  It is important to create clarity based upon the visibility provided to A la carte fees and the ethics associated with sales.
- Integrating the selling message
  It is important to sell ancillary services by being persistent, not obnoxious. By this, the chance of selling airline seats should not be lost as well.
- Engaging the employees as supporters
  It is also important to engage employees easily and during the design process in order to have sales-oriented employees to support the ancillary revenue movement.

Source: Adapted from Parker (2018).

ancillary items such as checked baggage, on-board food, premium seat selection, and extra legroom" (Boin et al., 2017). The following practices are visible in the online airline product distribution.

- There are separate prices for choosing the seat. Front row seats have different prices. Separate price options are given for the window seat, aisle seat, seats near emergency window space, etc. Seats can be finalized at the time of booking itself, and rates are different based on the features of the seats.
- Meals, breakfast, snacks and beverages can be chosen with an additional price while booking.
- Baggage pricing: An additional amount needs to be paid for extra baggage. Usually, a certain amount of weight is offered as free baggage allowance. For every additional amount of weight margins, extra charges are taken.

15.9 Promotion and other marketing mix elements

Promotion is an important element in marketing mix. The eventual function of promotion is a form of communication to inform, remind, or persuade the consumer to buy the product and services offered by the organization. Blythe (2005) states the below:

> Advertising, public relations, sales promotion, personal selling and all the other communications tools should put across the organization's message in a way that fits what the particular group of consumers and customers would like to hear, whether it be informative or appealing to the emotions.

The tools and measures used as part of marketing communication are used "to make prospective customers aware of products, to whet their appetites, stimulate demand and generally provide incentives to purchase, either direct from a producer or through a channel of distribution" (Middleton & Clarke, 2001). Marketing communication can be focused on a particular segment, individual or groups, by giving specific information about the tourism product and the value that is provided to the consumer. Promotion influences the consumer attitude and behaviour that create interest, desire and attention to purchase the product at a particular price (Norman, 1984). Promotion mix is the term used to represent various tools used as part of a promotion. "The promotional mix is like a recipe, in which the ingredients must be added at the right times and in the right quantities for the promotion to be effective" (Blythe, 2005). Advertising, public relations, sales promotion, personal selling, etc. are the major elements in the promotion mix.

   In the marketing mix concept, a place is an element, and it is all about making the product easily and conveniently accessible to the consumer. The place is generally referred to the location and accessibility of the products (Bisht et al., 2010). Accessibility is ensured through a distribution system. Distribution is all about a "downstream" section of the supply chain, and the players involved in it are also called marketing channel partners. A service provider should pay attention to channel marketing decisions owing to the inseparable characteristics of the services. Owing to inseparability, the production of the product (service) and

---

Table 15.6 Mobile Marketing: Tips to Maximize the Customer Contact Using Mobile Solutions

---

- Use mobile solutions to personalize communications, marketing efforts, brand recognition and online booking and servicing options.
- Use a Web-to-mobile friendly browser, apps or hybrid solutions, coupled with Search Engine Optimization (SEO)-enriched online and mobile content to increase ranking and exposure to target consumers.
- Create a mobile community that enables airlines to meet customer needs – anywhere, anytime.
- Promote mobile-only offers to your e-client database, send relevant specials to past fliers (based on their preferences and travel history) and participate in Groupon (e-commerce marketplace) offers.
- Become a passenger's companion by offering e-alerts, messages, promos, tips and the most current flight information.
- Ensure last-minute auctions to help fill those vacant seats.

Source: Amadeus (2013)

consumption occur at the same time and at the same place, a place that delivers all evidence to customer (Copley, 2004).

> Distribution channel members can help in information and market intelligence gathering, engage in persuasive marketing communication, ensuring customer interaction, matching of consumer needs and modifying the product as per needs, negotiation of price and other terms, storing and physical distribution of the products, financing as part of distribution activities and risk taking with regard to the distribution and sales.
>
> (Dileep, 2019)

The distribution management can involve forward flow, backward flow and flow in both directions. Forward flow enables the movement of products, title, promotion, etc. from the company to the customer. In the backward flow, some functions such as ordering, payment, etc. flow from consumers to the company. Flow of some aspects such as information, negotiation, finance, risk-taking, etc. takes place at both the directions. The airlines distribute the product, promotional aspects, etc. through the distribution system to the final customers. They receive the payments, market intelligence, etc. also through the same system. The airlines make use of a multichannel system to distribute their products. Both online and traditional intermediaries are depended on the airlines to ensure the accessibility of their products. Mobile marketing is also widely practised by the airlines now. ICT-enabled distribution by the airlines is described further in Chapter 17. Although online and mobile distribution have started to dominate in the airline distribution, intermediaries such as travel agencies and tour operators are still having a significant role in it.

Table 15.7 Airline Distribution System

Traditional Channels	Electronic Channels
Airline's own sale's offices	Airline websites
City ticket sale offices	Global distribution systems
Other airline's sales offices (mainly of alliance members)	Call centres
Travel agents	Online travel agents/mobile travel agents
Wholesalers	New distribution capability
Tour operators	Centralized reservation offices
Joint airline ticket offices	GDS new entrants
	Other online e-mediaries such as metasearch engines, aggregators, opaque sites, product review sites, etc.

An airline is a service industry in which the presence of people is so significant in the service delivery and in getting customer satisfaction. Although the role of physical elements such as the aircraft and airports is important, the airline is a high-contact service as the service delivery depends on the personnel involved. Employees, especially the operational and delivery personnel, contribute directly to the effectiveness and consumer satisfaction level. A direct interaction between consumers and employees, which strongly influences how customers perceive service quality and contribute in customer satisfaction, is there in the airline sector. The cabin crew staff, for instance, has a great role in making the journey pleasurable, safe and comfortable. "Moments of truth" has extreme significance in the travel and tourism sector, as Middleton and Clarke (2001) point out "it is the 'moments of truth' that stay in the consumer's mind and signify quality and satisfaction". The airlines, hence, have to prepare themselves and ensure quality employees with the necessary skills and knowledge for serving the customers.

Physical evidence, as suggested by Hoffman and Bateson (1997) in the case of services and products, has significance in the airline sector as well. The airline service involves tangible and intangible elements although the airline product is considered as a typical service. An airline seat and its features have a role in the passenger's travel comfort. The airport terminal and the facilities within it too have a great role in the traveller's satisfaction. The service provider must ensure tangible evidence of a firm's service quality that has a deep impression on passengers regarding the quality (Lovelock & Wirtz, 2007). The airport ambience, the aesthetics, the physical layout, décor, employee's appearance, equipment used, background and other services-cape contribute significantly to the customer's quality judgment, experience and satisfaction with a service and expectations of the service.

The airlines operate air services through a very complicated set of processes with utmost care and diligence. The set of procedures, measures and activities in a sequential order for the service delivery and operation can be termed as a process. The process implements, controls and assures the flow of activities to achieve the desired result.

15.10 Customer relationship management and frequent flier programme of the airlines

The concept of the customer relationship management (CRM) has been discussed in another chapter. Definitely, it is a strategy used as part of marketing by the airlines to retain their customers for future selling which can enable the airlines to not only retain profitable customers but also reduce the cost and increase the profit. A range of CRM practices are undertaken by the airlines. Relationship marketing, a terminology used interchangeably with CRM "is a marketing philosophy whereby a firm gives equal or greater emphasis to the maintenance and strengthening of its relationships with its existing customers as it does to the necessary search for new customers" (Wensveen, 2007). The same aims to ensure that customers come back and keep coming back (Blythe, 2005). Maintaining a relationship with customers is considered the utmost importance in businesses nowadays. Of late, mobile platforms are also used by airline to interact with passengers. Frequent updates are given to them so that the passengers will be well informed about the changes, etc.

The airlines undertake different types of customer retention strategies. Frequent flier programmes (FFPs) are part of this. American Airlines was the first to launch the FFP in 1981, and it was soon followed by United Airlines with its MileagePlus programme. It, simply, is as follows:

> an air carrier program that allows frequent fliers to earn free tickets after accumulating a certain number of miles flown on the carrier.... It was a marketing program originally aimed at creating flyer loyalty in response to price competition in the early 1980s.
>
> (Wensveen, 2007)

The ICAO describes the FFP as something "... in which members earn free or reduced-fare transportation or other benefits on the basis of the amount of their travel on certain airlines or for their purchase of certain goods and services" (ICAO, 2004). Since 1981, the programme has been an inevitable part of airline marketing. Passengers prefer to have FFP memberships. "The lure of air travel is, however, sufficient to encourage large sections of the general public to become members of these schemes, with many people often having active membership in two or more airline programmes simultaneously" (Williams, 2018). On each trip, passengers will get a mileage credit, and it will be accumulated to get incentives of different sorts, mainly the rewards such as free tickets, upgrades and free car rental services (Mark & Go, 1995). FFPs became a key measure of attracting and retaining travelling customers. Camilleri (2018) specified the following aspects of airline FFPs, which help us to understand the concept and nature of these schemes well.

- Users, the passengers, are usually rewarded for the air miles they have travelled, through points and/or fringe benefits.
- The passengers can redeem certain incentives, such as free flights or upgrades when they accumulate enough points.
- It is like an incentive scheme that links the needs and wants of passengers.

- Loyalty schemes encourage frequent buying behaviours.
- It, at times, is extremely influential in terms of the passengers' choice of full-service airlines.
- The ultimate aim of the FFPs was to improve the consumers' retention and loyalty.
- It is a sophisticated way of retaining customer information within CRM systems.
- The database can be used for providing personalized services to passengers as well.
- Recently, airline loyalty programmes are also used in conjunction with other firms, such as hospitality businesses.
- Those who accumulate miles/points outside the airline are offered attractive incentives from different businesses to accumulate their rewards.
- Lately, there may be a shift in focus from "customer satisfaction" to "revenue optimization".

FFP passengers will get a range of other benefits, such as entry in airport longue and class upgrades, as well. Of late, FFPs reward passengers not just with miles on air travel but with different types of incentives and retail purchase schemes. Revenue optimization is one of the aims of FFPs and that led to turn FFPs into profit centres. Apart from rewarding frequent fliers, a CRM programme intends to undertake targeted marketing campaigns and to learn about the customers and their buying behaviour. The airline sells miles or points to programme partners such as hotel chains, car rental companies, co-branded credit cards, online malls, retailers, etc. (Parker, 2018). This is a good source of revenue for the airlines. The airlines, nowadays, use mobile applications, and social media are used to communicate with passengers. Special offers, upgrades, etc. can be sold via mobile devices.

15.11 Conclusion

As a service industry, airline marketing can be a daunting task. In this chapter, we discussed the key marketing strategies used by the airlines to motivate potential customers and the steps they have taken to stay competitive and manage the business profitably. Passenger buying behaviour is influenced by lots of factors, and the prime concern for many travellers is the attractive price. The purchasing behaviour of travellers is influenced by many factors. The majority of the travellers place great importance on attractive prices. The "moment of truth" associated with the flying begins from the check-in time and ends when the journey completes. The passenger should feel comfortable and at ease throughout the process and should be able to enjoy the flight. The application of "marketing mix" components primarily acts as tools for creating and delivering airline services that meet customer needs which is the core of airline marketing.

The two sections of airline services include the ground services and in-flight services. The airlines currently want to sell ancillary services along with the main product and increase the ancillary revenue. The airline pricing policy mostly based on the classes of the service, mainly the first class, business class and economy class, and there will be differences in services and product features offered in different classes. The in-flight services offered to the passengers are based on the flight's distance and the booked class of service. Currently, the airlines are keen to add a varied kind of seating comfort on board, which attracts the afflu-ent members and business travellers. The airline's profit depends mainly on the revenue from passenger ticket sales and from freight transportation. Although the airlines use different pricing approaches, they primarily opt dynamic pricing, which is a part of the revenue management and yield management to deal with the unique features of this sector. Revenue optimization is a strategy to add the ancillary revenue to the airline. The airlines use a multichannel system to adver-tise, distribute their products and rely on online and traditional intermediaries to ensure the accessibility of their products. The "moments of truth" are so im-portant in the travel and tourism sectors, and these industries need to prepare themselves and ensure the quality employees with the right skills and knowledge needed to serve the customers. The airline undertakes a range of CRM practices, one of which is FFPs, which have become an important criterion for attracting and retaining travel customers. The airlines currently use mobile applications and social media to communicate with passengers frequently and doing post-travel follow-ups with the customers.

Sample questions

Short/medium answer type questions

- Distinguish between the airline customer and consumer.
- Explain the various factors that affect the buying behaviour of airline customers.
- Discuss how we can segment airline markets.
- Elucidate different product components in the airline sector.
- What are ancillary services?
- Write in detail about the airline distribution system.
- Describe the promotion strategies undertaken by the airlines.
- Discuss the importance of frequent flier schemes in the airlines.
- Discuss the revenue sources of the airlines.
- Write the various terms used to represent the performance of the airlines.
- Discuss why airline pricing is a difficult task.
- What are the factors that influence airline pricing?
- What are the different types of dynamic pricing practices in the airlines?
- Discuss in detail the revenue management in the airline industry.
- Discuss the differences in the services and features in different classes of service.

Essay type questions

- Write an essay on the marketing tools and strategies used by the airlines to attract and retain travellers.
- Write an essay on the revenue management practices followed by the airlines.

Suggested readings

Graham, A. (2018). *Managing Airports: An International Perspective.* London: Routledge.

Kotler, P., Bowen, J., & Makens, J. (2014). *Marketing for Tourism and Hospitality*, 9th ed. London: Prentice Hall.

Middleton, V.T.C., & Clarke, J. (2001). *Marketing for Travel and Tourism*, 3rd ed. Oxford: Butterworth-Heinemann.

O'Connor, W. (2001). *An Introduction to Airline Economics.* London: Praeger Publishers.

Shah, S. (2017). *Airline Marketing and Management.* Hampshire: Ashgate.

Chapter 16

Airport operations

Learning outcomes

After reading this chapter, you will be able to:

- Comprehend the structure, elements and subelements of an airport.
- Narrate airport ground operations.
- Explain passenger handling.
- Describe baggage handling and delivery.
- Comprehend ramp-handling activities.
- Discuss the safety and security measures in airports.

16.1 Introduction

The success of the air transport system depends greatly on efficient airport operations as well. Experience from airports has significant impacts on the overall tourist experience. Airports are facing an increasing number of challenges recently, particularly because of the sudden surge in the air transport demand and the changes in the air transport environments, both external and internal. The increasing number of flights and passengers strains airport operations, sustaining punctuality and performance, and safety is ever more difficult for airports. Airports are now transforming into business hubs than just offering the space and facilities for airlines to operate flight services. On the one hand, airports have to offer efficient services to airlines to undertake smooth and safe air transport services and provide facilities for other aeronautical and non-aeronautical agencies to perform their functions, and on the other hand, airports have to face the growing needs of their customers without causing social and environmental consequences. Airport expansion is imminent in many locations, and it is challenging to keep up the quality of services high to attract tourists as well as other types of passengers. There are a number of operations that are to be performed

 DOI: 10.4324/9781003136927-16

time-bound and with extreme meticulousness. Efficient administration is critical in the functioning of airports. The following describes the structure, various aspects and functions of airports in detail.

16.2 Structure of the airport

An airport is a complex transportation facility, designed to serve the aircraft, passengers, cargo and surface vehicles. Each of these users is served by different areas of an airport. The three areas of an airport are typically placed into the following:

- The airside
- The landside
- The terminal(s)

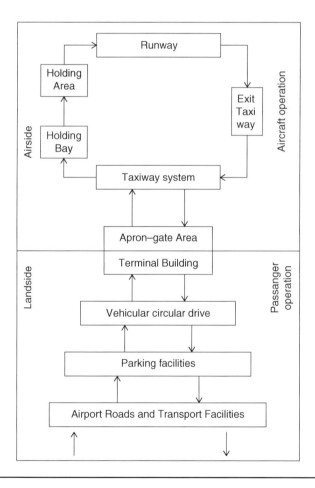

Figure 16.1 Airport components and flow of movements
Source: Adapted from Wells & Young, 2004.

Some experts do not use this tripartite classification. For example, Horonjeff and McKelvey (1983) distinguish only between the airside and the landside, making the division at the passenger boarding gates.

16.3 The airside

Airside components, sometimes called the aeronautical surfaces, or more simply the airfield, are those on which an aircraft operates. This is the most secured area in an airport. The International Civil Aviation Organization (ICAO) (2005) defines it as "the movement area of an airport, adjacent terrain and buildings or portions thereof, access to which is controlled". Early airports were just airsides, and the remaining facilities and structures were evolved over time. Principally, they are the runways where aircraft take off and land, the taxiways used for movement between the runway and the terminal, and the apron and gate areas where passengers embark and disembark and where aircraft are parked. The airside of an airport is meant for the movement of aircraft around the airport and landing and take-off. It is the most important area where all the technical aspects of flying take place in an airport. The aircraft can access only in this area. The major facilities in it include runways, taxiways, aircraft parking areas, navigational aids, lighting systems, signage and markings, air rescue and firefighting facilities, snow ploughing and deicing facilities and fuel service centres. The following are the major components of the airside:

- Runway
- Taxiways
- Path markings
- Pathway signs
- Apron/ramp area
- Hangar
- Air traffic control tower
- Support services and facilities
- Airport lighting system

16.3.1 Runway

A runway is the most important part of an airside. According to Wells and Young (2004), "Perhaps the single most important facility on the airfield is the runway. After all, without a properly planned and managed runway, desired aircraft would be unable to use the airport". The principal purpose of an airport is to facilitate the landing and take-off of flights to ensure the boarding/loading as well as offloading of passengers and cargoes for the movement of them into the next location. According to ICAO, a runway is "a defined rectangular area on a land aerodrome prepared for the landing and take-off of aircraft" (ICAO Definitions/ UVS international). Collins Dictionary gives a similar definition. According to it, runway is "the long strip of ground with a hard surface which an airplane takes off from or lands on" (www.collinsdictionary.com). Runway lengths and widths may vary; yet, a typical one can be about 3,200 meters long with essential width

Figure 16.2 Landing of an aircraft: Boeing 757 landing at Toncontín International Airport (TGU)

Source: Enrique galeano morales – Flickr, https://commons.wikimedia.org/w/
index.php?curid=3247096

to accommodate the wide-bodied aircraft. Latest aircraft such as A380 need farther and wider runways. Based on runway markings, three types of runways can
be seen, such as visual, non-precision instrument and precision instrument runways. Under the instrument runway category, two major types, non-precision
approach runway and precision approach runway, are there. A runway can be
composed of asphalt or concrete, depending on factors such as location, size and
types of aircraft. Lately, runways are made up of cement concrete and shoulders
with asphalt, or both are built with asphalt.

Strict rules are followed in the making of runways. Those can be pertaining to
the required length, width, direction configuration, stops, pavement thickness,
lightings, markings and signage. Aircraft characteristics, such as the maximum
gross take-off weight, acceleration rate, aircraft type, distance to fly for take-off
and wingspan influence in the making of runways. The determinant in the width
of a runway is usually the wingspan, of the largest operating aircraft. It usually
varies from 50 to 200 feet. Wind direction is a factor in the landing of aircraft,
and the primary runway will be oriented to the prevailing winds. Runways are
also sometime built "crosswind" directions. In large airports, parallel runways are
there, which are additional runways. In addition, they can have both parallel and
crosswind runways.

16.3.2 Taxiways

A taxiway is the route built to connect a runway with another area of an airport.
Similar to the runway, taxiways are also made of concrete or asphalt. A taxiway

connects runway either with a terminal or with a hangar, i.e., they are to ensure safe, smooth and expeditious movement of aircraft between the runways and the apron or other areas in the airport. Markings, signs and coloured lights are featured along taxiways and runways of major airports. The aircraft is supposed to taxi to the terminal/gate and hangar through the taxiway. At very busy airports, the taxiway system can be extensive and complex in geometry. Usually, in large airports, a multi-taxiway system will be there along with high-speed exit taxiways. Taxiways also have shoulders and strips.

16.3.3 Path markings

Markings in aircraft paths, usually in yellow, are used to differentiate between types of surfaces or paths. Operational guidance signs on the surfaces indicate specific meanings. Yellow on a black background identifies the runway or taxiway currently on or entering. Black on yellow indicates the intersecting taxiways the aircraft is approaching, with an arrow indicating the direction to turn. Many airports use conventional traffic signs, such as stop and yield signs, throughout the airport. White on red shows entrances to runways or critical areas; vehicles and aircraft are required to stop at these signs until the control tower gives clearance to proceed. In runways, white on red shows a runway intersection ahead. A single solid yellow bar across a taxiway indicates a position where the ground control may require a stop. If two solid yellow bars and two dashed yellow bars are encountered, this indicates a holding position for a runway intersection ahead; runway holding lines must never be crossed without permission. At some airports, a line of red lights across a taxiway is used during low visibility operations to indicate holding positions. Yellow taxiway centreline markings and aircraft stand markings are meant for the safe manoeuvring of aircraft. White apron markings are for the safe manoeuvring of vehicle traffic and vehicle parking.

16.3.4 Pathway signs

Yellow and black signs along a taxiway provide the location and directional information. A black sign with yellow letters or numbers indicates where the aircraft is located. A letter represents the taxiway (such as Taxiway A or Taxiway B). A number represents the nearby runway (such as Runway 4 or Runway 5). A yellow sign with black letters or numbers shows the names of the various paths leaving an intersection. Arrows indicate which path the sign refers to. Arrows may point left, right, diagonal left or diagonal right and will be accompanied by a number or letter to indicate what the path is named.

16.3.5 Apron/ramp

Apron is the area within the airside, which is intended for the loading and unloading of passengers and cargo and the rest of the activities as part of turn-around activities. The major activities that are being undertaken in the apron may include the refuelling; servicing; maintenance and parking of aircraft; maintenance; catering; loading/unloading baggage and cargo; aircraft servicing; boarding bridge manoeuvring; passenger boarding/deplaning; aircraft docking/pushback; and any movement of aircraft, vehicles and pedestrians necessary for such purposes. This area is usually a very active area and at times congested particularly in busy airports. The ramp area also denotes the specific space where aircraft park near to a terminal to load passengers and cargo. The term "ramp" is hardly used, and instead, the term "apron" is in frequent use. An apron is not just meant for turnaround activities of a flight for passenger transportation. It can be for similar other activities as well, such as for cargo loading and unloading. Considering such diverse activities, aprons can be classified into different types. Some of the common types of aprons are the following:

- Terminal apron
  The terminal area apron is meant for the enplaning and deplaning of passengers or loading and unloading of cargoes from an aircraft adjacent to the terminal. This can be connected directly to the gate. Otherwise, if they are away from the gates, then air stairs are used for boarding and deplaning passengers. Two types, the passenger apron and cargo apron, are there in this category.
  o Passenger apron
    This area is near to the terminal where gates are there, usually, and where passengers can board and deplane from an aircraft. Here is where the usual turnaround activities take place, as mentioned above.
  o Cargo apron
    This type of apron is meant exclusively for cargo loading and unloading along with other required activities that are needed for enabling the aircraft for the next flight. Such apron areas are typically near a cargo terminal building.
- Remote apron
  This apron, which is at a distance from the terminal apron, is meant for the aircraft to be secured and serviced for an extended period. In commercial airports, a parking apron may be there to accommodate aircraft that are not scheduled for the operation particularly at night, to keep the gate positions available for scheduled flights.
- Parking apron
  Unlike the remote apron, the parking apron is closer to the terminal apron, and in it, the aircraft can be parked for a specific period of time for regular light servicing and maintenance.
- Hangar apron
  This is near the hangar in an airport and meant for the movement of an aircraft into and out of a storage hangar.
- Service and hanger aprons
  Aprons where maintenance and repairing of aircraft are carried out under a hanger.
- General aviation apron
  This is dedicated to general aviation flight activities.
- Deicing aprons
  The purpose is for deicing operations, particularly in the winter seasons, and these are seen only in some countries where extreme cold conditions occur during winter seasons.
- Holding bay
  A holding bay can also be there, where an aircraft can be held or bypassed, to enable efficient surface movement of aircraft.
- Helipads

In commercial airports, helipads may also be there for helicopter operations. The layout, marking, lighting, access for vehicles, fixed or mobile services for aircraft servicing, etc. should follow quality industry standards. The apron layout is another reason for the classification of aprons. Designing an apron, as part of the airport design, is a crucial activity. Access easiness for aircraft; safety requirements and the nature of the terminal; the area needed for parking an aircraft considering the wingspan; geographical features of the airside; etc. are the prime considerations in the apron layout design. Different types of apron layouts are seen:

- Linear
  Individual stands for aircraft parking are arranged in a row along the terminal building or around it. Aircraft can be parked at gates immediately adjacent to the terminal itself. These are connected to the airport terminal building so that the passengers can directly board the aircraft. Air bridges can be there.
- Open
  Akin to the linear types, the open apron type also has stands in rows in front of the terminal building. The difference is that these stands are not connected to terminals. Usually, they are adjacent to terminals, and hence, passengers can walk across to board the flight. Depending on the distance from the terminal building, vehicles may be used to transport passengers to board the flight.
- Pier
  In the pier terminal design, stands in the apron are connected to the sides of extensions from the terminal. The stands can be in rows or in more complex forms.
- Satellite
  In this layout, the stands are arranged away from the terminal and the shape of the construction can be like a satellite. Because these are away from the terminal, some link has to be there to reach there, such as by underground tunnel or by overhead corridors.

The position of aircraft parking in stands makes different stand types depending on the nature of the parking of the aircraft as follows:

- Nose-in
- Angled nose-in
- Nose-out
- Angled nose-out
- Parallel stands

16.3.6 Hangar

The hangar is primarily meant for maintenance activities of an aircraft. The size, nature and facilities of it can vary depending on the size and nature of operations of airports. In the hangar, the storage of active aircraft, assembly of aircraft under construction, maintenance, repair or refurbishment of aircraft and storage of aircraft handling equipment can be performed. In a hangar, the following areas may be seen:

- Hangar area
- Shop area

- Warehouse area
- Office/administration and specialty areas
- Building utility area (McLaughlin, 2017)

16.3.7 Air Navigation Services and air traffic control

An air traffic control (ATC) tower is an inevitable element of air navigation facilities. Air Navigation Services (ANSs) are having the task of ensuring the security and facilitate safe, regular and efficient air traffic operations. The ANSs of a country, according to the Directorate of Airspace and Air Navigation Services Standards, India (www.dgca.in), is responsible for the following areas:

- Air traffic services
- Aeronautical Information Services
- Meteorological services for air navigation
- Communication, navigation and surveillance
- Airspace management
- Air traffic flow management
- Search and rescue

Air traffic controllers are vested with the task of ensuring safe aircraft operations while the flight is in the air and at the time of landing and take-off. A wide range of technological elements are vital in the coordination of controlling of flight operations. Such elements may consist mainly of communication and information technologies. Radio beacons; satellite systems; and other aids to landing, weather forecasts, airports, computer terminals, etc., are certainly part of them. Satellites and associated technology have altered the navigation systems as satellite technology has brought in accuracy and flexibility to navigation along with increasing the range and quality of communication. It is important to keep aircraft set distances apart while moving them from airport to airport using set routes. During the take-off, air traffic controllers will look after the aircraft while it is on the ground and permit it to take-off. As it moves up, another controller, using a radar screen, will track the aircraft's progress through the airway. Another set of controllers will take over the task coordinating with the progress of the aircraft smoothly and safely. They interact with the pilots to enable them to operate the flight smoothly. Frequent updates on various aspects of flying will continue from the side of the air traffic controllers until it reaches the destination. For landing also, necessary instructions will be provided by the respective controllers over there.

A wide range of support services that are vital for the smooth and efficient functioning of the air transport system are there in an airport. Fuel services and fire and rescue services are some examples. A fixed base operator ensures the aircraft maintenance, pilot services, aircraft rental and hangar rental tasks. The airport lighting system is another important component of the airside of an airport. This is more important for flight operations at night-time. Centreline lights, centreline reflectors, edge lights, edge reflectors, airport beacon and approach lighting (approach lighting system) are the major components in it.

16.4 The terminal

The terminal is the most visible part of an airport, which is primarily an interface between land and air modes of transport. Simply, it is a building that enables the processing of the departing passengers to board the flight, the arriving passengers to leave the airport and the cargo for transporting to another place. It can also be considered as a pathway between the landside and the airside through which both departing and arrival passengers have to go for boarding an aircraft for a flight to the destination, and while disembarking from aircraft to leave the airport to the landside. A terminal consists of the access system to board a flight or to leave from an airport after a flight; a system with necessary facilities and services for processing of passengers, baggage and cargo; and the system for airport administration, operations and maintenance. A wide range of facilities and services are placed within a terminal to enable the smooth processing of both passengers and cargoes for air transportation. In the early stages of the evolution of air transportation, the significance of the terminal was much less, and hence, there were limited facilities within the terminal. Of late, the importance of terminal is on the steady increase and a lot of investment is required for setting up the facilities within the terminal.

16.4.1 Structure and components of a terminal

The ultimate task of a terminal is to provide the required facilities for passenger and cargo processing as part of air transportation. To ensure the passenger and cargo processing, a wide range of facilities and services are to be offered within the terminal. An airport can have only one or many terminals, and concourses depend on the size of the airport, but they all serve the same functions. Such facilities and services may include check-in facilities and services, passenger loading and waiting areas, ticket counters, baggage handling facilities, restaurants, shops, security screening mechanism, emigration clearance facilities and services, customs clearance service areas, baggage claim area, commercial centres such as duty-free shops, car rental facilities and currency exchange centres. Loading, handling and storage areas for air cargo and mail, often separately located, are also part of the terminal complex. Depending upon the quantum of passenger and cargo movement, the size of the terminals will also vary. There can be centralized and decentralized terminals depending on the location of passenger processing. The trend of having more than one terminal, sometimes, separate terminals for domestic and international flights, is continuing. The major functions of terminals summed up, according to Kazda and Caves (2000), are as follows:

- Provide a convenient facility for the change of mode transport from ground to air and vice versa.
- Provide security to the airside by screening and checking of passengers, luggage, cargo, other people moving inside airports and items taken into the airside.
- Provide space and facilities for the airlines and cargo agencies to function their airport activities.

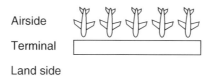

Airside

Terminal

Land side

Figure 16.3 Linear terminal

- Ensure facilities for shopping, refreshments and relaxation, and other needs of the travelling population while inside the airport.
- Provide facilities for restricting the carriage, the banned and restricted items, inwards or outwards of a country

The structure of the terminal building can also vary. Corresponding to the apron layout, terminals can also have different structures, such as simple, linear, satellite, pier and semicircular terminals. Simple terminals are seen nowadays in smaller airports having one building with a common ticketing and waiting area with multiple exits leading to an apron for boarding. A linear or curvilinear terminal, depending on the shape of the building, is larger than the simple terminal, with more gates and more rooms. In a pier finger terminal, "pier" is an extended path that leads to the space where aircraft are parked in the "finger" slots or gates for boarding. After the passenger processing at the simple terminal, they are led to a "pier". A pier satellite terminal or remote satellite terminal can also be there. There can be a terminal, which is connected to many satellite structures by separate concourses. Gates are seen at the tip of the satellite-like structures, and aircraft are parked in a cluster at the end of the concourses with the gates. Transporter terminals are with remote aircraft parking and passengers are transported using low-floor buses or similar vehicles to and from the building to the parked airplane. The mobile lounge can also be used as holding rooms for waiting passengers at gate positions where aircraft are parked in parallel rows (Table 16.1).

Terminals provide the necessary ground service facilities, using which the airlines can undertake passenger and cargo processing activities as part of their air transport service operation. The airlines hire the facilities of airports to enable the passengers to obtain boarding passes, clear security, claim luggage and board aircraft through gates. According to Dileep (2019), the following are the functions/activities that take place in a terminal, as part of commercial air transportation (Figure 16.4):

- Passenger processing to board flight
- Arriving passengers can enter the intended destination
- Baggage handling for departing and arriving passengers
- Services and facilities for the entry and exit of foreigners coming to or leaving a country
- Safety and security services
- Cargo handling
- Shopping, entertainments and refreshments
- Restricting the carriage of banned and restricted items while flying

> **Table 16.1** Common Terminal Types: Advantages and Disadvantages

Advantages	Disadvantages
Pier/Finger Terminal	
Centralized resources	Long walking distances
Economies of scale (resources and facilities)	Kerbside congestion
	Limited expansion capability
Facilitates passenger management	Reduced aircraft circulation and manoeuvrability
Economical to construct	Limited compatibility of future aircraft
Efficient land utilization	
Linear Terminal	
Shortest walking distances	Duplication of terminal facilities/amenities
Clear orientation/directions	Longer minimum connecting time
Simple construction	Longer walking distances for transfer passengers
Adequate kerb length	Special logistics for handling transfer bags
Shorter closeout times	Less flexibility in the terminal and apron for
Easier for moving or sorting baggage	future changes
Transporter Terminal	
Easy compatibility of the terminal/ apron geometry and future aircraft design development	Higher instances of passenger delays
	Early closeout times
	High capital, maintenance and operating costs
Ease of aircraft	Prone to industrial disputes with vehicle drivers
Manoeuvrability	Increased vehicular movements on airside with
Expansion potential for aircraft stands	aircraft
	Kerbside congestion
Simple and smaller central terminal	Increased minimum connecting times
Cost savings	
Satellite Terminal	
Centralized resources (human and facilities)	Requires high technology, underground transportation system
Facilitates passenger management	High capital, maintenance and operating cost
Additional satellites can be added to accommodate future aircraft design developments	Kerbside congestion
	Limited expansion possibility at main terminal
	Increases minimum connecting times
	Early closeout times

Source: Poh (2007).

The following sections/components can be seen in the departure area of a terminal in an international airport.

- Baggage screening: There can be an X-ray screening or similar mechanism that can screen the luggage (check-in baggage) of the departing passengers. Only

Air side

Terminal

Land side

Figure 16.4 Pier satellite terminal

the check-in luggage needs to be checked over there to verify whether any restricted items are carried in the luggage. In some airports, this check may be performed after collecting the luggage at the check-in counter.

- Check-in counters: A large linear area or separated sections with a number of check-in counters can be seen in a hall just after the entry location in the departure area. The departing passengers have to move to the respective counters where their airlines' check-in service is listed. There may be separate check-in counters for the business-class/first-class passengers. Usually, passengers have to be in the queue for the check-in. The staff will verify the documents and weigh the baggage. If the documents are fine for the travel, the boarding pass will be issued and the luggage will be taken in after attaching the tag in the luggage. The hand baggage will be handed back to the passenger for carrying along with them.
- Passport control/emigration service: Every international passenger has to pass through the emigration service centre. The officials will verify all the travelling documents, and exit from the country will be permitted electronically or manually by stamping in the passport.
- Security check: This is a vital area in air transportation. One of the primary functions of airport itself is to ensure the security of the travellers. A separate system will be there for checking the hand baggage as well as for the body. Metal detector wands and equipment will be used. Personal checking may also be there.
- Concourse: This is a large hall in which passengers can relax after passing through the due process for travel. From here, the passengers can move to the respective gates at the time of boarding. The path to the gate can vary depending upon the structure of the terminal building. Most of the commercial centres targeting the departing passengers are situated in and around this hall. Duty-free shops, restaurants, lounges, gift shops, currency exchange centres, etc., are commonly seen in concourses. Seating areas, restrooms and waiting areas are also there within it.
- Gates: Gates are the space through which the departing passengers can enter into the airside for boarding aircraft. Usually, there will be waiting areas and they can proceed for boarding when the announcement for the same is heard. The gates are usually manned by the airline/airport personnel to check the boarding passes again and to lead them to the aircraft (Figure 16.5).

Figure 16.5 Cologne Bonn Airport terminal. Mixed terminal-pier satellite, along with linear terminals. Courtesy: Borsi112- Own work, CC BY-SA 3.0, https://commons.wikimedia.org/w/index.php?curid=1313207

The arrival area will have the following components.

- Arrival gates: After landing, the passengers will be led to the arrival gates. Through there, they can enter into the airport.
- Transit/transfer passage: Some of the passengers in the arriving flight may have to wait for the connecting flight for travelling to the final destination, depending on their itinerary. In such cases, the passengers, usually called transit passengers, will be led to the transit passenger waiting area and from there they can move as departing passengers (without emigration).
- Passport control/immigration service: For an incoming international passenger, getting emigration clearance and necessary permission to enter into the destination country is important. The officials over there will verify all the travel documents and issue an entry permit. If it is manually performed, then there will be stamping done in the passport of the beholder. Nowadays, electronic measures are used widely.
- Baggage claim area: This area will consist of different conveyor belts through which the incoming baggage will come. The passengers can collect their baggage after verifying the tag.
- Customs clearance area: Two channels are there usually in airports. The green channel permits the incoming passengers to move out directly if there is no dutiable item carried. Nowadays, most of the luggage are checked through the scanning mechanism to see whether any restricted items are carried into or

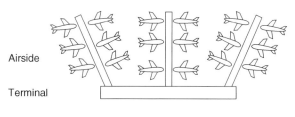

Airside

Terminal

Land side

Figure 16.6 Pier finger terminal

not. The red channel is the other way through which the passengers may have to approach officials for paying the duty, etc.

- Arrival concourse: This is another large area through which the passengers can move out. Within this area, a number of commercial centres targeting the incoming passengers are there. Currency exchange centres, rental car outlets, outlets of hotels, pre-paid taxi counters, bank counters/ATMs, gift shops, etc. are commonly seen in this area in almost all international airports (Figure 16.6).

16.5 The landside

An airport has to be considered an interchange where different modes of transportation connect. Because the airport itself is not a primary destination, consideration must be given to access by surface vehicles. As the terminal acts as an interface between land transportation and air transportation, it needs a system of access with the city using the land mode of transport. The landside, another component of an airport, ensures this access and it is devoted to surface transportation. In fact, the access system can consist of road as well as the rail mode of transportation. "The landside components of an airport are planned and managed to accommodate the movement of ground-based vehicles, passengers and cargo" (Wells & Young, 2004). Customarily, even though they are integrated with the city/regional transportation network, only roadways and transportation facilities in front of the terminal, on the airport property, are included in the landside. This denotes that the landside represents the system of transportation consisting of road and rail

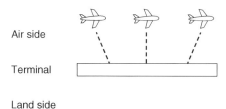

Air side

Terminal

Land side

Figure 16.7 Transporter terminal

networks that link the airport with the urban as well as regional transport network and the rest of the facilities and amenities, including the parking area, within the airport premises other than the terminal and airside. The landside provides the entry and exit for vehicles to move in and out of the airport. Passengers usually access airports using the land mode of transport through the landside. In large airports, ground access system can be complex, involving combinations of highway and train stations located under passenger terminals (Figure 16.7).

16.5.1 Physical components of the landside

This area provides the amenities and facilities for the safe and adequate passenger and cargo drop-off facilities. In addition, the arriving passengers can move out to reach the city or any other part in the region through this area. Usually, the landside is with relatively lesser security measures compared with the terminal and airside. In some regions, the landside also has strict security measures. The following are the components of the landside:

- Entry roadways
- Exit roadways
- Rail link (in some airports)
- Parking
- Commercial firms (e.g., car rental offices, prepaid taxi counters, bank outlets, restaurants).

16.6 Airport ground operations

When we are about to travel by an airplane, we carry out a series of actions that are familiar: we first book an airline ticket; approach the check-in area, where a staff member awaits us to hand over a boarding card to us after the verification of necessary travel documents; and accept our luggage. After passing through security checks, we arrive at the boarding gate, where another employee makes sure our boarding card and other travel documents are in order. Later, another employee takes us to the aircraft by bus if it is parked at a distant location. In the meantime, other workers have filled the airplane with fuel, other agents have provided the catering and the baggage has been loaded onto the hold and so on. Varieties of such services are provided during this time, including the following:

- Check-in
- Boarding
- Ramp handling
- Maintenance
- Cleaning
- Catering
- Fuelling

Usually, there are different personnel and equipment around the aircraft to service the aircraft. Hence, coordination must be there between different departments and safety and security are two crucial elements to dispatch an aircraft on time during a scheduled stopover. Along with punctuality, service quality levels are to be met, and for the same, service level agreements (SLAs) are established to be followed by airports. Through the airport handling manual, the International Air Transport Association (IATA) sets a series of standards for safe, secure and efficient airport operations. The IATA is also responsible for innovating and re-searching new handling policies and security guidelines on a day-to-day basis. The company providing such services, to ensure the quality levels, can size and adjust its own resources to its client's needs. SLAs are monitored during the provision of these services to assess their quality and detect any possible deviations, and the client can, in such case, demand corrective measures. Economic penalties may, in some cases, be triggered if there are significant deviations. All these will contrib-ute in enhancing the image of the airport as well.

16.7 Passenger handling

Before going into the details of passenger handling, it is important to understand the various types of passengers an airport will have to deal with. An introduction to major categories is in the following sections.

16.7.1 Types of passengers

Passengers are the final consumers of the air transport services that are provided by the airlines in association with the airports. Passengers using an airport may be divided into several subgroups that behave quite differently while circulating throughout the terminal building. The most common passenger segments are de-scribed below.

- International passengers: Passengers travelling between different countries.
- Domestic passengers: Passengers travelling within the country.
- Transfer passenger: They are the passengers moving to the final destination via an intermediary airport, for getting a connecting flight and have a transit stop for less than 24 hours. They will continue their travel with the same or a different airline company.
- Transit passenger: Passengers who land in an intermediary airport for a con-nection to the final destination airport with the same flight number.

   Some other common terms used to represent different types of passengers are given below.

- **Important passengers/very important person (VIP):** Some passengers are treated as VIP passengers based on their official, social or commercial status, and some special privileges and care are given to them by the airlines. It can be a preference in seat allocation, immunity from downgrading and denied boarding, upgrade priority, priority in check-in and baggage delivery, meal preferences, meet and greet services on special request, etc.
- **Frequent flyer passenger:** Frequent flyers are valuable customers for airlines. They are usually entitled to get bonus mileages as per airline rules, check-in

Figure 16.8 Check-in counters: JFK New York Terminal 5. Courtesy: Wikipedia Commons

priority via business-/first-class counters, preferential seating, excess free baggage allowance, access to airport lounges and chauffeur service (for first-class passengers).

- **Expectant mothers:** They are permitted against a medical certificate according to the duration of pregnancy, confirmation of fitness to travel and the airline policy and procedures.
- **Newborn babies:** Babies of more than 7 days old are permitted to travel. Restrictions are there for babies with illness, etc.
- **Infants:** Children of less than two years old can travel with a separate ticket on the applicable infant fare, but without a separate seat. If two infants are carried, a child ticket and a child restraint device (car-type infant seat) for the second infant are needed.
- **Children:** Children of age between 2 and 11 years can travel with separate tickets issued on the applicable child fare.
- **Unaccompanied minors** (UMs): A child of age between 5 and 12 who travels alone is called a UM. They have to be handed over to airline staff by parents or authorized persons, and on return, they have to be handed over back to the parents or authorized persons. For all these, necessary intimation and arrangements should have been completed earlier by parents.
- **Passenger with reduced mobility** (PRM): A passenger needs some degree of special assistance owing to varied reasons.
- **Medical case passengers:** This category needs medical clearance and may need medical attention and/or special equipment to maintain health during the flight. This case has to be approved by the respective airline's medical department. Medical escort (a qualified doctor/nurse/paramedic) may be needed in some cases. For those who need a stretcher, it can be arranged on specific aircraft.

- **Wheelchair passengers**: They are of different kinds, like, a wheelchair passenger who can use the stairs by himself/herself (wheelchair ramp), one who is unable to use the stairs and must therefore be assisted up (wheelchair steps), and a wheelchair passenger is unable to walk down (wheelchair cabin seat).
- **DPNA passengers:** Those with intellectual or developmental disability and needs the assistance of an escort.
- **Blind or deaf passengers:** Blind or deaf passengers are escorted to the gate if requested.
- **Emotional support animal:** A passenger may travel with an emotional support dog.
- **Service animals:** A passenger may travel with a trained service dog.
- Revenue passengers: A term used to refer to those passengers who travel with commercial or award tickets.
- Non-revenue passengers: These are those who travel with an industry discount ticket (e.g., for airline staff, travel agents, government discount and corporate discount).

There can be deportees and inadmissible passengers as well among normal passengers. At times, there can be unruly or disruptive passengers as well.

In accordance with international aviation and government regulations, all passengers travelling on international flights shall be in possession of the following:

- Valid air tickets
- Passport documentation
- Visa/transit visa
- Health documentation.

It is the responsibility of the passengers to ensure that all travel documentation applicable to their journey is in order before presenting themselves for check-in formalities. Should travel documentation not be adequate or appear not to be adequate, the passage shall be refused. The airlines that carry passengers to foreign countries with inadequate travel documentation have to face serious issues from the authorities. It is mandatory that the travel documentation of all passengers has been validated before acceptance, to verify full compliance with travel and visa regulations for points of transit and final destination. A reliable source for information on all the above is the travel information manual (TIM). Automated version of the TIM known as the travel information manual automatic (TIMATIC) is also available, which are used by the airlines. This is available in both the airline departure control system (DCS) and the reservation system. This automated version provides the following critical services:

- Passport requirements and recommendations
- Visa requirements and recommendations
- Health requirements and recommendations
- Airport tax to be paid by the traveller at either the departure or arrival airport
- Customs regulations relating to import/export of goods and small pets by a passenger.
- Currency regulations relating to import and export by a passenger

The TIM database is supported by the airlines around the world, to ensure that all of the latest information is present.

Table 16.2 Travel Documents

Passports
An official document issued by a competent government authority to prove citizenship of the respective country. In addition to normal passports, the following are different types of passports:

- *Joint passport (family passport):* Persons travelling together may hold joint passports that may be used to cover either: holder of the passport and child/children under a certain age or two or more children.
- *Diplomatic or consular passports:* Issued to diplomatic, consular and other government officials on missions.
- *Official, special or service passports:* Issued to government officials or other persons on government missions.
- *Temporary/emergency passports:* Issued in emergency cases and usually have the same legal effect as normal passports.
- *Alien passports:* Alien passports are issued to alien residents of the issuing country.

Other identification travel documents with limited acceptance include the national identity card, merchant seamen ID/passports and military ID.

Medical or Health Certificates
While travelling, it is essential to check the health documents requirements in the following:

- The country of destination
- The country of departure (also for returning if applicable)
- Transit stations.

A certificate stating the health status issued by the authorized category of the physician may be required at times when such are demanded. Some countries demand the proof of certain vaccinations and/or health certificates in an international format as legislated by the World Health Organization containing confirmation of these vaccinations.

Letter of Guarantee
A document stating the name of the sponsor and guarantees any incurred expenses if the passenger is subject to immigration refusal.

Visa
Although exceptions are there, this is a basic necessity to enter into a foreign country. Simply, it is an authorization given to non-citizens to enter the territory for which it was issued, subject to permission of an immigration official at the time of actual entry. This is usually a stamp endorsed in the applicant's passport. A visa can be revoked at any time. There are different types of visa, and the most common are introduced below.

Table 16.2 (Continued)

- *Work/employment visa:* Issued to people who are legally allowed to work in the country.
- *Transit*: Issued for short visit while the traveller is on a trip to another destination and having a break in the visited country.
- *Business visa:* For engaging in commerce in the country, not for permanent employment.
- *Student visa*: For the purpose of study at an institution of higher education in the issuing country.
- *Tourist visa*: Issued for a limited period of leisure travel, primarily for the purpose of visiting; no business activities and honorarium are allowed.
- *Visa for medical reasons:* This is to undergo diagnostics or a course of treatment in the host country's hospitals.
- *Residence visa:* This enables the incoming person to obtain long-term residence in the host country. It may be a prerequisite for getting the status of a permanent resident.
- *Immigrant visa:* This is granted for those intending to immigrate (status of a permanent resident) to the issuing country.
- *Diplomatic visa:* Issued to the bearers of diplomatic passports. On the contrary, *courtesy visa* may be issued to the eligible representatives of foreign governments or international organizations those who do not have diplomatic status.
- *Spouse visa or partner visa:* Issued to the spouse, civil partner or de facto partner of a resident or citizen of a given country to authorize the couple to settle in that issuing country.
- *On-arrival visa /visa on arrival (VOA)*: Issued at the port of entry for the citizens from those countries that are listed to be given a VOA option.
- *Electronic visa:* Visa issued based on electronic documentation and the visa is recorded electronically, till the entry time when the sticker or stamp is placed in the passport before travel.

Although the visa is issued in advance, the authority for permitting the bearers of visa to enter into a country is vested with the emigration officials at the port of entry. Even if visa is issued, there can be limitations in the number of entries into the countries. While some visa enables multiple entries, some others may permit single entry only using once issued visa.

16.7.2 Passenger check-in

Passenger check-in consists in carrying out all the procedures foreseen by the airline regulations related to the IATA and ICAO civil air transport regarding flight safety, to provide passengers with a boarding card. Passengers arrive at the airport on their own, enter the terminal and go to the check-in counter to receive a boarding card and to hand over their baggage. Afterwards, they go towards the security control area where their unchecked bags go through the X-ray control and then proceed towards the foreseen gate, following the signs. They wait for the departure announcement for their flight and, upon boarding, hand over their boarding cards with an ID and then cross a bridge or use a bus to board the aircraft. Nowadays, the **DCSs** are there which enable smoother and quicker processing of passengers. This is described in the last chapter. The following types of passenger check-in can be seen in airports.

- **Manual check-in:** This is performed in airports, which do not have automated systems. Manual stationery (boarding cards, baggage tags and seat chart) is used and manual close out (postflight)action is undertaken as part of this.
- **Automated check-in:** Airports with an automated system will follow this type. In this, automated stationery, for boarding card, baggage tags, seat chart, etc., is used; and close out (postflight messages) action is also carried out automatically.
- **Off-site check-in:** This allows convenient check-in from a place and time of their choice. This can be performed via Internet (online check-in) and mobile connectivity. Airlines' websites and mobile phone apps are some of the sources for this. The printout of the online boarding passes can be used for boarding.
- **Self-check-in kiosks:** Using the common-use self-service or check-in kiosk, passengers can get the boarding pass directly issued by entering the travel details. They do not have to approach check-in counters and in the queue for getting boarding passes. These are provided by either the airlines or airports. For those with baggage, they can deliver the baggage in the baggage drop space near the check-in counters of the respective airlines.
- **Through check-in:** This is for those who are moving on to the connecting flight and got the boarding passes for the whole journey issued from the first airport (the port of origin) itself for the whole journey, although breaks are there in between in stopover, transfer or transit points. The passengers and their baggage are processed onto the onward flight/s.

Airports and even the airlines have to display the notices regarding the non-permitted items to carry in both hand baggage and check-in baggage. Nowadays, messages regarding such carriage restrictions and security aspects to follow are sent electronically as well to the passengers.

Every passenger has to be allotted a seat except for those who have not attained two years of age. Priority and convenience are given for the unaccompanied minors (UMs), mothers with infants, children, invalids, sick and persons with reduced mobility. Seats adjacent to emergency exits are allotted for adults without handicap, expectant mothers, elderly people, deportees or prisoners, obese passengers, passengers with pets, etc.

16.7.3 Arrival and transfer services

When a flight lands, it will be driven to the apron to deplane passengers for entering into the arrival gate. A wide range of services are to be provided for the arriving passengers as well. Passengers have to be led to the arrival gate, and if transfer or transit passengers are there, they have to be directed to the passage for the same. If any passengers are there who need assistance, such as a UM and physically handicapped, the needed assistance has to be provided. A transfer passenger will have a confirmed or requested reservation on a flight scheduled to depart within 24 hours after arrival at the point of transfer. Moreover, the baggage might have been checked through to the connecting flight directly. In some cases, stopover is there which is a deliberate interruption of the journey by the passenger at an intermediate point in between the origin port and the destination.

16.8 Baggage handling and delivery

Baggage handling is a crucial task. Carry-on and checked baggage have to be security screened before acceptance on board an aircraft. Owing to security reasons, a number of items are forbidden to carry on board. This can include guns, firearms and other devices that discharge projectiles, stunning devices, objects with a sharp point or sharp edge, workmen's tool, blunt instruments (e.g., baseball and softball bats, clubs and batons and billy clubs), liquids on board (exceptions are there for certain items with limited quantity), liquid duty-free goods, and explosives and incendiary substances and devices. Items such as knives and lighters in the carry bags are refused at the security check.

Priority baggage is there in air transportation, which will be given priority for offloading delivery in the baggage claim area, and an indication label will be there in it. Priority baggage service may be given to VIP baggage, first-class/business-class/VIP baggage, etc. **Expedite baggage (rush baggage)** is a category of baggage which is sent on a flight other than the flight taken by the passenger who travelled in the previous flight or was lost in the transit. This has priority. Mishandled baggage shall be forwarded free of charge by the fastest possible means, using the service of any carrier to the airport nearest to the passengers' address. Wheelchair and mobility devices of passengers can also be carried. Musical instruments are included in the free baggage allowance. Extra baggage fee may be charged when the allowance is exceeded. Crew tags must be used for baggage carried by operating crew or dead head crew, which must be offloaded first and given priority to be delivered in the baggage claim area along with the other priority baggage. Urns with human ashes are also carried either as checked baggage or as carry-on baggage. Certain sports equipment can be considered as the part of the free baggage allowance. The size and weight limitations of free baggage allowance will be applicable. Carrying arms and ammunition has more restrictions. The arms, such as real arms, small defence arms (e.g., knives and daggers) and lookalike arms, are transported as checked baggage. Armed bodyguards or law enforcement officers may have different rules applicable. Similarly, some of the car or motorcycle parts can be transported as checked baggage in many airlines. Handling of pets should be in accordance with operating airline policy with local customs requirements, animal age and health requirements. Pets are carried either in a cabin or baggage compartment. Domestic animals of unusual size or wild animals and rodents must be transported as a cargo. The following are the categories carried in a cabin:

- **PETC (Pet in Cabin)**: Pets in an approved container are carried in the passenger cabin, in adherence to operating airline acceptance policy.
- **SVAN (Service Animals)**: Service animals, such as dogs trained to give support to passengers with disabilities.
- **ESAN (Emotional Support Animal)**: Emotional assistance dog for assistance to passengers with the specific need.

Excess baggage fees per kilogram or piece or special item are generally applied at the time of checked baggage acceptance. The overall rule is that a passenger who carries excess baggage must pay excess charges. He does, however, have the option of leaving the excess baggage behind. Excess baggage fees are applied as per operating airline specifications. The airline agent at check-in is responsible for determining the excess baggage rate that the passenger must pay. Before determining the amount of excess baggage, the check-in agent shall check the free baggage allowance in the ticket of the passenger. The allowance which is entered in the ticket always has to be accepted. If a passenger has a connecting flight, excess baggage has to be charged up to the point where his baggage is checked through.

Baggage labels enable the baggage handlers to sort and load easily. The airline's policy does matter in this connection. The baggage tag varieties can be different as below:

- Priority baggage
- Crew baggage
- Connection baggage
- Heavy baggage
- Late baggage
- Sporting equipment
- Mobility aids or devices
- Fragile baggage
- Items containing dangerous goods
- Standby baggage
- Items with limited release tag
- Animals in hold

Dangerous goods are not allowed to be carried on board by passengers or crew, except in certain cases when they can be safely transported under specific conditions. Passengers are to be informed about dangerous goods that they are forbidden to transport aboard an aircraft in text and pictorial form, electronically or verbally.

Baggage delivery has to be efficient and smooth. After unloading, the same has to be quickly moved to the baggage claim area at the terminal so that the checked baggage of all passenger groups is available for pickup as soon as possible after disembarkation. Priority has to be given to priority baggage. Checked baggage of VVIPs, VIPs and commercially important passengers (CIPs) along with other priority baggage and crew baggage has to be delivered first and that has to be followed by the first-class, business-class and frequent flyers. The baggage of passengers who require special handling such as UM, handicapped and wheelchair passengers has to be delivered along with the priority baggage before the delivery of economy baggage. If possible, crew baggage may be delivered separately from passengers' baggage. Complaints regarding missing or damaged baggage must be handled expediently by the staff available at the baggage claim area.

Cargo handling is another important aspect that takes place in dedicated areas within the airport. The cargo is a term representing various types of goods that are carried by ships, airlines, trucks, etc. for transporting them to the intended locations. It includes all articles, goods, materials, merchandise or wares carried onboard of such vehicles per the needs of the people who are sending them.

Dangerous goods, a distinctive category in the cargo, represent the articles/substances that are capable of posing a significant risk on health, safety or property when transported. Explosives, inflammable gases, flammable liquids and solids, and radioactive materials are the major elements in the dangerous good category.

16.9 Aircraft ramp handling

The ramp refers to the area in an airport where the aircraft are parked. Ramp-handling services ensure the efficient turnaround of aircraft so that flights stay on schedule. Ramp operations are a very important part of the whole operation of an aircraft. It covers the loading and unloading of baggage, air cargo and airmail onto the aircraft and transportation between the aircraft and the passenger terminal, air cargo terminals and the airmail centre. In addition to this, ramp-handling services cover preparations for the delivery onto aircraft of bulk baggage and baggage containers, aircraft loading bridge operations and passenger stairs operations. As we can see, it is a very complex situation where delivery precision and safety are very important issues. The successful turnaround procedure of an aircraft can be broken down into the following five steps of handling:

*   Preparation
*   Arrival
*   Unloading
*   Loading
*   Departure

A large number of people and vehicles work at the airport every day. Ensuring safety in every activity is very important owing to the existence of hazards and unsafe conditions. Regulations and procedures are implemented by regulators and operators with a view to minimize or eliminate the risk and there is no excuse for not observing them. All employees engaged in the ground handling activities at the airside must carry out their duties mindful of the need for safety and security. Vigilance, safety and security are matters of priority. Individuals at all levels within the departments have a duty to be familiar with and to apply safety and security measures relevant to their specific duties. They also have an obligation to develop awareness about the sense of responsibility towards safety and security among others.

Ground support equipment (GSE) is the support equipment found at an airport to support the operations. Training on the GSE operation includes the type of equipment to be used on each aircraft type based on the manufacturer recommendation. Types of ground service equipment can be varied. The following categories can be seen commonly:

*   Non-powered equipment
    *   Dollies and baggage carts
    *   Chokes
    *   Aircraft service stairs
    *   Aircraft tripod jack
    *   Unit load devices

- Powered equipment
  - Container loaders
    - Lower deck loaders
    - Main deck loaders
  - Medical high-loaders or ambulift
  - Conveyor belts or belt loaders
  - Forklifts
  - Tractors and tugs
  - Air starter unit
  - Pickups and cars
  - Refuellers
  - Ground power unit (GPU)
  - Buses
  - Catering vehicle
  - Transporters
  - Lavatory service vehicles
  - Potable water trucks
  - Passenger boarding steps/stairs
  - Pushback tugs and tractors
  - Deicing/anti-icing vehicles
  - Aircraft rescue and firefighting

Non-powered equipment is handled manually, without an engine's support. Dollies and baggage carts are used for the transportation of loose baggage, over-sized bags, mail bags, loose cargo carton boxes, etc. Chocks, kept at the front or back of the wheels, are used to prevent an aircraft from moving while parked. Aircraft services stair enables the maintenance technician to reach the bottom of the aircraft. Aircraft tripod jack supports the some of the parked aircraft to prevent their tail part from bending or dropping down. A unit load device is a pallet or container used to load luggage, freight and mail into an aircraft.

Powered equipment is with some mechanical force to undertake the tasks. Container loaders enable the efficient loading and unloading of containers and pallets into and out of aircraft. Its platforms raise and descend independently. Lower deck loaders (for loading into lower deck) and main deck loaders are the common types of them. Medical high-loaders or ambulift enable the disabled passengers to board and disembark easily. Belt loaders are used for unloading and loading of the baggage and cargo onto the aircraft. A forklift is a mechanized truck used to lift and move materials. Tractors and tugs are used to move all equipment such as bag carts, mobile air-conditioning units, air starters and lavatory carts. An air starter unit is used to start an aircraft's engines when the auxiliary power unit is not operational. Refuellers are either a self-contained fuel truck or a hydrant truck or cart. Fuel trucks constitute the former category, which can carry a large amount of fuel and have their own pumps, filters, hoses and other equipment. A hydrant cart or truck hooks into a central pipeline network and provides fuel to the aircraft. A GPU is a vehicle capable of supplying power to aircraft parked on the ground. GPUs may also be built into the Jetway, making it even easier to supply electrical power to aircraft. The GPU enables aircraft parked to have electricity supply when it is on the ground if needed.

Catering services include the loading of fresh food and drinks for passengers and crew and the unloading of unused food and drink from the aircraft; the meals are typically delivered in standardized carts. Meals are prepared mostly on the ground to minimize the preparation (apart from chilling or reheating) required in the air. The catering vehicle consists of a rear body, lifting system, platform and electro-hydraulic control mechanism. The vehicle can be lifted up and down, and the platform can be moved to the place in front of the aircraft. The transporter represents cargo platforms that can be used for transporting, loading and un-loading containers. Lavatory service vehicles are those vehicles used to empty and refill lavatories onboard aircraft after a flight. Potable water trucks, fitted with pumps as well as water storing tanks, are the vehicles used to deliver quality wa-ter to an aircraft. Passenger boarding steps/stairs are the mobile equipment used for boarding/deplaning passengers to/from aircraft. Pushback tugs and tractors are the equipment and vehicle used to push an aircraft away from the gate when it is ready to leave. Deicing/anti-icing vehicles are used for deicing/anti-icing pro-cedures on aircraft during winter seasons. Aircraft rescue and firefighting equip-ment are meant for evacuation and possible rescue of passengers and the crew of an aircraft involved in an airport ground emergency.

16.10 Aircraft weight and balance (load control)

All airplanes have weight limits and balance limits. Take-off and landing may not be safe for an aircraft that is loaded beyond its permitted weight. There could also be problems if the load carried on the aircraft is not distributed properly. Therefore, a load sheet officer has to make sure that weight and balance limits are not exceeded. For this purpose, the load sheet document and balance charts are prepared which are graphic presentations of all factors involved in the aircraft loading. **Load control** is a function to ensure the optimum use of the aircraft

Table 16.3 Phonetics to Follow in the Air Transport Sector as per the ICAO

Alphabet	Pronunciation	Alphabet	Pronunciation
A	Alpha	N	November
B	Bravo	O	Oscar
C	Charlie	P	Papa
D	Delta	Q	Quebec
E	Echo	R	Romeo
F	Foxtrot	S	Sierra
G	Golf	T	Tango
H	Hotel	U	Uniform
I	India	V	Victor
J	Juliet	W	Whisky
K	Kilo	X	X-ray
L	Lima	Y	Yankee
M	Mike	Z	Zulu

capacity and distribution of load as per the instructed safety and operational requirements. There are some load control principles to follow. Correct weight and
balance calculations are conducted before an aircraft's departure. A description
of aircraft load control was given in an earlier chapter.

Ramp safety rules and procedures promote safe ground handling. Therefore,
the minimum safety rules and procedures shall always be applied and understood
by all personnel working on the ramp. Aircraft damage can endanger passengers,
employees and aircraft. Disruptions may also negatively impact safe airline operations. Even a slight scratch or dent on an aircraft may result in a serious accident.

16.11 Airport security measures

Being the hub of the aviation security, a wide variety of measures is taken in the
airports to avoid safety and security issues. The ICAO (2005) defines security as
"Safeguarding civil aviation against acts of unlawful interference. This objective
is achieved by a combination of measures and human and material resources".
According to Arnold Barnett, security measures are of different kinds and are
generally classified into three: They are the measures to protect the passenger
cabin and cockpit; prevent explosions in the baggage compartment; and prevent
threats external to the aircraft (Barnett, 2009). Aviation security measures are
undertaken to safeguard the following:

- Passengers
- Crews
- Ground personnel
- General public
- Aircraft
- Airports
- Navigation facilities

Airports, together with the airlines, have a great role in ensuring all of these
categories. For baggage compartments, a variety of activities are undertaken to
ensure safety and security. Explosion detection equipment and canine teams involving trained dogs can be used to ensure that there are no dangerous materials
are loaded along with the cargo or checked-in bag into the baggage compartment. This exercise is performed when the cargo and baggage are there in the
airport. Consignments will be verified, and if it needs additional security measures, it will be verified manually/using "sniffer" dogs/metal detectors, explosive
vapour detectors, etc. The luggage is also screened using the X-ray mechanism
before collecting or loading into the aircraft. For carry-on/hand baggage screening, the airline counter may issue a tag for hand baggage. Hand baggage will
be screened using radioscopic (X-ray) equipment. In addition, explosive vapour
detectors may be used to check carry-on items. For checked baggage screening,
all such items have to pass through an automated screening device (usually X-ray
machine). It is basically performed to check whether unauthorized carriage of
weapons, explosives and dangerous goods is transported or not. A manual search
is also performed. Positive passenger bag matching is a recent measure, which
refers to a process by which the airline ensures that all checked bags on an aircraft

have their respective "owners" also on board. Checked luggage is cross-matched with passenger manifests to ensure that no baggage is there unless its owner is on board. To avoid external security threats, a wide range of measures are in place in and around an airport.

16.11.1 Passenger security

Each and every passenger needs to be identified properly to prevent any unlawful interference by the passengers. Certainly, every passenger's identity by verifying documents is done at different points. Moreover, passengers can be interrogated in a gentle way to have an initial personal verification. At the time of check-in, the passengers are asked to answer the following questions:

- Do you own this baggage?
- Was your bag(s) packed by anyone not travelling on this flight?
- Are you certain that nothing has been added since you packed?
- Did anyone give you anything to carry in it?
- Do you carry any dangerous goods items in your bag?

A wide range of security of documents such as boarding passes and baggage tags for every passenger and baggage are provided. These documents have to be retained with them till the end of the journey. By this, the entry of unauthorized people/baggage can be restricted as well. Every departing as well as transfer passenger, crew members, flight engineers and loadmasters and their cabin baggage/belongings are screened before boarding. All other persons and items entering the protected areas shall be authorized by security personnel and subject to

---

Table 16.4 Devices Used in Security Check/Screening

- Metal detectors: They are used for identifying weapons, magnetic materials, composites or metals. Enhanced walk-through metal detectors and handheld metal detectors are there.
- Holding stations: These are used for physical verification of passengers, whenever needed.
- X-ray units: Different types and varieties are available. Modern X-ray machines with a microprocessor are also used. Carry-on baggage X-ray machine is used to scan the items placed on the belt when it moves through the machine. Freight X-ray machines are also there.
- Neutron activation analysis: It is thermal neutron analysis, used to find out the composition of any object in the baggage.
- Explosive trace detector (ETD): The ETD is used to trace explosives in baggage, while passengers are in the queue, etc.
- Explosive trace portal (ETP): The ETP is used to detect explosive traces on passengers.
- Gas analyzers: These are used particularly to discover the plastic explosives.
- Dogs: Trained sniffer dogs are very common to discover explosives.
- Whole-body scanners: Two types are seen, such as backscatter X-ray scanners (soft X-ray scanners) and terahertz scanners (use high-frequency radio waves).

---

security control. All gates and departure areas are kept secured by keeping doors closed and use appropriate barricades when directing passengers. Man theses points and let the staff direct passengers to the aircraft. Only authorized personnel and screened passengers are allowed to board the vehicle. It is also important to assess each passenger in terms of the security risk by looking for anomalies and observing certain emotional characteristics and/or body language. If any potential problem is detected, it is important to protect the passengers first. Moreover, it is important to ensure that all security threats are immediately reported to the flight crew, airline authorities and other relevant authorities. Furthermore, it is critical to ensure that the passengers and baggage are handled properly.

16.11.2 Baggage security

The personnel have to ensure that all baggage is protected against unauthorized access from the check-in point until loading. Also, proper security measures are to be implemented for storage, handling systems and loading to ensure prevention of unauthorized access, tampering or introduction of prohibited articles in hold baggage. All baggage is kept under surveillance using closed-circuit television, etc., all the time. Proper screening mechanism is must in the baggage handling. Screening is "The application of technical or other means which are intended to identify and/or detect weapons, explosives or other dangerous devices, articles or substances which may be used to commit an act of unlawful interference" (ICAO, 2005). The following are the measures taken:

- X-ray machine screening of the baggage before entering of the beholder along with the baggage to the check-in zones.
- Screening by security personnel of the departing passengers and their cabin baggage before passing passport control and before accessing the departure passengers holding area at the gate.
- Screening of all transit passengers and their cabin baggage before the access of them to the departure passengers holding area.

Staff assisting the special category passengers shall ensure that the appropriate security screening is carried out by the airport security personnel before being permitted to board the aircraft.

In the case of transfer passengers, when passengers have to collect their hold baggage, the same may be treated as the originating baggage. Due procedure of baggage checking will be undertaken in such cases. If the baggage is collected and transferred in the sterile area, re-screening may not be necessary. Otherwise, if the baggage has come out of the airside or airport, the screening should be undertaken.

Weapons are to be kept carried in the hold or kept secured at all times either by approved personnel or locked away in a secure location. The authorized passengers such as air marshals/security personnel can carry weapons on board in the performance of their duties. For handling dangerous goods, the clauses in the IATA Dangerous Goods Regulations for handling and acceptance procedures are to be followed.

Security threat is there at different levels, such as the basic-level threat, intermediate-level threat and high-level threat. At the basic-level threat, there is a low-level security issue condition available. There may not be any chance of attack on the operator or airport. It may be due to the unlawful interference by individuals or groups owing to varied reasons. At the intermediate level, proper intelligence information may point to the possibility of attack on one or more operators and/or airports. At high level, the verifiable intelligence information indicates one or more operators and/or airports have specifically been targeted for attack. Based on and in collaboration with the authorities, necessary steps will be taken by the airlines and airports to nullify the threat. In short, baggage re-screening, passenger additional frisking procedures and all passengers may be taken for passenger processing activities from check-in to boarding. In the case of severe threats, passengers will be disembarked with the cabin baggage, all hold baggage will be returned, the cargo will be returned for identification and screening, etc. Passengers can identify their baggage and can be asked for an inspection. If unaccompanied baggage is there, it will be taken for further investigation. For cargo, manual inspection, use of specially trained dogs, metal detectors and explosive vapour detectors are employed when a serious threat is identified. The storing facilities are guarded and proper security measures are followed throughout the freight movement process until boarding. The employee restriction is also undertaken as per the rules and regulations. There may be a permit system prevailing. A background check before issuing the permit is undertaken. For each entry and exit, the ID is verified. Validity is there for all the permits given. There may be different zones where different groups of employees can access.

16.12 Conclusion

Airports are an important part of the air transport system and are now becoming business hubs rather than just their main function. The three areas of a typical airport are the airside, landside and one or more terminals. The airside of an airport is for the movement, landing and take-off of the aircraft, and it is the most important area where all the technical aspects of flying at an airport take place. The major components of the airside are the runways, taxiways, path markings, pathway signs, apron/ramp area, hangar, ATC tower, support services and facilities and airport lighting system. The ultimate task of the terminal is to provide facilities for passengers and cargo processing as part of the air transport. Currently, the terminals at major airports look like mini-cities, are aesthetically designed and have different apron layout structures. The landside, another component of the airport, ensures city access from the airport and is reserved for the surface transportation. In fact, the access system can cover both road and rail transport.

Airport ground operation functions must be carried out in coordination between different departments, and safety and security are two crucial elements to dispatch an aircraft on time during a scheduled stopover. Passenger handling is a part of ground handling, and it is mandatory that the travel documentation of all passengers has been validated before acceptance, to verify full compliance with travel and visa regulations for points of transit and final destination. The TIM is a reliable source for this, and an automated version of the TIM known as TIMATIC is available and used by the airlines. The airlines are using the DCS to enable smoother and quicker processing of passengers at the airport. Arriving passengers also need to be provided with a number of services. Baggage handling and delivery is a crucial job at the airport. Cargo handling is yet another important aspect that takes place in dedicated areas within the airport. Aircraft ramp handling is another crucial task, where delivery precision and safety are very important issues. GSE is the support equipment found at an airport to support the operations and has varied kinds. Ramp safety rules and procedures promote safe ground handling. Airport regulators and operators enforce regulations and procedures of safety and security to reduce or eliminate risk and there is no excuse for not observing them. Airports, together with airlines, have a great role in ensuring security and safety of the passengers and strict security control to be enforced for the passenger and baggage security.

Sample questions

Short/medium answer-type questions

- Describe the activities during the turnaround time.
- What do you mean by ramp-handling activities?
- Explain the process of deplaning and boarding of passengers.
- What are ANSs?
- Describe the components of an airport.
- Explain the activities in a terminal.
- What are the parts of the airside of an airport?
- Discuss the various aspects of cargo loading in aircraft.
- Explain the push back operations.
- Discuss the security measures in an airport.
- Explain the landside of an airport.
- Describe different types of check-in.
- What are the major equipment and vehicles used in airport ground handling?
- List the activities involved in passenger handling for an arriving passenger.
- Describe the ANSs provided for a flight after take-off until landing

Essay type questions

- Explain the ground handling operations in an airport.
- Explain the structure of an airport.
- Describe the passenger handling process in airport terminals.

Suggested readings

Ashford, J.N., Stanton, P.H, Moore, A.C., Coutu, P., & Beasley, R.J. (2013). *Airport Operations*. New York: McGraw Hill.
Graham, A. (2014). *Managing Airports: An International Perspective*, 4th ed. London: Routledge.
Kazda, A., & Caves, E.R. (2000). *Airport Design and Operations*. Oxford: Elsevier.
Young, S., & Wells, A. (2019). *Airport Planning & Management*, 7th ed. New York: McGraw-Hill.

Chapter 17

Air transport information technology

Learning outcomes

After reading this chapter, you will be able to:

- Understand the intricate relationship between air transportation and information technology (IT).
- Describe the significance of the information and communication technology (ICT) application in enhancing the tourists' experience.
- Explain the IT application in airports.
- Describe the ICT application in the airlines.
- Identify the emerging trends in the ICT application in the airlines and airports.
- Learn about the disintermediation and reintermediation in air travel.

17.1 Introduction

Certainly, ICTs are inseparable in most of the functions that enable efficient, smooth and safe air transportation. As of now, ICT is deeply pervaded into air transport operations of all sorts. Over the years, operations by various elements within the air transportation system have been transformed dramatically owing to the impact of the ICT application. Each element has to perform crucial functions in a time-bound manner. All those functions are facilitated greatly by ICT solutions. The influence of it has transformed the way how the sector has been interacting with the customers. Product distribution has been recording significant changes since the advent of Internet. Product access for the customers became so easy and convenient as any of the air transport product can be booked at any point of time from anywhere using a smartphone. Moreover, the passenger can immediately know any changes in flight schedules, etc. Airports depend much on

DOI: 10.4324/9781003136927-17

the ICT solutions to manage passenger and cargo processing. Sophisticated passengers seek high-end technology solutions, and the service providers have to be equipped well to generate customer satisfaction. ICT applications have benefited all the functional departments within the airlines and airports, particularly by increasing efficiency and reducing the cost. Certainly, ICT is a determinant in the efficient, profitable, competitive and successful air transport operations and management. The following is a description on the application of ICT in the form of technology solutions or information systems in the operation and management of airports and airlines.

17.2 ICT and tourist experience

This chapter describes the ways through with ICT solutions directly or indirectly influence the travel experience. In tourism, the role of IT in shaping the tourists' experience is on a steady ascend. Wang et al. (2017), opine,

> In recent years, information technologies (e.g., the Internet and the mobile phone) have become prevailing service conduits that influence tourist perceptions of destinations and travel behaviours. As necessary tools for travellers to acquire information at different stages of their trips, technology based services (e-commerce) are indeed critical for the tourism industry, as they promote the interactions between providers and tourists while rendering service experiences in a cost-effective and efficient manner.

According to Papatheodorou and Zenelis (2013), "The majority of ICT applications in air transport have a direct or an indirect effect on customer satisfaction and the overall tourism experience". In fact, every application, in one or the other way, contributes in making the journey smooth, comfortable and enjoyable. Some of those applications are inevitable in the functioning of various components of the air transportation system. Some others are making the interactions between travellers and service providers more comfortable. Some of them enhance the quality of the journey. Some technologies are meant for providing better safety and security. Overall, the combined effects of all those technology solutions lead to a better travel experience for the tourists as well as other travellers. Moreover, the travel experience is a major component in the tourist experience, and therefore, air transport–related ICTs too play a major role in tourists' experience. Increased personalization, digital interface at every touchpoints, operational efficiency and enhanced delivery of services take the travel experience to the next level.

Tourists' use of transportation-related ICT starts from the early stages of buying decision-making itself.

> For airlines, customer interactions start way before the flight is even boarded; the test begins when the flyer is looking for a flight and extends way after they unboard the plane. It can be a daunting task to keep up with the changing customer demands and provide a seamless and delightful experience throughout the passenger journey.
>
> (Chatterjee, 2017)

At the time of need recognition, tourists are stimulated by the image or perceptions of the air transport and that can trigger the need for choosing a particular airline or airport as part of the travel. Information search has become so easy. From Internet-based sources to mobile apps can now enable the potential buyer to get the needed information rather quickly. Artificial intelligence (AI)–based chatbot service enables the buyer in getting suggestions quickly. Evaluation of alternatives is much easier nowadays as varied online sources would certainly help the buyer in getting the comparisons, recommendations and opinions. Thus, before the purchase of air transport products itself, ICT plays a key role in providing a favourable experience. Buying a flight ticket is a matter of seconds now and can be done at any point of time, sitting anywhere. Making payment for the purchase is also quite easy.

The passenger experience within airports has improved greatly with the assistance of ICTs. Airport operations are transformed by the use of new technologies. Travellers of varied kinds are experiencing advantages owing to the new technologies. The ICTs can be defined as follows:

> facilitate and enable airport operations to take place at different geographical places, to become knowledge based and to be managed in real-time and to be streamlined, whilst also providing self-service possibilities to passengers who are simultaneously provided with additional value added personalized services and information. For airport management, ICT fosters and enables major reengineering efforts and the reorganization of processes which manage passenger flows and airport assets.
>
> (Sigala, 2008)

Personalization became easier for airports and the airlines. Using an app-based "luggage tag notifier" enables the traveller to deposit his/her baggage easily immediately after the entry into the airport. Facial recognition enables a smooth flow of the passenger within the terminal. Personalized airport shopping is also possible nowadays. Early check-in with the assistance of online/mobile-based platforms always relieves the traveller. Airports have different types of self-service check-in counters, of which some are mobile as well which can be placed conveniently. Increasing use of biometrics is revolutionizing the travel documentation and processing possibilities, and it eases the burden of passengers in getting checks of varied kinds as part of the international air travel. Airports have started to provide 5G Internet connectivity as well. For assisting differently abled passengers, airports are now venturing to provide personal mobility self-driving electric wheelchairs. Better control, shorter queues and higher satisfaction are possible with those sorts of ICT applications. Use of the latest technologies reduced the scope of missed luggage, and tracking of the luggage became easier.

From marketing perceptive, ICTs have an increasing impact nowadays. Tourists are influenced by ICT tool-based sharing and marketing of tourism experiences.

> Development of information and communication technologies has provided passengers more opportunities to share their flight experience on social networks and on-line platforms. Through electronic word-of-mouth, they can exchange their feedback and opinion on the quality of the service and their flight experience. Not only is this information fruitful for future passengers,

but it is considered an invaluable resource in the airline industry to assess the airline performance from the passenger's point of view.

(Punel et al., 2019)

Sharing of the travel and tour experiences is always a cherishing thing for the tourists, and social media platforms give plenty of opportunities for them. This can inspire others too to take part in tourism. The airlines particularly use every possible digital platforms and electronic means to interact, attract and persuade the potential buyers.

In-flight use of technology is an experience enhancer. Advanced technologies are now being used. For instance, virtual reality (VR) and immersive experiences can be a trend soon as this can enhance the journey more enjoyable by having VR-enabled in-flight entertainments (IFEs). By having in-flight connectivity, some of the airlines are trying to digitize the passengers' in-flight experience. After reaching the destination airport also, every service needed can be arranged with the help of ICTs. Taxi bookings, transfers, hotel booking, etc., are easy. Information access is also quite easy and that can reduce the strangeness in the destination.

The following is a detailed discussion on the application of ICTs in the airline and airport sector, which altogether make the travel smoother, enjoyable and rememberable.

17.3 Technology solutions in airports

A wide range of functions are there to be performed by the airport for the efficient air transportation. In fact, although flight operations are performed by the airlines, airports are crucial in enabling the airlines to operate services. Every function is to be performed within the specified time limit and delays can lead to irreversible impacts. Essentially, ICT is part and parcel of many of the airport functions. Information systems form the core of ICT application in any organizations, and here, the ICT application in airport functions is described using either information systems used in specific functions or by detailing the technology solutions used to perform particular tasks.

17.3.1 Baggage and cargo handling systems

Baggage and cargo handling is a crucial task in air transportation. The cargo and baggage movement process begins from the check-in area to the aircraft. The aircraft will have baggage and cargoes of so many people. The destination points of the cargo also vary. Owing to these complexities, the chances for misplacing, using wrong off-loading, etc., are very high. The computer technology has a lot of roles in this context. Also, if any item is lost, it has to be tracked. All such tasks can be accomplished with a combination of systems of databases and IT-based equipment. The baggage collection is an important task, and there, in the check-in area, delay can be possible when more passengers are there in the queue. Bag check-in systems help in easy and quick check-in of the passengers' luggage. It has a stand-alone scanning facility which ensures only conveyable bags with a readable bag tag are entered into the system of baggage acceptance and movement to the sorting area. These automated systems will ensure the weight, issue readable tags, options for payment of excess baggage, etc. Now Radio Frequency Identification (RFID) baggage tags are also used. Baggage tags are the most important identification materials, and they have optical barcodes that record the tag number, flight segments and destinations; this record is the ultimate source to retrieve the baggage, and the centralized database will record data from this tag, which will be used for handling and retrieving baggage. Here also, the tags that are attached to the baggage are the ultimate information source. Optical scanning technology in electronic eyes reads bag tags as they move along conveyor belts, on which the baggage moves. Drop technology solutions are provided by some airports. These can be used by the airlines and ground handlers as well. Using this, the service of traditional check-in counters can be reduced. Complete baggage management systems are there that can provide real-time information. The cloud-based baggage reconciliation solution is also in use in many airports, which has the capacity to reduce misplaced bags, resulting in fewer flight delays and happier passengers.

Baggage messaging software is another type of the technology solution used in the air transport. It is a type of baggage-monitoring software. It can monitor messages and bags, and it can generate the pseudo-baggage source message. The bag message system is designed for the airlines and airports for sending baggage messages. The bag messaging mechanism can keep track of the baggage, by exchanging multiple messages at each touchpoint, from bag drop, sortation and loading systems. Amadeus offers a messaging mechanism that can connect to any baggage handling systems via the Amadeus platform, routing messages from any departure control systems (DCSs) to every touchpoint in real time. Baggage source messaging solutions for errant transfer bags and fallback sortation solutions are also there in use. A fallback sortation bag tags-on-demand software is also there that can print authorized fallback tags on demand. The baggage tracking software is common these days. Bar tracking systems are there which can locate the lost baggage. A powerful baggage tracking software helps to get the precise picture of a bag's current location. There are also global tracing and matching services of delayed bags using the global tracking software. A net/mobile-based tracking application is also there. A networked connectivity providing mechanism is also there being developed for efficient corporate communication within the multiple units of corporates. Baggage tracing systems of advanced levels can now trace and match the misplaced baggage. Passengers can have more personalized services, and mobile agents can roam the airport to help passengers at different locations to report mishandled baggage and trace their status. Passengers can check the status of their bags via the Internet, and notifications are provided at the right time.

IT-enabled systems are there in use to handle reservations and tracking of cargoes. Cargo systems also use optical barcodes. IT-based cargo movement systems are there, and they use automated guided vehicles to move cargoes. Cargo movement is also a complicated procedure, and the possibility for loss of cargoes is very high. The cargo movement system helps the airlines to carry out the information of cargo movement very efficiently.

17.3.2 Check-in automation and self-service kiosks

Automation in check-in has been there for a long. Usually, this can be a part of a more comprehensive system used within an airport. Airline systems may have an interface with this as well. Self-service check-in is in vogue in almost all airports in the world. Multipurpose kiosks can be used in airports that can be used by passengers for various purposes such as check-in, booking and changing a reservation. Automated ticket machines (ATMs) are a measure to offer travel database consumers and are usually located in the check-in areas of airports (Sheldon, 2004). The following are the uses of ATMs:

- Access flight schedules
- Make seat reservations
- Print itineraries, tickets and boarding cards

ATM terminals will be linked to computerized reservation systems (CRSs) of the airlines. These are very much useful to travellers on single carriers and shorter flights and businesses travellers without check-in luggage on commuter flights. The self-service check-in applications for kiosks and the Web check-in arrangements are in practice nowadays. Using this can help in an integrated approach to implement and manage check-in processes, and the airlines can react quickly to their operational needs by making and scheduling their own standard configuration changes using an intuitive Web-based configuration console. It is now possible to check in using mobile devices with the assistance of geo-fencing of airports. It is predicted that virtual service agents guide the passenger through check-in at the airport. (Benckendroff et al., 2014). Along with the global positioning system (GPS), near-field communication and Bluetooth Low Energy are also now in use.

17.3.3 Departure control and passenger processing systems

DCSs constitute one of the most important systems used within the airports. The airlines and ground handlers can use this for efficient functioning of passenger processing in the airport until boarding. Automated DCSs are there that facilitate the airlines, airports and ground handlers to perform the check-in and boarding processes. This helps in automated check-in, boarding and load planning which are very crucial activities in airports. Modern systems of this kind facilitate different types of self-service options, including Web, mobile and kiosk check-in. These can be installed by airports and provide the airlines and ground handlers access to passenger processing applications on dedicated or shared common-use equipment. For example, SITA's (Société Internationale de Télécommunications Aéronautiques) AirportConnect Open provides the standard communications between all the peripherals required for passenger processing and that consists of passport readers, payment terminals, boarding pass and bag tag printers, and boarding gate readers (BGRs) and supports self-bag drop and self-boarding gates. Biometric technology is increasingly used for identification and documentation purposes. Facial recognition, eye iris patterns and fingerprints are also being used for identification purposes. Passenger handling systems are integrated systems that enable ground handlers to access multiple DCSs. These are usually more user-friendly with graphical user interface (GUI) features. The following are the modules and features of modern DCSs in general:

- Check-in
- Boarding pass issuing
- Seat allocation

- Checked baggage
- Load control calculation
- Passenger identification verification (e.g., passport screening)
- Denied boarding of the circumstances arise
- Handling no-shows and stand-by passengers
- Interline connections
- Interoperability with other systems (Benckendroff et al., 2017)

17.3.4 Gate management

IT support is there in the effective use of gate for arriving flights, depending on their characteristics. On arrival, each flight needs a gate assignment and it has to be coordinated with airport facilities to avoid delays in other flights. In determining the best use of gates, computerized systems are in use.

Of late, **self-service gates** are used by modern airports. This can help in self-boarding and access control to the airline lounges and other facilities. This may be with barcode readers, which can interact with the airline system and helps for automatic gate opening, and after the passing of the passenger, the gate closes. Usually, such systems may have sensors, lights, barrier arms, an integrated BGR and a receipt printer, and the data are communicated with the airline system for recognizing the genuineness of the boarding pass. The boarding pass validation solution is another innovation in this area. A bar-coded boarding pass verification system is there in place. Agents can verify the boarding passes more quickly. Boarding alerts are given via mobile devices as well.

Pre-departure authorization systems provide a technology solution for pre-departure travel authorization and consist of a full e-visa issuance and management system, as well as the ability to issue electronic travel authorizations. The real-time denial of boarding is also there. Also, technology solutions are there that enable the authorities to access information as a complete set of data, validated and in a usable format, and with enough time to process it before travellers arrive at their border. DCSs constitute one of the most important systems used within the airports. The airlines and ground handlers can use this for the efficient functioning of passenger processing in the airport until boarding. This helps in automated check-in, boarding and load planning which are very crucial activities in airports. Modern systems of this kind facilitate different types of self-service options, including Web, mobile and kiosk check-in. Border automation systems are becoming common in airports. These are the systems with self-service gates and kiosks for border control. The biometric kiosks can replace the traditional mechanism of travel documents verification, etc., and can automate the process. Biometric data, such as face, fingerprint and iris, can be used for the verification of the identity of the passenger as part of emigration checks, etc.

The immigration procedure is an important responsibility in an international air travel to be undertaken together by the governmental agencies with the assistance of airports. Technology systems are nowadays used to make the processes faster and easier. **Passport control kiosks** are an addition in many airports. This enables travellers from some countries to complete their customs declaration form on its touch screens. Travellers' passports are read and their fingerprints and facial images are captured by the kiosks, and hence, the long queues in the immigration counters can be reduced substantially. Travel documents are turning electronic along with the advancements in technology. New machine readable travel documents are becoming inevitable. Modern passports are becoming electronic, so that e-passports are emerging. The e-passport "has a contactless circuit embedded in the passport and is able to support biometric identification of the traveller" (Lucas, 2018).

17.3.5 Systems support airport management

Complete resource management systems are there which can not only help in managing the human resource but also help even the rest of the resources in use in the airports. It can coordinate the real-time management of equipment and human resource. The management aspects cover even the departure gates, baggage carousels, check-in desks, mobile resources for ground handling, etc. This is suitable for large airports with millions of passenger handling. Digital workspace can be provided within airports. The latest IT management service systems enable flexibility of the employees by permitting them to work from any space wherever desktop of IT-enable systems are available to do the work. Revenue/property management systems are also used in airports. These are useful for managing agreements, property, activity statistics and billing. The revenue management activities and back-office data consolidation are fully automated by this.

The digital workspace service is offered for the convenience of the employees. The latest IT management service systems enable flexibility of the employees by permitting them to work from any space wherever the desktop of IT-enabled systems are available to do the work. For the convenience of the staff in the airport, the **airside apps** are developed. These are apps created for the staff in the airport belonging to airline, airport and ground handling agencies. This will help to have the information to be the collected and shared in real time among the staff concerned. This can be used in tablets, mainly for coordinated information access among all the needed staff in real time and for enabling situational awareness, as well as emergency and disruption management communications.

17.3.6 Data processing solutions

The data from the airline including the flight timings and passenger load details are available in different formats, and these are transformed into an Extensible Markup Language (XML)–based data format as per the need of the airport and ground handling staff. A data analyzing software is also there. Data from various sources are gathered and analyzed and the reports are made, and such systems can provide key performance indicators (KPIs). Data explorer systems are there that can enable fast access to data so that the managers concerned within the airports can make more informed and faster decisions. **Operational information repository** is available which can provide multiple users to access data management tasks and automated functions of gathering, processing and distributing data. The **data connecting software** is there that can enable airlines, airports and other air transport industry partners to connect their host applications to messaging distribution networks. This acts as middleware and ensures efficient messaging services wherever needed.

The passenger flow analyzer is an innovative technology solution. These kinds of systems analyze passenger flows by departures, arrivals, transfers and visits at different locations in the airport. The output can be accurate flow patterns, dwell times, path analysis reports, etc. Similar systems can be there that can forecast accurate passenger flow for the next day, and this could help to have proactive management of the airport environment.

17.3.7 Flight movement predicting assistance

IT-based support services can be performed for the airlines and airports to assist in taking measures to manage irregular operations. Advanced predictions about the forthcoming flight movements can be made using such applications so that the operators concerned can take proactive measures. Past data, ATC information, climate updates, etc., are used, and predictions are conducted using AI as well. **Flight dispatch systems** can monitor flight progress, weather conditions and other aspects related to the flying of the flight from the origin to the destination.

17.3.8 Communication enhancement systems

Stakeholder communication facilitation systems are also there, like a system that is an entry-level Internet Protocol (IP) connectivity for common-use terminal equipment and kiosks, based on shared devices. Cost reduction can be possible through minimizing investment for infrastructure for establishing such a traditional communication mechanism and by increasing capacity and efficiency. Web-based applications are also possible now for faster and cheaper communication among all the stakeholders span over larger areas. Moreover, global conference services are also available which can support real-time, feature-rich voice and data sharing. The number of participants that can participate also increased substantially. Technology solution providers also offer cellular mobile connectivity services. Secured global connectivity for the required personnel of the industry is also provided using external services.

A messaging software is also there. Some software performs operational mail service now. In addition, technology solutions are there so that the messages can be received from any location via the Web. Message switching service solution is also offered by technology forms now. A secure XML data exchange service is also provided. Voice and data-integrated services are also offered in the market. Messaging services are provided with the assistance of the latest technologies. Air traffic control (ATC) messaging services are made easy with the air navigation service providers (ANSPs). Necessary modifications are made so as to make it easy for communication by the user with ATC organizations throughout the flight operations process.

17.3.9 Geo-location applications

Airport operations are time-bound, and the presence of passengers at the right time is inevitable in ensuring prompt services. Passengers need to know the exact times and changes in timings, etc. Different types of technology solutions now support airports in these areas. Virtual geo-fencing is now possible, and it is primarily used to track passengers. The airport can track the passengers using GPSs when the passenger is en route. The distance, time to reach airport, etc., can be understood. Triggers are there to sense the arrival at a specific location. Passengers can get necessary information about parking availability, etc. Geo-location apps are available in the market now. Indoor and outdoor geo-location technologies are being integrated into the modern location apps, which can provide up-to-date information on the flight status, the best route to their gate, how long it will take to get there and the like. Digital maps are a part of this, and Bluetooth beacon and proximity marketing are also integrated.

17.3.10 Flight Information Display Systems

Passengers need information on facilities and services within airports. In addition, they need information on the flight status, etc. All information of flight operations, particularly the flight status, are provided by flight information display systems (FIDSs), which are now essential in airports. These systems display flight departure and arrival schedules, gate assignment and baggage carousel (Sheldon, 1997). These have a large display, and multimedia and graphic displays are also there in these systems. The latest FIDSs can combine graphical, video and textual information as per the needs of the situations. Liquid-crystal display monitors, light-emitting diode signs and mobile terminals are part of such advanced systems and those can support multimedia content as well. Nowadays, these systems can combine graphical, video and textual information as per the needs of the situations. Entertainment options are there in airports using the latest technology. Self-service entertainment systems are an advanced version of it. These enable passengers to use entertainment options. These can be made available at different customer touchpoints and can be accessed via mobile devices as well wherever they are. The airline can provide such to the passengers while they are at the boarding gate, lounge, concourse, etc. Advanced audiovisual public addresses as well as media manager systems are in use, which can simultaneously display texts on video screens to correspond with the audio message. This may have content creation, recording, volume adjustment based on the situation, etc.

17.3.11 Airport apps

Airport apps can provide the essential and timely information as per the need of the passengers. Many airports nowadays like to distribute information about the happenings, particularly the flight delays, flight status notification, etc., to the consumers via apps. Advanced apps are turning to be context- and location-aware to assist passengers based on their needs in real time. The following are the essential features of such apps:

- Maps
- Navigation tools
- Information on airport commercial services, facilities and special offers
- Link to flight information display system
- Facilitate social media information between passengers (Benckendroff et al., 2014)

17.3.12 Point of sale systems

Point of sale (POS) systems are the common simple systems used at the points of sale in airports. An airport consists of different commercial centres and shopping units. Automated sale points are needed for efficient and quick transactions. Sale at the duty-free shops is now linked to the boarding passes as well. While payment collection, the boarding passes are scanned to identify the passenger. At some commercial centres, POS systems are linked with airports' passenger information system.

There are a number of ICT applications and solutions that are used for technical aspects of the air transportation. IT systems used in ATC, according to Benckendroff et al. (2014), are communication systems, navigation systems, surveillance systems and flight and weather information systems. Energy management systems are also used within airports. Many other areas are there where systems are used. Because this book focuses more on commercial aspects of the air transport and tourism, these are not included in this.

17.4 Airports and ICT: emerging trends

The emerging trends in the ICT application in airports are summarized below:

- **Biometrics:** It is increasingly being used in airports nowadays. It helps in easy and touch-free identity verification. Facial recognition mobile apps are in trend, which can make the check-in process easier for passengers. Biometric terminals are there in some airports now.
- **Robotics:** It is a trend in the airport sector. It acts as an automated labour-intensive operation and has a role in different areas such as baggage loading/unloading. The self-driving guide robot, automated vehicles on the airfield, baggage-related robots and delivery drones are also started to be used by airports. Autonomous baggage handling carts or baggage robots are there in some airports.
- **Augmented reality (AR):** It can be used in airports for different purposes such as for helping passengers to navigate the complex layout of the airport and to assist air traffic controllers with the vital job of keeping planes safe. Immersive experience solutions are also in vogue.
- **Beacons technology:** It can be used for making navigation easy for travellers between different terminals at the airport. Moreover, it can be used by help airports and vendors at the airport premises to know where passengers are and then send them personalized and relevant information accordingly.
- **Chatbot:** It enables assistance through enquiry services, and these are offered through social media, mobile apps, websites, etc. An AI-powered chat platform is there now for chatbots.
- **5G network connectivity**: Airports have started to provide 5G network connectivity as well to have better online experiences for the passengers.
- **Blockchain**: Airports can use this in improving passenger identification processes, in part by reducing the need for multiple ID checks.
- **Big data analytics:** They enable predictive maintenance within baggage systems, operational data insights and passenger behaviour analysis.

- **Mobile solutions**: Various types of mobile solutions are used by airports. Apps of different types are in use nowadays.
- **AI:** Currently, AI-powered products such as chatbots and virtual assistants are there. However, efforts are there in the increased use of it in every layer of the operational infrastructure.
- **Video analytics:** Airports can efficiently manage queues, crowds, baggage-trolley movements, unattended bags, etc., using video analytics.
- **Assistive technology**: Different types of technology solutions are being used for the disabled category of passengers and others who need special assistance. It can include an app, which can enable passengers to personalize the assistance they require and that can be requested in advance. Smart glasses and apps can assist the blind and low-vision travellers.

17.5 ICT application in the airlines

An airline is a large commercial organization with a wide variety of time-bound tasks to perform every now and then. The need for advanced ICT-based systems and solutions is so high for competitive survival. Being a commercial organization, most of the management information systems are used by the airlines, although some have specific terminologies associated with airline operations. The airline is one of the pioneers, which used transaction processing systems. Computer reservation systems developed by the airlines are considered as revolutionary transaction processing systems in the 1960s. They got advanced, and now, their cope and functions got expanded manifold. The major information systems/IT solutions used by the airlines, according to Benckendroff et al. (2014), are the following:

- Airline reservation system
- Decision support systems
  - Fleet management system
  - Flight scheduling and crew scheduling systems
  - Flight operating system
  - Revenue management system
- Global distribution systems (GDSs)
- Marketing information system
- Customer relationship management system
- DCSs
  - Gate control systems
  - Flight dispatch systems
- In-flight systems
  - Entertainment systems
  - Crew support systems.

17.6 Airline reservation systems

The airlines are using such reservation systems within them to distribute, sell and service their products. The airlines have to distribute flight schedules, seat availability and fare information (Cook & Billig, 2017). Airline reservation system is "the heart of the airline's operations" (Belobaba et al., 2009). These systems are fed with revenue management, crew scheduling, schedule optimization and pricing, all of which will be processed to give the required information to the GDSs. By linking with GDSs, these can provide better inventory and rates to end customers and travel agencies with online availability of 24/7 along with real-time bookings. Such systems consist of the exchange of data through the GDSs. Major GDS companies and similar firms do offer standard airline reservation systems also. The following components, according to Dileep (2019), are common in airline reservation systems

- Flight schedules: Days and times for flights operated by the airline.
- Fares: Fare and the corresponding rules for journeys are stored and provided as per need.
- Availability: Seat availability on a flight by service class.
- Passenger information: It is stored by using the passenger name record (PNR) format. This can be retrieved for various purposes such as reservation, ticketing and check-in.
- e-Tickets: The system provides e-tickets as well for each reservation for further use by the passenger during the entire process of the travel.

Moreover, apart from using reservation systems just for the product distribution, the advanced systems can be used for the key functionality for flight and schedule management and inventory control. Other stand-alone systems in the associated areas such as those in pricing, ticketing, and check-in are being associated for the efficient managing of bookings. These can be a part of passenger services systems as well. The reservation data managing software is also there which can gather the needed inventory, passenger records, departure control activities and booking details. These data will be beneficial for analysis and demand forecasting and the like. The data and the reports generated will be beneficial for customer relationship management, strategic management and other higher level managerial decisions. e-Ticketing generation is another task that is performed along with booking and reservation. Separate software can be used for this, and thus, the direct distribution of the airline product and ancillary services is possible using this.

Airfare managing systems are there. These identify market trends in air fares and provide quick responses. This will be beneficial for dynamic pricing. It is important to provide the right price at the right time. The market update is a key in it. The airfare pricing software is there to manage large volumes of pricing requests from various parts of the world. Using the updates and the rules of fare construction along with needed add-ons including taxes, these technology solutions quickly generate accurate prices in a particular situation. The airfare distribution system is also there. This can distribute the fare information to the GDSs and other channels of product distribution. Quick changes in prices can thus be intimated to the various channels of selling of the airlines. All these can be a part of integrated systems that deal with airline reservations or can function separately.

Different types of decision support systems (DSSs) are used by the airlines. DSSs are designed in such a way that they have more analytical power than other systems. They are built explaining with a variety of models to ATC messaging services are made easy with the ANSPs. Necessary modifications are made so as to make it easy for communication by the user with ATC organizations throughout the flight operations process. A DSS must have greater flexibility than other systems. These systems can perform functions such as handling large amounts of data from different sources; providing report and presentations flexibility; offering both textual and graphical orientation; supporting drill down analysis; and performing complex, sophisticated analysis and comparisons using advanced software packages (Stair & Reynolds, 2001).

17.7 Fleet management systems

It is important for the airlines to have punctual and time-bound flight operations. Irregular operations can lead to the loss of costumers in the future. The airlines cannot afford to mismanage these occurrences. The airlines realize the need for smart technologies that seek an optimal balance between operational reliability, cost efficiency and crew satisfaction. Sabre, another leading airline technology solution, illustrates its fleet managing software in the following way.

> Sabre Air Vision Fleet Manager is a global schedule-optimization system that considers operational constraints and uses patented technology to model passenger flows across the network so capacity is assigned to maximize profitability. Fleet Manager assigns the most appropriate aircraft type to each flight leg, thereby minimizing the effects of both spoilage (flying empty seats) and spill (failing to accommodate passengers). It combines economic and operational information from across the airline to create fleet recommendations that are robust, feasible and profitable.
>
> (Sabre, 2018)

Fleet consists of the most expensive resources in the airlines, and effective and utmost utilization is a key in the efficiency of the airline management.

17.8 Systems for flight and crew planning and scheduling

Deciding when and where to fly is a key to the profitability and success of the airlines. Flight scheduling is a complex task for large airlines as a number of factors such as the examination of most profitable routes, the number of aircraft to be flown in each route and the identification of route structure are involved in it. Varied objectives are there before the planners and decision-makers to look into, such as profitability, demand, available fleet and availability of crew. Many environmental, socioeconomic and political factors are also involved in flight scheduling and planning; certainly, IT has many things to do in these aspects, and flight schedule systems are there in use (Sheldon, 2004). It is important to optimize the entire network. Now, sophisticated and high-end information systems are there to assist the airline in optimized flight scheduling.

These flight scheduling system offers "IT solution to model various scheduling scenarios using these inputs and outputs. A sophisticated flight scheduling system allows decision-makers to adjust the inputs to model the effects as load factors, revenue and costs" (Benckendroff et al., 2017). Advanced systems are there with added features and functionalities and are integrated systems also. For instance, Amadeus's integrated system titled "The Amadeus SKY Suite By Optym" includes "breakthrough capabilities for schedule optimization, fleet optimization, demand forecasting, schedule reliability and route-frequency planning that can help airlines unlock tens to hundreds of millions of dollars annually in additional profits from their flight schedules" (http://www.amadeus.com).

Crew scheduling is an important task. Diverse aspects have to be taken care of while crew scheduling is performed. Computerized systems are in use to determine the best assignment of crew to a flight (Sheldon, 1997). Scheduling the pilots and flight attendants for each flight is an important aspect in the airline operation. Such systems have to optimize crew utilization, ensure cost control and adhere to long-term plans as well. The basic systems enable the airlines to plan and monitor crew rosters so that the right crew will become available at the right services. Moreover, the legal and safety aspects of crew members are also taken care while crew scheduling is performed by modern systems. Necessary changes can be made on crew rosters as and when needed, like at the time of flight delays and emergencies. Making cost-effective pairings is a major focus area in crew scheduling, and in some systems, these are undertaken by separate modules or systems. Producing efficient crew pairings, assigning operational and non-operational duties and publishing the roster are the primary outcomes of an integrated crew scheduling system. Some of the advanced crew scheduling systems may have crew-training scheduling modules as well. A crew scheduling system benefits the airlines, mainly by making the scheduling function easier and by reducing the cost associated with crew management. The crew can get support with a range of systems, through mobile apps, Web-based access systems, etc. Crew support systems are there that enable navigation, communication and maintenance of flight logs as well (Benckendroff et al., 2017).

ICT systems are used for planning and development activities associated with airline operations as well. For instance, ICT-based solutions are there for network planning of the airlines. According to HCL technologies,

> such solution entails a powerful user interface, simulation capabilities, customizable rules/workflows, and integration with a variety of existing internal & external systems. Primary objectives are to enhance business intelligence, minimize unprofitable flights, improve schedule quality, and reduce time involved with schedule plan creation.
>
> (HCL-www.hcltech.com)

17.9 Flight operation systems

A wide range of ICT applications are there that facilitate flight operations. Some are used within the aircraft, and some are operated from airports and airline bases. IT applications inside the aircraft are for major two aspects. One is to improve the services offered to the passengers, and the other is to ensure smooth operation of the flight. Flight operation technical systems are there that can assist the cockpit crew to operate the flight efficiently. Communication systems are there to interact with navigation service providers and the ATC tower. Moreover, many of the functionalities within the cockpit are automated. The Aircraft Communication Addressing and Reporting System is being used, and it helps in providing instructions between flight dispatcher and flight crews.

IT has a role to play in safety, which is a major concern in all aspects of airline operation. Safety systems are there of use in airline operations. Maintenance is the crucial aspect in relation to safety, and lack of proper and timely maintenance will lead to safety issues. These systems will help to ensure whether an aircraft gets maintenance properly or not. The database will have details on all aircraft pasts and the time schedule for maintenance (Sheldon, 1997). These systems benefit the airlines by reducing repair costs and increasing safety. The databases of such system will also have details on other safety aspects inside the airline by keeping records of all incidents that took place.

Flight catering systems are commonly used by the airlines as part of the in-flight passenger service. A catering system "captures special meal requests and manage the ordering, storage, preparation and delivery of meals. A range of systems order and track the ingredients required and monitor freshness, quality and quantity of ingredients, so that the order meets passenger demand" (Benckendroff et al., 2017). Load planning and distribution is an important task as part of flight operation functions. The load planning system provides the support in load planning for the functionalities needed to load and dispatch an aircraft. Moreover, it helps in getting the legally required documentation. This can enable an aircraft's weight and the centre of gravity to change with fuel consumption.

Inside the cabin, POS systems are used as a part of in-flight selling. The application of IT is in connection with offering services such as the sale of beverages and duty-free products. The visual geographic information system displays that show the location of the aircraft and some other details on the video screen along with the details on speed arrival time temperature outside, etc., are also there in aircraft. An aircraft situational display (ASD) is used to identify the location of the aircraft precisely while on flight. Now, the ASD is there in flights.

17.10 Revenue management systems

The fundamental aspect in revenue management is that "Airlines can maximize revenue and load factors by selling the right seats, at the right price to the right people, at the right time" (Benckendroff et al., 2014). This kind of systems tracks demand and sales on each and every flight. It has the ability to identify the dips in demand at any point of time. Automatic changes to the inventory, optimizing settings and discounted seats are made available by the system automatically. Amadeus, one of the leading airline technology solution providers, describe their revenue management system functionalities in the following way: Revenue management systems

> drive more revenue on your routes by optimizing fares and availability. Amadeus Revenue Management solutions help you maximize revenue opportunities across all your sales channels, for individuals and groups. Our tools use real-time data to accurately forecast demand, taking into account customer purchasing behaviour, competitor pricing and yield capacity. You can also

manage fare families and fenceless fare structures, giving you more flexibility to customize flight offers and avoid the buy-down effect.

(Amadeus- www.amadeus.com)

These systems "automatically update booking limits and forecasts at regular intervals leading up to flight departure. Historical data are combined with actual booking information to determine whether demand for different fare categories is consistent with forecasts" (Benckendroff et al., 2017). Technology solutions are there for analyzing, challenging and removing duplicate bookings and enabling

---

Table 17.1 Features of Revenue Management Systems

The features of the revenue management system of Maxamation Aviator, offered by SITA, have the following features:

Optimization

Each day, the airline reservation system sends the sales, inventory and scheduling data for all future flights. This system then reforecasts and analyzes each flight, calculating optimal class levels, and adjusts the inventory in the reservation system to maximize your revenue.

Automation

By automating processes, 90% of flights are handled automatically, and the airline team needs to just concentrate on special or new flights. Single flights can be easily adjusted, and whole blocks of flights can be modified in one hit, at the highest pace.

Forecasting

This system uses a vast amount of flight, segment (or leg) and class data to produce accurate forecasts of the upcoming and final demand. To get accurate forecasts, historical booking patterns of the demand are grouped by the route, day of week and departure time bands, unconstrained automatically, and then blended with present sales activity. Seasonality can be applied automatically or custom-made by flight analysts to suit local events. The forecasts are fed into the optimization logic that can generate recommended inventory settings to maximize revenue.

Reporting

A report engine helps to generate reports and graphs, all of which can be used to review data by the flight number, flight range or route – or for the whole network quickly. By this, it is easy to spot trends then zero in on flights that reflect specific criteria and enable the concerned to find and seize revenue opportunities with incredible efficiency.

Integration

This system facilitates the integration of it with the existing systems, helping to maximize the revenue and minimize lost profits through automated analysis, inventory adjustments and availability optimization for every flight.

Source: SITA.

airlines to resell seats while demand is still strong. This can help in increasing the revenue. Revenue management systems are capable to provide the following:

- Historical data: For identifying patterns and trends
- Forecasting: Demand forecasting
- Modelling: For recommendations regarding booking levels
- Decision support: With regard to booking and overbooking limits (Belobaba et al., 2009).

Revenue management has been a key in the profitability of the airlines, particularly since the airline industry was featured with a thin profit margin. Efficient systems can certainly enable the management to use demand fluctuations efficiently to survive competitively.

17.11 DCSs and flight dispatcher systems

Departure Control Systems are explained above, and the airlines too can use such systems. It eventually enables the airlines to perform the passenger processing in an airport until boarding efficiently. Flight dispatcher systems ensure an automated, intelligent digital dispatch process. Such systems can also verify certain safety matters, airworthiness factors and critical maintenance discrepancies. The flight path development is automated using this. While doing this, various factors will be taken into consideration, such as the aircraft performance and loading, climate variations, airspace restrictions and airport conditions. The movement of the flight will be pursued, and information provision to the pilot will be undertaken along the route whenever needed. Its airfield watching modules can generate the needed picture of both Meteorological Aerodrome Report and Terminal Aerodrome Forecast information. Having this system can reduce the uncertainties, greatly enhance safety and minimize human errors.

17.12 Marketing information system and customer relationship management

The marketing information system is more of a common system used in corporates. It eventually intends to seek the level of satisfaction of the customers. Organizations find ways to get closer to their present customers and understand the marketplace better. The scope of the systems starts from identifying the need of customers, evolving the product concept, designing the product, placing the product in the market and selling at an appropriate price. Marketing managers need information to help them in anticipating demand patterns of the product, increase selling and keep tight control over sales and distribution expenses. The information system specific to marketing gathers and processes data to provide a variety of reports to marketing managers and personnel concerning their budgets, sales performance, sales force management, marketing research and intelligence, product analysis, advertising and promotion, logistics and distribution, and customer service. The airlines use a number of systems, and dedicated marketing information systems can get inputs easier with the assistance of other connected systems to provide the output as per the need. The customer relationship management (CRM) is one of the major emphases of marketing by the airlines.

In this modern highly competitive business environment, it is indispensable that business entitles will create and maintain a close and cooperative relationship with customers (Parvatiyar & Sheth, 2001). It is a common saying that retaining a customer is much more economical than attracting a new customer. The CRM is defined as "the infrastructure that enables the delineation of an increase in the customer value and the correct means by which to motivate valuable customers to remain loyal-indeed to buy again" (Dyche, 2003). This points that customer retention is an important aspect in any kind of business. The CRM is basically a business strategy. The CRM uses information systems to coordinate all the business processes surrounding the firm's interactions with its consumers. According to Laudon and Laudon (2004), an ideal CRM system provides end-to-end customer care from receipt of an order through product delivery. Usually, CRM systems consolidate customer data from a variety of sources and give analytical tools for answering questions related to customer care and retention.

The CRM system is defined as the system that enables an organization to increase the retention of their most profitable customers, reduce cost and increase the value of customers' interactions, thereby maximizing the profit (Jaiswal & Mital, 2004). The airlines undertake different types of customer retention strategies. Frequent flyer programmes are part of this. The CRM has become an essential ingredient in the overall marketing of the airlines. The airlines nowadays use mobile applications, and social media are used to communicate with passengers. Special offers, upgrades, etc., can be sold via mobile devices.

17.13 ICT application by airlines: emerging trends

Recently, the airlines started to use a number of advanced ICT solutions to enhance the travel experience and ease the operations. The major are introduced below:

- **Biometrics**: For a faster check-in process, self-service biometric-enabled baggage drop, etc., biometrics is used. Also, the increased number of airlines is in the attempt to use facial recognition mobile apps, etc.
- **VR and immersive experiences**: The airlines also use these for providing a better travel experience while flying. Motion sickness-free VR IFE solution, VR headset services in airport lounges, VR-based training solutions, etc., are used by the airlines.
- **Voice technology or voice recognition technology**: The voice recognition technology is being used by the airlines as well, for voice check-in, etc.
- **Onboard connectivity**: More airlines are planning to have in-flight Internet connectivity to provide a better travel experience.
- **Blockchain technology**: The airlines are realizing the potential of it in terms of operational efficiency, enhanced security and passenger experience.
- **AI**: The airlines are now adopting AI for voice-activated digital assistance, predictive analysis, recognition tool, etc.

- **Robotics**: The airlines can make use of it for performing diverse tasks such as customer management and baggage handling.
- **Chatbots**: The airlines also make use of chatbots and AI-powered chat platforms to interact with passengers. The provision of real-time information can enhance the traveller experience. For instance, if any delay is there, it can be communicated immediately. Chatbots are used in air transportation mainly for the following:
  o Customer service
  o Check fares
  o Reservation and bookings
  o Cross-selling and upselling
  o Retailing
  o Track lost/mishandled baggage
  o Servicing customer bookings
- Wearable technology: This is used for storing data and information in devices. HoloLens of Microsoft is an example which can be used for training the mechanics. Smart earpiece technology is another example which can simplify communication between flight attendants on board. Apps for the Apple Watch can help the passengers to store boarding passes and receive real-time updates on their wrist.
- Internet of Things: Aircraft performance, functioning, etc., can be updated using real-time data with the help of the Internet of Things.
- Big data and analytics: The big data analysis technology is used to process voluminous data about customers and to provide the more personalized services.
- Mobile applications: These can help passengers to have real-time information, and the airlines can be in touch with passengers to make their travel more enjoyable.

Table 17.2 Advantages of Using Blockchain Technology for the Airlines

The airlines can use the blockchain technology to enhance operational efficiencies, security systems and customer experiences:

- By this, the airlines can do away with the need to rely on physical ID proofs by saving passengers' data that are kept in a virtual decentralized database.
- Flying miles can be turned into a more valuable asset that can be used to offer increased benefits to the customers, by tokenizing these points and providing them a chance to accrue these points through a community of partners.
- It can be extremely beneficial in building a robust security system for managing customer data.

Source: Robosoft Technologies Nov 10, 2017, 10 emerging technologies that are reshaping the flying experience for the airline industry, https://medium.com/@Robosoft/10-emerging-technologies-that-are-reshaping-the-flying-experiences-for-the-airline-industry-4af86995315

17.14 ICT application in airline distribution

Disintermediation, due to the advent of Internet, began a few decades ago. But without much delay, reintermediation began. While disintermediation points to the move of eliminating the intermediaries from the distribution system, reintermediation describes the trend of the emergence of additional or new electronic intermediaries into the distribution channel by using ICTs. Currently, a variety of ICT intermediaries that are actively involved in the airline product distribution are there. The GDS, as of now, is the chief electronic system that acts in the airline product distribution, but these are not directly distributing the products to the customers; instead, they make the distribution easy and more convenient for other intermediaries to sell the products to the final consumers. The most revolutionary development in the airline product distribution is the development of the new distribution capability (NDC). Yet, that also acts in between the airlines and intermediaries to make the system of the airline distribution more efficient. According to Benckendorff et al. (2014), the following are the online intermediaries:

- Online travel agents (OTAs)
- Metasearch engines
- Aggregators
- Trip-planning sites
- Affiliates
- Group buying sites
- Opaque sites
- Product review sites.

17.15 GDS

Global distribution systems are the modern incarnation of CRSs that were created for handling seat booking data many decades ago. The term GDS refers to a network of one or more CRSs for distributing product offers and functionalities of the participating organizations in different countries across the world (Werthner & Klein, 1999). The GDS consists of basically a super switch connecting several airline CRSs. A GDS will be powered by a large main-frame computer that performs many of the end-user functions that are delivered to travel agents using PC-based terminals (Inkpen, 1998). In the 1980s and 90s, GDSs were emerged as strong players dominating the airline product distribution worldwide. Amadeus was formed by Air France, Lufthansa, Iberia and Scandinavian Airlines System (SAS) in 1987 and later became a leading GDS. Delta Automated Travel Account System (DATAS) was formed by Delta Air Lines in 1984. In 1990, PARS II merged with DATAS II to form Worldspan. Galileo International became another leading GDS by having two separate systems; one is Apollo (in the USA) and Galileo (for the rest of the world). Abacus, another system, was owned by Singapore Airlines, Cathay Pacific and Dragon Air. In 2007, Travelport bought Galileo and Worldspan. Sabre remains strong, and currently, Amadeus, Travelport (Galileo and Worldspan), and Sabre are the leading GDSs. In China, TravelSky is there, and in Latin America, KIU is there as a leading GDS.

According to Benckendroff et al. (2017), the core functions of a GDS are availability, booking, passenger information, rates and conditions, e-ticketing, and itinerary management. Secondary functions include booking ancillary services, provision of information on passenger document requirements, integrated support system for decision-making, provision of e-commerce tools for retailers, corporate travel management, and communication and scheduling functions (Benckendorff et al., 2014). According to Amadeus, GDS refers to the following:

> the reservation tool travel agents use when making an air, hotel, car or other travel service booking. And not only do GDSs power the content of 'traditional' travel agency platforms, but they also provide pricing, availability and reservation functionality to many online travel agencies.
>
> (www.amadeus.com)

GDSs display flight schedules of different airlines and show available options for booking airline seats as well as other services. A booking request can be made at any point of time via the GDS, which will be either managed by the GDS itself or transmitted to the airlines for managing. The PNR is created by it. Once booking is confirmed, the e-ticket is created or summary of booking record is produced by the GDS.

Three different types of making reservation are there, such as sell on status, direct access and seamless connectivity (Werthner & Klein, 1999). In the first type, GDSs receive the availability and flight status from the airlines through SITA. On receiving of the reservation request by a travel agent, the GDS will contact the airline inventory system. When the airline replies, the GDS will send confirmation to the travel agent. In direct access, when a travel agent makes a request, it will be handled at the GDS itself. After the same is performed, the reservation will be transmitted to the airline's system. Here, the most important thing is that the GDS's inventory should be consistent with that of the carriers. In the last type, seamless connectivity mode, all the transactions carried out at the GDS are duplicated immediately on the carrier's system. According to Vialle (1995), the major functions of a GDS include the following: search facilities for flight schedules and availability; information on other travel and tourism products and their availability, such as package holidays, car rentals and ferries; seat reservation and selling; issuing tickets; maintenance of user information based on the PNR; maintenance of and search facilities for fare quotes and rules; and management functions both for intermediaries like travel agents and for airlines. Every GDS has a central data hub for data processing throughout the day, on all days, at a quick pace. Although travel consultants interact with a GDS using a GUI, user interfaces are traditional command-driven using formats and codes (Benckendorff et al., 2014).

17.16 OTA and Mobile Travel Agent

The concept of the online travel agency began during the mid-1990s. The first OTA was Travelocity, started in 1996. Sooner, in the same year, Expedia was formed. In 2015, Expedia bought Travelocity. Orbitz is also a subsidiary of Expedia now. They are Internet-based travel agencies that provide almost all the services similar

Traditional Airline Distribution System

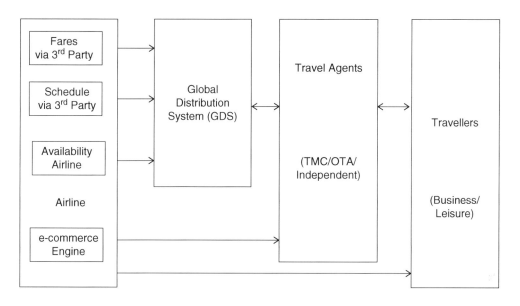

Airline Distribution System with NDC

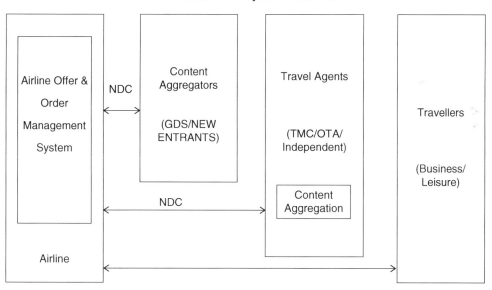

Figure 17.1 Airline distribution system: before and after NDC
Source: IATA, data available online at https://www.iata.org/contentassets/
6de4dce5f38b45ce82b0db42acd23d1c/ndc-standard-presentation.pdf

to those of a travel agency. OTAs can sell much wider variety of services, that too from various parts of the world. In addition to the airlines, OTAs sell products of other industries such as hotels, resorts, car rentals, tour operators and cruises. The mobile travel agent (MTA) is a term representing the distribution of travel products via mobile devices such as smartphones. The trend of the developing mobile-based travel distribution mechanism is on the increase. Customers can access and purchase any travel products at any point of time via smartphones, etc. According to Rossini (2014), MTAs are described as follows:

> currently niche players focusing on tonight-only bookings made by travellers on the go. However, in an increasingly competitive mobile travel arena, the most successful mobile-only players are expected to reach the mainstream market in the next few years, gaining share at the expense of traditional OTAs.

Very soon, it is predicted that most of the travel intermediaries have to have mobile applications as well for selling the products (Figure 17.1).

17.17 NDC

It has been predicted that the airline distribution is going to face a revolutionary change owing to the establishing of NDC. It has been envisaged as a technology solution for the travel product distribution in the most efficient manner by eliminating all the limitations that other technology systems, such as the GDS, were having. According to the International Air Transport Association (IATA), NDC is a travel industry–supported programme (NDC programme) launched by them for the development and market adoption of a new XML-based data transmission standard (NDC standard). This can enhance the communication channel between the airlines and intermediaries, particularly the retailers. This IATA-led collaborative industry initiative to build an open Internet-based data exchange standard primarily supports the present and enhanced airline distribution capability. (www.iata.org).

> Airlines, using modern-day Internet Language XML (Extensible Markup Language) to build their websites, can make very user-friendly sites to sell their multitude of new unbundled products. Airlines can also customize travel packages based on their customers' travel history and stated desires. Their services are either totally unavailable, or at best not easily, available to travel agents using EDIFACT GDS.
>
> (Cook & Billig, 2017)

This new technology solution can eliminate the current distribution limitations, such as the lack of scope for product differentiation and time to market, limited access to full and rich air content, lack of transparent shopping experience and high distribution costs. (www.iata.org). Parker (2018) has identified the following advantages of using NDC.

> **Table 17.3** Some of the Leading Online Travel Intermediaries

Expedia	Travelocity
Booking.com	Priceline.com
ebookers.com	Travelstart.co.za
Opodo	FlightHub
Justfly.com	eDreams
Kayak	FlightSite.co.za
lastminute.com	Flyin.com
Webjet	Orbitz
MakeMy Trip	Wotif.com
	Travelgenio

Source: Dileep (2019).

- Enhances communication between airlines and travel agents.
- Facilitates a more efficient airline distribution system.
- Addresses the end-to-end airline distribution process, such as shopping and booking.
- Delivers enhanced customer experiences.
- Provides options for product differentiation.
- Broadens display format and content (Parker, 2018).

17.18 Other online intermediaries

Other online intermediaries are introduced here. A **GDS new entrant (GNE),** also known as the global new entrant, is another airline distribution mechanism with advanced technology solutions emerged relatively recently. Farelogix, G2 SwitchWorks and ITA Software are the leading GNEs. Cook and Billig (2017) described the uses of GNEs using the example of ITA Software in the following way: "ITA Software, best known for a fare-shopping metasearch engine, promised as alternative with all capabilities of a traditional GDS-display of flight availability, schedules and passenger information; making reservations; and issuing tickets, refunds and exchanges" (Cook & Billig, 2017). These GNE companies "target low-cost distribution with their systems which recognizing the need to aggregate contents for all kinds of different sources" (Merten, 2008). Such systems intend to provide sophisticated technology solutions for airlines for distribution at cheaper rates, have a direct link with the airline inventory also, and have access to all fares, both public and Web fares (Dileep, 2019). **Metasearch engines** too have a role in the distribution of travel and tourism products. They primarily enable the customer to search, compare and choose the best option and then lead the customer to the respective sites where booking can be made. These, also called vertical search engines, "do not sell travel services at all – they search airline websites and redirect the customer to the airline or OTA for final purchase of a ticket" (Cook & Billig, 2017). Examples of this include Kayak, Trivago, Webjet and Flight Centre.

Travel aggregators exhibit all the best deals on a single platform and aggregate inventories of various travel and tourism industries from diverse sources. The users can access these products through these aggregators. **Affiliate** market online travel intermediaries' contents and offers drive bookings to them, and they usually charge for driving bookings to the clients (Dileep, 2019). Product review sites enable customers to have a comparison of the products they wish to purchase. **Opaque sites** are also booking channels which enable the unsold/distressed travel offers. "The so–called Opaque online travel agents are OTAs that do not fully disclose certain information about the flights before booking" (Cook & Billig, 2017). The primary focus of opaque sites is to sell the distressed inventory with a higher discount. Opaque sites will lead the customer to the supplier only at the last minute of the transaction.

17.19 Systems that enable easier product access and consumptions

Different types of other electronic solutions that enable easy access of the airline products or facilitate the smooth functioning of passenger processing are there. Personalized booking and check-in applications using personal computers and mobile platforms are also there. Desktop-, tablet- and smartphone-based applications are now being used for enabling the customers to access airline products based on their needs, for instance, SITA's Horizon. This system, according to SITA, is developed in such a way that it can provide booking, making changes, storing preferences, ancillary purchasing, loyalty processes and payment services through it. Booking can be made easily with calendar shopping, cabin options and upsell opportunities in clear sight. Moreover, check-in is easy with boarding passes as well as reminders delivered by the application (www.sita.aero). Mobile applications software is very common. This can be used in smartphones so as to enable the users to book flights, check-in, check frequent flyer accounts, scan credit cards and passports, etc.

Integration solutions are there nowadays. Traditional product distribution systems still have limited capacity to make use of the latest applications, and hence, an integration platform is inevitable for the efficient functioning of them. Technology solution providers now offer integration platforms to connect traditional systems such as central reservation systems and GDSs with a new application so that airlines, travel agencies, etc., can make use of them as a middleware. Contact centre services are another technology solutions that enable the airlines to streamline multiple call centres. The airlines usually have different contact centres as part of the product distribution. Call centres constitute an example. Systems are there in place to streamline the contact centres to make integrated functioning of multiple contact centres.

e-Commerce solutions are also used by the airlines. These can be used by the airlines to distribute products directly to the customers. These can provide options for multiple currency transactions, agent modules, customized offerings, graphical seat maps, etc. These can be used in addition to the distribution through GDSs. A content delivery network mechanism is used which can enable the organizations to optimize the e-commerce applications, and hence, most effective content delivery optimization can be made possible. Business intelligence systems are being used by the airlines. This is also a data analysis mechanism to identify, evaluate and act on trends, challenges and opportunities. Using this, the airlines can understand opportunities to improve the passenger experience and to make intuitive strategic decisions.

17.20 Conclusion

ICT is an integral part of aviation operations and is critical to efficient, profitable, competitive and successful aviation operations and management. Increased personalization, digital interface at every touchpoints, operational efficiency and enhanced delivery of services by the most modern ICT innovations take the travel experience to the next level. The passenger experience at the airport has been greatly enhanced by biometrics, facial recognition, VR and other immersive experience. The baggage management systems at the airport can provide real-time information and perform baggage reconciliation effectively. Advanced levels of baggage tracking systems can now detect and match mishandled luggage. IT-based cargo handling systems help the airlines to process cargo handling information more efficiently. Self-service check-in applications for kiosks and the Web check-in arrangements are in practice nowadays. The airlines and ground handlers use automated DCSs, which assist with critical operations at airports, such as automated check-in, boarding and load planning. Biometric data such as face, fingerprint and iris are used to verify the identity of the passenger as part of the emigration check. Complete resource management systems can coordinate real-time management of equipment and human resources. Data from various sources are gathered and analyzed, and the reports are made by data processing solutions, and such systems can provide KPIs. IT-based support services for flight movement–predicting assistance, communication enhancement systems, geolocation applications and FIDSs are revolutionary services at airport ICT. Many airports now like to provide users with information about events, especially flight delays and flight status notifications, through apps.

The emerging trends in the ICT application in airports are biometrics, robotics, AR and VR, beacons technology, chatbot, 5G network, blockchain, big data analysis, mobile solutions, AI, video analytics and various assistive technologies. The airlines' CRSs are fed with revenue management, crew scheduling, schedule optimization and pricing, all of which will be processed to give the required information to the other linked GDSs. Airfare managing systems detect market trends in airfares and provide quick responses for dynamic pricing. The important DSSs used by the airlines are fleet management systems, crew planning and scheduling systems, flight operation systems, revenue management systems, DCSs and flight dispatcher systems, and marketing information system and CRM. The GDS refers to a network of one or more CRSs that distribute product offers and activities of participating organizations around the world. In addition to airline services, the OTA and MTA also sell products from other industries, such as hotels, resorts, car rentals, tour operators and cruises. The NDC will increase the communication between the airlines and intermediaries, especially retailers. The GDS New Entrant (GNE), also known as the Global New Entrant, aims to provide the airline with innovative technology solutions for low-cost delivery and has direct access to the airline inventory and access at all rates, public and Web rates. Through the data analysis of business intelligence systems, airlines are able to identify, evaluate and work on trends, challenges and opportunities.

Sample questions

Short/medium answer type questions

- Write about the importance of information systems in air transportation.
- What are baggage handling systems?
- Write the trends in the ICT application in an airport.
- Give a brief account of information systems used in aircraft.
- Discuss the use of information systems in enhancing safety in air transportation.
- Give a brief account of flight handling systems.
- Discuss in detail the use of information systems in crew scheduling and management.
- What are gate management systems?
- Write about DCSs.
- What are the uses of automated ticket machines?
- What is a flight information system?
- What are the new ICT applications targeting passengers in the airline sector?
- Discuss the applicability of information systems in immigration services in airports.
- Discuss the advantages of DCSs.
- Distinguish between disintermediation and reintermediation.
- Describe the NDC of the IATA.
- Discuss the role of GDSs in the airline distribution
- Give a brief account on diverse online intermediaries in air transportation

Essay type questions

- Discuss how did the advent and developments in IT influence air transportation to become a modern industry.
- What are the information systems used in the air transportation sector? Discuss the benefits and advantages of using those systems.
- Discuss the use of ICT in enhancing the travellers' experience.

Suggested readings

Benckendorf, J.P., Sheldon, J.P., & Fesenmaier, R.D. (2014). *Tourism Information Technology*, 2nd ed. Oxfordshire: CABI.

Buhalis, D. (2003). *e-Tourism: Information Technology for Strategic Tourism Management*. Essex: Prentice Hall.

Buhalis, D. (2004). eAirlines: Strategic and tactical use of ICTs in the airline industry. *Information and Management*, 41(7), 805–825.

Buhalis, D. (2008). IT and Management information systems in tourism. In Bech, J. & Chadwick, S. (Ed.), *The Business of Tourism Management*. Harlow: Pearson.

Xu, F., & Buhalis, D. (Eds.). (2021). *Gamification for Tourism*. Bristol: Channel View Publications.

Chapter 18

Air transport and tourism: impacts, challenges and the future

Learning outcomes

By the end of this chapter, you will be able to:

- Comprehend the environmental impacts of air transport.
- Learn about the contribution of air transport in climate change.
- Outline the impacts of tourism in general.
- Explain the challenges faced by the air transport sector.
- Recognize the emerging trends in travel and tourism.

18.1 Introduction

Tourism has turned to be an inevitable economic sector in the world. The same is the case with air transport as well. Countries are increasingly interested in the development of tourism in order to bring economic benefits and socio-economic transformation to the destinations. It can lead to direct, indirect and induced impacts on local economies, and they are much dependent on the link of the tourism activities with the local economy. Greater linkages generally translate into higher levels of local economic activity. Despite having immense economic potentials, tourism is often criticized for its consequences. Air transport too is instrumental in the socio-economic progress of places. Air accessibility is considered critical for businesses and tourism. Yet, that too results in varied impacts, particularly on the environment. Sustainability hopes have been at stake due to the increasing impacts on nature. Air transport is a major contributor to tourism's carbon emissions that cause climate change as well. Ameliorating the impacts is a major challenge to both the tourism and air transport sectors. This chapter discusses the impacts of tourism and air transport and the challenges faced by both the sectors.

DOI: 10.4324/9781003136927-18

18.2 Environmental impacts of air transport

A key issue for any airport operator is how to optimize the economic potential of an airport while providing acceptable environmental protection. This may be a particular problem when the economic benefits of airport development may be perceived as being the most relevant within a regional or national context.

The main environmental impacts can be divided into five categories:

a   **Noise**: Aircraft noise has traditionally been considered the most important environmental problem at airports and, in many cases, public tolerance of aircraft noise has been diminishing. This is in spite of the fact that over the years, the noise levels associated with aircraft movements have been declining. This reduction has been primarily due to the development of less noisy aircraft and the pressure of more stringent requirements for noise certification of new aircraft types. Current aircraft types are typically 20 dB quieter than aircraft of 40 years ago (Air Transport Action Group, 2008). Noise certification was first introduced in 1969 by the United States in the Federal Aviation Regulations Part 36 (FAR Part 36). The International Civil Aviation Organization (ICAO) adopted similar international standards in 1971. These standards were included in the Environmental Protection Annex 16 of the Chicago Convention. Through the combination of the development of quieter aircraft and noise abatement operating procedures, most airports have managed to contain many of the problems arising from aircraft noise.

ICAO agreed with the concept of a "balanced approach" to noise management, which is comprised of four principal elements:

   o   *Reduction of aircraft noise at source.* This has been brought about by international certification and has an impact on reducing overall aircraft noise levels. The newest generation of aircraft such as the A380 and Boeing 787 are the quietest yet, and research continues for inventing new technology solutions in reducing noise from jet engines.
   o   *Land-use planning and management measures.* This involves defining a certain area, or noise buffer, around an airport where the construction of new houses and other noise-sensitive buildings is not allowed.
   o   *Noise abatement operational procedures.* This is usually done by directing aircraft away from the most densely populated areas. Airports may also choose to place restrictions on flight procedures by requiring, for example, reduced power and flap settings for take-off or approach.
   o   *Local noise-related operating restrictions.* A common measure is a night curfew or limitations on night flights. Many airports also impose noise surcharges for noisier aircraft and an incentive to use quieter aircraft.

b   **Emissions**: By consuming fuel, the aircraft are producing emissions of carbon dioxide (CO_2), nitrogen oxides (NOx), particles of sulphur oxides, carbon monoxide and various hydrocarbons. It is generally agreed that future global air traffic will increase at growth rates, which will outperform the impact of any technology improvements, which will reduce engine emissions. The details of this aspect are given later in this chapter.

c **Water pollution and use**: Water pollution at airports can occur for a number of different reasons. Surface water discharge or run-off that goes into local watercourses from runways, aprons, car parks and other land development may be contaminated by anti-icing and de-icing fluids such as glycol, which are used during the winter months. The chemicals used in maintaining and washing aircraft and vehicles, as well as fire training activities and fuel spillages, can also contribute to this pollution. Leakages from underground tanks and pipes, and grass fertilizers used in landscaping activities can contaminate the soil. Then, there is the normal wastewater from buildings and facilities such as domestic sewerage. An increasing number of airports now monitor water quality as well as air quality and have adopted various measures to minimize this water pollution. These include revised operational practices to reduce the use of harmful chemicals, to improve cleaning processes and to minimize spillage and leakages.

d **Waste and energy management**: The waste at airports is generated by airlines, airport operators and other airport-related companies. While most of the waste comes from airlines, usually the airport operators have overall responsibility for waste management for the entire airport activities. Improvements can usually be brought about by an assessment of on-airport treatment methods and the scope for reducing, reusing or recycling waste. In-flight catering waste, with the disposable nature of most of the packaging, is considered to be a particular problem. Off-airport disposal methods, which typically involve incineration and landfill, also need to be considered. Many airports now have recycling initiatives.

    Energy management, associated with the provision of heating, ventilation, air conditioning and lighting, is also very important. Many airports undertake energy audits. With energy conservation, as with waste and water management, there are good financial reasons why airports should address these issues since environmental improvements may bring about considerable cost savings. Some airports have installed solar panels, whereas some have wind power generators.

e **Wildlife, heritage and landscape**: There is also a need to protect the wildlife, flora and fauna, heritage and the landscape of the local environment particularly during the construction of a new airport or during airport expansion. Landscapes can be radically changed by airport development, which can disturb the ecosystem and can be visually intrusive. To compensate for this, some airports have established "green areas", which cover many hectares and include features such as walking paths, playgrounds and planted areas (Graham, 2003).

18.3 Impacts of travel and tourism: an overview

Indeed, it has been well stated that tourism instigates the impacts of varied kinds on nature, culture and society. Though tourism is economically very significant for a place, it also causes some economic consequences, say inflation and migration of labour. Sociocultural impacts also mar the image of tourism as a clean industry. Many examples can be cited worldwide for the negative impacts of tourism in the social and cultural spheres of human life. Adopting pseudo-behaviours, involving in drug and mafia activates, inspiring prostitution tendency, loss of local and traditional culture, etc., are considered the major menaces of tourism. Commercialization of art and art forms is another one that can be added to the negative impacts of tourism. On the contrary, the preservation and maintenance of culture and cultural features are highlighted as significant positive impacts of tourism. Apart from the impacts on economy, society and culture of the host population, environment and ecology is another important area where tourism causes varied impacts. Different kinds of tourism activities affect the natural and built environment. There is a complex relationship between tourism and the environment. Environmental impacts are inherently multidimensional, and the impacts are more irreversible. In other words, tourism tends to destroy tourism itself.

Among the impacts, environmental consequences are having far-reaching consequences. Tourism causes changes in the ecosystem wherever it is being developed. As Cooper et al., pointed out, as soon as tourism activity takes place, the environment is inevitably changed or modified either to facilitate tourism or during the tourism process (Cooper et al., 2008). The fragility of the destination can worsen the environmental impacts due to tourism. Impacts on rural areas are usually higher than those in the urban regions. Some forms of tourism cause more damage than other forms. For instance, ecotourism is envisaged to promote tourism in a sustainable manner with a low level of interventions on nature's features. On the other hand, tourism that needs much physical development can dampen the scope for preserving the ecological balances over there. Increased infrastructure development ends up in ecological imbalances and loss of vegetation. The more the destination is physically developed, the more is the scope for environmental impacts. The number of tourists too is a contributing factor in damaging the natural features. Much of the damage done to the environment as a result of tourism is caused simply by the volume of tourists arrivals. Absence of scientific planning and improper development of infrastructure can augment the environmental consequences due to tourism. If a destination crosses its carrying capacity by the visitors, the damages could be severe and of different types. Low seasons/off-seasons may be refreshing periods for nature, yet if the peak season is longer, then the impacts also can be more.

Tourism is a sector that consumes resources profoundly. The natural resource consumption rate is often alarming in the tourism sector. On the other hand, it generates wastes of all sorts, and many of the destinations lack proper waste management mechanisms. According to United Nations Environment Programme (UNEP),

> the tourism sector's consumption of key resources – energy, water, land and materials (such as fossil fuels, minerals, metals and biomass) – is growing commensurately with its generation of solid waste, sewage, loss of biodiversity, and greenhouse gas emissions. In a 'business-as-usual' scenario, tourism would generate through 2050 an increase of 154% in energy consumption, 131% in greenhouse gas emissions, 152% in water consumption and 251% in solid waste disposal.

A brief discussion on the environmental impacts of tourism is given below.

Depletion of natural resources: Water, fossil fuels, etc., are excessively used as part of tourism. The use of water is much higher by the tourists than by the local people. Water is overused by tourism enterprises, i.e. for tourist use, swimming pools and garden maintenance. Tourism transportation consumes fossil fuels greatly. Other types of natural resource consumption are also high. As a result of tourism growth, there can be pressure on resources such as energy, food and raw materials. The effect of this is usually higher in some locations where scarcity of resources is seen. Even tourist–local people conflicts occur due to such reasons.

Physical deterioration and ecological imbalance: The infrastructure development and tourism activities can lead to damage to the natural features. All sorts of tourism activities can cause irreversible consequences on the ecosystems over there. Construction of roads and other facilities and services will certainly damage the environment. Erosion can increase due to the development activities and tourist movements. Surface run-off and erosion are common in many tourist destinations. Landslides can also be possible due to the increasing rate of construction activities. A reduction in biodiversity due to regular tourism for several years can also be expected.

Littering, soil pollution and water contamination: Littering is a common problem in tourist destinations across the world except in some locations that have strict measures to minimize the threat of littering. Waste disposal at convenience is a nuisance, and its impacts are severe as it can lead to soil pollution as well as chemical issues deep down the Earth and even in the underground water sources. Wastewater management is another major issue. Many of the tourism establishments lead wastewater and sewage water directly to water bodies nearby. Tourist activities cause littering and waste disposal on rivers, scenic areas and roadsides.

Aesthetic pollution and visual pollution: Unplanned infrastructure and superstructure growth causes building of varied types, which are not compatible with the environmental aesthetics and traditional architectural practices. Such developments can impair one's ability to enjoy a vista or view. Issue of visual clutter, loss of traditional aesthetics of the location, loss of natural beauty due to constructions, graffiti and other visual defacement are part of aesthetic pollution as well as visual pollution of destinations. Large hotels and resorts of disparate design can look out of place in any natural environment and may clash with the traditional structural design as well.

Impacts on flora and fauna: Tourism developments in certain areas can severely affect the flora and fauna over there. Tourism in forests and nearby areas can have adverse effects on the wildlife and the plant species when the tourism takes place beyond a threshold limit of capacity. Animals' free life can be affected badly. Their breeding habits can be disturbed. Due to regular tourist presence, some of the animals may migrate to other locations. Some of the animals may get domesticated, which can affect their behavioural patterns. A rise in the souvenir trade can lead to the killing of, for example, small animals to make some items. The green cover can reduce drastically over a period of time.

Pollution: Pollution, particularly air pollution, is a common issue of tourism and is mainly due to transportation. Sound/noise pollution, water pollution and soil pollution are some other types of pollution. Pollution is the menace of mass tourism, and the rate is increasing day by day. Tourism is a phenomenon that arises out of movement of people, and naturally, transportation is a crucial activity in it. Among the transport activities, the pollution aspect is associated more with air transportation as it emits more amount of harmful and greenhouse gases (GHGs). Therefore, air transport is the major contributor to carbon emissions in the tourism sector. This aspect is discussed in detail later in this chapter.

18.4 Tourism's threat to climate change and the role of air transport in it

The threat of climate change is looming large over us, and it is poised to increase. It is a concern for every industry as each of them is affected by climate change directly or indirectly. On the contrary, most of the industries contribute a share in the global climate change. Climate simply refers to the general features of the weather experienced in any region. Tourism and climate have an inextricable linkage. Many a time, climate is a major attraction in tourism as well. Climate change involves changes in weather patterns and corresponding changes in oceans and other ecologically sensitive geographical features of the Earth. The statistical properties of the climate system that had been there for several centuries are being changed, rather quicker in recent times. While global temperature increases, precipitation, wind patterns, rain status and other measures of climate can experience sudden changes. As average temperatures are forecasted to increase significantly, up to as much as four degrees, tourism needs a strategic approach, instead of having a short-term plan. Though a few types of gains are predicted from climate change, the negative impacts of it outweigh them greatly. GHG effect keeps the Earth's atmosphere warm, facilitates the photosynthesis process of plants and, thus, supports the survival of living beings in this world. The increase in GHGs is causing global warming. GHG emissions pose the biggest threat to the environment. Carbon dioxide, methane and nitrous oxide are the major GHGs. Fossil fuel burning is the most important factor that causes climate change. GHGs are the prime reason for climate change. Changes in the ozone layer, sulphate emissions, aviation exhaust and solar radiation changes are some other causes. According to the UN, the following facts are associated with climate change:

- The concentration of GHGs in the Earth's atmosphere is directly connected to the average global temperature on Earth;
- Since the time of industrialization, the concentration of GHGs has been rising steadily, along with the rise in average global temperatures;
- Carbon dioxide (CO_2), the most abundant GHG, accounting for about two-thirds of GHGs, is largely the product of burning fossil fuels (www.un.org).

The last point, which tells about the role of the burning of fossil fuels, leads to the fact that transportation, which primarily depends on fossil fuels, is a great contributor to carbon emissions. As tourism encourages transportation greatly, it is blamed for the contribution of GHGs in large quantity. The effects of climate change are varied. Some of them are more common. According to the report of the first international Conference on Climate Change and Tourism (United Nations World Tourism Organisation, UNWTO, 2003), the obvious effects of climate change reported are as follows:

- Rising average temperature
- Rising sea level (mainly due to thermal expansion as it gets hotter)
- Increased frequencies of extreme climatic events, notably storms, associated precipitation changes and sea urges.

Certainly, a change in climate will definitely affect tourism in an adverse manner, as climate is a crucial element in the success of a nature-based destination. The effects of climate change on tourism can be diverse with varied dimensions. It is predicted that global climate change will have significant impacts on all such factors at the regional level. Leisure tourism, mostly nature based, is going to be the most affected by the climate change. Effects on other forms of tourism vary in importance. Business tourism and visiting friends and relatives (VFR) are relatively less affected by the climate change. Changes in water availability, biodiversity loss, reduced landscape aesthetic, altered agricultural production (e.g., wine tourism), increased natural hazards, coastal erosion and inundation, damage to infrastructure and the increasing incidence of vector-borne diseases will all impact tourism to varying degrees.

The rise in temperature can eventually lead to a rise in seawater level as well. This can severely affect the beach tourism in many locations across the world. Damages may be in different forms such as beach erosion, higher sea levels, sea surges and storms and reduced water availability. Some beach destinations may face an existential crisis, whereas some others may emerge based on the changing geographical conditions of coastal regions in the wake of climate change. Many other natural features can face crises of varied kinds. For instance, coral reefs can face extinction due to the continued effects of climate change. Global warming is heating seawater, which leads to coral bleaching, an affliction that causes normally colourful corals to turn white and also white plague. According to the Great Barrier Reef Foundation,

> Two of the greatest challenges brought by climate change—an increase in ocean temperatures and acidity levels—are creating severe knock-on effects, jeopardizing the Reef's survival. Tropical sea surface temperatures have risen by 0.4–0.5°C since the late 19th century, with rapid, human-induced climate change the greatest overall threat to the long-term future of the Great Barrier Reef.
>
> (www.barrierreef.org)

Mountain regions form another major geographical area that would be badly affected. Winter sports occur in mountain regions where the presence of ice/snow matters. Rising temperature will result in fast melting of ice, and ultimately, it will result in further social, economic and environmental consequences. Study reports say that as a result of climate change, the season will shorten in mountain regions and the demand pressure on more high altitude will increase. The summer season will lengthen further and generate an increase in demand. These would definitely cause further environmental damage to those areas. In the Arctic region, where longer summer season is there, cruise tourism, with activities like whale watching, will flourish. On the other hand, shorter winter and regular tourist arrivals over there will result in environmental impacts such as a reduction in the range of Arctic fauna and flora. Less snow, receding glaciers, melting permafrost and landslides are some possible effects of climate change in the mountain areas. Skiing and snowboarding are the winter sports that will be affected badly by climate change. The financial viability of winter tourism largely depends upon sufficient snow conditions. The travel demand pattern may also change due to climate change because a new destination will emerge as the existing destinations may

> **Table 18.1** Environmental Impacts in Air Transport and Mitigating Measures

Some Environmental Impacts	Measures to Mitigate Impacts
• Greenhouse gas emissions causing global climate change, mainly carbon dioxide (CO_2), aerosols with sulphates and contrail formation along with enhanced cirrus cloudiness. • Local air pollution due to emissions of nitrogen oxides (NOx), particulate matter (PM) and volatile organic compounds (VOCs). • Noise pollution: It deteriorates the quality of life of the people and other living beings in the airport surroundings. • Issues to the biodiversity due to conversion of land to paved areas or ecological monocultures, damage to the habitats of different living beings and soil and water contamination. • Sustainability concerns due to large-scale fossil fuel and water consumption, alteration of water sources and soil and water contamination.	• Technological measures, which include improvements on airframe, engine, navigation system, apron services, etc. • Regulatory and legislative measures with regard to noise, emissions certification, air quality standards and emissions. • Improvements on operational measures, particularly on take-off and landing efficiency, climb efficiency, cruise efficiency, approach efficiency and ground movement efficiency. • Improved land-use planning, eco-friendly airport design and environmental performance-based fleet planning. • Initiating economic measures, such as environmental taxes and carbon offset. • Use of environmental management system and performance indicators. Initiating environmental reporting and environmental auditing. • Adopting community approaches, including community liaison, community development and partnership approaches.

Source: Modified from Daley, Dimitriou and Thomas (2008).

be affected by climate change. This will have different social and economic consequences also as the situation will pose issues such as employment-related issues.

Ironically, tourism is a great contributor to the climate change phenomenon as well. Of the various causes that lead to climate change, air transport emissions have the largest share. A brief discussion on the role of air transport in climate change is given below.

18.5 GHG emissions from air transport and climate change

UNWTO in Davos Declaration (2007) mentioned that the share of tourism in global carbon emission is 5% (reported in Hares et al., 2010). Within tourism, transport is the largest contributor to climate change. As air transport dominates in the share of transport's contribution in carbon emissions, A. Bows et al. (2009) opine,

The tourism sector is taking a risk, by (apparently) aiming for air transport to become its dominant means of transport. Though this development is determined to some extent by market demand, it is clear that the sector could avoid commercial risks by starting to invest more in low-carbon tourism products.

An alarming estimation is that the travel and tourism industry may generate up to 40% of total global CO_2 emissions by 2050 (Gössling & Peeters, 2007). Gössling et al. (2010) reported that in the case of tourism, aviation has a share of 40% in carbon dioxide emission and 75% in "radiative forcing". Water vapour from aircraft also has a contribution to the climate change phenomenon as most of it is emitted by aircraft at an altitude of 10,000 to 14,000 metres, where these gases play a role in the forming of contrails and cirrus clouds, with strong but poorly understood effects on climate (Penner et al., 1999; Williams, 2002). Apart from carbon dioxide, there are also other components in the aircraft emissions, such as nitrogen oxides (NOx) and water vapour.

The degree of impact of aviation emissions is high since the emissions are deposited at high altitudes, on an average between 8 and 12 km above the Earth, and hence, it is deemed potential to influence the radiative balance of the Earth system in complex ways (Unger, 2011). Moreover, air transport leads to "radiative forcing" (an indicator of the warming due to the whole range of GHGs) of climate as well through emitting carbon dioxide, nitrous oxide, particles and water vapour in high altitudes and impacts cloudiness on the upper strata through contrails and aircraft-induced cirrus (Lee et al., 2009). Dube and Nhamo (2019), in a study on the role of aviation in climate change, revealed that there exists a significant positive relationship between aviation and climate change, and though there are some measures being undertaken to reduce the carbon emissions, they are found inadequate to reduce the GHG emissions in a considerable manner. Aviation's contribution to climate change is poised to continue as well. An analysis by Gudmundsson and Anger (2012) on CO_2 emission situation in line with IPCC storylines stated "….aviation CO_2 emissions are generally expected to grow faster than the overall global economy". The global pandemic has stopped the progress of both tourism and air transport for rather a long period of time. Yet, the world will not remain idle. People will overcome the situation, and the world will surge ahead again. Air transport too will grow at a remarkable rate. Along with the rise of air transport, the carbon emissions will also increase.

We have to keep in mind that the energy efficiency per tourist day is not on the increase, but rather on the decline, as a result of two important reasons, such as a hike in the distance covered per vacation and the relative decrease in the length of stay (Peteers & Dings, 2007). More than 5% increase in environmental efficiency per year is estimated for attaining sustainable development targets (Peteers & Dings, 2007). According to Peteers and Dings, (2007), climate change reduction measures and strategies being implemented and in ideas include mainly evolutionary technology, revolutionary technology and operational efficiency, along with policy interventions. Evolutionary technology includes bettering fuel efficiency by way of enhanced engine efficiency, better aerodynamics and a reduction in aircraft construction weights. Revolutionary technologies such as the use of biofuels (carbon dioxide emission can be reduced drastically, even up to 0% at certain conditions; still other components' emissions may remain) and the use of hydrogen (it can have a significant reduction in emissions) can be introduced. Operational efficiency can be enhanced through a reduction in flight holding time, optimization of routes, optimization of flight path and speed/altitude schedules and network optimization and fleet composition. Policy intervention can be on volume reduction and initiating technical standards strictly. Improvement of air traffic control is another strategy to avoid useless fuel burn. Market-based options and economic incentives constitute another strategy, which consists of ticket charges (e.g., VAT), taxes of fuel, emission charges and emission trading schemes.

18.6 Air transport challenges

There are a number of challenges that loom large over tourism and air transportation. According to Elamiri (2000), the major challenges facing the international air transport in the new millennium include safety, security, environment, infrastructure, information technology and economic regulations. The following constitute a description on major challenges faced by the air transport sector globally.

18.6.1 Recovering from the COVID-19 pandemic crisis

Aviation plummeted into an unprecedented crisis, and the current challenge is to overcome its impacts. Certainly, the sector was shattered, and the passenger transport sector was paralysed for many days. Regaining the passenger confidence in engaging in international air travel is a major challenge. Though the cargo transport sector somehow managed, the passenger sector had devastating impacts, which led to job loss of millions of professionals working directly as well as indirectly with the air transport sector. Tourism too had similar impacts. As the demand started falling along with the fast spread of the pandemic, countries came up with policies in restricting air transport into the countries. The industry may see consolidation to the highest level as many of the airlines might have faced a severe economic crisis. The revival of international tourism is also significant for the airline industry to have better demand. As the business travel faced severe consequences due to the pandemic, the virtual meetings became more convenient for the business sector, and this can have serious consequences on business tourism as well. There may be a decline in the meeting-related travel as the virtual meeting options gain increased significance. For airlines, coming back to profit level is a distant dream; rather, the focus may be to recover from the plummet. Between bankruptcies and consolidation, the number of airlines may decline when consolidation marches ahead in the airline industry. The recovery will take months, and regaining the growth rate that it had previously may take a few years of time.

18.6.2 Overcapacity and rising competition

The pandemic has created a situation where the passenger air transport sector is facing overcapacity as the demand will rise slowly only for a few years since the pandemic era. The supply side will remain strong and the demand may remain sluggish. Many airlines may go out of business due to issues such as overcapacity. The air transport market will experience severe competition among the existing airlines. Competition has been a major hurdle among airlines for several years which caused a decline in air travel costs as well. In the wake of increased completion and overcapacity, airlines have to suffer from rock-bottom fares, which will eventually lead to profit-related consequences. Competition among airlines has caused existential issues to airlines in history as well. Subsequent to the introduction of deregulation in the US market way back in the 1970s, the air transport sector faced immense dynamism and competition erupted along with the entry of new airlines and easing of restrictions. Eventually, the completion caused a significant decline in travel costs. In the post-COVID era also, the supply will remain strong though some of the airlines will face an existential crisis.

18.6.3 Environmental concerns

Environmental concerns have been a major threat in this new millennium. Infrastructure requirement has been on a steady increase, including airport facilities, Air Traffic Control (ATC) and navigation systems. Generally, demand is more, but opposition is also there due to social and environmental concerns. Even if fuel efficiency is getting increased, it is not sufficient to compensate for the damages the rising demand can cause. Climate change is possibly aviation's biggest environmental challenge. The quantity of carbon emissions has been increasing along with the growth of air transportation for some decades. The pandemic has stalled its progress for a short duration; still, it is poised to increase only. Carbon emissions constitute the major reason for the growing environmental challenge of the air transport sector. Air transport infrastructure expansion poses another major environmental challenge for the sector. The air transport sector has been engaged in making increased fuel-efficient engines. There is remarkable transformation in engines that the current ones are much more fuel-efficient compared to the engines decades ago. Still, they are not capable enough to come out of the significant contribution of GHGs and radiant effect. Aircraft manufacturers have been engaged in research and development in order to have better fuel-efficient engines and to have engines that can use alternative fuels, such as biofuels and solar cells. ICAO is also working on the objective of reducing carbon emissions from civil aviation, and the following strategies are identified:

- Technology and standards related to aircraft
  - New aircraft type designs from 2020
  - Aircraft type designs that are already in production in 2023, with a 2028 production cut-off date for non-compliance
- Improved air traffic management and operational improvements
  - Use of the most fuel-efficient route for taxiing and flying
  - Operating at the most economical altitude and speed
  - Maximizing the load factor
  - Avoiding extra fuel loading for a flight
  - Reducing the number of non-revenue flights
  - Maintaining clean and efficient airframes and engines
- Development and use of sustainable alternative fuels
- Market-based measures (ICAO/www.icao.int).

18.6.4 Technology

Every now and then newer technologies are emerging, and air transport has to adopt them. There is a growing demand for easing regulations for air transport due to economic reasons. In the wake of the pandemic situation, the air transport sector faced a different technological challenge. It had to embrace the latest technological solutions to ensure social distancing among the passengers as well as to offer touch-free services. "Digital transformation" is another area that is needed to improve productivity, enhance operational efficiency and increase profits. Digitizing paper processing, using mobile and social media platforms for customer interaction, the use of latest technologies for providing a better travel experience, etc., come into play. The use of artificial intelligence (AI), augmented reality, etc., became mandatory. Even otherwise, the air transport sector is challenged by the innovations emerging in information and communication technology every now and then. Simplifying travel through ICT innovations is a trend, which airlines and airports have to follow. Ensuring technology-enhanced services can reduce the interactions between passengers and the staff, which can minimize the possibility of friction between them. Technology can assist airlines in having increased customer-centricity around lifestyle and identity. Moreover, airlines have to initiate increased digitization, and big data analysis has become a matter of concern for them. Also, the consumers of airlines are a more advanced group and their use of technology is much higher than that of many other sectors. Providing connected/Internet-native services such as proposing personalized offers or providing immediate information and services linked to the travel context is a challenge to airlines. Therefore, it is of paramount significance for airlines and airports to utilize the latest ICT to communicate, deliver services and enhance travel experience.

18.6.5 Infrastructure expansion

The phenomenal growth of air transport demand during the last three decades or so resulted in the attempts to expand the infrastructure to meet the increasing requirements. Entry of new airlines demanded increased slots within airports. The problem of lack of and/or unfair slot distribution at airports can lead to managerial challenges. Airports face difficulty to provide suitable slots for new airlines/schedules, which poses challenges for increased tourist flow. The rise in passenger numbers led the airports world over to expand the terminals or to construct new ones. As the flight landing frequency increased, the number of runways required also had to be increased. The airside of airports recorded considerable expansion, and there is a need for expanding the airside and increasing the facilities within it. Moreover, airport expansion is always confronted with environmental and social issues. Expansion needs increased land acquisition, and that may require displacement of local residents, which can cause serious social consequences. Environmental issues are also common, and many a time, there are mass agitations against such initiatives. The need for massive investment is another hurdle in airport infrastructure development.

18.6.6 Safety, security and terrorism

These constitute some primary concerns of air transportation. Regarding security, the main issue is maintaining an adequate global security network. There are two contradictory aspects of aviation security. The air transport sector has to ensure utmost care and to take effective strategies and practices to ensure security to the best level. On the other hand, it is of paramount importance that those measures should not be at the cost of passengers' travel experience. Indeed, it is a real challenge for the air transport sector to execute effective security measures with little disturbance to passengers in having a pleasant journey. Screening, passenger data analysis, close surveillance, etc., are fundamental security measures. Security is depending upon the diligent mix of intelligence, information, technology, procedures and people designated for it. Security is nowadays more associated with terrorism issues. Commercial aviation has been an attractive target for terrorists and similar categories of people. For example, plane hijacking started from the early era of aviation itself. It continued, and the September 11 attacks were a turning point. After that, the change in security measures in air transport was dramatic. Now, the latest information and communication technologies are also used in ensuring tight security measures. Surveillance solutions nowadays do have the latest analytical capabilities embedded in video and access control systems. In fact, global standards, being imposed under the leadership of ICAO, are there for both safety and security aspects in air transportation. Therefore, the challenge here is to ensure the highest level of security with the lowest level of screening discomfort for passengers and to implement the safety and security procedures efficiently so as to have a comfortable, enjoyable and safe trip.

18.7 Tourism and air transport in the post-COVID era: an assessment

Tourism has to bounce back. The duration it may take to regain the previously anticipated growth rate is yet to be predicted. Vaccines will have an increased role in international tourism. Currently, there is a panic that similar viruses can erupt at any point of time. It can shatter the industry again, and if the fatality rate of those viruses is more, the effect can be furthermore devastating. The effect will be the same in both air transport and tourism. Moreover, an effect on one will have an equal response on the other as well. The following trends may prevail in the parlance of global tourism for a few years in the post-COVID era:

- Domestic tourism gains increased significance: Currently, domestic tourism is gaining ground, and it may have an increased role in the near future, which may have changes in the future. People may prefer shorter distances and safer choices. "Staycations" also get an increased role in tourism. Destination managers will try to tap domestic tourism potential more.
- Slump in business travel and incentive may continue: Corporate travel tendency is expected to have a setback even in the post-COVID era, as online meetings will continue to have a role in businesses. Moreover, due to the recession, companies may try to reduce business travel as well. MICE, a segment of business tourism, altogether have to wait for more years for a complete recovery. This can affect full-service carriers (FSCs) as well, since the business travel segment depends more on FSCs for their travel. Holding mega-events may not be that much feasible compared to the pre-corona stage.

- The norm of vaccination: Destinations would prefer to ensure safety first. Vaccination norms will prevail for years in the realm of international tourism. Fear of repeat of pandemics may remain in the air for some more time. In addition, people are afraid that more virus types may emerge at any point of time. As news about a new virus or the spread of some diseases can immediately cause panic, movements will be quickly reduced.
- Less crowded outdoor tourism to gain strength: Outdoor tourism would be increasingly attractive than the indoor recreations. Rural tourism can have increased priority among leisure tourists. Even in outdoor attractions, crowding may deter people to stay away from there.
- Automobile tourism to increase: Air transport can have a slight blow with regard to international tourism since more people will prefer to have journeys by automobile at least for some time. Near-city travel is likely to see an uptick. Cars may play a better role in international tourism in the immediate future, as more tourists may prefer journeys by car to move to nearby destinations, even abroad. In the long term, that trend may vanish. Cars may be preferable for more people for family trips to nearby destinations.
- Online product distribution will get strengthened further: The number of people who prefer to buy travel and tourism products will increase. The potential buyers shall use multiple online platforms for bookings.

Table 18.2 Interlinked Trends in International Tourism

World Travel and Tourism Council (WTTC) in collaboration with Oliver Wyman identified the following trends in connection with the COVID-19 consequences in the travel and tourism sector:

- Demand evolution: People are more oriented towards the familiar, predictable and trusted choices for travelling. The tourism sector will see more domestic vacations, extensive planning and the outdoors. The industry is already adapting to it.
- Health and hygiene: Health, safety and trust are prime concerns. Personal experiences, the fear of being stuck in another country, and concerns for distancing can drive consumer behaviour in the short-to-mid-term. Increased close collaboration is required by the businesses with their extended value chains to ensure readiness.
- Innovation and digitization: Quest for innovation and the integration of new technologies has increased tremendously. Digital adoption and consumption are on the surge, and consumers are now expecting contactless technologies, among others, as a basic prerequisite for a safe and seamless travel experience.
- Sustainability: There is an increased urge to tackle social, environmental and institutional sustainability. In particular, intensified public awareness of wildlife markets and poaching has boosted advocacy for wildlife protection.

Source: WTTC, The Recovery and Beyond, September 2020, data available online at https://wttc.org/Research/To-Recovery-Beyond

- Revival of leisure travel: The international leisure tourism segment is anticipated to revive, yet with a slow growth rate. Tourism has always shown resilience to come back to the growth trajectory. This time, it may take more years. As tourism depends on discretionary income, it will take several months for tourism to regain the previous level of international tourist arrivals. One major issue may be with the group travel as it may face severe issues in the near future as well. The mature travel segment may hesitate for engaging in tourism due to the psychological effects that may prevail for a couple of years more.
- Increased sustainability scope: While destinations were closed down, nature had great relief, as the tourist pressure was not there on it in the natural destinations. As transportation was restricted, emissions were also less. Furthermore, a lot of time is at the disposal of the destination managers to plan effectively, to undertake carrying capacity analysis and environmental impact assessment and to ensure visitor management practices. This is an ideal time to plan ahead for destinations having serious concerns about sustainability.
- Price slump: The low rates for tourism products may continue for a few more years as demand pressure is not there. As survival becomes the prime concern, the price levels may be compromised. The luxury hospitality segment may have no choice but to reduce tariffs. Lower occupancies and lower room rates will be a double whammy for the rated hotels and resorts. Every sector in the tourism industry amalgam will also have this effect.
- Shopping tourism to face slump: The forthcoming recession and the lack of disposable income can dampen the scope of shopping tourism in the years to come as well. Overseas shopping may remain a luxury until the economic levels regain the previous status.

18.8 Conclusions

Air accessibility is crucial for businesses and tourism. Despite the huge economic potential, the consequences of tourism are often criticized. Air transport is a major contributor to the carbon emissions of tourism that also contribute to climate change. The main environmental impacts caused by air transportation are aircraft noise, carbon emissions, water pollution, waste and threat on wildlife, heritage and landscape. Tourism is an area where resources are used profusely. Natural resource consumption rates are often a concern in the tourism sector. Climate change certainly affects tourism in an adverse manner, especially in a nature-based destination. Of the various causes leading to climate change, air transport emissions carry the most. The degree of impact of aviation emissions is high since the emissions are deposited at high altitudes. Measures and strategies to mitigate climate change mainly involve evolutionary technology, revolutionary technology and operational efficiency and policy interventions.

There are many challenges in tourism and aviation. The major challenges facing international aviation in the new millennium are security, safety, environment, infrastructure, information technology and economic regulations. Aircraft manufacturers have been involved in research and development to obtain better fuel-efficient engines and to install engines that can use alternative fuels such as biofuels and solar cells. Utilizing the latest ICT to communicate, provide services and enhance the travel experience is paramount for airlines and airports. Because of the extraordinary growth in the demand for air transport, efforts and large-scale investment are needed to develop infrastructure that results in environmental and social issues as well. The recovery of the aviation and tourism industry from the COVID-19 pandemic will take months, and it is expected to take a few years to achieve the growth rate.

Sample questions

Short-/medium-answer-type questions

- What are the environmental impacts of air transport?
- Identify the measures for reducing the issue of noise associated with air transportation.
- Discuss the impacts of tourism in general.
- Give a brief account on carbon emissions from aviation.
- Elucidate the role of air transport in the climate change challenge of tourism.
- Identify the contemporary challenges of air transportation.
- Write about the emerging trends in the post-COVID era.

Essay type questions

- Write an essay on the strategies that a tourist destination can undertake to ameliorate the environmental impacts of tourism.

Suggested readings

Belobaba, P., Odoni, A., & Barnhart, C. (2015). *The Global Airline Industry.* West Sussex: John Wiley & Sons.

Bows, A., Anderson, K., & Peeters, P. (2009). Air transport, climate change and tourism. *Tourism and Hospitality Planning & Development*, 6(1), 7–20.

Cento, A. (2010). *The Airline Industry: Challenges in the 21st Century.* Physica.

O'Connell, J.F., & Williams, G. (2016). *Air Transport in the 21st Century: Key Strategic Developments.* London: Routledge.

References

Abou-Ragheb, L. (2020). How is Covid-19 changing airports? *World Economic Forum*, data available online at https://www.weforum.org/agenda/2020/09/how-is-covid-19-changing-our-airports/

Acar, Y., & Altas, A. (2017). New solution suggestions for the development of Aksaray tourism: Hot air balloon tourism. *Journal of Academic Social Science*, 63, 134–138.

ACI (2018). Airport Council International: Economic Impact Study, data available online at https://airportscouncil.org/intelligence/economic-impact-study/ (accessed on 25 November 2018).

ACI (2018a). Airport Council International: Annual World Airport Traffic, data available online at https://aci.aero/wp-content/uploads/2018/11/WATR_WATF_Infographic_Web.pdf (accessed on 20 November 2018).

ACI (2020). ACI Advisory Bulletin, https://store.aci.aero/wp-content/uploads/2020/08/COVID19-4th-Economic-Impact-Advisory-Bulletin.pdf

Adler, N., Martini, G., & Volta, N. (2013). Measuring the environmental efficiency of the global aviation fleet. *Transportation Research Part, B*, 53, 82–100.

Airbus, www.airbus.com, data available online at https://www.airbus.com/aircraft/passenger-aircraft/a380.html#longdistancetravel.

Air India, Code Share-FAQs, http://www.airindia.in/code-share-faqs.htm

Airlines of America, data available online at http://airlines.org/industry/

Airport Technology, www.airporttechnology.com, https://www.airport-technology.com/contractors/consult/crowdvision/

Air Transport Action Group (ATAG). (2008). enviro.aero facts and figures, data available online at www.enviro.aero.

Albers, S., & Rundshagen, V. (2020, January-May). European airlines: Strategic responses to the COVID-19 pandemic. *Journal of Air Transport Management*, 87, 101863.

Alderighi, M., & Gaggero, A.A. (2019, November). Flight availability and international tourism flows. *Annals of Tourism Research*, 79, 102642.

Altus, S. (2009). AERO - Effective Flight Plans Can Help Airlines Economize, in Boeing, data available online at https://www.boeing.com/commercial/aeromagazine/articles/qtr_03_09/article_08_1.html.

Amadeus (2013). How airlines can attract more customers-Amadeus Blog, data available online at http://www.amadeus.com/nablog/2013/08/how-airlines-can-attract-more-customers/airlines

Amadeus-www.amadeus.com, data available online at http://www.amadeus.com/web/amadeus/ru_1A-corporate/Airlines/Airline-Systems/Airline-Core-Systems/Amadeus-Airlines-Revenue-Optimisation/Amadeus-Revenue-Management/1400000041600-Categorizable_P-AMAD_CategoryDetailPpal-1319637765587?industrySegment=1259068355670

AOPA. What Is General Aviation, data available online at https://www.aopa.org/-/media/files/aopa/home/advocacy/what_ga.pdf

References

Ash, L. (2020). Airports are becoming more like tourist destinations. Simple Flying.com, data available online at https://simpleflying.com/airports-tourist-destinations/

Ashford, D.M. (1990). Prospects for space tourism. *Annals of Tourism Research*, 11(2), 99–104.

Ashford, N.J.S., Mumayiz, S.A., & Wright, P.H. (2013). *Airport Engineering: Planning Design and Engineering of 21st Century Airports*, 4th ed. New York: John Wiley & Sons.

Ashford, J.N., Stanton, P.H., Moore, A.C., Coutu, P., & Beasley, R.J. (2013). *Airport Operations*. New York: McGraw Hill.

ATAG (2017). Aviation Benefits 2017, Air Transport Action Group (ATAG), data available online at https://www.icao.int/sustainability/Documents/AVIATION-BENEFITS-2017-web.pdf

ATAG (2018). ATAG: Aviation beyond Borders, data available online at https://www.aviationbenefits.org/media/166344/abbb18_full-report_web.pdf

Avery, P. (2018). Aircraft load planning and control. In Bruce, P.J., Gao, Y., & King, J.M.C. (Eds.), *Airline Operations: A Practical Guide*. London: Routledge, pp. 220–238.

Ayazlar, A.R. (2015). Flow phenomenon as a tourist experience in paragliding: A qualitative research. *Procedia Economics and Finance*, 26, 792–799. doi: 10.1016/S2212-5671(15)00845-X

Bakhshi, B. (2007). The Impact of Tourism Marketing Mix on Attracting Domestic and Foreign Tourists in Kish Island. Master Thesis, Tehran, Islamic Azad University.

Banhart, C. (2009). Airline schedule optimization. In Belobaba, P., Odoni, A., & Barnhart, C. (Eds.), *The Global Airline Industry*. West Sussex: John Wiley & Sons, pp. 183–210.

Barnes, A.B. (2012). Airline pricing. In Özer, Ö., & Philips, R. (Eds.), *The Oxford Handbook of Pricing Management*. Oxford: Oxford University Press, pp. 45–92.

Barnett, A. (2009). Aviation safety and security. In Belobaba, P., Odoni, A., & Barnhart, C. (Eds.), *The Global Airline Industry*. West Sussex: John Wiley & Sons, pp. 313–341.

Barret, A. (2008). The emergence of LCC sector. In Graham, A., Papatheodorou, A., & Forsyth, P. (Eds.), *Aviation and Tourism: Implications for Leisure Travel*. Hampshire: Ashgate, pp. 103–118.

Bartsch, R. (2018). Regulatory framework. In Bruse, P.J., Gao, Y., & King, J.M.C. (Eds.), *Airline Operations: A Practical Guide*. London: Routledge, pp. 3–17.

Bateson, J.E.G. (1979). Why we need service marketing. In Ferrell, O.C., Brown, S.W., & Lamb, C.W. (Eds.), *Conceptual and Theoretical Developments in Marketing*. Chicago, IL: American Marketing Association, pp. 131.

Bateson, J.E.G., & Hoffman, K.D. (1999). *Managing Services Marketing: Text and Readings*, 4th ed. New York: The Dryden Press.

Bauer, B.L., Bloch, D., & Merkert, R. (2020). Ultra Long-Haul: An emerging business model accelerated by COVID-19. *Journal of Air Transport Management*, 89, 101901.

Bauman, Z. (2007). *Consuming Life*. Cambridge: Polity Press.

Bazargan, M. (2010). *Airline Operations and Scheduling*, 2nd ed. Hampshire, UK: Ashgate Publishing.

Becken, S., & Carmignani, F. (2020). Are the current expectations for growing air travel demand realistic? *Annals of Tourism Research*, 80. doi: 10.1016/j.annals.2019.102840

Becken, S., & Hay, E.J. (2007). *Tourism and Climate Change: Risks and Opportunities*. Clevedon: Channel View Publications.

Belobaba, P., & Odoni, A. (2009). Introduction and overview. In Belobaba, P., Odoni, A., & Barnhart, C. (Eds.), *The Global Airline Industry*. West Sussex: John Wiley & Sons, pp. 1–17.

Belobaba, P, Odoni, A.R., & Barnhart, C. (2009). *The Global Airline Industry*. West Sussex: John Wiley & Sons.

Belobaba, P., Odoni, A., & Barnhart, C. Airline Economics, Centre for Air Transportation Systems Research, George Masons University, data available online at https://catsr.vse.gmu.edu/SYST660/Chap3_Airline_Economics[2].pdf

Belobaba, P.P. (2009). The airline planning process. In Belobaba, P., Odoni, A., & Barnhart, C. (Eds.), *The Global Airline Industry*. West Sussex: John Wiley & Sons, pp. 153–180.

Benckendorff, J.P., Sheldon, J.P., & Fesenmaier, R.D. (2014). *Tourism Information Technology*, 2nd ed. Oxfordshire: CABI.

Bertan, S. (2020). Key success factors for doing business in hot air balloon riding. *Journal of Tourism and Services*, 20(11), 124–131. doi: 10.29036/jots.v11i20.131

Bieger, T., Döring, T., & Laesser, C. (2002). Transformation of business models in the airline industry—impact on tourism. In Keller, P. & Bieger, T. (Eds.), *Air Transport and Tourism*. St. Gallen: AIEST, pp. 34–42.

Bieger, T. & Laesser, C. (2001). The role of the railway with regard to mode choice in medium range travel. *Tourism Review*, 56 (1/2), 33–39. https://doi.org/10.1108/eb058354

Bieger, T., & Wittmer, A. (2006). Air transport and tourism – Perspectives and challenges for destinations, airlines and governments. *Journal of Air Transport Management*, 12(1), 40–46. doi: 10.1016/j.jairtraman.2005.09.007

Bieger, T., & Wittmer, A. (2011). From the aviation value chain to the aviation system. In Wittmer, A., Bieger, T., & Muller, R. (Eds.), *Aviation Systems: Management of the Integrated Aviation Value Chain*. New York: Springer, pp. 61–76.

Bisht, S.S., Mishra, V., & Fuloria, S. (2010). Measuring accessibility for inclusive development: a census based index. *Social Indicators Research*, 98, 167–181.

Black, T. (2020). Safe-Flying Vision: Virus-Killing Robots, Fever Checks by Camera, Bloomberg, data available online at https://www.bloombergquint.com/business/honeywell-pitches-virus-killing-bot-air-sensors-for-safe-flying

Bloch, D. (2020). What Are the Unique Stakeholder Management Challenges Posed in Ultra Long-Haul Aviation Projects? IE University, data available online at https://www.blochaviationadvisory.com/publications/stakeholder-management-ulh/.

Blythe, J. (2005). *Essentials of Marketing*, 3rd ed. Essex: Pearson Education.

Boeing (2016). Boeing Current Market Outlook 2016-2035, data available online at http://www.boeing.com/resources/boeingdotcom/commercial/about-our-market/assets/downloads/cmo_print_2016_final.pdf.

Boeing (2018). Commercial Market Outlook-2018-2037, data available online at https://www.boeing.com/commercial/market/commercial-market-outlook/#/interactive-forecast

Boeing. Boeing-International Traffic Rights-Freedoms of the Air, data available online at https://www.boeing.com/resources/boeingdotcom/company/about_bca/pdf/Startup-Boeing_Freedoms_of_the_Air.pdf

Boin, R., Coleman, W., Delfassy, D., & Palombo, G. (2017). How airlines can gain a competitive edge through pricing, McKinsey and Company, data available online at https://www.mckinsey.com/industries/travel-transport-and-logistics/our-insights/how-airlines-can-gain-a-competitive-edge-through-pricing

Boniface, B., & Cooper, C. (2009). *Worldwide Destinations. The Geography of Travel and Tourism*, 5th ed. Oxford: Butterworth-Heinemann.

Booms, B.H., & Bitner, M.J. (1981). Marketing strategies and organisation structures for service firms. In Donnelly, J., & George, W.R. (Eds.), *Marketing of Services*. Chicago, IL: American Marketing Association, pp. 47–51.

Booth, S. (1993). *Crisis Management Strategy, Competitionand Changes in Modern Enterprises*. London: Routledge.

Bows, A., Anderson, K., & Peeters, P. (2009). Air transport, climate change and tourism. *Tourism and Hospitality Planning & Development*, 6(1), 7–20. doi: 10.1080/14790530902847012

Brilha, M.N. (2008). Airport requirements for leisure travellers. In Graham, A., Papatheodorou, A., & Forsyth, P. (Eds.), *Aviation and Tourism: Implications for Leisure Travel*. Hampshire: Ashgate, pp. 167–176.

Brueckner, J.K., & Pels, E. (2007). Cost functions in transport. In Button, K. & Hensher, D. (Eds.), *Handbook of Transport Modelling*. Amsterdam: Elsevier, pp. 381–393.

References

Buchanan (2018). Operational Planning and Control. In Bruce, P.J., Gao, Y., & King, J.M.C. (Eds.), *Airline Operations: A Practical Guide*. London: Routledge, pp. 116–124.

Budd, L., Francis, G., Humphreys, I., & Ison, S. (2014). Grounded: Characterising the market exit of European low cost airlines. *Journal of Air Transport Management*, 34, 78–85.

Butler, R. W. (1980). The concept of a tourist area cycle of evolution: Implications for management of resources. *The Canadian Geographer*, 24(1), 5–12.

Caetano, J.D., & Fares Gualda, D.N. (2010). A Flight Schedule and Fleet Assignment Model, data available online at https://www.researchgate.net/publication/315496349_A_FLIGHT_SCHEDULE_AND_FLEET_ASSIGNMENT_MODEL

Castillo-Manzano, J.I., L'opez-Valpuesta, L., & Gonz´alez-Laxe, F. (2011). The effects of the LCC boom on the urban tourism fabric: The viewpoint of tourism managers. *Tourism Management*, 32, 1085–1095.

Celata, F. (2007). Geographic marginality, transport accessibility and tourism development. In Celant, A. (Ed.), *Global Tourism and Regional Competitiveness*. Bologna: Patron, pp. 37–46.

Chang, L.Y., & Hung, S.C. (2013). Adoption and loyalty toward low cost carriers: The case of Taipei-Singapore passengers. *Transportation Research E: Logistics and Transportation Review*, 50, 29–36.

Chang, C-L., McAleer, M., & Ramos, V. (2020). A charter for sustainable tourism after COVID-19. *Sustainability*, 12, 3671. doi: 10.3390/su12093671

Chatterjee, G.S. (2017). How technology is flight to customer experiences in the airline industry. *Robosoft Technologies*. https://www.robosoftin.com/blog/technology-in-airline-industry

Cho, Y-H., Wang, Y., & Fesenmaier, R.D. (2002). Searching for experiences. *Journal of Travel & Tourism Marketing*, 12(4), 1–17. doi: 10.1300/J073v12n04_01

Chung, J.Y., & Whang, T. (2011). The impact of low cost carriers on Korean island tourism. *Journal of Transport Geography*, 19(6), 1335–1340.

CIM. UK Chartered Institute of Marketing, https://www.cim.co.uk/qualifications/get-into-marketing/

Clarke, L., Johnson, E., Nemhauser, G., & Zhu, Z. (1997). The aircraft rotation problem. *Annals of Operations Research*, 69, 33–46.

Clerk, P. (2007). *Buying Big Jets: Fleet Planning for Airlines*, 2nd ed. Hampshire: Ashgate.

Cole, S. (2015). Space tourism: Prospects, positioning, and planning. *Journal of Tourism Futures*, 1(2), 131–140. https://doi.org/10.1108/JTF-12-2014-0014

Collier, A. (2007). *Principles of Tourism: A New Zealand Perspective*. New Zealand: Pearson Education.

Collier, M., & Smith, S. (2017). The Flight Dispatch Process, https://www.faa.gov/about/office_org/headquarters_offices/ato/service_units/systemops/ato_intl/documents/cross_polar/CPWG23/CPWG23_Brf_AAL_Dispatch_Process.pdf

Collins, P. (2006). Space tourism: From Earth orbit to the Moon. *Advances in Space Research*, 37(1), 116–122.

Cook, A.R., Yale, L., & Marqua, J.J. (2007). *Tourism: The Business of Travel*, 3rd ed. Harlow: Pearson Education.

Cook, N.G., & Billing, G.B. (2017). *Airline Operations and Management: A Management Textbook*. London: Routledge.

Cook, N.G., & Goodwin, J. (2008). Airline networks: Comparison of hub and spoke and point to point systems. *Journal of Aviation/Aerosoace Education and Research JAAER*, 17(2), 51–60.

Cooper, C., Fletcher, J., Fyall, A., Gilbert, D., & Wanhill, S. (2008). *Tourism: Principles and Practice*. London: Pitman Pearson Education.

Copley, P. (2004). *Marketing Communications Management: Concepts and Theories, Cases and Practice*. Oxford: Elsevier Butterworth-Heinemann.

Costa, A.C., & Chalip, L. (2005). Adventure sport tourism in rural revitalisation—An ethnographic evaluation. *European Sport Management Quarterly*, 5(3), 257–279. doi: 10.1080/16184740500190595

Cristina, S. (2017). New perspectives of the tourism and air transport relationship. *Cactus Tourism Journal*, 15(2), 24–32.

Cristina, S., & Monica, C.G. (2017, July). "Hybrid" airlines – Generating value between low-cost and traditional. *Proceedings of the International Conference on Business Excellence, Sciendo*, 11(1), 577–587.

Cross, R. (1997). *Revenue Management: Hard-Core Tactics for Market Domination*, 1st ed. New York: Bantam Doubleday Dell Publishing Group.

Crouch, G.I. (2001). The market for space tourism. *Journal of Travel Research*, 40(2), 213–219.

Crouch, G.I., Divinney, M.T., Louviere, J.J., & Islam, T. (2009). Modelling consumer choice behaviour in space tourism. *Tourism Management*, 30(3), 441–454.

Daley, B., Dimitriou, D., & Thomas, C. (2008). The environmental sustainability of aviation and tourism. In Graham, A., Papatheodorou, A., & Forsyth, P. (Eds.), *Aviation and Tourism: Implications for Leisure Travel*. Hampshire: Ashgate, pp. 239–254.

Davidson, R. (1994). *Tourism*. London: Pitman.

Dennis, N. (2009). Airline trends in Europe: Network consolidation and the mainstreaming of low-cost strategies. In Gössling, S., & Upham, P. (Eds.), *Climate Change and Aviation: Issues, Challenges and Solutions*. London: Earthscan.

Dezhbankhan, F., & Dezhbankhan, S. (2014). Safety Implications of Air Transport Liberalization, The First Conference on Safety in Air Transportation, Iran, Tehran, 24th & 25th June-2014, data available online at https://www.researchgate.net/publication/305467353_Safety_Implications_of_Air_Transport_Liberalization

Dileep, M.R. (2011). *Information Systems in Tourism*. New Delhi: Excel Books.

Dileep, M.R. (2018). *Tourism: Concepts, Theory and Practice*. New Delhi: I.K International.

Dileep, M.R. (2019). *Tourism, Transport and Travel Management*. London: Routledge.

Divisekera, S. (2003). A model of demand for international tourism. *Annals of Tourism Research*, 30(1), 31–49.

Dobruszkes, F., & Mondou, V. (2013). Aviation liberalization as a means to promote international tourism: The EUeMorocco case. *Journal of Air Transport Management*, 29, 23–34.

Doerr, L., Dorn, F., Gaebler, S., & Potrafke, N. (2020). How new airport infrastructure promotes tourism: Evidence from a synthetic control approach in German regions. *Regional Studies*. doi: 10.1080/00343404.2020.1714022

Doganis, R. (2005). *The Airline Business in the Twenty First Century*. London: Routledge.

Doganis, R. (2006). *The Airline Business*, 2nd ed. London: Routledge.

Donzelli, M. (2010). The effect of low-cost air transportation on the local economy: Evidence from Southern Italy. *Journal of Air Transport Management*, 16(3), 121–126.

Doshi, V. (2017). The incredible power of placing the traveler at the center of the airport experience, Sabre, data available online at https://www.sabre.com/insights/the-incredible-power-of-placing-the-traveler-at-the-center-of-the-airport-experience/

Dresner, M. (2006). Leisure versus business passengers: Similarities, differences, and implications. *Journal of Air Transport Management*, 12(1), 28–32.

Drummond, G., Ensor, J., & Ashford, R. (2001). *Strategic Marketing: Planning and Control*. Burlington: Butterworth-Heinemann.

Dube, K., & Nhamo, G. (2019). Climate change and the aviation sector: A focus on the Victoria Falls tourism route. *Environmental Development*, 29, 5–15.

References

Dubois, G., & Ceron, P.J. (2006). Tourism/leisure greenhouse gas emissions forecasts for 2050: Factors for change in France. *Journal of Sustainable Tourism*, 14(2), 172–191. doi: 10.1080/09669580608669051

Duval, T.D. (2013). Critical issues in air transport and tourism, tourism geographies. *An International Journal of Tourism Space, Place and Environment*, 15(3), 494–510. doi: 10.1080/14616688.2012.675581

Dyche, J. (2003). *A Business Guide to Customer Relationship Management*. Singapore, Delhi: Pearson Education.

Echevarne, R. (2008). The impact of attracting low cost carriers to airports. In Graham, A., Papatheodorou, A., & Forsyth, P. (Eds.), *Aviation and Tourism: Implications for Leisure Travel*, Hampshire: Ashgate, pp. 117–192.

Elamiri, M. (2000). Major challenges for air transport in the 21st century, WTO Seminar on Tourism and Air Transport, World Tourism Organization. Madrid, Spain.

ELFAA (European Low Fares Airline Association). (2004). Benefits of LFAs. http://www.elfaa.com/documents/ELFAABenefitsofLFAs2004.pdf.

Elliott, K.J. (2020). Tourists flock to Great Wall of China in post-coronavirus holiday rush. *Global News*. https://globalnews.ca/news/7383893/great-wall-of-china-coronavirus-photos/

Engel, J.F., Blackwell, R.D., & Miniard, P.W. (1995). *Consumer Behavior*, 8th ed. Forth Worth, TX: The Dryden Press.

Eno Centre for Transportation (2017). What effect does airline consolidation have on passengers?, data available online at https://www.enotrans.org/eno-resources/effect-airline-consolidation-passengers/

Eurofound (2010). European Foundation for the Improvement of Living and Working Conditions- Representativeness of the European social partner organizations: Civil aviation, data available online at https://www.eurofound.europa.eu/sites/default/files/ef_files/docs/eiro/tn0809027s/tn0809027s.pdf

European Space Agency ESA (2008). Space tourism: ESA's view on private suborbital spaceflights. ESA Bulletin, 135, Paris: ESA Institutional Matters and Strategic Studies Office. http://www.esa.int/esapub/bulletin/bulletin135/bul135c_galvez

Evans, N., Campbell, D., & Stonehouse, G. (2003). *Strategic Management for Travel and Tourism*. Oxford: Butterworth-Heinemann.

Evans, N., & Elphick, S. (2005). Models of crisis management: An evaluation of their value for strategic planning in the international travel industry. *International Journal of Tourism Research*, 7(2), 135–150.

Everis/UNWTO (2012). Conclusions, Global Report on Aviation: Responding to the needs of new tourism markets and destinations, World Tourism Organization (UNWTO), Madrid, Spain.

FAA (Federal Aviation Administration) (2015). Airport Categories, data available online at http://www.faa.gov/airports/planning_capacity/passenger_allcargo_stats/categories/ (accessed on 14 December 2016).

FAA handbook, Gliders and Sailplanes, data available online at https://www.faa.gov/regulations_policies/handbooks_manuals/aircraft/glider_handbook/media/gfh_ch01.pdf

FAA (2005). Human Error and General Aviation Accidents: A Comprehensive, Fine-Grained Analysis Using HFACS, Federal Aviation Administration (FAA), data available online at https://www.faa.gov/data_research/research/med_humanfacs/oamtechreports/2000s/media/0524.pdf

FAA (2012). General Aviation Airports: A National Asset, Federal Aviation-US Department of Transportation, data available online at https://www.faa.gov/airports/planning_capacity/ga_study/media/2012AssetReport.pdf

FAA (2014). The Federal Aviation Administration: The Economic Impact of Civil Aviation on the U.S. data available online at https://www.faa.gov/air_traffic/publications/media/2014-economic-impact-report.pdf (accessed on 16 February 2016).

FAA, https://www.faa.gov/airports/airport_safety/part139_cert/airports-affected/general-aviation-airports/

Fageda, X., Jimenez, J.L., Perdiguero, J., & Marrero, K. (2017). Does market exit of a network airline affect airline prices and frequencies on tourist routes? *Tourism Management*, 61, 465–471.

Fageda, X., Suau-Sanchez, P., & Mason, J.K. (2015, January). The evolving low-cost business model: Network implications of fare bundling and connecting flights in Europe. *Journal of Air Transport Management*, 42, 289–296.

Fageda, X., Suárez-Alemán, A., Serebrisky, T., & Fioravanti, R. (2019). Air transport connectivity of remote regions: The impacts of public policies. *Regional Studies*. doi: 10.1080/00343404.2018.1556391

Fasone, V., Kofler, L., & Scuderi, R. (2016). Business performance of airports: Non-aviation revenues and their determinants. *Journal of Air Transport Management*, 53, 35–45.

Faulkner, B. (2001). Towards a framework for tourism disaster management. *Tourism Management*, 22(2), 135–147.

Fayos-Solà, E., & Marín, C. (2009). *Tourism and Science Outreach: The Starlight Initiative*. Madrid: World Tourism Organization.

Fennell, P. (2018). Crew Planning. In Bruse, P.J., Gao, Y., & King, J.M.C. (Eds.), *Airline Operations: A Practical Guide*. London: Routledge, pp. 125–139.

Fernández, L.X., Coto-Millán, P., & Díaz-Medina, B. (2018). The impact of tourism on airport efficiency: The Spanish case. *Utilities Policy*, 55, 52–58. https://doi.org/10.1016/j.jup.2018.09.002

Filson, T. (2017). Irregular operations: Planning for the unplanned to recover operations efficiently, SABRE, data available online at https://www.sabre.com/insights/irregular-operations-planning-for-the-unplanned-to-recover-operations-efficiently/

Flight International (2002). Rebel Skies – The Future, April.

Forsyth, P. (2006). Martin Kunz memorial lecture. Tourism benefits and aviation policy. *Journal of Air Transport Management*, 12, 3–13.

Forsyth, P. (2010). Tourism and aviation policy: Exploring the links. In Graham, A., Papatheodorou, A., & Forsyth, P. (Eds.), *Aviation and Tourism: Implications for Leisure Travel*. Aldershot: Ashgate, pp. 73–84.

Foxall, G.R., & Goldsmith, R.E. (1994). *Consumer Psychology for Marketing*. London: Routledge.

Franke, M. (2018). Network design strategies. In Bruse, P.J., Gao, Y., & King, J.M.C. (Eds.), *Airline Operations: A Practical Guide*. London: Routledge, pp. 44–61.

Fu, X., Oum, H.T., & Zhang, A. (2010). Air transport liberalization and its impacts on airline competition and air passenger traffic. *Transportation Journal*, 49(4), 24–41.

Gallet, C.A., & Doucouliagos, H. (2014). The income elasticity of air travel: A meta-analysis. *Annals of Tourism Research*, 49, 141–155.

GAMA (2017). 2016 General Aviation Statistical Data Book and 2017 Industry Outlook, General Aviation Manufacturer's Association, data available online at https://gama.aero/wp-content/uploads/2016-GAMA-Databook_forWeb.pdf

Garcia, I. (2020). Hilton, Hyatt, and Marriott Will Introduce New Cleaning Protocols, data available online at https://www.housebeautiful.com/lifestyle/a32367701/hilton-hyatt-and-marriott-new-cleaning-protocols-coronavirus/

Gerardi, K., & Shapiro, H. (2007). The effects of competition on price dispersion in the airline industry: A panel analysis. Web site of the Federal Reserve Bank of Boston.

Gershkof (2016). Airline Disruption Management: A Complex Problem Seeking Solution, Travel Technology Research Ltd-Amadeus, data available online at https://amadeus.com/documents/en/blog/pdf/2016/09/airline-disruption-management-whitepaper-2016.pdf

Getz, D. (2008). Event tourism: Definition, evolution, and research. *Tourism Management*, 29, 403–428.

References

Goeldner, R.C., & Ritchie, J.R.B. (2003). *Tourism Principles, Policies and Practices*. New Jersey: John Wiley & Sons.

Goeldner, R.C., & Ritchie, J.R.B. (2011). *Tourism Principles, Practices, Philosophies*. New Delhi: John Wiley & Sons.

Google Trends, data available online at https://trends.google.com/trends/explore?q=staycation&date=all

Gopalan, R., & Talluri, K. (1998). The aircraft routing problem. *Operations Research*, 46(2), 260–271.

Gössling, S., Hall, M.C., Peeters, P., & Scott, D. (2010). The Future of Tourism: Can Tourism Growth and Climate Policy be Reconciled? A Mitigation Perspective. *Tourism Recreation Research*, 35(2), 119–130. doi: 10.1080/02508281.2010.11081628

Gössling, S., & Peeters, P. (2007). 'It does not harm the environment!' an analysis of industry discourses on tourism, air travel and the environment. *Journal of Sustainable Tourism*, 15(4), 402–417.

Gourdin, K. (1988). Bringing quality back to commercial travel. *Transportation Journal*, 27(3), 23–29.

GRA Inc. (2017). Impact of Airline Consolidation on Consumer Choice, data available online at https://eutraveltech.eu/wp-content/uploads/2019/11/Airline-consolidation-limits-competition-and-reduces-consumer-choice-study-confirms.pdf

Graham, A. (2003). *Managing Airports: An International Perspective*, 2nd ed. Oxford: Butterworth Heinemann.

Graham, A. (2014). *Managing Airports: An International Perspective*, 4th ed. London: Routledge.

Graham, A., Papatheodorou, A., & Forsyth, P. (2008). Introduction. In Graham, A., Papatheodorou, A., & Forsyth, P. (Eds.), *Aviation and Tourism: Implications for Leisure Travel*. Hampshire: Ashgate, pp. 1–5.

Gross, S., & Klemmer, L. (2014). *Introduction to Tourism Transport*. Oxfordshire: CABI.

Gudmundsson, V.S., & Anger, A. (2012). Global carbon dioxide emissions scenarios for aviation derived from IPCC storylines: A meta-analysis. *Transportation Research Part D*, 17, 61–65.

Gunn, C.A. (1994). *Tourism Planning: Basics, Concepts, Cases*. Washington, D.C: Taylor & Francis.

Gunn, C.A., & Var, T. (2002). *Tourism Planning: Basics, Concepts, Cases*. London: Routledge.

Gupta, R., & Ganesh, L. (2017). Dynamic pricing in airline industry. *Asian Journal of Research in Business Economics and Management*, 7(1), 15–29.

Gursoy, D. Chen, M., & Kim, H.J. (2003). The US airlines relative positioning based on attributes of service quality. *Tourism Management*, 26(1), 57–67.

Haaland, W.L., Shanahan, D.F., & Baker, S.P. (2009). Crashes of sightseeing helicopter tours in Hawaii. *Aviation, Space, and Environmental Medicine*, 80, 637–642.

Haanappel, P.P. (1980). Bilateral air transport agreements -1913–1980. *Maryland Journal of International Law*, 5(2), 242–273.

Hall, D.R. (1999). Conceptualising tourism transport: Inequality and externality issues. *Journal of Transport Geography*, 7(3), 181–188.

Halpern, N. (2010). The marketing of small regional airports. In Williams, G., & Bråthen, S. (Eds.), *Air Transport Provision in Remoter Regions*. Aldershot: Ashgate.

Halpern, N., & Bråthen, S. (2011). Impact of airports on regional accessibility and social development. *Journal of Transport Geography*, 19, 1145–1154.

Halpern, N., & Graham, A. (2016). Factors affecting airport route development activity and performance. *Journal of Air Transport Management*, 56, 69–78. doi: 10.1016/j.jairtraman.2016.04.016

Halpern, N., Graham, A., & Dennis, N. (2016). Low cost carriers and the changing fortunes of airports in the UK. *Research in Transportation Business & Management*, 21, 33–43.

Hao, F, Xiao, Q., & Chon, K. (2020). COVID-19 and China's hotel industry: impacts, a disaster management framework, and post-pandemic agenda. *International Journal of Hospitality Management*, 90. https://doi.org/10.1016/j.ijhm.2020.102636

Hardingham-Gill, T. (2020). Hong Kong airport brings in cleaning robots and disinfection booth. CNN Travel, https://edition.cnn.com/travel/article/hong-kong-airport-cleaning-robots-wellness-scn/index.html

Hares, A., Dickinson, J., & Wilkes, K. (2010). Climate change and the air travel decisions of UK tourists. *Journal of Transport Geography*, 18, 466–473.

Harteveldt, H.H. (2016). The Future of Airline Distribution: 2016–2021, Atmosphere Research group/International Air Transport Association, data available online at https://www.iata.org/contentassets/6de4dce5f38b45ce82b0db42acd23d1c/ndc-future-airline-distribution-report.pdf

Harvey, G. (2007). *Management in the Airline Industry*. London: Routledge.

HCL, https://www.hcltech.com/white-papers/engineering-rd-services/airline-network-planning

HCL (2013). Network Planning-WhitePaper, HCL Technologies. https://www.hcltech.com/white-papers/engineering-rd-services/airline-network-planning

Henderson, L.I., & Tsui, K.H.W. (2019). The role of niche aviation operations as tourist attractions. In Graham, A., & Dobruszkes, F. (Eds.), *Air Transport: A Tourism Perspective*. Elsevier.

Herrmann, N., & Hazel, B. (2012). *The Future of Airports*. New York: Oliver Wyman.

Higgins-Desbiolles, F. (2020). Socialising tourism for social and ecological justice after COVID-19. *Tourism Geographies*. doi: 10.1080/14616688.2020.1757748

Hindley, B. (2004). *Trade Liberalization in Aviation Services Can the Doha Round Free Flight?* Washington, D.C: The AEI Press.

Hobe, S. (2007). Legal aspects of space tourism. *Nebraska Law Review*, 86(2), data available online at https://digitalcommons.unl.edu/nlr/vol86/iss2/6

Hobe, S., & Cloppenburg, J. (2004). Toward a new aerospace convention? - Selected legal issues of 'space tourism'. In *Proceedings of the International Institute of Space Law: 47th Colloquium on the Law of Outer Space*, Vancouver, Canada. (October 2004), pp. 377–383.

Hoffman, K.D., & Bateson, J.E.G. (1997). *Essentials of Services Marketing*. Dryden Press.

Holloway, J.C. (2006). *The Business of Tourism*, 2nd ed. England: Pearson Education.

Holt, J.M., & Poyner, J.P. (2006). *Air Carrier Operations*. New Castle: Aviation Suppliers and Academics.

Horner, S., & Swarbrooke, J. (2005) *Leisure Marketing: A Global Perspective*. London: Elsevier Butterworth-Heinemann.

Horner, S., & Swarbrooke, J. (2007). *Consumer Behaviour in Tourism*, 2nd ed. Oxford: Butterworth-Heinemann.

Horonjeff, R., & McKelvey, F.X. (1983). *Planning and Design of Airports*, 3rd ed. New York: McGrawHill.

Horswell, (2018). A flight attendant's perspective. In Bruse, P.J., Gao, Y., & King, J.M.C. (Eds.), *Airline Operations: A Practical Guide*. London: Routledge, pp. 287–310.

Howie, F. (2003). *Managing the Tourist Attractions*. London: Continuum/Thomson Learning.

http://www.amadeus.com/web/amadeus/en_1A-corporate/Hotels/Amadeus-LinkHotel/About-GDS-Distribution/1319593371760-Page-AMAD_DetailPpal?industrySegment=1259068355773

http://www.amadeus.com/web/amadeus/ru_1A-corporate/Airlines/Airline-Systems/Airline-Core-Systems/Amadeus-Airlines-Revenue-Optimisation/Network-Planning-and-Scheduling/1319696287072-Categorizable_P-AMAD_CategoryDetailPpal-1319637765587?industrySegment=1259068355670

https://www.maliat.govt.nz

References

https://www.unwto.org/glossary-tourism-terms#:~:text=Tourism%20is%20a%20 social%2C%20cultural,personal%20or%20business%2Fprofessional%20purposes

Hudson, S., & Miller, A.G. (2005). The responsible marketing of tourism: The case of canadian mountain holidays. *Tourism Management*, 26(2), 133–142.

Hunziker, W., & Krapf, K. (1941). *Grundriß Der Allgemeinen Fremdenverkehrslehre (in German)*. Zurich: Polygr. Verl.

IATA (2007). International Air Transport Association Annual Report 2007, https://www.iata.org/about/Documents/ar2007.pdf.

IATA Press Release No: 56, 02 Oct. 2018, data available online at https://www.iata.org/en/pressroom/pr/2018-10-02-01/

IATA Press Releases (2020). International Air Transport Association, data available online at https://www.iata.org/en/about/sp/pressreleases/

IATA Program Strategy (2016). Simplifying the Business-Innovating Better Together, data available on https://www.iata.org/whatwedo/stb/Documents/2016-White-Paper.pdf

IATA (2006). *Aviation Training Programme – Introduction to the Airline industry course Text Book*, 1st ed. Montreal: IATA.

IATA (2013). 3 June 2013 Strong Performance Sustains Profitability, IATA Presse Release, https://www.iata.org/pressroom/pr/Pages/2013-06-03-02.aspx

IATA (2013a). Air Travel Demand, https://www.iata.org/whatwedo/documents/economics/air_travel_demand.pdf

IATA (2014). Operations Control (OCC), data available online at https://www.iata.org/whatwedo/workgroups/documents/acc-2014-gva/occ-3-occ.pdf

IATA (2017). Press release 55, dated 24 October 2017, https://www.iata.org/en/pressroom/pr/2017-10-24-01?__prclt=1vWh6x5L

IATA (2018). IATA Forecast Predicts 8.2 billion Air Travelers in 2037, IATA Press Release No.62, Dtd.24/10/2018, data available online at https://www.iata.org/pressroom/pr/Pages/2018-10-24-02.aspx

IATA (2018a). Traveller Numbers Reach New Heights, IATA Press Release No.51, Dtd.6/09/2018, data available online at https://www.iata.org/pressroom/pr/Pages/2018-09-06-01.aspx

IATA (2018b). Press Release No.: 5, Date: 7 February 2019 https://www.iata.org/pressroom/pr/Pages/2019-02-07-01.aspx

IATA (2019). https://www.iata.org/contentassets/a686ff624550453e8bf0c9b3f7f0ab26/wats-2019-mediakit.pdf

IATA-WATS (2019a). Air transport Statistics 2019, https://www.iata.org/contentassets/a686ff624550453e8bf0c9b3f7f0ab26/wats-2019-mediakit.pdf.

IATA. https://www.iata.org/en/iata-repository/pressroom/fact-sheets/fact-sheet---industry-statistics/

IATA. https://www.iata.org/en/programs/stb/e-ticketing

IATA/Colehan, T. Montreal Convention 1999: A global standard, ICAO and IATA, data available online at https://www.icao.int/Meetings/LegalSeminar/Documents/TC_Montreal%20Convention%201999.pdf

IATA/History, growth and development, IATA, https://www.iata.org/en/about/history/history-growth-and-development/

Iatrou, K., & Oretti, M. (2007). *Airline Choices for the Future: From Alliances to Mergers*. England, Burlington: Ashgate.

Iatrou, K., & Tsitsiragou, E. (2008). Leisure travel, network carriers and alliances. In Graham, A., Papatheodorou, A., & Forsyth, P. (Eds.), *Aviation and Tourism: Implications for Leisure Travel*. Hampshire: Ashgate.

ICAO (2003). Aircraft Nationality and Registration Marks, Annex 7 to the Convention on International Civil Aviation, International Civil Aviation Organization (ICAO): Montreal.

ICAO (2004). Manual on the Regulation of International Air Transport, International Civil Aviation Organization, Doc 9626, data available online at https://www.icao.int/Meetings/atconf6/Documents/Doc%209626_en.pdf

ICAO (2005). Amendment No.11 to the International Standards and recommended Practices, data available online at https://www.icao.int/SAM/Documents/GREPECAS/2006/AVSCOMM05/avseccomm05wp03.pdf

ICAO (2007). Global aviation leadership. *The ICAO Journal*, 62(4), data available online at https://www.icao.int/environmental-protection/Documents/Publications/6204_en.pdf

ICAO (2009). International Civil Aviation Organization: Review of the classification and definitions used for civil aviation activities, data available online at http://www.icao.int/Meetings/STA10/Documents/Sta10_Wp007_en.pdf (accessed on 25 March 2016).

ICAO (2009a). ICAO Working Paper on 10th Session of the Statistics Division, Montréal, 23 to 27 November 2009, data available online at file:///F:/Airline/ICAO%20sefinitions%202.pdf

ICAO (2010). Aviation's Contribution to Climate Change, International https://www.icao.int/environmental-protection/documents/environmentreport-2010/icao_envreport10-ch1_en.pdf

ICAO (2013). International Civil Aviation Organization: Sixth Worldwide Air Transport Conference - Letter of Transmittal (ATCONF/6), Montréal, 18 to 22 March 2013.

ICAO (2013a). Working paper on Airport Competition, presented by the Airports Council International (ACI), data available online at https://www.icao.int/Meetings/atconf6/Documents/WorkingPapers/ATConf.6.WP.090.en.pdf

ICAO (2015). Continuing Traffic Growth and Record Airline Profits -Highlights 2015: Air Transport Results, Press Release of International Civil Aviation Organization dated 22nd December 2015.

ICAO (2017). Annex 17 to the Convention on International Civil Aviation, http://dgca.gov.in/intradgca/intra/icao%20annexes/an17_cons.pdf

ICAO (2017a). Fleet Planning and airline route evaluation, ICAO https://www.icao.int/MID/Documents/2017/Aviation%20Data%20and%20Analysis%20Seminar/PPT4%20-%20Fleet%20Planning.pdf

ICAO (2020). Effects of Novel Coronavirus (COVID-19) on Civil Aviation: Economic Impact Analysis, https://www.icao.int/sustainability/Documents/COVID-19/ICAO_Coronavirus_Econ_Impact.pdf

ICAO/Aircraft Engine Emissions, International Civil Aviation Organization (ICAO), https://www.icao.int/environmental-protection/Pages/aircraft-engine-emissions.aspx

ICAO Air Transport Reporting Form A and A-S plus ICAO estimates, data available online at https://www.icao.int/annual-report-2016/Documents/ARC_2016_Air%20Transport%20Statistics.pdf

ICAO-Chicago Convention, Manual on the Regulation of International Air Transport (Doc 9626, Part 4), International Civil Aviation Organization (ICAO), data available online at http://www.icao.int/Pages/freedomsAir.aspx and

ICAO, data available online at https://www.icao.int/about-icao/Pages/default.aspx

ICAO Definitions - UVS International, data available online at http://www.uavdach.org/aktuell_e/3_UVSI_ICAO-Definitions_V01_120813.pdf (accessed on 30 August 2016).

ICAO. Public Private Partnership (PPP), data available online at https://www.icao.int/sustainability/Pages/im-ppp.aspx

ICAO/www.icao.int. On board sustainable future, https://www.icao.int/environmental-protection/Documents/ICAOEnvironmental_Brochure-1UP_Final.pdf

IHLG (2017). Industry High Level Group (), Aviation Benefits 2017, https://www.icao.int/sustainability/Documents/AVIATION-BENEFITS-2017-web.pdf

References

IHLG (2019). Aviation Benefits Report 2019, Industry High Level Group (IHLG), https://www.icao.int/sustainability/Documents/AVIATION-BENEFITS-2019-web.pdf

IKA, International Kite boarding Association, data available online at https://www.kite-classes.org/the-sport/disciplines-classes-equipment

ILO (2013). Civil aviation and its changing world of work, International Labour Organisation- Sectoral Activities Department, data available online at http://www.ilo.org/wcmsp5/groups/public/@ed_dialogue/@sector/documents/meetingdocument/wcms_201282.pdf

Inkpen, G. (1998). *Information Technology for Travel and Tourism*. London: Pitman Publishing.

InterVistas (2015). IATA Report on 'Asia Pacific Commercial Air Transport: Current and Future Economic Benefits', data available online at https://www.iata.org/contentassets/5d4c3f78802248378497cc561ca019b0/intervistas-report-aspac-dec2015.pdf.

Ivanova, M. (2017). *Air Transport – Tourism Nexus: A Destination Management Perspective*. Varna: Zangador.

Jaiswal, M., & Mital, M. (2004). *Management Information System*. New Delhi: Oxford University Press.

James, G. (2012). An interdependent relationship for developing new tourism markets, Global Report on Aviation: Responding to the needs of new tourism markets and destinations, World Tourism Organization (UNWTO), Madrid, Spain.

Kaspar, C. (1993). The competitiveness of long haul destinations. 35th AIEST Congress Publication. In AIEST (Eds.), *Competitiveness of Long Haul Tourist Destinations*. St. Gallen: AIEST.

Kaul, R.N. (1985). Dynamics of tourism: A trilogy, Vol. 111. New Delhi: Transportation and Marketing.

Kazda, A., & Caves, E.R. (2000). *Airport Design and Operations*. Oxford: Elsevier.

Keller, P. (2000). Structural changes in the market for air transport and impact on tourism, WTO Seminar on Tourism and Air Transport, World Tourism Organization. Madrid, Spain.

Khadaroo, J., & Seetanah, B. (2008). The role of transport infrastructure in international tourism development: A gravity model approach. *Tourism Management*, 29, 831–840.

Khan, S.A.R., Qianli, D., SongBo, W., Zaman, K., & Zhang, Y. (2017). Travel and tourism competitiveness index: The impact of air transportation, railways transportation, travel and transport services on international inbound and outbound tourism. *Journal of Air Transport Management*, 58, 125–134. doi: 10.1016/j. jairtraman.2016.10.006

Khisty, C.J., & Zeitler, U. (2001). Is hypermobility a challenge for transport ethics and systemicity? *Systemic Practice and Action Research*, 14, 597–613. https://doi.org/10.1023/A:1011925203641.

Kim, G. (2018). Dispatch and flight following. In Bruce, P.J., Gao, Y., & King, J.M.C. (Eds.), *Airline Operations: A Practical Guide*. London: Routledge, pp. 239–253.

King, M.C.J. (2018). Business strategy and airline models for operating managemers. In Bruse, P.J., Gao, Y., & J.M.C. King (Eds.), *Airline Operations: A Practical Guide*. London: Routledge.

Kirk, P., Harrison, A., Popovic, V., & Kraal, B. (2014). Deconstructing expected passenger experience in airports. In DRS2014 International Conference of the Design Research Society Proceedings. Umea, Sweden

Kiser, J. (2003). The Multilateral Agreement on the Liberalization of International Air Transportation, Presented in ICAO Preparatory Seminar for the Worldwide Air Transport Conference, held in Montreal, March 22, 2003, data available online at https://www.icao.int/Meetings/ATConf5/Documents/Kiser.pdf

Klophaus, R., Conrady, R., & Fichert, F. (2012). Low cost carriers going hybrid: Evidence from Europe. *Journal of Air Transport Management*, 23, 54–58.

Koontz, H., & Weihrich, H. (1990). *Essentials of Management*. Singapore: Mc Graw Hill.

Kotler, P., & Armstrong, G. (2013). *Principles of Marketing (Global Edition)*, 15th ed. Harlow: Pearson Education.

Kotler, P., Bowen, J., & Makens, J. (2003). *Marketing for Hospitality and Tourism*. London: Prentice Hall.

Kotler, P., Bowen, J., & Makens, J. (2014). *Marketing for Tourism and Hospitality*, 9th ed. London: Prentice Hall.

Laming, C., & Mason, K. (2014). Customer experience—An analysis of the concept and its performance in airline brands. *Research in Transportation Business & Management*. http://dx.doi.org/10.1016/j.rtbm.2014.05.004

Lappan, S., Malaivijitnond, S., Radhakrishna, S., Riley, P.E., & Ruppert, N. (2020). The human–primate interface in the New Normal: Challenges and opportunities for primatologists in the COVID-19 era and beyond. *American Journal of Primatology*. https://doi.org/10.1002/ajp.23176

Laudon, K., & Laudon, J. (2004). *Management Information System-Managing the Digital Firm*, 8th ed. India: Prentice Hall.

Lederer, M.E. (2020). UN: Global tourism lost $320 billion in 5 months from virus, data available online at https://news3lv.com/news/coronavirus/un-global-tourism-lost-320-billion-in-5-months-from-virus?fbclid=IwAR2D0twrYAMzzHusiS9cfnX-toYmDfgxIJO-LBVw0qE_rp1ucxQ6bMKYXykg

Lee, S.D., Fahey, W.D., Foster, M.P., et al. (2009). Aviation and global climate change in the 21st century. *Atmospheric Environment*, 43, 3520–3537.

Lee, S., Oh, C-K., & O'leary, T.J. (2005). Estimating the impact of the September 11 attacks on the US air transport passenger demand using intervention analysis. *Tourism Analysis*, 9(4), 355–361.

Leiper, N. (1979, October-December). The framework of tourism. *Annals of Tourism Research*, VI(4), 390–407.

Leiper, N. (1990). Tourism Systems, Department of Management Systems, Occasional Paper 2, Auckland: Massey University.

Li, G. (2008). The nature of Leisure travel demand. In Graham, A. Papatheodorou, A., & Forsyth, P. (Eds.), *Aviation and Tourism: Implications for Leisure Travel*. Hampshire: Ashgate.

Litman, T. (2008). Evaluating accessibility for transportation planning, data available online at http://trid.trb.org/view.aspx?id=859513.

Livingston, M.D. (2010). *Space Tourism, in Encyclopedia of Aerospace Engineering*. West Sussex: John Wiley & Sons.

Lohmann, G., Albers, S., Koch, B., Pavlovich, K. (2009). From hub to tourist destination – An explorative study of Singapore and Dubai's aviation-based transformation. *Journal of Air Transport Management*, 15(5), 205–211.

Lohmann, G., & Duval, D.T. (2011). Critical aspects of the tourism-transport relationship. Oxford: Goodfellow Publishers.

Lohmann, G., & Duval, D.T. (2014, October). Destination morphology: A new framework to understand tourism–transport issues? *Journal of Destination Marketing & Management*, 3(3), 133–136.

Lohmann, G., & Vianna, C. (2016). Air route suspension: The role of stakeholder engagement and aviation and non-aviation factors. *Journal of Air Transport Management*, 53, 199–210. doi: 10.1016/j.jairtraman.2016.03.007

Lovelock, C., & Wirtz, J. (2007). *Service Marketing- People, Technology, Strategy*. London: Pearson-Prentice Hall.

Lucas, P. (2019). A glimpse at emerging markets. ACI Insights, https://blog.aci.aero/a-glimpse-at-emerging-markets/

Lucas, S. (2018). Facilitation, immigration, customs, and quarantine. In Bruce, P., Gao, Y., & King, J.M.C. (Eds.), *Airline Operations: A Practical Guide*. London: Routledge.

References

Lumsdon, L. & Page, S.J. (2004). Progress in Transport and Tourism Research: Reformulating the Transport-Tourism Interface and Future Research Agendas. In Lumsdon, L., & Page, S.J. (Eds.) *Tourism and Transport Issues and Agenda for the New Millennium.* Oxford: Elsevier, pp. 1–26.

Ma, S., Zhao, X., Gong, Y., & Wengel, Y. (2020). Proposing "healing tourism" as a post-COVID-19 tourism product. *Anatolia*, 1–4. doi: 10.1080/13032917.2020.1808490.

Magloff, L. (n.d.).Dynamic pricing strategy. Small Business - Chron.com, http://smallbusiness.chron.com/dynamic-pricing-strategy-5117.html

Mak, B. & Go, F. (1995). Matching global competition. *Tourism Management*, 16(1), 61–65.

Maker, A. (2020). "Maldives Border Miles" launched, Business Traveller, https://www.businesstraveller.com/business-travel/2020/09/29/maldives-border-miles-programme-launched/

Market Research Future (2017). Global Helicopter Tourism Market Information Report by Tourism Type, https://www.marketresearchfuture.com/reports/helicopter-tourism-market-4495

Market Research Future/www.marketresearchfuture.com, data available online at https://www.marketresearchfuture.com/press-release/helicopter-tourism-market

Mason, P. (2009). *Tourism Impacts, Planning and Management.* Oxford: Butterworth-Heneimann.

Mathaisel, F.X.D. (1997). Decision support for airline schedule planning. *Journal of Combinatorial Optimization*, 1(2), 251–275, https://pdfs.semanticscholar.org/ba56/fe19d-b6a9cb0f60e6ed1bb3a07f3beff8bea.pdf

Mathieson, A., & Wall, G. (1982). *Tourism: Economic, Physical and Social Impacts.* London: Longman.

Matisziw, T.C., Lee, C.-L., & Grubesic, T.H. (2011). An analysis of essential air service structure and performance. *Journal of Air Transport Management*, 18, 5–11.

Maul, B., & Spear, B./Olivew Wyman. (2018). For European airlines, consolidation has become both necessary and inevitable. *Forbes*, https://www.forbes.com/sites/oliver-wyman/2018/10/30/for-european-airlines-consolidation-has-become-both-necessary-and-inevitable/#4399f2802ce5.

Maurer, P. (2006). *Luftverkehrsmanagement – Basiswissen*, 4th ed. Oldenbourg, Munich, Germany.

Masson, S. & Romain, P. (2009). Can the high speed rail reinforce tourism attractiveness? The case of the high speed rail between Perpignan (France) and Barcelona (Spain). *Technovation*, 29 (9), 611–617. doi:10.1016/j.technovation.2009.05.013

May, M., & Hill, S.B. (2002). Unpacking aviation travel futures and air transport. *Journal of Futures Studies*, 7(1), 41–65.

McAfee, R.P., & Velde, T.V. (2005). Dynamic pricing in the Airline industry, Working Paper, data available online at https://mcafee.cc/Papers/PDF/DynamicPriceDiscrimination.pdf

McCabe, V., Poole, B., Weeks, P., & Leiper, N. (2000). *The Business and Management of Conventions.* Melbourne: John Wiley and Sons.

McCarthy, E.J. (1987). *Basic Marketing: A Managerial Approach*, 9th ed. Homewood, IL: Irwin.

McLaughlin, D. (2017). Aviation Hangar, WBDG, https://www.wbdg.org/building-types/aviation/aviation-hangar

Mekinc, J., & Music, K. (2015). Elements of safety in paragliding. *Annales Kinesiologiae*, 7(1), 67–80, http://ojs.zrs-kp.si/index.php/AK/article/view/97.

Merten, P.S. (2008). Transformation of the distribution process in airline industry empowered by information and communication technology. In Van Slyke, C. (Ed.), *Information Communication Technologies: Concepts, Methodologies, Tools and Applications.* London: IGI Global.

Middleton, V.T.C., & Clarke, J. (2001). *Marketing for Travel and Tourism*, 3rd ed. Oxford: Butterworth-Heinemann, pp. 254–283.

Midkiff, H.A, Hansman, J.R., & Reynolds, G.T. (2009). Airline flight operations. In Belobaba, P., Odoni, A., & Barnhart, C. (Eds.), *The Global Airline Industry*. Sussex: John Wiley & Sons, pp. 213–251.

Milde, M. (2008). *International Air Law and ICAO*. Montreal, Canada: Eleven International Publishing.

Milioti, C.P., Karlaftis, M.G., & Akkogiounoglou, E. (2015). Traveler perceptions and airline choice: A multivariate probit approach. *Journal of Air Transport Management*, 49, 46–52.

Mindell, D. (2015). The Science and Technology of World War 2, data available online at http://www.learnnc.org/lp/editions/nchist-worldwar/6002 (accessed on 25th November 2015).

Mo, C.M., Howard, D. R., & Havitz, M.E. (1993). Testing an international tourist role typology. *Annals of Tourism Research*, 20 (2), 319–335.

MOCA (2020). About Air transport Bubbles, Ministry of Civil Aviaiton, Govt. of India, data available online at https://www.civilaviation.gov.in/en/about-air-transport-bubbles

Morley, C. (2006). Airline alliances. In Dwyer, L., & Forsyth, P. (Eds.), *International Handbook on the Economics of Tourism*. Cheltenham: Edward Elgar, pp. 209–223.

Morley, C.L. (2003). Globalisation, airline alliances and tourism: A strategic perspective. *Asia Pacific Journal of Tourism Research*, 8(1), 15–25. doi: 10.1080/10941660308725452

Moss, L. (2020). Colombia Launches Covid-19 Biosafety Certification for Tourism Sector, Finance Columbia, data available online at https://www.financecolombia.com/colombia-launches-covid-19-biosafety-certification-for-tourism-sector/

Movig, R. (2018). Baggage process. In Bruse, P.J., Gao, Y., & King, J.M.C. (Eds.), *Airline Operations: A Practical Guide*. London: Routledge, pp. 195–207.

NASA (1996). Assignment: Design a Spaceship, https://www.nasa.gov/centers/langley/news/factsheets/Design-Spaceship.html.

NASA (2003). Spacecraft classification, https://www.nasa.gov/audience/forstudents/post-secondary/features/F_Spacecraft_Classification.html

NASA (2010). What Is a Rocket? https://www.nasa.gov/audience/forstudents/5-8/features/nasa-knows/what-is-a-rocket-58.html

NASA and Virtual Skies, Airport Design, National Aeronautics and Space Administration and Virtual Skies, data available online at http://virtualskies.arc.nasa.gov/airport_design/7.html (accessed on 23 September 2017).

NASA/www.grc.nasa.gov, How does a jet engine work? National Aeronautics and Space Administration–NASA, https://www.grc.nasa.gov/www/k-12/UEET/StudentSite/engines.html

Nathan, M. (2000). The paradoxical nature of crisis. *Review of Business*, 21(3/4), 12–16.

NBAA (1997). *National Business Aviation Association. The Real World of Business Aviation*. Washington, DC: National Business Aviation Association.

Nenem, S., Graham, A., & Dennis, N. (2020). Airline schedule and network competitiveness: A consumer-centric approach for business travel. *Annals of Tourism Research*, 80. https://doi.org/10.1016/j.annals.2019.102822.

Nguyen, T. (2017). U.S. airline consolidation no good for consumers. *National Consumers League*, https://www.nclnet.org/u_s_airline_consolidation.

Nilsson, H.J. (2009). Low-cost Aviation. In Gössling, S., & Upham, P. (Eds.), *Climate Change and Aviation: Issues, Challenges and Solutions*. London: Earthscan, pp. 113–130.

Nolan, J., Ritchie, P., & Rowcroft, J. (2005). Small market air service and regional policy. *Journal of Transport Economics and Policy*, 39(3), 363–378.

Normann, R. (1984). *Service Management*. Kobenhavn: Schultz Forlag.

References

North American Industry Classification System, www.bls.gov, data available online at https://www.bls.gov/iag/tgs/iag481.htm

NSS. (2009). Space tourism: Opening the space economy, National Space Society. Positional Paper on Space Tourism, data available online at http://www.nss.org/tourism/position.html

O'Connor, W.E. (2001). *An Introduction to Airline Economics*, 6th ed. Westport: Praeger Publishers.

Odoni, A. (2009). Airports. In Belobaba, P., Odoni, A., & Barnhart, C. (Eds.), *The Global Airline Industry*. West Sussex: John Wiley & Sons, pp. 343–375.

Olipra, Ł. (2011), Low cost airlines – New "quality" in the air transport in the European Union. In Klamut, M. (Ed.) *Wroclaw University of Economics' Research Papers, PN 211, Economics*, 4 (16), Wroclaw 2011, pp. 368–389.

Page, J.S. (2003). *Tourism Management, Managing for Change*. Oxford: Butterworth-Heinemann.

Page, J.S. (2009). *Transport and Tourism Global Perspectives*, 3rd ed. Essex: Pearson Education.

Papadakos, N. (2009). Integrated airlines scheduling. *Computers and Operations Research*, 36(1), 176–195.

Papatheodorou, A. (2008). The impact of civil aviation: regimes on leisure travel. In Graham, A., Papatheodorou, A., & Forsyth, P. (Eds.), *Aviation and Tourism: Implications for Leisure Travel*. Hampshire: Ashgate.

Papatheodorou, A., & Iatrou, K. (2007). Leisure Travel: Implications for Airline Alliances, 2007 World Conference of the Air Transport Research Society, Berkeley, United States.

Papatheodorou, A., & Lei, Z. (2006). Leisure travel in Europe and airline business models: A study of regional Airports in Great Britain. *Journal of Air Transport Management*, 12(1), 47–52.

Papatheodorou, A., & Zenelis, P., (2013). The importance of the air transport sector for tourism. In Tisdell, C.A. (Ed.), *Handbook of Tourism Economics: Analysis, New Applications and Case Studies*. Singapore: World Scientific Publishing Co. Pvt. Ltd, pp. 207–224.

Paraschi, P.E., Georgopoulos, A., & Kaldis, P. (2019). Airport business excellence model: A holistic performance management system. *Tourism Management*, 72, 352–372. https://doi.org/10.1016/j.tourman.2018.12.014.

Park, D., Nam, T-J., & Shi, C-K. (2006). Designing an immersive tour experience system for cultural tour sites. In Extended Abstracts Proceedings of the 2006 Conference on Human Factors in Computing Systems, CHI 2006, Montréal, Canada, April 22–27, 2006, 1193–1198. https://doi.org/10.1145/1125451.1125675

Parker, G. (2018). Customer points of contact. In Bruse, P.J., Gao, Y., & King, J.M.C. (Eds.), *Airline Operations: A Practical Guide*. London: Routledge, pp. 62–73.

Parmentier, A. (2013). Aircraft routing: Complexity and algorithms, data available online at http://cermics.enpc.fr/~parmenta/ROADEF/Rapport_MPRO_Axel_Parmentier.pdf-Strauss, 2017 (accessed on 25th March 2018).

Parvatiyar, A. & Sheth, N.J. (2001). Customer relationship management: Emerging practice, process, and discipline. *Journal of Economic & Social Research*, 3(2), 1–34.

Pearce (1995). *Tourism Today: Geographical Analysis*, 2nd ed. Harlow: Longman.

Peeters, P., Gössling, S., & Becken, S. (2006). Innovation towards tourism sustainability: Climate change and aviation. *International Journal of Innovation and Sustainable Development*, 1(3), 184–199.

Penner, J.E., Lister, D.H., Griggs, D.J., Dokken, D.J., & McFarland, M. (Eds.) (1999). *Aviation and the Global Atmosphere; A Special Report of IPCC Working Groups I and III*. Cambridge: Cambridge University Press.

Peteers, M.P., & Dings, J. (2007). Climate change, tourism and air transport – Global sustainable tourism requires sustainable air transport. In Amelung, B., Blazejczyk, K., &

Matzarakis, A. (Eds.), Climate Change and Tourism – Assessment and Copying Strategies, Institute of Geography and Spatial Organization, Polish Academy of Sciences, Maastricht – Warsaw.

Petersons, B. (2018). 5 New Planes That Will Change the Way You Travel, Conde Nast Traveller, https://www.cntraveler.com/story/new-planes-that-will-change-the-way-you-travel

Pforr, C., & Hosie, J.P. (2008). Crisis management in tourism. *Journal of Travel & Tourism Marketing*, 23(2–4), 249–264.

Piermartini, R., & Rousova, L. (2008). Liberalization of Air Transport Services and Passenger Traffic, World Trade Organization-Economic Research and Statistics Division, 2008, data available online at https://www.wto.org/english/res_e/reser_e/ersd200806_e.pdf

Pintarelli, F. (2017). What are yield and revenue management? *Genetica*, data available online at https://www.genetica.marketing/en/what-is-yield-and-revenue-management/

Poh, E. (2007). Airport Planning and Terminal Design, Strategic Airport Management Programme, LACAS and Civil Aviation Authority of Singapore (CAAS), data available online at http://clacsec.lima.icao.int/Reuniones/2007/Seminario-Chile/Presentaciones/PR07.pdf

Pompl, W. (2006). *Luftverkehr: Eine Okonomische und politische einfuhrung.* Berlin: Springer.

Poon, A. (1993). *Tourism, Technology and Competitive Strategies.* Oxford: CAB International.

Prideaux, B. (2000). The role of the transport system in destination development. *Tourism Management*, 21, 53–63.

Prideaux, B. (2000a). The resort development spectrum — a new approach to modeling resort development. *Tourism Management*, 21(3), 225–240. doi: 10.1016/S0261-5177(99)00055-2

Prideaux, B., &Whyte, R. (2014). Implications for destinations when low-cost carrier operations are disrupted: The case of tiger airlines Australia. *Advances in Hospitality and Leisure*, 9, 99–118.

Punel, A., Hajj Hassan, L.A., & Ermagun, B. (2019). Variations in airline passenger expectation of service quality across the globe. *Tourism Management*, 75, 491–508.

Qiu, R.T.P., Park, J., Li, S., & Song, H. (2020). Social costs of tourism during the COVID-19 pandemic. *Annals of Tourism Research*. https://doi.org/10.1016/ j.annals.2020.102994

Ralph, S., & George, R. (2001). *Principles of Information System.* Singapore: Thomson Learning.

Reddy, M.V., Nica, M., & Wilkes, K. (2012). Space tourism: Research recommendations for the future of the industry and perspectives of potential participants. *Tourism Management*, 33(5), 1093–1102.

Renshaw, M.B. (1997). *The Travel Agent.* Great Britain: Business Education Publishers.

Rey, B., Myro, L.R., & Galera, A. (2011). Effect of low-cost airlines on tourism in Spain. A dynamic panel data model. *Journal of Air Transport Management*, 17(3), 163–167.

Rifai, T. (2012). Foreword in Global Report on Aviation: Responding to the needs of new tourism markets and destinations, World Tourism Organization (UNWTO), Madrid, Spain.

Riley, M., Ladkin, A., & Szivas, E. (2002). *Tourism Employment: Analysis and Planning.* Clevedon: Channel View Publications.

Rossini, A. (2014). The Rise of Mobile Travel Agencies, Euromonitor, data available online at https://blog.euromonitor.com/2014/01/the-rise-of-mobile-travel-agencies.html

Sabre (2008). Sabre study shows "hybrid" airlines edging out traditional LCCs, Sabre Press release, May 8, 2008, https://www.sabre.com/insights/releases/sabre-study-shows-hybrid-airlines-edging-out-traditional-lccs/

Sabre (2018). Airline Solutions Dictionary, https://assets.sabre.com/files/AS_Product_Dictionary_2018_Final.pdf

Sabre (2018a). Open digital transformation: The technology evolution. Sabre, Texas, data available online at https://go.sabreairlinesolutions.com/open-technology-article-thankyou

References

Sabre, efficient operations efficient airlines capitalize on integrated solutions and processes, https://www.sabreairlinesolutions.com/images/uploads/Efficient_Operations_
Brochure.pdf

Sabre, https://www.sabre.com/files/Sabre-History.pdf

Sabre, www.sabreairlinesolutions.com

Samuel, J., Rahman, M.M., Ali, G.G.M.N., Samuel, Y., & Pelaez, A. (2020). Feeling Like It Is
Time to Reopen Now? COVID-19 New Normal Scenarios Based on Reopening Sentiment
Analytics. Preprints 2020. doi: 10.20944/preprints202005.0318.v1

Santana, G. (2004). Crisis management and tourism. *Journal of Travel & Tourism Marketing*, 15(4), 299–321.

Schano, R. (2008). A 'balanced approach' to airport marketing: The impact of low-cost
airlines on tourism in Salzburg. *Airport Management*, 3(1), 54–61.

Scheyvens, R. (2002). *Tourism for Development*. Harlow: Prentice Hall.

Schiffman, L.G., & Kanuk, L.L. (2009). *Consumer Behaviour*, 9th ed. New Jersey: Pearson
Prentice Hall.

Schlumberger, E.C., & Weisskopf, N. (2014). Ready for Takeoff? The Potential for Low-Cost
Carriers in Developing Countries, International Bank for Reconstruction and Develop-
ment/The World Bank, Washington DC.

SeatMaestro, www.seamaestro.com, data available online at https://www.seatmaestro.
com/top-5-modern-airport-terminals/

Security Magazine (2020). https://www.securitymagazine.com/articles/93095-gerald-r-ford-
airporttestsuv-autonomousrobot

Seetaram, N., Forsyth, P., & Dwyer, L. (2016). Measuring price elasticities of demand for outbound tourism using competitiveness indices. *Annals of Tourism Research*, 56, 65–79.

Segal, T. (2020). The North American airline industry: Is it an oligopoly? *Investopedia*, https://
www.investopedia.com/ask/answers/011215/airline-industry-oligopoly-state.asp

Seidenstat, P. (2004). Terrorism, airport security, and the private sector. *Review of Policy
Research*, 21(3), 275–291.

Serrano, F., & Kazda, A. (2020). The future of airport post COVID-19. *Journal of Air Transport Management*, 89, 101900.

Shah, S. (2007). *Airline Marketing and Management*. Hampshire: Ashgate.

Shaw, S. (2008). Aviation Marketing and the leisure travel demand. In Graham, A., Papatheodorou, A., & Forsyth, P. (Eds.), *Aviation and Tourism: Implications for Leisure Travel*.
Hampshire: Ashgate.

Sheldon, P. (2004). *Tourism Information Technology*. Oxon: CABI Publishing.

Sherali, D.H., Bish, K.E., & Zhu, X. (2006). Airline fleet assignment concepts, models, and
algorithms. *European Journal of Operational Research*, 172(1), 1–30.

Shin, H., & Kang, J. (2020). Reducing perceived health risk to attract hotel customers in
the COVID-19 pandemic era: Focused on technology innovation for social distancing
and cleanliness. *International Journal of Hospitality Management*, 91. https://doi.
org/10.1016/j.ijhm.2020.102664.

Sigala, M. (2008). Applications and implications of information and communication technology for airports and leisure travellers. In Graham, A., Papatheodorou, A., & Forsyth,
P. (Eds.), *Aviation and Tourism: Implications for Leisure Travel*. Hampshire: Ashgate.

Simillon, P. (2017). Top ten common causes of airline disruptions, Amadeus data available online
at https://amadeus.com/en/insights/blog/top-ten-common-causes-airline-disruptions

SITA, https://www.sita.aero/solutions-and-services/product-finder

Slutsken, H. (2020). Five ways Boeing's 747 jumbo jet changed travel. *CNN Travel*, https://
edition.cnn.com/travel/article/boeing-747-jumbo-jet-travel/index.html

Smith, K. (2015). Drone Racing: What is it?, data available online at https://myfirstdrone.
com/blog/drone-racing-what-is-it

Spasojevic, B., Lohmann, G., & Scott, N. (2017). Air transport and tourism – a systematic literature review (2000–2014). *Current Issues in Tourism*, 21. doi: 10.1080/13683500.2017.1334762.

Spector, S., & Higham, E.S.J. (2019). Space tourism in the Anthropocene. *Annals of Tourism Research*, 79. https://doi.org/10.1016/j.annals.2019.102772.

Spisto, M. (2018). Airline. In Jafari, J., & Xiao, H. (Eds.), *Encyclopedia of Tourism*. New York: Springer, p. 36.

Stainton, H. (2020). Virtual tourism explained: What, why and where, Tourism Teacher, data available online at ttps://tourismteacher.com/virtual-tourism/#1-definitions-of-virtual-tourism

Stoenescu, C., & Gheorghe, M.C. (2017). Hybrid" airlines – Generating value between low-cost and traditional. *Proceedings of the International Conference on Business Excellence*, 11(1). doi: 10.1515/picbe-2017-0062

Suau-Sanchez, P., Voltes-Dorta, A., & Cugueró-Escofet, N. (2020). An early assessment of the impact of COVID-19 on air transport: Just another crisis or the end of aviation as we know it? *Journal of Transport Geography*, 86. doi: 10.1016/j.jtrangeo.2020.102749.

Swann, A. (2018). Maintenance planning. In Bruse, P.J., Gao, Y., & King, J.M.C. (Eds.), *Airline Operations: A Practical Guide*. London: Routledge, pp. 140–151.

Swissport-www.swissport.com, data available online at http://www.swissport.com/products-services/products-services/ground-handling/ (accessed on 15 April 2017).

Szakal, A. (2013). Interline and code-share agreements, http://www.aviationlaw.eu/wp/wp-content/uploads/2013/09/Interline-and-code-share-agreements.pdf

Tang, C., Weaver, D., & Lawton, L. (2017). Can stopovers be induced to revisit transit hubs as stayovers? A new perspective on the relationship between air transportation and tourism. *Journal of Air Transport Management*, 62, 54–64.

The Department of Infrastructure, Regional Development and Cities of Australian Government, https://infrastructure.gov.au/aviation/international/bilateral_system.aspx

The Free Dictionary, https://encyclopedia2.thefreedictionary.com/airline+industry

The Insight Partners (2002). Helicopter Tourism Market to 2027, data available online at https://www.theinsightpartners.com/reports/helicopter-tourism-market

The World Bank, https://www.worldbank.org/en/topic/transport/brief/airtransport#:~:text=Air%20transport%20is%20an%20important,tourism%2C%20and%20create%20employment%20opportunities

Thompson, K., & Schofield, P. (2007). An investigation of the relationship between public transport performance and destination satisfaction. *Journal of Transport Geography*, 15(2), 136–144.

Timothy, D.J. (2005). *Shopping Tourism, Retailing Andleisure*. Clevedon: Channel View.

Torrez, C., & Kozak, B. (2019). Limitations of helicopter training within 14 CFR Part 147. *Collegiate Aviation Review International*, 37(1), 107–116. http://ojs.library.okstate.edu/osu/index.php/CARI/article/view/7794/7213

Tóth, G., & Dávid, L. (2010). Tourism and accessibility: An integrated approach. *Applied Geography*, 30(4), 666–677.

Truitt, L., & Haynes, R. (1994). Evaluating service quality and productivity in the regional airline industry. *Transportation Journal*, 33(4), 21–32.

Truonga, V.N., & Shimizu, T. (2017). The effect of transportation on tourism promotion: Literature review on application of the Computable General Equilibrium (CGE) Model. *Transportation Research Procedia*, 25, 3096–3115.

Tsui, H.W.K. (2017). Does a low-cost carrier lead the domestic tourism demand and growth of New Zealand? *Tourism Management*, 60, 390–403.

UN & WTO (1994). Recommendations on Tourism Statistics, United Nations Department for Economic and Social Information and Policy Analysis Statistical Division and World Tourism Organization, New York.

References

UN & UNWTO (2008). International Recommendations for Tourism Statistics 2008, Department of Economic and Social Affairs: Statistics Division, United Nations Publications.

UN, Strategic Planning Guide for Managers, https://hr.un.org/sites/hr.un.org/files/4.5.1.6_Strategic%20Planning%20Guide_0.pdf

UNEP-IE. (1993). Environmental Codes of Conduct for Tourism. Paris: UNEP.

Unger, N. (2011). Global climate impact of civil aviation for standard and desulfurized jet fuel. *Geophysical Research Letters*, 38(L20803), 1–6.

UNWTO (2000). https://www.e-unwto.org/doi/pdf/10.18111/9789284403745

UNWTO (2002). https://www.e-unwto.org/doi/epdf/10.18111/9789284406876

UNWTO (2012). Global Report on Aviation: Responding to the needs of new tourism markets and destinations. World Tourism Organization (UNWTO), Madrid, Spain.

UNWTO (2013). *Tourism Highlights*. Madrid: World Tourism Organization.

UNWTO (2017). UNWTO Tourism Highlights 2017, data available online at https://www.e-unwto.org/doi/pdf/10.18111/9789284419029 (accessed on 15 December 2017).

UNWTO (2018). Overtourism? Understanding and Managing Urban Tourism Growth beyond perceptions, https://www.e-unwto.org/doi/pdf/10.18111/9789284420070

UNWTO (2018a). https://www.e-unwto.org/doi/pdf/10.18111/9789284419876

UNWTO Glossary, Glossary of Tourism Terms by United Nations World Tourism Organizations, data available online at http:// media. unwto.org /en/ content / understanding-tourism- basic-glossary (accessed on 15 June 2018).

UNWTO Glossary of tourism terms, https://www.unwto.org/glossary-tourism-terms#:~:text=Tourism%20is%20a%20social%2C%20cultural,personal%20or%20business%2Fprofessional%20purposes

UNWTO International Tourism highlights, 2019, data available online at https://www.e-unwto.org/doi/pdf/10.18111/9789284421152

UNWTO News September 20, https://www.unwto.org/news/unwto-highlights-potential-of-domestic-tourism-to-help-drive-economic-recovery-in-destinations-worldwide

UNWTO World Tourism Barometer, 18(5) (2020, August/September).

Urfer, B., & Weinert, R. (2011). Managing airport infrastructure. In Wittmer, A., Bieger, T., & Muller, R. (Eds.), *Aviation Systems: Management of the Integrated Aviation Value Chain*. New York: Springer, 103–134.

US DOT, US Department of Transportation, https://www.transportation.gov/policy/aviation-policy/licensing/code-sharing

US DOT-FAA (2016). Aircraft Weight and Balance Handbook, U.S. Department of Transportation-Federal Aviation Admininstration, https://www.faa.gov/regulations_policies/handbooks_manuals/aviation/media/FAA-H-8083-1.pdf

USPA (2018). Skydivers Information Manual, United States Parachutes Association (USPA), data available online at https://uspa.org/Portals/0/files/Man_SIM.pdf

Uysal, M. (1998). The determinants of tourism demand: A theoretical perspective. In Loamides, D., & Debbage, K. (Eds.), *The Economic Geography of the Tourist Industry: A Supply Side Analysis*. London: Routledge, pp. 79–98.

Vialle, O. (1995). Global Distribution Systems in the Tourism Industry, WTO, Spain.

Vogt, C. The Difference Between the Aviation Industry and the Aerospace Industry, https://smallbusiness.chron.com/difference-between-aviation-industry-aerospace-industry-26208.html

Vojvodić, K. (2006). Europsko tržište niskotarifnih zračnih prijevoznika. *Suvremeni promet*, 26(5), 363–366.

Voltes-Dorta, A., & Pagliari, R. (2012). The impact of recession on airports' cost efficiency. *Transport Policy*, 24, 211–222.

Wang, W., Cole, T.S., & Chen, S.J. (2017). Tourist innovation in air travel. *Journal of Travel Research*, 57(2), 164–177. https://doi.org/10.1177/0047287516686724

Wattanacharoensil, W., Schuckert, M., & Graham, A. (2016). An airport experience framework from a tourism perspective. *Transport Reviews*, 36(3), 318–340.

Weiss, T. (2004). Tourism in America before World War II. *The Journal of Economic History*, 64(2), 289–327.

Wells, T.A. (1988). *Air Transportation: A Management Perspective*. California: Wadsworth Publishing Company.

Wells, T.A., & Young, S. (2004). *Airport: Planning and Management*, 5th ed. New York: McGraw-Hill.

Wensveen, J. (2009). *Air Transportation: A Management Perspective*, 6th ed. Aldershot: Ashgate.

Wenzel, M., Stanske, S., & Lieberman, M.B. (2020). Strategic responses to crises. *Strategic Management Journal*, 41, V7–V18.

Werthner, H., & Klein, S. (1999). *Information Technology and Tourism-A Challenging Relationship*. New York: Springer Wien.

Whyte, R., & Prideaux, B. (2007). Impacts of low cost carriers on regional tourism. Paper presented at the CAUTHE 2007: Tourism e Past achievements, future challenges (Sydney, Australia).

Williams, G., Mason, K., & Turner, S. (2003). Market Analysis of Europe's Low Cost Airlines, Report 9- Air Transport Group. Cranfield: Cranfield University.

Williams, M. (2002). *Climate Change Information Sheets*. Geneva: UNEP/UNFCCC.

Williams, R. (2018). Market, product, consumer. In Bruce, P., Gao, Y., & King, J.M.C. (Eds.), *Airline Operations: A Practical Guide*. London: Routledge, pp. 18–30.

Williams, W.P., & Hunter, G. (2002). Assessing stakeholder perspectives on HeliSkiing's socio-economic impacts in British Columbia's Rocky Mountains: Applying a tourism impact scale. *Tourism Recreation Research*, 27(3), 67–82. doi: 10.1080/02508281.2002.11081375

Wind, Y. (1984). Going to market: New twists for some old tricks. *Wharton Magazine*, 4(3), 34–39.

Wirtz, J., Heracleous, L., & Pangarkar, N. (2008). Managing human resources for service excellence and cost effectiveness at Singapore Airlines. *Managing Service Quality: An International Journal*, 18(1), 4–19. https://doi.org/10.1108/09604520810842812

Wober, L. (2003). Postal communication, international regulation. In Max Planck Institute for comparative Public Law and International Law (Ed.), *Encyclopedia of Public International Law*. Amsterdam: North Holland.

WTO (1980). https://www.e-unwto.org/doi/pdf/10.18111/unwtogad.1981.1.l5l7gmm0252 20756#:~:text=These%20results%20are%20chiefly%20due,3.6%20per%20cent%20 over%201980

WTO (1981). World Tourism: 1979–1980. World Tourism Organisation, https://www.e-unwto.org/doi/pdf/10.18111/unwtogad.1981.1.l5l7gmm025220756

WTTC (2020). WTTC, Economic Impacts, data available online at https://wttc.org/Research/Economic-Impact#:~:text=330%20million%20jobs%2C%201%20in, 4.3%25%20of%20 total%20investment.

Wu, H-L. (2010). *Operations and Delay Management: Insights from Airline Economics, Networks and Strategic Planning*. Surrey: Ashgate Publishing.

www.aci.aero, data available online at https://aci.aero/news/2020/09/30/up-to-46-million-jobs-at-risk-due-to-covid-19-aviation-downturn/

www.aci.aero/news, data available online at https://aci.aero/news/2020/10/01/aci-publishes-alternatives-to-physical-distancing-at-airport-security-checkpoints/

www.africanaerospace.aero, data available online at https://www.africanaerospace.aero/seychelles-takes-one-step-back-to-move-forward.html

www.airbus.com, data available online at https://www.airbus.com/company/we-are-airbus.html

References

www.atraircraft.com, data available online at http://www.atraircraft.com/about-atr/cor-porate-overview/company-profile.html

www.boeing.com, data available online at https://www.boeing.com/company/

www.bombardier.com, data available online at https://www.bombardier.com/en/aviation/commercial-aircraft.html

www.britania.com, https://www.britannica.com/technology/spacecraf

www.casa.gov.au, data available online at https://www.casa.gov.au/aircraft/sport-aviation/gyroplanes

www.collinsdictionary.com, https://www.collinsdictionary.com/dictionary/english/runway

www.dgca.in, http://dgca.nic.in/manuals/PM_ANS.pdf

www.dubaiairports.ae, data available online at https://www.dubaiairports.ae/corporate/about-us/dwc-dubai-world-central/

www.dubai-online.com, data available online at https://www.dubai-online.com/essential/tourism-statistics/

www.embraer.com, data available online at https://embraer.com/global/en/about-us

www.globalsecurity.org, Basics of Aircraft Load Planning, https://www.globalsecurity.org/military/library/policy/army/fm/55-9/ch5.htm#bplp_5

www.gov.au

www.heliusa.com, data available online at https://www.heliusa.com/tour-companies/

www.iata.org, data available online at http://www.iata.org/whatwedo/airline-distribu-tion/ndc/Pages/default.aspx.

www.icao.int, https://www.icao.int/sustainability/Pages/eap-fp-forecast-scheduled-pas-senger-traffic.aspx

www.khaleejtimes.com/, data available online at https://www.khaleejtimes.com/business/aviation/dubai-airport-retains-top-position-as-worlds-busiest-airport

www.revfine.com, https://www.revfine.com/space-tourism/

www.surftoday.com, https://www.surfertoday.com/kiteboarding/what-is-kiteboarding

www.tupolev.ru, data available online at https://www.tupolev.ru/en/about/

www.un.org, data available online at https://www.un.org/en/ga/search/view_doc.asp?symbol=A/RES/2148%20(XXI))

www.un.org, data available online at https://www.un.org/en/sections/issues-depth/climate-change/

Yale, P. (2001). *The Business of Tour Operations*. Essex: Pearson Education.

Yan, C., & Kung, J. (2015). Robust Aircraft Routing. Transportation Science, Forthcoming, data available online at https://ssrn.com/abstract=2518028

Yun, A/Changi Airport, Singapore Changi Airport Preparation For & Experience with the A380, data available online at http://www.aci.aero/Media/aci/file/2008%20Events/ASQ%20Speeches/YUN_presentation.pdf (accessed on 15 June 2018).

Yuswohady. (2020). 30 prediksi perilaku konsumen di NEW NORMAL. Yuswohady.com. Diun-duh dari, https://www.yuswohady.com/2020/04/23/perilakukonsumen-di-new-normal/

Zhang, Y., & Findlay, C. (2014). Air transport policy and its impacts on passenger traf-fic and tourist flows. *Journal of Air Transport Management*, 34, 42–48. doi: 10.1016/j.jairtraman.2013.07.010

Zheng, Y., Goh, E., & Wen, J. (2020). The effects of misleading media reports about COVID-19 on Chinese tourists' mental health: A perspective article. *Anatolia*. doi: 10.1080/13032917.2020.1747208.

Index

Note: **Bold** page numbers refer to tables; *italic* page numbers refer to figures

Printed in the United States
by Baker & Taylor Publisher Services